Jahrbuch für Rechtssoziologie und Rechtstheorie IV

Jahrbuch für Rechtssoziologie und Rechtstheorie

Herausgegeben in Verbindung mit
Erich Fechner, Arthur Kaufmann, Ulrich Klug,
Niklas Luhmann, Peter Noll, Heinrich Popitz, Manfred Rehbinder,
Rüdiger Schott, Paul Trappe

von Werner Maihofer und Helmut Schelsky

Band IV

Westdeutscher Verlag

Zur Soziologie des Gerichtsverfahrens (Sociology of the Judicial Process)

Herausgegeben von
Lawrence M. Friedman und Manfred Rehbinder

Westdeutscher Verlag

Softcover reprint of the hardcover 1st edition 1976
Satz: Klaus Grüßner, Krefeld
Buchbinderische Verarbeitung: Langelüddecke, Braunschweig

ISBN 978-3-322-96983-5 ISBN 978-3-322-96982-8 (eBook)
DOI 10.1007/978-3-322-96982-8

Inhalt

Einleitung der Herausgeber

Manfred Rehbinder

Zur Soziologie des Gerichtsverfahrens

Die rechtssoziologische Erforschung des Gerichtsverfahrens, so sehr sie heute wie alle Rechtssoziologie noch in ihren Anfängen steckt, ist in Deutschland schon recht früh begonnen worden. Die erste mir bekannte größere Erhebung gehört in den Bereich dessen, was wir heute als impact research bezeichnen würden. Als nämlich nach der Gründung des Deutschen Reiches im Jahre 1871 die einzelstaatlichen Verfahrensgesetze in den sogenannten Reichsjustizgesetzen vereinheitlicht wurden, die am 1. Okt. 1879 in Kraft traten, beschloß einer der damals führenden Prozeßrechtler, der Leipziger Professor Adolf Wach, die Auswirkungen der neuen Zivilprozeßordnung auf die tägliche Gerichtspraxis zu erheben. Insbesondere interessierte ihn, wie sich „bei den erstinstanzlichen Kollegial-Civilgerichten die sogenannte Mündlichkeit des Verfahrens ausgebildet hat", die in den früheren Gebieten des gemeinen und preußischen Prozeßrechts bis dahin nicht die Regel war. Sieben Jahre nach dem Inkrafttreten der ZPO versandte er an 172 deutsche Landgerichte detaillierte Fragebogen (1)*. Er erhielt 194 ausführliche Berichte von 101 Landgerichten in einem Gesamtumfang von 2.400 Seiten (2), die er in einem ausführlichen Bericht von 168 Seiten auswertete und über dessen Ergebnisse er mit einem anderen bedeutenden Prozessualisten in Streit geriet (3). Zwar war ein einheitliches Prozeßgesetz wie die ZPO gegenüber dem früheren regional zersplitterten Rechtszustand ein Vorteil und in vielen Punkten auch in der Sache ein Fortschritt. Aber die an das Mündlichkeitsprinzip geknüpften Erwartungen hatten sich nicht erfüllt. So heißt es heute in einem führenden Kommentar zur ZPO: „Die ZPO von 1877 war ein geradezu ideales Werkzeug der Prozeßverschleppung; eine förmelnde Handhabung im Geist der Begriffsjurisprudenz machte ihre Mängel unerträglich. Schon früh setzten daher Bestrebungen ein, das Verfahren, wenigstens dasjenige vor den Amtsgerichten, den Lebensbedürfnissen besser anzupassen" (4).

So kam es, daß die ersten deutschen Rechtssoziologen, die die Begriffsjurisprudenz als sogenannte Freirechtler bekämpften, sich zu Fragen der Prozeßreform äußerten. Im Jahre 1911 zeigte Hermann Kantorowicz, der sich später in der Emigration an den amerikanischen Diskussionen um den Rechtsrealismus beteiligte (5) und schon im Jahre 1906 unter dem Pseudonym Gnaeus Flavius eine entscheidende Attacke der Freirechtslehre gegen die Begriffsjurisprudenz geritten hatte (6), was die Freirechtslehre an Forderungen an eine Prozeßreform zu stellen hatte (7). Ein Jahr später veröffentlichte Eugen Ehrlich, der mit seiner Programmschrift „Freie Rechtsfindung und freie Rechtswissenschaft" aus dem Jahre

* Anmerkungen auf den Seiten 9 f.

1903 (8) der Freirechtsbewegung ihren Namen gegeben hatte, eine Stellungnahme zur Reform der Gerichtsverfassung, die er auf Bitten des Deutschen Richterbundes diesem abgegeben hatte (9). Ebenfalls in diesen Zusammenhang gehören viele der Arbeitern der Freirechtler Ernst Fuchs (10) und Ludwig Bendix (11).
Allerdings vermissen wir bei den Freirechtlern meist die Anwendung der Methoden empirischer Sozialforschung. Ihre oft beträchtliche praktische Erfahrung und die beispielhaften Mitteilungen einzelner Fakten reichen nicht aus, um ihre Kritik oder ihre Reformvorschläge wissenschaftlich abzusichern., mögen sie inhaltlich noch so berechtigt und voller Anregungen für die weitere Arbeit sein. Das gilt auch für den 1928 erschienenen, interessanten Vortrag des Münchener Prozessualisten W. Kisch über die soziale Bedeutung des Zivilprozesses (12), dessen Überlegungen erst in unseren Tagen von Johann J. Hagen fortgeführt wurden (13). Die Freirechtler stellten zudem die Richterpersönlichkeit in den Mittelpunkt ihrer Untersuchungen, äußerten sich also mehr zur Richtersoziologie und Richterpsychologie als zur Soziologie des Gerichtsverfahrens. Diese eindimensionale Fixierung auf die Richterpersönlichkeit beherrschte lange auch die Szene, als in den USA mit dem Einsatz empirischer Methoden bei der Untersuchung des Prozesses begonnen wurde (14). Erst als man die verhaltenswissenschaftlichen Modelle, die den ersten größeren Untersuchungen zugrunde lagen, zugunsten systemtheoretischer Ansätze aufgab, wurde die Richtersoziologie zu einer umfassenderen Justizsoziologie erweitert. Welche Fülle ganz anderer Faktoren als nur die Richterpersönlichkeit in der Prozeßwirklichkeit eine Rolle spielen, wird Gegenstand unserer gemeinsamen Arbeit sein.
In Deutschland setzte die empirische Richterforschung erst zu Beginn der 60er Jahre ein. Aufgrund sozialstatistischer Erhebungen von Walther Richter über die Richter an den Oberlandesgerichten kam es zu umstrittenen Interpretationen von Ralf Dahrendorf, insbesondere zu dem Vorwurf, daß in den Gerichten „die eine Hälfte der Gesellschaft über die ihr unbekannte andere Hälfte zu urteilen befugt" sei. Schwerpunkt der folgenden Untersuchungen war immer wieder das Sozialprofil der Richter und anderer Rechtsberufe und ihre gesellschaftspolitischen Einstellungen, insbesondere in den Arbeiten von Zwingmann, Weyrauch, Kaupen und Görlitz (15). Gegen die Art der Datenerhebung sowie vor allem die daraus hergeleiteten überzogenen Interpretationen, ferner gegen den mangelnden Nachweis einer Auswirkung von Sozialprofil und Einstellung auf die Urteilspraxis sind heftige Vorwürfe erhoben worden (16). Zu recht werden daher zur Zeit andere Forschungsansätze gewählt, so die teilnehmende Beobachtung der richterlichen Tätigkeit (17) oder die Beurteilung fiktiver Fälle durch Richter in schriftlicher Befragung (18). Immer aber handelt es sich schwerpunktmäßig um die Soziologie der richterlichen Entscheidungstätigkeit, nicht aber um eine Soziologie des Verfahrensrechts.
Das ist nur anders, wo man wieder dort anknüpft, wo Adolf Wach gegen Ende des vorigen Jahrhunderts begonnen hatte, nämlich bei der Untersuchung von Teilaspekten der Prozeßwirklichkeit unter dem Blickwinkel einer Reform des Verfahrensrechts. Die erste größere Untersuchung dieser Art nach dem letzten Kriege ist die Untersuchung der Ursachen für Fehlurteile im Strafverfahren durch Karl Peters, der in der Zeit von 1951 bis 1963 1.100 Akten auswertete (19). Beachtliche Arbeiten sind ferner die im Zusammenwirken mit dem Bundesjustizministerium durchgeführten Untersuchungen über die Ursachen der Prozeßverzögerung von Baumgärtel und Mitarbeitern (20) und die Untersuchung über die

Rolle von Musterprozessen am Lehrstuhl von Arens, über die dieser berichten wird. Noch in vollem Gange sind die Arbeiten im Institut für Rechtstatsachenforschung von Bender und Mitarbeitern und von Blankenburg über Fragen der Prozeßreform sowie die Untersuchung über die Rolle der Sachverständigen von Pieper, über die im Verlauf der Tagung ebenfalls berichtet werden wird.
Soziologische Untersuchungen der Prozeßwirklichkeit stoßen zur Zeit in der BRD auf großes Interesse in Fachkreisen. Die sozial-liberale Koalition hat nämlich eine große Justizreform in Aussicht genommen, deren Entwürfe zum Teil auf erhebliche Kritik stoßen. Die Diskussion um die Reformprojekte kreisen meist um die erwarteten Auswirkungen dieser oder jener Regelung. Fast überall fehlt es hier an gründlichen Voruntersuchungen. Andererseits wird man nicht verlangen dürfen, daß die Reform bis zur Beendigung der eigentlich notwendigen Rechtstatsachenforschung verschoben wird. Dazu sind die Mängel des gegenwärtigen Rechtszustandes zu drückend. Aber es gehen doch vom Zwang zur Reform erfreuliche Impulse für die Forschung aus, die in diesem Punkte sicher sein kann, die erwünschte Resonanz zu finden. Das läßt erwarten, daß auch die Bemühungen unserer Tagung (21) mit Aufmerksamkeit verfolgt werden.

Anmerkungen

1 A.Wach/J.Weismann: Eine civilprozessualische Enquête, in: ZZP 10 (1887), S. 181–193.
2 Wach: Die civilprozessualische Enquête. Ergänzungsheft zu ZZP, Bd. 11, 1887, S. 4. Ganz anders war die Reaktion, als 6 Jahre nach dem Inkrafttreten des Bürgerlichen Gesetzbuches Martin Wolff in einigen Punkten erheben wollte, welche Auswirkungen das neue Zivilrecht auf die Praxis gehabt hatte. Die Untersuchungen mußten eingestellt werden, da es an der Bereitschaft der Praktiker zur Mitarbeit fehlte, vgl. M. Wolff: Das bürgerliche Gesetzbuch und die deutschen Lebensgewohnheiten. Eine Umfrage bei Praktikern, zumal Notaren und Richtern der freiwilligen Gerichtsbarkeit, in: JW 1906, S. 697–700, und den Bericht von Martin Segall: Das bürgerliche Recht und die Lebensgewohnheiten, in Archiv für bürgerliches Recht 32 (1908), S. 410–457.
3 Vgl. Otto Bähr: Die Prozeß-Enquête des Professor Dr. Wach, Kassel 1888; Wach: Die civilprozessualische Enquête im Lichte Bährscher Kritik, in: ZZP 12 (1888), S. 172–177. Bähr warf Wach „Mündlichkeitsschwärmerei" vor.
4 Baumbach-Lauterbach: ZPO, 30. Aufl., 1970, Einleitung I, S. 1.
5 H. Kantorowicz: Some Rationalism about Realism, in Yale Law Journal 43 (1934), S. 1240.
6 Gnaeus Flavius: Der Kampf um die Rechtswissenschaft, Heidelberg 1906.
7 Kantorowicz: Methodenreform und Justizreform, in: DRiZ 1911, Sp. 349 ff.
8 Erneut abgedruckt in Eugen Ehrlich: Recht und Leben, hrsg. von M. Rehbinder, 1967, S. 170–202.
9 Eugen Ehrlich: Die Neuordnung der Gerichtsverfassung, in: DRiZ 1912, Sp. 437–465, 563.
10 Vgl. z.B. Ernst Fuchs: Gerechtigkeitswissenschaft, ausgewählte Schriften zur Freirechtslehre, hrsg. von seinem Sohn Albert S. Foulkes, Karlsruhe 1965, und Ernst Fuchs: Gesammelte Schriften über Freirecht und Rechtsreform, hrsg. von Foulkes, 3 Bde., Aalen 1970 ff.
11 Ludwig Bendix: Zur Psychologie der Urteilstätigkeit des Berufsrichters, hrsg. von Manfred Weiss, Neuwied 1968.
12 W. Kisch: Die soziale Bedeutung des Zivilprozesses, in: Judicium 1 (1928/29), S. 1–37. Immerhin ist derart soziologisch aufgeschlossene Arbeit ein deutlicher Fortschritt gegenüber rein dogmatisch-spekulativen Erörterungen. Vgl. als positives Beispiel aus neuerer Zeit Eberhard Henke: Judicia perpetua oder: Warum Prozesse so lange dauern, in: ZZP 83 (1970), S. 125–167.

13 Johann Josef Hagen: Die soziale Funktion des Prozesses, in: ZZP 84 (1971), S. 385–395.

14 Vgl. den Bericht von Manfred Weiss: Die Theorie der richterlichen Entscheidungstätigkeit in den Vereinigten Staaten von Amerika, Frankfurt/M. 1971. Der erste Schritt waren aber auch hier statistische Erhebungen, vgl. den Bericht über die Arbeiten des Johns Hopkins Institute (Baltimore), in: M. Rehbinder: Entwicklung und gegenwärtiger Stand der Rechtstatsachenforschung in den USA, 1970, S. 18–22.

15 Klaus Zwingmann: Zur Soziologie des Richters in der BRD, 1966; Walter O. Weyrauch: Zum Gesellschaftsbild des Juristen, 1970; Wolfgang Kaupen: Die Hüter von Recht und Ordnung, 1969; Axel Görlitz: Verwaltungsgerichtsbarkeit in Deutschland, 1970.

16 Z.B. Walther Richter: Zur Bedeutung der Herkunft des Richters für die Entscheidungsbildung, 1973.

17 Rüdiger Lautmann: Justiz – die stille Gewalt, 1972.

18 Karl Dieter Opp/Rüdiger Peukert: Ideologie und Fakten in der Rechtssprechung, 1971.

19 K. Peters: Untersuchungen zum Fehlurteil im Strafprozeß, 1967.

20 Gottfried Baumgärtel/Peter Mes/Gerhard Hohmann: Rechtstatsachen zur Dauer des Zivilprozesses, 2 Bde., 1971/72; ferner Max Vollkommer: Die lange Dauer der Zivilprozesse und ihre Ursachen, in: ZZP 81 (1968), S. 102–135.

21 Die nachfolgenden Beiträge sind die überarbeiteten Fassungen der Referate einer Arbeitstagung zur Soziologie des Gerichtsverfahrens, die vom 24.–28. September 1973 im Zentrum für interdisziplinäre Forschung der Universität Bielefeld stattgefunden hat.

Lawrence M. Friedman

Introductory Remarks

The social study of law is in most senses a new field of learning. It has its classics, to be sure, but basically the field is in the process of construction, from the ground up, so to speak. Most of the work that has been done is relatively recent. A natural scientist recently remarked that 90 percent of all natural scientists who have ever lived are still alive. By this he meant not that scientists live long lives, or are preserved in formaldehyde, but rather that natural science, while it goes back at least to the ancient Greeks, is essentially recent, and has been growing explosively. Similarly, almost everyone who would be cited in the footnotes in a general study of law and sociology would be contemporary – Max Weber, Durkheim, Eugen Ehrlich might be exceptions, Otherwise the world would belong to the living.

What has this recent growth accomplished? In one sense an enormous amount, in another sense, very little. Compared to what had gone before, the bulk is enormous. Despite many dreary pages, one sees a body of data in process of growth, and even the glimmering of general theory. But such theory – and even theories of the middle range – still seems far off. Another problem, which is perhaps particularly apropos for us here, is the particularism and national isolation of most of the work. Much of the impetus for social study of law comes from the hearts and minds of reformers. Reform of legal institutions often requires meticulous, particular study. If one sets about to improve the civil courts of Honduras, one gets little help from Max Weber, with all due respect. One must begin with exact knowledge of what actually goes on in the courts. Those people most likely to have a taste for reform, and an intimate knowledge of the practice are not, as a matter of fact, likely to construct general theories of law and society. National barriers are particularly acute because so much empirical work in law and society comes out of the United States. Americans have many virtues, but a gift for languages is not one of them; few scholars in the United States are aware of any work done in other countries, unless it appears in English. For many countries, there is nothing to be aware of, but it is hard to see how they could know this *a priori*; in others there is a growing body of work.

It seems to me of particular importance to break down, somehow, the national barriers. Or course, one cannot ship simultancous translators all over the world. to aid in this enterprise. But it is important to communicate across boundaries, to pool resources and knowledge. If scholars uncover anything at all that has general validity, or suggests broader hypothesis, there must be some way to disseminate it, so that we do not waste time, going over the same ground. This collection of essays aims to bridge, in some small way, the communication gap. It aims at comparison, exchange of ideas, mutual learning. From these essays, one extracts a sense of what is going on in many countries, in many schools of thought. This knowledge helps us at least to grope toward generalizations in the middle range. The subject of the following essays is the sociology of the judicial process. This is not the whole domain of law and society, but is a crucial part of it. Courts have been at the core of the practice of law, at the core of the ethnographic study of law, at the core of law reform efforts in various countries. For common law scholars, the judicial process seems a natural focus, because of traditional emphasis (some think overemphasis) on courts and judges in common law thought. But "courts" have been defined largely as appellate courts. Conventional legal scholars studied little else but official reports of appellate courts, making no attempt to go beyond and investigate how lower courts worked, and what impact courts made on society. Here, to the contrary, in every essay, for every country, the focus is on the system as a system, on the actual work and effect of courts and court-like institutions, as molded by general and particular social forces.

I. Der Einfluß allgemeiner gesellschaftlicher Kräfte auf die Formen gerichtlicher Verfahren

Torstein Eckhoff

The relationship between judicial and political branches of government

I. Classical Separation of Power Theory

Since the times of Montesquieu (1) and the Federalists (2) it has been usual to regard government as composed of certain powers whose function is to "check and balance" each other. In Montesquieu's scheme these powers were the King, the nobility and the people. A balance between them should be obtained by vesting the executive function in the King and dividing the legislative power between the nobility and the people. Montesquieu did not regard the courts as power-holders because he conceived judicial decisions as passive reproductions of the will of the legislator (3). The Federalists, however, assigned a more active role of the courts. They considered the judiciary as the third power of government, besides the legislature and the executive. Courts of justice should, in the words of Alexander Hamilton, be "the bulwarks of a limited constitution against legislative encroachments", and it was therefore important that the judges possessed an "independent spirit" (4).
It is questionable whether the classical theory of separation of power offers an adequate description of present day government. It does not take into account the complexities of the modern state, where administrative agencies have taken over many of the functions previously left to the courts, and it leaves out of consideration centers of power outside the state apparatus, as for instance political parties, trade unions, business organizations and multinational companies. For a more detailed analysis of balance of power in our societies it would certainly be appropriate to take into consideration a much larger number of actors than the classical three branches of government.
However, for purposes of this paper it is not necessary to take these complications into account. My aim is to discuss the relationships between the judicial branch of government and the political branches. The latter expression is here used as a common designation of the legislature and the executive. It is not my intention to imply anything about the functions of courts through the use of the terms "political" and "judicial". For instance, I would not deny that the courts may also act "politically" in some broader sense of that word.
Another weakness of the classical division of power theory is that it gives a one-sided picture of the relationship between the different branches of government. Montesquieu's point of departure was the assumption that power has a tendency to be misused. Therefore "things must be so arranged that power is checked by power" (5). The main purpose of dividing power between different

* Notes on pages 22 f.

organs was in other words to enable them to prevent each other from doing harm. This negative aspect of the relationship was emphasized also in the writings of the Federalists.

To be sure, it has been one of the functions of courts to prevent the executive and legislative branches of government from misusing their power. But this is only one aspect of the relationship, and it is probably not the most important. There is, after all, much more cooperation than conflict between the different branches of government. The courts get much of their resources from the legislature and executive and they render services in return. My suggestion is therefore that we look upon the relationship as a kind of exchange (6). In the following section an attempt will be made to describe some of the services and counter services which are exchanged. In the two last sections I will discuss whether conceptions of balance – and lack of balance – in the exchange relationship can help to explain conflicts between courts and other organs of the state as well as gradual changes over time in judicial activities.

II. The Exchange Model

Let us first take a look at the courts' resources, i.e. the factors which enable them to make decisions and to get these respected.

Some of the resources have their basis in the heritage of legal ideals, principles, and ways of reasoning that judges are supposed to master during the course of legal education and professional training. Whether or not legal learning is a powerful resource depends upon the prestige of law in the society and upon the reputation of judges within the legal profession. This source of power is only indirectly and slowly affected by actions of the political branches of government. In addition to the *informal* authority, which the judges possess because they are learned and respected members of the legal profession, there is also their *formal* authority to make final decisions backed by a threat of force. These power-resources stem to a large extent from constitutional or statutory provisions enacted by the political branches of government. Courts may be able to extend their own jurisdiction, or to restrict it, since they have the power to interpret the provisions determining the scope of their authority. But to some extent at least they are dependent on the willingness of the legislature and executive to recognize their power as legitimate and to enforce their decisions. Much of the formal authority vested in the courts and the apparatus for enforcement of court decisions can therefore be regarded as resources given to the courts by the legislative and executive authorities. And the underlying expectation is usually that the courts will render certain services in return.

Another resource is the body of rules, principles and policies which serve as premises of judicial decisions. It may sound strange to characterize the substantive rules of law as a resource, since these rules limit the freedom of decision-making. It should, however, be born in mind that rules not only set bounds but also give guidance, support and protection. They facilitate decision-making by pointing to relevant factors and by giving the decision-maker the right to dismiss, as irrelevant, a multitude of arguments and considerations which might have confused and bothered him. The rules also serve to protect the judge by limiting the scope of relevant criticism, and they make it easier for him to resist undue influence because he can defend himself by referring to his duty to follow the law.

To be sure, not all the rules, principles and policies on which courts base their decisions stem from the political branches of government. But some of them do. And judges have developed a technique of argumentation which enables them to pretend that they find the law even when they actually make it. For instance, references to a more or less fictious "intention of the legislator" may serve to conceal the decision-makers own value judgments. Thus, the responsibility can be placed on the legislature, and authority can be transmitted from the norm-system to the individual decision, even when there is much latitude for judicial discretion.

We will now turn to some of the services rendered by the courts.

One central judicial task is to decide in individual cases what is right and wrong according to law. Many administrative agencies have similar tasks, but administrative application of law is – at least in most Western countries – the object of judicial control, whereas the courts' determination of right and wrong cannot be contested by any organ outside the court system.

The authority of courts to make these final decisions has particular importance where there is a question of applying force. It is necessary for the government to be able to use force in order to secure the fulfilment of private and public obligations and discourage deviant behaviour. But the use of force is frightening and will easily meet resistance if it is not considered legitimate. And unless the rulers are considered infallible there will always be a suspicion that those who are interested in using power may misuse it. To leave the final decision to independent and impartial courts therefore helps to make the application of force appear more legitimate. By serving as a guarantee against arbitrariness and partiality the courts make it easier for the political branches of government to carry through their policies – through force if necessary.

To determine what is right and wrong can also be a way of settling disputes – between individuals, or between an individual and the government, or between different state organs, or (in a federal system) between state and federation. Judicial procedure is certainly not the only way of resolving conflicts. We have different forms of negotiation and mediation where the emphasis is not on questions of right and wrong but on adjusting the interests of the parties. There are also types of arbitration and of administrative decision-making where methods of conflict resolution more or less similar to the judicial may be applied.

The extent to which conflicts are brought before the courts depends upon a variety of factors (7). Among other things it is important whether there exist other ways of getting the conflict resolved. Sometimes the courts are given a monopoly to authorize certain actions or to change statuses, for instance to inflict punishment and to grant divorce. But in many instances there is a choice between different means of settlement, and when that is the case the effectiveness and costs of the alternatives will play a role. What is considered an appropriate way of getting the dispute settled, depends again on the attitudes of the persons concerned. The more stress they lay on the moral value of being right, the more likely it is that they will go to the courts. Their attitudes towards the courts are also of significance. Particularly important is whether or not they consider judges to be more qualified to determine what is right and wrong and more impartial than other decision-makers.

The effectiveness of the different kinds of conflict resolution will also vary according to the type of conflict concerned. And what kinds of conflicts are likely to occur in a society depends on its social, economic and political structure. One point which I want to mention in this connection is that courts may be particularly useful in federations and in states where the legislative and executive branches of government are independent of each other, because conflicts between federation and state or between different branches of government may be difficult to resolve by means other than adjudication.

It is obviously useful to society to have an apparatus for conflict resolution. But something must be said to account for the fact that it may be advantageous to the political branches of government to be able to leave the settlement of certain disputes to independent courts, rather than give these tasks to administrative or executive officers.

Firstly, the disposition of conflict cases may be a burden on the administrative apparatus, hinder the execution of other tasks, and create difficulties in relation to clients. Moreover, an independent organ will sometimes better be able to resist pressure from the parties. Threats and promises can make a greater impression on those who are responsible for carrying out administrative or executive tasks than on an independent organ. Secondly, from the point of view of the parties it may be more satisfactory that the conflict is resolved by independent courts, because these often will appear more impartial and inspire more confidence than administrative or executive agencies. This is especially true if the state itself is a party or has party interests. And even if there is no clear party interest, political authorities may easily be suspected, out of regard for the solution of other tasks, of having interest in the outcome of the conflict which weaken their impartiality. Courts of law will therefore in many instances be more effective resolvers of conflicts.

In the history of Western nation-states it has been a rather general trait that judicial power was originally vested in the King, or his council, or some other governing body, and was only gradually transferred to independent courts. Something similar has happened in many large organizations. For instance, the international maritime conferences established "neutral bodies" some years ago, to settle certain types of disputes between the organization and its members. Previously these disputes had been settled by the conference's board (8). General Motors has similarly set up an impartial umpire to resolve disputes between the company and its dealers (9). The United Nations by resolution in 1949 established a domestic tribunal to decide conflicts between the organization and its employees (10).

These examples give some support to the assumption that the political leadership of a state or an organization sometimes find it convenient to be able to hand over to an independent organ the power to settle certain disputes and to decide when force can be applied.

It follows that independence is a crucial aspect of the judicial system (11). It makes the courts better suited to legitimate the application of force, and it may – at least in some cases – make them more suited to settle disputes. In other words, the political branches of government can, by giving the courts a certain amount of independence, secure more valuable services from them. The ways in which independence is guaranteed differ from one country to another. A usual pattern is, however, that judicial decisions are final (i.e. not subject to review by any organ outside the court system) and that judges are protected in their decision-making against interference from the executive as well as from political parties, pressure-groups and others.

Judicial independence can be conceived as an additional resource given to the courts. It has consequences not only for their capacity to perform the functions already mentioned, but offers them also an opportunity to set policy and make law. The scope of judicial policy-making varies from one system of law to the next, depending upon such factors as the amount of legislative acitivity, the kind of language used in statutory provisions, the methods of statutory interpretation, the weight laid on precedents, etc. But even more important than the latitude for discretion thus left to the courts is the way in which they use their discretionary power. In some countries the courts have not been afraid of counteracting the policies of the legislative and the executive powers, whereas in other countries they have shown a high degree of loyalty or deference to the political branches of government.

Judicial policy-making can in some instances be conceived as a service rendered the political auhtorities. It is often convenient for a legislator to use broad and unspecified language in the statutory provisions and leave to the courts to work out in detail the ways in which social interests should be promoted. But this presupposes that legislators and judges by and large share the same values. The situation is quite different if political and judicial authorities pursue incompatible policies. In that case judicial policy-making will not be a service to the political authorities but will on the contrary hinder them in carrying out their own objectives.

III. Conflicts between judicial and political branches of government

Where political and judicial authorities pursue incompatible policies tension and, in some cases, open conflict may result.

In the U.S.A., in the first part of the 19th century, beginning with the presidency of Thomas Jefferson, there was considerable conflict between political and judicial authorities (12). In the background was considerable popular dissatisfaction with the courts – particularly among farmers. Many of them were heavily in debt. They felt judges represented the wealthy classes and that they favoured creditor interests. One cure was to democratize the courts. Judges were to be elected by popular vote, for a definite term, rather than appointed for long terms or for life. This reform was never instituted in the federal courts; but by 1850 most of the states had provided for election of some or all of their judges.

Political-judicial conflict did not, however, cease. Among others, President Roosevelt came into conflict with the Supreme Court in the 1930's after the court invalidated important parts of the president's New Deal legislation (13). Roosevelt proposed to "pack" the court by appointing a number of new judges to sit alongside the old ones. But the plan met strong resistance and was never authorized by Congress. Meanwhile, the court changed its course – perhaps because it felt the pressure – and ultimately, deaths and retirements gave Roosevelt a court more to his liking.

A somewhat different course of events took place in South Africa in the

1950's (14). A legislative enactment limiting the political rights of the black population was declared unconstitutional by the Supreme Court in 1952. In response to this, the legislature created a special appellate court – composed of members of Parliament – to hear appeals from judgments of the ordinary courts which invalidated enactments of the legislature. This special court reversed the judgment of the Supreme Court. In turn the Supreme Court declared that the legislation creating the special court was invalid, and the judgment of that "court" was a legal nullity. The government did not resubmit the invalidation to the special court. But it did not give in. In 1955, a bill was passed increasing the quorum in the Appellate Division of the Supreme Court from five to eleven in any case where the validity of an Act of Parliament was considered. The government characterized the bill as a purely administrative measure to "ease and smoothe the functions of the Court." But the real purpose was to make it possible for the six new judges to outvote the other five. Next the government dissolved and reconstituted the Senate on a basis which secured the government a two-thirds majority. A new Separate Representation Bill was introduced; it obtained the necessary two-thirds majority. And when this Act was brought before the Supreme Court in 1956 it was upheld by a 10 to 1 vote.

The last example I want to mention is a conflict still going on in Finland. President Kekkonen gave a newspaper interview on his 70th birthday, in 1970, in which he criticized the courts and the legal profession. His accusations were much the same sort as those that were made against the American judiciary in the first half of the 19th century. His point of departure was a study made by the Finnish sociologist Raimo Blom concerning public attitudes toward courts (15). The study disclosed that a considerable minority of the population lacked confidence in the impartiality of the judiciary. President Kekkonen maintained that this lack of confidence was due to the conservatism of the legal profession. The judiciary was among other things accused of sabotaging progressive legislation. The reform program advocated by Kekkonen was substantially the same as that advanced over a century before, in the United States: namely, that judges should be elected for a term of years.

Kekkonen's attack on the courts led to a discussion in the Parliament and later to the appointment of a small committee to work out a reform program. The committee finished its work in December 1971. Its report (16) starts out with a historical survey of the development of courts in Finland and other countries and a critical analysis of the classical theory of the separation of powers. Montesquieu's program was, according to the committee, historically conditioned by the fact that the kings had misused their absolute power. It was a step in the right direction to divide the power, because it opened up the possibility of development toward more democratic government. But the time had now come for completing this development by bringing the judiciary under democratic control. Judicial policy-making should be controlled by political authorities, although the independence of courts in deciding individual cases should be preserved. The committee did not explain how this combination of dependence and independence can be put into practice. Indeed, the distinction between "policy" and "nonpolicy" decisions is quite a shaky one. Judges make policy and create new law in the course of deciding individual cases.

The committee realized that democratization of the judicial system had to be carried out in stages. It suggested among other things reform of legal education and of the legal aid system. With regard to the judiciary the committee proposed as a first step towards democratization that judges should be appointed for a term of years and not, as at present, for life.

The president's initiative and the committee's report gave rise to intense discussions. Those who oppose the proposals regard them as attacks on judicial independence, and fear that rule of law will be undermined. This criticism has mostly come from bench and bar, and from conservative politicians; left wing groups have approved of the proposal, or have found it too moderate. The discussion is still going on; and it is uncertain whether any part of the program of democratization will be actually carried out.

It is common in the conflict-situations described that courts are accused of being too conservative. Additional examples of situations where courts are said to lag behind in the process of social change could easily be adduced. On the other hand, some courts have been more willing than other branches of government to initiate social change, for instance the United States' Supreme Court during the Chief Justiceship of Earl Warren. The South African court tried to protect the political rights of the underdogs. But judicial conservatism still seems to be the most usual cause of conflict.

Another lesson we can learn from the examples is that courts are likely to lose when they engage in open conflict with the other branches of government. When the political branches make use of their power to amend the constitution, enact new laws, and if necessary appoint new judges, the courts will, as a rule, have to yield.

But the strength of the judicial branch of government varies a great deal from one society to another. Courts will have a stronger position where there is a division of power between the legislature and the executive – as in the United States – compared to countries where these powers are joined as is usually the case in parliamentary states. For the same reason, a divison of power between federal and state organs tends to strengthen the position of federal courts. Ideological factors are also important, in particular the strength of the rule of law ideology compared to the strength of a strict democratic principle of majority rule.

Even though the political branches of government sometimes have reasons to be dissatisfied with court decisions, open conflicts of the kinds mentioned above occur relatively rarely. Both the legislature and the executive seem to be interested in avoiding such conflicts, and there is good reason for this caution. The political costs of a struggle with the judiciary can be high; and such a struggle could also reduce the future usefulness of the courts if they were forced to conform. They could, as already mentioned, become less fitted to settle disputes and to legitimate the use of governmental force if they lost too much of their independence. Becauce of the advantages derived from leaving these matters to independent courts, it may be worthwhile to tolerate judicial independence even if legislative and executive policies to some extent are impaired or frustrated by court decisions. How much is worthwhile to tolerate may vary with the relative strength of the different branches of government, with the value of the services rendered by courts to the political authorities, and with the degree to which deviant judicial policy-making upsets the plans or the feelings of the other branches. In other words, it is a question of balance in the exchange relationship.

IV. *Changes over time in the business and functions of courts*

I now leave the instances where open conflict between courts and political authorities has occurred and turn to a development which has taken place in my own country (Norway) (17).

In the last 150 years the number of judges in Norway has doubled, while the population has quadrupled. Public administration has grown rapidly in the same period. A great number of administrative boards and agencies are today engaged in law enforcement and conflict resolution. And arbitration has more or less replaced litigation as a means of settling certain commercial disputes. Thus a great deal of the tasks previously performed by the courts are handed over to other organs.

The courts are instead charged with certain new tasks. They have since the beginning of the nineteenth century assumed the power to control the legality of administrative action, and toward the end of the century they also began to review Acts of Parlimanent. In the years between 1890 and 1920 several statutory provisions were declared unconstitutional. But after that time the courts gradually became more tolerant of legislation, and in the last 40 years only two laws have been invalidated. Judicial control over administration is, however, exercised to a greater extent than previously. But in administrative cases, too, the courts take care to avoid conflicts with the highest political organs of government.

The increased importance of judicial control over administration cannot compensate for the diminishing part courts have come to play in other fields. Courts are used less than before to resolve conflicts, and their importance as policy makers is probably also reduced. The decline has not been the result of any outspoken dissatisfaction with the work of courts. Public administration has been much more subject to criticism than the judiciary. Still, when new tasks arise, they are given to the administration and not to the courts. And the courts have become more and more reluctant to interfere with policies pursued by the other branches of government.

The exchange model offers a possible explanation of the development. Changed social conditions seem to have reduced the value of the kinds of services which the courts can render. The demand for these services has therefore decreased, and they are less important than they previously were for the political branches of government. The position of the courts is thereby weakened. But they have been able to adapt themselves to the new conditions. They have, for one thing, taken care not to deviate too much from the policies pursued by the political authorities, and no serious conflict has occurred.

The development which I have outlined is probably not peculiar to Norway. Data from other Western countries seem to indicate a general decline of judicial activities – in spite of the fact that the number of legal issues to be resolved has certainly increased (18). The question therefore arises whether some common feature in the development of Western nations in the last century has reduced the usefulness of judicial services. It is of course difficult to answer this question. But my guess is that industrialization has been the most important factor.

In a modern industrialized society traditional legal methods of regulating behavior lose much of their importance. Financial and monetary measures, subsidies and concessions are by and large more efficient means of exerting influence than rules of law backed by force. And since the political branches of government therefore are less dependent on application of force than they once were, judicial legitimation of the use of force has diminished in importance. Industrialization has probably also reduced the popularity of judicial conflict resolution. Most other ways of getting conflicts resolved take less time than litigation, and they are as a rule cheaper and less likely to injure the relationship between the parties. In an industrialized society the time factor becomes increasingly significant, and so do economic calculations which often make a compromise much to be preferred to litigation. The moral value of establishing who is right and who is wrong, which has been one of the main motives for going to court, is probably more important in a stable peasant society than it is in a changing world, where people are oriented more toward the future than toward the past.

Summary

Der Artikel wird eingeleitet von einer Kritik der klassischen Lehre zur Gewaltenteilung. Das Verhältnis zwischen Gerichten und politischen Organen wird nicht vorwiegend von gegenseitiger Beschränkung, von Verhinderung des Mißbrauches von Macht, sondern von gegenseitiger Dienstleistung geprägt. Es wird also vorgeschlagen, diese Beziehung als ein Tauschverhältnis anzusehen – die verschiedenen in den Tausch eingebrachten Leistungen und Gegenleistungen werden aufgezählt. Danach wird das Tauschmodell zur Erklärung des Verlaufs bestimmter Konflikte zwischen Gerichten und politischen Organen in den USA, Südafrika und Finnland herangezogen. Abschließend wird eine Entwicklung untersucht, die in den letzten 100 bis 150 Jahren in Norwegen und wohl auch in anderen westlichen Ländern beobachtet werden kann: daß nämlich die Bedeutung der Gerichte teilweise reduziert wurde. Es wird versucht, dies unter Zuhilfenahme des Tauschmodells als Folge der Industrialisierung zu erklären – ausgehend von der Annahme, Industrialisierung trage zur Verminderung des Wertes judizieller Dienste bei und stelle daher die Gerichte im Tauschverhältnis schlechter: sie können nicht mehr so große Gegenleistungen in Form von Einfluß und Macht beanspruchen wie früher.

Notes

1 Montesquieu, De l'Esprit des Lois (1748).
2 Alexander Hamilton, John Jay, James Madison, The Federalist (1788).
3 "Mais les judges de la nation ne sont .... que la bouche qui prononce les paroles de la loi, des être inanimés qui n'en peuvent modérer ni la force ni la rigueur" (op. cit., Tome I, Livre XI, Ch. VI).
4 The Federalist, No. 78.
5 Op. cit., Tome I, Livere XI, Ch. IV.
6 On the use of exchange theory in sociology and social psychology see e.g. George Caspar Homans, Social Behaviour, its Elementary Forms (London 1961), Peter M. Blau, Exchange

and Power in Social Life (N.Y. 1964), John W. Thibaut and Harold H. Kelley, The Social Psychology of Groups (N.Y.1959) and Torstein Eckhoff, Justice: Its Determinants in Social Interaction (Rotterdam 1974).

7 Cf. Torstein Eckhoff, "The Mediator, the Judge and the Administrator in Conflict-resolution", Acta Sociologica, Vol. 10, 1966, pp. 148–172 (also in B–M. Blegvad (ed.), Contributions to the Sociology of Law, Copenhagen 1966).

8 Cf. Arvid Frihagen, Linjekonferanser og kartell-lovgivning (Shipping Conferences and Anti-trust-Laws), Oslo 1963, pp. 139–41.

9 Cf. Stewart Macaulay, Law and the Balance of Power, The Automobile Manufacturers and their Dealers (1966), p. 203.

10 The events leading to the establishment of this tribunal are analysed by Yehezkel Dror, "Organizational Functions of a Domestic Tribunal: A Case Study of the Administrative Tribunal of the United Nations", The British Journal of Industrial Relations, vol 2, 1964, pp. 42 ff.

11 The importance of judicial independence is discussed more in detail in Torstein Eckhoff, "Impartiality, Separation of Powers and Judicial Independence", Scandinavian Studies in Law, vol. 9, 1965, pp. 11-48.

12 Cf. Lawrence M. Friedman, A History of American Law (New York 1973) pp. 109–121 and J. Williard Hurst, The Growth of American Law (Boston 1950), pp. 134–140.

13 Cf. Fred Rodell, Nine Men (New York 1955), pp. 213–254.

14 Reported in Geoffrey Marshall, Parliamentary Sovereignty and the Commonwealth (Oxford 1957), pp. 139 ff.

15 Some of Blom's findings are reported in English in Jette Moller Nielsen (ed.), Retssociologi i Norden, II (Sociology of Law in the Nordic Countries, II), (Copenhagen 1970).

16 Rettsväsendekommissionens betänkande (Report of the Administration of Justice Committee) (Kommitteebetänkande 1971: B 112, Helsingfors 1971).

17 The development is described in greater detail by Vilhelm Aubert, "Law as a Way of Resolving Conflicts: The Case of a Small Industrialized Society" in Laura Nader (ed.), Law in Culture and Society (Chicago 1969).

18 See e.g. Friedman's and Toharia's papers in this volume, where data from U.S.A., England and Spain are presented.

Lawrence M. Friedman

Trial Courts and their Work in the Modern World*

The topic of this essay, at its broadest, is, what effect does social change have on the courts and the way they work?
This is, of course, a question which we cannot even tentatively answer. We will confine ourselves to a few remarks on changes that have taken place during the last century, in several Western countries that have undergone rapid economic growth. First, we will explore the meaning of the question itself. What *is* a court? We will discuss the functions of courts, advance some propositions about the way they have responded to social change, and, finally, set out some relevant facts and figures.

I. At the threshold, we meet the question, what exactly do we mean when we ask about the effect of social change on "courts." What a "court" is, is not self-evident. Indeed, it is in every sense a problem. Courts are not objects in the real world, but social institutions. Different societies label quite a diverse array of institutions as "courts." There are almost as many definitions as there are societies.
Generally speaking, a "court" can be defined in one of two ways: First, in terms of the function of courts, that is, what they do. Second, one can also define as a court any institution that has a particular structure or form. For example, one might make the presence of an independent third party, the judge, part of the definition of a court.
A good functional definition is quite hard to frame. This is because it is hard to think of a distinctive and unique function, which is carried on only by a set of institutions that we can or do conveniently call by the name of "courts." Of course, we can always sidestep this difficulty by calling *any* institution that performs a courtlike function, a "court." But if we stretch too far the common meaning of the word "court," we run the risk of robbing ourselves of any meaningful boundary for the term. For example, if we decide on dispute-settlement as our function, and call any agency that settles disputes a court, then a father runs a "court" when he stops a fight between two quarreling children and gives a toy to one and not the other. For some purposes, it might make sense to study this father, along with the Cour de Cassation or the House of Lords-if we were studying dispute settlement in general, for example. For other purposes, to study family disputes might be quite inappropriate. A functional definition can be made more precise, and more useful, by bringing in additional

* Research underlying this paper was supported by Grant GS 33821, National Science Foundation, U.S.A. The opinions expressed are of course my own.

elements – for example, by restricting the term "courts" to institutions of a certain formal or structural character. This, however, verges once more on institutional definition.

Institutional definitions themselves vary. The common image of a court induces some kind of picture of a small system, with three roleplayers. Two are "parties," who share some question or dispute; the third is an outsider, the judge, who resolves the issue between them. Usually, we think that a judge is a man with authority; he can issue binding orders, backed by some element of force; usually too we think that a court is distinctive, in that the judge bases his decision at least partially on principles or rules. In other words, he has not invented his criteria on the spot, nor have the parties themselves wholly stipulated them. They have some sort of prior or independent existence. This is the idea of *law*. None of these elements is absolutely vital, or to be taken as dogma. In many "cases" in "courts" only one party appears; this party goes to the judge for some ruling, or advice, or for some change of status – an uncontested adoption, or a petition for a change of name.

Many jurists doubt the necessity of an element of sanction or force. If we insisted too literally on this point, we would exclude from the concept of "court" many institutions which look and act like courts, but which do not have the backing of an organized state. This is particularly true of "courts" in some preliterate societies. These "courts," however, invoke other sanctions – perhaps public esteem or disapproval, or the judgment of the gods.

More important is the fact that this rough definition does not and cannot distinguish between "courts" and administrative tribunals, not to mention the work of arbitrators in labor and commercial disputes. A hearing before an English rent tribunal, or before the National Labor Relations Board in the United States, would fit the definition exactly. On the other hand, the definition does not fit well the routine work that many "courts" constantly perform – probating wills, processing uncontested claims. These are cases where the court does not adjudicate anything in the ordinary sense of this word.

We will ignore this second point for now. But the first point is crucial. Try as we might, it is hard to draw a rational line that will separate "courts" from other tribunals. In plain fact, the word "court," in the United States, or Great Britain, or France, is used to refer to specific institutions, with a specific history and tradition. Social scientists studying legal systems do not include, in their definition of a "court," the idea that judges should hold appointments for life, or should be trained in law schools, or should come from a certain class background, or must be barristers, or members of the bar, or must have served an apprenticeship, or memorized certain parts of a civil code; or that judges are bound to decide cases by looking at precedents, or by subsuming the facts of a case under some section of a code, or whatever. But these are among the things that some people in some societies do understand as essential to a "court"; these are ideas that have at least folk-validity, like the idea that a whale is a fish, or that English is descended from Latin. Folk-notions about courts are, of course, highly relevant *social* facts.

If we ask, then, about the fate of "courts" in the modern world, we are asking not one but two questions. First, what is the fate of certain institutions which people in particular countries call courts – whose specific histories and traditions cling to them like barnacles; and, second, what is the fate of "courts" in the broader sense of our general definition? The two questions will very likely have different answers, just as, if one asked what had become of executive power in Great Britain since 1800, one gets a different answer than if one asked, what became of the power of the king.

II. We turn now to the question of the *functions* of courts. The word function is somewhat ambiguous here. It can refer to what courts actually do, regardless of anybody's intent, and it can also refer to some sort of mandate of "courts," imposed by society (or less vaguely, by people who count in society). Then again, it can mean both in some sort of combination; both meanings refer to important aspects of courts in society. We will try to list a few major headings that meet both criteria: they describe what courts do, and also what people seem to expect of them.

Dispute settlement is clearly one of the great and historic functions. It is the one that most clearly fits the traditional, usual picture of a court, and the standard definition. One thinks of King Solomon and the two women arguing over the baby both claimed; or the judges among the Barotse, described by Gluckman (1)*; or closer to home, two quarrelling neighbors, each claiming title to a piece of land, or a couple locking horns over alimony and custody, or a seller suing a buyer for refusal to pay the price of a carload of lumber; or an action for libel and slander.

At the outset, one should note that the idea of dispute "settlement" has rather different overtones in some of these examples, compared to others. What is different is the kind of dispute. Let us take a typical modern example: a woman falls to the floor in a bus, and injures herself; later, she claims the driver had been negligently driving, and she sues his company. She will of course either win, lose, or settle out of court. In this sense, the dispute will come to an end. But was it ever a "dispute"? Not if the word carries some overtone of conflict, acrimony, disharmony. That would be dispute settlement as described by many anthropologists: putting an end to a feud, restoring social harmony, setting things right again in society – and never mind winners and losers. This kind of "dispute settlement" simply does not fit most of the work of formal courts in Western nations. These courts will, to be sure, decide which party is right and which is wrong, who wins and who loses. But they have no particular talent for or interest in the expressive, personal aspects of the case, if any. Indeed, most cases will have no such aspects. If they do, the court will studiously ignore them, at least in that part of their work that leaves a formal residue behind (2). Rather, the court will seem to be trying to narrow the issues, in a businesslike way – to clear away underbrush, the better to resolve some precise legal point. The village court, on the contrary, will try to arrange the case to gather and keep in much of what the Western court leaves out – all sorts of smoldering disputes and feelings that lie at the root of the problem. The striking contrast between the two styles, of course, is no accident; a small, face to face society cuts its court to a different pattern of social need, compared to a society of big cities and heavy industry.

Despite this, there are some similarities, regardless of the society, among all cases of "dispute settlement." For one thing, the litigants, on both sides, act as private

* Notes on page 38.

parties; whether roughly equal in wealth and power (as two neighbors tend to be) or unequal, as, for example, in actions by individuals against insurance companies or international oil cartels, in tort; or when a large department store sues a customer for the money he owes. The parties do not represent the collectivity, the state, or act in a collective capacity (3). One or both will have invoked the court, appealed to its authority, in an attempt to get the dispute resolved. Presumably, both parties expect a fair, impartial decision; certainly the plaintiff does. The parties will be at odds over some matter of fact, or over some duty or right. Or they will disagree about what some norm means, or whether it really applies to their situation; but nominally at least they both adhere to the norm. They do *not* (in our definition) expect the rules to change in the middle of the case; and they do not challenge the legitimacy of the court, or the judge, or the rules. They expect stability; they expect legal process to stand still, at least during their lawsuit. Actually, people in litigation, in all societies, expect this kind of stability; exceptions – which we will discuss – are few and are rare.

We stipulated that in a case of *dispute settlement*, both parties were private, or acting in a private capacity. But there are cases in which the party who brings a case represents the state or the general community; or claims to act on its behalf. This litigation forms a type and fills a function we will call *social control*. The clearest example is the ordinary criminal trial.

The parties – state and individual – here too do not expect rules to change in the course of the trial. What is distinctive about cases of social control is the locus of initiative: it lies in a public agency, acting in the public behalf. And the point of the case, as a general rule, is to support or enforce general or public norms of the community, which the defendant or the accused has violated.

This last sentence has a naive ring to it; criminal justice, in many countries, is on the whole, a dreary, repetitive system, processing hundreds of small thieves and drunks at a time; so grand a phrase as "community norms" in the Durkheim sense, hardly suits it at all; what some see is merely the dull, mindless cruelty of the modern state, a ruling class, or a thoughtless bourgeoisie; or the narrow mind of the police; or at worst the will of a tyrant. Nonetheless, in the background of each case are real rules and norms. They are not necessarily the same as the paper rules, but *some* form of social control is imposed, *some* kind of norm is enforced.

Furthermore, one can draw, for criminal law, a distinction similar to that drawn for cases of dispute settlement. Different types correspond to different kinds of society. Some criminal trials will be narrowly directed at one precise issue – did John Smith, the accused, really break into this house on Oak Street, on October 9, and steal the silver? In many countries, indeed, it would be grossly improper to bring in evidence of anything else. Side issues, and what Smith did in the past, are not "relevant." On the contrary, in face to face societies, and in the Socialist countries, courts may pay more attention to the context, will search for the social meaning of what happened, will want to look at the accused as a whole person, and the situation as a total situation. This is because the theory of social control, which guides the court, stresses deterrence or "education" or rehabilitation in some broad sense. The court feels it is vital to show the accused how wrong he has been; how his deeds have hurt society, or himself, or some important value. If he does not or cannot see it, at least the audience in the coutroom should learn to act or learn to fear, or society at large must draw some lesson.

Social control in the courts of the West is in some ways more mysterious. Why the elaborate procedures? Why the deliberate blindness to context? Why is punishment furtive and private? It is easy to understand what public hanging was supposed to accomplish; much harder to see what is accomplished when a man is put to death in the middle of the night, alone except for a handful of reporters and the official witnesses. Perhaps the very absurdity of this system has helped to weaken the death penalty. The trial of offenders no longer carries the main burden of deterrence, hence of social control. The police, for example, are far more important. Full trials (which only a tiny minority of the accused go through) are almost an afterthought.

Social control is, of course, more than criminal law. In the modern state, there are literally thousands of regulatory norms, many of them primarily enforced by administrative agencies. It is part of the social control system to enforce these norms, when necessary, through "courts." Indeed, it is quite a usual practice. The formal, traditional courts have some share in this business; administrative tribunals adjudicate an immense number of cases. In all of these, the norms are known in advance, and are expected to be stable in the short run.

Increasingly, in modern times, lawsuits are also brought *against* the state, by a private individual or company (4). The claim is that the government has failed to follow its own rules, thus depriving the plaintiff of one or more of his rights or impairing some item of value. For example, a veteran might complain that the government has improperly refused to give him a pension; a land-owner can complain that the city wrongfully denied him the right to convert his house into apartments, a food company can complain that the Food and Drug Administration was wrong to seize a shipment of canned soup and condemn it. These cases, brought in court or before administrative tribunals, are the reverse of (regulatory) social control. They are cases of *review of governmental actions.*

So far we have assumed some level of *stability of norms.* The litigants expect the rules – of procedure and substance – not to change in the middle of a trial. How can we tell this? We can measure it, simply if roughly, by taking plaintiff (and defendant) at their word: do they *ask* for any change in rules? Are claims or defenses radical or innovative in tone?

Overwhelmingly, they are not. But once in a while, a plaintiff files a claim with a difference. He may ask that the court declare some statute unconstitutional, or overrule a line of cases, or adopt some grand new course of action. Theoretically, this can occur in *any* of the three types of cases mentioned (private party suing private party, government as plaintiff, government as defendant). This gives us, then, three additional types of litigation. Plaintiff can demand a new rule (of products liability, for example) in an ordinary lawsuit. Government can try to use criminal process to introduce new norms, or new ways to handle old norms – in a political show trial, for example. And a private litigant can attack the government in an innovative way. These cases are never common; but when they occur, they tend to be far more important than ordinary cases. The United States Supreme Court hears many cases in these three categories; courts in other states and countries far fewer; trial courts hardly any at all.

One last type of case should be mentioned. Courts in many countries handle great masses of routine matters – making or keeping records, registering formalities, stamping approval on claims or on changes of status. Courts process uncontested divorces by the thousands; they grind out judgments in petty, undisputed cases of debt, they probate wills, they grant petitions for change of name. In almost none of these matters is there any real "dispute." These matters may have an important effect, in the mass; but in the particular case, what the court does hardly fits the usual understanding of "adjudication."

It is true that sometimes, in these routine matters, a more serious issue arises, which calls for the skill and training of a learned judge. Most probate proceedings are utterly routine; but once in a while there is a will contest, or a disputed claim. Arguably the judge must stand by, like a doctor at a hospital, in case of emergency. No doubt some other arrangement could be made than to have these routine matters handled by a "court." Many of them are fossilized forms of what were once areas of more vigorous adjudication. Yet these matters are a distinctive and important type of judicial activity, in the traditional courts of many countries. We will refer to them as *routine administration.*

It is one thing to sketch out "functions," another to measure them. To talk about the "functions" of courts often means to talk about what court proceedings are *supposed* to accomplish. "Function" thus assumes some sort of purpose or intent, assigned by society to courts. It is almost hopeless to try to get at such an intent. It is simpler to count *outcomes* of the work of the courts, and treat these as indicators of functions. (Murderers go to jail, for example, which fulfils the function of social control.) Another crude indicator, suggested here, is the identity of the plaintiff.

III. Can we frame hypotheses about the relationship between social change and the functions of courts? We may begin by drawing a picture, somewhat idealized, of the way courts behave in a face-to-face society, far from modern economy and society. In such a society, judges are wise men, elders, respected chiefs; they sit in "court" to settle quarrels between members of the group. Trials are open, and the public eagerly attends. Access is free; there are no fees, or very small ones; procedure is simple and non-technical; ritual, where it exists, is not the mystery of a learned profession; there are no "legal" norms and rules distinct from other norms and rules in society, that is, nobody makes much about the difference between "legal" and non-legal norms. Justice will probably be quick; judgments will aim to restore harmony within the social group; the court will cast its net widely to encompass the whole situation, rather than trying to distill a single "issue" between the parties. An "issue," would be only a symptom; the court will want to deal with the causes of a dispute, not with the symptoms.

In simple societies, this is a clearly useful kind of court. Society is kept on an evem keel; conflicts do not get out of hand. Disputes get settled; at the same time, trials and proceedings are a kind of open education, teaching the community its norms. Legal process draws normative boundaries for society, reaffirms the rules, structures the moral world of the community. Social control and dispute settlement march hand in hand; indeed, it is hard to tell them apart. The rules, though invested with traditional authority, are not entirely static; a certain amount of subtle change takes place. Perhaps no one is aware that rules are changing, except when the chiefs intervene and legislate.

This pattern, obviously, does not fit all societies. It takes a small, close-knit community, where everybody, or nearly everybody, knows what is expected, where roles are rather precisely defined, where people recognize the lines of authority, and assent to them. The most obvious examples come from simpler, non-literate communities, old and new, in various parts of the world. But there are many variations. The neighborhood and comrade courts of socialist countries have some points in common with these traditional courts; so too did local courts in colonial America, some courts in the ancient world, and courts on the manors and estates of medieval England. All of these, to be sure, deviate somewhat from the idealized picture.

To repeat; in these courts, justice is open, cheap, and swift. Public opinion encourages people to bring their troubles to the judges; and people make no strong separation between legal and non-legal rules.

By way of contrast, the courts in modern, industrial societies are expensive, technical and slow. Their norms are not widely known, and accessible mainly to a learned cult of lawyers. In this sense, then, justice is far from "open." Nor is justice "open" in the literal sense. To be sure, there are seats at trials for the public. A sensational murder trial will draw a crowd; but few people come to an ordinary trial. Judge and jury will deliberate in secret. Rules of evidence screen out all irrelevant evidence, under rigid standards.

Moreover, Western societies do not seem to want their citizens to air their troubles in court. Lawsuits are positively discouraged. It is an evil to "stir up" litigation. The law favors settlement; the public agrees. A popular American handbook of the 19th Century quoted this saying:

> It is . . . a wise child that knows enough to keep out of the fire, and I should think as much of the *man* who contrives to keep out of the law; for generally speaking, like the majority of prizes in a lottery, it is a losing game even when successful. A prudent man therefore will refrain from law as long as his wrongs are tolerable or endurable (5).

To prefer conciliation to trial is, to be sure, no novelty in legal culture. The Far Eastern systems of law share this trait. There, we are told, people are encouraged to avoid formal courts in favor of informal, traditional ways of settling disputes; and compromise and adjustment are the ideal. In modern society, settlement out of court simply means do-it-yourself; the passion for settlement is a passion for throwing people back on their own resources.

The modern world did not invent this slow, expensive system, full of mysterious technicality, which we call "law." Indeed, English law (for example) is far faster and more transparent than its ancestor, the medieval common law. Medieval common law, as it appears in the sources, was basically that law which the royal courts applied to tangled land disputes among the gentry. The common law, like medieval society, was rigid, hierarchical, ceremonial, superstitious. The people who litigated had enough time, status, patience, power and gullibility to wrangle over their "estates" year after year in the courts. That a legal system should be rational (meaning clean, clear and efficient) was an idea that had not yet taken hold of people's minds. The system did not, however, *discourage* litigation; it preferred litigation to lawless, armed self-help.

Modern Western law does discourage recourse to courts, in word and in deed, at least, recourse to settle disputes. Formal court proceedings, on the whole, move very slowly, cost a lot of money, and proceed by rules that are a closed book to the average man – indeed, to the average businessman, civil servant, or the average anyone, except perhaps the average lawyer. Yet all this occurs in an age that claims to worship efficiency, rationality and science.

How are we to explain this trait of legal culture? One theory is to fix the blame on 19th century individualism. The self-reliant man was the ideal of that age. People were supposed to manage on their own, rather than to run crying to court. This explanation strikes one on the whole, as far less likely than an economic explanation – or at least what people of the time would have considered an economic explanation.

Let us, for simplicity, assume economic growth as a goal widely shared in 1800 or 1850. How might the law contribute to this end? First of all, by dismantling restrictions, and freeing trade. Second, by taking positive steps to encourage commerce and manufacture. These two aims have one key characteristic in common: they favor the sheer *volume* of transactions. The more of society's goods that are traded on the market, the better; the more traders, the better; the higher the turn-over, the better.

The economy, then, should be left as free as possible, not for its own sake, but because free trade would foster prosperity. Business, left to its own devices, would develop tools – forms and techniques – to permit and encourage rapid trade. Such forms would have a routine, standard look; their use would be as trouble free as humanly possible. A vigorous market is one in which people absorb losses in the short run, and continue to trade. They do not break off commercial relationships, in the midst of a competitive situation, nor do they funnel transactions through courts. Any legal agency, which exercises discretion, and is careful, slow and individuating, cannot help but interrupt the flow of trade. Court must therefore be a last resort.

The basic tool to discourage litigation is *cost*. Where law is technical and slow, it is expensive, even apart from dollar costs (which also rose). As costs rose, so did the threshold at which litigation became worthwhile, driving out ordinary, middle-class disputes.

But "legal" activity as a whole does *not* decline, in a developing country; quite the contrary. As the economy expands, the number of contracts, notes, and deeds increases astronomically; more corporations and other business associations are formed; more people make out wills, and leave estates to be probated. As a society modernizes, its population leaves farm and village for factory and city, commerce quickens, and the market touches the lives of more and more people. The number of transactions which need legal form goes up correspondingly. Every indicator of economic activity is reflected also within the legal system. This is only to be expected, once we admit that legal change follows and is dependent on social change. But this does *not* mean more "trials", and more use of the formal courts. In modern society, most transactions are private, that is, they take place without the intervention of employees of the state. But these transactions are nonetheless affected by law; they make use of forms or formalities specifically validated by positive law, or they depend on the advice or consent of a lawyer or notary; wills, contracts, and articles of incorporation, for example (6). Thousands of other transactions do use the courts, but routinely, to collect debts, legitimize status, and so on. Indicators of *private* legal transactions should grow faster than the population, in a period of rapid economic growth. We have no *a priori* view about what should happen to routine administration, in such a period. Debt collection, for example, may become an important industry. Somebody will do this dirty work, but whether routine debt collection will pass through a "court" depends on the legal tradition, and the inherited legal structure. Lastly, we expect the number of full, formal trials – the classic dispute settlements – to rise with the rising middle class, and then, at some point in economic development, to begin a long, slow decline.

The relationship, then, between law and economic development, in modern society, is complex; but it may show the following pattern:

(1) As a traditional society transforms itself, many changes will take place in the working rules of law. Those rules and institutions that do not fit a market economy – or, for that matter, a planned economy – and which cannot adapt, will fade away or be abolished. An ever-increasing percentage of the population will make use of formal legal instruments, and engage in formal legal transactions; the gross volume of such transactions will obviously rise. The number of litigated cases may also go up, because the *number* of consumers of law is increasing so rapidly; and a feudal legal system will be changed into a legal system for the merchant and the middle class.

(2) With industrial maturity, the rate of formal trials will level off. Costs will be permitted to rise, and this, among other things, will discourage use of the courts. Delays in trials become intolerable. The number of judges remains more or less static. The system is rationalized and "improved;" nonetheless, it is and remains foreign for the average citizen – and to the average *potential* litigant. The volume of legal transactions continues to increase very rapidly; the litigation rate, however, is now static or declining. At the trial level, formal court systems gradually lose their share of dispute settlement cases. Their work becomes, in large part, *routine administration.*

(3) Certain dramatic uses of the courts, in the United States, suggest at least the possibility of a further phase in the history of courts. Interest groups have come to make use of the courts as instruments for introducing new, sometimes startling norms. The cases that serve this function are relatively few; but they are unusually important. It is not entirely clear why this development has taken place; in any event, it can occur only when certain preconditions are met – for example, a tradition of activism among at least *some* judges and lawyers. The preconditions are absent in most countries. Even in the United States, federal courts and a few high state courts are responsible for almost all of these cases; and the cases are not particularly common. It is possible, however, that a vaguely similar development may take place in other countries, despite very different legal traditions.

(4) Courts continue to play an important part in the system of social control. Here too, routinization and mass production have elbowed aside the full, formal trial, in criminal justice (7). Regulatory aspects of social control by-pass the traditional "courts." Modern societies assign much of the work of regulation to administrative tribunals. These are supposed to have a better grasp of the subject matter; and are free from many technicalities which bind the traditional courts. In the impersonal, large-scale societies of today, social control is a far different task than in small face-to-face societies. Society cannot depend on the peer group to punish, or augment or enforce a punishment. Social control shifts emphasis to detection and punishment, away from education and community control. Socialist societies, however, try to reverse this trend.

Many of these hypotheses can be tested. They at least imply quantitative indicators. In most cases, the necessary research is still lacking. In the last part of this essay, however, we will examine some evidence bearing on the volume of litigation in civil cases, in modern nations; and the role of the formal courts in settling disputes.

IV.The evidence on volume of litigation is fragmentary and in part ambiguous, though pointing in one definite direction. The evidence on legal activity as a whole is rather scanty, too. Professor Toharia has made a careful study of data on the Spanish legal system in the recent period of rapid economic growth. He contrasts formal court proceedings with legal activity in general; for these he used notarial acts as indicators. He found that, as the Spanish economy grew, so did the gross volume of legal activity. Moreover, the volume of notarial documents showed the greatest gains in the most urban, industrial regions of Spain. Formal court proceedings did not show comparable results; these remained static or declined (8). Blegvad, Bolding and Lando have studied the volume of civil litigation at first instance in Sweden and Denmark, between 1930 and 1970. In Sweden the volume actually decreased; in Denmark, litigation grew in absolute numbers, but not in proportion to population (9).

From the late 1850's on, published judicial statistics are available for Great Britain. We are able to trace, with some accuracy, the total number of lawsuits begun in England and Wales, year by year, in the country courts, and in the High Court. These two figures, taken together, comprise all except the most petty civil cases. Until about 1900, the gross number of cases begun in court rose, both in absolute terms, and relative to population. During the four year period, 1889–1893, for example, plaintiffs brought 1,184,794 proceedings on the average. This came to 41 per 1,000 population. In 1904, 1,518,527 proceedings were begun, or about 45 per 1,000 (10). But by 1910, the statisticians reported that litigation was not keeping pace with population growth. The total cases for 1910, for all courts of first instance, amounted to 1,473,940, or 41 per 1,000 population. The rate of litigation remained static until quite recent times. In 1938, the aggregate figure for cases begun in all courts of first instance was 1,476,684 – less than in 1904; by 1962 it had increased to 1,881,829; thereafter, the number of proceedings declined once more. It was not until 1969 that the 1962 figure was bettered (1,968,678); there was a big jump in 1970, to 2,132,442, but in 1971 the totals once more declined to 1,873,911; and the figure for 1972 was 1,986,146 (11).

One can, of course, ask many questions about these figures – how they are gathered, and what they mean. Many, if not most of the county court "cases" are, as we shall see, routine debt-collection cases. There are many mysteries, large and small, in the ebb and flow of caseloads. Changes in rules of law, and in modes of procedure, also may have had an effect. But the overall impression is clear. In modern England, the rate of civil litigation simply does not keep pace with economic growth. After the turn of the century, we find an actual decline. Tremendous changes in the economy, since the second World War, have left a faint impact at best on the volume of civil litigation.

Figures for the United States are more difficult to gather, and to assess. No aggregate statistics are published for trial courts. I have gathered data for five sample years (1890, 1910, 1930, 1950, 1970), for a rural California county, San Benito. The county is sparsely settled, and its volume of litigation is tiny. In 1890, 6,412 people lived in the county. They brought 31 cases in Superior Court, or 4.8 per 1,000 population. This is less than one-eighth the English rate, which in itself warns us about the comparability of the data (12). In 1930, when the population was 11,311, there were 101 cases; or roughly 8.9 per 1,000. By 1970, though the population had grown to 18,226, only 147 cases were begun in Superior Court, that is, the rate had dropped to 8 per 1,000. The litigation rate, in short, rose proportionately until about 1930, and then began to decline. In Alameda County, much more densely populated, there were 7.6 cases per 1,000 in 1890; in 1910, this had risen to 13.5; by 1950, the volume had sunk to 9.5, rising to 11 per 1,000 to 1970, when the county had more than a million inhabitants.

It would be important, too, to take a look at the *kind* of cases that these various courts decided. In 1970, in San Benito County, most of the 147 "cases" had little to do with dispute settlement. Indeed, most were entirely routine. Eighty-two of the 147 cases – about 55 percent – were petitions for the dissolution of marriage. Almost all were completely cut and dried. Any "dispute" had been settled long before the case reached the court. Many more than half of the cases from 1970 can be safely assigned to the category of *routine administration*. Besides uncontested divorces, there were six adoption petitions. In these cases, too, the family (and social agencies) had made the real decisions long before the perfunctory business in court. The few contract cases were almost equally routine.

In 1890, too, there were many routine cases; but there were somewhat more cases of genuine disputes, and the work of the court was on the whole less stereotyped (13). In general, the *routine administrative* role of the court has grown, while its *dispute settlement* role is steadily shrinking. Despite the rise in sheer *numbers* of cases, the urban counties, on close analysis, seem to show a similar decline.

English data suggest that their local courts, that is, the county courts, have long played predominantly a *routine administrative* role. It is common knowledge that these courts are mostly used today to collect uncontested debts. They are a kind of public collection agency. This function goes far back in time. In the trial court in Shoreditch, on London's East Side, in October, 1859, out of 777 cases, plaintiffs won 746 cases, defendants only 11, and there were 20 nonsuits. The total amount recovered was £1594/10/6, so that the *average* recovered by the 746 winners was only slightly more than £2. £2 made more of a splash in the 1850's than it does today; nonetheless, it is clear that the courts were engaged mainly in processing petty claims in the mass (14).

In general, the percentage of cases in which plaintiff wins is a good indicator of whether or not a "case" is perfunctory or not. If plaintiffs win an overwhelming percentage of the cases, there is a strong suggestion that these plaintiffs are using the court to process routine cases routinely. Where there are genuine disputes, one might still expect plaintiffs to win *most* of the cases; but not 90 to 95 percent of the time. Yet the figures of the English county courts for more than a century, consistently show a tremendous success rate. In the Durham County Court, plaintiffs won 80 of 111 cases entered in the record books on February 13, 1911; seven cases were marked "paid", which can also be assigned to plaintiff's column. In 12 cases, defendant was not served; in eight, the case was struck out or withdrawn. Judgment was entered for defendant in only three cases (15). Aggregate data support the Durham findings. Plaintiffs are recorded as winning the overwhelming majority of their cases, from the earliest published statistical records on. In 1870, for example, 912,795 cases were entered in county court. 523,340 of these went to judgment. Plaintiffs won 505,744 of these judgments; there were 8,185 non-suits and only 9,411 judgments for defendant (16).

It is good to be a plaintiff in the United States as well. In San Benito County, plaintiffs or petitioners are bound to win most of the cases, if only because so much of the docket consists of uncontested suits for dissolution of marriage, and other routine matters. Craig P.Wanner studied trial court cases in three American cities, Baltimore, Milwaukee, and Cleveland for 1971 and 1972. Plaintiffs, he found, won huge majorities of the cases that went to judgment (17).

Another sign of the routine nature of legal process, is the low percentage of cases in which anything resembling a "trial" is held. Here again, some English figures are revealing. In the year 1904, a total of £6,637,186 was recovered by plaintiffs in the High Court. Presumably, then, these were not the trivial matters litigated in the county courts. But more than half of this figure was recovered through default judgments – £3,921,613; another £1,943,467 was recovered under special summary proceedings ("Order XIV"). Only £200,820 was recovered after trial by jury, about 3 percent of the total. Insignificant percentages of *cases* actually went to trial – in 1908, .06 percent of the cases went to the jury; and only 2.93 percent were even heard by a judge without jury (18).

Indeed, wherever we look, in records of English litigation, we receive the same impression. Despite the tremendous changes in English society, the number of *cases* passing through the courts does not keep pace with growing population, and growing economic complexity. "Cases" are vastly outnumbered by routine administration. In England, merchants make use of the county court to collect small debts, most often for unpaid merchandise (19). In Shoreditch County Court, 138 cases were reported for April 29, 1930. 113 of these were debt collection cases brought by sellers and listed under the rubric of "goods sold and delivered." Of the 138, cases, almost half (62) were for less than £1. 8 cases were for arrears of rent; in one, the amount sought was 2s 6d! In these cases, almost all the defendants are workers, while the plaintiffs are shopkeepers, doctors, artisans. The minute books usually record the occupations of plaintiff and defendent; in Durham County Court, in 1911, out of 94 such cases, in 76 the defendant was identified as a "miner." Most of the rest were also working class ("laborer," "coke drawer" and so on). But only three of the *plaintiffs* were miners. The rest were grocers, boot dealers, drapers, warehousemen, house furnishers, and the like. They sued for small amounts; 49 of the 94 actions were for less than £1.

In this coal mining area, the business of the courts was largely a matter of debt collection – small merchants suing working men who owed them money. In the county court of Newport and Hyde, on the Isle of Wight, there were 170 cases brought in 1890, 97 of them actions to collect for goods sold. In this rural district, however, the litigants were small merchants suing other merchants; and on the whole, larger amounts were at stake than in Durham. There was even one case where a tailor sued a "gentleman," for £5/10; a colliery proprietor sued another "gentleman" for £2/15/6 (20).

In the California counties studied, these cases of petty debt do not appear. Many of them are drawn off now into the small claims court which, though presumably designed as the poor man's court, quickly turned into the court in which the poor man is (inexpensively and routinely) sued (21). The English county courts had a strikingly similar history. Abel-Smith and Stevens state flatly that "Though it was often ... claimed ... that County Courts were for the benefit of the poor man, it is clear that the major demand for them came from the middle classes," and in operation, they simply allowed an expansion of credit and "conferred benefits not on the working man but on the small tradesman (22)."

The evidence presented here is, of course, quite fragmentary. But it does tend to confirm the general picture of the evolution of court systems in industrializing societies. More comparative data would be useful.

Clearly, court systems in modern Western nations still perform many roles. In some ways they perform them well. Courts help in the solution of many *social* problems. But they are almost totally irrelevant for resolution of disputes between individuals; and it is virtually impossible for the small man, the average man, to use them for any but a few aberrant purposes (23). For most problems and disputes, the citizen is relegated to other agencies, or to his family or group or, as is so often the case, left entirely on his own. This situation represents a social judgment, a collective decision. It is not wholly irrational. But neither is it free from social cost.

Summary

Welchen Einfluß hat sozialer Wandel auf erstinstanzliche Gerichte und deren Arbeitsweise? Zur Beantwortung dieser Frage müssen wir zuerst den Begriff „Gericht" definieren, der sich auf bestimmte historische Typen von Entscheidungsinstanzen oder auf jede Form der Intervention Dritter bei Streitigkeiten beziehen kann. Dieser Beitrag versteht unter „Gericht" die formale Gerichtsinstitution der westlichen Nationen.

Derartige Gerichte können eine Reihe von Funktionen erfüllen, nämlich

– Konfliktbereinigung (Klagen Privater gegen Private)
– Soziale Kontrolle (Staatsmacht gegen Private)
– Überprüfung von Hoheitsakten (Private gegen den Staat)

Dies alles setzt Stabilität der Normen voraus; jedoch können auch Neuerungen bewirkende Verfahren in jedem dieser drei Verfahrenstypen vorkommen. Gerichte leisten ferner ein großes Maß von routinemäßiger Verwaltungsarbeit.

In den westlichen Gesellschaften scheinen sich die Gerichte von der Rolle der Konfliktbereinigung zurückzuziehen. Dieser Prozeß korreliert mit der wirtschaftlichen Entwicklung und Industrialisierung. Ein Indikator dafür ist der zahlenmäßige Rückgang förmlicher Prozesse und die Schwerpunktverschiebung von der Konfliktsbereinigung zur routinemäßigen Verwaltung. Beweismaterial für diese Tendenzen wird aus verschiedenen Ländern untersucht.

Notes

1 Max Gluckman, The Judicial Process Among the Barotse of Northern Rhodesia (1955).
2 This is certainly true of appellate courts; less true perhaps of trial courts. Clearly, too, we are not speaking of hidden or subconscious motives which may move the court in its decisions. That is another and quite different matter.
3 Government owns property and makes contracts, and there are, therefore, many lawsuits, in which government is a party, as landlord, or tenant, or contracting party, that are cases of dispute settlement, because the governmental litigant is not acting in a governmental capacity.
4 Some of these, of course, are actions against the state in its capacity as land-owner or contracting party; these are simply treated here as dispute settlement cases. See n. 3 supra.
5 This remark is found in James Hewson, Every Man His Own Lawyer (1841), p. 6, among other places.
6 See the essay of José J. Toharia, this volume.
7 See the essay by Herbert Jacob, this volume.
8 See the essay of José Juan Toharia, this volume.
9 Britt-Mari Blegvad, P. O. Bolding, Ole Lando, Arbitration as a Means of Solving Conflicts (1973), pp. 103–105.
10 Civil Judicial Statistics 1904, p. 18.
11 Civil Judicial Statistics 1972, p. 19.
12 In California, many petty cases were brought before justice courts. Most of these records do not survive. A few cases may have been drained off into federal court, though the number is probably nor significant. See Lawrence M. Friedman and Robert V. Percival, A Tale of Two Courts, Litigation in Alameda and San Benito Counties, 10 Law and Society Rev. (1976).
13 In 6 of the 31 cases in 1890, the judge in this trial court wrote an elaborate opinion, citing authority and discussing the facts and the law rather thoroughly.
14 Shoreditch Minute Book, August-October 1859.
15 Durham County Court, P.R.O. AK2, No. 10, Plaint and Minute Book B, 1910-11, p. 18 ff.
16 Civil Judicial Statistics, 1870, xi. Plaintiffs won most first instance cases in High Court, too, but the percentages were not so overwhelming. Out of 2,319 cases in 1876, plaintiffs won a verdict in 1,341, defendants in 423; the remainder were held over, or nonsuited or withdrawn. Civil Judicial Statistics 1876, p. xxi.
17 The study is Craig P. Wanner, "The Public Ordering of Private Relations", 9 Law and Society Rev. 293 (1975).
18 Civil Judicial Statistics, 1908, p. 18.
19 This is probably why the volume of litigation per thousand population is so much higher than in California counties.
20 Cnty. Ct., Newport and Hyde, Plaint. Bk. C., 1888–92, P.R.O. AK6, No. 23, pp. 51 ff. By 1916, the county had come to resemble Durham, in that many of the defendants were identified as "laborers." P.R.O., AK6, No. 27.
21 Beatrice A. Moulton, "The Persecution and Intimidation of the Law Income Litigant as Performed by the Small Claims Courts in California", 21 Stanford L. R. 1667 (1969).
22 Brian Abel-Smith and Robert Stevens, Lawyers and the Courts, A Sociological Study of the English Legal System. 1750–1965 (1967), pp. 33–35.
23 See further on this point the essays of Rolf Bender and Christoph Strecker, and of Marc Galanter, this volume.

José Juan Toharia

Economic Development and Litigation: The Case of Spain

Spain has undergone during the last decade an impressive process of economic development which has begun to change dramatically the social structure of the country (vid. infra, section 2). In principle it can be expected that such a deep process of change must have some impact on the structure and functioning of the Spanish legal system. That is, it can be expected that new socio-economic conditions will affect in some way the volume of legal and judicial activity. By *legal activity*, I mean the voluntary and spontaneous utilization by private parties of civil norms in effect; by *judicial activity*, the legal activity before the Courts, i.e., the flow of litigation brought to them. Consequently what I am suggesting is simply that the process of socio-economic change can be expected to have some effect on the use of laws and Courts by private parties.

The literature on law and development is not rich in hypotheses about the effects of economic development on those two legal dimensions (1).* Lack of theory stems no doubt from lack of empirical, quantitative data on specific societies, from which one might build explanatory hypotheses. This essay will attempt to construct some theory, and document it with data drawn from Spain.

The main theme of this paper can be phrased as follows: what is the effect – if any – of the process of economic development (and subsequent social change) on the volume of cases brought to the Courts, i.e., on litigation, in comtemporary Spain? This basic question should not be read, however, as implying that economic development or industrialization is the only relevant factor determining the volume of litigation in a country. Countries with similar levels of development may differ widely in their rates of litigation.

The particular legal system, its norms of substance and procedure, its legal culture, the structure of its judicial institutions, and so on, all act as a basic screening device between legal or potential legal conflict and the actual level of litigation. Consequently, to establish meaningfully the possible impact of industrialization on the volume of litigation one must first try to control for the effect of the legal system on the rate of litigation. In other words, the action of the economic variable is filtered, channeled and even at times annuled by other intervening variables, related to the nature of the legal system. Section 1 of this study will be devoted to an exploratory inventory of these variables, for contemporary Spain. Only then will the specific effect of economic development on litigation in Spain be examined. Section 2 will briefly document the process of economic growth and its consequences in Spain since the early 1960's; sections 3 and 4 will be devoted to analysis of changes in legal and judicial

* Notes on pages 80 ff.

activity since that date. The last three sections (sections 5 to 7), relying on data drawn from a survey of a sample of Spanish lawyers and judges, will attempt to document the actual volume of "cases" which by-pass the courts; and the judges' perception of – and reaction to – this practice.

1. Legal Systems and Litigation (2)

a) The first and most abvious factor to consider with respect to the determination of the flow of litigation is the *legal culture* of the country under study. I use the term legal culture in Friedman's sense, as "the values and attitudes which bind the (legal) system together . . . (and which) determine what structures are used and why, which rules work and which do not, and why" (3). Attitudes and values toward litigation, held in a particular society, influence decisively the parties' proneness to bring or not bring their cases before the Courts (4). Attitudes towards litigation may also vary sharply within a single society. Linz and De Miguel, for instance, found that in Spain the businessmen whose factories are located in industrialized areas are more likely to bring labor conflicts to Labor Courts than those whose factories are located in predominantly rural areas (5). For the latter, the recourse to court was regarded as a personal failure, as a loss of moral ascendancy over employees. Court action tended consequently to be seen as an intrusion into purely private matters of a third, totally extraneous, party. Also, in *Gemeinschaft*-like social settings community social control may make the use of judicial instances unnecessary or ill considered (6). In any case it hardly seems debatable that cultural factors play a decisive role in determining the volume of litigation. Legal culture, of course, does not remain static; it evolves over time. For our purpose, however, we will treat it as stable in the short-run.

b) Generally speaking-cultural factors aside – litigation is possible only when there exists a doubt which of two or more parties would prevail. Thus, litigation is conceivable only in cases of legal indeterminacy, which must be resolved by a third, neutral party, whose right to interpret the law authoritatively is recognized beforehand. Legal indeterminacy may be due to the level of *technical quality of the law.* In principle, the more technically perfect a law (we do not concern ourselves here with its ethical merits), the less room it leaves for litigation. Under a technically perfect law, any conceivable situation arising under the law is so clearly and carefully treated, that a person involved in conflicts concerning its provisions will know beforehand, without litigation, if his legal position is superior to that of his opponent. The terms of such a law leave little room for speculation. Each party will clearly know his rights. Few actions will be brought, since claimants will always know if they will win, and, if so, the other party will know too that it is senseless to resist. Similarly, if the technical quality of the law is poor, it will abound in gaps, ambiguities and imprecisions. Parties, unable to know their rights beforehand, will often litigate to find out their rights. Outcomes will be highly unpredictable, since the imprecision of the law allows the judge maximum room for interpretation.
Many factors account for the level of technical excellence of a law. For our purposes, it will suffice to hypothesize that laws reflecting hard-to-reach compromises between conflicting groups, and which were debated in the

legislature line by line, *will* probably show a low degree of technical quality, internal consistency, terminological precision, and so on. Laws relating to bitterly controversial topics, and those which undergo deep changes during the legislative process can thus be expected to be among those with a low degree of technical quality.

The idea of a link between litigation and the technical quality of the law is not new. We find it in the ideology lying behind the European codification movement, which aimed at producing systematic, comprehensive law, easy to understand, so that any individual could find the solution to his legal problems for himself (7).

Most sociologists of law have tended to neglect the technical aspects of law, perhaps because of a sociological bias. The sociological perspective sees law as a set of institutions devised to solve specific kinds of conflicts arising in society. This identification of law with conflict-resolution ignores the vital regulatory function of law (to which conflict resolution is only ancillary: if the laws were perfect, there would be few conflicts to solve). Conflicts often arise out of technical shortcomings in the law. The fact that they seem unavoidable (since it would be utopian to think of enacting laws that were technically perfect) should not confuse us, however, about their relation to the legal system (8).

c) Another factor, which can influence the flow of litigation, is the *modernity or antiquity of the body of existing laws* (9). It is possible that the younger a legal system, the higher the propensity to litigate, since each new law seems to bring with it a flow of new cases (possibly the unresolved cases accumulated due to the shortcomings of the prior legislation). But this seems to be a transitory phenomenon: once this first wave of cases is gone, there is no reason to expect that new law will encourage litigation.

An alternative hypothesis might be that new laws are more likely to be in tune with social reality than older laws, leaving less room for ambiguity or extensive interpretation and, as a result, providing less incentive for litigation. That is, a legal system whose laws are periodically renewed to match changes in society can be expected to generate less litigation, other things being equal, than a legal system whose laws are predominantly old.

Any such relationship between modernity of the legal system and volume of litigation does not necessarily hold, however, for the volume of *legal activity* (as defined above). The modernity (or lack of modernity) of a body of laws does not necessarily mean an increased (or decreased) use of it by private parties.

In fact, one may imagine four different type-situations:

(1) the laws are old and unused. This is the case of an obsolete body of norms, which private parties will rarely find useful in their social lives but which, because of legal indeterminacy, have a tendency to foster litigation. In such a case, strong pressures for changes are to be expected (unless the state of affairs benefits legal or political elites).

(2) the laws are old, but are used by people in their daily activities. Here, legal fictions may develop, to overcome the obsolescence of the laws and to use them to regulate new situations.

(3) the laws are both new and used: this would be society with a body of laws fully adjusted and adequate to social needs. The private parties will make use of the laws in force, and will have little recourse to courts.

(4) the laws are new, but not used: an indication of the extent to which they are inadequate (for whatever reasons) to the social and cultural context.
Of course, these four ideal-typical situations will never be found as such in reality. Most societies will fall somewhere in between. Also, some laws may be new, some obsolete, some used, some others not, in a society.

d) Another aspect which can contribute to the flow of litigation is the extent to which a legal system can be said to be *formally-or substantively-oriented.* A legal system is formally-oriented when formal aspects and considerations predominate; substantively-oriented when causes and intentions predominate over form in legal relations. Of course, no legal system is purely and totally of one type or the other. But, one or the other aspect may predominate in a legal system, at least compared to certain others.
A formally-oriented legal system does not encourage litigation. There is little room for argument or debate: either the act (or contract, or relation) has complied with formal requirements, or it has not. If it has, its provisions are totally valid or binding; if not, the legal act or relation is void and no claim can be based upon it. In either case, the parties involved will know beforehand whether they are legally (i.e., formally and not substantively) right or wrong.
Early Roman law can be considered an example of a formally-oriented system: legal formulae determined the nature and contents of a contract, regardless of underlying intentions. A system placing so much emphasis on formal aspects thus allows for institutionalization of experts in the use of legal formulae. European legal systems have inherited a certain degree of formal orientation from Roman and medieval law, hence the striking role played in them by the Notary.
On the other hand, a more substantively-oriented legal system leaves more room for litigation, since formal aspects can always be challenged on the grounds that they do not correspond to the true "cause" of the legal relation or the purpose behind it. This primacy of the substantive components protects the parties' true intentions, but increases unpredictability into legal relations, since subjective factors can be introduced at any time. Thus, those legal fields directly connected with economic and commercial life (where predictability is a decisive factor) have tended, in most European countries at least, to be formally oriented. Other things being equal, the more formally-oriented a legal system, the less likely it is to evidence a large volume of litigation.

e) Another aspect, closely connected with the one just discussed, is the way in which the role of the judge is defined in a given legal system. The role of the judge may be defined as mechanical application of the law, leaving the judge no room for extensive or creative interpretation. In such a case (normally associated with a general formal orientation of the legal system) a lower level of litigation may be expected compared to the case (most likely associated with a general substantive orientation) in which the judge has a flexible role, allowing, a high degree of flexibility.

f) Finally, *costs* of litigation (both in money and time) can play a decisive role in determining the volume of litigation (10).

From these six factors, we can construct the chart presented in table 1. The typologies offered by the chart can be applied to whole legal systems, or to specific legal areas within a given legal system. For the sake of simplicity, I will discuss here only their application at the level of whole legal systems.

Tab. 1: Factors Determining the Amount of Litigation in Legal Systems

		Case A	Case B	Case C	Case D	Spain	
Legal Culture	=favors litigation	*		*			
	-does not favor litigation		*		*	*	
Technical Quality of the Laws	-high		*	*			
						*	
	-low	*			*		
The Laws In Force Are	-old and used	*			*	*	
	-old and not used						
	-new and used		*	*			
	-new and not used						
The general Orientation of the legal System is	-formal		*				
						*	
	-substantive	*		*	*		
The role of the Judge is	-mechanical		*			*	
	-flexible	*		*	*		
The costs of Litigation are	-high		*	*		*	
	-low	*			*		

Case A in table 1 may be said to represent the case of a legal system maximally prone to litigation: its legal culture predisposes individuals to have recourse to the courts; the technical quality of the laws is low; laws tend to be inadequate to the social conditions; the system is substantively-oriented, the role of the judge is flexible, and the costs of litigation low.
Case B represents the opposite situation, where no factor encourages litigation.
Most actual legal systems will probably tend to be more like Cases C or D (where the factors do not tend in the same direction), or like other combinations, which the chart would allow us to construct. Also, it could well be that some laws in force in a given legal system would be old and not used, others old and used, or the costs of litigation (in time or money) would vary according to fields of law – all of which would increase the number and complexity of types suggested by the chart.

The chart does, however, suggest how misleading it may be to speak of the effects of economic development on litigation, without having examining other intervening factors. Indeed, if we now introduce into Table 1 our independent variable (i.e., economic development) we can easily see that its potential effects on litigation will vary sharply from case to case. Let us examine, for instance, Case A. What are the likely effects of economic development on such a legal system? One possibility would be that the process of change brings with it a wave of deep, far-reaching reforms, as a result of which the body of laws becomes attuned to new social conditions, their technical quality is improved and the costs of litigation considerably raised. If so, then the high rate of litigation would decrease.

But if the process of change does *not* bring with it any of these reforms, and the legal system remains as described, increase in all economic and commercial relationships, occasioned by the process of economic growth, will cause an increase in legal activity. Yet, at the same time, the uncertainty of the legal system will tend to deter people forming new legal relations from having recourse to the courts to settle conflicts. Thus the rate of litigation will decline.

On the other hand, what would the effects of economic development be on a legal system like Case B (assuming no major structural changes)? In such a case (where laws of a high technical quality are continually re-adapted to social conditions) new types of social relations will have no major difficulty in using the existing body of laws; but the highly formal character of the legal system will prevent them from noticeably changing the rate of litigation.

Thus, the effects of economic development on litigation can vary sharply from case to case, depending on the nature of the other intervening factors. We should not think of a single, universally valid relationship between economic development and litigation. We should, rather, try to establish predictions and hypotheses valid for specific types of legal systems.

Let us note that, in discussing proneness to litigation in Case A or B, we meant not the absolute numbers of lawsuits, but the ratio between legal relations and litigation. We expect, for instance, one out of ten legal relations in Case A, compared to one out of every hundred in Case B (the figures are purely illustrative), to result in litigation. Supposing now an increase (both for Cases ,A and B) in the volume of legal activity, we can in principle expect that ten per cent of the new legal relations in Case A, and one per cent in Case B, will result in litigation. That is, unless some new factor intervenes, an increase in legal activity should mean for both cases (though in very different proportions) an increase in the amount of litigation. But when economic development intervenes, bringing with it an increase in legal activity, we would expect a *decrease* in the percentage of legal relations that result in litigation in Case A; the old ratio for Case B should continue.

The Spanish Legal System

Before turning to an analysis of the ways in which economic development has affected (both at the national and subnational level) legal and judicial activity in Spain, we will attempt to describe, in terms of the chart in Table 1, the Spanish legal system as it existed in 1960.

Though conclusive data on the point are lacking, available information seems to indicate that in general (probably with some regional differences) the Spanish legal culture does not favor litigation. Popular stereotypes and proverbs regard the judicial machine with deep distrust and view litigation as an evil. In a sense, we shall see later, this attitude is shared by Spanish lawyers, reinforcing the cultural tendency.

The technical quality of the laws is difficult to evaluate. In general, the laws enacted during the 19th century seem to be technically superior to those enacted in recent decades. Overall the body of laws seems of high quality (I have, in the chart placed the star close to the dividing line between high and low technical quality). Moreover, many important bodies of norms (Civil Code, Code of Commercial Law, Criminal Code, Procedural Code) were enacted in the 19th century; hence the body of laws in force can in general be considered rather old. However, they seem to possess a remarkable vitality, as will be seen later. Consequently, we can describe the laws in force in 1960 as old and used.

As for the general orientation of the legal system, it can be said to be predominantly (though not exclusively) formal (a situation which I have attempted to express by placing the star close to the dividing line between formal and substantive orientation). The role of the judge, according to procedural norms, is predominantly mechanical. Finally, costs of litigation were high in 1960 in terms of time and, since 1959, in terms of money.

In summary, this is a legal system which allows relatively little room for litigation. Any potential encouragement to use of the courts, implied by the possible obsolescence of an old body of laws, was in all likelihood counterbalanced by the formal orientation of the legal system, the mechanical definition of the judge's role, the high costs of litigation and, more than anything, by cultural attitudes and values that discouraged litigation.

I will now proceed to analyze the relationship between the process of economic development in Spain since 1960, and changes in legal and judicial activity, at the national and subnational levels, in that country.

2. *The Spanish process of economic development*

An American economist has called the "dramatic pace" at which Spain, since the early 1960's, has modernized her economy and improved the standard of living an "economic miracle". He contrasts this to "two decades of economic isolation and stagnation," and adds that:

- since 1961 there was a more rapid pace of economic development than in any period of comparable length in Spain's recent history, with real GNP growing on average by 7.3 % a year. Per capita GNP rose, according to official data, to about $ 1,130 in 1972. . . .
- Substantial structural changes transformed Spain into an essentially industrial country; and
- Balance of payments constraints on growth have ceased to exist, at least for the time being (11).

The social consequences of such a revolutionary process of economic growth have been intensively examined by Amando de Miguel and associates (12). The best single summary of such changes is perhaps that presented in Table 2 and Graph 1. As can be seen, the percentage of active population employed in agriculture (the best single indicator of industrialization for the Spanish case) (13) has dramatically dropped from 42 % in 1960 to 26 % in 1970, and is expected to be well below 20 % in 1975.

Of course, the "Spanish economic miracle" has not affected the whole country in the same way. Its effects are concentrated in some regions, leaving others largely unaffected. Since our main interest is evolution during the so-called "development decade" (the 1960's), we will measure the degree of variation of the percentage of active population employed in agriculture (APA) between 1950, before the process of development had started, and 1967, almost a decade after the beginning of the process of change. (This is also the last date for which fully reliable data are available). We will employ a five-fold typology, in which we will consider fully industrialized, or post-industrial, those provinces showing an APA of less than 15 %; industrial, those with an APA between 15 % and 25 %; semi-industrial, those with an APA between 25 % and 35 %; sub-industrial, those with an APA larger than 50 % (14).

Graphic 1: Evolution of the Percentage of A.P.A. In Spain, 1900–1975 (———————: estimations)

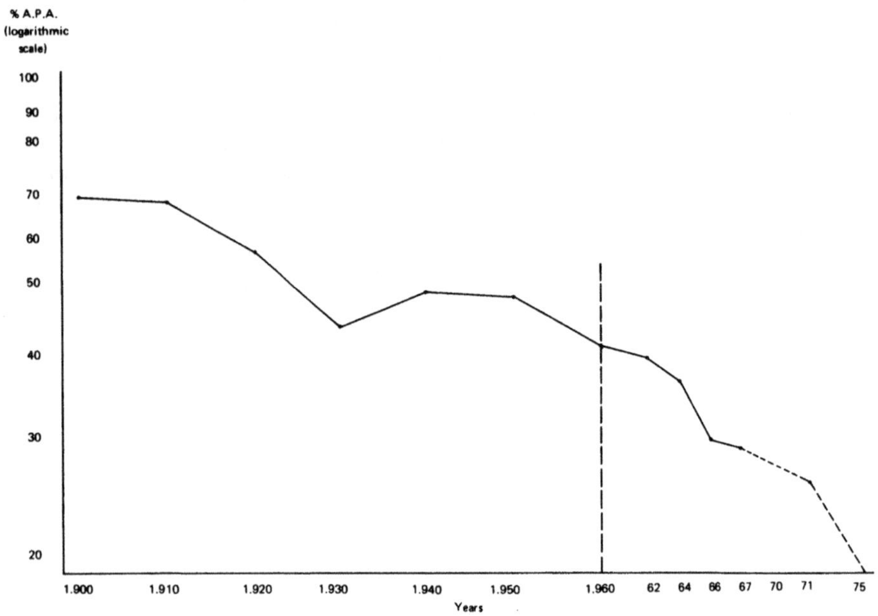

Since we are not interested in the volume of the APA at a given date, but rather in the way in which it has evolved over the period considered (1950-67), we will classify the 50 Spanish provinces as follows:

(a) in the first category are those provinces which, since 1950, have had and APA smaller than 15 %. These are the provinces of Madrid, Barcelona, Guipuzcoa and Vizcaya, which we will now consider as Post-Industrial Spain.

Tab. 2: Evolution of the Occupational Structure of the Spanish Population, by Sectors (1900–1970)

Year	Agriculture		Industry		Services	
	Thousands	%	Thousands	%	Thousands	%
1900	4.558	68	1.019	15	1.151	17
1910	4.220	64	1.074	16	1.281	20
1920	4.557	59	1.673	22	1.472	19
1930	4.041	47	2.674	31	1.858	21
1940	4.781	52	2.168	24	2.260	25
1950	5.271	50	2.652	25	2.698	25
1960	4.803	42	3.572	31	3.148	27
1961	4.729	40	3.694	32	3.271	28
1962	4.634	39	3.867	32	3.377	28
1963	4.538	38	4.022	33	3.493	29
1964	4.140	34	4.082	34	3.974	33
1965	3.935	32	4.244	34	4.096	33
1966	3.796	30	4.472	36	4.134	33
1967	3.690	29	4.568	37	4.315	34
1970	3.400	26	4.900	38	4.700	36

Source: II Informe sobre la situación social de España (Madrid, Euramérica, 1970), p. 169.

(b) the second category consists of those provinces which between 1950 and 1967 have changed from a sub-industrial (35 % to 50 % APA) to an industrial (15 % to 25 % APA) stage. These are the provinces of Alava, Alicante, the Balearic Islands and Gerona, which can be said to have been most dramatically affected by the process of economic growth. They will be referred to as "Industrial Spain".

(c) the third category will include those provinces which, during the period considered, changed from a sub-industrial (35 % to 50 % APA) or a pre-industrial (more than 50 % APA) stage to a semi-industrial (25 % to 35 % APA) one. Nine provinces (Navarre, Huelva, Cadiz, Oviedo, Santander, Valencia, Valladolid, Zaragoza and Tarragona) fall within this category, which we can label as "Semi-Industrial Spain".

(d) the fourth category (referred to henceforth as "Sub-Industrial Spain") groups those 19 provinces which, during the period, changed from a pre-industrial to a sub-industrial stage (Almeria, Albacete, Burgos, Castellon, Santa Cruz de Tenerife, Ciudad Real, Cordoba, Huesca, Leon, Logrono, Lerida, Segovia, Malaga, Murcia, Sevilla, Valencia, Las Palmas, Pontevedra and Salamanca).

(e) finally, the fifth category includes the remaining 14 provinces, unaffected by economic development, and remaining at a pre-industrial level (that is, with a APA of more than 50 %). We will refer to them as "Pre-Industrial Spain" or, simply, as "Underdeveloped Spain".

Table 3 shows us these five national sub-contexts.

Tab. 3: The "Five Spains"

APA in 1967 \ APA in 1950	More than 50 %	Between 35 % and 50 %	Between 25 % and 35 %	Between 15 % and 25 %	Less than 15 %
Less than 15 %					Post-Industrial Spain
Between 15 % and 25 %		Industrial Spain			
Between 25 % and 35 %	Semi-Industrial Spain				
Between 35 % and 50 %	Sub-Industrial Spain				
More than 50 %	Pre-Industrial Spain				

3. *Legal activity and economic development in Spain*

Our key indicator for legal activity will be the number of instruments each year authorized by a notary. The importance of the notary, in civil and commercial life in a Civil Law country, has already been indicated. The number of instruments he authorizes provides an excellent indication of the volume of legal activity in society, since practically no significant legal transaction is arranged in a Civil Law system without his intervention.

A common stereotype links the notary to rural society: but in fact industrial or industrializing contexts seem to require his functions most. In rural areas, face to face relationships predominate; the community acts as a binding force, making recourse to the notary almost unnecessary (15). As the frequency of transactions with strangers increases, the presence of the notary becomes more necessary, to give formality and impersonality to relationships (16). The notarial function seems, thus, in a Civil Law country, to be related to the level of development. In principle, as society develops, the volume of notarial activity should increase proportionately. And in truth, in Spain the percentage of the population employed in agriculture (APA) appears to be negatively correlated with the volume of notarial activity. These negative correlations are as follows: -0.50 for 1900, -0.56 for 1910, -0.50 for 1930, -0.58 for 1940, -0.64 for 1950, -0.80 for 1960 and -0.82 for 1967.

As can be seen, though always significantly negative, the correlation becomes especially sizable after 1960, the conventional date for the beginning of the process of development. The correlations show that the the larger the percentage of active population employed in agriculture, the lower the level of notarial activity. Development leads to an increase in legal activity (measured here by the volume of notarial activity).

Consider the data in Table 4. As can be seen, it is only after 1960 that, for Spain, the volume of notarial activity increases markedly. The growth in eight years – 1960–68 – was 210 %; greater than the growth registered for the period 1940–59 (200 %). The same phenomenon appears in Italy, too. Only after 1950

Tab. 4: Evolution of Notarial Activity in Spain and Italy (1900–1970)

	Italy	Spain	
Year	Absolute Numbers	Absolute Numbers	Ratio per 1,000 Inhabitants
1.900	1.051.126	544.837	–
1.905	1.067.767	570.716	–
1.910	1.233.762	561.033	28,1
1.915	1.151.780	541.561	26,2
1.920	1.452.955	665.793	30,7
1.925	1.601.359	839.795	37,4
1.930	2.030.844	948.275	40,2
1.935	1.605.611	771.931	31,2
1.940	1.409.466	619.432	23,9
1.945	1.208.276	904.432	33,5
1.950	3.239.190	1.263.576	45,1
1.955	6.623.739	1.428.529	48,9
1.960	8.907.875	1.820.406	59.8
1.965	12.217.682	2.740.058	85.7
1.968	14.518.271	3.838.136	199,0

Sources: For Italy, Sumario di Statistiche Storiche Italiane
For Spain, Anuario Estadistico de España, for the corresponding years.

(the beginning of rapid economic recovery and growth) does the volume of notarial activity increase drastically. In Spain, in 1940, the ratio of notarial instruments per 1,000 inhabitants was 23.9, in 1960 59.8, in 1965, 85.7, in 1968, 199.0. Consequently, it seems safe to assert that in Spain economic development and volume of legal activity are positively associated.

Table 5 shows which types of legal activity have shown the most growth. The smaller increases (and the only decrease) are registered for those types of notarial instruments directly related to the Civil Code (items 1,2,3, and 5: civil status, testaments, contracts on the occasion of marriage, estate successions); the largest by far are registered for notarial instruments specifically related to commercial

Tab. 5: Relative Increase of the Different Kinds of Notarial Acts (1950 = 100)

	1950		1960	1969
Relative to civil status	(4,316)	100	111.3	158.6
Testaments	(119,177)	100	119.6	151.8
Contracts in the occasion of marriage	(2,996)	100	68.2	38.0
Contracts in general	(283,199)	100	116.9	232.3
Division of estates	(33,019)	100	115.0	143.2
Creation, modification and dissolution of corporations	(4,641)	100	153.9	412.5
Mortgages, loans	(31,852)	100	107.2	203.4
Dissolution of obligations	(26,180)	100	108.4	209.3
Proxies of all kinds	(164,519)	100	115.7	187.2
Authentications in general	(69,870)	100	146.9	222.6
Actions for failure to pay negotiable instruments	(521,717)	100	181.1	482.2
Total Notarial Instruments	(1.263,576)	100	144.0	346.5

Source: I.N.E., Anuario estadistico de España, for the corresponding years.

Tab. 6: Evolution of the Relative Weight of Each Kind of Notarial Instrument Out of the Total Number of Notarial Instruments, for 1950, 1960 and 1969 (in percentages)

	1950	1960	1969
Instruments relative to civil status	0.3	0.2	0.1
Testaments	9.4	7.0	4.0
Contracts in the occasion of marriage	0.2	0.1	0.02
Contracts in general	22.4	18.2	15.0
Division of estates	2.4	2.0	1.0
Creation, modification and dissolution of corporations	0.3	0.3	0.4
Mortgages, loans	2.5	1.8	1.6
Dissolution of obligations	2.0	1.5	1.2
Proxies of all kinds	13.0	10.4	7.0
Authentications in general	5.5	5.6	3.5
Actions for failure to pay negotiable instruments	41.0	51.0	57.5
Total Notarial Instruments	100.0	100.0	100.0

law (items 6 and 10: creation, change and dissolution of corporations; and actions for failure to pay negotiable instruments). The rest of the items (4,7,8,9, and 11) can relate either to civil or commercial law; they show an intermediate degree of growth.

The increase in the volume of legal activity seems due mainly to the increase in actions for failure to pay negotiable instruments. This category accounnted for 57.5 % of the notarial activity in 1969; compared to 41.0 % in 1950. (Table 6). Since this category refers to a conflict (one party did not comply with obligations imposed by the original agreement), this datum provides us at the same time with an indication of an increase in legal conflicts potentially objects of litigation (notarial *protesto* is a pre-requisite for bringing a lawsuit, though most of the time it is used only to intimidate the debtor).

This tremendous increase in legal activity is not homogeneous for the whole country. In Tables 7a and 7b we see the varying evolution of notarial activity by province, and in each of the five socio-economic sub-contexts we have identified. First of all, we note an enormous change in the differences between the minimum and maximum figures for notary acts per 1,000 inhabitants. In 1910, the maximum was 51.0, the minimum 7.6, a difference of 43.4; in 1967, the minimum was 31.2, the maximum 248, the difference 216.8. That is, between 1910 and 1967 the gap between the maximum and minimum number of notarial instruments per 1,000 inhabitants increased 425 per cent. This seems to indicate that in 1967 the differences between provinces are much more marked than in 1910 – a reflection of the uneven effect of economic growth on the various provinces.

If we group the fifty provinces into our five socio-economic contexts (Table 7b) we can see those differences more clearly. The more industrialized the context, the larger the volume of notarial activity. Moreover, while the number of notarial instruments per 1000 inhabitants increased in Post-Industrial Spain by 104.4 between 1910 and 1967, the increase was a mere 30 in Pre-Industrial Spain.

For the period 1960-67, the following are the differences in the number of notarial instruments per 1,000 inhabitants, for each context, between the two dates:

–	Post-Industrial Spain	:	+61.5
–	Industrial Spain	:	+96.7
–	Semi-Industrial Spain	:	+47.6
–	Sub-Industrial Spain	:	+35.0
–	Pre-Industrial Spain	:	+15.9
–	National average	:	+48.6

Tab. 7 (a): Evolution of Notarial Activity, by Provinces
(The figures represent number of notarial instruments per 1,000 inhabitants)

	Years							
Provinces	1910	1920	1930	1940	1950	1960	1964	1967
Alava	30,1	24,9	29,5	21,2	40,5	53,0	74,0	114,8
Albacete	14,2	17,0	37,2	14,9	37,5	55,9	66,9	78,8
Alicante	39,4	48,9	63,4	34,5	78,7	90,9	148,7	194,0
Almeria	30,1	28,0	35,5	25,5	34,5	44,1	64,2	83,4
Avila	14,3	14,4	20,1	13,0	19,4	30,0	40,7	44,7
Badajoz	21,3	21,2	28,6	19,9	33,1	39,4	48,0	50,7
Baleares	51,0	57,2	65,4	49,2	71,7	83,8	105,7	248,0
Barcelona	42,5	54,4	54,9	34,9	70,9	87,5	136,8	165,5
Burgos	17,9	14,8	16,6	12,8	25,9	42,6	43,5	62,8
Cáceres	15,0	14,1	19,3	16,0	38,0	29,0	39,3	41,0
Cádiz	20,8	24,1	43,7	16,3	41,1	62,8	83,8	91,5
Castellón	36,9	42,4	55,6	39,7	57,7	66,9	91,4	108,4
C. Real	23,0	23,9	42,6	32,0	44,4	48,5	64,3	65,3
Córdoba	26,1	24,1	39,0	22,3	38,2	45,2	72,0	68,0
Coruña	30,9	29,4	30,8	20,9	29,8	35,7	49,5	62,0
Cuenca	8,4	6,9	13,3	6,3	19,2	23,7	30,5	35,6
Gerona	38,5	39,6	36,2	32,0	52,5	66,9	105,4	124,6
Granada	23,4	23,1	30,8	20,8	36,6	43,9	61,5	71,3
Guadalajara	7,7	7,2	11,9	6,5	22,1	25,1	34,5	44,8
Guipúzcoa	42,0	46,3	45,0	30,5	50,5	67,8	81,8	109,2
Huelva	16,6	17,5	24,1	12,1	29,7	56,3	67,3	77,0
Huesca	22,6	27,0	28,0	17,8	33,0	47,2	64,0	64,6
Jaén	28,6	29,8	45,1	23,5	45,1	43,8	56,6	65,0
León	12,5	12,5	19,7	10,7	23,5	33,4	40,7	43,9
Lérida	39,0	43,1	47,2	30,8	57,5	91,0	95,8	110,5
Logrono	21,9	21,6	30,1	20,0	39,3	50,2	71,9	88,7
Lugo	34,6	38,2	35,5	26,7	35,5	40,2	49,2	51,4
Madrid	40,4	45,7	72,2	32,0	62,5	104,6	131,7	161,4
Málaga	19,7	29,4	37,8	18,7	44,3	44,0	76,8	115,5
Murcia	37,5	32,4	54,6	25,4	59,8	77,7	110,9	121,6
Navarra	29,1	33,2	30,4	27,7	39,9	50,0	69,4	98,9
Orense	15,4	17,4	15,8	10,2	19,0	21,1	27,7	31,2
Oviedo	26,2	27,8	31,6	20,8	33,7	47,0	53,2	64,6
Palencia	26,8	30,7	27,3	26,5	36,7	50,9	61,3	64,9
Palmas (Las)	24,2	27,7	41,9	19,0	42,8	57,3	111,4	146,1
Pontevedra	30,4	27,4	30,3	18,4	36,1	44,0	60,4	73,7
Salamanca	18,8	19,8	22,8	20,7	34,1	43,9	59,1	65,7
S. Cruz Tener	--	--	31,9	19,5	53,2	55,9	136,1	136,5
Santander	25,1	26,7	29,6	20,7	42,3	55,3	77,0	88,7
Segovia	15,8	19,0	18,7	13,1	20,7	26,6	38,5	45,8
Sevilla	24,6	31,4	48,9	23,1	44,4	55,1	82,6	101,3
Soria	7,6	6,6	9,0	6,9	11,5	17,7	26,8	33,9
Tarragona	48,3	51,7	60,6	46,2	65,1	83,1	123,0	165,0
Teruel	15,0	15,3	14,5	9,4	19,1	24,0	32,7	38,8
Toledo	16,1	18,7	27,6	20,1	34,3	42,6	50,8	51,4
Valencia	42,0	56,1	69,7	39,1	64,0	75,6	103,6	133,2
Valladolid	29,6	24,7	36,2	21,5	40,0	52,2	75,1	127,5
Vizcaya	30,9	35,0	37,4	29,3	45,7	67,3	110,0	137,2
Zamora	14,9	15,7	20,8	14,6	33,1	32,9	42,6	50,4
Zaragoza	20,6	23,4	31,3	17,3	40,2	61,5	84,1	126,0
Total	28,1	31,2	40,1	23,9	45,1	58,9	88,2	107,5

Tab. 7 (b): Evolution of Notarial Activity in the "five Spains," 1910–1967 (ratios per 1,000 inhabitants)

	Years							
	1910	1920	1930	1940	1950	1960	1964	1967
Post-Industrial Spain	38.9	45.4	52.4	31.7	57.4	81.8	115.1	143.3
Industrial Spain	39.8	42.7	48.6	34.2	48.7	73.7	108.5	170.4
Semi-Industrial Spain	28.7	31.7	39.7	24.6	44.0	60.4	81.8	108.0
Sub-Industrial Spain	23.3	24.9	35.0	21.6	40.2	51.6	74.3	86.6
Pre-Industrial Spain	18.1	18.4	23.1	15.3	28.3	32.1	42.2	48.0
Total Spain	28.1	31.2	40.1	23.9	45.1	58.9	88.2	107.5

4. *Judicial activity and economic development in Spain*

The increasing volume of legal activity, shown above, might be accompanied by an increase of litigation before first instance tribunals. However, this does not seem to be the case. In Table 8 we see that the number of "voluntarios" (voluntary) and "contencioso" (contested) cases per 1,000 inhabitants has remained remarkably constant over the past seventy years, and at a rather low level. This low level of litigation was predictable from the factors in Table 1, and is scarcely surprising. Indeed, what is surprising is that the process of economic change does not seem to have affected the rate of litigation (in fact, the 1969 rate is slightly lower than the 1960 rate).

If we consider now just the "contencioso" cases, those which involve two conflicting parties, we find the same pattern (see Table 9): the proportion of cases brought to court is suprisingly stable and rather low (the peak is 3.01 cases per 1,000 inhabitants in 1940). Judicial activity seems little affected by major changes in society – such as the process of economic growth of the 1960's. The difference between judicial and legal activity is shown dramatically in Graph 2.

Table 10 shows the evolution (in rates per 100,000 inhabitants) since 1953 of the four main categories of "contencioso" cases, which accounted for 83.6 % of the total in 1960 and 89.5 % in 1967. As can be seen, the rate of large and small claims rose slowly from 1958 to 1963, and then began a slow downward trend; cases concerning actions for failure to pay negotiable instruments show a somewhat similar pattern of rise and fall, though they reached a peak in 1964 and ended in 1967 well above their 1958 level – in a sense, a surprising pattern, which does not correspond to what could have been expected from the great increase in disputes over negotiable instruments (at the notarial level); finally, cases concerning estates – a pre-industrial type of litigation – are the only ones which show to some extent, and always relatively speaking, a pattern of sustained increase.

Tab. 8: "Contenciosos" and "Voluntarios"* Cases Brought to the Courts, In Absolute Numbers and In Ratios per 1,000 Inhabitants

Year	Absolute Number	Ratio	Year	Absolute Number	Ratio
1906	56.485	2,92	1949	90.305	
1909	53.260	2,66	1950	90.045	3,18
1914	46.262	2,23	1951	89.930	3,20
1915	45.134	2,14	1952	87.981	3,11
1916	43.803		1953	79.685	2,79
1917	47.054	2,22	1954	85.468	2,96
1932	93.996	3,95	1955	84.187	2,85
1933	82.477		1956	81.363	2,78
1934	41.221		1957	80.429	2,72
1935	41.800	1,67	1958	85.970	2,89
1936**	24.882		1959	87.729	2,92
1937**	18.685		1960	84.873	2,74
1938**	20.855		1961	84.179	2,75
1939**	34.200		1962	85.916	2,78
1940	106.336	4,06	1963	91.017	2,92
1941	61.335	2,34	1964	86.899	2,78
1942	61.970		1965	88.327	2,78
1945	74.133	2,72	1966	87.918	2,76
1946	77.134		1967	84.174	2,65
1947	78.002		1968	88.943	2,74
1948	81.963		1969	82.983	2,53

Source: INE, Estadisticas Judiciales de Espãna.

* "Contencioso" cases are those in which two (or more parties) confront and oppose each other; "voluntario" cases are those in which no dispute between parties is involved a person asks the Court for an interpretation of the law or clarification of a legal situation.

** The data for these four years probably refer only to the Nationalist side (the Civil War started July 18, 1936 and ended April 1, 1939).

Tab. 9: "Contencioso" Cases Brought to the Courts, in Rates per 1,000 Inhabitants

Year	Absolute Number	Ratio	Year	Absolute Number	Ratio
1906	28.985 (X)	1,44	1960	56.894	1,87
1940	78.836 (X)	3,01	1961	57.611	1,89
1945	46.633 (X)		1962	59.556	1,93
1950	62.545 (X)	2,20	1963	65.436	2,10
1953	50.190	1,76	1964	67.093	2,14
1954	55.035	1,91	1965	67.256	2,12
1955	53.710	1,85	1966	67.105	2,10
1956	51.542	1,76	1967	64.384	2,00
1957	50.105	1,70	1968	57.808	1,71
1958	53.415	1,78	1969	62.483	1,83
1959	55.987	1,86			

(X) Estimations

Graphic 2: Profiles of the Evolution of the Rates of Notarial Instruments and of Cases Brought to Courts
––––: Missing Information

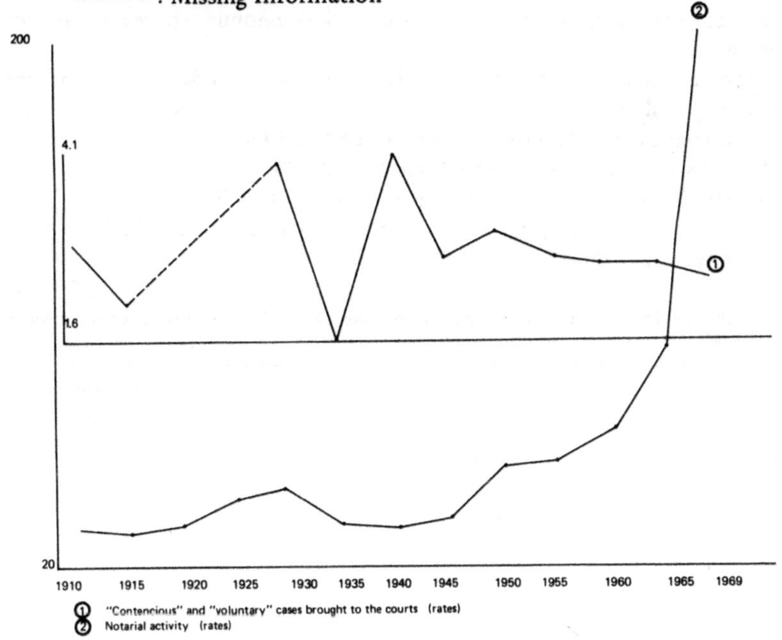

Tab. 10: Evolution Since 1953 of the Four Main Categories of "Contencioso" Cases (in rates per 100,000 inhabitants)

Year	Total	Large Claims*	Small Claims**	Estates	Affairs referring to negotiable instruments	Percentage represented by the four categories out of the total
1953	125,6	5,7				
1954	133,2	7,2				
1955	131,6	6,5	7,6	49,2	39,0	
1956	124,5	4,0				
1957	119,5	4,0				
1958	125,5	3,6	10,4	57,0	31,3	
1959	127,3	3,8	10,3	50,4	40,0	
1960	128,7	4,0	11,3	45,1	46,9	83.6 %
1961	129,0	4,1	12,1	41,7	48,3	
1962	131,9	4,3	12,4	45,0	50,6	
1963	142,3	4,6	12,9	46,2	61,3	
1964	147,0	4,2	11,2	45,9	68,0	
1965	142,4	4,1	11,4	47,6	63,3	
1966	142,9	4,5	12,2	47,6	62,3	
1967	134,3	3,6	10,5	47,9	58,1	89.5 %

* Over 500.000 pesetas
** Between 150.000 and 500.000 pesetas

In short, the categories most directly related to economic life do not experience any increase corresponding to the process of development.
If we now examine variations between 1960 and 1967 in the rate of cases brought to courts in each of the five socio-economic contexts, we see the following:

- in Post-Industrial Spain, the rate increases by 0,77 %, that is, it remains practically stable;
- in Industrial Spain, the rate increases a notable 39.4 %;
- in Semi-Industrial Spain the rate increases 22.5 %
- in Sub-Industrial Spain, the rate decreases slightly (−1.9 %);
- in Pre-Industrial Spain, the rate decreases markedly; in 1967 it is 15.9 % smaller than in 1960 (Table 11).

Tab. 11: **Changes in the Ratio of "Contencioso" Cases Brought to Courts Between 1960 and 1967**

	1960	1967	Percentual Increase
Post-Industrial Spain	25.8	26.0	+0.77 %
Industrial Spain	21.1	29.4	+39.3 %
Semi-Industrial Spain	20.0	24.5	+22.5 %
Sub-Industrial Spain	15.4	15.1	− 1.9 %
Pre-Industrial Spain	11.3	9.5	−15.9 %

The general pattern can be stated as follows: economic growth does not seem to be significantly refleced in the flow of judicial activity in those provinces which are the most advanced in the country (i.e., in Post-Industrial Spain). On the other hand, in those provinces which seem to have entered a phase of economic take-off, the process of growth does seem to have a substantial effect on the flow of cases. Finally, those provinces least affected by the process of change (Sub- and Pre- Industrial Spain) show a decrease in the volume of judicial activity. How are we to explain these facts?
Between 1906 and 1931, litigation slowly declined; then, in 1931, judicial life suddenly boomed (the inauguration of a new regime, the Second Spanish Republic, may have contributed somewhat); however, by 1935 judicial activity sank to the lowest point of the century (a rate of just 1.67 per 1000); in 1940 – probably due to normalization of judicial activities after the disruptions of the Civil War (1936-39) – judicial activity reached a peak; ever since, and until 1960, the pattern was one of fluctuating stability; from 1960 to 1964, probobly as a consequence of the process of economic development, judicial activity somewhat quickened; since 1964, the trend seems to be toward a slow but sustained decrease of the rate of cases brought to courts.
It appears that the process of development will at first stimulate judicial activity. This is what happened between 1960 and 1964 in the country as a whole, and what seems to have been happening in 1967 in Industrial and Semi-Industrial Spain. At a later point, however, judicial activity levels off. This phase was experienced by the country as a whole after 1964, and experienced by Post-Industrial Spain in 1967. We can assume a third and final phase – sustained

decrease in the rate of litigation, though not in legal activity. This seems to be the stage reached by Italy today (Table 12), and the one which Post-Industrial Spain may shortly reach.

Tab. 12: Evolution of the Rate of Litigation (expressed in number of civil cases brought to Courts per 1,000 inhabitants) for Spain and Italy

Year	Italy	Spain
1901	71,49	
1906		2,92
1936-40	21,20	4,06 (1940)
1947	6,64	
1948	8,76	
1951	10,62	3,20
1959	11,49	2,92
1966	8,43	2,76

Source for Italy: Consiglio Superiore della Magistratura, Realtá Sociale e Amministrazione della giustizia, 1970, p. 43.

This descriptive model is, of course, built on the assumption that the higher the degree of economic development (in a country already endowed with a modern legal system, but economically non-developed), the higher the use of substantive norms, the higher the numer of legal conflicts, but the *lower* the number of such conflicts brought to court. Of course, such a model is suggested, not proved by the Spanish experience. More information is needed for similar societies, undergoing similar processes of development.
In any case, the data indicate that in Spain, for the last decade, extensive by-passing of the courts has taken place while, on the contrary, legal activity has increased enormously. This seems to suggest that while the new types of legal relations brought about by economic development can adapt themselves to existing substantive norms, the new types of legal conflicts derived from those relations find the formal mechanisms of conflict resolution outmoded and inadequate – and avoid them. What we can call the "procedural component" of the legal system may thus be the one most called into question by economic development.

Changes in the work load of judges

The fact that large numbers of legal conflicts seem to be avoiding the Courts, especially in the more industrialized areas, should not induce us to think that the work pressure and work load of the judges, expecially in those areas, is small or decreasing. For the previous analyses we have used ratios (proportions between the number of cases and the number of inhabitants) as a way to control for the increase of the population over the years being considered. But such a measurement concealed the exact amount of cases to be actually solved by each District Court.

Tab. 13: Distribution of the Case-Load in the District Courts of the "Five Spains"

	Mean Number of Cases Brought to Each of the District Courts Existing in the Context		Total Number of District Courts Existing in the Context	
	In 1960	In 1967	In 1960	In 1967
Post-Industrial Spain (four provinces)	212.3	219.4	79	89
Industrial Spain (four provinces)	113.6	157.1	31	35
Semi-Industrial Spain (nine provinces)	94.0	137.0	116	108
Sub-Industrial Spain (mineteen Provinces)	69.7	87.75	198	173
Pre-Industrial Spain (fourten provinces)	53.2	53.6	152	135
Total for the whole country:	97.8	127.3	576	540

As we can see in Table 13, the mean number of cases brought to Spanish District Courts was 97.8 in 1960, versus 127.3 in 1967. Of course, the case-load is not distributed evenly over the country. While in Pre-Industrial Spain each District Court had to resolve, on the average, only 53.2 cases per year in 1960, the Courts in Post-Industrial Spain had to face, in the same period, an average number of 212.3 cases, that is four times more work.

The process of economic development after 1960 does not seem to have made things much worse for the courts in Post-Industrial Spain (their average number of cases in 1967 and 219.4, that is, just 7.1 more cases, on the average, than in 1960), but this seems to be due mainly to the fact that new District Courts were created there during the period. As for Industrial Spain, in spite of the creation of four new District Courts to help reduce the work load, the average number of cases to be resolved by each court reached a total of 157.1 in 1967 (that is 43.5 more cases per court on the average). For Semi- and Sub-Industrial Spain the work load of the Courts seems to have increased over the period 1960–67, but the average amounts reached in 1967 are hardly crushing and seem due mainly to the reduction in the number of District Courts. As for Pre-Industrial Spain, not even the reduction in the number of courts caused an increase in the average work load, which by 1967 was still about four times smaller than that of Post-Industrial Spain.

There are also tremendous differences in the work load in different kinds of tribunal. As can be seen in Table 14, among the judges of the sample, those serving in District Courts located in large cities seem to have a heavier work load : 53.4 % of them indicate that over the past year they had handled more than 1,500 cases (versus 13 % for judges serving in villages, 19 % for magistrates serving in Provincial – Criminal – Audiencias and 20 % for magistrates serving in

Territorial – Civil – Audiencias); only 10 % (versus 42 %, 56 % and 71 % respectively for the other three categories) had to resolve less than 500 cases over the past year.
However, as will be seen, and contrary to what might logically be expected, work load does not seem to make any significant difference in the perception by judges of the avoidance of the courts by potential litigants.

Tab. 14: Case-Load by Type of Tribunal Served (in percentages)

Answer that Their Annual Case-Load is. . . .	District Judges in Villages	District Judges in Capitals	Provincial (Criminal) Audiencias Magistrates	Territorial (Civil) Audiencias Magistrates
Below 500 cases	42	10	56	71
Between 501 and 1,500 cases	42	37	25	10
Over 1,500 cases	13	53	19	20
No answer	2	.		
(N)	(45)	(73)	(16)	(55)

Source: My own 1972 survey to a national sample of Spanish Judges and Magistrates.

5. *Lawyers and Litigation*

The process of economic development in Spain since 1960 seems to have considerably increased the volume of legal activity, and caused a certain decrease in judicial activity. This suggests a sizable degree of avoidance of courts by potential litigants, in civil and commercial cases. The *size* of this avoidance phenomenon is impossible to determine, without a systematic national survey of practicing lawyers. At present, the only information on this point comes from a survey of a sample of practicing lawyers in Madrid (17). The following question was asked: "Of the affairs of which you were personally in charge during last year, what proportion ended up in court for resolution? ". As can be seen in Table 15, 33.3 % of the interviewees answered "very few, almost none", 13.5 % "a fourth, approximately", 9.3 % "a third, more or less", 14 % "fifty per cent, approximately", 12.8 % "about three fourths" and 16.9 % "almost all or all".
To a certain extent the data indicate a bi-modal distribution: 46.8 % appear as not litigation-prone, 29.7 % as litigation-prone and the remaining 23.3 % fall in the middle. The distribution seems to suggest that there are three rather clearly identifiable groups of practicing lawyers: those who practically never litigate (largest group), those who constantly litigate, and a smaller group who sometimes litigate and sometimes do not.
What can first be noted is that, contrary to a widely held folk image which labels lawyers as *picapleitos* (a derogatory term to describe those who encourage litigation for its own sake), the dominant group of Spanish lawyers, at least in Madrid, appear to avoid litigation systematically. Lawyers no longer see litigation as their prototypical occupation. Other activities – such as counselling – seem to

Tab. 15: Inclination Towards Litigation Among Madrid Practicing Lawyers (in percentages)

"Of the affairs you were personally in charge of during last year, what proportion ended up in court for resolution?"		
Very little, almost none	33.3	not litigation prone: 46.8 %
A fourth approximately	13.5	
A third more or less	9.3	No fixed policy: 23.3 %
Fifty percent, approximately	14.0	
About three fourths	12.8	litigation prone: 29.7 %
Almost all or all	16.9	
(N)	(171)	

Source: Zaragoza's survey (1972)

occupy most of the time of the largest group of lawyers engaged in practice. Furthermore, large sectors of the legal profession treat litigation almost as a disease to be prevented. One lawyer wrote: "legal counsel is like prophylaxis: it helps prevent litigation which is a morbid situation among men... Litigation is unanimously considered a disaster...A transaction achieved through the attorney's efforts constitutes one of his biggest triumphs" (18). Legal folklore abounds in proverbs depicting litigation as the utmost evil – for example, "Vale mas un mal pacto que un buen pleito" (a bad deal or transaction is better than a good lawsuit), "Pleitos tengas y los ganes" (May you litigate and win – a somewhat cryptic way of implying that the only thing possibly worse than litigating is to win the litigation, since the costs will in any case exceed the possible benefits).

One important consequence is that lawyers in Spain no longer rely exclusively – or almost exclusively – on litigation for a living. In Table 18, we see that, among lawyers earning over 50,000 pesetas a month, 51 % are not litigation-oriented; 27.3 % are litigation-oriented – a clear indication that lawsuits are not longer the best source of income for lawyers. Income considerations do not seem to be working today among Spanish lawyers as an incentive for litigation (except perhaps in the lowest levels of the profession). The decision to bring a case to court, or not, seems clearly to result from other factors. Unfortunately, we lack any information on the dynamics of the decision to bring a case to Court. However, it seems safe to guess that the nature of the legal conflict is an important factor; the general pattern of propensity to litigate depicted in Table 15, cannot be expected to apply evenly to every type of case. Table 16 confirms this hypothesis. The inclination is examined from the point of view of the specialized field of practice in which the respondent is engaged. The differences found are indeed remarkable. Among the lawyers devoted to civil law, 50.5 % are not litigation oriented (20.8 % are prone to litigation). Among lawyers devoted to corporate affairs, the differences are even higher: 65.1 % are not litigation-oriented; 20.9 % are prone to litigation. The trend among lawyers devoted to other fields of legal practice is completely different: an orientation towards litigation clearly predominates (among lawyers devoted to criminal law, administrative law and labor law, 66.6 %, 50.0 % and 60.0 %, respectively, are litigation prone; only 11.1 %, 14.3 %, and 10.0 %, respectively, are not).

Tab. 16: Inclination to Litigate Among Practicing Lawyers of Madrid, by Main Specialized Field of Practice (in percentages)

Proportion of the Affairs Handled Over Last Year Resulting In Litigation	Civil Law	Corporation Law	Criminal Law	Administrative Law	Labor Law
Very few, almost none	34.7	53.5	–	14.3	10.0
A fourth Approximately	15.8	11.6	11.1	–	–
A third more or less	9.9	2.3	–	7.1	20.0
Fifty percent, approximately	16.8	11.6	16.6	21.4	–
About Three fourths	13.9	2.3	33.3	21.4	30.0
Almost all or all	6.9	18.6	33.3	28.6	30.0
D.K., N.A.	2.0	–	8.8	10.0	10.0
(N)	(101)	(43)	(18)	(14)	(10)
Not litigation oriented	50.5	65.1	11.1	14.3	10.0
No clear orientation	26.7	13.9	16.6	28.5	20.0
Litigation prone	20.8	20.9	66.6	50.0	60.0

Such remarkable differences can hardly stem from lawyers' personal inclinations or whims. Instead, what must be assumed is that, within each of these legal sub-fields, some structural mechanisms cause different predispositions towards litigation. Lawyers devoted to criminal law can hardly avoid court; in the Spanish legal system most criminal offenses must be prosecuted *ex-officio,* and public prosecutors can make no deals with the defense. The normal path of a criminal case goes through the judicial route, with the possible exception of "private crimes" (*delitos privados*) some of which (for instance, adultery) are not prosecuted *ex-officio,* and thus leave room for extra-judicial settlement.

As for lawyers devoted exclusively to administrative law, their situation is similar. According to the European tradition of public law, the State can make no deals with private individuals or enities. Anyone involved in conflict with any branch or institution of public administration has no choice but to challenge in court the resolution of his case by the administration.

As for labor cases, parties resort to private lawyers only when conciliation has been unsuccessfully attempted at the local office of the official labor unions. In a sense, labor conflicts are screened; only those which fail to be resolved at this first stage of conciliation (and, consequently, those showing a higher level of conflict) get to the lawyers, which to a large extent may explain the large number which end up in litigation.

For these legal fields, then, we have built-in institutional mechanisms that act as constraints on the chances of extra-judicial settlement. Similar mechanisms can not be found in civil or commercial law: in these two legal fields no internal predisposition of the law favors one way of conflict resolution over the other. Traditionally, civil and commercial law have been considered proper realms for litigation. However, it is precisely in these two legal specialties that the propensity for litigation among lawyers seems to be at its lowest. When left to themselves, with room to maneuver and without any institutional constraints, the lawyer's reflex today is to attempt informal, extra-judicial settlement, rather than go the path of litigation.

It is worth noting that the tendency for extra-judicial settlement among Madrid lawyers seems to be noticeably higher among those specialized in corporate affairs. The lawyer devoted to civil affairs will as a rule have individuals as clients; the lawyer devoted to corporate affairs, will have business entities. This may affect the way in which they handle their cases. An individual who agrees with his lawyer to press for a lawsuit does not have to account for his action; he will be the only one affected by the outcome of judicial process. A corporation, however, is normally represented by the general manager, who will have to account for his decisions to the Board of the corporation. Since trials are slow, and their outcome always uncertain, and since the manager will have to give embarrassing explanations to the Board if he loses, the manager will, as a rule, be inclined to conciliate. He would rather make some concessions than enter the dangerous all or nothing game of judicial process. Furthermore, whatever the costs of a settlement, they are apt to be balanced by the time and effort saved. In this situation, both the lawyer and the client will tend to want to avoid judicial settlement.

The fact that the large majority of lawyers devoted to civil or corporate cases appear not to be litigation-oriented should not make us forget, however, that a sizable minority (about 21 % in both cases) *is* litigation-prone. To a certain extent we have here again a bi-modal distribution, which seems to suggest a second stage of specialization. Lawyers tend to specialize by field of law; within each specialized field, lawyers seem also to specialize further, as courtroom lawyers (the minority of lawyers devoted to civil or corporate affairs, but the majority among the rest) or in counseling (the majority of lawyers devoted to civil and corporate cases, the minority among the rest).

There are, to be sure, in corporation and commercial law, instances in which recourse to court is hardly avoidable (for instance, in *quiebras* – bankruptcies – or *juicios ejecutivos* – actions related to unpaid negotiable instruments). The fact that two out of every ten lawyers devoted to corporate affairs are litigators may mean that they have specialized in these specific kinds of cases. The others occupy themselves exclusively with those cases which do not require court action. In such cases, litigation comes very rarely, only when that is the determined, unshakeable desire of the client, perhaps for irrational motives, or when used as a dilatory – or intimidating – tactic in the client's interests (19). Even then, two courses of action may be open to the lawyer: personally to take the case to court, or to turn it over to a corporation lawyer specialized in court work.

On the other hand, in most conflicts over corporation law, the parties will hire lawyers of equivalent status and prestige. This factor will further strengthen the chances for settlement, since the weakness or incompetence of the other part's legal counsel will not act as an incentive to press for total victory.

The data in Table 16 confirm what an outside observer would gather from interviews with practicing lawyers, some of whom boast that they have never set foot in a courtroom. The intermediate groups of lawyers, who do not show any clear tendency to seek or avoid litigation may constitute old-fashioned lawyers who understand legal practice to include both litigation and counseling.

The data in Table 17 allow us to estimate the actual amount of work carried out by each type of practicing lawyer. As can be seen, 31.6 % of the lawyers devoted to civil affairs and 48.6 % of those devoted to corporate affairs handle more than 100 cases per year (the corresponding percentages for lawyers devoted to criminal, labor and administrative affairs are respectively 44.5 %, 30.0 % and 21.4 %). That is, the proportion of lawyers having more than 100 cases per year is larger among those who are less likely to have recourse to courts. Or to put it differently, lawyers that litigate less have in their hands a large proportion of the legal conflicts (and moreover they are by far the more numerous: 144 out of 176 in the sample).

Tab. 17: Number of Cases Handled Yearly, Among Practicing Lawyers of Madrid, by Specialized Field of Practice (in percentages)

	Civil Law	Criminal Law	Administrative Law	Corporation Law	Labor Law
More than 200	6.1	16.7	7.1	21.6	10.0
From 100 to 200	26.5	27.8	14.3	27.0	20.0
From 25 to 100	38.8	38.9	57.1	24.3	20.0
Less than 25	20.4	–	7.1	13.5	50.0
D.K., N.A	8.2	16.6	14.3	13.5	–
(N)	(98)	(18)	(14)	(37)	(10)

All this seems to confirm the initial hypothesis we had advanced: litigants and lawyers are avoiding the courts, especially in civil and commercial law. This means that, in a country undergoing rapid economic development, fewer legal conflicts relating to economic life are being brought to the forum which in principle should resolve them: the courts. That key legal elite, the judiciary, is losing any substantial influence on important aspects of social life.

The amount of litigation: an attempt at estimation

Since we do not have figures on the number of legal conflicts and cases handled by all Spanish practicing lawyers, it is impossible to calculate accurately the amount of litigation and the amount of avoidance of litigation.

On the basis of data contained in Table 19, an estimation can be attempted, however, for practicing lawyers in Madrid, assuming that for all the interviewed lawyers answering that they had handled up to 25 cases during the past year (35 answers) or between 25 and 100 cases (62 answers), the mean number of cases effectively taken care of was around 50. Similarly, for those answering "between 100 and 200" (41 answers) and "more than 200" (19 answers), we will guess at a mean of 150 cases.

Tab. 18: Tendency to Litigate, Among Practicing Lawyers of Madrid, By Declared Monthly Income

Proportion of cases handled during last year resulting in litigation	Over 50,000 Pesetas	Up to 50,000 Pesetas
Very few, almost none	41.8	28.0
A fourth approximately	9.1	12.8
A third more or less	12.6	9.7
Fifty percent approximately	7.2	15.0
About three fourths	11.0	14.0
All or almost all	16.3	18.2
D.K., N.A.	2.0	2.0
(N)	(55)	(93)
Not litigation oriented	50.9	40.8
No clear orientation	19.8	24.7
Litigation oriented	27.3	32.4

Tab. 19: Propensity to Litigation By Number of Cases Handled Yearly, Among Madrid Practicing Lawyers (in absolute numbers)

"Of the affairs you were in charge of personally during last year, what proportion ended up in court for resolution?"	Number of cases handled			
	More than 200	Between 100 and 200	Between 25 and 100	Less than 25
Very few, almost none	7	8	17	21
A fourth approximately	3	4	9	2
A third more or less	0	2	10	3
Fifty percent approximately	0	12	7	4
About three fourths	2	6	10	2
Almost all or all	6	8	9	3
Do not know, do not answer	1	1	0	0
Total	19	41	62	35

Source: Zaragoza's survey (1972)

Accepting these estimations, the following computations can be carried out: Of those sixty lawyers who handled an estimated average of 150 cases yearly (41 who had answered "between 100 and 200" and 19 who answered "more than 200"),

- 15 said that practically no case resulted in litigation;
- 7 said that one fourth did, that is $\frac{7 \times 150}{4} = 262$ did;

- 5 said that one third did, that is
  $\frac{5 \times 150}{3} = 250$ did;
- 12 said that one-half did, that is
  $\frac{12 \times 150}{2} = 900$ did;
- 8 said that three-fourths did, that is
  $\frac{8 \times 150}{4} \times 3 = 900$ did;
- finally, 14 said that practically all their cases resulted in litigation, that is
  14 x 150 = 2,100 cases did.

Adding these figures suggests that for the sixty lawyers with more than 100 cases per year an estimated 4,412 cases out of 9,000 led to litigation. Similarly, for the 97 lawyers handling less than 100 cases yearly, 1,237 cases out of 4,850, we estimate, resulted in litigation. Adding the two figures, we have a total of 5,649 cases, or some 40 %, of the total of 13,850, which led to litigation (20). Roughly, then, between one-third and one-half of all legal conflicts reaching the offices of the lawyers in the sample ended up in litigation.

6. *The perception of court avoidance*

We now turn our attention to analysis of the way in which the judges, the legal elite most directly affected by trends in litigation, perceive those trends. I asked the judges in my sample: "Generally speaking, what proportion of all conflicts with legal implications that arise in Spanish society would you say are brought to court for resolution? " (see Table 20). The answers show a high awareness of the phenomenon of court avoidance:

– very few, almost none	19.7 %
– one Fourth,	22.9 %
– a third,	13.3 %
– fifty per cont,	20.2 %
– three fourths,	8.5 %
– all or almost all,	3.7 %

Actually, most judges seem to perceive the situation as rather worse than our own estimates. According to our calculations, about 40 % (that is, between one third and one half) of all legal conflicts result in litigation before the courts. If so about 20 % of the judges in the sample (those answering "very few, almost none") see the situation as much worse (21) than it really is, an additional 23 % (those answering "one-fourth") see it as somewhat worse, 33.5 % (those answering "one-third" or fifty per cent") see it as we have estimated it to be; only 8.5 % (those answering "three-fourths") see it as somewhat better than it is; and just 3.7 % (those answering "all or almost all") see it as much better.
To simplify our analysis, we grouped the answers in three groups:
a) the first group consists of those who perceive the evasion of cases (22) from courts as much larger than it is. These judges overestimate the number of conflicts settled out of the courts, and, consequently, the loss of judicial

Tab. 20: Perception of the Proportion of Legal Conflicts Brought to Court, Among Spanish Judges (in percentages)

Proportion of all legal conflicts perceived as brought to the Courts for resolution	N	%
Very few, almost none	37	19.7
One fourth approximately	43	22.9
A third more or less	25	13.3
Fifty percent approximately	38	20.2
About three fourths	16	8.5
Almost all or all	7	3.7
D.K., N.A.	22	11.7
	188	100.0

Typology according to the perception of conflicts brought to Court		
Critical (1+2)	80	42.6
Aware (3+4)	63	33.5
Uncritical (5+6)	23	12.2

influence. We can call this group "critical", since their answers seem to imply a critical outlook on the present state of the judiciary.

b) The second group consists of those whose responses seem close to our own data. Those judges we label as "aware", since their perception seems not to be distorted one way or the other.

c) A third and last group can be formed with respondents whose answers are clearly unrealistic. Their perception of reality seems distorted by an optimistic bent, which makes them think that practically no conflict is resolved outside the courts. To the extent that such answers imply the belief that the judicial structure is fully effective, and fully adapted to social reality, these judges can be called "uncritical".

The critical group accounts for 42.6 % of the respondents, the aware group 33.5 %, and the uncritical group only 12.2 %. In short, there is a high degree of awareness among Spanish judges.

What variables determine whether a judge will be aware, critical or uncritical? Are purely personal or ideological factors decisive, or can these attitudes be traced to specific experiences? Many factors which, in principle, could be expected to affect perception, such as case-load, turn out not to be significant. Perceptions do not seem to result from professional experiences, but rather from ideological preconceptions. I constructed a dichotomized typology of judges, on the basis of their perception of characteristics which the ideal judge should possess. I offered the judges whom I interviewed the following list of characteristics, from which they had to select a maximum of four:

a) a high level of legal and technical preparation,
b) capacity to contribute through his decisions to the evolution of the law,
c) a constant concern about his independence,
d) a great dedication to his work,
e) a constant interest in protecting the rights and freedoms of the citizens,
f) a deep sense of equity enabling him to interpret the law flexibly
g) an unimpeachable private life,
h) a constant concern for the formal and procedural aspects of the cases brought to him,
i) a clear sense of the consequences (social, human, political, economic) that his decisions may have,
j) a great religiosity.

Of these ten characteristics, two (a) and (d) may be taken for granted and, for our purposes here, considered as neutral (besides, most respondents mentioned them). The remaining eight characteristics can be classified in two groups: those which imply involvement and active participation in the dynamics and processes of the society (characteristics b, e, f and i) and those which, on the contrary, imply a withdrawal from social affairs (characteristics c, g, h and j). Characteristics b, e, f and i can be said to imply an *active* conception of the judge's role; characteristics c, g, h and j seem to point to a *passive* conception, in which aloofness from society is a judge's greatest possible virtue, and his strongest possible safeguard against outside influences. We will assign a value of +1 to each of the four active-oriented characteristics, a value of −1 to each of the passive-oriented ones and a value of 0 to the two neutral characteristics. For each respondent we will thus have a score which can range from a maximum of +4 (if he mentions all four active features) to a minimum of −4 (if he mentions all four passive characteristics). For our purposes here we will consider as active all those with a total score of +1 or more; all the rest will be labeled passive.
As can be seen in Table 21, the judge's role conception explains, at least to some extent, perceptions of court avoidance. Those who tend to think that the judge should play an active role in the life of society are more likely to overestimate

Tab. 21: Perception of the Proportion of all Legal Conflicts Brought to Court Among Spanish Judges, By Conception of the Role of the Judge (in percentages)

Proportion of all legal conflicts perceived as brought to the Courts for resolution	Active conception of the role of the Judge	Passive conception of the role of the Judge
Very few, almost none	24.0	14.1
One fourth approximately	26.9	17.6
One third more or less	16.0	9.4
Fifty percent approximately	15.4	25.9
About three fourths	6.7	15.3
All or almost all	1.0	7.1
D.K., N.A.	12.5	10.5
(N)	(104)	(85)
Critical	50.9	31.7
Aware	31.4	35.3
Uncritical	7.7	22.4

the amount of legal conflicts that avoid the courts. Passive judges are more likely to feel that they are handling the bulk of the legal conflicts which arise in society. The proponent of an active orientation would preach involvement to his colleagues; the proponent of passive orientation, retirement. All this, of course, affects perception of the legal conflicts in society and of the rate of litigation. Passive judges, not very aware of the processes going on in society, nor motivated to perceive shortcomings in the administration of justice, tend to think that most conflicts end up in court – as it should be. Active judges, more critical about a situation which does not allow them to influence social affairs as they might like, will, on the contrary, perceive the avoidance of court and the resulting loss of power or influence. Their general orientation may even induce them to dramatize the situation beyond reality. In short, perception of court avoidance seems linked more to ideological than to contextual factors.

The perception of litigiousness through time

If we ask judges to compare the present amount of litigation with that of ten years earlier, 32.6 % state that the earlier amount was larger, 33.2 % that it was more or less the same, and 30.0 % that it was smaller (Table 22).
The feeling that there is less litigation today is somewhat stronger among District Judges and among magistrates serving in Territorial *Audiencias*. Magistrates serving as District Judges (in cities which are provincial capitals) or in Provincial (Criminal) *Audiencias* are more likely to perceive an increase in litigation (Table 23). One possible explanation for these differences may lie in actual changes in volume of litigation in various courts. As has already been pointed out, the largest increase in case load, in absolute numbers, during the last ten years, has affected mainly District Courts located in large cities, and some Criminal *Audiencias*. First instance civil tribunals located in small urban areas, or

Tab. 22: Perception of Present Amount of Litigation, As Compared With That of a Decade Ago, Among Spanish Judges

Proportion of legal conflicts resulting in litigation ten years ago was	(N)	%	
Much larger	8	4.3	32.6
Larger	53	28.3	
More or less the same	62	33.2	
Smaller	42	22.5	30.0
Much smaller	14	7.5	
D.K., N.A.	8	4.3	
Total	187	100.1	

Tab. 23: **Perception of Present Amount of Litigation, As Compared with That of a Decade Ago, Among Spanish Judges, By Present Professional Category (in percentages)**

The amount of litigation ten years ago was		District Judges in villages		District Judges in cities		Provincial Audiencias Magistrates		Territorial Audiencias Magistrates	
Much smaller	Smaller	9.0	25.0	11.0	35.7	0.0	38.0	4.0	24.0
Smaller		16.0		24.7		38.0		20.0	
More or less the same		31.0		30.1		31.0		38.0	
Larger	Larger	33.0	37.0	21.9	26.0	19.0	25.0	35.0	39.0
Much larger		4.0		4.1		6.0		4.0	
D.K., N.A.		6.0		8.2		6.0		–	
(N)		(45)		(73)		(16)		(55)	

second instance civil tribunals (and some Provincial *Audiencias*) have experienced little or no change in the volume of litigation.

The association between work load and perception of changes in the volume of litigation is further documented in Table 24. The heavier the case load, the higher the tendency to consider today's volume of litigation larger than that of a decade ago. We have seen that the perception of the amount of avoidance of litigation is determined mainly by ideological factors. A judge does not normally have in his professional life any way to assess the actual number of conflicts arising, and the percentage that evades litigation. But when judges are asked to compare the present volume of litigation with that of a decade ago, they are comparing two real and experienced quantities. Hence they can rely much more on their professional experience and, as a consequence, purely ideological components play a lesser part in determining their opinion.

It is, however, interesting to observe the consistency between the two evaluations. 30 % of those who think that litigation has increased are critical versus 52.5 % of those who think litigation has decreased. On the other hand, among those who think that the volume of litigation has been increasing in the past ten years, 17.8 % are uncritical; only 1.6 % of those who think that the amount of

Tab. 24: **Perception of Present Amount of Litigation, As Compared With That of a Decade Ago, Among Spanish Judges, By Current Case Load (in percentages)**

The amount of litigation was ten years ago	Up to 500 cases per year	More than 500 cases per year
Smaller*	22.9	35.9
More or less the same	35.6	28.3
Larger**	40.2	27.1
(N)	(87)	(92)

* Groups answers "much smaller" and "smaller."
** Groups answers "larger" and "much larger."

litigation has been decreasing are uncritical (Table 25). This seems to indicate that judges feel that the proportion of conflicts avoiding the courts has increased over the decade (this is clearly indicated by the fact that 52.5 % of those who think that today's volume of litigation is less than that of ten years ago also think that practically no legal conflict today ends up in litigation). The critical-minded not only think that te present situation is bad, they also feel that it has been deteriorating over the years.

Tab. 25: Perception of Present Amount of Litigation, As Compared With That of a Decade Ago, Among Spanish Judges, by Perceived Volume of Legal Conflicts Resulting Today in Litigation (in percentages)

Orientation towards the volume of litigation	The amount of litigation was ten years ago		
	Smaller	The same	Larger
Critical (say that a fourth or less of legal conflicts result in litigation)	30.3	43.5	52.5
Aware (between a third and 50 % result in litigation)	33.9	30.7	39.3
Uncritical (three fourths or more result in litigation)	17.8	19.3	1.6
(N)	(56)	(62)	(61)

The Judges' attitude towards Court avoidance

Up to this point we have been concerned with perception rather then with evaluation. We now turn to the way in which the judges assess the situation, as they perceive it. Do they consider the decline of litigation a potential threat to the stability of society and the administration of justice? We asked those who believed that 50 % or less of all legal conflicts resulted in litigation to assess the situation "from the point of view of the administration of justice". 38.3 % answered that they considered it damaging, 33.7 % considered it neither damaging nor beneficial, and 22.5 % considered it beneficial (see Table 26). This high dispersion of answers seems to indicate that judges take different aspects or factors into consideration. In principle, two main factors may be assumed to be at work: the perceived amount of court avoidance; and, the fields of law in which the avoidance is perceived as taking place.

As can be seen in Table 27, the larger the volume of perceived court avoidance, the more likely that it will be found damaging and the less likely that it will be considered beneficial. Family cases and cases relating to economic and commercial life form the largest proportion of the legal conflicts that judges consider less likely to result in litigation (Table 28). Those perceptions are fairly accurate. That avoidance takes place in one field of law rather than another should make – and in fact does make – a difference in evaluation: only 29 % of those judges who perceive the avoidance of courts to affect mainly civil cases find it

Tab. 26: Spanish Judges' Attitude Towards the Avoidance of Courts of Potential Cases

Consider the avoidance	N	%
Very damaging	23	16.6
Rather damaging	30	21.7
Neither damaging nor beneficial	52	37.7
Rather beneficial	29	21.0
Very beneficial	2	1.5
D.K., N.A.	2	1.5
Total	138	100.0

Tab. 27: Spanish Judges' Attitude Towards the Avoidance of Courts of Potential Cases, By Perceived Volume of Legal Conflicts Resulting In Litigation (in percentages)

	Perceived amount of conflicts resulting in litigation	
Consider the avoidance	Very few, almost none	Other answers
Damaging	54.0	32.1
Neither damaging nor beneficial	27.0	41.3
Beneficial	18.9	24.8
(N)	(37)	(109)

Tab. 28: Types of Legal Conflicts Perceived by Spanish Judges As Less Likely To Result In Litigation (in percentages)

Family cases	29.4
Economic, commercial corporations cases	18.2
Estate successions	4.7
Labor cases	1.1
Tenancy cases	1.8
Sexual offenses	6.5
There is not a specific type of case	3.5
Others	28.2
Do not know	6.5
(N)	(170)

damaging, and 32.2 % beneficial; among judges who perceive avoidance to occur mainly in other areas (especially commercial law and criminal law) 43 % find it damaging, only 17.2 % beneficial. That is, avoidance of cases affecting two private parties tends to be considered less damaging than that of cases affecting (directly or potentially) the collective interest (as criminal and commercial cases do) (Table 29).

These answers seem to reveal an implicit classification of legal conflicts and cases

Tab. 29: Spanish Judges' Attitude Towards the Avoidance of Courts of Potential Cases, By Type of Legal Conflict Mainly Perceived As Avoiding the Recourse to Court (in percentages)

Consider the avoidance	Civil Cases	Other types of legal conflicts
Damaging	28.8	44.9
Neither Damaging nor beneficial	40.0	36.2
Beneficial	32.2	16.9
N.A., D.K.	–	3.8
(N)	(59)	(105)

according to their importance, measured by their social implications, a criterion somewhat surprising for judges of a legal system which defines the task of the judge as the abstract application of norms to concrete cases. This is but one more indication of the extent to which a sizable proportion of the members of the Spanish judiciary seem to feel uneasy with the basic passivity of their role as presently defined.

From avoidance to escape

So far, we have just considered legal conflicts which could have gone to court, but did not, because of the slowness and inflexibility of judicial processes. That is, avoidance may be traced to shortcomings and inadequacies of procedural norms.

There may be, however, avoidance of a different nature: acts or situations which cannot be made in object of litigation for lack of substantive norms. There may be intentional acts which, though damaging legitimate interests of innocent persons cannot, however, be considered as criminal since no law so classifies them. This is likely to occur where the body of substantive norms has not kept pace with social change, creating a kind of legal vacuum (23). Since Spain has undergone rapid economic development, in the last decade, it would be interesting to see if, from the judges' perspective, the changing social and economic conditions have made this "vacuum" more likely or more frequent. We asked the following question: "It is often said that in modern, industrialized societies intentional act difficult to classify as crimes but which, however, cause serious damage to legitimately acquired rights, are more and more frequent. Such actions, it is argued, escape justice, because they cannot be subsumed under existing norms. How often would you say that this takes place presently in Spain? " Only 0.5 % of the judges interviewed answered "never", only 10.6 % "seldom". 86.8 % seem to be aware, with varying degrees of intensity, that such a situation exist (see Table 30). Generally speaking, then, Spanish judges seem to feel that industrialization has created such legal vacuums. We will refer to this second cause of avoidance as the "escape" phenomenon.

Once again, the perception of the judges seems to be strongly rooted in ideological inclinations. One could have expected, indeed, that judges serving in industrial areas would be more sensitive to the "escape" phenomenon, if

Tab. 30: Perception of the Existence of Intentional Acts which Should Be the Object of action of the Courts, But Which Escape because of Lack of Appropriate Legal Classifications Among Spanish Judges (in percentages)

Such kinds of action take place in present-day Spain	
Very often	15.9
Quite often	39.7
Sometimes	31.2
Seldom	10.6
Never	0.5
D.K.	1.6
N.A.	0.5
(N)	(189)

Tab. 31: Perception of Conflicts and Actions Escaping Control of the Courts, By Character of the Socio-economic Context Where Serving (in percentages)

Actions escaping control by the Courts happen	Industrial Context	Non-Industrial Context
Very or quite often	54.5	57.1
Sometimes	28.6	35.1
Seldom or never	14.3	6.5
(N)	(112)	(77)

perception were based on experience rather than on ideology. But Table 31 shows that there are not significant differences in perceptions between judges serving in industrial and non-industrial contexts. Judges' opinions on the matter, therefore, may well be determined by ideological pre-conceptions. On the other hand, judges' opinions on this subject are consistent with their perceptions about avoidance of courts; the more avoidance they perceive, the more they also see the "escape" phenomenon (Table 32).

This close association between the two perceptions seems to suggest that the judges who are most aware of avoidance are also those who show sensitivity to "escape," – or, in other words, perception of procedural shortcomings is associated with perception of substantive shortcomings. In both cases the higher sensitivity seems to reflect ideology rather than experience. Active judges perceive more "escape" than passive judges. (62.5 % of the former say that these occur "very often" or "quite often", only 17 % of the latter). At the same time, 15.3 % of the passive judges feel that "escape" occurs "seldom" or "never", and only 7.7 % of the active judges. The conception of the role of the judge seems to influence the perception of what we have called "escape" (see Table 33). On the other hand, surprisingly, since an active-orientation seems to imply less satisfaction with the present situation of the judiciary than a passive-orientation, the higher the degree of satisfaction with their present situation, the lower the awareness of "escape" of actions of the type we are considering (see Table 34).

Tab. 32: Perception of Conflicts and Actions Escaping the Control of the Courts, By Perception of the Degree of Court Avoidance (in percentages)

Proportion of all legal conflicts perceived as brought to the Courts for resolution	Actions escaping to the control of the Courts happen					
	Very Often	Quite Often	Sometimes	Seldom	Never	N.A.,D.K.
Very few, almost none	36.7	17.6	10.2	20.0	(1)	(2)
A fourth approximately	16.7	28.4	25.4	5.0		(1)
A third more or less	6.7	20.3	11.9	5.0		
Fifty percent approximately	20.0	14.9	20.3	45.0		
About three fourths	3.3	6.8	13.6	10.0		
Almost all or all	–	2.7	6.8	5.0		
D.K., N.A.	16.7	17.6	13.6	5.0		(1)
(N)	(30)	(74)	(59)	(20)	(1)	(4)

Tab. 33: Perception of Conflicts and Actions Escaping the Control of the Courts, By Conception of the Role of the Judge (in percentages)

Actions escaping control by the Courts happen	Active-oriented	Passive-oriented
Very or quite often	62.5	47.1
Sometimes	28.8	34.1
Seldom or never	7.7	15.3
N.A., D.K.	1.0	3.6
(N)	(104)	(85)

Tab. 34: Perception of Conflicts and Actions Escaping the Control of the Courts, By Satisfaction With Present Social Position of the Judge (in percentages)

Actions escaping control by the Courts happen	Satisfied	Neither satisfied nor dissatisfied	Dissatisfied
Very often	11.6	18.0	33.3
Quite often	37.5	42.0	42.9
Sometimes	36.6	26.0	14.3
Seldom	11.6	12.0	4.8
Never	(1)	–	–
D.K., N.A.	–	(1)	(2)
(N)	(110)	(49)	(20)

The possibilities for action

Can the judiciary do something to close the gaps in the law, and end the "escape" phenomenon? 30.6 % of the respondents thought there was nothing they could do to remedy the situation, 51 % considered that they could do "something" in this respect, and 17.8 % said that they could do "much" or "very much" (Table 35). That is, two out of every three judges in the sample

Tab. 35: **Spanish Judges' Perception of What the Courts of Justice Could Do To Have Actions and Conflicts Escaping Their Control Subject To It (in percentages)**

The Courts could do			
Very much	much	8.1	17.8
Much		9.7	
Rather	something	20.4	51.0
Something		30.6	
Nothing		30.6	
N.A.		0.5	
(N)		(186)	

seemed to believe that there was, in principle, something they could do to remedy the situation. At first sight, one might be tempted to interpret such answers as symptoms of utter optimism or unreality (especially when one considers the judge's narrow roledefinition in Spanish law), or as a proof of active-orientation. However, the data in Tables 36 and 37 puts these answers in the proper perspective.

Table 36 records answers to the question: "What could the courts of justice do to make such actions subject to their control? ". 39.1 % give answers suggesting direct action (22.7 % mention extensive interpretation of existing law, 16.4 % suggest harshness in sentencing as a way of setting an example). 46.1 % give answers suggesting indirect action (23.4 % mention the possibility, expressed in Article 2 of the Criminal Code, that the Judicial Council – *Consejo Judicial* – call the attention of the Government to legal deficiencies or shortcomings; 22.7 % mention more general forms of calling attention to the problem). In short, 46.1 % indicate that what they can do is look for outside help; 39 % think that judges could solve the problem themselves. We can call the former outside-oriented (they think that something can be done – but only from the outside), and the latter inside-oriented (they seem to think that the judiciary can solve the problem by itself, by redefining the tools at its disposal). The percentage of respondents who say that the judiciary can do much or something is essentially the same, among both outside and inside-oriented judges (Table 37). For some respondents, to make use of Article 2 of the Criminal Code seems, then, to be doing "much" To solve the situation; for others the solution may be, instead, to use extensive interpretation. The use of a specific adverb does not thus seem directly connected to outside or inside-orientation. In a sense, what

Tab. 36: Spanish Judges' Perception of the Specific Actions That the Courts Could Take to Have Conflicts and Actions Escaping Their Control Subject To It (in percentages)

Use extensive interpretation of the existing law	22.7	inside-oriented
Investigate them thoroughly, be harsh in sentencing	16.4	inside-oriented
Make use of article 2 of the Criminal Code	23.4	outside-oriented
Call to the attention of the society and government (through annual reports, etc.)	22.7	outside-oriented
Other answers	12.5	
D.K., N.A.	2.3	
(N)	(128)	

(The question was asked only th those answering that the Courts could do very much, much, rather or something to remedy the Situation.)

Tab. 37: Spanish Judges' Perception of the Specific Actions That the Courts Could Take to Have Conflicts and Actions Escaping Their Control Subject To It, By General Evaluation of What the Courts Could Do In This Regard (in percentages)

The specific actions suggested imply an	Very much, much	Rather, something
Inside orientation*	42.9	46.3
Outside orientation**	57.1	53.7
	(28)	(80)

* Answers referring to extensive interpretation and harsh sentencing.
** Answers referring to calling the attention of the government and society at large.

could be concluded from this analysis, is that the data referring to what the courts could do tend to reflect more what the judges wish for, than a description of reality: some 70 % answer that the courts could at least do something with respect to "escapes", but only 39 % (of that 70 %) indicate real potential actions by the courts. In other words, the general, abstract wish to be able to do something dominates actual possibilities to take action.

7. Conclusion: Economic Development and Its Effects on the Judge's task

So far, we have concerned ourselves exclusively with the judges' perception of the quantitative changes brought about in their work by economic development. Judges vary in their perceptions of the amount of cases which avoid the courts; such perceptions seems to be related mainly to the judge's concept of the ideal role of the judge. The way in which judges *evaluate* avoidance of the courts seems to depend on how *much* avoidance they perceive; and the field of law in which the avoidance is seen to occur.

One last point remains to be examined: the possible *qualitative* differences, which the process of social change may have introduced. Is the task of the judge, regardless of volume, more or less difficult after a decade or two of rapid industrialization?

There seems to be a remarkable consensus among Spanish judges (71.4 %); the judge's task is more difficult today; only 23.8 % see it as more or less the same as before, and a remarkably low 3.1 % describe it as easier (Table 38). The main reason given for this increase in difficulty rests in the fact that social and commercial life have become much more complex. A minority (23.7 %) Refer to purely legal dimensions, such as an increase in the volume of legislation or the appearance of new contractual forms (Table 39). Interestingly, judges serving in non-industrial areas ascribe the difficulty of their task to industrialization in even larger proportions that those serving in industrial areas – an indication that attitudes on the topic result from stereotypes rather than experience (Table 40). If we combine the data in Tables 40 and 22 we can build a typology of the

Tab. 38: Spanish Judges' Perception of the Way in Which Industrialization Has Affected the Difficulty of the Judge's Task

In comparison with what it was some ten or twenty years ago, the task of the judge has become	N	%
Much more difficult	58	30.7
Somewhat more difficult	77	40.7
More or less equally difficult	45	23.8
Somewhat easier	5	2.6
Much easier	1	0.5
N.A., D.K.	3	1.6
Total	189	100.0

Tab. 39: Reasons Causing An Increase in the Difficulty of the Judge's Task, As Perceived by Spanish Judges

	N	%
Increase of the volume and complexity of legislation	14	10.4
Social and commercial life have become much more complex, and so have legal cases	88	65.2
New contractual forms have appeared, most of which are atypical	18	13.3
The work load has increased enormously	9	6.6
Other reasons	4	3.0
D.K., N.A.	2	1.5
Total	135	100.0

Tab. 40: Spanish Judges' Perception of the Way in Which Industrialization Has Affected the Difficulty of the Judge's Task, By General Character of the Socio-economic Context in Which Serving (in percentages)

In comparison with what it was ten or twenty years ago, the task of the judge has become	Industrial Context	Non-Industrial Context
Much more difficult	25.9	37.0
More difficult	41.7	39.5
More or less equally difficult	25.9	21.0
Less difficult	2.8	2.5
Much less difficult	0.9	–
D.K., N.A.	2.8	–
(N)	(108)	(81)

forms of complexity which (in the view of judges), economic development may bring to judicial activity, combining qualitative and quantitive aspects. The amount of litigation may be perceived as having grown both in volume and in difficulty; or simply in volume, but not in difficulty; or simply in difficulty, but not in volume; or in neither respect. Each possible perception implies a different degree of overall complexity of judicial activity brought about by economic development.

The first type (Type I) corresponds to views of those judges who perceive an increase in judicial activity both of volume and in difficulty, as a result of the development process. As can be seen in Table 41, 44 respondents fall within this category (Cell A).

Type II includes 51 respondents, who see the overall complexity of judicial activity to have increased somewhat (whether as a result of an increase in difficulty, volume remaining the same, or as a result of an increase in volume, difficulty remaining basically the same; Cells B and D in Table 41).

Type III includes those 60 judges who consider that, basically, the overall complexity of judicial activity has remained as before, either because, although difficulty is greater, volume has tended to decrease, thus compensating for the

Tab. 41: Spanish Judges' Perception of the Way in Which Industrialization Has Affected the Difficulty of the Judge's Task; By Perception of the Evolution of the Amount of Litigation (in absolute numbers)

In comparison with what it was some ten years ago the amount of litigation is today	In comparison with what it was ten or twenty years ago, the difficulty of legal cases is today		
	Greater	The Same	Smaller
Larger	44 (A)	7 (D)	2
The same	44 (B)	17 (E)	1
Smaller	43 (C)	16 (F)	2
Total	131	40	5

other factor, or because both volume and difficulty of legal cases are perceived as stable. Respondents in Cells C and E in Table 41 form this category.

Finally, Type IV Includes respondents who seem to feel that complexity of judicial activity has lessened somewhat in the course of economic development. This category embraces 16 judges who perceive the amount of litigation presently reaching the courts, and the difficulty of the cases, as less than they were some ten years ago (Cell F, Table 41).

We can therefore, establish four principal types of judges, depending of the way in which they perceive that the volume of litigation and the difficulty of legal cases has varied with industrialization. Of the two dimensions we have used to build the typology, one (the qualitative one) responds to purely subjective evaluations. However, the quantitative measure can be treated objectively, and compared with respondents' estimations. As we have seen, the process of industrialization does *not* seem to have caused an increase in the relative volume of litigation. With this in mind, we can attempt the following interpretation of the four types of judges.

Type I judges see litigation as increased, which objectively does not seem to be the case; they are overwhelmed by volume and complexity. Judges of Type I seem *overcome* by a challenge they are unable to meet.

Type II judges could be described as *responsive:* most of them feel that the volume of litigation has remained substantially the same, but feel that legal conflicts have gained in complexity. They seem, in short, to perceive the situation much as it really is.

Type III judges, on the contrary, could be termed, in the main, *unresponsive:* they do not seem to perceive any effect of industrialization either on the volume or on the difficulty of legal cases.

Finally, Type IV judges form what we could call the marginal sector of the Judiciary: their perception of the amount of litigation is more or less in accordance with what we know it to be. However, they associate the decrease in litigation with a decrease in difficulty of cases. They probably have in mind certain classic types of cases, predominant in a non-industrial society, but declining in an industrializing one, whose difficulty consequently can hardly be said to increase. If my assumption is correct, they appear alienated from changes taking place, and as such, *marginal* to the new socio-economic condition.

This typology is advanced here in a tentative way. However, we can provisionally accept it, as a useful device for analyzing the Spanish judiciary. In terms of the typology, 25.7 % of the Spanish judges would be considered *overcome*; 55 % *responsive*, 9.9 % *unresponsive,* and 9.4 % *marginal.* About half of the judges appear to be attuned with new socio-economic reality, the other half unattuned – a rather plausible estimate in the light of the data presented.

The present paper constitutes a shortened and revised version of Chapters 9 to 12 of my doctoral dissertation, The Spanish Judiciary: A Sociological Study. The Administration of Justice in a Civil Law Country Undergoing Social Change under an Authoritarian Regime, submitted to the Department of Sociology at Yale University on December 1, 1974. The research on which it is based was made possible by a research fellowship from the Foreign Area Fellowship Program, of New York. A number of persons have helped me with their comments and suggestions, but my main intellectual debt is to Juan J. Linz (Yale University), my thesis director. I want also to thank Cristina Blanco, Gloria de Sagarra, Katharina Horter, Alberto Soteres, Luis Toharia, Manuel Garcia de Belza, Jaime Vegas and

Juan Manuel Rodrigo, all of them students at the time in the Universidad Autonoma, and Maria del Mar Teran, for their research assistance in different phases of the study, as well as the directive team of DATA SA. (Madrid) for their assistance and permission to use their facilities in the processing of the survey data. Finally, Professor Angel Zaragoza (Universidad Autonoma de Madrid) graciously authorized me to use data from his survey of a sample of practicing lawyers in Madrid (still in process of analysis), for which I am deeply grateful.

Summary

Es gibt bis jetzt wenig zusammenhängende empirische Kenntnisse über die Faktoren, die die Prozeßhäufigkeit beeinflussen, welche sogar in Ländern mit vergleichbarem Rechtssystem unterschiedlich ist. Nach einem kurzen Überblick über einige allgemeinere Faktoren, die wahrscheinlich die Prozeßhäufigkeit beeinflussen, versucht der Beitrag die Art und Weise zu klären, auf die einer dieser Faktoren, nämlich die ökonomische Entwicklung, in einem bestimmten Untersuchungsgebiet, nämlich dem heutigen Spanien, die Prozeßhäufigkeit beeinflussen kann.

Als erstes wird die Auswirkung der unterschiedlichen Entwicklung auf den Umfang der rechtlichen Aktivität untersucht (worunter der freiwillige Gebrauch geltender Normen durch private Parteien verstanden wird, gemessen am Umfang notarieller Beurkundungen), um einen Bezugsrahmen für Vergleiche zu finden. Dabei wird festgestellt, daß der Umfang rechtlicher Aktivität enorm zunahm, als Spanien sich ökonomisch entwickelte. Das Anwachsen rechtlicher Aktivität scheint aber nicht, wie man vielleicht hätte erwarten können, mit einer parallelen Zunahme der Prozeßtätigkeit einherzugehen. Dies wird erklärt als ein Anzeichen für ein weitverbreitetes Meiden der Gerichte, sobald das Land sich industrialisiert. Aufgrund von Daten einer Erhebung über Rechtsanwälte in Madrid wird versucht, das Verhältnis zwischen denjenigen Fällen, die die Praxis der Anwälte erreichen, und denjenigen abzuschätzen, die schließlich in einem Prozeß vor den Gerichten enden. Dieses Verhältnis variiert deutlich je nach Art der Praxis.

Die letzten Abschnitte des Beitrages untersuchen das Ausmaß, in dem spanische Richter sich der Meidung von Gerichten bewußt sind. Aufgrund einer Erhebung unter Richtern erster und zweiter Instanz wird festgestellt, daß die Mitglieder der Gerichte bestimmte Modelle der Vermeidung von Prozessen durchaus wahrnehmen. Diese Wahrnehmung ist wesentlich von ideologischen Faktoren abhängig: aktivorientierter Richter (d.h. Richter, die ihre Aufgabe in einem weiten und flexiblen Sinne verstehen, mit möglichst großem Bewegungsspielraum) können am ehesten das Phänomen der Vermeidung des Gerichts erkennen.

Notes

1 John H. Merryman's A First Essay on Law and Development, February 1972 (mimeographed) constitutes a seminal exception. My own previous work Cambio social y vida juridica en Espana, 1900–1970, Madrid, cuardernos para el dialogo, 1974; originally, my Ph. D. dissertation at Madrid Law School, attempts to document the effects of economic development on the legal system of Spain. The research project, Studies in Law and Development, conducted at Stanford University under the direction of John H. Merryman, and with

the participation of scholars from Mexico, Peru, Chile, Costa Rica, Italy and Spain, should increase enormously our knowledge on the specific effects on the legal system, of the process of economic growth.

A general review of the literature on law and social change can be found in D. Trubeck, "A Critique of the Law and Development Literature" (paper no. 10, Working Papers, Program in Law and Modernization series, Yale Law School).

2 This portion of the paper is much indebted to Juan J. Linz, whose comments and suggestions contributed enormously to it.

3 Lawrence M. Friedman, "Legal Culture and Social Development," in Verfassung und Recht in Übersee, ed. H. Kruger (1969), pp. 265–266.

4 See T. Kawashima, "Dispute resolution in Japan" in V. Aubert (ed.), Sociology of Law (Baltimore, Md., Penguin Books, 1969).

5 Juan J. Linz and A. de Miguel, "El empresario ante los problemas laborales" in Revista de Politica Social (October-December, 1963), pp. 5–106.

6 On attitudes toward recourse to courts of justice for the settlement of a conflict, in a rural, traditional context, see J. Pitt-Rivers, The People of the Sierra (London, Weidenfeld and Nicolson, 1954), Chapter X: even when morally right, the party who brings the case to court is looked upon with reprobation by the whole village, which considers his action mannerless.

7 For a summary of the concepts and implications of the European codification movement, see John H. Merryman, The Civil Law Tradition (Stanford University Press, 1969). The basic idea that the law should have no lags or vacuums could allow us to hypothesize that in principle, and controlling for the economic variable, the amount of litigation would tend to be smaller in a civil law system than in a common law system (where the law is to a larger extent worked out through confrontation and contest).

8 Lawrence M. Friedman and John H. Merryman have helped clarify my thinking on this point.

9 I use the terms in Max Weber's sense. Cf. Max Weber on Law in Economy and Society (Cambridge, Harvard University Press, 1954), p. 63. See also R. Bendix' discussion in Max Weber, an Intellectual Portrait (Anchor Books, 1962), pp. 398–400.

10 Of course, a number of other factors may also intervene, for example, the average technical quality of the lawyers. But to the extent that these have a secondary importance (i.e., they are somewhat subordinated to the factors we have analyzed) they can be ignored for our purposes.

11 W. Wipplinger, "Spain's Economic Development Path," paper presented at a two day conference on Spain in the Seventies: Problems of Change and Transition, held in Washington, D.C., June 13–14, 1973, mimeographed draft, p. 1.

12 Amando de Miguel et al., II Informe sobre la situacion social de Espana (Madrid, Euramerica, 1970).

13 Ibidem, p. 99 and ff.

14 I follow Amando de Miguel's terminology in II Informe ... op. cit.

15 A. de Miguel, II Informe ... op. cit., pp. 92–93.

16 Ibidem.

17 The survey was carried out by Professor Angel Zaragoza (School of Law, Universidad Autonoma de Madrid) to whom I am grateful for permission to use his data.

18 A. Fernandez Serrano, La Abogacia en Espana y en el mundo (Madrid, 1955) pp. 374–375.

19 I am grateful to Messrs. Alzaga and Montero, Attorneys at Law in Madrid, for information they provided me on this point.

20 Another possible – and probably more refined – way to make such an estimate would be to use as the mean number of cases handled by the lawyers with less than 25 cases per year, some 20 cases (it is indeed hardly conceivable for a full-time practicing lawyer to handle less than such an amount yearly, as an average). For those handling between 100 and 200 the mean can be estimated to be 150. For those handling between 25 and 100, we can estimate a mean of some 62 cases. Finally for those handling more than 200, that is for the fully successful members of the profession, a mean of some 300 cases can be safely estimated (since several of them will in all likelihood handle well over three or four times this figure). Making the same computations as before, with these new means, we reach the result that some 45 percent of the legal conflicts reaching the lawyers' offices result in litigation, an estimate close enough to the previous one to reinforce its plausibility.

21 The use of the adverbs "worse" and "better" in this context (and in the following pages) does not carry any ethical or value implication. When I say that the judges perceive the situation as worse than it really is, what I am assuming is that they resent the avoidance of courts, not that such an avoidance is necessarily something evil.

22 The same can be said of the expression "evasion of cases" or "case evasion" which sometimes will be used as an alternate for "court avoidance" or "avoidance of recourse to the courts." The expressions are used in a purely descriptive sense, not in a normative sense.

23 An example of a legal "vacuum" is the case of devices to prevent electric meters from working properly. In post-war Spain, such cases were frequent but could not be prosecuted, because the narrow provisions of the Criminal Code made it impossible to treat stealing energy as a crime against property.

II. Politische und soziale Determinanten richterlicher Tätigkeit

Erhard Blankenburg

Der Anteil gerichtlicher Verfahren bei der Austragung sozialer Konflikte

Gerichtliche Verfahren sind durch eine Reihe von Merkmalen gegenüber anderen Regelungsmechanismen für soziale Konflikte hervorgehoben. Verfahrensregeln, Einlassungs- und Erwiderungsfristen, die Notwendigkeit, mehrere Personen zu einem Termin zu koordinieren, die festgelegten Rollenzuweisungen bei dieser Verhandlung – all dies bedeutet, daß sich die Parteien auf mehrere Monate, manchmal sogar Jahre des Wartens einrichten müssen, wenn sie die Entscheidung in ihrem Konflikt vor Gericht tragen. Verfahrensweisen und Rollenmerkmale sind symbolisch überhöht, was neben der Legitimationsfunktion die Wirkung hat, daß zu den Parteien eine soziale Distanz aufgebaut wird.

Diese Merkmale des Verfahrens haben zur Folge, daß nur eine bestimmte Art von Konflikten, und diese nur von seiten bestimmter sozialer Gruppen vor Gericht gebracht werden. Soziale Mechanismen treffen eine Selektion unter der Vielzahl rechtlich relevanter Konflikte, so daß nur ein Bruchteil tatsächlich vor Gericht gelangt. Hinzu kommt, daß von allen sozialen Konflikten schon das Gesetz nur eine Auswahl justiziabel gemacht hat: Teilweise, weil sie jenseits einer Privatheitsschwelle liegen, über die hinaus nicht für vertretbar gehalten wird, daß der staatliche Sanktionsapparat in Interessenkonflikte hereingezogen wird (so etwa, aber nicht nur, im Bereich „besonderer Gewaltverhältnisse"). Teilweise aber auch können Konflikte deshalb nicht justiziabel gemacht werden, weil sie jenseits einer politischen Relevanzschwelle liegen: Wenn Interessengegensätze groß und die Machtmittel beträchtlich sind, ist die Konstellation sehr häufig, daß sich keine der Parteien einer richterlichen Entscheidung fügen würde (so etwa bei Tarif- und Arbeitskonflikten).

Sicherlich hängt die Art der Konflikte, die in einer Gesellschaft auftreten, von der jeweiligen Gesellschaftsstruktur ab: Industrielle Gesellschaften weisen andere Konflikte auf als agrarische, kapitalistische andere als sozialistische. Darüber hinaus aber unterscheiden sich auch die Relevanzkriterien und die Auswahl dessen, was einer gerichtlichen Konfliktlösung zugeführt wird: Hier müssen wir sowohl die gesellschaftlichen Bedingungen der Entscheidungen betrachten, nach denen bestimmt wird, was justiziabel gemacht wird, als auch die gesellschaftlichen Bedingungen der Selektivität dessen, was innerhalb der rechtlichen Regeln tatsächlich vor Gericht gebracht wird.

Wir wollen im folgenden aufzeigen, wie man die Rolle der Gerichte bei der Austragung sozialer Konflikte in der Bundesrepublik beschreiben könnte. Dabei soll als erstes ein Vergleich mit einem anderen Rechtssystem eine Vorstellung von der Größenordnung vermitteln, den die gerichtliche Tätigkeit in unserem Land hat. Im weiteren diskutieren wir die verfügbaren Daten aus verschiedenen Gerichtszweigen, sowie diejenigen Informationen, die uns Schlüsse auf die vorgerichtliche Selektion beim Zugang zum Recht erlauben. Durchgehend verfolgen wir dabei die Fragestellung, wieweit die Gerichte der Funktionszuschreibung gerecht werden, in Bezug auf soziale Machtverhältnisse kompensatorisch zu wirken.

1. *Häufigkeit justizieller Konflikte in verschiedenen Gesellschaften*

Eine Methode, die Rolle der Justiz in einer Gesellschaft zu bestimmen, ist der Vergleich zwischen verschiedenen Gesellschaften. Schon wenn wir den Geschäftsanfall der Gerichte auf die Bevölkerung beziehen, erhalten wir eine Vorstellung davon, wieviele Konflikte in einem Land gerichtlich geregelt werden. Für den Vergleich der Prozeßgegenstände liefert uns die Statistik leider nur sehr grobe Daten, die zudem durch Unterschiede im materiellen Recht schwer vergleichbar sind.
Um die Zahl der variierenden Variablen zu reduzieren, wollen wir Gesellschaften vergleichen, die einen ähnlichen wirtschaftlichen Entwicklungsstand und einen ähnlichen Grad der Industrialisierung haben. Jede historische Analyse wird zeigen, daß die Zahl und die Arten der gesellschaftlichen Konflikte sich mit der wirtschaftlichen Struktur verändern: Industrielle Gesellschaften mit einem hohen Grad an Bürokratisierung haben andere Konflikte, die gelöst werden müssen, sie haben andere Selektionsmechanismen, nach denen es sich entscheidet, welche Konflikte vor Gericht getragen werden, als weniger komplexe Gesellschaften.
Wir haben sowohl einen strukturellen als auch einen historischen Aspekt bei dem Vergleich der Rolle der Justiz in verschiedenen Gesellschaften zu beachten. Wenn wir die Bundesrepublik Deutschland (BRD) und die Deutsche Demokratische Republik (DDR) hierzu heranziehen, dann haben wir eine Reihe von Faktoren kontrolliert: Beide sind industriell entwickelt, beide zeigen hohe und konstante wirtschaftliche Wachstumsraten, beide haben eine rechtliche Tradition gemeinsam. Jedoch sind in der DDR in den vergangenen 20 Jahren rechtliche Institutionen und Regelungen allmählich gemäß sozialistischen Rechtsvorstellungen geändert worden.

	Strafjustiz (1970)	Ziviljustiz (1970)			
	Täter je 100.000 strafmünd. Einwohner	Zahlungsbefehle	Zivilrechtsprozesse	Ehescheidungsklagen	sonstige Familienrechtssachen
BRD	3.924	6.928	1.567	207	146
DDR	640	767	187	273	120

Quellen: Materialien zum Bericht zur Lage der Nation 1972, Bundestagsdrucksache VI/3080 S. 236
Stat. Bundesamt Wiesbaden: Rechtspflegestatistik Reihe 9, I, 1970
(als Zivilrechtsprozesse sind für die BRD alle „gewöhnlichen" Prozesse gezählt)
Stat. Jahrbuch der DDR 1972 S. 3, S. 486, 490 (bei Strafverfahren einschließlich, bei Zivilrechtsprozessen ohne Verfahren vor Konfliktkommissionen)

Für die Zivil- wie in der Strafrechtspflege liegen die Raten gerichtlicher Konfliktlösungen in der DDR wesentlich niedriger als in der BRD. Mit Ausnahme der Ehescheidungsklagen, die in der DDR etwas häufiger sind, werden in der BRD alle gewöhnlichen Zivilprozesse und Mahnverfahren fast 9 mal so häufig, Strafverfahren mehr als 6 mal so häufig geführt. Sowohl im Zivilrecht als auch im Strafrecht gibt es in der DDR mit den Konfliktkommissionen Substitute für gerichtliche Verfahren (1) * – ob diese noch in die Statistik aufgenommen werden sollten, ist eine Frage der Definition dessen, was wir „gerichtliches Verfahren" nennen wollen. Selbst unter Einschluß der Tätigkeit der Konfliktkommissionen bleibt die Häufigkeit von Prozessen in der DDR weit unter der der BRD. Diese Zahlen jedoch ermöglichen noch keinen Rückschluß auf die Häufigkeit gesellschaftlicher Konflikte insgesamt. Wir benötigen weitere Informationen, um zu entscheiden, ob die niedrigen Prozeßraten in der DDR ein niedriges Konfliktniveau in zivilen Streitigkeiten und einen hohen Grad an Konformität mit den Strafrechtsnormen anzeigen, oder ob sie einfach eine Folge von Konfliktregelungen unterhalb der Schwelle des Gangs zum Gericht sind. Was das Strafrecht angeht, so wissen wir, daß beide Effekte kumulieren: In der DDR sind viele Bagatelldelikte (insbesondere Bagatelldiebstähle) entkriminalisiert und lediglich einer administrativen Sanktion unterworfen. Dies bedeutet für unseren Zusammenhang: Diese Delikte sind nicht mehr Gegenstand gerichtlicher Verfahren. (Sollte man diese Fälle allein zum Vergleich der Kriminalstatistiken in Rechnung stellen, so bliebe jedoch immer noch eine bedeutend geringere offiziell registrierte Kriminalitätshäufigkeit in der DDR als in der BRD (2).

Über die Gründe der unterschiedlich hohen Prozeßhäufigkeiten können wir bislang leider wenig aussagen. Hierzu bedürfte es vergleichender Untersuchungen, die nicht nur Rechtsregeln, sondern auch ihre institutionelle Realisierung, die Häufigkeiten von Konflikten in verschiedenen Bereichen und die Formen der Austragung zueinander in Beziehung setzen. Bei einem solchen Verständnis von „Rechtsvergleich" könnte die Statistik der Prozeßhäufigkeiten der Schlüssel zu wichtigen Strukturmerkmalen von entwickelten Gesellschaften sein.

Insbesondere der Vergleich zwischen sozialistischen und kapitalistischen Staaten muß weiter geführt werden. Ob die geringeren Prozeßraten, die sich auch in anderen sozialistischen Ländern zeigen, für ein „Absterben des Staates" sprechen, oder ob sie sogar auf einen geringeren Grad an „gesellschaftlichen Widersprüchen" hindeuten, läßt sich nur durch einen auch materiellen Vergleich der Streitgegenstände, sowie der funktionalen Äquivalente für Konfliktregelungen entscheiden. Fest steht, daß die Rolle der Gerichte in sozialistischen Ländern nicht annähernd so bedeutend ist, wie in westlichen Industriegesellschaften.

2. Selektive Sanktionierung durch die Strafjustiz

Im strafrechtlichen Bereich ist die Selektivität der Sanktionen durch eine Reihe von Untersuchungen thematisiert worden. Verschiedene Studien zeigen, daß die Zahl der unregistrierten Delikte bei weitem größer ist als die offiziell registrierten Delikte. Selbst dann jedoch, wenn wir uns auf solche Fälle beschränken, die zur Kenntnis einer Kontrollinstanz gekommen sind, bleibt die weitere Verfolgung

* Anmerkungen auf den Seiten 96 f.

selektiv. Welchen Bedingungen diese Selektivität unterliegt, zeigt sich, wenn wir den Weg eines Delikts durch die verschiedenen Kontrollinstanzen verfolgen:

- Der Torhüter des Kriminalisierungsprozesses ist die Polizei. Da Informationen über abweichendes Verhalten aktiv gesucht werden müssen, unterliegt die Informationsgewinnung strategischen Entscheidungen: Polizeikontrollen konzentrieren sich auf bestimmte Teile einer Stadt, die als „verdächtig" angesehen werden, sie beschränken sich auf Verhalten, das auf öffentlichen Straßen und Plätzen beobachtbar ist. Strafbare Verhaltensweisen, die hinter geschlossenen Türen oder an einem Schreibtisch begangen werden (sowie manche Arten des Betrugs, der Unterschlagung), haben daher eine sehr viel geringere Wahrscheinlichkeit, entdeckt zu werden, als physische Aktionen, die in der Öffentlichkeit stattfinden (wie z.B. Diebstahl oder Körperverletzung) (3). Sehr oft jedoch bleibt das Verdachtschöpfen nicht der Polizei alleine überlassen. Bei Streitereien, einer Rauferei oder Ruhestörungen wird die Polizei gewöhnlich von einer der Parteien oder einer beteiligten dritten Person herbeigerufen. Sie kann in diesen Fällen nicht umhin, von dem Konflikt Kenntnis zu nehmen – jedoch hat sie faktisch eine große Entscheidungsmacht, ob sie das Geschehene als strafrechtlich relevant ansieht oder nicht.

Verhalten der Polizei in Situationen des Konflikts
(Teilnehmende Beobachtung von 52 Fällen, ohne Verkehrsunfälle) (4).

Formale Reaktion (Festnahme, Verwarnung)		16 %
Verweis auf den Privatklageweg		44 %
Informelle Konfliktlösung		40 %
		100 %
	N	(52)

Nur bei einem kleinen Teil der beobachteten Fälle leitet die Polizei tatsächlich strafrechtliche Sanktionen ein, sehr viel öfter erweist sie sich als schlichtende – und damit auch als letzte – Instanz. Auch in den Fällen, wo „auf den Privatklageweg verwiesen" wird, handelt es sich häufig um ein „Abwimmeln" der Kenntnisnahme von Situationen, an denen durchaus ein „öffentliches Interesse" zu begründen wäre (3).

- Der größte Teil der Strafanzeigen bei klassischer Kriminalität gelangt zur Polizei durch private Anzeigen – auch hier sind selektive Mechanismen am Werk. Bei privaten Anzeigen ist die Zahl der Delikte groß, bei denen gar keine Strafverfolgung beabsichtigt ist (etwa bei Diebstahlanzeigen gegen unbekannte Täter die in erster Linie aus versicherungsrechtlichen Gründen aufgegeben werden) (5). Private Anzeigen sind je nach Opfersituation und nach Art des Deliktes selektiv: Von privater Seite werden Vermögens- und Eigentumsdelikte angezeigt, selten jedoch Verkehrsdelikte oder kaum je Vergehen gegen öffentliche Güter; selektive Anzeigenneigung zeigt sich darin, daß die Strafverfolgung des Verkaufs verdorbener Lebensmittel oder von Umweltverschmutzung auf die Entdeckung durch Ermittlungsorgane angewiesen ist.
- Sobald ein polizeiliches Einschreiten oder eine Anzeige einmal in das „Vorkommnisbuch" der Polizei eingetragen ist, so ist diese in der Bundesrepublik gemäß dem Legalitätsprinzip verpflichtet, den Vorgang an die Staatsanwalt-

schaft weiterzuleiten. Nur diese kann entscheiden, ob ein Fall zu Gericht getragen wird oder nicht. Jedoch hat der Staatsanwalt kaum eigene Informationsquellen: Er bleibt auf die Ermittlungstätigkeit der Polizei angewiesen. Staatsanwälte verrichten ihre Arbeit in erster Linie am Schreibtisch, hauptsächlich damit beschäftigt, die große Zahl der kleinen Fälle für die Anklageerhebung vorzubereiten. Es ist außergewöhnlich, wenn sie selbst an einer Ermittlung teilnehmen, und es geschieht auch nicht häufig, daß sie einen Fall an die Polizei „zur weiteren Ermittlung" zurückschicken.

In der Regel bringen die Staatsanwälte vor Gericht, was von der Polizei erfolgreich aufgeklärt werden konnte, sie stellen diejenigen Fälle ein, bei denen die Polizei nicht genügend Beweismittel hat herbeischaffen können. Die Anklagequote (Anteil der Klagen und Strafbefehle an allen staatsanwaltschaftlichen Ermittlungsverfahren) ist sehr gering: Sie variiert von 15 % bei einigen großstädtischen Staatsanwaltschaften bis zu 40,% in einigen ländlichen Regionen. Ein Teil dieser Differenzen ist auf die verschiedenen Verfahren des „Nummernschindens" zurückzuführen, die der Legitimierung von Stellenanforderungen bei den Ministerien dienen. Ein Teil kann darauf zurückgeführt werden, daß in Großstädten Vergehen mit geringer Aufklärungschance besonders häufig sind (z.B. ist hier der Anteil von Diebstählen besonders hoch). Jedoch selbst wenn alle diese Faktoren kontrolliert sind, bleibt immer noch ein bemerkenswerter Unterschied in den Anklagequoten in einer städtischen und einer ländlichen Region bestehen.

Erledigung von Diebstahlsfällen
Vergleich zweier Staatsanwaltschaften 1970 (6)

	Anklage Strafbefehl	Einstellung	Begründung in % aller Einstellungen	
			Täter unbekannt mangels Beweises (§ 170 StPO)	Sanktionsverzicht (§ 153 StPO)
städtische STA	12 %	88 %	98 %	2 %
ländliche STA	22 %	78 %	90 %	10 %

Bei beiden Staatsanwaltschaften ist die Anklagequote für Diebstähle sehr niedrig: In dem ländlichen Gebiet unserer Untersuchung jedoch mit 22 % erheblich höher als in dem städtischen Gebiet mit 12 %. Dieser Unterschied ist eine Folge der polizeilichen Ermittlungstätigkeit: Die Staatsanwälte in dem ländlichen Gebiet haben eine niedrigere Einstellungsquote, außerdem sind auch unter den eingestellten Verfahren mehr aufgeklärte Fälle – die Staatsanwälte zeigen sich jedoch großzügig im Gebrauch des § 153 StPO – ihre Anklagequote wäre noch höher, wenn sie nicht von der Möglichkeit des Sanktionsverzichts Gebrauch machte.

– Es scheint, daß die Kontrollinstanzen, die ein Delikt passieren muß, bevor es vor Gericht gelangt, die meisten Zweifelsfälle herausgefiltert haben. Nur wenige

Fälle werden vor Gericht eingestellt oder sogar freigesprochen – die wichtigste Funktion des Gerichtsverfahrens scheint die Legitimierung des langen, vorhergegangenen Entscheidungsprozesses zu sein (7).
Das Resultat dieses Prozesses trägt schichtspezifische Züge: Unter allen verurteilten Delinquenten sind Arbeiter überrepräsentiert. Wie groß das Maß der schichtspezifischen Ungleichverteilung allerdings ist, läßt sich aus keiner Statistik ersehen; lediglich bei Jugendlichen und Heranwachsenden läßt die Verurteiltenstatistik einen Schluß auf die Schichtzugehörigkeit zu:

	% der Studenten und Schüler (Höhere- bzw. Realschule) in der Altersgruppe von 18 - 21 Jahren	
	unter den Verurteilten des Jugendstrafrechts	in der Gesamtaltersgruppe
Diebstahl/Unterschlagung	7,5 %	
Verkehrsdelikte	11,9 %	17,5 %
alle übrigen Delikte	9,4 %	

Quellen: Statistisches Bundesamt, Rechtspflegestatistik, 1970 Reihe 9 A, Tabelle 9
Statistisches Jahrbuch der BRD 1972

Jugendliche aus den oberen Schichten sind unter den Verurteilten unterrepräsentiert. Dies ist deutlicher, wenn wir klassische Vergehen betrachten (Diebstahl, Unterschlagung), weniger deutlich bei Verkehrsdelikten. Mit den klassischen Delikten kriminalisiert das Strafrecht die Verhaltensweisen am stärksten, die in den unteren Schichten häufiger anzutreffen sind. Selektive Entdeckungschancen und Sanktionsverzichte bewirken, daß die Strafverfolgungsinstanzen das schichtspezifische Bild der Kriminalität noch verstärken (8).

3. *Der soziale Zugang zur Ziviljustiz*

Die Selektivität des strafrechtlichen Entscheidungsprozesses, ob ein Fall vor Gericht gebracht wird oder nicht, ist durch eine Reihe von Institutionen strukturiert, deren Vorentscheidungen rechtlich gebunden sind. Vor einem Zivilprozeß muß ein ähnlich langer Entscheidungsweg durchmessen werden, jedoch

Länge d. Klonflikts vor u. während d. Zivilproz. (Basis: 40 Fälle vor (9) dem Amtsgericht)

	Konfliktentstehung bis zur Klageerhebung	Prozeßdauer 1. Instanz	vom Urteil bis zur Klageerhebung 2. Instanz	Prozeßdauer 2. Instanz
Eine Instanz	10 Monate	5 Monate		
Zwei Instanzen	12 Monate	6 Monate	2 Monate	6 Monate

sind es hier die Parteien (und ihre Anwälte), die entscheiden, ob und wann der Weg zum Gericht gegangen wird. Durchschnittlich hat ein Prozeß vor dem Amtsgericht eine Vorgeschichte von 10 Monaten – länger als die durchschnittliche Prozeßdauer in erster Instanz. Fälle, die später in Berufung gehen, haben 1 Jahr von der Konfliktentstehung bis zur Klageerhebung gebraucht – so lang wie die Prozeßdauer in beiden Instanzen zusammengenommen.
Wenn fast ein Jahr vergeht, ehe eine der Parteien Klage erhebt, dann müssen dem Prozeß einige Versuche der Konfliktregelung vorangegangen sein. Wir wissen darüber wenig, da sie außerhalb des formalen Verfahrens stattfinden, und wir wissen folglich auch nicht wie viele potentielle Konflikte dem Gericht erspart geblieben sind. Wir können nur einige spekulative Versuche machen, aus Merkmalen der tatsächlichen Gerichtsverfahren darauf zu schließen, welche sozialen Bedingungen zu Gerichtsprozessen führen.
Bei mehr als der Hälfte der Parteien, die eine Berufungsklage erheben, steht eine Versicherung hinter dem Prozeß – sei es, daß es um einen Schadenersatzanspruch geht, den letztlich nicht die Partei, sondern die Versicherung begleichen muß, sei es, daß die Kosten des Verfahrens von einer Rechtsschutzversicherung getragen werden müssen. Auch steigt die Berufungshäufigkeit, wenn die Parteien durch einen Rechtsanwalt vertreten sind. (Von wievielen Prozessen der Anwalt allerdings schon vor einer Klage in erster Instanz abgeraten hat, wissen wir nicht.)
Es hängt also von der Hartnäckigkeit ab, mit der die Parteien schon vor dem Gang zum Gericht gestritten haben, und von der Zahl der in den Prozeß einbezogenen Drittpersonen, wie lange der Prozeß geführt wird. Selbst dort, wo ein Prozeß gemäß der Akte wie ein Konflikt zwischen Privatpersonen aussieht, stellt sich im Interview häufig heraus, daß in Wirklichkeit „institutionelle Hintermänner" den Prozeß führen. Auch bei Betrachtung der Parteienkonstellation, wie sie aus den Gerichtsakten ersichtlich wird, zeigt sich, wie selten Zivilprozesse von Privaten ausgehen, wie viele von juristischen Personen oder von Geschäftsleuten angestrengt werden:

Status der Parteien Kläger	– Beklagte	% der Amtsgerichtsprozesse (10)
Juristische Person/ Geschäftsleute	– Private	45 %
Private	– Private	27 %
Juristische Person/ Geschäftsleute	– Juristische Person/ Geschäftsleute	19 %
Private	– Juriszische Person/ Geschäftsleute	9 %
		100 %
		(N = 489 %

Am Amtsgericht überwiegen die Zivilprozesse der Geschäftswelt – wobei eher kleine Firmen prozessieren, meist um Forderungen aus einem Kaufvertrag geltend zu machen. Die umgekehrte Konstellation – daß Private gegen eine Firma klagen, um eine Leistung einzufordern oder die Mängel einer Ware zu beanstanden, kommt dagegen nur selten vor. Hierfür lassen sich zwei Erklärungen geben:

Entweder kann der Kunde seinen Anspruch auch ohne die Hilfe des Gerichts durchsetzen, da die Firma ihm entgegenkommt, oder aber er verzichtet auf den Prozeß, aus Mangel an Information oder Vertrauen, mit Hilfe des Gerichts zu seinem Recht zu kommen: Die weite Verbreitung von „Allgemeinen Geschäftsbedingungen", denen sich der Kunde bei einem Kaufvertrag unterwirft, spricht eher für die zweite Erklärung.
Nimmt man zu den Kauf-, Werk- und Dienstverträgen noch die Prozesse hinzu, die aus einem Verkehrsunfall entstanden sind, haben wir schon mehr als zwei Drittel aller Zivilprozesse am Amtsgericht erfaßt.
Die Zivilgerichtsbarkeit am Amtsgericht ist überwiegend mit Konfliktregelungen beschäftigt, die sich aus dem Straßen- oder Warenverkehr (einschließlich der Dienst- und Werkverträge) ergeben.
Anders die Landgerichte, die allerdings einen sehr viel niedrigeren Geschäftsanfall haben. Hiervon sind 42 % Ehescheidungen – die häufigste Konfliktart wenn Private gegen Private prozessieren. Bei allen anderen Landgerichtsprozessen sind die Gegenstandsverteilungen ähnlich wie am Amtsgericht.

Prozeßgegenstände in erster Instanz	Amtsgericht	Landgericht
Zahl der Zivilprozesse insgesamt+)	742 381	311 504
Ehesachen	–	42 %
Unterhalts-, Kindschaftssachen	7 %	–
Mietsachen, Räumung	8 %	–
Sonstige gewöhnliche Prozesse	85 %	58 %
	100 %	100 %
darunter (bei streitigen Urteilen++)		
Kaufverträge	35 %	30 %
Dienst-Werkverträge	21 %	21 %
Bausachen	1 %	6 %
Verkehrsunfälle u.ä.	14 %	23 %
Sonstiges	29 %	20 %
	100 %	100 %

Quelle: +) Statistisches Bundesamt, Rechtspflegestatistik Reihe 9, I, 1971 (Berücksichtigt sind hier nur gewöhnliche Prozeß- und Ehesachen)
++) G. Baumgärtel, P. Mes, Rechtstatsachen zur Dauer des Zivilprozesses, Köln 1972

Angesichts dieser Verteilung von Prozeßgegenständen wundert es nicht mehr, daß die Prozeßhäufigkeit mit der städtischen (und wirtschaftlichen) Ballung stark ansteigt: Während in einigen ländlichen Gebieten auf 100.000 Einwohner lediglich etwa 700 Zivilprozesse kommen, sind es in städtischen Ballungsgebieten bis zu 4000 (11).
Für Zivilverfahren gibt es eine ähnliche Tendenz der Konzentrationen in städtischen Zentren wie wir sie im Bereich des Strafrechts beobachten können. Schaut man sich die Konstellation von Klägern und Beklagten an, so sind die Zivilgerichte mit Dienstleistungsfunktion für die Wirtschaft und mit den Integra-

tionsproblemen der Familie beschäftigt. Die geringsten Zugangssperren, mit einer Klage vor Gericht zu ziehen, haben „professionelle Prozeßparteien": Geschäftsleute, Firmen und andere juristische Personen. Soweit man dies am Status der Parteien – und insbesondere des Klägers – erkennen kann, scheinen die Zivilgerichte keine kompensatorische Wirkung auf die soziale Machtverteilung auszuüben (12).
Angesichts der Abhängigkeit der Zivilprozeßtätigkeit von wirtschaftlicher Aktivität ist es erstaunlich, daß in der Bundesrepublik von 1955 bis 1971 der Geschäftsanfall der Zivilgerichte etwa konstant geblieben ist: Gegenüber den Zeiten der Weimarer Republik oder des Kaiserreiches ist die Zahl der Zivilprozesse je Kopf der Bevölkerung sogar erheblich gesunken. Kaupen (13) ist im Oberlandesgerichtsbezirk Hamm den Abhängigkeiten des Zivilprozeßaufkommens von der ökonomischen Struktur detaillierter nachgegangen. Sein Untersuchungsgebiet umschließt ländliche Räume Westfalens ebenso wie industrialisierte Stadtregionen im Ruhrgebiet, und industrielle Umland mit vorwiegend kleineren Gewerbebetrieben (z.B. Zulieferungsindustrien). Hier sind es nicht die am meisten industrialisierten Städteregionen (und natürlich schon gar nicht die ländlichen), sondern diejenigen mit einer wettbewerbsintensiven Industrie, die in einer Vielzahl von kleineren Firmen organisiert ist. Man kann hieraus den Schluß ziehen – der allerdings durch weitere vergleichende Untersuchungen erhärtet werden müßte – daß die *Zivilgerichtsbarkeit in erster Linie Dienstleistungen für mittelständische Unternehmen* bietet, daß ihre Inanspruchnahme ein Kennzeichen einer wettbewerbsmäßig orientierten Wirtschaftsordnung ist (14).

4. Grenzen der Konfliktbereiche, in denen die Gerichte tätig sind

Bislang haben wir den Begriff „Konflikt" für verschiedene Arten von Fällen benutzt. Die ordentlichen Gerichte in der Bundesrepublik sind mit Aufgaben der normativen Kontrolle, der Konfliktregelung in ökonomischen Beziehungen und bei Desintegration von Familien beschäftigt. Sie greifen kaum in Konflikte regulierend ein, die für den Produktionsprozeß zentral sind: Auseinandersetzungen um Löhne, Arbeitsbedingungen und Fragen des beruflichen Status. Sie stellen die Herrschaftsbeziehungen im Produktionsprozeß ebenso wenig in Frage wie die zwischen Produzenten und Konsumenten.
Dies wird noch deutlicher, wenn man sich die Ansprüche anschaut, die vor den Arbeitsgerichten geltend gemacht werden. Hier ist die Parteienkonstellation in der Tat arbeitnehmerfreundlich: 90 % aller Kläger sind Arbeitnehmer, die gegen ihren (früheren) Arbeitgeber klagen. Insgesamt kann man daher die Tätigkeit der Arbeitsgerichte sehr viel eher als „kompensatorisch" bezeichnen als die der Zivilgerichte. Zudem ist der Geschäftsanfall der Arbeitsgerichte seit Jahren ständig wachsend. Jedoch reduziert sich der Anspruch bei einem Drittel aller Fälle auf Zahlung, in der Hälfte aller Klagen geht es dem Arbeitnehmer nach Auflösung des Arbeitsverhältnisses nur noch um die Herausgabe der Papiere, das Ausstellen eines Zeugnisses u.ä. Sehr selten sind Beschlußsachen, also Fälle, in denen Arbeitnehmer kollektiv für bessere Arbeitsbedingungen oder Beteiligungsrechte streiten: So ist z.B. die Einrichtung eines Betriebsrats für Betriebe mit mehr als 5 Beschäftigten gesetzlich verankert, aber dennoch haben etwa in Baden-Württemberg nur 46 % aller Betriebe eine solche Einrichtung (15). Weder

die Gewerkschaften noch einzelne Arbeitnehmer versuchen auf dem Weg über die Gerichte ihre Beteiligungsrechte zu erstreiten.

Es gibt also noch eine andere, tiefergehende Selektivität dessen was die Gerichte tun. Ihre Legitimität beruht offensichtlich auf den Grenzen, die ihnen gesetzt sind: Sie können Konflikte nur regulieren solange sie individualisiert sind – sobald ein Konflikt zu einem Kampf zwischen organisierten Interessen wird, scheint er über die Kapazität justizieller Institutionen hinauszugehen. Da die Gerichte nicht aktiv versuchen, Gesetze in Kraft zu setzen, sondern vielmehr darauf warten, daß von den Parteien Ansprüche mit ihrer Hilfe durchgesetzt werden, hängt ihre Tätigkeit von der Perzeption der Parteien ab, wieweit sie die Macht der Gerichte hoch genug einschätzen, um soziale Verhältnisse zu ändern. Ein guter Indikator hierfür ist, welche Konflikte von den Parteien als „politische Frage“ perzipiert werden. – Die Definition dessen, was als „politisch“ betrachtet wird und was nicht, unterliegt einem ständigen Bewertungs- und Umwertungsprozeß – das Resultat jedenfalls ist, daß mit diesem Begriff den Gerichten Grenzen gezogen werden, innerhalb welchen Bereichs sie legitim tätig werden können, und in welchem Bereich nicht.

Per definitionem reicht die Verwaltungsgerichtsbarkeit am weitesten in den Bereich politischer Entscheidungen. Immer ist hier mindestens eine staatliche Verwaltungsbehörde Prozeßpartei, in der Regel versuchen einzelne Bürger oder juristische Personen gegen einen Verwaltungsakt (oder dessen Unterlassen) mit Hilfe des Gerichts anzugehen. Auch hier kann man per Definitionen von einer kompensatorischen Parteienkonstellation sprechen, auch hier beobachten wir seit Jahren zunehmenden Geschäftsanfall. Eine Aufteilung der Prozeßgegenstände zeigt wiederum welche Art von Konflikten hier vor Gericht gelangen.

Von allen Klagen beim Verwaltungsgericht Freiburg 1972 betrafen:

Baurecht:	
Bauplanung, -genehmigung	
Verkehr, Wasser, Wege	27 %
Ausbildung:	
Schule, Universität	17 %
Wehrrecht	15 %
Personal im öffentlichen Dienst (Beamtenrecht)	9 %
Polizeimaßnahmen	6 %
Soziale Dienste, Gesundheitswesen	5 %
Sonstiges	21 %
	100 %
N	(1287)

Quelle: Angaben des Verwaltungsgerichts Freiburg

Zu den klassischen Aufgaben der Verwaltungsgerichte gehören die Bausachen: Anlieger, die sich gegen eine Bauplanung wehren, Bauherren, die ihre Genehmigung zu erstreiten versuchen, Nachbarn, die wiederum gegen eine Baugenehmigung kämpfen oder für Wasser- und Wegerechte streiten. Teilweise stehen hinter solchen Prozessen Nachbarschaftsstreitigkeiten, in die die Behörden nur mittelbar hineingezogen sind. Teilweise stehen hier jedoch auch individuelle Eigentümerinteressen gegen die einer öffentlichen Bauplaung. Der nächstgrößere Konfliktbereich, der vor die Verwaltungsgerichte gelangt, ist seit einigen Jahren in schnellem Anwachsen begriffen: Einsprüche gegen die Entscheidungen von Lehrern und Schulbehörden, gegen Zulassungsbeschränkungen und für Partizipationsrechte an den Universitäten. Hier, ebenso wie bei Prozessen aus dem Bereich des Wehrrechts entstehen Konflikte im Rahmen eines schnellen gesellschaftlichen Wandlungsprozesses bei dem das Verhältnis von individuellem Anspruch und sozialer Verpflichtung neu definiert wird („Bildung ist Bürgerrecht"). Wie sich z. Zt. an den Diskussionen um Umweltschutz oder Polizeirecht bei Demonstrationen zeigt, ist das öffentliche Recht am stärksten gesellschaftlichen Interessenkonflikten und damit Veränderungen ausgesetzt. Das öffentliche Recht mit seinen Ermessens- und Zweckmäßigkeitserwägungen ist in weiten Bereichen nicht konditional programmiert wie andere Rechtsgebiete. Daher erwachsen den Verwaltungsgerichten mehr als allen anderen Zweigen der Gerichtsbarkeit rechtsfortbildende Aufgaben.

5. Selektion von Konflikten als Strukturmerkmale der Justiz

In verschiedenen sozialen Bereichen und bezogen auf die Tätigkeitsfelder der Justiz überhaupt, ist ihr Beitrag zur Lösung von Konflikten von einer Vielzahl sozialer Bedingungen abhängig. So unterschiedlich die aufgezählten Phänomene auch sein mögen, gemeinsames Merkmal jeder Justiz ist die Selektion die unter möglichen regulierungsbedürftigen Konflikten getroffen wird.
Die Gesetzmäßigkeiten von denen es abhängt, ob eine Gerichtsbarkeit tätig wird, unterscheiden sich ebenso stark wie die sozialen Bereiche in die sie regelnd eingreifen. Verallgemeinernde Aussagen, von welchen Bedingungen es abhängt, ob ein sozialer Konflikt vor Gericht gelangt, lassen sich daher nur für die einzelnen Rechtsbereiche getrennt machen. Gemeinsam ist ihnen jedoch, daß die Gerichte selbst kaum darin eingreifen, welche Art von Geschäftsanfall zu ihnen kommt. Der Umfang ihrer Tätigkeit hängt von Kräften und Institutionen ab, die den Zugang zur Justiz regulieren:

- In der Strafjustiz sind es die Bedingungen der Entdeckung von Straftaten, die sich weitgehend aus den Interessen und Verhaltensregelmäßigkeiten von Anzeigern und Polizei erklären lassen. Immer noch muß hierbei allerdings zu der bloßen Entdeckung der Wille zur Kriminalisierung hinzukommen: Sowohl potentieller Anzeiger, als auch die Polizei und bürgerliche Staatsanwaltschaft kennen Spielräume, innerhalb deren sie sich für einen Sanktionsverzicht entscheiden können. Die Verhaltensweisen, die jeweils kriminalisiert werden, und die Prozesse der Selektion wirken zusammen, daß vor dem Strafrichter die Angehörigen der unteren Schichten überrepräsentiert sind.
- Der Zugang zur Zivilgerichtsbarkeit muß im wesentlichen aus den Interessen und sozialen Merkmalen der Parteien erklärt werden, wobei hierbei vermutlich schon der erste Schritt eine große Rolle spielt: die sozialen Barrieren, die der Inanspruchnahme eines Rechtsanwalts entgegenstehen mögen. Wenn man von Ehescheidungen, Kindschafts- und Unterhaltsprozessen absieht, dann werden die Zivilgerichte in erster Linie von Angehörigen der Mittelschicht in Anspruch genommen. Diese Charakterisierung bestätigt sich auch, wenn man

juristische Personen und Geschäftsleute betrachtet, die den Rechtsweg beschreiten: es sind überwiegend mittlere und kleine Unternehmen, und es sind typisch Konflikte, die gegenüber dem Endverbraucher entstehen, die vor Gericht getragen werden. Vermutlich entzieht sich ein großer Teil von – durchaus rechtsfähigen – Auseinandersetzungen bei längerfristigen ökonomischen Beziehungen, dadurch daß sie auf dem Wege von Verhandlungen und ökonomischer Machtausübung geregelt werden.

– Schon bei der Zivilgerichtsbarkeit, aber noch deutlicher bei gesonderten Gerichtsbarkeiten wie den Arbeits- oder Verwaltungsgerichten, stößt die Diskussion von Zugangsvoraussetzungen auf eine logische Schwierigkeit: Es ist nirgends ableitbar und kaum empirisch feststellbar, welches das Universum von „rechtsrelevanten Konflikten" ist, innerhalb dessen man Bedingungen der Selektivität gerichtlicher Verfahren bestimmen könnte. Bei allen diesen Gerichtsbarkeiten fällt jedoch auf, daß es in der Bundesrepublik kaum Bewegungen gibt, mit Hilfe der Gesetze soziale Veränderungen durchzusetzen. Fragen müssen hier notwendig spekulativ sein, auf Denkmöglichkeiten verweisen, die bestenfalls durch Beispiele aus anderen Rechtssystemen plausibel gemacht werden können: Warum gibt es etwa angesichts so vieler Prozesse von Verkäufern, die ihr Geld eintreiben, so wenige von Käufern, die Mängelrügen oder andere Konsumenteninteressen gerichtlich durchzusetzen versuchen? Sollte man sich hier mit der Antwort der geringen Organisationsfähigkeit von Konsumenteninteressen zufrieden geben, dann ließe sich jedoch mit der Frage fortfahren, warum etwa Gewerkschaften bislang nicht die Gerichte in Anspruch genommen haben, um den Partizipationsrechten der Arbeitnehmer im Betriebsverfassungsgesetz Geltung zu verschaffen? Wie läßt es sich erklären, daß es in der Bundesrepublik kaum Bemühungen gibt, die Interessen von ausländischen Arbeitern und ihren Familien auf dem Gerichtswege durchzusetzen (deren Diskriminierung am Arbeitsplatz, gegenüber dem Vermieter oder durch Behörden durchaus Parallelen zu der rechtlich prekären Situation von ethnischen Gruppen in den USA aufweisen und deren sich dort gerade Anwälte mit Hilfe gerichtlicher Anti-Segregations-Kampagnen und Einrichtungen der „Rechtshilfe für Arme" angenommen haben)?

Die Zahl der Gerichtsverfahren (pro Kopf der Bevölkerung) ist in der Bundesrepublik vergleichsweise recht hoch. Doch bleiben die Konflikte, die hier ausgetragen werden, im Rahmen der gesellschaftlichen Machtverhältnisse: abweichendes Verhalten wird vorwiegend dort kriminalisiert, wo es Unterschichtsverhalten ist; die „gewöhnlichen Prozesse" vor den Zivilgerichten bewegen sich meist im Bereich der Friktionen im Rahmen des Waren- und Straßenverkehrs; die Prozesse vor den Arbeitsgerichten berühren kaum die gesellschaftlich relevanten Interessen zwischen Arbeitnehmern und Arbeitgebern; allenfalls bei den Verwaltungsgerichten läßt sich eine „politische" Bedeutung konstatieren, da sich hier Interessen melden, die sich gegen staatliche Entscheidungen zur Wehr setzen, auf einem Rechtsgebiet, bei dem immer wieder erneut die Grenzen zwischen privaten und öffentlichen Interessen gesteckt werden.

Der Richter mag zwar im Rahmen des Rechts „unabhängig" urteilen, jedoch bleibt er abhängig davon, welche Konflikte vor ihn getragen werden.

Die soziale Bedeutung der Gerichte läßt sich nicht nur von dem bestimmen, was im einzelnen Prozeß verhandelt wird, sondern sie liegt weitgehend schon vorher in der Selektion von Konflikten, die (nicht) vor Gericht kommen. Wer in der

Justiz eine Gewalt sieht, die die Macht der Mächtigen beschränken und die Rechte der Schwachen schützen soll, mag hierfür zwar durchaus Beispiele finden, durch eine Betrachtung empirischer Häufigkeiten aber muß er enttäuscht werden: Der Großteil dessen, was die Gerichte tun, ist nicht sozial kompensatorisch, sondern es bestärkt bestehende Machtverhältnisse.

Summary

The role of the courts in handling social conflicts.

It depends on a number of cultural and social conditions, whether a conflict is submitted to judicial courts or not. Comparisons of litigation rates of civil and criminal processes per capita show extreme differences from one country to the next – this may be illustrated by a comparison between the two German states: In the Federal Republic there are much higher rates both of civil and criminal processes than in socialist Germany.

The comparison of legal cultures is not developed enough, to differentiate whether this is due to an actually lower level of conflict in socialist countries or whether it indicates that there are other than judicial patterns of regulation. However, within one country we can see already, that it depends on a number of factors, whether a conflict is taken to court or not: First of all, the law does not regard all types of conflict as manageable by judicial treatment, either because they are below a level of privacy or beyond a level of "politisation". Besides that every law has its dark field: i.e. conflicts which fall into the competence of justice, but there is nobody to take the issue to court. Social barriers discriminate lower classes in criminal procedures as well as in civil litigation.

Judicial courts do not actively seek their cases, they are thus dependent on the types of conflict which are brought before them. In criminal process there are agencies of social control (police, prosecuters) which function as gatekeepers. In civil and in special courts access is determined by social capabilities of the litigants. In addition there may be some reluctance of parties to take issues to court which are regarded as being "political" – i.e. not manageable by court procedure, even if they could be subsumed under the rule of law. These cases of non-litigation are indicators of the "legal culture" as well as the cases of litigation. Together they determine the role of the courts in handling social conflicts.

Anmerkungen

* Die Überlegungen dieses Aufsatzes bildeten den Ausgangspunkt von Forschungen, die seit Abschluß des Manuskripts im Jahr 1973 zum Teil weiter geführt werden konnten. Vergleiche hierzu meine Veröffentlichungen: Studying the frequency of civil litigation in Germany, in: Law and Society Review 9, 1975, S. 307–319; sowie: Nicht-Kriminalisierung als Struktur und Routine, Verhandlungen des Deutschen Kriminologentages 1975, erscheint demnächst.

1 Ein geringer Teil der Unterschiede kann durch unterschiedliche Führung der jeweiligen Statistiken erklärt werden: In der Kriminalstatistik der DDR werden die Verfahren bei

einem rechtskräftigen Urteil oder bei vorläufiger Einstellung gezählt, Freisprüche und endgültige Einstellungen werden im Gegensatz zur Kriminalstatistik in der BRD also nicht aufgeführt. Ein großer Teil der Straftaten wird an gesellschaftliche Gerichte abgegeben – diese werden bei der Abgabe (also vor einer Entscheidung) statistisch erfaßt. Die Verfahren vor gesellschaftlichen Gerichten sind somit in der Statistik der Strafrechtspflege enthalten. Bei der Zivilrechtspflege weist die Statistik nur „gerichtliche Verfahren" aus, hier sind somit offenbar Verfahren vor Konfliktkommissionen nicht enthalten. Nach Angaben des Berichts zur Lage der Nation 1972, Bundestagsdrucksache VI/3080, S. 305 führen diese jährlich 15.000 Einigungen in zivilrechtlichen und anderen Rechtsstreitigkeiten herbei. Bei einer Erfolgsquote von 80 % bedeutet dies, daß etwa auf je zwei gerichtliche Zivilrechtssachen ein Verfahren vor einer Konfliktkommission entfällt. Unter Einschluß dieser Verfahren liegt die Zivilrechts-Prozeßrate bei 298.

2 Materialien zum Bericht zur Lage der Nation 1972, Bundestagsdrucksache VI/3080, S. 234. Vgl. insbesondere auf S. 236 die Kriminalitätsrate vor der Änderung der StPO in der DDR (1968), sowie auf S. 238 die Veränderung der Deliktstrukturen.

3 Vgl. Johannes Feest, Erhard Blankenburg, Die Definitionsmacht der Polizei, Düsseldorf 1972, besonders Kapitel 3 und 5.

4 Ebenda, S. 133–134, vgl. auch Fernand Kirch, Die Polizei in Situationen des privaten Konflikts, M.A. Arbeit, Freiburg 1973.

5 Vgl. Kurt Weis, Renate Müller-Bagehl, Private Strafanzeigen. In: Kriminologisches Journal 1971, S. 185–194.

6 Eigenes Manuskript 1973: Max-Planck-Institut für internationales und ausländisches Strafrecht – Forschungsgruppe Kriminologie – Freiburg. Vgl. auch E. Blankenburg, Die Rolle des Staatsanwalts im Prozeß sozialer Kontrolle, in: Kriminologisches Journal 1973, S. 196. Die hier durchgeführte Regressionsanalyse zeigt allerdings große Streuungen der Erledigungsquoten sowohl bei ländlichen als bei städtischen Staatsanwaltschaften. Wenn hier eine städtische einer ländlichen Staatsanwaltschaft gegenübergestellt wird, so sollte das Stadt-Land-Gefälle als ein wichtiger Faktor herausgestellt werden, keineswegs aber von hier auf alle städtischen oder alle ländlichen Staatsanwaltschaften verallgemeinert werden: Bezieht man die Fälle des § 153 StPO auf alle anklagereifen Fälle (wo „die Ermittlungen genügend Anlaß zur Klage ergeben"), so ergeben sich auch bei großstädtischen Staatsanwaltschaften z.T. sehr hohe Einstellungsquoten.

7 Mit Freispruch enden 4,7 % aller Strafprozesse. Einstellungen des Verfahrens durch das Gericht erfolgten bei 6,9 %. Vgl. Stat. Bundesamt Fachserie A, Reihe 9 (Rechtspflege) 1971 Tab. 1 Einstellungen und Freisprüche, die mit Maßregeln verbunden sind, sind nicht als solche berücksichtigt, da hier effektiv eine Sanktion verhängt wurde.

8 Vgl. Dorothee Peters, Richter im Dienst der Macht, Stuttgart (Enke) 1973 kann zur Ungleichbehandlung der Strafverfolgungsorgane zwar nur Daten von geringer Gültigkeit liefern, sie belegt jedoch, daß Einstellungsmuster und Täterbilder von Strafrichtern eine schichtspezifische Beurteilung implizieren. Vgl. meine Rezension im Krim. Journal 1974, S. 150.

9 Vgl. Erhard und Viola Blankenburg, Hellmut Morasch. Der lange Weg in die Berufung, in: Rolf Bender (Hrsg.) Tatsachenforschung in der Justiz, Tübingen (C. B. Mohr) 1972, S. 81–104.

10 Ebenda.

11 Vgl. Prognos Gutachten „Struktur der Zivilgerichtsbarkeit", Tübingen (J.C.B. Mohr) 1974, hrg. von der Bundesrechtsanwaltskammer.

12 So treten selbst in Mietprozessen zu 3/4 die Vermieter, und nur zu 1/4 die Mieter als Kläger auf. Vgl. H. Koch, G. Zenz, Erfahrungen und Einstellungen von Klägern in Mietprozessen, in: Schelsky-Rehbinder (Hrsg.). Jahrbuch für Rechtssoziologie und Rechtstheorie, Bd. 3, Düsseldorf 1972. Allerdings ist zu beachten, daß die Untersuchung 1970 (also vor der Novellierung des Mietrechts) durchgeführt wurde.

13 Wolfgang Kaupen, unveröffentlichtes Manuskript, Köln 1972.

14 In einem Land am Beginn seiner industriellen Entwicklung wie Spanien steigt die Zivilprozeßtätigkeit parallel zum Wirtschaftswachstum, ohne jedoch bislang auch nur annähernd die Prozeßhäufigkeiten in der Bundesrepublik zu erreichen – in spätkapitalistischen Ländern wie in der Bundesrepublik Deutschland oder den USA bleibt sie trotz hohen Wirtschaftswachstums konstant. Vgl. Toharia, in diesem Band S. 39 ff., sowie Friedman, in diesem Band S. 25 ff.

15 Vgl. J. Feest/G. Metzger-Pregizer, Betriebskriminalität und Betriebsjustiz, in: Kriminologisches Journal, 2/1972, S. 89.

Joel B. Grossman

Political Justice and System Maintenance: An Overview of Some Major Variables*

The concept of political justice is as important to understand as it is difficult to define. Clearly it involves the use of the legal process to affect the balance of political power in a society. Often, though not always, it involves the use of the courts and is equated with what are popularly denominated as "political trials." Although legally only individuals are charged with crimes, we may distinguish political justice from ordinary criminal justice by stressing its focus (direct or indirect) on a range of group or class (1)** interests other than the individual interests of the defendant.

The traditional focus of political justice studies has been on criminal trials. It might be more comprehensive and more functional to define political justice as an alternative authority enforcement device, an auxiliary weapon to protect consensus, enhance authority and bolster minimum levels of regime support, where ordinary political and legal means are inadequate. Political justice, through legal process, seeks to impose sanctions, disadvantages and constraints on groups or individuals whose activities represent an actual or potential threat to public order and to the maintenance of the authority of the regime.

Political justice is especially relevant to dynamic societies whose traditional bounds of social order are being questioned. It is a way of managing change before other, more permanent, arrangements can be made; a method of mediating conflict and reducing tensions as the balance of power between groups and interests shifts and the capacity of more formal institutions to fulfill this role according to previously agreed-upon rules lags behind. Not only is political justice an important means of both adjudicative and nonadjudicative conflict resolution, but in times of stress it may be used to mediate conflicts at a relatively low level of visibility, utilizing mostly short-term solutions, which are not too uncomfortably far from the political center (2).

This approach to political justice is functional and nonideological. We are interested, as political analysts, in understanding and explaining the existence of a widespread phenomenon – why, when and how it occurs, and its impact. Most studies have treated political justice as a lamentable pathology or as a sign of

* This is a revised version of a paper presented at the Conference on the Sociology of the Judicial Process, Bielefeld, West Germany, September 24–29, 1973. The useful comments of the other participants in the Conference, especially Lawrence Friedman and also of Murray Edelman, Robert Booth Fowler, Mary H. Grossman, and Austin Sarat, are gratefully acknowledged. The larger study of which this essay is a part has been supported by the Institute for Research on Poverty of the University of Wisconsin.

** Notes on pages 117 ff.

political decay. One of the enduring myths of the liberal democratic state is that political justice is an aberration – inconsistent with the rule of law and contrary to the norms and ideals of liberal democracy. But political justice need not be viewed as an abnormality. Indeed, political justice is not unrelated to the existence and to the maintenance of the very liberal principles of which it is said to be subversive (3). While incidents of political justice often do represent individual excesses, more often and more importantly they are the product of systematic forces at work in a society. Yet, as Balbus has perceptively noted, theories of the liberal state are particularly unreceptive to this notion (4). The orthodox deny that legal repression is possible, so long as the norms of the liberal state are faithfully adhered to. Of course such repression does or may occur; they attribute this fact to a failure of individuals to conform to the norms of due process. On the other side, the radical critics simply assert that repression is inherent in capitalist liberalism, and confine themselves to a condemnation of the entire system, including its law and courts (5). Both views do not help us understand the persistence and compatibility of liberalism *and* political justice.

Another explanation for the aberrational myth of political justice lies in the subjectivity of the terms involved. In American society there is a common tendency to attribute a negative connotation to anything described as "political." The terms political and justice are viewed as antithetical. A "political" solution is one which emphasizes bargaining, compromise, expediency and value relativism. "Justice" represents a different set of values. Whatever one's choice of definition, justice is associated with such concepts as fairness and rightness – a moral constant in a world of declining and relativistic virtue (6). The emotive discordancy between the two terms is acute.

Lack of agreement .on a definition of justice is also part of the problem of defining political justice. It may be, as John Rawls has suggested, that "justice is the first virtue of social institutions" (7). But this primacy is, if anything, enhanced because it is a relatively vague "cluster" concept, difficult to operationalize and available as an important political symbol to those on both sides of many important issues. Rawls argues that justice provides a necessary (though not exclusive) set of principles for assigning rights, duties, and advantages in a society, and that it serves as a standard for evaluating governmental action. Of course the existence among individuals of a "shared conception of justice" makes the process of allocation and evaluation substantially easier. But it is not the only value for which a commonly shared conception is an important parameter of social cohesion and integration. Common religious beliefs, shared economic goals and statuses, and common adversaries are just three of many other possible values or conditions which may underwrite consensus and harmony in a society. Moreover, observers often presume a shared conception of "justice" because of some consensus (or lack of express dissensus) which in fact results from other factors. But even assuming that Rawls is correct, the real virtue of justice may be precisely that it is widely available as a symbol of reassurance – to society and self. Also, though people may agree on an abstract formulation of justice, in concrete operational terms, and in a particular situation they may reveal great stress, disagreement and conflict. (The same is true of such ideals and basic norms as free speech.) It may be that effective justice is always, in the broad sense, political.

Political justice may, and often does, involve misuse of governmental power. But it is not *per se* dependent on illegal actions by governmental officials. Nor is all government illegality to be described as political justice. Law-breaking on the part of public officials obviously does occur, but political justice may be most effective when it occurs within the limits – though perhaps near the margins – of legality. Edelman has noted the imprecision of legal language, and its consequent impact on the behavior of citizens and public officials alike. Legality and illegality are not dichotomous variables but merely formal representations of the end points of a continuum which defines the acceptability and legitimacy of the acts of citizens and public officials (8). The law-abidingness of private citizens is often judged according to situational factors, and allowances made (both by law enforcement officials and individual citizens themselves) for conditions which made obedience to law impractical, impossible, immoral or in derogation of other widely held values (9). So too the legality of official acts is often ambiguous and a matter of degree. The prevailing political climate, the source and degree of threats to its hegemony which a regime perceives, the importance of certain goals, the clarity and enforceability of applicable legal or constitutional standards, and the perceived costs and benefits of pursuing a particular policy are all to be considered in determining the legitimacy of governmental action. This is not to deny the importance of formal legal rules or standards of justice in guiding official behavior; it merely recognizes their limitations and inherent inflexibility.

Law itself often specifies conditions under which otherwise prohibited government actions are permitted. In the United States, constitutional provisions for the establishment of martial law and suspension of the writ of habeas corpus come to mind. A vast array of less obvious statutes and precedents provide for invocation or exercise of emergency powers by the executive (10). Some of these are of particular importance to the question of political justice, because they empower the government to deal with groups or individuals in what otherwise would be clearly illegal ways. The removal of Japanese Americans from their westcoast homes during World War II was a blatant and large scale example (11). Few today would support a similar action by the government. Yet in upholding portions of President Roosevelt's executive order, the Supreme Court approved the concept that emergency situations might legitimize even so blatant a repression of individual rights (12). Similar arguments were made by the government in the recent domestic wiretap case (13), and by the Nixon Administration in defense of some of its internal security policies (14). The Supreme Court's rejection of the government's argument – that it had the right to wiretap without judicial warrant in domestic security investigations – may have set some fresh limits (15). It remains to be seen how effective such limits are in practice. Even where the law does not specifically provide for exceptions to its rules, it often invites exceptions through ambiguity, and in the complex relativity of means and ends. The chief executive is charged with major responsibility for protecting national security; the prosecutor and policeman with preserving the public order. It is not difficult to understand how these (valid) ends are frequently invoked to justify (invalid) means.

When one moves away from the federal government's concern with "national security" – admittedly a gray area in which the limits of executive power are most difficult to define – to the more mundane relations between government and citizens, and from relatively formal government actions to the murky waters of administrative decisions, the definition of legality is not significantly clearer. Here the discretion of officials is greatest, the visibility of government policies low, and opportunities for misuse of power maximized (16). Misuse of power is often equated with brutality or overzealousness in prosecuting the opponents of a regime. But, paradoxically, the American tradition of underenforcement of the law may be an equally effective weapon of political justice. Political justice should be seen not only as what government does to its enemies, but also in the disparity between the treatment accorded to enemies and friends.

Our view of political justice does not depend on the *motivation* of policymakers Questions of motivation are, in any case, almost totally resistant to objective classification, in the absence of explorations at the individual level (17). Motivation is also difficult to define. In any event, political justice is an institutionalized phenomenon (18). It can exist and be effective without "bad intent" on the part of individual actors, and it can fail to have any substantial impact even where such intent is present.

Political justice is rarely the purposive and rational enterprise which is often implied or attributed to it. It shares with other governmental policymaking the common characteristics of incrementalism, mixed motivation, confusion of ends and means, inadequate calculation of political policy impact, inadequate informational base, inadequate resources, lack of cohesiveness and lack of control over outcomes. Indeed these problems may be particularly acute in the case of policies of political justice because, by their very nature, they usually cannot be articulated and defended as legitimate government actions.

Our exploration of political justice in this paper will also stop short of a full assessment of its impact. The outcomes of particular political trials are easily observed in terms of the fate of individual defendants. But our view of political justice encompasses more than political trials. It covers a wider range of governmental activities, and the impact of these activities is diffuse and difficult to measure (19).

The remainder of this paper is a theoretical exploration of the main attributes and functions of political justice. Necessarily it stops short of denoting precise boundaries. For the sake of convenience and conceptual clarity, we will discuss first the goals and strategies of political justice, and then some of the variables most likely to structure its use.

I. Political Justice – Goals and Strategies

Political justice is an instrument of government policy, not an end in itself. In its different forms it is most likely to be utilized as a tactic in the achievement of three categories of goals (20). In the first category are goals which emphasize deterrence, rehabilitation or reintegration of target groups. The assumption is that the targeted deviance is largely individual and reparable. In this context the focus of political justice is likely to be cooptative and even ameliorative. Relatively innocuous concessions made by members of target groups, such as symbolic acts of contrition or other reaffirmations of the faith, may satisfy the government. A rehabilitative policy may also take the form of positive rewards granted in return for political acquiescence and support; more subtly it may involve increasing dependency through resource redistribution.

The second category emphasizes containment. It is a more group-oriented policy which may depend on relatively informal restraints but which may also require more formal measures such as the imposition of mild sanctions or disqualification from certain offices, privileges and benefits. It may also involve the passage or use of laws and other tactics by law enforcement officials to harass groups by forcing them to exhaust their resources in self-defense.

The third, most severe, and often most visible category of goals which involves the use of political justice tactics emphasizes repression, retribution and, ultimately, extinction. It is directed at groups or individuals whose very existence is so threatening to the regime that co-existence is impossible. Rehabilitation or containment are rejected for either practical or ideological reasons.

These categories are not mutually exclusive, either in the definition of goals or in the choice of means. The use of a particular tactic or strategy is as likely to depend on available resources or "traditional" responses to certain types of provocations as it is to reflect carefully planned policies. As with many other governmental policies, means become instrumental in the determination of goals; goals are often articulated belatedly to explain means. And as with other policies, the public explanation of a government's behavior may be designed to meet external standards, such as legality, regardless of the operative tactical goals. The choice of tactics is also dictated by the perceived imminence and severity of threat of the target group and the possibilities of resolving the group's differences with the government by less formal and less drastic means. The more dangerous a group, the more it is perceived as committed to its anti-system goals, the lower the threshold at which increasingly more repressive countermeasures are likely to be initiated. Conversely, no matter how far apart a group is from prevailing norms, it is not likely to face repressive government action if its behavior, ideology, and life style are not perceived as imminent or credible threats – at least not beyond some mild form of stigmatization or low level harrassment. The role of government at this end of the continuum may be limited to intelligence gathering through surveillance or informers.

Most studies of political justice have focused on the courts, and especially on the "political trial" as the primary form of political justice. Yet Kirchheimer was undoubtedly correct in viewing the political use of the courts as essentially a middle range policy, "neither the most incisive nor the most frequent form." He saw the role of the courts as particularly useful in completing repression or harrassment, in the dramatization of the legitimacy of a regime's policies, and in rallying political support (21). Political trials may be particularly useful in affirming official policies, stigmatizing those who oppose them, and developing popular support for those policies and encouraging distrust of and perhaps privately organized measures against, regime opponents. We refer here to their potential; political trials can be quite risky to a regime. They may backfire badly; thus the motivation to undertake such trials must be quite strong (22).

Kirchheimer also noted that where large numbers of persons were involved, administrative procedures might be more effective than political trials (23). Courts are simply not set up to handle mass trials (witness the difficulties, even with prior planning, in processing and in justifying the processing of persons arrested in the course of urban riots) (24). The shortcuts which must be taken, and the high visibility of images conveyed by such procedures, produce enough negative symbols to effectively undercut whatever gains in regime legitimacy and support might otherwise be realized. Besides, courts are limited to those situations where regime opponents have committed, or can be charged with, criminal violations. Even allowing for the flexibility which the government has in defining crimes such as conspiracy, this still leaves a considerable range of "subversive" activity which cannot be packaged into a criminal charge. The bureaucratization of political justice offers one rather underexplored alternative. It is likely to be particularly efficacious if we are concerned not only with the overt, obvious and easily identified political crime, but with a range of less visible, less overt, and less easily definable acts which, additively, may have an equally profound and disturbing effect on the maintenance of the system.

Alan Wolfe has classified "repressive laws" in such a way as to to accommodate a range of strategies wider than use of criminal law alone (25). Wolfe recognizes that the forms of legal repression may be judicial, administrative and executive. Wolfe distinguishes among the following: [1] harrassment laws, such as vagrancy statutes, whose original intent was more neutral than its current repressive use (he ignores the long-time repressive use of the law of vagrancy); [2] obligatory laws, such as the selective service act, which impose obligations generally but which fall most heavily upon certain disfavored groups; [3] inclusion laws, which are designed to affix labels which might form the basis for later discrimination, e.g. laws about aliens; [4] process laws, such as the conspiracy statutes, which punish not illegal acts but the process of planning illegal acts; [5] public order laws, which criminalize riotous and other forms of disorderly conduct or require permission for parades or otherwise limit political expression; [6] preventive laws, designed to control those who are potentially disruptive; and [7] explicitly political laws, such as the various espionage and sedition statutes which, in Wolfe's view, tend to follow rather than cause the repression and devitalization of deviant groups (26).

Suggestive as they are, Wolfe's categories are too legalistic and confining. Laws can be put to different uses, depending on the situation and the objects of attack. For example, containment may be achieved in a number of ways, and may include tactics of harrassment. Containment may succeed merely by discrediting ideological foes; or it may capitalize on intra-group conflicts or differences in the vulnerability of group members. Weak group members may be coopted into informer roles, or into accepting some mainstream values and working for these values within the group. Thus it seems better now simply to recognize that there are clusters of strategies which may contribute to harassment, containment, or retribution, and that the success of particular strategies is an empirical question very much dependent on circumstance and situation.

II. Major Variables Defining Selection of Strategies

Allowing that political justice is not a perfectly rational enterprise, it is helpful to assess how close it does – or might – come to such a standard. Ideally, some form of cost-benefit analysis would precede any decision to pursue a particular strategy of political justice. Such a calculus would necessarily involve agreement on what a particular regime would require to maintain authority. How much authority might be gained – or lost – from following a particular strategy? What are the consequences of failure – or only partial success? Is failure more costly than mere inaction? Will a particular tactic provoke the sort of resistance that strengthens the opposition and requires further – and perhaps excessive and even more costly – government action? What about backlash? Tactics of political justice are often pursued not so much for their effect on target groups as for their value in providing symbolic reassurance to supporters of the government. Government acts as an agent of one group in trying to repress another. But there is always the risk of losing some support. Tactics which exceed acceptable norms of procedure may alienate one segment of support, while tactics which are insufficiently positive and authoritarian may alienate another. Efforts to meet both types of criticism would be contradictory and might serve to expose the weaknesses of a regime, instead of adding to its authority. And there is always the problem that intensive efforts to eliminate deviant groups may escalate into a much larger sphere or more intense conflict which the regime is not equipped to handle.

At the foundation of any determination of strategy is a set of assumptions about existing levels of regime support, about popular commitment to compliance with law, about popular tolerance for marginally legal tactics (which, of course, may depend on who, and how dangerous, the opposition is perceived to be), and about the utility and efficacy of coercive sanctions. How do subjects generally, and dissidents in particular, view the regime? Are we talking about fully allegiant citizens, or citizens who may comply but not really support the political order? In Richard Rose's terms, is the regime seen as fully legitimate in the eyes of its dissident subjects (27)? Is their opposition to specific policies, to the regime generally, or both? These are important questions which are not canvassed adequately in strategic planning, yet which may powerfully affect the autcome. Rose argues, in the context of his study of Northern Ireland, that in a regime which is not fully legitimate the institutions of law may contribute mainly to disorder (28). It remains an important empirical question to determine if this observation is applicable in the United States. But there is enough partial evidence to suggest that it is (29). In communities where the police or courts are viewed as repressive, even "proper" law enforcement techniques are viewed as provocative efforts of repression. There are many implications of this observation. For our purposes it serves mainly to remind us first that law is not *per se* an alternative to or a means of preventing political justice. A "legal" or "legalizing" solution may be viewed very differently by those who accept or reject the basic legitimacy of legal institutions. Second, the observation serves to emphasize the convergence of roles and perceptions that constitutes one of the main operative components of political justice. Political justice is not just what government does to its enemies, but what grows out of a set of relationships between government and its opponents (30).

Within this framework we extend our inquiry by concentrating on two sets of variables: societal norms of justice and fairness which limit the options of political justice; and the nature and perception of threats. *Norms of Justice and Fairness.* In any society there are likely to be a set of norms which define the boundaries of acceptable use of the legal process, and of political action generally. In the United States the most important is the emphasis on the rule of law itself and the notion of fairness which not only pervades the legal process but contributes importantly to those perceptions of legitimacy which underwrite support of political regimes. As we have seen, the concept of justice is very complex, but certain fundamental aspects stand out. For example, one can differentiate conceptually between procedural and substantive justice. The former is concerned with rules and processes by which public and private decisions are made. The latter is concerned with outputs and outcomes, and focuses on the distribution of commodities like wealth, honor, status, and material goods. It is often called distributive justice, and may include also a negative or corrective component such as punishment or penalty for the commission of a wrongful act, and the assessment of compensation for damages done to others.

Procedural and substantive justice are often separated analytically, but in practice they are interrelated. Procedural rules may be neutrally applied to all fit cases, but they are rarely neutral in the sense of valuefree. It is more than theoretically possible, as Edmond Cahn has noted, for fair procedures to mask substantive injustice (31). Typically this is one of the forms of what is called political justice. Law is not so much a set of rules for the control of private interests as it is a reflection of such interests as have acquired dominance in political, social and economic life. What one group sees as fair another may view as oppressive. What the law enforces is likely to be the set of interests which is most powerful in a community, or for which adequate supporting resources exist. The quest for justice is not an armchair undertaking in logic, but a real and often brutal competitive undertaking in which abstract conclusions about what is right play but a limited role.

Even where nominally fair procedures exist they are not likely to produce equitable results when applied to individuals of markedly different resources (32). Under certain conditions recourse to the courts may narrow the gap or reduce the advantages caused by unequal resources. But it may also favor those already advantaged. However advantages are computed, the government is almost always advantaged when it goes to court. Thus, theoretically fair procedures may not only mask substantive injustice but exacerbate it (33).

In the United States, procedural justice is most often symbolized by the evolving concept of "due process of law." In its legal context, due process is associated with the right to a fair hearing, to adequate notice and opportunity to defend oneself against charges, and the right to be judged by an impartial arbiter according to a set of previously determined rules (34). It is also the right of equality of treatment by agents of the government – equality in relation both to how others are treated, and to one's individual capacities and needs.

The thrust of the idea of just procedures is not limited to government action. The idea pervades many social processes, and governs a wide variety of private relationships and efforts at dispute settlement. It has become a forceful standard of judgment for the law and official action, constituting, in Lon Fuller's phrase, the "inner morality" of law and the basis of its legitimacy (35). Indeed so pervasive is the idea (even allowing for differences in its basic formulation) that, under the rubric of "legality" it has become an ideology; for some it is almost a secular religion (36).

Legality is often equated with justice. As Fuller has said in another context, "If we do things the right way, we are likely to do the right thing" (37). Yet it seems clear that legality and justice are not indistinguishable. Internally consistent rules may not be just in every case. And such rules may not produce just results. To equate legality with justice is to make the untenable assumption that the law has only one end and aim, and that is justice. Yet there are other social functions of law, which may depend on the appearance of justice, rather than on its actual achievement.

Indeed, justice and law are by no means identical. One must remember the distinction between two central strains in the concept of law: law as enhancing and upholding governmental institutions, and law as upholding and protecting individual rights. The chief function of law in many societies is simply to sustain the ruling authorities: this conception is often associated with a culture in which citizens are reluctant to press claims for individual rights. Rights-consciousness is considered vulgar and disharmonious to social unity, and social unity is more important than individual satisfactions (38).

The idea of law as the embodiment of individual rights is, of course, central to Anglo-American law and it is that conception on which the alleged unity of law and justice is based. But the first strain is also present, as indeed it – or some substitute – would have to be in any viable system of legal governance. It is seen most obviously in the criminal law, and in the extensive laws and rules which support the operations of government and government officials, and enhance their legitimacy and claim to the right to govern. The arguments in favor of a strong sense of civil obligation and obedience to law rest on the implicit assumption that the government itself is bound by the law. Yet in the final analysis it is the government or its agents which decide what the law means.

The clash between these two strains of law is often resolved explicitly by judicial decisions which weigh the claim of citizen rights against the needs of officials to carry out their tasks. More often perhaps it is resolved implicitly when public officials make discretionary decisions which take into account local customs and pragmatic needs of governance as well as the formal law. Daniel Boorstin has reminded us of the ambivalence with which Americans have traditionally viewed the law (39). Those who equate law and justice have resolved at least part of that ambivalence by treating law and justice in their most idealistic and complementary form.

It is widely recognized that general rules which appear just may in particular instances produce obvious injustice. Here too the equation of law and justice is less than perfect. In a legal system composed of rules, justice requires some provision for discretion, some leeway for individualization of cases. Rules must be both uniform and equitable. As Harold Ofstad has noted,

> Am impartial judge may be unjust because he sends everybody to the gallows. The kind judge may be intolerably partial if he is kinder to his friends than to his enemies. Impartiality is necessary but not sufficient for justice. Or, in other words, it is sufficient for – and perhaps identical with – *formal* justice; but formal justice is only necessary and by no means sufficient for the realisation of *material* justice (40).

The optimal balance between rule inflexibility and official discretion is not uniformly or objectively ascertainable. It may be, as the Supreme Court of the United States has recently decided, that the absence of any rationalizing principle in the application of the death penalty makes its imposition unjust and unconstitutional. Yet it would seem open to serious question whether uniform and unremitting application of the death penalty would be more just (although perhaps in the view of some of the current justices it would be more in accord with the constitution) (41).

Kenneth Davis has argued that the application of rules is "principled" while unfettered discretion opens the door to "emotions, favoritism, and politics" (42). His is another version of the ideology that justice is best served in a regime of strict adherence to rule. He may be correct in observing that the legal system contains far too much broad discretion, erring on the side of increasing the risks of arbitrariness (though also the capacity for individualization) rather than on the side of making law too narrow and inflexible to take account of individual differences. The tendency to broad discretion probably reflects the need to accommodate conflicting social norms in a multi-cultural society, blending these into a system of laws that is nominally uniform. Discretionary power is an important variable in the allocation of advantages to individuals and groups, and a critical component of political justice.

The relationship of social justice to individual justice is also a difficult problem of defining the boundaries of our subject (43). Justice for individuals is closely related to procedures and the capacity for individualization; social justice, however, is more than the sum of individual cases of justice; it takes into account the needs of the society as a whole. In so doing, it may have to violate norms which, in an individual context, are highly legitimate. Individual justice and social justice are often competitive if not mutually exclusive. Individual justice requires restraint on state power; social justice is a distributive concept. The notion of equality is important to both. Some argue that equality suggests uniformity. The state must confer upon persons such resources as will produce a high degree of uniformity in possessions and equality of resources and advantages (or withdraw from those with excess resources). A more restricted view is that social justice requires equality of opportunity or access, but not necessarily uniformity in outcome. Each of these views, of course, expresses a different conception of human nature, genetic endowments, and of the relationship of the individual to the state. Though political justice can sometimes be measured by the degree of unequal treatment of groups or individuals, much inequality is unrelated to political justice; certainly the two are not synonymous.

Considerations of what is just for the individual and what is just or possible within the social unit raises the issue of political obligation and consent. These in turn evoke questions about the legitimacy of governing institutions and law, and those who exercise governmental power. Concepts of justice are important standards for evaluating the legitimacy of a regime or of particular policies or acts. Satisfying the norms of justice is an important political resource and a powerful symbol. To assert the justness of one's regime or cause is to deny legitimacy to those who oppose it. For those in opposition the claim of injustice is a potent battle cry. More important, it may serve to weaken the loyalties of citizens and justify, if not promote, attempts at regime change.

The sources of claims of injustice are numerous. To be most meaningful and politically useful they must be defined within the structure of a political system. For example, the rights of individuals, though often stated in universalistic terms, must relate to the purposes of the political organization of which they are a part. The western democratic liberal tradition of governance is relatively limited in scope. Its aims are to maximize individual justice and freedom of choice, although as some critics have pointed out. liberalism seeks to strike a delicate balance between liberty and order, which necessitates some ambiguity toward the range of permissible individual acts and the appropriate governmental actions needed to maintain order.

Except where the interests of the state are claimed to be paramount, as in security matters, or in the maintenance of public order, the preservation of individual rights is seen as the essence of justice. Where the goals and purposes of the state are greater than the sum of individual satisfactions, as reflected in greater state involvement in economic and social planning (and possibly in official ideology to which all must subscribe), then justice is likely to be defined and measured in social or meta-social terms. In the first instance law may be seen (however inaccurately) as the embodiment of justice. In the second, justice may be achieved through law but is not dependent on it.

Concepts of justice affect the goals and strategies of political justice by establishing standards by which to measure the legitimacy of government action. Yet the complexity and ambiguousness of the subject assures the government some flexibility in its actions. It is at least open to government, under some conditions, to argue for the right to deviate from the rules where the resulting harm may be sufficiently great. Or the government may be able to sustain the position that attainment of certain ends legitimizes the utilization of means which, in the abstract, would be prohibited. The concept of justice is normally a brake on repressive government action; but it may also provide a rationale and a means for sustaining such action under certain circumstances.

One of the strongest assets of "political justice" is that it can often capitalize on this ambiguity to legitimize what might otherwise be easily recognized as repressive action. Relying on the system of justice requires the government to make certain concessions to norms of fairness and law. This reliance may have a payoff which more than justifies whatever concessions must be made. Government reliance on the system of justice may actually increase the dependence of citizens on existing institutions, and increase the manipulative social control capacity of the government. To invoke the protection of the courts, one must acknowledge their legitimacy – at least to the point of playing by the rules. Due process can effectively exist only within an institutional context. Hence due process serves to promote citizen attachment to existing authority, while limiting government and protecting individual rights. If justice is equated with rules, legality and law, interests and grievances may be deflected away from a focus on substantive issues which, in the long run, the government may find more threatening (44).

Edelmann noted continued strong support for the norm or myth of justice even among those least favorably treated by the justice system, reflecting "the tenacity of widespread cognitions" resistant to change. If this is indeed so, it is strong evidence of the utility and flexibility of the concept of justice in achieving stability (45). The desirability of maintaining public support for existing patterns of justice may serve to check some excesses or misuse. On the other hand, the limits within which governmental action is perceived as just are probably broader than most people have heretofore imagined.

Ideally, a regime should follow policies widely perceived as "just" but which at the same time maximize internal order and regime support. A key sustaining function of government is to control the constant – and possibly creative – tension between order and justice. The actions of government officials and government policies, are among the most important inputs into what citizens may view as justice received – or justice denied. Since justice is not always zero-sum enterprise it is possible to maximize citizen satisfactions across a broad spectrum of the electorate. This is more true of the "symbolic" than the material dimensions of justice, and government policy is likely to be structured accordingly. It is probably not necessary for all governmental acts to be perceived by any single individual or group as uniformly "just". A group or individual assesses justice in relative terms, across a whole band of governmental policies and symbols which concern the individual or group.

Whether or not government chooses to conform, or how closely it chooses to conform, to a legalistic model in dealing with any particular threat is itself a variable of some complexity. Kuykendall has suggested that "legalistic behavior" is emphasized in periods of order and stability while suppressive behavior is emphasized in time of stress (46). His observation lacks precision but it does effectively focus on the interplay of variables. Justice and order are sometimes symbiotic, at other times almost mutually exclusive. Justice – both real and apparent – may promote order; and claims of injustice may promote disorder, by withdrawing legitimacy from the government.

Yet justice and order are not always congruent. Cultural factors may be important, as suggested by Goethe's observation that "if there has to be a choice between injustice and disorder ... the German prefers injustice" (47). Whether or not this is true of the Germans, it does suggest an endemic dilemma of all societies. At those times when order is viewed as most important, the likelihood of political justice is increased – at least in those societies which also wish to maintain a commitment to justice and individual rights.

Nature and Perception of Threat. A second group of variables likely to determine goals and strategies of political justice is the type of threat and the way it is perceived by the relevant authorities. Obviously subjective questions of magnitude and timing are involved here. Evaluating the severity of a particular threat and the appropriate response is rarely an exercise in objective logic, any more than a regime's self perceptions about its own needs or its prediction about the possible benefits – or costs – to be expected from a particular course of action. A widely pursued course of political justice that is ineffective or that backfires may be far more costly than mere inaction. A particular tactic may provoke the sort of escalated resistance that only strengthens the hand of the opposition and requires escalated – and perhaps ill-considered and excessive – government action. There is also the need to consider a regime's supporters. The goals of a particular strategy may be primarily directed at providing symbolic reassurance to a regime's friends rather than actually doing away with its enemies. Yet what happens if that symbolic reassurance only provokes more demands by supporters to take more repressive and more risky action against its opponents?

At the heart of this problem of perception is the lack of a consensus on how much public order is needed, how the establishment or maintenance of order relates to the authority needs of a regime, or how to predict the acceptable costs of attempting to achieve one or the other. All this differs between societies, and within a society. What may be threatening under one set of circumstances may be tolerable under another. As Matthew Holden has observed, it is a problem of the "critical mass" (48). A dozen violent crimes in a short time span may provoke demands for stern government countermeasures. A similar number of crimes over a longer period of time, or more widespread geographically, may cause less alarm. Today governments accept a level of verbal criticism and abuse which would have been treated as seditious and libelous in the period after World

War I, and regarded as disloyal after World War II. The boundary between political rights and political crime is constantly shifting. Since World War I the trend has been toward enlargement of political rights. This has resulted in new limitations on formal government responses to signs of political disaffection. As a result there may have been some shift in emphasis to less formal and visible tactics of political justice (49).

The government's definition of acceptable "disorder" today is very much dependent on, but also the creator of, citizen perceptions of what is acutely threatening and what is merely disagreeable. The widespread perception that violent crime is rising and that life in big cities is less safe makes it possible to create a political issue out of "law and order", which engenders support for repressive government action, and for candidates who advocate such measures. A climate is created which encourages "maximum" penalties for those convicted of crime. And it provides a partial, if self-serving, rationalization for the invocation of other government actions close to the margins of legality.

How the government defines a particular act or series of events is important in several ways. First, its initial response may be critical in shaping citizen perceptions about the acts in question and about its own role in regard to them. Second, as Rose and Miller remind us, the government may limit or define its own response by the way it defines an act initially (50). If it dismisses a protest demonstration as "merely hooliganism" or as the solitary work of a few dissidents it will not have provided sufficient justification for calling out the National Guard or declaring a state of martial law or otherwise suspending constitutional guarantees. On the other hand, if the government defines the same event as a riot this has more serious and more political overtones, and government will be expected to react with a greater show of force. But at the same time it will be admitting the existence of widespread dissatisfactions with its policies and greater threats to its power and authority. For the same reasons a government may be reluctant to label an "ordinary anti-social act" (51) as a political crime, especially when it is precisely this label which is coveted by the perpetrators of the act; they see it as a defense (or at least a good appeal to a jury) against charges of illegal acts where the facts are not in dispute and the law itself does not provide an exception for political motivation. If by its verbal cues the government contributes to citizen unrest and insecurity, then by its actions it must seek to alleviate those feelings.

Similarly, flag burning, destruction of draft cards, marijuana consumption, pornography, homosexuality, abortion, petty gambling and prostitution may not directly threaten the public order or regime stability, but their indirect impact on the political system is considerable. Such practices, even if they do not directly challenge the political system, are often associated with life styles and values which some citizens regard as immoral and as threats to legitimate authority; they may be regarded as more threatening than crimes of violence or "clean" crimes which result in serious economic loss to individuals or to the society.

Such "crimes without victims" often reflect stratification in wealth and power as well as differences in norms (52). It is not the act itself so much as the fact of deviance that elicits a hostile response and stimulates recourse to the criminal sanction. The President's Crime Commission recently pointed out that Americans see crime in moral rather than social terms; Americans believe that man is responsible individually for his actions (53). Crime is seen as the result of moral failings rather than as the result of unfavorable environments. This view of crime, associated with what Francis Allen has called the "rehabilitative ideal," has obvious conservative consequences (54). It ignores the relationship of a particular "criminal" act to its social background, and tends to divert attention from the social consequences of determining what is and what is not criminal. Since the problem is perceived as one of individual deviance, social responsibility is denied, the criminal law is deemed the most appropriate response, and the threats to legitimacy of the regime which the act might precipitate are minimized. Furthermore, the use of "excessive force," or other departures from the norms of enforcement behavior, are more easily justified – both morally and politically – when the cause of deviance is assumed to lie within the individual. At the same time actions against deviant individuals will indirectly affect the broader causes or groups which represent the real "threats".

Legislatures will typically define deviant acts as criminal offenses. Of course, there is a wide gap between legislative prohibition and judicial enforcement. Buth the successes or failures of criminal sanctions are not to be judged entirely by the numbers of people charged with crimes. Far more people in the United States who are involuntarily confined to an institution are undergoing "treatment" rather than "punishment". Criminalization of deviant acts (including political crimes) stigmatizes those acts, and brands their associated subcultures as immoral or inferior. It allows those who disapprove to feel morally superior because they refrain from similar indulgences and because they see themselves as acting or thinking in the public interest. This results in a form of symbolic confirmation of values. Many people are less interested in the efficacy of enforcement than in the symbolic satisfaction of knowing that they are on the side of the law, that they, as Berkowitz and Lutterman put it, are "socially responsible" (55). That the acts of which they disapprove are legally condemned may lull critics into a state of quiescence and relatively passive regime support; or it may act positively to increase levels of trust, support and efficacy by assuring citizens that at least some of their complaints are being dealt with. Paradoxically the criminal statute (and associated enforcement effort) which condemns a particular form of behavior may have a greater suppressant or support-inducing effect on its "sponsors" than on its intended objects.

Joseph Gusfield noted the importance of the law as a device by which those needing reassurance about their own values stigmatized the values of others. He argued that Prohibition, while it may not have controlled the consumption of alcohol, did allow rural Protestant America to stigmatize urban immigrants and Catholics who, because of their greater affinity for alcohol, could be labeled less worthy (56). Much the same sentiment was expressed earlier by Thurman Arnold:

> Most unenforced criminal laws survive in order to satisfy moral objections to established modes of conduct. They are unenforced because we want to continue our conduct, and unrepealed because we want to preserve our morals (57).

The imposition of criminal sanctions upon those who not only violate certain norms but oppose them as well may constitute severe political repression. But the toleration of systematic evasion of such laws by the deviant subcultures they are designed to suppress, while dominant groups continue to proclaim their virtue, may in fact be a far more subtle and effective, if unintended, weapon for achieving order and stability in a multi-cultural or multi-class society. Conflict between groups is reduced to tolerable levels when each group obtains some measure of satisfaction. Those who oppose the behavior in questions receive symbolic reassurance that they are right and additional satisfaction from believing that deviants are suffering the consequences. At the same time, the practicalities of law enforcement, including the gap in values between those who support a law and those who enforce it, and the protections of due process rules, allows the controversial behavior to continue relatively uninhibited. Direct contact between the groups is minimized. Because the law is underenforced deviants receive some assurance that their values or conduct are not entirely illegitimate. In Gusfield's words:

> Conflict between the two groups is thus minimized. The existence of divergent and potentially conflicting cultures "does not necessarily constitute any particular problem for the society as a whole so long as the two groups are not in direct interaction and do not directly confront one another's differing orientation" (58).

Conversely, where systematic evasion of such norms is not tolerated, and where important resources are directed to full enforcement, conflict may be exacerbated. The risks of promoting alienation through enforcement or nonenforcement, must be balanced against the possibility that use of the criminal sanction will actually narrow the moral gaps between groups.

Systematic evasion is particularly useful in reducing conflict where open political compromise is difficult or impossible to obtain, as is frequently the case where there is conflict over fundamental values. Compromise is much less difficult where there is conflict over material goods which can be translated into monetary terms and are inherently more susceptible to bargaining.

Gusfield points to another phenomenon: relabeling a particular deviant act to make it more acceptable to the group opposing it. The nation is already prone to use euphemisms in commercial and political discourse. Drug users can be labeled "sick" rather than "evil". The moral dimensions of prostitution, abortion, and excessive use of alcohol are absorbed into the concern over health. The offender becomes the object of solicitude rather than punishment. The acts or values remain unacceptable, but concern shifts to the personal or social forces which brought the acts about. Treatment becomes the appropriate response, although deviants who are "treated" may in fact be dealt with more harshly than those who are "punished". More important, relabeling can often succeed in depoliticizing the acts, or the motivations of the actors. The drug offender is the best example. By labeling him as sick, use of drugs as a means of political protest is obscured. His flaunting of disobedience to the law and his rejection of prevailing norms, need not be considered as part of an aggregate form of deviance, but as an individual, and less threatening, form (59).

Relabeling, of course, can also be applied to governmental acts or policies, which become "sick" or evil, or repressive, or fascist, or the like. Such labels rationalize withdrawal of support – perhaps even the commission of unlawful acts.

Relabeling is less effective against acts of open political dissidence. For one thing the threat to dominant interests may be perceived as more direct, and compromise less practicable. Where the possibility of conversion is low, the appropriate response may be to deal harshly. Formal political reeducation is always a possibility and is openly practiced in some countries. But it is doubtful that political deviance can be effectively eliminated or curtailed in this way in a nontotalitarian society, apart, perhaps, from surface recantations under threat of sanction. Individuals may conform but ideas are more difficult to suppress. A more common approach is to place greater emphasis on inculcating and socializing others in the population to the desired values, and devising conformity rituals such as loyalty oaths. The need to stigmatize political dissidence often diminishes as events which caused it fade into history or as the dominant ideology absorbs – and thus legitimizes – what once was the radical's creed.

Groups – or values – which are not openly in defiance of the law or in opposition to prevailing values but which are nonetheless considered as potential threats to order and authority, are difficult to deal with. The difficulty is compounded when what is threatening in the action of such groups is the claim that, as applied to themselves, society and the government have failed to live up to their own ideals. Here the strategy and tactics must be considerably more subtle. It is simply impossible to "explain" or accept the disparity between rich and poor, or black and white, without admitting contradictions between the ideal and reality. One typical response is to attack the methods by which such groups seek a redress of their grievances as contrary to other fundamental values, e.g. poverty or racism should be eliminated but not by civil disobedience. Another response is to undercut the worthiness of members of such groups, for example, by distinguishing between the "deserving" and the undeserving poor, or by exposing leaders of such groups as immoral, unethical or power-hungry. Finally, a less acceptable but still utilized alternative is to challenge the legitimacy of a group's aspirations, by asserting that its leaders (almost never its rank and file members) have been taken in by, or more explicitly are servants of, a foreign ideology or some other sinister conspiracy to subvert the established order.

The criminalization of morals offenses – with or without toleration of norm evasion – relabeling, political surveillance and harassment, and conformity rituals are among the less open and more indirect methods of dealing with political dissidence, or with conditions of group conflict that have some potential for causing disorder and eroding support of the regime. Beyond these, there always lies the possibility of resort to more formal legal actions, including political trials. Use of such tactics will vary according to whether the threat consists of [a] a deliberate political crime, such as espionage or sedition; [b] politically motivated violations of essentially nonpolitical criminal laws; and [c] other threatening conditions including the existence of dissident groups, or their activities, or those of highly visible individual dissidents.

Balbus suggests that resort to formal law has both advantages and disadvantages (60). Short-run threats are best dealt with less formally, outside the official framework of legally prescribed remedies. Many have noted the dilemma inherent in efforts to enforce both law and order. More serious threats, particularly if they fall into categories *a* and *b*, may provoke "legal" responses. There are advantages to the government in following ordinary legal procedures and, perhaps even more important, in depicting the threatening actions as ordinary crimes without political motives. "Criminalizing" an act immediately deprives it of some legitimacy. The government gains tactical advantages when it forces those who committed certain acts to defend themselves in an arena chosen by the government. This is especially true where the procedural rules to be applied (e.g., the rules of evidence, and legal definitions of the crimes), serve to focus attention on facts, and turn attention away from the political justifications which may have motivated its commission. Thus, in the conspiracy trial of Dr. Spock, the defense was prohibited from arguing the illegality of the war in Vietnam. The charge was conspiracy to obstruct the draft. The evidence consisted of showing certain otherwise legal acts by Dr. Spock and his co-conspirators – speeches and the delivery of surrendered registration certificates to the Department of Justice – which amounted to such obstruction. The judge decided, that, as a matter of law, the alleged (and admitted) acts constituted a crime. The jury was left only to decide if the defendants had done what they said they had done – and it so decided (61). The conviction was later overturned on appeal (62), but the case aptly illustrates the point that the most successful political prosecutions are those which are ostensibly least political. Formally, there are few political crimes in American law, but it is almost always to the interest of defendants to claim that their prosecution is politically motivated (63).

We have argued that often it is to the government's advantage to treat political dissidence as ordinary crime, clothed, as Balbus notes, in the language and procedures of formal rationality (64). Yet there are also risks. Losing political cases, or enough of them, may result in a long run withdrawal of legitimacy both from the government and from the legal system. The government must decide if this risk is worth the achievement of shorterrun goals. Use of the courts to control political dissidence is undoubtedly inefficient, costly, and time consuming. Yet its advantages as a strategy often outweigh its disadvantages. Recourse to the courts also gives dissidents an unparalleled forum for advancing their own views and exposing what they regard as the corruptness of the government. Legitimacy is a critical political resource – for both sides – and its enhancement or preservation is an important strategic consideration.

III.

Political justice is a specialized form of social control. Like other forms of social control the dimensions and frequency of its occurrence reflect certain key features of the society – its commitment to the use of the law, or legal forms, in social control, its definition of justice and other norms which may limit government action, the degree of dissensus and the perceived relationship between dissensus and legitimacy, and the availability and efficacy of other, perhaps less costly, strategies. Political justice is not an isolated phenomenon and cannot be understood apart from its cultural milieu. We have suggested that it is usually a residual strategy called into being to supplant or reinforce more routine strategies of social control.

There are many other strategies or devices of social control. Two in particular require mention, as especially relevant to an understanding of political justice. In a liberal, pluralist society, stability and order depend on involving citizens in activities which promote their stake in, and allegiance to, the dominant regime. The unarticulated premise is that such activities should absorb their interests and divert their attention from government. Duverger has suggested that depoliticizing events favors the established order (65). And Kornhauser has noted how an overlapping group structure tends to keep people absorbed in nonpolitical activities (66). But not all involvement is order producing or allegiance reinforcing. The legitimacy of group action makes groups a useful device and focus for dissident activity. The group's very existence becomes a potential source of conflict which may threaten the regime. In such situations, where a primary mechanism of control and order has failed, alternatives will be sought. Political justice provides a major option in such circumstances because it helps to break down political deviance of groups into individual transgressions, which are then punished by law; this gives government a controlled, manageable, yet potentially effective, response.

Social control is also promoted by widespread dissemination of norms such as justice, equality, and legality which imply that under certain circumstances government will protect its citizens, grant them benefits, and recognize their basic "rights". Yet, as Lawrence Friedman has observed, the interest of the government in promoting the concept of "rights" is balanced by the need to limit excessive exercise of rights: "if everybody suddenly claimed his due the system would be gravely overloaded" (67). The unwillingness or inability of government to fulfill its promises would become apparent. Many "rights" conflict with each other in practice, if not in principle; others would lose value in the process of bureaucratic enforcement or distribution. Accepting as fact the proposition that all theoretically valid rights could not actually be granted or enforced, it is important to government to pursue a course of action which maximizes citizen belief in these rights but minimizes the chances that they will in fact all be claimed. One way of doing this is by promoting rights abstractly; the greater the level of abstraction at which they are recognized, the less chance they will be operationalized.

Protest movements and dissident groups are often at their most threatening, when they demand the actualization of rights. Political justice, with its reliance on legal forms, is often thought to be an appropriate strategic response. For reasons already suggested, it may also be a risky maneuver, serving only to expose the very contradictions between theory and practice which the dissident group is advertising. Both the effectiveness and the risks of political justice are dependent on the level of rights consciousness which characterizes a particular culture or society.

In a very important sense all justice is political. This impedes, though it does not deny, the possibility of efforts to isolate and understand the pervasive phenomenon of political justice in the modern democratic state. The objective of this essay was to begin the process of transforming the term from a largely subjective and pejorative concept to a tool of analysis capable, ultimately, of guiding empirical reserarch. We have described some legal, social, and political parameters which move us closer to a more concrete definition and a more realistic view. Yet the concept remains elusive. It remains difficult to separate political justice from mere government illegality, though we know the two are not the same. Certainly, not all injustice is the result of political justice, yet surely much of the impact of political justice is, by any standards, unjust.

Political justice may, in certain circumstances, be a force for good. It preserves the form and structure of political authority while at the same time it allows a level of conflict among competing groups and ideologies that may be, on the whole, relatively healthy. Even the passage of a criminal statute which, on its face appears repressive, must be recognized for what it often is: a compromise between those who counsel more severe measures and those who seek to decrease

the repression potential of government action by subjecting it to the limits of legal process. Alan Wolfe has written that repressive political laws often follow rather than precede the demise of a target group; the law proclaims the victory (or compromise) but is not the prime generating force behind it (68).
Perhaps the key to understanding political justice is the recognition that it is a pervasive phenomenon, made up of many different kinds of acts. These are usually designed to be temporary (often symbolic) solutions, rather than more permanent regulatory policies. They are most likely to occur at times of great political stress, often when a prior consensus about certain values or a heretofore stable balance of power is disintegrating. Political justice, like judicial lawmaking, is an interstitial process, which arises more out of perceived necessity than out of conviction.

Summary

Thema ist die Untersuchung einiger wichtiger Variablen, die die politische Justiz in einer Gesellschaft definieren und ihre Grenzen festlegen. Unter politischer Justiz wird der Gebrauch des Gerichtsverfahrens zum Zwecke der Vergrößerung von Macht und Autorität eines Regimes verstanden. Sie wird oft gebraucht, um Sanktionen, Nachteile oder Zwangsmaßnahmen bestimmten Gruppen oder einzelnen aufzuerlegen, deren Aktivitäten eine aktuelle oder potentielle Bedrohung für das Fortbestehen der herrschenden Macht bedeuten.
Politische Justiz ist örtlich beschränkt auf nicht-totalitäre Gesellschaften. Gebrauch und Erscheinungsformen variieren je nach:

1. der Vorstellung über den bestehenden Grade der Anerkennung des Regimes,
2. der Vorstellung von Umfang und Schwere der Bedrohung für die Autorität des Regimes,
3. Art der Gruppen und einzelnen, die als Ursprung dieser Bedrohungen betrachtet werden.
4. Variablen einer Gesellschaft wie Grad des Konsenses und des sozialen Zusammenhaltes und
5. Normen über Gerechtigkeit und Billigkeit, von denen behauptet werden kann, daß sie für den Gebrauch oder Mißbrauch des Gerichtsverfahrens bestimmend sind und ihm Schranken setzen.

Notes

1 Many have made observations along this line, yet a more precise characterization remains elusive. This is the reciprocal of Angela Davis' distinction between ordinary crime and political crime. Se Angela Y. Davis, et al., If They Come in the Morning (New York: Signet Books, 1971), p. 29. Otto Kirchheimer's classic definition of political justice is that it is "the utilization of judicial proceedings for political ends." He recognizes that courts inevitably play a political role and distinguishes political justice because of its concern with destroying the power or legitimacy of the opposition and/or building up the power of the existing authorities. See Kirchheim, "Politics and Justice", in Burin and Shell (eds.), Politics, Law and Social Change: Selected Essays of Otto Kirchheimer (New York: Columbia University Press, 1969), p. 408.

2 For a recent discussion of the strategies and consequences of conflict resolution, see Joel B. Grossmann and Austin Sarat, "Courts and Conflict Resolution: Problems in the Mobilization of Adjudication", American Political Science Review (1976).

3 Otto Kirchheimer, "Political Justice," in International Encyclopedia of the Social Sciences, Vol. XLL (New York: Crowell and Collier, 1968), pp. 246–248. See also Alan Wolfe, The Seamy Side of Democracy: Repression in America (New York: David McKay, 1973), p. 208.

4 Isaac D. Balbus, The Dialectics of Legal Repression: Black Rebels Before the American Criminal Courts (New York: Russell Sage Foundation, 1973), p. 1 and passim.

5 See, for example, Edgar Friedenberg, "The Side Effects of the Legal Process," in Wolff (ed.), The Rule of Law (New York: Simon and Schuster, 1971), pp. 37–53. And generally see the essays in Jonathan Black (ed.), Radical Lawyers (New York: Avon, 1971).

,6 John Rawls, A Theory of Justice (Cambridge: Harvard University Press, 1971), pp. 11–17, 30–33.

7 Ibid., p. 3.

8 Murray Edelman, The Symbolic Uses of Politics (Urbana: University of Illinois Press, 1964), pp. 138–142; and, generally, Politics as Symbolic Action (Chicago: Markham, 1971). Also see Jethro K. Lieberman, How the Government Breaks the Law (Baltimore: Penguin Books, 1973).

9 For an interesting recent study of the phenomenon of "rule exception" and the utility of compliance, see Harrell Rodgers and Charles Bullock, Law and Social Change (New York: McGraw-Hill, 1972), pp. 182–185.

10 For example, a recent study has revealed that there are 470 emergency power statutes either in force or available to the President to use at his discretion. The study further showed that the Declarations of National Emergency of 1933 and 1950 are still in force. See "Summary of Emergency Power Statutes: A Working Paper by the Special Committee on the Termination of the National Emergency," U.S. Senate, October, 1973.

11 Jacobus Ten Broek, Edward M. Barnhart, and Floyd M. Matson, Prejudice, War and the Constitution (Berkeley: University of California Press, 1954).

12 Korematsu v. United States, 321 U.S. 760 (1944).

13 United States v. United States District Court, 407 U.S. 297 (1972). Pending are congressional efforts to further tighten the limitations on governmental use of wiretaps and electronic eavesdropping. On the other hand, the Supreme Court has been less willing to inquire into the constitutionality of nonelectronic snooping on the political activities of private citizens. Laird v. Tatum, 408 U.S. 1 (1972).

14 Press reports of the statements of several principals charged in the Watergate burglary of Daniel Ellsberg's psyhiatrist, Dr. Lewis Fielding, indicate that one defense to those charge will be that the operation was required by national security considerations.

15 Op. cit., Note 13.

16 There are numerous studies which detail the scope of official discretion in "low-visibility" decision-making. See Jerome Skolnick, Justice Without Trial (New York: Wiley, 1966), and James Q. Wilson, Varieties of Police Behavior (New York: Atheneum, 1968) on the police.

17 It is possible to conceive of politically motivated acts which are sufficiently camouflaged so as to "pass" for ordinary activities. And there undoubtedly are acts of government officials which lack this motivation and yet are widely perceived as acts of political justice. Thus there may be real differences, both theoretical and real, between the governmental and consumer perspectives.

18 I have in mind here a parallel to the distinction between "overt" and "institutional" racism which is drawn by Rodgers and Bullock. Most of what has been written about political justice has tended to focus on its more "overt" manifestations: relatively little has been said about its more covert or "institutionalized" qualities. See Harrell Rodgers and Charles Bullock, Racial Equality in America: In Search of an Unfulfilled Goal (Pacific Palisades, Cal.: Goodyear Publishing Company, 1975), chapter 1. Also see Bertram M. Gross, "Friendly Fascism: A Model for America", Social Policy, (Nov/Dec, 1970), 44–52.

19 By its very nature political justice is likely to produce ramifications – on the immediate target groups, of course, but also on the legitimacy of the regime, the attitudes of officials toward further use of similar tactics, and the adoption of alternate strategies if those initially chosen do not work.

20 Our emphasis in this paper on a governmental perspective should not be read to exclude the very important role of target groups in bringing about the conditions, and, indeed, even the overt acts, of political, if that is to their advantage.
21 Otto Kirchheimer, Political Justice (Princeton: Princeton University Press, 1961), p. 3.
22 I know of no compilation yet available to support this point. But certainly the nearly universal negative result (e.g. acquittal) of recent trials involving the Black Panthers and many groups and individuals opposed to the Vietnam War suggests the validity of this observation. Political trials often generate sympathy and support for the target group – and help to publicize its goals. This point is amplified later in the paper.
23 Kirchheimer, op. cit., Note 21, p. 96.
24 See Balbus, op. cit., Note 4; "Criminal Justice in Extremis" (Chicago: American Bar Foundation, 1969); and the Report of the National Advisory Commission on Civil Disorders, Ch. 13.
25 Alan Wolfe, op. cit., Note 3, pp. 95–102 and passim.
26 Ibid., pp. 99–100.
27 Richard Rose, Governing Without Consensus: An Irish Perspective (Boston: Beacon Press, 1971), pp. 191, ff.
28 Ibid., p. 113.
29 Certainly the best evidence on this point comes from studies of police behavior which show that enforcing the law and maintaining order are often regarded as mutally exclusive strategic alternatives. Strict law enforcement during urban riots, when perceptions of regime legitimacy by rioters might be expected to be at a low ebb, has often been eschewed in favor of benign neglect.
30 There are many examples of this relationship. Inter alia, see Kenneth Dolbeare and Joel B. Grossman, "LeRoi Jones in Newark: A Political Trial?," in Becker (ed.), Political Trials (Indianapolis: Bobbs-Merrill, 1971), pp. 227–247.
31 See Edmund Cahn, "Justice," in International Encyclopedia of the Social Sciences, Vol. 8 (New York: Crowell and Collier, 1968), pp. 343–344.
32 This point is especially well made in Marc Galanter's essay, this volume.
33 Use of the courts to solve disputes may be a double-edged sword. There are circumstances in which those with resources may take advantage of nominally neutral judicial procedures; on the other hand invoking the legal system is a classic tactic by which the "have nots" try to reduce the impact of greater resources of their adversaries.
34 Due process – entirely apart from its specific meaning – is a notion of great political appeal. The current trend in the United States is to extend the concept to new groups, institutional settings, and walks of life. Thus we find variations of a due process model extended from criminal trials for adults to the juvenile courts, to processes of involuntary civil commitment, and to the internal decisions of institutions as diverse as prisons and universities (students and faculty).
35 Lon Fuller, The Morality of Law (New Haven: Yale University Press, 1964), Ch. 2. For a more extended analysis, see Robert Booth Fowler and Joel B. Grossman, "Law, Liberalism and Social Change: A Preface", American Politics Quarterly 1974, 276–311.
36 See Judith Shklar, Legalism (Cambridge: Harvard University Press, 1964). For an interesting discussion of the consequences of "legalisation," see Jeffrey Jowell's essay, this volume.
37 Lon Fuller, "What the Law Schools Can Contribute to the Making of Lawyers," 1 Journal of Legal Education (1948), 204.
38 See Galanter, op. cit., Note 33, and Grossman and Sarat, op. cit., Note 2.
39 Daniel Boorstin, "The Perils of Indwelling Law," in Wolff, op. cit., Note 5, p. 76.
40 Harold Ofstad, "Impartiality," in Legal Essays: A Tribute to Frede Castberg (Stockholm: Scandinavian University Books, 1963), p. 135.
41 Furman v. Georgia, 408 U.S. 238 (1972).
42 Kenneth Davis, Discretionary Justice (Urbana: University of Illinois Press, 1971), p. 52. See also Mortimer Kadish and Sanford Kadish, Discretion to Disobey (Palo Alto: Stanford University Press, 1973).
43 See generally Richard Brandt (ed.), Social Justice (Englewood Cliffs, N.J.: Prentice-Hall, 1962).
44 Edelman has noted the potential reassuring and tranquilizing effect of the rhetoric of justice and equality in Politics as Symbolic Action, op. cit., Note 8, p. 81. But the

hypothesis that due process norms can promote regime support both positively (by increasing its legitimacy) and negatively (by absorption of interests and increasing dependency) is considerably more provocative and deserving of extensive empirical attention.

45 Ibid., p. 47.

46 Jack Kuykendall, "Toward a Theory of Negative Contacts," in Reasons and Kuykendall (eds.), Race, Crime and Justice (Pacific Palisades, Cal.: Goodyear Publishing Company, 1972), p. 231.

47 Quoted in Barbara Tuchman, The Guns of August (New York: Macmillan 1962), p. 355.

48 Matthew Holden, Jr., "The Quality of Public Order," in Schmandt and Bloomberg, The Quality of Urban Life (Beverly Hills: Sage Publications, 1969), p. 436.

49 Kirchheimer appears to make a contrary observation, but it is in reference to western societies generally, op. cit., Note 3, p. 246. With regard to the contemporary United States the point seems self-evident, although I am aware of the frequently large gap between the formal definition of rights by courts and legislatures and (a) the individual perception of rights as an operative concept; and (b) the extent to which the exercise of political rights is actually protected.

50 Richard Rose and William Miller, "What Are the Odds on Justice? Or, The Limits of the Law", unpublished pap, 1972, p. 5.

51 Ibid.

52 Distinctions of social class do not come into play in the official definition of such crimes, but frequently do affect how and against whom they are enforced. The impossibility of equal enforcement is one of the main arguments in favor of decriminalization. See Edwin Schur, Crimes Without Victims (Englewood Cliffs, N.J.: Prentice-Hall, 1965); and Dallin Oaks, "Studying the Exclusionary Rule in Search and Seizure," 37 University of Chicago Law Review (1970), 665–757.

53 President's Commission on Law Enforcement and Administration of Justice, The Challenge of Crime in a Free Society (Washington, D.C. U.S. Government Printing Office, 1967), p. 50.

54 Francis Allen, The Borderland of Criminal Justice (Chicago: University of Chicago Press, 1964), pp. 25–41.

55 Leonard Berkowitz and Kenneth G. Lutterman, "The Traditional Socially Responsible Personality," 32 Public Opinion Quarterly (1968), 169–185.

56 Joseph Gusfield, Symbolic Crusade (Urbana: University of Illinois Press, 1963), pp. 122–126 and passim.

57 Thurman Arnold, The Symbols of Government (New Haven: Yale University Press, 1935), p. 160.

58 Gusfield, op. cit., Note 60, p. 115.

59 Joseph Gusfield, "Moral Passage: The Symbolic Process in Public Designations of Deviance," 15 Social Problems (1967), 175–188.

60 Balbus, op. cit., Note 4, p. 3.

61 Jessica Mitford, The Trial of Dr. Spock (New York: Knopf, 1969), pp. 195–201.

62 Spock v. United States, 416 F 2d. 165 (1969).

63 The crime of treason, defined by the Constitution, is an exception. So too, possibly, are those crimes which penalize acts which could only be crimes if directed towards, or committed against, the government, e.g. directly advocating the overthrow of the government by force and violence, or obstruction of the draft. Most crimes with political motives are, however, treated by the government as nonpolitical; the political motivations of the defendants are normally not allowed to be argued as a justification for illegal acts. Obviously, the interests of the government in denoting an act as an ordinary criminal offense may clash with the motivations of the defendants in labeling the act as political. It might even be argued that all crimes are political, though not perhaps in the explicit or articulated motivations of the criminal. Certainly it would be difficult to ignore the political component in crimes committed in the context of social adversity, e.g. in the urban ghetto or out of despair because of economic depression.

64 Balbus, op. cit., Note 4, pp. 7–15.

65 Maurice Duverger, The Study of Politics (New York: Crowell, 1972), p. 253 and passim.

66 William Kornhauser, The Politics of Mass Society (New York: Free Press, 1959), p. 64 and passim. See also Jack L. Walker, "A Critique of the Elitist Theory of Democracy," 60 American Political Science Review (1966), 285–295; Peter Bachrach, The Theory of

Democratic Elitism: A Critique (Boston: Little, Brown, 1967); and Theodore Lowi, The End of Liberalism (New York: Norton, 1969).

67 Lawrence Friedman, "The Idea of Right as a Social and Legal Concept," 27 Journal of Social Issues (1971), 189–198.

68 Wolfe, op. cit., Note 3, p. 214. Kirchheimer seems to make the same point which, among other things, expresses the paradox that political justice may work best against relatively weak opposition groups.

Thomas Raiser

Zum Problem der Klassenjustiz

I. Der Begriff der Klassenjustiz kommt in der Bundesrepublik seit einiger Zeit in der Rechtssoziologie und der sich mit der Justiz beschäftigenden Publizistik immer stärker in Gebrauch (1)*. Soweit der Begriff, was nahe liegt, in polemisch propagandistischer Form und offenkundig politischer Zielsetzung verwendet wird, braucht er die Wissenschaft nicht zu beschäftigen und namentlich nicht Gegenstand einer Tagung zu sein, die sich mit der Soziologie des Gerichtsverfahrens beschäftigt. Indessen würde man den Absichten der Autoren, die ihn benutzen, durchaus nicht gerecht, wenn man es dabei beließe, sie dem Verdacht auszusetzen, derartige Intentionen zu verfolgen. Zwar ist kaum zu verkennen, daß der Begriff häufig eine kritische Spitze aufweist und sein Reiz sich nicht zuletzt aus seinem Potential für den politischen Meinungskampf erklärt. Aber neben und ungeachtet dieses Elements wird der Begriff als Instrument zur soziologischen Beschreibung und Erklärung des richtlichen Entscheidungsprozesses oder doch wichtiger in ihm auftretender Phänomene verwendet, und der Anspruch kann sogar so weit reichen, ihn als Instrument der wissenschaftlichen Analyse mit gleichem Rang neben die bisher gebräuchlichen Norm-, Rollen- und systemtheoretischen Ansätze zu stellen, die in der Justizsoziologie sonst, namentlich auch in den Vereinigten Staaten, üblich sind (2). Dieser Umstand nötigt dazu, sich mit seiner wissenschaftlichen Aussagekraft und Tragweite kritisch auseinanderzusetzen. Seine Herkunft aus dem marxistischen Vorstellungsschatz ist offenkundig und braucht hier nicht im Einzelnen belegt zu werden (3). Sie hat zur Folge, daß ihm, mindestens atmosphärisch, die Marx'schen Lehren von der Dichotomie der Gesellschaft (Kapitalisten- und Arbeiterklasse bzw. Bourgeoisie und Proletariat), vom Klassenkampf, der Selbstzerstörung des Kapitalismus, der proletarischen Revolution und schließlich vom Endzustand der klassenlosen Gesellschaft unlöslich anhaften. Wieweit er in diesem Sinn tatsächlich verstanden und gebraucht wird, ist weiter unten zu erörtern (4). In die rechtssoziologische Begriffswelt wurde er in Deutschland durch Ernst Fraenkel in den 20er Jahren eingeführt (5), nachdem ihn bereits vorher namentlich Karl Liebknecht in seinen Reden und Schriften gebraucht hatte (6). Zu der Publizität, die er gegenwärtig besitzt, hat ihm aber vor allem Ralf Dahrendorf verholfen, der ihn in seinem Buch „Gesellschaft und Demokratie in Deutschland" (7) für die Beschreibung der westdeutschen Justiz und ihrer Eigenarten einführt und im Duktus seiner Darstellung auffallend stark betont.

II. Versucht man den Begriff der Klassenjustiz ohne Rückgriff auf die historischen Hintergründe aus sich selbst heraus zu verstehen, so zeigt sich alsbald, daß er

* Anmerkungen auf den Seiten 133 ff.

außerordentlich unscharf ist und sich einer prägnanten Definition entzieht. Er läßt offen, ob mit Justiz, dem strengen Wortsinn entsprechend, nur die Rechtsprechungsorgane gemeint sind, oder ob er sich darüber hinaus auf die gesamte Rechtspflege unter Einschluß von Gesetzgebung, Kautelarpraxis und Rechtswissenschaft bezieht. Ferner läßt er sich sowohl auf die Tätigkeit und das Verhalten einzelner Personen (z.B. einzelner Richter) wie auf die Struktur und Zielfunktionen rechtlicher Institutionen (der Gerichte, der Rechtsprechung) als solcher beziehen. Noch weit schwerer fällt ins Gewicht, daß der Inhalt des Klassenbegriffs nicht feststeht, sondern schon bei Marx selbst in unterschiedlichen Schattierungen erscheint (8) und heute sowohl im bürgerlichen wie im marxistischen Sprachgebrauch differenziert und uneinheitlich gebraucht wird (9). Schließlich erweist sich die Verbindung der Begriffe „Klasse" und „Justiz" zum Schlagwort als problematisch, denn sie suggeriert, daß klassenspezifische Diskriminierungen, was immer dies sei, hauptsächlich in der Rechtspflege vorkommen, während andere Bereiche der Gesellschaft, z.B. die Wirtschaft oder das politische System, und die Interdependenz des Rechts mit diesen Bereichen außerhalb des Gesichtskreises bleiben. Alle diese Umstände wiegen deshalb besonders schwer, weil sich die Mehrzahl der rechtssoziologischen Autoren nicht auf den Versuch einläßt, den Begriff genauer zu umschreiben oder zu definieren, sondern an einer begriffsgeschichtlichen oder -theoretischen Analyse und vollends an einer exakten, operationalen Definition uninteressiert zeigt. Aus diesen Gründen empfiehlt es sich auch hier nicht, von den theoretischen Problemen auszugehen, welche seine Verwendung aufwirft, sondern den Blick zunächst auf die Phänomene zu richten, die in der Literatur als Beispiele und Erscheinungsformen von Klassenjustiz hervorgehoben und gebrandmarkt werden.

III. Für die Einteilung der in Betracht kommenden Fälle gibt es keine übergeordneten Gesichtspunkte, sie ist vielmehr in gewissem Sinne beliebig. Karl Liebknecht (10) hat eine Klassifikation benutzt, die sich am Verlauf des Gerichtsverfahrens orientiert, und vier Stationen aufgezählt, bei denen klassenspezifische Unterscheidungen auftreten können: in der Kommunikation zwischen Richter und Parteien; in einer einseitigen Aufnahme und Würdigung des Sachverhalts durch das Gericht; bei der Auslegung der Gesetze; schließlich bei der Strafzumessung. Die Einteilung leistet nützliche heuristische Dienste, weshalb wir uns im folgenden an sie anlehnen können, ohne sie schematisch zu befolgen:

1. In einer Reihe von Arbeiten finden sich Hinweise darauf, daß der Umgang des Richters mit dem Angeklagten bzw. mit den Parteien klassenspezifische Unterschiede aufweisen könne (11). Es wird festgestellt, daß manche Richter den Ton ihrer Verhandlungsführung ändern, je nachdem, ob sie es mit Angehörigen der Oberschicht, der Mittelschicht oder der Unterschicht zu tun haben, und z.B. einem angeklagten Unternehmensleiter oder Professor höflich, zurückhaltend und verständnisvoll begegnen, während sie Arbeitern gegenüber autoritär und barsch auftreten (12). Wenn derartige Verhaltensmuster bestehen, liegt die Vermutung nahe, daß sie sich nicht in Äußerlichkeiten erschöpfen, sondern auch in der rechtlichen Beurteilung des Sachverhalts niederschlagen. Häufiger und prinzipiell wichtiger dürften indessen Positionsunterschiede auf der Seite der Prozeßparteien selbst sein: Angehörige der Unterschichten verfügen regelmäßig über ein niedrigeres Bildungsniveau als Mitglieder der höheren Schichten. Sie haben es daher

schwerer, die Vorgänge im stark formalisierten Gerichtsverfahren zu durchschauen, die Rechtssprache zu verstehen, zu erkennen, worauf es ankommt, nicht zuletzt sich selbst verständlich und genau auszudrücken. Der dadurch entstehende Effekt einer mangelhaften Verständigung wird durch die Kompliziertheit des Rechts und die im Volk weit verbreitete Reserve gegenüber dem Rechtswesen sowie durch die psychischen Hemmungen, die eben daraus erwachsen, noch weiter verstärkt. Auch Richter, die sich nicht die Mühe machen, die Vorgänge mit der nötigen Ausführlichkeit zu erklären, tragen in solchen Fällen zu einer Verzerrung der Kommunikation bei. Hinzu kommt ferner, daß die gleichen Personen im allgemeinen auch über geringere finanzielle Hilfsmittel verfügen und daher nicht imstande sind, das Bildungsgefälle durch den Beistand guter Anwälte und den Einsatz sonstiger Hilfsmittel, wie etwa kostspieliger Gutachten und Sachverständiger auszugleichen. Selbst der Zugang zum Gericht wird durch hohe Prozeß- und Anwaltskosten für die armen Leute erschwert, wenn nicht unmöglich gemacht, und desgleichen ist ihr Vermögen, längere, sich über mehrere Instanzen hinziehende Prozesse durchzuhalten, gering. Die Instrumente, welche das deutsche Recht zur Abhilfe solcher Notstände vorsieht, funktionieren nur unvollkommen und geben zu wachsender Kritik Anlaß (13). Im Strafprozeß sieht das Gesetz zwar vor, daß bei schweren Delikten dem Angeklagten, der außerstande ist, selbst einen Verteidiger zu engagieren, ein Pflichtverteidiger beigeordnet werden muß, aber zum einen stellen sich die guten und erfolgreichen Anwälte für diese Aufgabe meist nicht zur Verfügung, und zum anderen treffen den Angeklagten, der nicht freigesprochen wird, auch in diesem Fall die Verteidigungskosten (14). Ähnliches gilt für das Zivilverfahren, in dem das sogenannte Armenrecht den Begünstigten nur vorläufig von den Prozeßkosten entbindet (15).

2. Im Zusammenhang mit dem Stichwort „einseitige Würdigung des Sachverhalts" wird vor allem auf Selektionsprozesse hingewiesen, die dazu führen, daß Arbeiter ein höheres Risiko laufen, strafrechtlich verfolgt zu werden als Angehörige der Mittel- und Oberschichten (16). Bereits die Polizei verfahre einseitig, wenn sie verdächtigen Personen oder Gegenden eine erhöhte Aufmerksamkeit widme, denn ein Verdacht falle infolge sozial fixierter Vorurteile vorzugsweise auf Personen aus dem Unterklassenmilieu und auf die von diesen besiedelten Wohngebiete. Es sei statistisch belegt, daß Verbrechen in dieser Schicht relativ zu ihrem Anteil an der Gesamtbevölkerung weit häufiger aufgedeckt werden als in anderen Schichten (17). Ähnliche Mechanismen setzten sich auf höherer Ebene fort. Wenn das Strafrecht die Gewaltkriminalität stärker betont als die „Intelligenz"-Delikte, benachteilige es einseitig die unteren Schichten. Derselbe Vorgang wiederhole sich im Strafverfahren, weil die Staatsanwaltschaften und Gerichte mit den Tatbeständen der Gewaltkriminalität leichter fertig werden als mit den regelmäßig komplizierter und klüger angelegten und daher schwerer aufzuklärenden Wirtschaftsvergehen, die deshalb auch im Vergleich zu ihrer Sozialschädlichkeit viel zu wenig erfolgreich bekämpft werden (18). Hierher gehörende Tatbestände werden ferner aus dem Arbeitsrecht berichtet, wo u.a. Ramm (19) darauf hingewiesen hat, daß das Bundesarbeitsgericht in seiner Judikatur zum Arbeitskampf die tatsächlichen Hintergründe von Streiks usw. einseitig zu ungunsten der Arbeitnehmer aufgeklärt und beurteilt habe. Anzufügen sind Beobachtungen aus unterschiedlichen Rechtsgebieten, wonach Richter außerstande waren, ein für die Beteiligten verständliches und „brauchbares" Recht zu sprechen, weil sie die

Lebensbedingungen des Arbeitermilieus und die Mentalität der Arbeiter nicht kennen oder nicht richtig beurteilen konnten (20).

3. In einer dritten Gruppe von Fällen wird die klassenspezifisch ungleiche Interpretation und Anwendung von materiellen Rechtsvorschriften gerügt. Es liegt auf der Hand, daß Vorwürfe dieser Art der Grundlage entbehren, soweit die Gesetze dem Richter präzise Anweisungen für seine Entscheidung geben, denn insoweit kann eine Diskriminierung nur im Gesetz selbst liegen, nicht dagegen dem das Gesetz anwendenden Richter zum Vorwurf gemacht werden. Als Einfallstor für eine diskriminierende Auslegungspraxis kommen aber allgemeine Rechtsbegriffe, gesetzliche Generalklauseln und Blankettvorschriften in Betracht, die den Gerichten tatsächlich Spielraum für die eigene Beurteilung des Sachverhalts gewähren. Regelmäßig entstammen denn die Beispiele auch diesem Bereich. So wird vorgetragen, die Rechtsprechung, welche auf dem Weg über eine allzu weitherzige Auslegung der Regeln über den Vertragsschluß die Übernahme allgemeiner Geschäftsbedingungen in Einzelverträge zu Lasten der Verbraucher und des kleinen Mannes großzügig zugelassen habe, trage Klassencharakter (21). In Fällen einer engen Interpretation der gesetzlichen Schutzklauseln zuungunsten der sozial schwachen Mieter wird Ähnliches vermutet (22). Aus dem Baurecht wird ein Fall berichtet, in welchem ein Generaldirektor eine baurechtliche Befreiung erhielt, die einem Justizbeamten bei im wesentlichen vergleichbarem Sachverhalt vom gleichen Gericht versagt blieb (23). Weitere Fälle finden sich im Arbeitsrecht, das aus verständlichen Gründen im Zentrum der Aufmerksamkeit steht. Unter anderem wird ein Urteil gerügt, das dem Gesellschafter einer radiotechnischen Lehrwerkstatt, der zugleich Landtagsabgeordneter war, Schmerzensgeld gegen einen Religionslehrer zubilligte, der anläßlich einer Lehrlingsdemonstration skandalöse Zustände bei der Lehrlingsausbildung im Betrieb des Klägers gerügt hatte (24). Vor allem aber wird die rechtsschöpferische Judikatur des Bundesarbeitsgerichts zum Tarifvertrags- und Streikrecht angegriffen (26). Neuerdings wirft die Judikatur gegenüber den ausländischen Gastarbeitern in der Bundesrepublik einschlägige Probleme auf, da diese als Ausländer und Minderheiten am unteren Ende der sozialen Hierarchie stehen (26).

4. Was schließlich diskriminierende Praktiken in der Strafzumessungspraxis angeht, so wird darauf hingewiesen, Richter neigten zu dem Vorurteil, daß Arbeiter (27) besondere kriminelle Energie und besonders geringe Einsicht für die Strafwürdigkeit ihrer Handlungsweisen zeigten und daher nur durch harte Strafen beeindruckt und gebessert werden könnten (28). Der Sachverhalt ist durch Beispiele belegt; auch besitzen wir erste Versuche, ihn sozialwissenschaftlich-statistisch zu erfassen (29).

IV. Überblickt man die Literatur, so schält sich nach und nach ein Bestand von beobachteten Fakten heraus, die im Umkreis des Begriffs Klassenjustiz genannt werden und immer wiederkehren: Schranken im Zugang zum Gericht, Verständigungshindernisse im gerichtlichen Verfahren, Armenrecht und Anwaltskosten, schichtspezifische Begrenzung des Blickfelds der Richter, Selektionsprozesse und Diskriminierung im Strafverfahren, Mißstände im Arbeits- und Mieterschutzrecht sowie in einigen anderen sozial relevanten Rechtsgebieten. In den meisten Fällen wird der Jurist der Kritik zustimmen können, sofern es nicht, wie überwiegend, von vornherein soziologisch versierte Richter oder Rechtswissenschaftler sind, von denen sie ausgeht (30), wenn auch anzuerkennen ist, daß ihnen vielfach erst die Perspektiven der Soziologie die Augen für Mißstände solcher Art geöffnet haben (31). Es ist auch nicht nötig, zur Begründung der Kritik den Begriff der Klassenjustiz zu bemühen, denn sie läßt sich mit anderen Argumenten ebenso stichhaltig untermauern. So widerspricht es, um ein bereits genanntes Beispiel zu nennen, unzweifelhaft dem im geltenden Recht verankerten Prinzip der Gleichheit vor Gericht, wenn ein Richter einen Arbeiter anders behandelt als einen Unternehmensleiter oder Professor. Desgleichen sind Einwände gegen eine engstirnige Interpretation der Sozialklausel im Mietrecht letztlich nicht aus der Perspektive der Soziologie, sondern nur der Interpretation des Gesetzes und der Absichten des Gesetzgebers selbst schlüssig darzulegen.

Auch aus anderen Gründen besteht Anlaß, die Tragweite der soziologischen Aussagen näher zu durchleuchten. Das von ihnen vorgelegte Material besteht hauptsächlich aus Einzelfällen, deren Signifikanz zweifelhaft ist, und die daher den Anspruch auf Allgemeingültigkeit, der in der theoretischen Aussage bei vielen Autoren mit ihnen verknüpft wird, nicht zu tragen vermögen. Hier stoßen wir auf eine auffällige Schwierigkeit: Auf der einen Seite betonen die Soziologen, man habe es nicht mit individuell vorwerfbarem Verhalten zu tun, namentlich sei es so gut wie ausgeschlossen, daß einzelne Richter unter Verstoß gegen das Gebot der formalen Rechtsgleichheit Angehörige der unteren Schichten des Volkes bewußt diskriminieren und dergestalt eine gezielte Klassenjustiz üben (32). Vielmehr handele es sich um „strukturelle Effekte" (33), schichtspezifische Verhaltensformen und Vorurteile des Richterstands bzw. der Juristen, die unbewußt oder unreflektiert in die Entscheidungen einfließen und sich im Ergebnis zum Nachteil sozial unterprivilegierter Bevölkerungsgruppen auswirken. Auf der anderen Seite bleibt der einwandfreie sozialwissenschaftliche Beleg für diese Thesen aber aus. Selbst die Beobachtung der angeführten Einzelfälle und -phänomene erfolgt oft nicht unter der sorgfältigen methodischen Kontrolle, die in den Sozialwissenschaften verlangt wird. Der Befund läßt demnach einen Überschuß an theoretischer Verallgemeinerung erkennen, der durch die Ergebnisse der Empirie nicht bestätigt wird und daher sozialwissenschaftlich bestenfalls als Vermutung oder Arbeitshypothese formuliert werden kann.

Dieser Stand der Forschung lenkt die Aufmerksamkeit auf die Probleme, welche sich der empirischen Verifikation einer Klassenjustiz prinzipiell entgegenstellen. Zwar ist die Herkunft und Schichtzugehörigkeit von Richtern, gemessen am Beruf und sozialen Status des Vaters und des Schwiegervaters, mit den Mitteln der sozialwissenschaftlichen Forschung exakt nachzuweisen. So steht heute fest, daß, wenn man das fünfgliedrige Schichtenmodell von Janowitz (34) zugrundelegt, die deutschen Richter überwiegend den Mittelschichten zugehören, und zwar mit 63 % der sogenannten oberen Mittelschicht und etwa 28 % der unteren Mittelschicht, während nur 5,7 % aus den Unterschichten der abhängigen Handwerker und Arbeiter aufgestiegen sind, die über 50 % der Gesamtbevölkerung ausmachen (35). Auch hat sich gezeigt, daß diese Situation seit 50 Jahren im wesentlichen konstant blieb (36) (37). Ferner lassen sich gewisse Eigenarten der berufsspezifischen Sozialisierung, wie sie in der deutschen juristischen Universitäts- und Referendarausbildung auftreten, sozialwissenschaftlich erfassen (38), und ebenso gelingt es, Merkmale einer typischen Berufsmentalität herauszuarbeiten (39). Der Nachweis einer Klassenjustiz würde jedoch erfordern, einen Zusammenhang zwischen Herkunftsmerkmalen bzw. Attitüden solcher Art und einer signifikanten Zahl von klassenspezifisch diskriminierenden Entscheidungen herzustellen und zu belegen. Daß dies gelingt, ist seit Rottleuthners eindrucksvoller Analyse der Struktur des Problems schon theoretisch kaum mehr zu erwarten (40). Der Nachweis klassenspezifischer Diskriminierung basiert auf der Behauptung, daß gleiche Fälle ungleich behandelt werden. Welche Fälle gleich, welche ungleich sind, hängt nun aber angesichts der richterlichen Argumentationsweise, die weniger mit logisch eindeutigen Schlüssen, als mit besseren und schlechteren Argumenten, einem höheren oder geringeren Grad von Plausibilität operiert, von Bewertungen ab, welche die Umstände des Einzelfalls reflektieren und sich daher der sozialwissenschaftlich-statistischen Verallgemeinerung weitgehend entziehen. Unter diesen Umständen kann es schwerlich gelingen, eine hinreichend große und aussagekräftige Zahl von Diskriminierungsfällen zusammenzustellen, die als Basis für die Analyse des Ursachenzusammenhangs dienen könnte (41). Der Begriff der Klassenjustiz erweist sich mit anderen Worten als sozialwissenschaftlich kaum operationalisierbar (42).

V. Die Erkenntnis, daß ein empirischer Nachweis von Klassenjustiz kaum zu erhoffen ist, schließt nicht aus, den Begriff in der Wissenschaft zu verwenden, sofern sich sein Nutzen für die Erkenntnis aus anderen Gründen namentlich der hermeneutischen Sinnerfahrung ergibt. Beschreiten wir diesen Weg, stoßen wir indessen sogleich auf die bereits eingangs bemerkte inhaltliche Unbestimmtheit des Begriffs. Seine Schwankungsbreite und Unschärfe in der rechtssoziologischen Literatur, ja in ein und derselben Arbeit, ist so groß, daß es fast regelmäßig nicht gelingt, ihn auf einen hinreichend präzisen Bedeutungsgehalt zu fixieren, womit für eine Wissenschaft, die sich nicht mit dem Nebel von Pauschalurteilen begnügt, das Todesurteil über ihn gefällt wird. So liegt, um den Ernst der Lage am Beispiel zu demonstrieren, ein grundlegender Unterschied darin, ob man mit Klassenjustiz die Struktur des Rechts als normativer Ordnung (Klassenrecht) und der rechtlich geordneten Gesellschaft (Klassencharakter des Rechts als Ausfluß des Klassencharakters der Gesellschaft) assoziiert oder spezielle Erscheinungsformen der Justiz, möglicherweise im Gegensatz zu einem klassenneutralen Gesetzesrecht. Die Stoßrichtung der Kritik ist in beiden Fällen grundverschieden, denn wer sich gegen die Klassenstruktur des Rechts oder der Gesellschaft wendet, muß seine Kritik an den Gesetzgeber oder an die Öffentlichkeit richten, während die Gerichte nur im zweiten Fall als geeignete Adressaten erscheinen. Wenn die Justizkritik sich zum Beispiel auf das gesetzlich geordnete, die Richter in allen wesentlichen Punkten bindende Armenrecht stützt, verkennt sie diese Situation und geht daher fehl, setzt sich unvermeidlich sogar dem Vorwurf der wissenschaftlichen Unredlichkeit aus. Nun dürfte es den Intentionen der meisten Autoren entsprechen, Klassenrecht und Klassenjustiz zugleich aufzudecken, und dagegen ist nichts einzuwenden, wenn man sich über das Verhältnis zwischen beiden peinliche Rechenschaft gibt. Es muß aber gesagt sein, daß das oft nicht geschieht, wodurch die Chance vertan wird, zwischen abhängigen und unabhängigen Variablen zu unterscheiden und einen Beitrag zur Erklärung des richterlichen Entscheidungsprozesses zu leisten.
Noch größere Verwirrung stiftet die mangelnde Reflexion des Begriffs der Klasse selbst in der rechtssoziologischen Literatur. Gelegentlich wird er einigermaßen präzis im ursprünglich marxistischen Sinn verstanden, der eine zweigegliederte,

antagonistische Struktur der Gesellschaft voraussetzt (43); an anderer Stelle bezieht er sich auf eines der Schichtenmodelle, die in der neueren „bürgerlichen“ Soziologie benutzt werden, namentlich das von Dahrendorf in die Rechtssoziologie eingeführte fünfgliedrige Modell von Janowitz (44); bei wieder anderen Autoren verliert er jegliche Konturen und dient ohne Anspruch auf inhaltliche Genauigkeit dazu, Mißstände, die man als kritikwürdig empfindet, auf einen gemeinsamen Nenner zu bringen (45). Ein mixtum compositum solcher Art muß zu Pauschalurteilen und ideologischen Verallgemeinerungen verführen, die den kritischen Ansprüchen wissenschaftlicher Erkenntnis nicht standzuhalten vermögen. Es ist auch nicht zu sehen, wie dem abzuhelfen wäre. Von der Empirie ist, angesichts der mangelnden Operationalisierbarkeit des Begriffs in diesem Punkt nichts zu erwarten. Sucht man aber Hilfe bei der soziologischen Theorie, so zeigen sich alsbald vergleichbare Differenzen, welche die Hoffnung auf einen Konsens schwinden lassen. Zwar werden die Wurzeln des Begriffs in der Marxschen Gesellschaftsanalyse nicht bestritten und dürfte auch Einigkeit herrschen, daß er für die Erklärung der sozialen Strukturen im letzten Jahrhundert einen bedeutenden Erkenntniswert besaß (46). Darüber hinaus scheint allgemein anerkannt, daß er sich zur Beschreibung der gegenwärtigen Gesellschaft in den westlichen Industrieländern nicht ohne Modifikationen eignet, weil sich in diesen neben und über die Dichotomie in zwei Klassen andere Differenzierungen vielfältiger Art gelagert haben, die sich einem so einfachen Schema widersetzen. Im übrigen aber bestehen tiefe methodische und tendenzielle Differenzen. Dabei fällt zunächst ins Gewicht, daß der Begriff class im angelsächsischen Sprachgebrauch, von dem Dahrendorf und andere Autoren beeinflußt sind, weniger im Sinn des deutschen Worts Klasse erscheint als im Sinn von sozialer Schicht oder Gruppe, und jedenfalls die Marx'sche Zweiteilung der Gesellschaf in Bourgeoisie und Proletariat nicht in sich aufgenommen hat (47). In der deutschen „bürgerlichen“ Soziologie wird dagegen im allgemeinen zwischen Klasse, Schicht und Gruppe unterschieden und im Zusammenhang mit dem Klassenbegriff danach gefragt, welche Komponenten der früheren Klassenstruktur sich bis in die Gegenwart hinein erhalten haben (48). Nur insoweit wird es für sinnvoll gehalten, den Begriff weiter anzuwenden. Marxisten setzen dagegen die Klassenstruktur der Gesellschaft regelmäßig voraus, konzentrieren sich auf die Suche nach Phänomenen, die in das Schema passen und lassen sich jedenfalls von der Vorstellung leiten, die Gesellschaft werde sich in Zukunft zwangsläufig (wieder) zu antagonistischen Klassenstrukturen entwickeln (49). Die soziologische Relevanz dieser unterschiedlichen Denkansätze ist hier nicht zu erörtern, denn der begrenzte Gegenstand der Soziologie des Gerichtsverfahrens nötigt nur zu der Frage, welchen Nutzen der Klassenbegriff für die Erklärung des richterlichen Prozesses stiftet. Die Antwort kann angesichts des Stands der Theorie nur negativ sein. Es ist nicht zu erwarten, daß er dazu beiträgt, sozialwissenschaftliche Erkenntnisse über die Natur des Gerichtsverfahrens oder seine heutige Gestalt zu gewinnen, welche die Chance in sich tragen, methodischer Kritik standzuhalten und in diesem Sinn objektiver Wissensbestand zu werden.

VI. Erweist sich die wissenschaftlich-analytische Brauchbarkeit des Begriffs demnach als ungenügend, so drängt sich die Frage auf, worin sein Reiz für die zahlreichen Autoren liegt, die ihn verwenden. Man könnte versucht sein, ihn als Modeerscheinung abzutun, doch wäre eine solche Erklärung zu billig. Auch seine

Eignung als Reizwort für die öffentliche Diskussion und als politische Parole erklärt nicht, warum er mit dem Anspruch wissenschaftlicher Potenz auftritt. Eine Antwort findet sich vielmehr erst, wenn man die Gerechtigkeitsidee ins Auge faßt, von der aus gesehen die als Klassenjustiz gebrandmarkten Phänomene als etwas Negatives und Kritikwürdiges erscheinen. Entschließt man sich dazu, so gelangen zunächst alsbald erneut Karl Marx und seine Lehre von der idealen klassenlosen Gesellschaft in den Gesichtskreis, in der die Parole gilt: „Jeder nach seinen Fähigkeiten, jedem nach seinen Bedürfnissen" und die erst die Chance schafft, den Menschen von der Selbstentfremdung durch die Arbeit zu erlösen und ihm zur wahren Freiheit zu verhelfen (50). Freilich bleibt diese Philosophie bei den meisten Autoren ein blasser und verschwimmender Horizont, denn sie äußern sich zu ihrem Gesellschaftsideal expressis verbis regelmäßig nicht, sondern zeigen sich eher uninteressiert, eine über die Kritik hinausreichende Aussage zu formulieren, und soweit sich zwischen den Zeilen ihrer Texte Andeutungen finden, klingt die ganze Fülle liberaler, demokratischer, sozialistischer und marxistischer Ideen und Reformprogramme an. Vordergründig erschöpft sich die Allianz, welche der Begriff der Klassenjustiz stiftet, demnach im Negativen, und jeder Autor ist auf sein Ideal der anzustrebenden gerechten Gesellschaftsordnung gesondert zu befragen.

Gleichwohl ist der Versuch geraten, den Sinn der „großen Negation", die sich im Stichwort Klassenjustiz artikuliert, vor der Kulisse marxistischer Zukunftsvisionen genauer zu untersuchen. Die Rechts- und Gesellschaftsordnung in der Bundesrepublik weist, wie jede Gesellschaft, eine spezifische Mischung von sozialer Gleichheit und Ungleichheit auf, die ihren Charakter prägt. In ihr herrscht politische Gleichheit, garantiert durch das allgemeine Wahlrecht, und formale Rechtsgleichheit im Verhältnis zwischen den Bürgern untereinander wie im Verhältnis von Bürger und Staat, gesichert durch die Grundrechte, das Rechtsstaatsprinzip und die im Zivilrecht vorausgesetzte allgemeine Rechtsfähigkeit. Zugleich schützt das geltende Recht, z.T. durch dieselben Rechte und Institutionen, die individuelle Freiheit und läßt es aus diesem Grunde zu, daß soziale Unterschiede und eine vielfältig gegliederte, in gewisssem Grad hierarchisch aufgebaute Gesellschaft entstehen, welche die Geltung des Gleichheitsgedankens einschränken. Auch das Recht spiegelt soziale Differenzierungen wieder, sei es, daß es sie – wie z.B. das Ausländerrecht – bestätigt und stabilisiert, sei es, daß es sie zu kompensieren sucht, wie die Schutzvorschriften zugunsten des jeweils Schwächeren im Privatrecht, sei es, daß es sie nicht zur Kenntnis nimmt und daher duldet. Insofern läßt sich sagen, das geltende Recht etabliere eine bestimmte, aus Elementen der Freiheit und der Gleichheit zusammengesetzte Sozialstruktur, den zugleich liberalen und sozialen Staat. Nun ist bekannt, daß die Prinzipien des Liberalismus und des Sozialismus in Spannung zueinander stehen und namentlich rechtlich verordnete Gleichheit regelmäßig nur auf Kosten der Freiheit zu verwirklichen ist (51). Im Plädoyer gegen Klassenjusitz und für die Aufhebung von schichtspezifischen Differenzierungen offenbart sich so gesehen eine – mehr oder weniger ausgeprägte – rechtsphilosophische und rechtspolitische Tendenz, die egalitäre Komponente des geltenden Rechts zu Lasten der liberalen stärker zu betonen und auszubauen. Dies ist der Kern, wie mir scheint, der Rede von der Klassenjustiz, der allerdings, da sollte nichts beschönigt werden, mit Soziologie nicht mehr allzuviel zu tun hat, jedenfalls wenn man Soziologie als Antithese zur spekulativen Sozialphilosophie versteht (52).

VII. Es sollte deutlich geworden sein, daß sich die im Vorstehenden entfaltete Kritik nicht gegen die speziellen rechtssoziologischen und juristischen Untersuchungen richtet, die eingangs referiert wurden, sondern nur gegen das Etikett, unter dem sie verkauft werden. Die Kritikwürdigkeit der gebrandmarkten Phänomene selbst wurde bereits mehrfach bestätigt. Es besteht auch kein Zweifel, daß, je bedenklicher sie sind, desto mehr daran liegt, sie sorgfältig aufzuklären und bekanntzumachen. Soweit die Rechtssoziologie hierzu beitragen kann, ist ihre Hilfe demnach dringend erwünscht. Sollen ihre Bemühungen aber von Erfolg gekrönt sein, so kommt es darauf an, das begriffliche Instrumentarium, mit dem sie arbeitet, gegenüber dem simplen Konzept der Klassenjustiz wesentlich zu verfeinern, denn nur dann können die speziellen Zusammenhänge durchsichtig werden, aus denen sich einzelne Fälle einer Diskriminierung sozial schwacher Personen vor Gericht erklären. Nur ein solches Verfahren eröffnet ferner die Chance einer interdisziplinären Verständigung zwischen Soziologen und Juristen, welche, wie die vorliegenden Untersuchungen selbst beweisen, auf diesem Gebiet besonders nottut, aber gefährdet ist, solange sich die Juristen nur angegriffen fühlen. In welchem Sinn ich von Verfeinerung und Differenzierung der Forschungsansätze spreche, läßt sich am besten an Beispielen zeigen:

1. Wenn die Neigung bestimmter Gerichte gerügt wird, die Sozialklauseln des Mietrechts zum Nachteil der vom Gesetzgeber für schutzbedürftig erachteten Mieter eng auszulegen, so mag sich die Erklärung aufdrängen, wir hätten es mit der klassenspezifischen Begünstigung des als Bourgeois und Kapitalist stilisierten Hauseigentümers und einer Diskriminierung des Mieters zu tun, der als armer Arbeiter und Proletarier erscheint. Die mitgeteilten Urteile erlauben nicht nachzuprüfen, ob eine solche Interpretation in den Tatsachen Rückhalt findet oder nicht. Indessen lehrt schon die Alltagserfahrung, daß sie, jedenfalls als generelle These formuliert, schwerlich zutrifft. Auch Arbeiter sind heute nicht selten und in wachsendem Maße imstande, Hauseigentum zu erwerben, während umgekehrt als Mieter auch dem Bürgertum zugehörige Personen, z.B. Studenten, Beamte usw. in Betracht kommen. Die stärkere Position des Vermieters ist nicht in seiner Klassenzugehörigkeit begründet, sondern erklärt sich aus dem ungedeckten Bedarf an Wohnungen, d.h. aus der Situation des Markts, um den es geht. Demgemäß lassen sich Versuche, Mieter auszubeuten, auch in allen Schichten der Bevölkerung finden, und es spricht nichts dafür, daß sie zwischen Bürgerlichen und Arbeitern häufiger sind als umgekehrt. Daraus folgt, daß auch ein Mietrichter, der seine Auslegung einer Gesetzesvorschrift ohne Rücksicht auf das soziale Milieu der Parteien in allen Fällen, die ihm vorgelegt werden, gleichmäßig handhaben muß, nicht klassen- oder schichtspezifisch differenziert. Die Konzeption der Klassenjustiz erweist sich in diesem Fall als eine schlechthin unangemessene und schiefe Kategorie. Statt dessen ist es geboten, für die juristische und soziologische Analyse des Falls beim gestörten Marktmechanismus und den typischen sozialen Rollen des Vermieters und Mieters anzusetzen.

2. Im Hinblick auf die Selektionsmechanismen in der Strafverfolgung wäre der klassen- oder schichttheoretische Ansatz nur brauchbar, wenn sich feststellen ließe, daß Kriminalpolizisten üblicherweise aus dem Bürgertum bzw. den höheren Schichten stammen, was nach dem vorliegenden Material nicht der Fall ist (53). Die soziale Zusamensetzung der Gruppen nötigt vielmehr dazu, das Phänomen der

schichtspezifischen Selektion, soweit es nicht vom Gesetz selbst bereits vorgezeichnet ist, mit anderen Mitteln zu erklären. Ich vermute, daß die wichtigsten Gründe in der berufsspezifischen Ausbildung und Sozialisation der Kriminalpolizei als Berufsgruppe und in den von der Gruppe gepflegten Verhaltensmustern zu suchen sind. Zur Klärung einer solchen These ist in erster Linie auf die Theorien des gruppenspezifischen Verhaltens und der Lern- bzw. Sozialisationsprozesse in sozialen Berufsgruppen zurückzugreifen.

3. Die berufs- und gruppenspezifische Ausprägung bestimmter Mentalitätsmerkmale und Verhaltensmuster kommt als Erklärungsmodell auch in Betracht, wenn es gilt, die auf Einzelbeobachtungen basierende Hypothese zu verfolgen, daß Richter mit Arbeitern anders umgehen als mit Professoren und Generaldirektoren. Da wir andererseits wissen, daß die Richter sich zur Hälfte aus der oberen und zu einem weiteren Viertel aus der unteren Mittelschicht rekrutieren (54), kommt statt dessen auch das allgemeinere Schichtenmodell der Soziologie als Grundlage in Frage, und es könnte sich sogar als nützlich erweisen, mit beiden Modellen zugleich zu operieren. Schließlich ist auch denkbar, statt in der Abstraktion von der Berufsgruppe zur sozialen Schicht aufzusteigen, umgekehrt vorzugehen, d.h. die soziale Hierarchie detaillierter zu gliedern und eine der Tabellen zu benutzen, welche den Rang der Berufe auf der Stufenleiter des Sozialprestiges vielgliedriger und differenzierter wiedergeben. Dagegen wäre es offenkundig wiederum schief, das zweiteilige Klassenschema zu übernehmen, und zwar ungeachtet aller weiteren Einwendungen schon deshalb, weil es schwerfällt und selbst orthodoxen Marxisten bis heute nicht gelingt, Beamte und Richter in diesem Schema überzeugend einzuordnen (55).

4. Am nächsten liegt endlich, um ein letztes Beispiel zu nennen, der Rückgriff auf das Klassenmodell im Arbeitsrecht, wo sich Arbeitgeber und Arbeitnehmer als die Nachfahren der Kapitalisten und Proletarier des letzten Jahrhunderts einander gegenüberstehen. Hier wird man in der Tat feststellen können, daß die Strukturen des Rechts bis heute von der Ausgangssituation des Klassengegensatzes geprägt wird, die im Zuge der Vermögensbildung und Mitbestimmung der Arbeitnehmer erst nach und nach überwunden werden (56). In der Ausgliederung der Arbeitsgerichtsbarkeit aus der allgemeinen Justiz und der Besetzung der Arbeitsgerichte mit Repräsentanten beider Seiten hat selbst der Gesetzgeber dem Rechnung getragen. Insofern kann es sachgerecht sein, in diesem Bereich auch bei der soziologischen Justizkritik mit dem Klassenschema zu arbeiten, jedenfalls wenn es gilt, kritisch zu fragen, inwieweit sich die überkommenen sozialen Strukturen in der Judikatur noch immer durchzusetzen vermögen.

Summary

The concept of class justice has for some time played a growing role in the sociology of justice in the Federal Republik of Germany. The concept has an assumed scholarly as well as a political value. It is applied to such phenomena as the following: barriers in access to court, blocks to understanding between judges

and accused persons or parties to civil cases, laws relating to the poor, the cost of lawyers, class-specific limitations on the outlook of judges, discrimination in the administration of criminal justice (especially inequalities in sentencing), misunderstandings in protective labor law, and laws to protect tenants, as well as in other socially relevant areas of law. But critique of such phenomena does not require the concept of class justice. The concept is in fact not operationalizable in a social science sense, since it presupposes showing that similar cases are regularly or frequently decided to the disadvantage of certain classes or groups, and that a causal connection exists between the class background of the judge and such discrimination. But judicial style and reasoning, in the particular case, make it impossible to establish this discrimination with sufficient certainty.
The concept of class justice is, moreover, very general and vague; there is no chance of any consensus about its meaning. But an agreed meaning is necessary for its use in rigorous study. Marxist and bourgeois uses differ; the German concept of "class" is narrower than the Anglo-American concept. Differences in definition reveal themselves, on closer look, to reflect different approaches to the philosophy and politics of law, going beyond the boundaries of empirical social science. For these reasons, the concept should not be used in sociology of law. Concepts such as role, social group, occupational group, and social stratum, among others, will better serve for sociology, and for the critique of legal institutions.

Anmerkungen

1 Vgl. namentlich Lautmann, Klassenjustiz?, in: Der Bürger im Staat, 1970, S. 155 ff.; ders., Soziologie vor den Toren der Jurisprudenz, Stuttgart 1971, S. 69 ff.; Rottleuthner, Klassenjustiz?, Kritische Justiz 1969, S. 1–26, neueste erweiterte Fassung in: ders., Rechtswissenschaft als Sozialwissenschaft, Frankfurt 1973, S. 42 ff.; ders., Richterliches Handeln, Zur Kritik der juristischen Dogmatik, Frankfurt 1973, S. 162–183; Geffken, Klassenjustiz, Frankfurt 1972; ders., Zur Kritik der Klassenjustiz, Demokratie und Recht 1973, S. 273 ff.; ferner die Aufsätze in: „Klassenjusitz heute" Heft 1/1973 der Zeitschrift „Vorgänge" mit Aufsätzen u.a. von Rasehorn, Rechtslosigkeit als Klassenschicksal; Wassermann, Gedanken zur Wirtschaftskriminalität; Kaupen, Klassenjustiz in der Bundesrepublik?, Lautmann/Peters, Ungleichheit vor dem Gesetz, Strafjustiz und soziale Schichten; Sack, Klassenjustiz und Selektionsprozesse; Ostermeyer, Justizreform – Quadratur des Kreises; Ott, Politische Benachteiligung eines Arbeitnehmers; Kupke, Soziale Benachteiligung in Mietrechtsprozessen. Vgl. dazu auch meine Besprechung in JA 1973, S. 433.

2 Vgl. etwa die Darstellung der verschiedenen Forschungsansätze bei Rottleuthner, Richterliches Handeln, a.a.O.; ferner Geffken, Klassenjustiz, a.a.O. Ein Überblick über die US-amerikanische Justizsoziologie findet sich bei Manfred Weiss, Die Theorie der richterlichen Entscheidungstätigkeit in den Vereinigten Staaten von Amerika, Frankfurt 1971; ferner in meiner Einführung in die Rechtssoziologie, 2. Aufl., Berlin 1973, S. 38 ff.

3 Marx und Engels haben zwar keine gesonderte Rechtstheorie entwickelt. Sie haben jedoch den Begriff der „Klasse" als einen Zentralbegriff ihrer Lehre benützt. Daneben ergibt sich aus ihrem Verständnis des bürgerlichen Rechts (vgl. „Das Kapital", MEW 23, S. 99, 351 f.) daß jede Rechtsanwendung durch den bürgerlichen Staat Klassenjustiz sein muß.

4 Vgl. Abschnitt V.

5 Fraenkel, Zur Soziologie der Klassenjustiz, 1927, Neudruck, Darmstadt 1968.

6 Vgl. Rechtsstaat und Klassenjustiz 1907, in: Gesammelte Reden und Schriften Bd. 2, Berlin 1960; ders., Gegen die preußische Klassenjustiz 1910, a.a.O., Bd. 3.

7 München 1965, S. 273 ff. Vgl. auch Dahrendorfs Werk „Soziale Klassen und Klassenkonflikte in der industriellen Gesellschaft", 1957; amerikanische Ausgabe: Class and Class Conflict in Industrial Society, Stanford/Cal. 1959.
8 Vgl. die Stichworte „Klasse", „Klassengesellschaft", „Klassenkampf" in: G. Claus und M. Buhr (Hrsg.), Philosophisches Wörterbuch, 7. Aufl., Bd. 1, Ostberlin 1970.
9 Besonders charakteristisch für die Uneinheitlichkeit des bürgerlichen Sprachgebrauchs sind die Beiträge in Heft 1/1973 der Zeitschrift „Vorgänge" (s. Anm. 1). Im englischen Sprachraum bedeutet das Wort class Klasse, Schicht und soziale Gruppe zugleich. Einen uneinheitlichen Gebrauch auf marxistischer Seite findet man schon bei Liebknecht, a.a.O., Bd. 2, S. 17, wo er die Begriffe Schicht und Klasse abwechselnd aber im gleichen Sinne gebraucht. Die Uneinheitlichkeit wird auch gerügt von Geffken, Demokratie und Recht, a.a.O., S. 273 ff. Vgl. ferner das Zitat Anm. 8.
10 Rechtsstaat und Klassenjustiz, a.a.O., S. 38 ff.
11 Vgl. bereits Liebknecht, a.a.O., Bd. 2, S. 38, 41, Bd. 3, S. 25. Ferner G. Winter und F. Schumann, Sozialisation und Legitimierung des Rechts im Strafverfahren, zugleich ein Beitrag zur Frage des rechtlichen Gehörs, in: Jahrbuch für Rechtssoziologie und Rechtstheorie, Bd. 3, S. 529–554, sowie A. M. Tausch und I. Langer, Soziales Verhalten von Richtern gegenüber Angeklagten, Zeitschrift für Entwicklungspsychologie und pädagogische Psychologie, 1971, S. 289.
12 Vgl. die zahlreichen Einzelbeispiele bei Rasehorn, a.a.O. (Anm. 1), S. 5 ff.; ferner bei Lautmann, Der Bürger im Staat, a.a.O., (Anm. 1), S. 158; Einzelbeobachtungen finden sich bei demselben Autor in: Justiz – Die stille Gewalt, Frankfurt 1972, passim.
13 Vgl. den Beitrag von M. Rehbinder in diesem Band und die dort in Fn. 1 genannten Autoren.
14 § 465 StPO in Zusammenhang mit § 92, Nr. 7 GKG.
15 §§ 114, 115, Abs. 1, Nr. 1, ZPO.
16 Zum folgenden vgl. Rasehorn, a.a.O., (Anm. 1) S. 9, unter Hinweis auf F. Sack, Neue Perspektiven in der Kriminologie, in: R. König und F. Sack (Hrsg.), Kriminalsoziologie, Frankfurt 1968, S. 431 ff.
17 Ebenda. Vgl. ferner M. Brusten, Determinanten selektiver Sanktionierung durch die Polizei, in: J. Feest, R. Lautmann (Hrsg.), Die Polizei, Soziologische Studien und Forschungsberichte, Opladen 1971, bes. S. 43 ff. m.w.N. in Fn. 37.
18 Vgl. Tiedemann (Hrsg.), Die Verbrechen in der Wirtschaft, Karlsruhe 1970, sowie Wassermann, a.a.O. (Anm. 1), S. 26–31.
19 JZ 1961, S. 273 ff.
20 Vgl. Liebknecht, a.a.O., Bd. 2, S. 31, Bd. 3, S. 6–15, und 24–26; insb. in Bezug auf die Moral von Angehörigen der Unterschicht siehe Rasehorn, a.a.O., S. 13–16. Hierzu gehört auch die von J. Limbach im vorliegenden Band S. 309 ff., herausgearbeitete Tatsache, daß Richter sich der Unwissenheit und Unerfahrenheit von sozial unterprivilegierten Verbrauchern bei Ratenkäufern nicht im klaren sind.
21 Kaupen, a.a.O., (Anm. 1), S. 33; ebenso Geffken, Demokratie und Recht, a.a.O., (Anm. 1), S. 279.
22 Kupke, Soziale Benachteiligung in Mietrechtsprozessen, a.a.O., (Anm. 1), S. 82 ff.
23 Berichtet bei Rottleuthner, Richterliches Handeln, a.a.O., (Anm. 1), S. 182.
24 KJ 1970, S. 479 – JZ 1972, S. 89 mit Anmerkung von Kübler.
25 Vgl. Xenia Rajewsky, Arbeitskampfrecht in der Bundesrepublik, Frankfurt 1970, und die zahlreichen Nachweise dort.
26 Vgl. für das Mietrecht Kupke, a.a.O. (Anm. 1), S. 85 f. Offensichtlich treten die oben S. 124 f. aufgezeigten Probleme der Unterschicht vor Gericht bei den sprachunkundigen und ungebildeten Ausländern noch stärker hervor.
27 Dagegen gehören Prozesse gegen politisch mißliebige Personen und Gruppen nicht in diesen Zusammenhang, weil bei den dort Angeklagten die Unterschicht unterrepräsentiert ist und selbst wo Arbeiter angeklagt werden, deren Selbsteinschätzung als „Speerspitze der Arbeiterklasse" nur subjektiv festzumachen ist, während offen bleibt, ob sie auch objektiv die Interessen der Arbeiter vertreten; vgl. zum Ganzen auch meine Einführung in die Rechtssoziologie (Anm. 2), S. 33.
28 Lautmann, Klassenjustiz? , a.a.O., S. 159.
29 Zum Beispiel Lewrenz u.a., Die Strafzumessungspraxis bei Verkehrsdelikten in der BRD, Hamburg 1968; Opp/Peuckert, Ideologie und Fakten in der Rechtssprechung. Eine soziologische Untersuchung über das Urteil im Strafprozeß, München 1971.

30 Kritisch dazu Geffken, Demokratie und Recht, a.a.O., der von marxistischer Seite aus kritisiert, daß die bisherige Klassenjustizdiskussion in der BRD überwiegend für und von Juristen geführt werde. Derartig determinierte Untersuchungen hätten „klassenmäßig bedingte Grenzen", denn die Juristen hätten es gelernt, sich selbst (und die Justiz) „als Zentrum des gesellschaftlichen Alls zu begreifen".

31 Unter den Richtern, die sich mehr oder weniger stark mit der Justizsoziologie beschäftigt haben, wären zu nennen R. Wassermann, T. Rasehorn, H. Ostermeyer, W. Richter und R. Schmid. Was die Rechtswissenschaftler betrifft, die sich mit Justizsoziologie beschäftigen, so kann man heute schon konstatieren, daß eine einigermaßen vollständige Aufzählung den hier zur Verfügung stehenden Raum sprengen würde.

32 Einen ähnlichen Gedanken vertritt schon Liebknecht, wenn er sagt, das Wesen der Klassenjustiz liege in „allgemeinen menschlichen Eigenschaften" (a.a.O., Bd. 2, S. 117). Vgl. ferner z.B. Dahrendorf, a.a.O., (Anm. 7), S. 273, und dezidiert Lautmann, Klassenjustiz? , a.a.O., (Anm. 1), S. 155, der in einer solchen Haltung einzelner Richter die „krasseste Form" von Klassenjustiz sieht. Vgl. schließlich auf einer abstrakten erkenntnistheoretischen Ebene Th. Adorno (Vorlesung zur Einleitung in die Erkentnistheorie, Frankfurt o.J., S. 117): „Das eigentlich logische allgemeine Subjekt, das man gewohnt ist als das konstitutive Objekt von Erkenntnis überhaupt anzusprechen, das ist in Wirklichkeit ein gesamtgesellschaftliches Subjekt; wir sind gleichsam nur die Träger dieser intersubjektiven gesamtgesellschaftlichen Rationalität, und wir sind als einzelne konkrete Individuen gar nicht unmittelbar identisch mit jener Vernunft".

33 Lautmann, a.a.O., Vgl. auch Liebknecht, a.a.O., Bd. 3, S. 39, und Kaupen, a.a.O., (Anm. 1).

34 KZfSS, Soziale Schichtung und Mobilität in Westdeutschland, 1958, S. 1 ff.

35 Die Zahlen wurden der bei Richter, Zur soziologischen Struktur der deutschen Richterschaft, Stuttgart 1968, S. 12, abgedruckten Tabelle entnommen.

36 Nach Kaupen, Die Hüter von Recht und Ordnung, Neuwied 1970, Tabelle 17, S. 78.

37 Das Ergebnis entspricht übrigens weitgehend den Feststellungen, die Schmidhauser für die Rekrutierung der Richter am Supreme Court der USA gefunden hat, vgl. John R. Schmidhauser, The Justices of the Supreme Court, 3 Midwest Journal of Political Science, 1959, S. 1–57.

38 Vgl. Kaupen, a.a.O., (Fn. 36).

39 Kaupen, a.a.O.

40 Rottleuthner faßt zusammen: „Der wissenschaftliche Nachweis von Klassenjustiz dürfte aber zumeist scheitern am ‚Argument des Einzelfalles': Es handele sich um Ausnahmen; es müßten Tendenzen Häufigkeiten nachgewiesen werden, aber es fehlt an der Häufigkeit vergleichbarer Fälle (Welcher Fall ist kein ‚neuer'?) und am ‚Argument der Eigenart des Falles', an der Narrativität des Sachverhalts. Es lassen sich immer Besonderheiten in jedem Fall herausheben, die eine differenzielle Beurteilung erlauben. – Dann geht es nur noch um Plausibilität – um plausible Begründung der Kriterien der Ähnlichkeit und der Unterschiedlichkeit. Der Nachweis von Klassenjustiz ist ein Kampf darum, wer Türhüter der Plausibilität sei" (Rottleuthner, Richterliches Handeln, a.a.O., S. 183).

41 Am ehesten in der Strafzumessungspraxis; s. dazu oben bei Anm. 30.

42 Im Ergebnis ebenso Rottleuthner, a.a.O., (Anm. 40).

43 So neben den „klassischen" Autoren Liebknecht und Fraenkel z.B. von Hannover, Politische Justiz 1918–1933, Frankfurt 1966, Kirchheimer, Politische Justiz, Neuwied/Berlin 1965, Geffken, a.a.O., (Anm. 1), Rottleuthner, a.a.O., und neuerdings auch Kaupen, a.a.O., (Anm. 1).

44 Vgl. neben Dahrendorf die Beiträge von Lautmann sowie von Rasehorn, Wassermann, Ostermeyer, in: „Vorgänge" (Anm. 1).

45 So besonders markant Rasehorn, a.a.O.; vgl. dazu meine Kritik, a.a.O., (Anm. 1), sowie die kritischen Bemerkungen Geffkens, Demokratie und Recht, a.a.O., S. 274 („beschränkte Diagnose – beschränkte Therapie").

46 Vgl. u. v. a. W. Abendroth, Ist der Marxismus „überholt"? , in: Antagonistische Gesellschaft und politische Demokratie, Aufsätze zur politischen Soziologie, 2. Aufl., Neuwied 1972, S. 344 ff.

47 Vgl. Stichwort Social Class in: Gould/Kolb (Ed.), A Dictionary of the Social Sciences. London 1964.

48 Vgl. u.a. Dahrendorf, Klassen und Klassenkonflikt in der industriellen Gesellschaft, a.a.O.; Popitz, Zum Begriff der Klassengesellschaft, Hamburger Jahrbuch für Wirtschafts- und

Gesellschaftspolitik Bd. 3, 1958; Schelsky, Die Bedeutung des Klassenbegriffs für die Analyse unserer Gesellschaft, 1961, in: Auf der Suche nach Wirklichkeit, Düsseldorf 1965, S. 352 ff.

49 So z.B. H. Jung, Zu den klassentheoretischen Grundlagen einer sozialstatistischen Analyse der Klassen- und Sozialstruktur der BRD, in: Klassen- und Sozialstruktur der BRD 1950–1970 (herausgegeben vom Institut für marxistische Studien und Forschungen, Frankfurt 1972, Teil 1); auch Geffken, a.a.O., (Anm. 1).

50 Karl Marx und F. Engels, Ausgewählte Schriften in zwei Bänden, 17. Aufl., Berlin 1966, Band 2, S. 17.

51 Vgl. z.B. den von Forsthoff herausgegebenen Sammelband „Rechtsstaatlichkeit und Sozialstaatlichkeit", Darmstadt 1968.

52 Vgl. meine Einführung in die Rechtssoziologie, a.a.O., S. 1–3.

53 Vgl. Rüdiger Spiegelberg, Einige Daten zur Rekrutierung und Ausbildung der Polizei, in: Die Polizei, herausgegeben von Feest und Lautmann, a.a.O., (Anm. 18), S. 109.

54 Siehe oben Abschnitt IV.

55 Vgl. Jung (Fn. 49) sowie Das philosophische Wörterbuch, Fn. 9.

56 Vgl. Th. Raiser, Marktwirtschaft und paritätische Mitbestimmung, Heidelberg 1973, S. 65 ff.

III. Richterliche Entscheidungsfindung

Johann J. Hagen

Eine entscheidungstheoretische Konzeption des Justizverfahrens

1. Die Anwendung der Entscheidungstheorie auf Probleme des Justizverfahrens ist geeignet, Mängel und Einseitigkeiten sowohl der rechtsdogmatischen Betrachtung wie auch der empirischen Rechtssoziologie zu beseitigen, da die Entscheidungstheorie synoptisch konzipiert ist, also deskriptive und präskriptive Prämissen in gleicher Weise berücksichtigen kann.

2. Verwendbar ist die Entscheidungstheorie nur in ihrer erweiterten Form als Theorie kognitiver und informationsverarbeitender Prozesse. Damit ist der weitgehende Verzicht auf mathematische Formalisierung der Modelle verbunden. An deren Stelle treten die Probleme der Informationsgewinnung und der heuristischen Techniken, die die Entscheidungsaufgaben an die gegebenen Beschränkungen anpassen.

3. Da juristische Fragen in der Regel zum Typus der schlecht-definierten und nicht-operationalen Probleme zählen, ist die eigentliche Entscheidung die Definition des Problems und die Schließung der offenen Beschränkungen. Die Informationsverarbeitungsprozesse dieser Art besitzen objektive Strukturen, die auch im gerichtlichen Entscheidungsprozeß ihre Gültigkeit haben. Die Besonderheit dieser Entscheidungsklassen liegt lediglich in ihrer Legitimation, also darin, daß die Lösungshypothesen, die in die offenen Beschränkungen eingesetzt werden, dem offiziellen Normensystem entnommen werden müssen.

4. Entscheidungshandeln kann wissenschaftlich nur durch einen Algorithmus oder ein heuristisches Programm erklärt werden, von dem es gesteuert wird. An die Stelle fehlender objektiver und offizieller Programme treten inoffizielle Programme, die aus der klassen- und schichtspezifischen Rekrutierung und Sozialisation der Entscheidungsträger hervorgehen.

5. Der gerichtliche Entscheidungsprozeß muß als soziales System erklärt werden, das über eine formale Organisation verfügt. Aus dieser Besonderheit ergibt sich für das Justizverfahren eine Reihe von Abweichungen gegenüber dem spieltheoretischen Modell der Nonkooperation.

6. In den entscheidungstheoretischen Modellen finden sich deskriptive und normative Elemente, die zusammen aus der praktischen Relevanz der Entscheidungstheorie zu erklären sind. Die allgemeine Intention der Entscheidungstheorie, nämlich Objektivierung und Optimierung des Entscheidungsverhaltens, kann im speziellen Bereich der Justiz technische und punktuelle Reformen einleiten.

1. Entscheidungstheorie und Rechtswissenschaft

Der Einsatz der Entscheidungstheorie im Bereich von Verwaltung und Rechtspflege trägt gewissen kritischen Einwänden gegen die traditionelle Rechtswissenschaft Rechnung, die sich im besonderen auf deren praktisch relevante Teile, nämlich Rechtsdogmatik und Methodenlehre, beziehen. Diese Kritik ist im wesentlichen im Rahmen der Rechtssoziologie formuliert worden und zielt auf den empirisch belegbaren Umstand, daß das Entscheidungs- und Verfügungsverhalten des Rechtsstabs von einer Summe variabler Faktoren abhängt, von denen die Dogmatik des materiellen und Prozeßrechts lediglich den formellen Legitimationsaspekt behandelt (1)*. Andrerseits enthält die Rechtssoziologie unter dem positivistischen Primat der empirischen Methode (Rechtstatsachenforschung) eine immanente Tendenz, die formelle Programmierung von Rechtsakten zu vernachlässigen oder überhaupt zu unterschlagen. Sie gewinnt dadurch einen ausgesprochen destruktiven Charakter, der den objektiven Verfall der bürgerlichen Gesetzlichkeit widerzuspiegeln scheint. Das allseits spürbare Unbehagen bezieht sich auf das Fehlen einer integrierenden Theorie, die sowohl die faktischen und informellen wie auch die normativen und formellen Prämissen des Entscheidens zu erfassen vermag. Von einer solchen Theorie wäre zu erwarten, daß sie einerseits an reale Handlungsabläufe anknüpft, andrerseits aber sich nicht in bloß beschreibender „Praxeologie" (2) erschöpft, sondern die Rechtspraxis auch mit rationalen Maßstäben versorgt.

Die Wissenschaftsorganisation bedient sich zur Abgrenzung der Disziplinen in zunehmendem Maße analytischer und nicht ontologischer Kategorien (3), d.h. bei unterschiedlichen Forschungsinteressen und Aspekten kann derselbe Gegenstand Erkenntnisobjekt verschiedener Disziplinen sein. Die praktische Jurisprudenz ist an ihrem Gegenstand im Hinblick auf den Konkretisierungszusammenhang von Normen verschiedener Stufen interessiert, der in der Entscheidung realisiert wird, während der kognitive Mechanismus dieser Transformationen als unproblematisch vorausgesetzt wird. In die Modelle der Entscheidungstheorie dagegen gehen Rechtsnormen als präskriptive Prämissen der Problemdefinition ein und bilden Beschränkungen der Lösungsalternativen. Beide verwenden danach einen scheinbar verschiedenen Entscheidungsbegriff: im einen Fall ist Entscheidung der Oberbegriff einer Reihe förmlicher und autorisierter Akte, im andern Fall die Auswahl einer aus der gegebenen Ausgangssituation mittels eines bewußten Kalküls ermittelten Handlungsalternative. Aber der anhand eines allgemeinen Methodenkanons bestimmte Legitimationsrahmen wird von der Rechtsdogmatik ebenfalls mit der Intention einer Beschränkung der Entscheidungsmöglichkeiten formuliert. Die Explikation von Normen durch die praktische Rechtswissenschaft dient dem Ziel, Kriterien anzugeben, gegen die Rechtsakte im Wege eines Kontrollverfahrens getestet werden können. Nicht der Entscheidungsbegriff ist somit verschieden, sondern der Aspekt, unter dem Rechtslehre und Entscheidungstheorie ihn analysieren: die juristische Betrachtungsweise verlegt sich nahezu ausschließlich auf den legitimierenden und kontrollierenden Bereich der Entscheidung, sie ist also überwiegend nur am Ergebnis interessiert; die Entscheidungstheorie bezieht das Zustandekommen des Ergebnisses dagegen mit ein und analysiert damit den Entscheidungsprozeß im Ganzen. Zwar bilden danach die juristischen Fragen, die von Gerichten zu lösen sind, eine spezielle

* Anmerkungen auf den Seiten 152 ff.

Entscheidungsklasse, aber die Rechtswissenschaft beinhaltet keine spezielle Entscheidungstheorie. Denn ihre Entscheidungsaufgaben sind unter den allgemeinen Entscheidungsbegriff subsumierbar, aber durch ihre normative Bindung wird aus der Gesamtmenge kognitiver Informationen das „offizielle Informationssystem" (4) ausgesondert und getrennt behandelt. In Wirklichkeit kann aber, wie die Theorie der Rechtsanwendung lehrt (5), der Entscheidungsprozeß nicht auf normative Operationen innerhalb des offiziellen Informationssystems reduziert werden.

Andere mehr fachspezifische Einwände betreffen die unzureichende Integration der verschiedenen Rechtsbereiche im Rahmen der Rechtswissenschaft. Das gilt im besonderen für die klassischen Gebiete des materiellen Rechts (Zivilrecht, Strafrecht, Verwaltungsrecht, Verfassungsrecht) und die entsprechenden speziellen Verfahrensbereiche. Es scheint, daß für deren Verhältnis mehr externe Kriterien des Wissenschaftsbetriebs als sachlich und praktisch zwingende Gründe ausschlaggebend sind. Auch der Lehre von der Doppelfunktionalität (6), die sich am ehesten um eine theoretische Explikation des gegenseitigen Verhältnisses bemüht hat, liegt im Grunde genommen die Trennung der Funktionen zugrunde. Die funktionale Bestimmung der präskriptiven und offiziellen Elemente organisierten problemlösenden Verhaltens, wie es auch das Justizverfahren darstellt, ist trotzdem im Ansatz richtig und entwicklungsfähig. Aber Aussagen über Funktionen als Abstraktionsklasse möglicher Zustandsformen können zulässigerweise nur im Rahmen eines Systems und von den Elementen dieses Systems gemacht werden. Unter einem kybernetischen Aspekt lassen sich Verfahren und Entscheidung, auf die sich die getrennten Normenbereiche beziehen, als System und zwar als dynamisches oder Verhaltenssystem darstellen. Als System gilt hier eine Menge von Elementen, die durch festgelegte Relationen eine Ganzheit bilden; der Terminus Verhaltenssystem charakterisiert jene Teilklasse von Systemen, die aktive Elemente mit Inputs und Outputs besitzen (7). Faßt man den Entscheidungsprozeß, wie es in der Entscheidungstheorie üblich ist, als dynamisches System auf, so sind die anzuwendenden Normen als Elemente und durch ihre Funktionen in diesem System definiert. Dadurch wird eine zugleich differenzierende und integrierende Betrachtungsweise möglich. Die diversen Normen prozessualer und materiellrechtlicher Natur sind im einzelnen als Sollwerte, Zielfunktionen, Präferenzen, heuristische Strategien, Entscheidungsregeln, Lösungsgeneratoren etc. zu bestimmen.

Eine weitere Schwierigkeit, die mit den Mitteln der traditionellen Rechtsdogmatik nicht befriedigend zu lösen ist, resultiert aus dem ungeklärten Verhältnis von Struktur und Funktion. Dieses Problem kann allerdings auch nicht von einer Entscheidungstheorie als Theorie der Individualentscheidung (8) gelöst werden, sondern nur unter Zuhilfenahme der Organisationstheorie. Im Justizverfahren geht es speziell um die Strukturierung des konkreten Prozeßgeschehens durch organisatorische Invarianten und um ihre Berücksichtigung im Entscheidungsprozeß. Handlungsabläufe, die bei Organen mit Rechtspflegefunktionen konzentriert sind, besitzen Massencharakter und bedürfen darum einer formalen Organisation, die für wiederkehrende Entscheidungen allgemeine Beschränkungen festlegt. Dieser strukturierende Effekt der Organisation wird von *Kosiol* (9) folgendermaßen charakterisiert: „Die Organisation schafft durch Grundsätze und generelle Entscheidungen das Gerüst oder den Rahmen, in dem sich laufende Dispositionen abspielen. Organisieren ist ein dem Disponieren vorgelagertes

Umweghandeln, in dem zuerst strukturierend für viele Fälle und dann, darin eingebettet, für den einzelnen Fall gehandelt wird. Beim Organisieren geht es um Dauerregelungen und Dauereinrichtungen, die das Gesamtgefüge festlegen, an das der Ablauf der Arbeitsprozesse gebunden ist." Durch die Prozeßrechtsdoktrin wird ein Teil der organisierten Strukturen als formale Zulässigkeitsbedingungen ausgegliedert, die in Form von Prozeßvoraussetzungen bzw. Prozeßhindernissen in die Einzelverfahren hineinwirken (10). Aber praktisch relevant ist das Verhältnis Struktur und Funktion, Organisation und Prozeß doch in dem Sinn, daß die organisierten Entscheidungssubjekte nicht zur Bewältigung einzelner Entscheidungsaufgaben, wie etwa private, ad hoc gebildete Schiedsgerichte, eingerichtet sind, sondern zur Erledigung ganzer Klassen von Entscheidungsaufgaben. In diesem Rahmen bilden alle Entscheidungen, die parallel oder seriell getroffen werden können, eine Einheit, die sich nicht in den formal festgelegten Teilen der Organisation, der „Verfassung" (11) also, erschöpft, sondern sich auch durch die Kapazität des Entscheidungsapparats und das gemeinsame Programmrepertoire verwirklicht. Erst durch diese Erweiterung wird die technische Reform der rechtlichen Entscheidungsprozesse einer wissenschaftlichen Behandlung zugänglich. Hier liegt neben der allgemeinen Konzeptualisierung das eigentliche Anwendungsfeld der Entscheidungstheorie: optimale Ausnutzung von Kapazitäten, Mobilisierung von Zeitreserven, die Entwicklung standardisierbarer und objektivierbarer Verfahren zur Informationsgewinnung und -verarbeitung, die entlastende Substitution von Routineakten (12) usw.

Denkbare Einwände gegen diesen Einsatz der Entscheidungstheorie könnten sich auf deren *formalen* Charakter beziehen. Denn unverkennbar ist die Entscheidungstheorie, die sich auch heute noch nicht eindeutig von der Operationsforschung abgrenzen läßt, durch die Verwendung mathematischer und kybernetischer Verfahren geprägt. Demgegenüber verfügt die Rechtswissenschaft nur in sehr bescheidenem Ausmaß über eine formalisierte Theorie, nämlich in Form der Deontik, die zudem noch in vielerlei Hinsicht in den Anfängen steckt (13). Daraus wird gelegentlich der Schluß gezogen, die Rechtswissenschaft habe es mit einer besonderen Form des gesellschaftlichen Überbaus zu tun, dessen Merkmale eine Formalisierung prinzipiell ausschließen. Die Natur ihres Gegenstandes soll also die Rechtswissenschaft auf Interpretations- und Harmonisierungsaufgaben von sprachlich-persuasorisch konzipierten Texten festlegen, deren „normative Sinn-Strukturen" nur hermeneutisch erschlossen werden könnten (14). Diese wissenschaftsfeindliche Argumentation ignoriert einmal die Entwicklung der Entscheidungstheorie aus einer geschlossenen Konzeption mit streng ökonomischer Anwendung zu offenen, kognitiven und informationsverarbeitenden Modellen, die auf eine vollständige Formalisierung zunehmend verzichten (15). Tatsächlich ist der Anwendungsbereich der Entscheidungstheorie durch diese Modifikationen erheblich erweitert worden und umfaßt damit alle informationsverarbeitenden Prozesse. Erst in der erweiterten Form einer Theorie informationsverarbeitender oder kognitiver Prozesse wurde die entscheidungstheoretische Behandlung von Problemen des Justizverfahrens sinnvoll. Im übrigen muß auf die Entwicklung der strukturalen bzw. mathematischen Linguistik, der generativen Grammatik, der Sprachstatistik und anderer formaler Disziplinen verwiesen werden, die zusammengenommen das Ziel einer Quantifizierung umgangs- oder fachsprachlich gebundener Ausdrücke als immer weniger unrealistisch erscheinen lassen (16). Aber zentral entkräftet werden die Thesen der Hermeneutiker durch

die Möglichkeiten der Simulation und Substitution von Informationsverarbeitungsprozessen. Denn dafür wird lediglich Analogie der Strukturen und Operationstreue verlangt, nicht jedoch die Überführung von Semantik in Syntaktik. So wird das Gedächtnis, das seine Inhalte assoziativ, also nach dem semantischen Gehalt aufruft, von einem Retrievalprogramm simuliert, das mittels Adressenaufruf, also syntaktisch arbeitet (17).
Die entscheidungstheoretische Betrachtungsweise, die synoptisch verschiedene, auch normative Aspekte vereinigt, muß sich durch den Nachweis rechtfertigen, daß sie die wesentlichen Bestandteile des justizförmigen Entscheidungsprozesses zu erfassen und auszudrücken vermag. Gesichert könnten diese Aussagen indes erst genannt werden, wenn sie sich auf eine Fülle von Einzeluntersuchungen stützen könnten und in einer Rückkoppelung durch praktische Anwendung bestätigt würden. Demgegenüber besitzt diese Studie nur einen konzeptionellen Charakter. Die Schwerpunkte dieser Konzeption sollen die Elemente des Entscheidungsmodells, der Informationsfluß, die Programmstrukturen und das soziale System bilden. Abschließend soll noch einiges zur praktischen Relevanz der Entscheidungstheorie und ihrer Anwendung im Justizbereich nachgetragen werden.

2. Elemente des Entscheidungsmodells

Das allgemeine Entscheidungsmodell umfaßt folgende Elemente: Aktor, Umwelt, Alternativen, Wertsystem, Entscheidungsregeln und technologisches bzw. soziologisches Modell der Umwelt. Dieses Basismodell muß durch kognitive Zusatzannahmen ergänzt werden, nämlich Problemdefinition, Einstellung und heuristische Programme. Der Aktor bezeichnet das Entscheidungssubjekt, also das aktive Element im Entscheidungssystem, das die subjektive Komponente (Wertsystem, Entscheidungsregeln) des Entscheidens liefert. Die objektive Komponente wird von Umwelt und Alternativen repräsentiert. Auch Entscheidungshandeln ist objektiv determiniert, aber nicht im mechanistischen Modus einer eindeutigen Zuordnung von Umweltfaktoren und Handlungsvarianten, sondern die Ausgangssituation definiert ein Möglichkeitsfeld mit einem bestimmten Freiheitsgrad, der vom Aktor entsprechend seinen präskriptiven Prämissen realisiert wird. Diesem Umstand wird durch die Differenzierung von Umwelt und Alternativen Rechnung getragen: Alternativen beziehen sich auf jenen Teil der Umwelt, der im Einflußbereich des Aktors liegt, der also durch seine Aktivitäten verändert werden kann. Die übrigen Teile der Umwelt, denen gegenüber das Entscheidungssubjekt sich nur adaptiv verhalten kann, werden auch als Daten bezeichnet. Um seinen Handlungsspielraum und damit die zulässigen Alternativen abschätzen zu können, bedarf der Aktor einer Menge von Informationen, mit deren Hilfe er die Umwelt und ihre objektiven Gesetzmäßigkeiten in einem technologischen oder soziologischen Modell abbildet. Durch die Unterscheidung von technologischem und soziologischem Modell kann auch berücksichtigt werden, ob der Aktor sich unter den Bedingungen einer passiven oder einer interagierenden Umwelt entscheidet. Entsprechend dem Ausmaß der verfügbaren Umweltinformation, anhand deren auch die Handlungskonsequenzen kalkuliert werden, können verschiedene Typen von Entscheidungssituationen klassifiziert werden, nämlich Entscheidungen unter Sicherheit, unter Risiko und unter Unsicherheit, auf die hier nicht weiter eingegangen werden soll (18). Durch dieses technologische (soziologische) Modell wird der zulässige Lösungsbereich festgelegt, in dem sich die Alternativen bewegen. Um aber zwischen den zulässigen Alternativen, die vom Möglichkeitsfeld freigegeben werden, wählen zu können, muß der Aktor über ein Wertsystem verfügen, das Kriterien zur Bewertung der einzelnen Alternativen liefert. Dieses Wertsystem ist mit einer Zielfunktion und einem Entscheidungsverfahren gekoppelt, durch das der Zielerreichungsgrad ermittelt werden kann. In der klassischen Entscheidungstheorie wurde dieser Teil - der ökonomischen Verwendung entsprechend - von der Nutzentheorie okkupiert. Die Entscheidungsaufgabe kann dann als gelöst gelten, wenn der Alternativen- und Ergebnisraum mittels Zielfunktion und Wertsystem präferenziell geordnet ist. Für Entscheidungssituationen mit unvollständiger Information wurden sogenannte Entscheidungsregeln (Bayes-Regel, Minimax-Regel, Hurwicz-Regel etc.) formuliert, die durch die kognitiven Erweiterungen dann mit den heuristischen Programmen zusammenfließen.

Dieses stark vereinfachte Basismodell ist einer speziellen Entscheidungsklasse mit vorgegebener Problemstellung (Profitmaximierung) und in der Regel quantifizierbaren Zielfunktionen adäquat, darüber hinaus aber völlig unrealistisch. In dieser weitgehend formalisierten Gestalt wäre die Entscheidungstheorie kaum geeignet, Probleme des Justizverfahrens zu analysieren. Zur Entwicklung einer allgemeinen und objektunabhängigen Entscheidungstheorie mußte eine Reihe realistischer Bedingungen eingebaut werden, während die Postulate des Basismodells nur als Normativ beibehalten werden können. Statt vollständiger Information wird eine relevante Informationsmenge nach einem Beschaffungsprogramm, das Real-Time-Bedingungen erfüllen muß, verlangt; an die Stelle einer vollständig, schwach transitiven Ordnung der Alternativen und optimaler Lösungen tritt das Prinzip der befriedigenden Lösung, die mit Hilfe der psychologischen Lehre vom Anspruchsniveau und von der Leistungsmotivation bestimmt wird; statt der rigorosen Fassung der Wertkonsistenz wird das Wertsystem informations- und zeitabhängig gesehen. Vor allem werden Entscheidungsaufgaben nicht mehr als vorgegeben betrachtet, sondern es stehen verschiedene Problemfassungen zur Verfügung, die gleichzeitig den Lösungsweg indizieren. Diese Betrachtungsweise ermöglicht über die Problemdefinition eine Anpassung der Entscheidungsaufgabe an gegebene Beschränkungen des kognitiven Apparats. Überhaupt rückt damit das Problem der beschränkten Informationsverarbeitungskapazität ins Zentrum einer realistischen Entscheidungstheorie. Der Sinn heuristischer Programme ist es, mit diesen Beschränkungen fertigzuwerden. Die Entscheidungstheorie ist damit keine ökonomische Theorie mehr, sondern eine Theorie der Ökonomie des Entscheidens. Die erweiterte Fassung der Entscheidungstheorie erlaubt es darüber hinaus, auch das Entscheidungssubjekt als Ensemble gesellschaftlicher Verhältnisse aufzufassen. Dies wird möglich durch die Erkenntnis kognitiver Mechanismen, die Erfahrungen, Lern- und Sozialisationsvorgänge in den konkreten Entscheidungsprozeß vermitteln. Gemeint sind Attitüden oder Einstellungen, die sowohl die Wahrnehmung, also die äußere Informationsrezeption selektiv organisieren wie auch die Überführung von gespeicherten Inhalten des Langzeitgedächtnisses (Begriffe, Werte, Verhaltensmuster) in das Kurzzeit- oder Arbeitsgedächtnis (19) besorgen.

Als allgemeine Theorie kognitiver und informationsverarbeitender Prozesse kann die Entscheidungstheorie auch die Klasse der juristischen Entscheidungen zu ihrem Anwendungsfeld rechnen. Zum Zweck einer entscheidungstheoretischen Konzeption empfiehlt es sich allerdings, zunächst die richterliche und meritorische Entscheidung (Sachentscheidung) herauszuheben und die Verfahrensschritte der übrigen Verfahrensteilnehmer analytisch zur interagierenden Umwelt zu rechnen (20). Diese Vereinfachung ist auch dadurch gerechtfertigt, daß in den meisten Justizverfahren der nonkooperative Entscheidungstyp überwiegt. Aus ähnlichen Erwägungen scheint es auch berechtigt, die Darstellung primär auf die prototypische Struktur des Zivilprozesses zu beziehen. Weitere Vereinfachungen ergeben sich aus der Annahme eines homogenen Entscheidungssubjekts, das nicht erst im Wege eines internen Entscheidungsprozesses durch Überredung, manipulative Taktiken oder gegenseitige Anpassung zu einer Beschlußfassung gelangt. Überhaupt können positiv normierte Besonderheiten, die sich aus der historisch bedingten Organisation der Rechtspflegefunktionen ergeben, nicht in diesem Rahmen berücksichtigt werden, sondern bedürften spezieller Untersuchungen. Die entscheidungstheoretische Konzeption bewegt sich damit etwa auf demselben Abstraktionsniveau wie die allgemeine Verfahrenslehre.

3. Der Informationsfluß

Die Sachentscheidung als das organisatorisch festgelegte Verfahrensziel ist das Produkt einer Reihe von informativen Verknüpfungen, die in der nachstehenden Abbildung schematisch dargestellt sind:

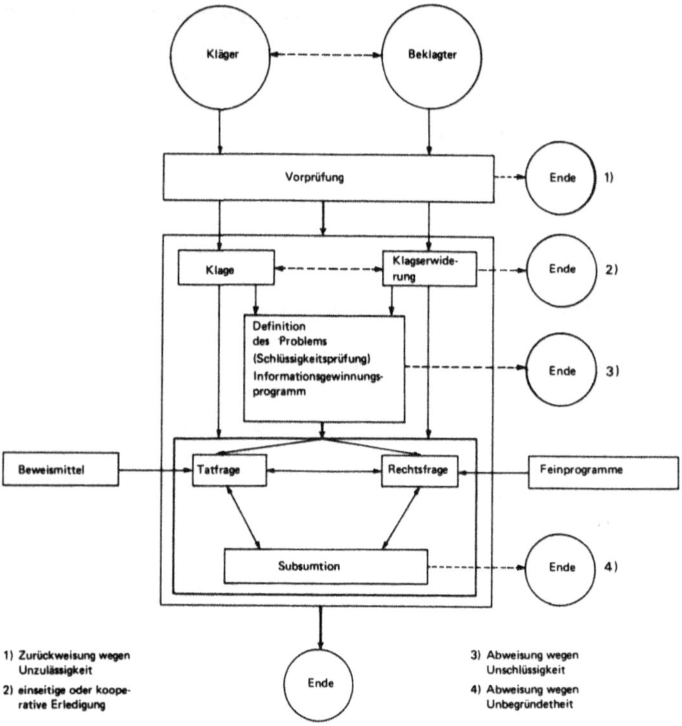

Ausgangsprämissen bilden die Tatsachenbehauptungen und Sachanträge der Parteien, die vom Entscheidungssubjekt als Daten zu behandeln sind. Nur ausnahmsweise können diese Prämissen durch gerichtliche Verbesserungs-, Berichtigungs- oder Ergänzungsaufträge verändert werden. Diese Primärinformationen fungieren als Inputs des Entscheidungssystems, die nach den Regeln des Justizverfahrens in Outputs transformiert werden müssen. Da das Entscheidungssystem nur für eine bestimmte Teilmenge von Entscheidungsaufgaben eingerichtet ist, hat der Verarbeitung der Inputs eine Vorprüfung voranzugehen, die nach formalen Kriterien über die Zulässigkeit entscheidet. Die zugelassenen Eingangsinformationen gehen in die Definition der Entscheidungsaufgabe ein und bilden dadurch Beschränkungen des zulässigen Lösungsbereichs. Das Ausmaß der Beschränkungen kann im einzelnen verschieden gestaltet sein. Soweit die adaptive Datenmenge nicht nur Tatsachenbehauptungen, sondern auch die Legitimationsgrundlage umfaßt, stellen die Eingangsinformationen eine Vorformulierung des Entscheidungsproblems dar, das in diesem Stadium lediglich auf formale Inkonsistenz zu überprüfen ist. In den Fällen, in denen die Eingangsinformationen lediglich aus Tatsachenbehauptungen und Urteilsantrag oder nur aus Tatsachenbehauptungen bestehen, verfügt der Aktor über einen weiteren Alternativenbereich; er kann nicht nur zwischen Abweisen und Stattgeben bzw. teilweisem Abweisen und teilweisem Stattgeben wählen, sondern muß sich auch zwischen verschiedenen rechtlichen Qualifikationen entscheiden. Es entspricht auf jeden Fall dem starken Einfluß der Dispositions- und Verhandlungsmaxime, daß die Parteien durch Festlegung oder Zurückhaltung von Informationen die Entscheidungsaufgabe aktiv mitgestalten.

Aus den Eingangsinformationen, die der kontradiktorischen Verfahrensstruktur wegen in der Regel inkonsistent und widerspruchsvoll ausfallen, muß der Aktor die Problemdefinition und das Informationsgewinnungsprogramm ableiten. Ein Nebenprodukt dieser Informationsverarbeitung ist die Schlüssigkeitsprüfung. Die Definition des Problems umfaßt alle Restriktionen, denen Entscheidungsvarianten zu genügen haben; sie liefert also die Extension des Lösungsbereichs (21). Die Problemdefinition kann operationale und nicht-operationale Elemente, sogenannte „open constraints" (22) enthalten. Operational sind die Problemdefinitionen dann, wenn ein Entscheidungsverfahren existiert, das eindeutig feststellen läßt, ob eine Entscheidungsalternative in die angegebene Extension fällt. Soweit die Eingangsinformationen einen formulierten Urteilsantrag enthalten, verfügt der Aktor zumindest über ein operational definiertes Problemelement. Von diesem Antrag ist darum auszugehen. Mittels logischer Zuordnungen der tatsächlichen Informationen kann ein Teil der offenen Beschränkungen geschlossen werden. Der Aktor kann anhand der operationalen Problemmerkmale entscheiden, welche von den angebotenen Informationen er als relevant ansieht, um in den eigentlichen Entscheidungsprozeß einzugehen. Es kann zudem durch logische Operationen Kongruenz und Widerspruch zwischen Kläger- und Beklagtenbehauptungen festgestellt und damit eine weitere Teilmenge von Informationen ausgesondert werden. Der Rest ist „Definitionsspielraum" (23). Die Problemdefinition erfüllt drei Funktionen: Deskription, Generation und Verifikation von Lösungen (24). Die Definitionsmerkmale des Problems liefern Kriterien, nach denen präsumtive Lösungen beschrieben werden. In der konkreten Anwendung heißt dies: die in die Definition der Entscheidungsaufgabe aufgenommenen Behauptungen beschreiben mögliche Beweisergebnisse. Als Verifikatoren bilden

die Restriktionen Bewertungskriterien, die als Bestandteil eines Entscheidungsverfahrens eine Kontrolle darüber zulassen, ob eine Lösung in den extensionalen Rahmen fällt. Die logische Zuordnung der akzeptierten Datenmenge erlaubt auch die Überprüfung der Schlüssigkeit der Sachentscheidung. Als Generatoren gewinnen die Beschränkungen der Problemdefinition einen programmierenden Charakter, der über die allgemeine Richtung des Suchverhaltens entscheidet.
Von der Problemdefinition hängt offenkundig die Entscheidung über das Informationsgewinnungsprogramm ab. Im Gegensatz zu den geschlossenen Modellen des Entscheidungsverhaltens kann realistischerweise nicht von einer gegebenen Informationsmenge ausgegangen werden, die mittels formaler Entscheidungsregeln auch bei Ungewißheit verarbeitet werden können, sondern die Informationsgewinnung wird hier selbst zu einem bedeutsamen Teil des Entscheidungsprozesses. Da aber rationales Handeln in Entscheidungen nur als determiniertes und zielstrebiges Verhalten denkbar ist, bedarf der Aktor eines Programms, das den Suchvorgang steuert. Ein solches Programm kann der Aktor aus der generativen Funktion der Problemdefinition ableiten. Dieser Zusammenhang wird prozeßtechnisch mit den Termini Beweisthema (= relevante Tatsachenbehauptung), Beweismittel (Urkunden, Zeugen, Sachverständige, Augenschein, Parteienvernehmung) und Beweiszulassung ausgedrückt. Es handelt sich dabei um eine Operation, für die der gemeinrechtliche Prozeß das Beweisinterlokut bestimmt hat und die von einigen geltenden Prozeßordnungen im Beweisbeschluß zu erledigen ist (25). Der entscheidungstheoretische Informationsbegriff umfaßt allerdings auch präskriptive Informationen (26). Soweit diese nicht in Form einer vorgeschriebenen Qualifikation des prozessualen Anspruchs zu den Beschränkungen zählen, muß das Informationsgewinnungsprogramm sich auch auf die Präskriptoren der Sachentscheidung beziehen. In dieser Form stellt sich die Entscheidungsaufgabe als typische nicht-operationale Problemdefinition dar. In die offenen Beschränkungen werden Lösungshypothesen eingesetzt, die im Suchvorgang gegen die Zusatzinformationen getestet werden. Als Lösungshypothesen im Justizverfahren fungieren normierte Tatbestände, die anhand der Beweisergebnisse auf Subsumtionsmöglichkeiten überprüft werden. Das so programmierte Verfahren stellt sich als Folge von Suchschritten und Rückkopplungsvorgängen dar und ist mit einer Art Stufenfunktion ausgestattet, die es erlaubt, ab einem bestimmten Informationsbetrag zu einer anderen Lösungshypothese überzugehen. Der Informationsprozeß verläuft dann, ausgehend von der Eingangsinformation (A), über das Informationsgewinnungsprogramm (a_j), den Suchvorgang (b_j) und den Test (c_j), der über Annahme und Subsumtion (S) bzw. Auslösung der Stufenfunktion entscheidet. Gesteuert wird der Prozeß von einer Lösungshypothese (R), die nach Maßgabe der zusätzlichen Informationen variiert werden kann. Dieser Regelungsprozeß kann folgendermaßen dargestellt werden:

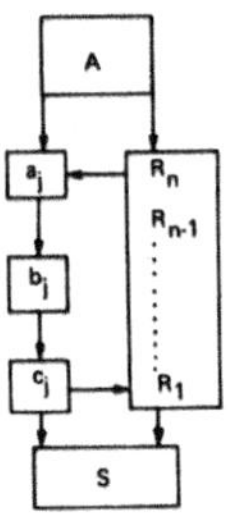

Auch in der juristischen Literatur ist die wechselseitige Abhängigkeit von Rechtsfrage und Tatfrage bekannt und wird unpräzise als hermeneutischer Zirkel oder als „zirkelhaftes Wandern des Blicks" (27) umschrieben. Aber es fehlt offenbar noch an einem objektivierbaren Verfahren, das den Ergebnissen den Charakter der Zufälligkeit nehmen würde. Rüdiger *Lautmanns* Untersuchungen des Justizverfahrens als „teilnehmender Beobachter" haben ergeben, daß die für die Hypothesenvariation erforderliche Rückmeldung in der Praxis häufig durch den Abwehrmechanismus der kognitiven Dissonanz und die Strategie der Perseveranz gestört wird: „Der Entscheider sucht *die favorisierte Alternative durch konsonante Argumente zu stützen.* Konkurrierende Alternativen werden dann nur mit ablehnenden Argumenten bedacht. Die ins Auge gefaßte Alternative gewinnt dadurch immer mehr an Attraktivität, während Gegenalternativen unattraktiv und schließlich ganz vergessen werden" (28). Der Informationsfluß nimmt dann tendenziell folgende lineare Form an:

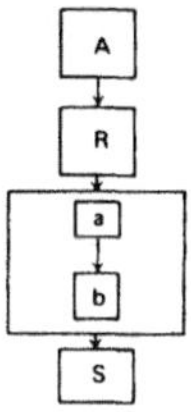

Der Zeitfaktor verlangt von jedem Informationsgewinnungsprogramm eine selektive Steuerung: aber hier findet Überselektion statt.
Der Suchvorgang der Informationsgewinnung tastet die Umwelt des Aktors nach deskriptiven (Beweismittel) und nach präskriptiven Informationen ab, wobei letztere die Feinprogramme liefern. Diese Feinprogramme, die aus Präjudikaten, Kommentaren und anderer Rechtsliteratur bezogen werden, ermöglichen eine allmähliche Schließung der offenen Beschränkungen. Sobald die Entscheidungsaufgabe hinsichtlich deskriptiver und präskriptiver Beschränkungen geschlossen, also operational definiert ist, kann mittels eines deontischen Algorithmus die Aufgabe gelöst werden.

4. Die Programmstruktur

Dem entscheidungstheoretischen Verständnis entspricht es, Entscheidungen als determiniertes und zielstrebiges Verhalten aufzufassen, das invariante Strukturen besitzt. Im Prinzip laufen alle Aussagen der Entscheidungstheorie darauf hinaus, Entscheidungsakte aus einer endlichen Menge von Programmen zu erklären. Damit steht die Entscheidungstheorie in krassem Gegensatz zu allen idealistischen Konzeptionen, die dem Entscheidungsakt einen dizisionistischen Charakter beimessen. Auch die auf *Katona* (29) zurückgehende Unterscheidung von *echten* und *routinemäßigen* Entscheidungen ist unter diesem Gesichtspunkt ebenso zu kritisieren wie die von *Simon* (30) in *programmierte* und *nicht-programmierte* Entscheidungen. Denn auch in sogenannten echten oder innovativen Entscheidungen werden für Teillösungen oder Ausführungshandlungen Subroutinen,

Schablonen oder gewohnheitsmäßige Verhaltensformen benutzt. Als lernendes System vermag der menschliche Informationsverarbeitungsapparat grundsätzlich Erfahrungen aus früheren Problemlösungen in den laufenden Entscheidungsprozeß wiedereinzuschalten. In diesem Sinn ist ein lernendes Verhaltenssystem durch seine Vergangenheit programmiert.
Die einzelnen Entscheidungsklassen differieren allerdings ganz erheblich in der Art der verfügbaren Programme. Üblicherweise wird zwischen Algorithmen und heuristischen Programmen unterschieden (31). Eine weitere Unterscheidung bezieht sich auf die Stufe des Programmierens und ergibt Objekt- und Metaprogramme bzw. Algorithmen 1., 2., 3. Stufe usw. Als Unterscheidungsmerkmale zwischen Algorithmen und heuristischen Programmen dienen (nach *Klein*) die Kriterien Lösungsgarantie und heuristische Kraft. Daraus ergibt sich folgendes Schema (32):

Kriterien	Lösungsgarantie	Verwendet heuristische Prinzipien und hat heuristische Kraft
Entscheidungsalgorithmus	conditio sine qua non	In aller Regel
Heuristisches Programm	Keine Lösungsgarantie. Findet für die Mehrzahl der Fälle Lösungen, die im Verhältnis zum erforderl. Aufwand als gut genug empfunden werden	conditio sine qua non

Ein Algorithmus setzt sich aus der Angabe der Operatoren, der logischen Bedingungen und der Reihenfolge zusammen, in der die Operationen vorzunehmen sind. Das Wesen heuristischer Programme ist nicht in gleicher Weise eindeutig bestimmt. Als übereinstimmendes Kennzeichen wird von den meisten Autoren die *Reduktion des Suchaufwands* genannt (33). Heuristische Programme, die als erlernbare und damit objektivierbare Methoden der Problemlösung gelten können, sind zum Teil an spezielle Problemklassen gebunden, zum Teil allgemeiner, objektunabhängiger Natur (34). Die Aufgabe der Entscheidungstheorie als gesellschaftlicher Produktivkraft ist es, durch empirische Untersuchungen die Programmstruktur sichtbar zu machen, die heuristischen Techniken zu objektivieren, zu formalisieren und sie letztlich einem Algorithmus anzunähern, der zur Entlastung in ein Automatenprogramm überführt werden kann.
Die Analyse des Justizverfahrens unter dem entscheidungstheoretischen Programmaspekt ist in allgemeiner Form kaum möglich. Denn die bei den gerichtlichen Entscheidungsträgern konzentrierten Entscheidungsklassen sind nicht nach der Programmstruktur gegliedert, sondern nach Kriterien des politischen Systems zusammengefaßt. Diese ungegliederte Entscheidungsmenge müßte darum zuerst unter entscheidungstheoretischen Gesichtspunkten klassifiziert und die einzelnen Teilmengen müßten getrennt auf ihre Programmstruktur analysiert werden. Allgemeine Aussagen dagegen müssen zwangsläufig einen pauschalen Charakter haben. So kann etwa allgemein gesagt werden, daß das Justizverfahren zwar überwiegend Routineakte umfaßt, aber nur sehr selten über einen

Entscheidungsalgorithmus verfügt. Von einem Algorithmus kann man am ehesten im Zusammenhang mit Entscheidungen numerischen Charakters sprechen, so etwa bei Kosten- und Kostenersatzentscheidungen oder bei anderen Entscheidungen, die mittels eines Rechenverfahrens durch unmittelbare Anwendung des Gesetzesprogramms zustandekommen (Steuerrecht, Besoldungsrecht, Förderungswesen etc.) (35). Dagegen ist die deontische Operation des Justizsyllogismus nur ein Ausführungsprogramm des umfassenden Entscheidungsprozesses; die eigentliche Entscheidungsaufgabe liegt in der Definition des Problems und der Schließung offener Beschränkungen. Die Verhaltensnormen der Verfahrensordnungen haben im allgemeinen keine heuristische Kraft, sondern sind organisatorischer Natur. Dagegen sind die Beweislastvorschriften technisch als Entscheidungsregeln aufzufassen, die (als Alternative zum *non-liquet*) Entscheidungen bei Ungewißheit erlauben.

Die Fragen, die im Justizverfahren zu lösen sind, zählen in der Regel zum Typus der schlecht-definierten und nicht-operationalen Entscheidungsaufgaben mit großen Definitionsspielräumen. Da die Entscheidungsträger im politischen System des bürgerlichen Rechtsstaats als weisungsungebundene Gesetzesvollziehung organisiert sind, hängt die Programmstruktur wesentlich von der determinierenden Qualität der anzuwendenden Gesetze ab. Im allgemeinen haben aber die gesetzlichen Parameter nur den Charakter von Metaprogrammen, die der Generierung von Unter- und Objektprogrammen dienen. Die Entwicklung dieser Feinprogramme ist Aufgabe der Rechtsdogmatik als praktischer Jurisprudenz. Aber eine gewisse rabulistische Grundtendenz der Rechtswissenschaft als einer Lehre, die Beliebiges begründbar macht (36), Kommunikationsschwierigkeiten mit Rechtspraxis und Rechtsstab sowie der allgemeine Abbau der bürgerlichen Gesetzlichkeit in der Spätphase des Kapitalismus lassen immer mehr Programmlücken offen, in die in steigendem Maße irrationale und dezisionistische Momente einfließen. Damit treten persönliche Merkmale der Entscheidungssubjekte in den Vordergrund, wie sie in der Richtersoziologie behandelt werden (37). Die *Sozialisation* der Aktoren wird für die Entscheidungstheorie in dem Maße relevant, in dem spezielle Entscheidungsverfahren und heuristische Programme fehlen. Der Suchvorgang tastet in diesen Fällen die im Langzeitgedächtnis gespeicherten Informationen nach schichtspezifischen und klassengebundenen Begriffen, Werten und Verhaltensmustern ab, um daraus ein Ersatzprogramm zu entwickeln (38).

5. *Der Entscheidungsprozeß als soziales System*

Die Kombination von Entscheidungstheorie und Organisationstheorie ermöglicht eine Auflösung des individualpsychologischen Reduktionismus, zu dem die kognitive Theorie tendiert. Sie erlaubt es, Entscheidungsprozesse mit mehr als nur einem Aktor darzustellen, mit anderen Worten, Entscheiden als soziales System aufzufassen. In diesem Sinn stellt sich auch das Justizverfahren als soziales und organisiertes System dar, in dem die Entscheidungsaufgabe nicht nur in Teilschritte, sondern auch auf verschiedene Aktoren nach festgelegten Regeln aufgeteilt wird. Das soziale Entscheidungssystem ist charakterisiert durch eine Mehrzahl von Entscheidungsträgern mit Entscheidungsinterdependenz (39). Die kombinierte Anstrengung von Organisations- und Entscheidungstheorie ist auf die

Erforschung der Strukturen dieses sozialen Systems gerichtet, also auf die invarianten Relationen zwischen den aktiven Elementen des Systems.
Die Ausprägung des Relationennetzes hängt entscheidend vom kooperativen oder nonkooperativen Charakter des Systems ab. In den verschiedenen Justizverfahren, insbesondere in dem als prototypisch bezeichneten Zivilprozeß, herrscht der nonkooperative Entscheidungstyp vor. Die Aktoren des Systems verfügen über kein technologisches System, mit welchem sie die Handlungsvariablen der interagierenden Umwelt zuverlässig bestimmen könnten; sie entscheiden, wie *Gäfgen* (40) sagt, unter „rationaler Indeterminiertheit". In den rechtlich ausgestatteten Verfahren vor Gerichten gilt dies allerdings nur mit Einschränkungen. Zum einen existieren auch im kontradiktorisch strukturierten Zivilprozeß partiell Elemente der Kooperation. Zwar müßte eine direkte Anwendung des Null-Summen-Paradigmas, wonach ein Aktor nur gewinnen kann, was der andere verliert, streng kompetitive Situationen ergeben und damit auch beschränkte Kooperationen ausschließen. Aber Rechtsunsicherheit, Zeitdruck und Kostenrisiko liefern unter Umständen integrative Bewertungskriterien, die etwa einen Vergleich oder andere Formen der prozessualen Kooperation als rationale Lösung erscheinen lassen. Zum andern sind die möglichen Handlungsvariablen der interdependenten Aktoren durch die verhaltensnormierende Funktion der Prozeßvorschriften stark eingeengt. Verfahrensnormen sollen im Entscheidungssystem eine möglichst zuverlässige Orientierung ermöglichen; das ist ihre eigentliche, ihre „Grundfunktion" (41). Überhaupt offenbart die Anwendung der nonkooperativen Spieltheorie, die üblicherweise als Modell von Entscheidungen unter rationaler Indeterminiertheit verwendet wird, deutliche Schwächen. Die unbefriedigenden Resultate spieltheoretischer Modellierungsversuche sind häufig auf eine unvermittelte Anwendung zurückzuführen, die den Grundsatz mißachtet, daß die spieltheoretisch formulierten Regeln nur im dialektischen Zusammenhang mit den Handlungen zu verstehen sind, in denen sie realisiert werden. Außerdem ist das gesellschaftliche Anwendungsfeld mit den explizit formulierten Voraussetzungen der Spieltheorie zu vergleichen. Eine Voraussetzung für die erfolgreiche Verwendung von Modellen der Spieltheorie ist die Möglichkeit der Strategienbildung. Eine Strategie ist ein vollständiger Verhaltensplan, durch den der Spieler für jede im jeweiligen Spiel vorkommende Situation eine bestimmte Entscheidung festlegt (42). Eine solche strategische Entscheidung läuft auf ein Verfahrensprogramm hinaus, das die Entscheidungssequenzen eines Aktors zur Gänze steuert. Die Entwicklung derartiger Programme kann man zwar auch auf dem Gebiet justizförmiger Entscheidungsklassen als Aufgabe entscheidungstheoretischer Forschungen bezeichnen, aber man darf keinesfalls von ihrem Vorhandensein ausgehen. Die bekannten prozessualen Verhaltensmöglichkeiten der Zermürbung, des Hinhaltens, der Verschleppung, der sukzessiven Information usw. stehen dagegen durchwegs auf einer taktischen Stufe.
Der gewichtigste Einwand gegen eine unvermittelte spieltheoretische Explikation des sozialen Entscheidungssystems betrifft die Kontingenz der Situationen und die Konstanz der Entscheidungsprämissen. Im Gegensatz zu den spieltheoretischen Annahmen müssen die Interaktionssituationen im Justizverfahren nicht notwendig als „Zufallssituationen" *(chance situations)*, sondern auch als „Geschicklichkeitssituationen" *(skill situations)* (43), genauer gesagt, als Verhandlungssituationen bezeichnet werden. Der Aktor bzw. sein professioneller Vertreter kann grundsätzlich damit rechnen, daß der Ausgang der einzelnen Entscheidungs-

situationen und des Entscheidungsprozesses überhaupt von seinem persönlichen Einsatz und seinen Fähigkeiten abhängt. Damit wird die ganze Skala manipulativer Techniken relevant, mit deren Hilfe die Aktoren gegenseitig ihre Entscheidungsprämissen beeinflussen können (44).

6. Die praktische Relevanz der Entscheidungstheorie

Die Verwendung der Entscheidungstheorie dient einem praktischen Ziel, nämlich der Objektivierung und Optimierung von problemlösendem Verhalten. Im Gegensatz zur Verhaltensforschung oder zur empirischen Soziologie erschöpft sie sich nicht in einer theoretischen Abbildung von Aktionsformen, sondern vermittelt praktische Anleitungen zu rationalem Handeln. Als praktische Disziplin umfaßt die Entscheidungstheorie deskriptive und normative Elemente. Dieser Unterschied läßt sich am besten anhand der Problembereiche Simulation und künstliche Intelligenz demonstrieren (45). Theorien über problemlösendes Verhalten können in verschiedener Absicht aufgestellt werden: einmal zur Entwicklung eines Computerprogramms, das reales Verhalten simuliert. Das Simulationsprogramm dient der Verifikation von Hypothesen über heuristische Entscheidungsmethoden. Man spricht hier von deskriptiven Programmen. Die theoretischen Konstrukte können andererseits als Vorbereitung eines Programms mit künstlicher Intelligenz aufgefaßt werden, das Probleme „besser" löst als natürliche Systeme. Diese Programme haben dann normativen Charakter. In der gesellschaftlichen Praxis greifen beide Elemente ständig ineinander. Es ist die Aufgabe einer Soziologie der Mensch-Maschine-Symbiose (46) über diesen Zusammenhang wissenschaftliche Aussagen zu liefern, die erst einen geplanten Einsatz von Entscheidungstechnologien gestatten. Zu den allgemeinen Beschränkungen des menschlichen Informationsverarbeitungsapparats (begrenzte Verarbeitungs- und Speicherkapazität, serielle Organisation, hohe Reaktivität und Ermüdbarkeit, Störanfälligkeit etc.) treten im Bereich des gerichtlichen Entscheidungsprozesses spezielle Mängel, etwa der verwendeten Programme, die teilweise einen anarchischen und unbewußten Charakter besitzen, Kommunikationsstörungen, fehlende Rückkopplungen, mangelhafte Zeitplanung usw. Im Gegensatz zur Rechtsdogmatik, die sich ebenfalls als praktische und normative Disziplin versteht, bezieht sich die Entscheidungstheorie sowohl auf die Analyse des tatsächlichen Entscheidungsverlaufs wie auch auf die Möglichkeiten seiner Verbesserung. Realistischerweise muß hinzugefügt werden, daß das Operationsfeld der Entscheidungstheorie als technisches Instrument der Rationalisierung äußerst beschränkt ist, solange die Strukturen einer Gesellschaftsformation die Sollwerte diktieren, die selbst keiner bewußten Gestaltung zugänglich und damit grundsätzlich nicht rationalisierbar ist. Die Möglichkeiten der Verbesserung des justizförmigen Entscheidungsverhaltens können unter diesen restriktiven Bedingungen nur technischer und punktueller Natur sein. Es geht einmal um die Entlastung vom Routineaufwand, aus dem auch die Justizarbeit zum großen Teil besteht. Dann wäre die Ausbildung des Justizpersonals stärker auf die Beschaffung der faktischen Prämissen auszurichten, wie es auch von *Lautmann* (47) gefordert wird. Schließlich muß die Erarbeitung und Verwendung eines objektiven Kalküls angestrebt werden, das die eindeutige Ableitung von Entscheidungen garantiert und den Entscheidungsprozeß transparent macht. Alle diese pragmatischen Zielsetzungen erfordern aber eine Fülle von Einzeluntersuchungen (48), die durch eine solche allgemeine Konzeption nur angeregt werden können.

Summary

1. Dicision theory is well suited to fill in gaps and to remedy failures of vision in traditional legal scholarship as well as in empirical legal sociology. This is because decision theory is synoptically conceived, and can at the same time take into account descriptive and prescriptive premises.
2. Decision theory is usable only in its broader form, as a theory of the processing of cognitions and information. To do so it must relinquish mathematical modeling, in favor of heuristic techniques which adapt decision tasks to given limitations.
3. Since legal problems as a rule are badly defined and non-operationalized, the true decision consists of defining the problem and closing open restraints. Data processing of this type has objective structure, which applies also to judicial decision processes. These latter are special only in their legitimation, that is, the solution hypotheses which are used to close the system must be taken from the official system of norms.
4. Decision behavior can scientifically be explained only through an algorithm or a heuristic program, by which it is guided. In place of objective and official programs, which are lacking, unofficial programs enter in, which proceed out of the fact that the decision-maker is recruited and socialized in a class-specific way.
5. Judicial decision process must be explained as a social system which presides over a formal organization. This characteristic explains the deviations (with regard to judicial process) over against the gametheoretical model of non-cooperation.
6. Decision theoretical models contain descriptive and normative elements which together make up the practical relevance of decision theory. The general purpose of decision theory, namely objectivization and optimization of decision behavior, can lead, in the system of justice, to the introduction of technical and other reforms.

Anmerkungen

1 Vgl. J.J. Hagen: Soziologie und Jurisprudenz. Zur Dialektik von Gesellschaft und Recht, München 1973, S. 31 ff.

2 E. Albrecht: Theoretische Fragen der Entwicklung der Leitungswissenschaft, DZfPh. 1973, S. 435.

3 Vgl. dazu G. Gäfgen: Theorie der wirtschaftlichen Entscheidung. Untersuchungen zur Logik und ökonomischen Bedeutung des rationalen Handelns, Tübingen 1968^2, S. 43 ff.

4 Vgl. B.J. Biddle: Roles, Goals, and Value Structures in Organizations, in: W.W. Cooper/H.J. Leavitt/M.W. Shelly (ed.): New Perspectives in Organization Research, New York – London – Sydney 1964, S. 150 ff.

5 Vgl. J.J. Hagen: Elemente einer allgemeinen Prozeßlehre. Ein Beitrag zur allgemeinen Verfahrenstheorie, Freiburg 1972, S. 72 ff.

6 Vgl. W. Niese: Doppelfunktionelle Prozeßhandlungen. Ein Beitrag zur allgemeinen Prozeßrechtslehre, Göttingen 1950; J.J. Hagen: Hauptprobleme des österreichischen Bestandverfahrens, München – Salzburg 1971, S. 12 f.; und ders.: Elemente einer allgemeinen Prozeßlehre, S. 122 ff.

7 Vgl. G. Klaus: Kybernetik und Gesellschaft, Berlin 1973[3], S. 131 ff.

8 So A. Etzioni: Soziologie der Organisationen, München 1971[3], S. 52.

9 E. Kosiol: Organisation der Unternehmung, Wiesbaden 1962, S. 28.

10 Vgl. J.J. Hagen: Elemente einer allgemeinen Prozeßlehre, S. 98 f., 139 ff.

11 Vgl. dazu E.S. Corwin: The Constitution and What it Means Today, Pinceton/N.J. 1954[11], und R. Eells: The Government of Corporations, Glencoe/Ill. 1962.

12 Vgl. J.J. Hagen: Fragen zur normativen Automation, DSWR 1973, S. 20.

13 Vgl. H. Wagner/K. Haag: Die moderne Logik in der Rechtswissenschaft, Bad Homburg – Berlin – Zürich 1970, und J.J. Hagen: Soziologie und Jurisprudenz, S. 157 ff.

14 So etwa H. Schelsky: Soziologiekritische Bemerkungen zu gewissen Tendenzen von Rechtssoziologen, in: M. Rehbinder/H. Schelsky (Hrsg.): Zur Effektivität des Rechts, Jahrbuch für Rechtssoziologie und Rechtstheorie, Bd. III, Düsseldorf 1972, S. 605.

15 Vgl. dazu W. Kirsch: Entscheidungsprozesse, Bd. I: Verhaltenswissenschaftliche Ansätze der Entscheidungstheorie, Wiesbaden 1970, S. 61 ff.

16 Vgl. dazu L. Reisinger: Automatisierte Normenanalyse und Normanwendung, Berlin 1972, S. 9 ff.; und J.J. Hagen: Fragen zur normativen Automation, S. 18 f.

17 Vgl. G. Klaus: Kybernetik und Erkenntnistheorie, Berlin 1972[4], S. 40 f.

18 Vgl. dazu G. Gäfgen: Theorie der wirtschaftlichen Entscheidung, S. 129 ff.

19 Vgl. A. Newell/H.A. Simon: Memory and Process in Concept Formation, in: B. Kleinmuntz (ed.): Concepts and the Structure of Memory, New York – London – Sydney 1967, S. 241 ff.

20 Vgl. J.J. Hagen: Elemente einer allgemeinen Prozeßlehre, S. 74 f.

21 Vgl. W.R. Reitman: Cognition and Thought. An Information Processing Approach, New York – London – Sydney 1965, S. 126.

22 W.R. Reitman: Heuristic Decision Procedures, Open Constraints, and the Structure of Ill-Defined Problems, in: M.W. Shelly/G.L. Bryan (ed.): Human Judgements and Optimality, New York – London – Sydney 1964, S. 282 ff.

23 W.R. Reitman, a.a.O., S. 293.

24 Vgl. W. Kirsch: Entscheidungsprozesse, Bd. II: Informationsverarbeitungstheorie des Entscheidungsverhaltens, Wiesbaden 1971, S. 148 f.

25 Vgl. dazu J.J. Hagen: Die Vorbereitung der Streitverhandlung. Ein Beitrag zur Aktivierung des Zivilprozesses, JBl 1970, S. 125; vgl. weiters K.-H. Beyer: Die Verfahrenskonzeption in Zivilsachen, NJ 1973, S. 383 ff.

26 Vgl. G. Klaus: Sprache der Politik, Berlin 1971, S. 84 ff.

27 Vgl. R. Leicht: Von der Hermeneutik-Rezeption zur Sinnkritik in der Rechtstheorie, in: A. Kaufmann (Hrsg.): Rechtstheorie. Ansätze zu einem kritischen Rechtsverständnis, Karlsruhe 1971, S. 73.

28 Justiz – die stille Gewalt. Teilnehmende Beobachtung und entscheidungssoziologische Analyse, Frankfurt/M 1972, S. 162.

29 G. Katona: Psychological Analysis of Economic Behavior, New York 1951, S. 64 ff.

30 H.A. Simon: The Shape of Automation for Men and Management, New York 1965, S. 58 ff.

31 Vgl. dazu H.K. Klein: Heuristische Entscheidungsmodelle. Neue Techniken des Programmierens und Entscheidens für das Management, Wiesbaden 1971, S. 39 ff.

32 H.K. Klein, a.a.O., S. 42.

33 Vgl. A. Newell/J.C. Shaw/H.A. Simon: The Processes of Creative Thinking, in: H.E. Gruber/G. Terell/M. Wertheimer (ed.): Contemporary Approaches to Creative Thinking, New York 1962, S. 78; E.A. Feigenbaum/J. Feldman: Computers and Thought, New York - San Francisco – Toronto – London - Sydney 1963, S. 6.

34 E.A. Feigenbaum/J. Feldman, a.a.O.

35 Vgl. H.J. Kerkau: Automatische Datenverarbeitung (ADV) – Kybernetik in Rechtswissenschaft und Praxis, Berlin 1970, S. 32 ff.; J.J. Hagen: Fragen zur normativen Automation, S. 20.

36 Vgl. J.J. Hagen: Soziologie und Jurisprudenz, S. 24 ff.

37 Dazu zusammenfassend E. Dingeldey: Unpolitische Justiz? Frankfurt/M 1971, S. 71 ff.

38 Vgl. dazu E.E. Jones/J.B. Gerard: Foundations of Social Psychology, New York – London – Sydney 1967, S. 76 ff.; I.S. Kon: Soziologie der Persönlichkeit, Köln 1971, S. 145 ff.

39 Vgl. W. Kirsch: Entscheidungsprozesse, Bd. III: Entscheidungen in Organisationen, Wiesbaden 1971, S. 61 ff.

40 Theorie der wirtschaftlichen Entscheidung, S. 176 ff.

41 J.J. Hagen: Elemente einer allgemeinen Prozeßlehre, S. 29 f.

42 Vgl. E. Burger: Einführung in die Theorie der Spiele, Berlin 1966², S. 10 f.

43 Vgl. N. Kogan/M.A. Wallach: Risk Taking, New York – Chicago – San Francisco – Toronto – London 1964, S. 7.

44 Vgl. dazu E.E. Jones/J.B. Gerard: Foundations of Social Psychology, New York – London S. 54 ff, 66 ff.

45 Vgl. dazu H.K. Klein: Heuristische Entscheidungsmodelle, S. 42 ff.

46 Vgl. dazu G. Klaus: Kybernetik und Gesellschaft, Berlin 1973³, S. 168 ff.

47 Justiz – die stille Gewalt, S. 49 ff.

48 Als erwähnenswertes Beispiel einer solchen Einzeluntersuchung kann etwa gelten K. Haag: Rationale Strafzumessung. Ein entscheidungstheoretisches Modell der strafrichterlichen Entscheidung, Köln – Berlin – Bonn – München 1970.

Herbert Jacob

Criminal Courts as Organizational Phenomena*

The study of courts – especially American courts – has attracted scholars from many disciplines in recent years. Lawyers, anthropologists, sociologists, and political scientists each bring their own perspective to bear and apply their own paradigms. Some scholars have analyzed trial courts chiefly in terms of legal phenomena and characteristics; they focus on the judge as decisionmaker and on the formal procedures of trial courts (1)**. As more behaviorally oriented researchers have taken an interest in courts, however, there has been a decided shift from the focus on formal legal procedures to the decision-making process. Attention has been directed to the whole range of decisions made in trial courts, and those who produce them. This has produced considerable research on social psychological traits of judges, and the sociology and psychology of juries (2).

More recently, scholars have emphasized that decision-making in trial courts is a group process even when juries are not involved and even if the judge sits alone. What masquerades as the judge's decision in a criminal case is really the outcome of bargaining between defense counsel and prosecutor, with occasional participation by the judge. Bargaining has replaced judicial decision-making as the dominant paradigm of trial court activity in the United States, at least for the criminal courts. Instead of focusing on the judge alone, scholars now study interactions of all those participating in the system of criminal justice (3).

At the same time, many observers claim that courts are mismanaged and inefficient; they view plea bargaining as one symptom of the breakdown of the adversary system. With management principles in mind, they bring organizational perspectives to bear on the analysis of courtroom activities. Exponents of the organizational perspective include both scholars trying to systematize observations of those who have perceived courtroom activity in social-psychological terms (4). and reformers who wish to rationalize the flow of business through the courts. In the following pages, I shall attempt to spell out some features of an organizational perspective for criminal trial courts. The perspective derives in part from observations of criminal courts in Baltimore, Chicago, and Detroit. Theory and illustrations are thus somewhat culture bound; but they may serve to stimulate further comparisons.

Judicial behavior in the criminal courts is an organizational phenomenon. While it is true that trial courts have a single judge (in contrast to multi-judge appellate

* This research was supported by a grant from the National Science Foundation (Grant Number 33965) to the author and to Professor James Eisenstein. This paper was completed while the author was a Fellow at the Center for Advanced Study in the Behavioral Sciences. However, responsibility for the views stated in this paper rests solely with the author.

** Notes on pages 171 f.

courts), criminal court judges do not act by themselves. Their decisions are the collective product of a courtroom team. The decision is the judge's only in the sense that it is announced and legitimized by him.

The members of the courtroom organization are the judge, prosecuting attorneys, defense counsel, clerks and bailiffs. They constitute a small organization – a small group, as it were, or, as some might have it, a small production unit. This small organization operates with considerable permanency and autonomy. As an organization, it has those traits which all organizations share: structure, common goals, and standardized ways of working on its raw materials to achieve those goals (5).

The structure of courtroom organizations is well defined; but it is not as hierachical as that of most organizations. Nominally, the judge is in charge, but he does not possess the usual supervisory powers of the head of a bureau. Rather, he is the most prestigious member of the courtroom team and makes final decisions on the disposition of cases. He does not, however, control the resources of the courtroom organization; he does not decide on job assignments and pay of the other members of the organization; and most of the work of these others goes on without his direct supervision. Yet all other members of the organization defer to the judge when he makes his wishes expressly known.

The basic relationship in the courtroom organization is one of collaboration, rather than hierarchy. This may strike an observer as ironic, since the court is best known as the site of adversary proceedings where conflict, rather than collaboration, occurs. Conflict certainly occurs; but it is carefully staged and controlled. It is an overlay on top of the more fundamental collaborative structure which is the foundation of the courtroom organization (6).

Evidence of this phenomena can be seen any day in court when a trial is scheduled to take place. Before the trial commences, the courtroom team engages in mutual banter and disposes of other business with mutual exchanges of favors and accommodations. During recesses, all are likely to withdraw to the judge's chambers to dispose of further business and to socialize together over a cup of coffee. Once the trial has commenced, however, each member of the team withdraws to his appointed place in the courtroom and plays his adversarial role, as if their previous collaborative relationships had not existed.

The courtroom organization is also marked by a high degree of specialization. Each member of the organization has a particular role; there is no exchange of roles among major participants, even though they have common experiences and training. This is partly because of the fact that most of the major participants represent another organization in the court. For instance, the defense counsel cannot take the part of the prosecutor, because prosecutors are part of the state's attorney's office. Over the course of several years, an individual lawyer may associate first with the state's attorney's office, then with the public defender's office; later he may become a judge. But he will be part of different courtroom organizations during this career; he will not play these various roles in the same courtroom organization. While a part of one organization, he will play one role only.

This specialization creates a high degree of stability in the organization. It permits each member of the team to become adept at the work routines associated with his role; and it allows the team to develop stable expectations about the actions of other members of the courtroom organization. Thus the routine business of the courtroom proceeds in a quite informal fashion, with many "understandings" that are never formally recorded, but which nevertheless lubricate much of the normal work of the court. In Chicago, for instance, it is not unusual for the public defender to attend plea conferences for defendants who are represented by private counsel; he may even indicate his opinion to the lawyers who are actively developing the bargain. In this way, he learns what kinds of deals private counsel are getting for their clients; he is able thus to gauge his own activities. He also lets others know what he might expect to obtain in a similar situation. Private counsel also attend conferences in which the Public Defender's clients are being discussed. The net result is a higher degree of uniformity in the outcome of such conferences, than would be the case if they were held among discrete participants who rarely witnessed any conferences other than their own.

The courtroom organizations also enjoy considerable staff support. Each courtroom is staffed by one or more clerks, a court stenographer, and several bailiffs. The clerks keep official records and in many instances manage the flow of cases. It is not unusual to see the clerk establish the order in which cases are called; in Chicago private attorneys often slip money to the clerks, in order to get their cases called early in courtrooms which are particularly crowded. This is, of course, illegal; but it is common practice nonetheless. The court reporter keeps a stenographic record of all formal proceedings. The bailiffs maintain order, control the flow of prisoners from the bullpen to the courtroom and back, and run whatever errands the judge or other personnel require. These staff members have no role in the disposition of cases; they serve only to facilitate the work of other members of the courtroom team. They are usually as numerous as the "line" workers in the courtroom and in many instances they are more numerous. In that sense, courtroom organizations are generously staffed.

Note that we have been speaking of a *courtroom* organization; the basic unit is the courtroom, not the court system. The courtroom is the work unit, the unit in which interactions occur, and the unit which produces an identifiable project. The court *system* is an intellectual construct, which may be useful for some purposes; but it is the courtroom that is the behavioral unit. The walls which enclose a courtroom isolate it from other courtrooms in a remarkably effective manner; there is little communication between one courtroom and another. The doors to the courtroom are almost always closed; there is almost no lateral communication between courtrooms. When court is in session, members of one courtroom team do not have a chance to speak with those of another. There are not even any regular lunch hours, in the cities of our study, where members of various teams can communicate informally. There is hierarchical supervision of individual role-players, but not of the team; members of the courtroom team belong to different parent hierarchies, and their nominal superiors almost never meet. Further, the various courtroom organizations systematically obscure the information on which such hierarchical supervision might be based.

The members of the courtroom team are immersed in the world of the law. The judge, prosecutor, and defense counsel are lawyers, products of formal legal education. Many have had years of experience in the criminal courts. This experience yields a rich lode of anecdotes reflecting a culture and a commitment to the norms that dominate the administration of criminal law. The non-lawyers who staff the courtrooms share in the culture. The clerks and bailiffs are non-professionals, usually from a working class rather than a middle class backround, with much less formal education than the lawyers around them. But they have also been immersed in the courtroom culture for a long time; they share experiances and folklore – if not the formal training – of the lawyers.

Members of courtroom organizations thus have something of a common occupational background. When they enter a courtroom organization, they already speak the technical language which sets the courtroom apart from most other work settings. They also are likely to share certain perspectives on their work and work surroundings – such as a belief in the guilt of defendants who appear in court, a cynicism about human behavior, a commitment (somewhat uneasy) to prescribed procedure, and an understanding of what "really goes on" in the courtroom. This means they understand how such devices as continuances and motions are used as tactics of delay, how the threat of a jury trial increases uncertainty, and how members of the team exchange information as part of their common striving for a reasonable disposition of cases. New members join as old ones die, transfer, or resign; but at any given time, most members are veterans; and most members of the courtroom organization are well versed in some aspects of the courtroom world before they become participants. The organization itself will have to commit few resources to formal training or socialization.

Another characteristic which sets the courtroom team apart from other organizations is that most of its members – and in some instances all of them – belong to other work organizations and must divide their allegiance between the courtroom and other organization. The prosecutor is part of the State's Attorneys Office; the defense counsel may be on the staff of the Public Defender's Office or a partner in a law firm; the judge is part of a larger court system; the clerk is part of the Clerk's Office; the bailiff probably belongs to the Sheriff's Department. Although each belongs to these other work organizations, most of them spend almost their entire workday in the courtroom, interacting with each other rather than with other members of their own occupational group. They are paid by their parent organization, but are not supervised closely by it. Their workload, working conditions, and their product result from their courtroom interactions rather than from directives of their parent organization. Their assignment to a particular courtroom is usually a matter of negotiation between the courtroom team and the parent organization. But initial recruitment is the responsibility of the parent organization and the pool from which a courtroom can draw is limited by the recruitment efforts of the parent organizations.

The dual allegiance of members of the courtroom organization means that to some extent each member is governed by norms peculiar to himself and not common to other members of the courtroom team. The degree to which this is true varies. Some prosecutors are more bound to the regulations of their office in negotiating pleas than others; the clerk and bailiff may be bound less by their own "professional" rules than by the courtroom's norms – in comparison with the prosecutor. Some defense counsel – especially those who are Public Defenders – are more bound to a parent organization than others. Private attorneys have commitments to their law firms and to norms of the legal profession; these may conflict with norms of the courtroom in which they happen to be operating. Consequently, the courtroom organization – more than most other organizations – must strive to reconcile or overcome competing orientations of its members. It is common for work organizations to command only a fraction of their member's allegiance; but they do usually command most of the allegiance that relates to employment. But courts must share work-orientations with other organizations.

Private defense counsel occupy a special position in the courtroom organization. Unlike other participants, they are not permanently assigned to the courtroom. They move from courtroom to courtroom and take part, then, in many "organizations". In Chicago, however, they attempt to cluster their workload in a handful of courtrooms, in part to minimize the strain of multi-organizational membership. Their anomalous position tends to make them more marginal members of the courtroom team than others. Defense counsel who are not "regulars" in the cortroom are still more peripheral. Many conflicts which occur in court come about because of the intrusion of these marginal members, into a routine established by others. Although it draws its members from other organizations, the courtroom has a set of identifiable goals which bind its members together in common enterprises. Following common usage among organizational analysts. we may distinguish between "production" goals (oriented toward producing the services demanded by the court's clientele) and "internal" goals, oriented toward maintenance of the organization itself (7).

Before examining the "production" goals, however, it is well to identify the court's clientele. Only in a vague sense is it the general public; for the most part, the public is unaware and uninterested in courtroom activities. The court has far more salient clients, which it must constantly strive to satisfy. The most significant of these are the State's Attorney and his staff, the police, the press, and the officials of the prison system. Each of these makes demands on the courts, although of varying kinds and degree.

The State's Attorney's office is concerned with the courts' output because the District Attorney himself is judged by that output and because he may to some degree control the inflow of cases. If the output of the courts is unsatisfactory to him, the District Attorney may attempt to pressure courtroom organizations to alter their outputs. In Chicago, a recent State's Attorney, Edward Hanrahan, placed the names of judges who gave lenient sentences on his bulletin board or his office door together with caustic comments. One of the principal subjects for workday gossip was which judge (and courtroom organization) was on the board that week. It was also the cause of considerable anxiety within the various courts. This kind of attention by Hanrahan invited press inquiries, threats of transfers, and posed other dangers to organizational stability.

The police department also has an interest in the courts' output although its concern is less immediate. The police focus on courtroom decisions which affect their own operations – such as the scheduling of cases requiring the presence of policemen, the release of defendants, the outcome of cases in which police violence is part of the charge. Police are less interested in other courtroom activity because police departments do not judge themselves by the ultimate fate of the persons they arrest. Police morale or attitudes may be affected if too many arrested people go free; but for the most part, police interest in cases ceases with an arrest, since that clears the crime as far as police statistics are concerned.

A third major client of the criminal courts is the press. The press has a more limited interest than the State's Attorney. Its concern is focused almost exclusively on major trials which may produce headlines and sell newsstand copies. Reporters typically make the rounds of the various courtrooms and ask the clerk or some other member of the organization whether anything interesting has happened during the day or is about to happen. This practice gives the courtroom organization the power to hide embarrassing incidents by simply not disclosing them to the reporter. In addition, the press occasionally spotlights "breakdowns" in the administration of criminal justice; courtroom organizations are keenly sensitive about becoming the object of such attention. The courtroom organization enjoys obscurity and attempts to satisfy its press clientele with only those spectacular cases which will insure favorable or harmless publicity, while its everyday operations remain inviolate.

The fourth specific clientele group consists of officials of the prison system. They are affected by court decisions to send convicted defendants to prison and must adapt themselves to the sentencing decisions of judges. Except in times of crisis – during waves of prison disorders and when the prisons are so overcrowded that they cannot accept additional inmates (as recently happened in Florida) – the demands of the prison system remain modest. Statutory constraints on judicial sentences affect the demands of the prison system. That system does have some interest in uniformity of sentencing.

The external goal of the courtroom organization is to satisfy each of these clientele groups in disposition of cases. Enough cases must be handled to make the record of the State's Attorney look respectable; and there must be enough convictions to show that he is in vigorous pursuit of the criminal. For the police, the same goals serve to some degree; police are also much concerned with the scheduling of cases. For the press, the courts must produce their disposition rate in a way which makes it appear legitimate to the general public. Thus there must not only be guilty pleas but jury trials, displaying the adversarial process at work for the benefit of the reading public. For prison officials, sentences must display some uniformity; and the flow of prisoners must not exceed the capacity of the prisons.

In addition to these "production" or externally oriented goals, courtroom organizations have a number of internally oriented, system maintenance goals. These are goals directed toward maintaining a flow of material and symbolic resources which will permit the courtroom organization to persist. Internal goals are closely linked, for the most part, to external goals. If clientele groups are satisfied, the courtroom organization's search for resources will be easier. However, some internal goals, and the means of attaining them, are not so closely linked to attainment of external goals.

One of these internal goals is minimization of uncertainty. It is highly desired because it helps maintain the stability and cohesiveness of the courtroom organization, and contributes substantially to the productiveness of the organization. As certainty increases. the organization can dispose of its caseload with less effort. The aversion to jury trials is a product of the desire to avoid uncertainty. Defense attorneys who routinely threaten a jury trial are disliked by other members of the organization; courtroom regulars rarely use this tactic, because, as regulars, they are closely integrated members of the organization and therefore share the goal of avoiding uncertainty. Jury trials are more likely to be demanded by peripheral members of the courtroom organization or by outsiders, except in those unusual cases where they appear inevitable because of the characteristics of the case, and where they serve the conflicting goal of providing the press with dramatic news.

The aversion to jury trials rests on the unpredictability of jury verdicts. Even the most experienced trial attorney sweats out the jury's deliberations, and afterwards professes ignorance of how the jury reached its verdict. Bench trials breed uncertainty to a lesser extent. The judge is a member of the courtroom organization and his proclivities are well known to other members. However, other uncertainties cannot be avoided in a bench trial. The behavior of witnesses, and the testimony they give, are always somewhat unpredictable. Even when witnesses have been extensively interviewed before the trials, attorneys cannot be sure about their testimony, or their demeanor, or the impression they will leave with the judge. That uncertainty is increased by the fact that witnesses are seldom thoroughly interviewed before a routine bench trial; much of the direct examination and all of the cross examination is often a freeform "fishing expedition".

The most direct way to reduce uncertainty is to control the outcome of cases through negotiation. In negotiation, conviction is a foregone conclusion and the sentencing outcome is subject to control. The parties deal with each other; they control the amount of information that will flow to the outside world; they discuss and weigh alternative outcomes before a decision is reached. They avoid outcomes which threaten working relationships within the organization; and each member of the organization can be provided symbolic rewards, which strengthen his allegiance to the organization. Disruptive elements of a case outcome are minimized.

A second internal goal is to minimize investment in single cases so that the entire caseload can be handled by the organization without disruption. In the short run – and possibly in the long run – the organization cannot expect substantial additions to staff or resources, or substantial reductions in its workload. Again, negotiations rather than trials are economical in time, staff, and money. Careful screening of cases also serves economy. Trials require great preparation and much courtroom time. A typical case can be disposed of through negotiation with an investment of less than an hour of courtroom time; a bench trial rarely takes less than two hours; a jury trial normally requires at least two days. Negotiations require little more than reading the files which associates have prepared for the principals; witnesses are usually not interviewed if it is clear that the case will be settled with a plea. Bench trials require some witness preparation and jury trials require elaborate witness preparation, and selection of a jury as well. All members of the courtroom organization recognize that if heavy investment is made in too many cases, their output would decline and their workload increase. It is therefore important for the organization to maximize negotiation and minimize trials.

A third and conflicting – system maintenance goal is to sustain the legitimacy of the output of the organization. The professional training of the principal members of the organization places a high value on procedural regularity and the adversary process. The lawyer members of the organization are formally committed to this process, to protection of the rights of defendants, to the due-process requirements of the Constitution, to the presumption of innocence. But these legal ideals foster uncertainty, and require greater investment per case than the organization can afford. Yet lawyer members of the organization profess allegiance to these values, because their professional peers demand it and because the legitimacy of courtroom outputs, in the eyes of the general public and other outsiders, requires this commitment. The dilemma is partly resolved by elaborate rituals which accompany deviations from the norm of full adversary trials. Guilty pleas and sentencing decisions are announced in rituals which have little relation to the actual events which preceded them. For instance, most guilty pleas are accompanied by a litany which requires the courtroom members to assert that no promises have been made and that the defendant is truly guilty of the offense charged, although the guilty plea in fact does rest on promises, and the charge to which he pleads may have little relationship to the offense actually committed. Occasionally a defendant is confused by these inconsistencies and gives the wrong responses to the litanay. The court then quickly recesses for a few moments while the defense attorney rehearses the litany with his client; when the session resumes, the same questions are asked and the proper responses are put into the public record in order to preserve the legitimacy of the verdict.

Both internal and external goals guide organizational behavior of the courtroom team. The goals are multiple, and sometimes inconsistent; the inconsistency leads to inconsistent verbal behavior and explains actions that would otherwise seem capricious. Courtrooms, like many organizations, are subject to conflicting demands; environments and perceptions change; goals change along with these elements of context and situation.

Organizational goals are not necessarily inconsistent with the professional values of the legally trained members of the courtroom team. The defense counsel's obligation is to *represent* his client to the best of his abilities. If the attorney finds it is in the best interest of the client to negotiate a plea rather than demand a jury trial, he can recommend acceptance of the bargain in good conscience. Likewise, the state's attorney has a responsibility to protect the innocent as well as to prosecute the guilty. He can justify bargaining as a way of reching the appropriate, though not the maximum sentence. Finally, the realities of courtroom organization do not require the judge to abdicate his role as a neutral arbiter; quite to the contrary, the judge may serve as a disinterested third party, a wise mediator and decision-maker, in ways that purely adversarial proceeding might foreclose. Thus the goals of the organization often mesh with the professional values of its chief members; their prior socialization reinforces rather than undermines its operations.

Courtrooms share with other organizations a third characteristic: development of work routines. Such routines are what organizational theorists call organizational technology; they vary widely with the kind of work an organization does. Criminal courts use three techniques of routinization: motions, the staging of hearings, and the negotiation of differences. Each of these techniques has characteristics unique to the legal system; but they also share traits in common with techniques of other organizations.

Filing motions is one of the most common routines in a courtroom. Motions are requests to the judge for a particular decision or for information from the other party. Motions for discovery, for instance, are requests for information that the other party holds: when the defense files such a motion. the prosecution must make some or all of its files available to the defense. A motion to suppress evidence requests the judge to declare that certain evidence has been seized illegally and should therefore not be used in the proceedings. The most common motion is for a continuance; this is a request to the judge to delay disposition of the case until a future date. Such a motion may be filed either by prosecution or defense.

Motions may be made orally or in writing. Some courts require that all motions be made in writing, but such rules are often ignored in practice. Many courtrooms set aside a designated part of the day or week to hear and rule on motions. The motion must be in specified form, indicating what is wanted and what the legal justification for the request is. Many motions are submitted by defense counsel, to convince the defendant that his lawyer is working hard for him, and to preserve rights in case of appeal. The judge rules on most motions on the spot, without further argument. However, sometimes the very outcome of the case hinges on the motion, and a formal hearing is staged before the judge rules upon it. Many cases are routinely dismissed when the prosecution so moves; if the prosecution moves to dismiss, the judge will grant the motion except in very unusual circumstances. Where illegal seizure of evidence is at issue, the outcome of a motion to suppress may well determine the outcome of the case. Without the contested evidence, the prosecution often has insufficient evidence to convict.

Prosecution and defense each submit motions which will promote dispositions favorable to their interests; each will oppose motions which lead to unfavorable results. Judges rule on the motions, deciding whether what the motion requests is authorized by law. Sometimes his decisions are purely ministerial. For instance, in Illinois charges must be disposed of within 120 days after the initial arrest, except when a delay has been requested by the defense. A motion for dismissal must be granted if 120 days have elapsed and the defense never requested a continuance. Other motions, however, may require the exercise of discretion; they turn on facts, or interpretation of events as presented in the courtroom. This is particularly true of motions to suppress evidence. Whether or not evidence was seized illegally may depend on an interpretation of circumstances facing a policeman on the street. The judge can believe the policeman's version, or the defendant's. Perhaps neither is the whole truth; but the judge has no way of gaining insight into the real events.

Hearings are another technique used in the courtroom. The prosecution and defense bring witnesses to testify about events of which they have knowledge. There are many different kinds of hearings, but all follow a highly stylized format. Usually the prosecution presents its witnesses first (because of the presumption of innocence); although in hearings on motions brought by the defense, defense witnesses testify first. Testimony proceeds through question-and-answers. The questions must meet certain rigid criteria. They may not "lead" the witness by suggesting a response. They must be directly relevant to the evidence. They often follow a carefully developed dequence, building a foundation for later testimony by the same witness or by others. Witnesses are required to give relatively direct answers and ordinarily may not testify to things which they did not themselves see or hear. After a witness has answered the questions of the attorney who called him to the stand, the opposing party may ask the witness questions. This is called cross-examination and must also conform to rigid standards. At any point in a hearing, the judge may interpose his own questions. All evidence is taken under oath; the giving of false evidence is a crime which may be severely punished. Witnesses are usually under court order (subpoena) to testify; if they refuse, and do not have strong legal grounds for their refusal (such as their constitutional right to avoid self-incrimination), they may be imprisoned for their failure to testify.

The party seeking a hearing has the responsibility for staging it. This usually means that the prosecution must make certain that its witnesses are present and that it is prepared to produce the evidence sufficient for a conviction. Yet, to a considerable degree, responsibility for staging the hearing is shared with the defense. The defense must also have its witnesses present, must be prepared to challenge the prosecution evidence, and perhaps must present evidence of its own. The judge, although nominal head of the courtroom organization, plays no role in preparation of the hearings. He presides over them; he is supposed to make sure that they follow prescribed form; he often makes decisive rulings at the end of the hearing. But he plays no formal role in the preparation of the hearings.

The skills required for staging hearings are quite different from those required for the making of motions. Motions require a knowledge of the legal requirements for the particular subject of the motion; but many of the motions themselves are so highly stylized that their preparation is now sometimes relegated to a programmed typewriter. Hearings require skill in asking questions, in sequencing testimony, in raising objections to questions asked by the other side, or to legally improper answers; they call for a degree of psychological insight into the emotional state of the witness and of the opposing attorney. For many witnesses, testifying in court is a terrifying experience and an astute lawyer can often shake their story by highlighting apparent inconsistencies or by questioning the motives of the witness. An attorney has a stake in protecting his own witnesses and destroying the credibility of witnesses for the other side. Adversary hearings are, of course, what the public associates with courtrooms and trials.

Negotiation is the third technique typically used by members of the courtroom organization. Every stage of the criminal prosecution process is subject to negotiation. Typically the negotiations are between the two parties to a case; the judge plays no role. Plea bargaining is one of the most significant forms of negotiation; but there are many others. Every morning most courtrooms are the scene of brief negotiations about the scheduling of cases – should one lawyer accede to the other's request for a continuance, or should he object to it? And what day shall the two agree upon for the next court appearance? The convenience of both sides is usually served by mutual agreement upon a date, rather than by letting judge or clerk arbitrarily assign a date. Both sides look at their calendars to see which days are relatively open, and far enough in the future to fulfill the purpose of the delay – e.g., obtaining additional evidence, bringing a witness back, getting payment of a fee, completing another case against the defendant, allowing the attorneys to make trips. The decision to hold a hearing is often the result of breakdown of prior negotiations; the defense has rejected a plea bargain – either tentatively, pending the outcome of an evidentiary hearing, or finally, forcing the case to go to trial. Long run objectives are often in the minds of the negotiators. Parties agree on a particular motion or on a plea bargain within the context of their knowledge that hundreds of other cases will be processed by the courtroom organization in the following weeks and months.

The skills required in negotiation are again different from those used in hearings and motions. Negotiation requires flexibility; it requires insight into the position of the other party; it often involves an element of bluff. Negotiations also require a different kind of knowledge. Legal knowledge sometimes is an valuable weapon in negotiations, since the relative strength of each side may be a vital factor. Knowledge of a judge's preferences and his likely actions are even more essential, because they define, practically speaking, the limits of any bargain that prosecution and defense may reach. While other courtroom techniques are formal and highly stylized, negotiations are very informal. They may occur at any time and at any place; they do not follow a rigid sequence of behaviors. They usually involve no written documents.

The techniques used by the courtroom organization to process its workload have much in common with techniques used by other organizations. It is only their setting and the special language of lawyers which make court operations appear so mysterious.

A courtroom which processes several dozen cases of armed robberies each month has some pretty firm ideas about the characteristics of armed robbery. But the legal tradition and the professional ethics of the principal participants deny the routine character of such cases and promote an official perspective which insists that each case is unique and calls for individual treatment. The participants may speak of "assembly line" justice, but they do not behave like assembly line workers. Even though there is a good deal of routine, the major participants must perform relatively complex operations, and have a great deal of discretion (9). Either prosecutor or defense attorney may initiate some complicated action requiring other people in turn to respond. If the defense submits, for example, a motion that challenges the validity of the arrest, the prosecutor must respond, witnesses must appear, a formal hearing will be held, and the judge will have to rule on the motion. Such motions are common in certain kinds of cases (for instance, concealed weapons cases); but they are not routine or simple. A conscious decision must be made to submit such a motion; the decision is based on calculations involving the likely effect on the outcome. the required investment of time by the initiator, the effect it will have on his client and on potential clients, and his perception of what is appropriate in the organizational context of the courtroom in which he is operating. Likewise, the prosecutor must decide how to handle the case – whether to offer a plea bargain and if so what kind of settlement to suggest. His decision rests on his reading of the particulars of the case – the seriousness of the incident (regardless of the legal label attached to it), his relations with judge and defense attorney in that courtroom, his prior recommendations in analogous cases. the pressures and policies emanating from his parent organization, and his state of preparation, should the case be called for a trial. These considerations are not novel to an experienced prosecutor; but none of them are simple or routine. Similarly, the judge – even when processing a typical guilty plea, or sentencing for a typical crime – has complex, discretionary acts to perform. He may ask more or less the same questions, and accept similar answers, but he need not do so; any deviation from the common ritual will have repercussions for all the other participants. Also, he must take care to build a formal record that can withstand the scrutiny of an appeals court.

The work in the courtroom involves a high degree of judgment. Potential trouble lurks in every case. Serious mistakes may be picked up by the media, or lead to complaints in the parent organizations, or generate rebuke by the appellate courts. Therefore each case is given at least a cursory examination, and the alternative courses which are available to the courtroom organization are explored at some length. A case may get this attention intermittently, over the course of the several weeks or months that it lies on the docket of the trial court. Few cases, however, must or can be treated in a *single* way. Discretion and judgment are always present, in processing cases.

Finally, the techniques utilized in the courtroom involve the members of the courtroom team intensely with one another. Few can be performed by a single member of the team, without collaboration or response. None can do their courtroom work in the isolation of their offices. Most require the attendance (and often the active participation) of other members of the team. The action of one member of the team has unavoidable repercussions for other members of the team; members are forced to interact.

Courtroom techniques structure interactions, just as an assembly line structures interactions among factory workers, or a laboratory structures interactions among research scientists. The various techniques structure interactions in somewhat different ways. The filing of motions requires the least interaction. It requires a certain amount of office staff, probably the staff of the parent organization. In court, it involves the clerk, the two opposing lawyers, and the judge.

At hearings and trials, the prosecutor and defense attorney take opposing roles. During hearings, the two attorneys address each other only formally; most of their interactions are with witnesses and with the judge, not with one another. The judge is placed in the position of a neutral arbiter. Although he may have opinions about the case (lawyers for the parties may be fully aware of these), he must maintain the appearance of open receptivity to facts and ideas. His interactions, too, are highly formal. He usually responds to initiatives from lawyers, rather than initiating interactions himself. In negotiations, few formal rules inhibit interactions. Hearings run to routine, but negotiations vary enormously in content and style. Some are quite adversarial; others are collaborative. In some the defense attorney is aggressive; in others the prosecutor is aggressive. Some are held in the presence of the judge, others occur in his absence. When the judge is present, he may actively promote agreement or simply give his approval to whatever agreement is reached.

Because all three techniques are used in most courtrooms (often in random sequence), courtroom organizations do not have a typical interaction pattern. What is typical of courtroom organizations is that they rapidly shift from one interaction pattern to another. Courtroom members must be flexible; they must be able to shift from one to another type of interaction, in order to accomplish their mission.

Motions, hearings, and negotiations are directed at two functions which criminal courts constantly perform: screening out cases and sanctioning defendants.

Cases flow in to court; and the organization must screen them, separating those to be handled from those which will be ignored. Almost every criminal court in the United States receives more cases than it can handle. The attrition in large city courts is enormous. In Chicago, for instance, the police made 65,682 felony arrests in 1972. But only 3,514 felony indictments were filed, and only 1780 convicted defendants were sent to the state penitentiary (10). Likewise, in suburban Westchester County, New York, the police made 2,718 felony arrests but there were only 347 felony convictions in 1970 (11).

What cases do the courtroom members screen out? The courtroom organization considers some offenses trivial – possession of marijuana, for instance, increasingly falls into this category; and many disorderly conduct arrests are so treated. Other cases involve essentially private disputes, settled between the disputants before the court can handle them; the complainant subsequently withdraws his complaint. In such instances, the complainant may have used arrest and courtroom appearances to force a private settlement. This often occurs when a creditor charges his defaulting debtor with theft, or when an estranged wife wants to be left alone by her former husband. In other instances, the offender compensates the victim in order to escape formal sanctions; his payment persuades the victim to withdraw the compalint. Screening can occur at many stages in the process. Many cases are dropped because the police do not consider them serious enough to pursue; when the police fail to show up at court proceedings, the cases are apt to be dismissed.

Positive decisions to drop prosecution of cases may result from motions submitted by the prosecution (large numbers of cases are dismissed on motions of various sorts); as a result of hearings – for instance, at a preliminary hearing, the judge may find "no probable cause" to hold the defendant – or as a result of negotiations (the defense may convince the prosecution not to proceed further; the case will then be dismissed by motion).

Other cases are screened out as a result of inaction. In Chicago, for instance, it normally takes two to three months after arrest before a preliminary hearing is held. During that interval, the case is called 3–5 times in the courtroom; but each time it is continued until a later date, either by motion of the defense or the prosecutor. Whenever the case is called, the complaining witness and arresting officer must appear. If they continue to appear, the courtroom organization will take it as a sign that they consider the case serious enough to merit the court's careful attention. If they stop appearing, the case will be dismissed. The assumption is that unless the pricipals consider the case serious enough to warrant investing time in court appearances, the courtroom organization need not consider the case worth their while.

The courtroom techniques also determine what sort of sanction will be imposed on the defendant. Sentences are usually more lenient when they emerge from negotiations rather than from trials. Trial judges usually give defendants who plead guilty a "bonus", a reward for not taking up too much of the busy court's time and for reducing the uncertainty of the work of the courtroom. Almost every court we observed admitted to such a practice under one guise or another. But part of the difference also stems from the different kinds of information likely to be exchanged in the two techniques. Mitigating circumstances are more likely to be brought out in a bargaining session than at a trial. At a trial the prosecutor must develop his case in full; he does so at a relatively leisurely pace. The defense is often hard pressed to make its case; the defense often hesitates to place the defendant on the stand for fear his prior criminal record will be revealed. By contrast negotiating sessions rarely last more than half an hour; the prosecutor outlines the bare bones of his case, while the defense attorney makes all sorts of assertions about defendant's situation, in mitigation of the sentence. While the defendant's prior record is almost always discussed, the defense can argue ameliorating circumstances, which often could not be proved in open court.

Sentences are not the only disposition which the courtroom organization disposes of. Acquittals restore the innocence of the defendant; a less positive form of this affirmation is dismissal of the charges. In addition, the judge may praise witnesses or (less frequently) defendants; he may lecture and criticize defendants (while at the same time dispensing a mild sentence in the form of probation).

The screening and sanctioning processes are important for achieving the goals of the courtroom organization. They serve to promote both the external production goals of the organization and the internal system maintenance goals. Consequently, the organization is reluctant to share these functions with outsiders. For instance, in Chicago, the penal code requires a presentence report by the probation department before sentencing, unless the report is waived by the defendant. The courtroom organization in most instances insists on the waiver as part of any plea bargain, in order to avoid sharing sentencing power with outsiders. It has been frequently suggested by reformers that more uniformity in sentencing might be achieved if outside judges shared the sentencing function; but judges and other members of the organization oppose this reform. Greater uniformity might interfere with the production rate in courtrooms; therefore, the courtroom organization resists any interference with the sanctioning function.

Implications of the Organizational Approach

The organizational scheme described here has been drawn from work done primarily with the criminal courts of Chicago, Illinois, U.S.A. The elements of the approach are variables, that help explain differences among the Chicago courts, as well as between courts in Chicago and courts in other cities.

Among the twenty-one Chicago courtrooms there is considerable variation in volume of dispositions, and in the ratio of trials to guilty pleas. We would expect the volume of dispositions to be positively related, in the first place, to the cohesiveness of the courtroom organization. Courtroom organizations whose principal function is screening rather than sanctioning will display different organizational characteristics. They will make less use of adversarial trappings, and will exhibit a high degree of consensus on goals and procedures. The judge will play a less dominant role than in courtroom organizations where sanctioning is the principal function.

The differences between courtroom organizations in Chicago and Baltimore, for instance, are striking. In Baltimore, there is relatively little plea bargaining; trials, especially jury trials, are more frequent. We can perhaps attribute that difference in large part to differences in organizational characteristics of courtrooms in the two cities. The public defender in Baltimore employs private attorneys who are assigned to particular courtrooms. There is also more movement from courtroom to courtroom among State's Attorneys. This is because, whenever a courtroom becomes available for a trial, the next case on the docket is moved to that courtroom regardless of its previous assignment. Thus participants in a case often do not know until the last moment which judge, state's attorney and courtroom they will confront. At the same time, there are fewer opportunities for members of the courtroom team to become a cohesive organization. Consequently, we observed much less camaraderie among courtroom members. Chambers are less frequently the scene of sociable gatherings among courtroom regulars during recesses. On the other hand, the allegiance of courtroom participants to their parent organizations is stronger than in Chicago. Judges confer with each other at least once a week at a lunch meeting. State's attorneys spend more time in their offices, and are more dependent on the work of other members of the office than in Chicago. Since trials are more frequent, the Baltimore courts seem to be more visible to the general public than the Chicago courts; and personnel of the Baltimore courts appear more sensitive to demands of the press than their Chicago counterparts. These differences support greater use of adversary proceedings, and less resort to plea bargaining.

In Detroit the importance of organizational characteristics also is evident. As long as all plea bargains went to only a few judges, the Detroit system of negotiating the pleas through a centralized pretrial section of the District Attorney's office worked smoothly. After a ruling of the Michigan Supreme Court, pleas had to be taken to all the judges of the Recorders Court on a random assignment basis. The plea system became markedly more complex. The pretrial section and the prior set of judges developed understandings which the new judges did not share. The new arrangement required a larger communication network. This, together with the larger number of participants, the absence of agreed upon operating procedures, and differences about the appropriate goals of the process, substantially disrupted the plea bargaining system. Under the new arrangements, plea bargains were less effective in reducing uncertainty.

Where courtroom organizations form cohesive working groups, plea bargaining is the norm, and full adversary trials the exception. This has important implications for our understanding of the trial process and the possibilities of reforming it. Negotiated pleas come about because of organizational characteristics, developed to cope with increasing caseloads. But to reduce caseloads would probably not substantially reduce pleas without other fundamental changes in the organizational pattern of courtrooms. Changes would also be required in the goals of organizational members, in their responsiveness to outside forces, and in their cohesiveness. If one wanted to increase the number of trials and adversary proceedings, the most effective way would be to disrupt courtroom organization, as occurred in Baltimore; by increasing uncertainty and preventing the development of stable relationships among courtroom regulars, one increases the incentive to ask for a trial, and decreases the attraction of plea bargaining. Such a course, however, would cost much more, because trials take more time in the courtroom and more work by courtroom personnel.

The organizational approach also directs us to focus our research on structural variables, goals, and characteristic technologies of courtroom organizations. The legal categories in which cases and defendants fit may be thought of as independent variables, which cue particular kinds of courtroom response. The legal categories are manipulated to achieve organizationally desired outcomes. For instance, the strength of the evidence against a defendant is often not tested in a formal trial, but it helps determine whether the case will be dismissed, disposed by a plea to a lesser offense, or by a plea to the original charge. The prior record of the defendant – legally inadmissable except to challenge the defendant's credibility as a witness – plays an essential role in the sanctioning process, long before the guilty plea is taken, because the organization uses it as a cue to classify the defendant and fit his case into one or another category of disposition. Likewise, as the clientele of the courtroom organization changes, we may expect changes in organizational goals and courtroom behavior. If the police, press, or prisons become more attentive to the courtroom's output, the organization will have to adapt its goals to meet the new demands. Much of the courtroom's behavior is defensive and insular. It can be best understood in terms of the groups to which the organization is responding and the groups from which it is protecting itself.

While traditional socio-legal research treated all trials as a single category, we may soon know enough about variations in trial court behavior to develop an typology of courtroom organizations. Such a typology will help explain various behaviors and their consequences. Viewed as organizations, some criminal courts may be more like certain civil courts, than they are like other criminal courts. Even the enormous differences between Continental and common law systems may narrow, when examined in this perspective.

Summary

Überlicherweise werden amerikanische Geschworenen-Gerichte analysiert, wie wenn sie Ein-Mann-Gerichte wären und die Untersuchung beschränkt sich auf den Richter und seine Beziehung zur Geschworenenbank, sofern eine benötigt wird. Das ist ein falscher Ausgangspunkt. Strafgerichte sind kleine Organisationen, die neben dem Richter auch Staatsanwälte, Strafverteidiger, Gerichtsschreiber, Gerichtsdiener und Gerichtsstenographen umfassen. Sie entwickeln sich zu mehr oder weniger zusammenhängenden Organisationen mit eigenen Zielen, Normen, Betriebsverfahren und Techniken. Obwohl der Richter das angesehenste Mitglied er Gerichtsorganisation ist, nimmt er selten eine hierarchische Spitzenposition ein. Seine Führungsfähigkeiten werden vielmehr gedämpt durch die Eigenheiten der Organisationsstruktur und die Gerichtsentscheidungen beruhen eher auf dem Zusammenwirken aller Mitglieder als auf der Tätigkeit des Richters allein.

Wie alle Organisationen, so wird auch das Gericht beeinflußt von der Zusammensetzung und der Sozialisation seiner Mitglieder, von den motivierenden Faktoren für deren Arbeit, von gemeinsamen Zielen und den zur Anwendung kommenden Techniken. Jedes dieser Elemente muß untersucht werden.

Alle wichtigen Teilnehmer der Gerichtsorganisation sind Juristen; die meisten von Ihnen kommen aus dem kleinen Teil des Anwaltstandes, der sich auf strafrechtliche Arbeit spezialisiert. Dies bedeutet, daß sie nicht nur die gleiche berufliche Ausbildung haben, sondern auch bedeutende gemeinsame Erfahrungen und Perspektiven. Nichtjuristische Mitglieder der Gerichtsorganisation (Gerichtsschreiber, Gerichtsdiener und Gerichtsstenographen) passen sich schnell der gerichtlichen Atmosphäre an und übernehmen in beachtlichem Umfang das Erscheinungsbild eines Juristen.

Berufliches Weiterkommen und Sicherheit des Arbeitsplatzes bewegen die Mitglieder eines Gerichtes, sich für die äußeren und inneren Ziele eines Gerichtes einzusetzen. Die äußeren Ziele sind darauf gerichtet, die „Kundschaft" der Gerichte zu befriedigen. Im Falle der amerikanischen Strafgerichte besteht diese Kundschaft hauptsächlich aus dem Staatsanwalt, den Polizeistellen, den Nachrichtenmedien und den Gefängnisbehörden. Die inneren Ziele sind darauf gerichtet, das Gleichgewicht der Organisation zu festigen.

Ein wichtiges Element der Festigung einer Organisation ist das Vermeiden von Unsicherheit. Dies findet man bei beinahe allen Organisationen. Im Strafgericht zeigt sich dies in der Vermeidung von Beweiserhebungen mit Hilfe der Geschworenenbank und der Begünstigung von Schuldgeständnissen. Schuldgeständnisse werden gefördert, weil sie das Resultat von Verhandlungen sind, die kontrolliert werden können, schwurgerichtliche Verfahren werden gemieden, weil sie Außenstehende in die Verhandlung verwickeln (Zeugen und Geschworene), die nicht kontrolliert werden können und die Unvorhersehbarkeiten in das Verfahren bringen. Dieser Wunsch nach Vermeidung von Unsicherheiten ist mindestens ebenso entscheidend für die Förderung von Geständnissen als die häufiger als Grund erwähnte Überlastung der amerikanischen Schwurgerichte. Dies funktioniert jedoch nur dann am wirksamsten, wenn die Gerichtsstruktur relativ straff und stabil ist, d.h. wenn dasselbe Personal über eine lange Zeitspanne regelmäßig zusammenarbeitet. Wenn Gerichtsstrukturen weniger stabil sind, können gemeinsame Normen und Ziele nicht so effektiv in Erscheinung treten und die Teilnehmer sind weniger fähig, die Unsicherheiten eines Schwurgerichtsverfahrens zu vermeiden.

Die von Gerichtsorganisationen angewandten Techniken sind das Stellen von Anträgen, die Durchführung von Beweisaufnahmen und das Abhalten von Verhandlungen. Jede dieser Techniken erfordert ganz verschiedene Fähigkeiten, alle aber ein hohes Maß von Urteilskraft, was es unmöglich macht, den Arbeitsfluß so zu strukturieren, wie dies am Fließband möglich ist. Vielleicht erscheinen Rechtsfälle als Routineangelegenheit, jeder von ihnen hat aber seinen individuellen Kniff und verlangt einige Ermessensausübung bei seiner Abwicklung. Obwohl Entscheidungen sehr schnell gefällt werden können, sind sie doch keine routinemäßigen Tätigkeiten im Sinne fabrikmäßiger Fließbandarbeit.

Diese allgemeinen Prinzipien einer Organisationsanalyse der Gerichte werden durch einige Beobachtungen einer Untersuchung von Strafgerichten in Baltimore, Chicago und Detroit veranschaulicht. Es ist zu hoffen, daß sie auch in anderen Kulturkreisen Gültigkeit haben.

Notes

1 See for example, Lewis Mayers, The American Legal System, revised ed. (N.Y.: Harper & Row 1955, 1964) Henry J. Abraham, The Judicial Process (2nd ed. (N.Y.: Oxford University Press, 1968).

2 For research on juries, see Harry Kalven Jr. & Hans Zeisel, The American Jury (Boston, Little Brown, 1966). For a summary of research on judges, see Herbert Jacob, Justice in America 2d ed. (Boston: Little Brown, 1972), pp. 105–112. Another line of research has examined sentencing decisions by judges; a brief discussion is given, ibid., pp. 177–78.

3 Abraham S. Blumberg, Criminal Justice (Chicago: Quadrangle Books, 1967); Albert S. Alschuler, "The Prosecutor's Role in Plea Bargaining", University of Chicago Law Review 36 (1968), 50–112. Also Maureen Mileski, "Courtroom Encounters: An Observation Study of a Lower Criminal Court", Law & Society Review 5 (1971) 473–538.

4 For example, see Malcolm Feeley, "Two Models of the Criminal Justice System: An Organizational Perspective", Law & Society Review 7 (1973) 407–426. My exposition of the organizational perspective differs from Feeley's in being more explicit about dimensions of organizations other than goals.

5 See Charles Perrow, Organizational Analysis: A Sociological View (London: Tavistock Publications, 1970), and James D. Thompson, Organizations in Action (N.Y.: McGraw Hill, 1967). For somewhat different statements of organizational theory see Herbert A. Simon, Administrative Behavior (N.Y.: Macmillan, 1957); James March and Herbert A. Simon, Organizations (New York: Wiley, 1958), and Amitai Etzioni, A Comperative Analysis of Complex Organizations (New York: Free Press of Glencoe, 1961).

6 Cf. Jerome H. Skolnick, "Social Control in the Adversary System" Journal of Conflict Resolution II (1967), 52–67, for an earlier statement of a similar view.

7 For an exceptionally lucid review of various concepts of organizational goals, see Lawrence B. Mohr, "The Concept of Organizational Goal", American Political Science Review 67 (1973), 470–81.

8 Cf. Thompson, op. cit., pp 67–70. Thompson uses the term "task environment" to encompass the role of such clients.

9 Ibid.

10 Chicago Crime Commission, Press Release March 19, 1973.

11 Crime and Service Study of Westchester County, Vol. I, pp. II–4 and II–8 (mimeo). For similar data for Los Angeles, Detroit, and Chicago see Isaac D. Balbus, The Dialectics of Legal Repression (New York: Russell Sage Foundation, 1973) pp. 47–97, 131–46, 210–16.

IV. Alternativmodelle für die Rechtspflege

Britt-Mari Blegvad

The Choice Between Litigation and Arbitration

I. Introduction

The use of commercial arbitration can be regarded as an alternative to litigation. I will in this paper report some results of a comparative study of this form of dispute settlement. This study has been carried out since the end of the sixties in Sweden and Denmark by a team of scholars from the two countries mentioned (1)*.

Arbitration is here regarded as an adversary method of dispute settlement, which we will take to mean that the parties to the dispute control [1] whether arbitration should be utilized at all; [2] what issues should be presented for decision; [3] what data should be presented; and [4] what arguments should be used. The procedure involves not only the disputants but also at least one third party, who functions as a conflict settling agent. This agent often is a commercial expert. The decision to use commercial arbitration, the decision as to content, and the third party's methods are all essentially private. Prior cases generally do not serve as authoritative sources to be used in arbitrary commercial cases.

Litigation in commercial cases is also an adversary method, with the same characteristics as those outlined above for arbitration. It, too, is a type of conflict settlement in which a third party is involved. But this third party is in Sweden and Denmark a public servant. Furthermore, dispute settlement by arbitration is final; commercial litigation can, however, be appealed.

Most research efforts regarding judicial decision-making have so far concentrated on criminal trials and criminal justice. Studies have been made of plea bargaining, pre-trial procedures, the role of the jury, etc. Research on the criminal courts is, of course, related to important social problems. On the other hand, the Swedish-Danish research team felt it would be useful to examine decision procedures used in commercial life as well. Arbitration is a common alternative to civil litigation. Many decisions here are significant for society as a whole as well as to the individual disputants. Our study has thrown light on the use of commercial arbitration, which had been obscure and subject to conflicting views beforehand.

The study itself was not easy to carry out. We met with problems in reaching parties who had used commercial arbitration. It was therefore decided to collect the material through lawyers in private practice (advocates) who function as important intermediary agents. They are the ones who suggest the use of arbitration to their clients (the eventual parties). We also contacted people who had been active as judges in arbitration tribunals.

* Notes on pages 183 f.

This form of strategy necessarily limits the scope of our study. Advocates only function as intermediary agents in certain kinds of conflicts. We have therefore studied arbitration in a restricted group of categories: conflicts regarding building and construction contracts, business contracts involving domestic and foreign parties, and disputes concerning tenancy and leases.
There are very few other socio-legal studies in this field, so to a great extent we had to start from scratch. *Smith* (1956) and *Mentschikoff* (1961) have reported on a similar study carried out in the fifties in the United states; *Lazarus* et al. (1965) give us some data from a follow-up study; *Bonn* published two articles in 1972, drawn from a doctoral dissertation covering mostly arbitration in the textile industry. All these studies use data from a special organization as their starting point, namely, the American Arbitration Association. This organization is stronger in the Eastern than in the Western portion of the United States. It is also my impression that the really "big" parties do not use the services of this organization. From Europe we know of one study – *Kohler's* investigation, published in 1967, dealing mostly with Frankfurt am Main (2).
The lack of comparative data had an impact on design of our study. It had to be mainly descriptive, convering *how* – and only to some extent *why* – commercial arbitration is used in some situations.

II. Legal Background

In Sweden as well as in Denmark, parties are free to submit disputes to arbitration, instead of bringing suits to the ordinary courts. If the parties have made an arbitration agreement, this agreement has an effect in two different ways. It can be invoked as an estoppel: if one of the parties, in spite of the agreement, goes to court, the court is supposed, if the other party so demands, to dismiss the case. Further, the agreement can lay the foundation for effective enforcement of the arbitration, resulting in an arbitral award which can, except in rare cases, be relied on to end the dispute definitively. In the period covered by our study (1963–1967), Sweden and Denmark differed slightly in the applicable law. In Sweden two statutes, from as early as 1929, covered the subject, and recommended a special procedure. In Denmark no rules of this kind had been enacted. The legal status of arbitration was similar here, but based on judge-made law (3).

III. The study

Commercial arbitration is a means of conflict settlement which (one assumes) is used as an alternative to litigation – an alternative which perhaps is becoming more and more popular.
Existing legal literature often takes for granted that commercial arbitration is quicker and less expensive than litigation. In arbitration, too, technical experts can participate at all stages of the proceedings. This should be advantageous when the facts are technical or complicated. It is moreover regarded as an advantage over litigation that arbitration is not public. One of the purposes of our study was to find out whether arbitration *in fact* was quicker, less expensive

and regarded as advantageous by the people involved in the ways here indicated. A Swedish scholar, *Per Olof Ekelöf*, instigated this study of arbitration. *Ekelöf* was interested in why arbitration was used – so he thought – to a growing extent in Sweden. A specialist in Swedish procedural law, *Ekelöf* could not understand why this development was taking place. The problem, he thought, was both theoretically interesting for socio-legal scholars, and important in bearing on the reform of the Swedish procedural system. Unlike the courts of some countries (e.g., the United States) Swedish courts had reasonable caseloads, and no waiting time of any importance. This could therefore not be the explanation of the growth of arbitration. On the other hand, it was assumed that arbitration was used less in Denmark than in Sweden (4).

A team composed of scholars with an interdisciplinary background from the two countries designed a comparative Swedish-Danish study of the use of commercial arbitration.

As very little was known about commercial arbitration, one of the most important aspects of the project was to achieve a better knowledge of the role of commercial arbitration as a means of conflict settlement, laying the basis for a more detailed and reliable evaluation of the legal problems connected with arbitration. A furhter aim was to elucidate the effectiveness and appropriateness of existing rules on arbitration, and the role and attitudes of lawyers and technical experts involved in this type of conflict resolution.

These rather generally formulated problems were reformulated during the initial stages of the research process (5). The conceptions about the general character of commercial arbitration were also regarded as keys to empirical indicators of the beliefs or values held by different groups. Several hypotheses were formulated on the assumed relations between these values, and the conflict solving mechanisms which different groups would prefer. In other words: if Swedish advocates *believe* that arbitration is *quicker*, this belief could influence their advices to their clients and therefore have an impact on the use of arbitration (6). Another problem is the "choice" between different forms of conflict resolutions and *how* and *when* this "choice" takes place. Our study shows that arbitration in Sweden and Denmark very often is initiated via a clause in a contract. This was reported by 58 per cent of the Swedish advocates who took part in arbitration in the research period. The corresponding Danish figure was 88 per cent. Even so, the parties – or their advocats – at the problem-defining phase of the conflict can often define themselves in or out of the clause. The clause can, for example, say that arbitration shall be used for technical disputes. The question then is: what is a technical dispute.

In addition to this, parties or their advocates may choose arbitration because they feel they can influence the composition of the arbitration tribunal. Different attitudes towards compromise might also have an impact. The study also concidered how arbitration tribunals treat evidence, and what substantive norms they use, compared to courts; also, the influence of macro-sociological factors, such as the level of economic development of the countries concerned.

In this paper I will mention only a few especially interesting results. But first, I would like to state briefly some facts about the methodology used.

IV. The Data Collecting Technique

The study used several data collection techniques. Documents provided a useful but limited source of information. In the initial phase, interviews were held with lawyers and other professionals, who could be regarded as experts on commercial arbitrations. In the second phase, a questionnaire was distributed to Swedish and Danish advocates. These lawyers are, as mentioned before, regarded as important intermediary agents in the process of structuring the conflict-solving mechanisms of commercial life. Their view on possible alternatives in dispute settlement, as well as their role in predicting consequences for business relations, are assumed to be essential to the decisions of the parties involved.
We therefore concentrated our efforts on this group. In Sweden, our return was about 60 per cent; when analyzed, the material shows that the response rate of more important groups such as advocates with a large practice was 72 per cent. The corresponding figures for Denmark were 50 and 58 per cent respectively. Since some judges participate in arbitration tribunals, the questionnaire was also sent to all Danish judges and about half of the Swedish ones. The return here was quite high. The average response rate of the Swedish judges is 73 per cent and of the Danish ones 85 per cent. We therefore feel that we have rather good survey material, as a basis for further analysis. This material has also to some extent been supplemented by interviews.

V. Some Factors Relevent to a "Choice" between Arbitration and Litigation

A. Type of Cases

As we have said, any arbitration clauses used in contracts both in Sweden and Denmark limit the use of this form of dispute settlement to conflicts with a strong technical element. Around 70 per cent of the Swedish and 60 per cent of the Danish advocates are of the opinion that it "is easier to reach an arbitral agreement on technical issues (e.g., questions of building techniques, bookkeeping or methods of distribution) than on purely legal issues". In Denmark this factor seems also to be linked with the use of arbitration in very big cases, i.e., cases concerning more than 1.500.000 D.Crowns.
We are, of course, aware that a study of the resolution of conflicts where advocates are used limits the scope drastically. Several investigations, both outside and inside Scandinavia, show that the organization of the legal profession is such that small businessmen would not be as likely to use its services. But the research team was surprised to find that the type of arbitration investigated was used to such an extent for contracts arising under building or construction contracts the value of 1.500.000 D.Crowns or more. We knew that the Danish Central Organization of Builders and the comparable Swedish organization recommended to their members that they use arbitration for certain conflicts, and even introduced arbitration clauses in their standard contracts. Around 50 per cent of the Swedish and the Danish advocates had taken part in arbitration in construction conflicts. In other words: the *type of issue* plays a bis role in the "choice" of arbitration.
Involved here are also the questions of the *money at stake* and the *time element.*

It is well known that construction firms are more dependent than many other businesses on a steady flow of money for financing. If arbitration is regarded as a quicker way of settling conflicts than litigation, a builder would tend to choose this way of settling his conflict in order to save money. It turned out that 35 per cent of the Swedish and 25 per cent of the Danish advocates had participated in settling big construction conflicts by arbitration. This practice was also confirmed through interviews.

In our material, the *technical complexity* of the issues was often mentioned as yet another element which contributed to the "choice" of arbitration rather than litigation. It is felt that judges could not unterstand technical details, and that it took too long a time to teach the judges enough about the technical problems involved. Though experts may be called in by the courts, they cannot, according to Swedish and Danish law, take part in the decision making process, and in the formulation of the judgment. If arbitration is used, one or two technical experts are as a rule part of a three person arbitration tribunal, and take an active part in formulating the award.

Considering the factors here mentioned – can we say anything about the number of cases where arbitration is used as compared to litigation (7)? My estimation – based on our data – is that arbitration was begun in 460 cases in Sweden and in 300 cases in Denmark per year in the period covered by our study. Of these, around 22 per cent in Sweden and 33 per cent in Denmark were conciliated, i.e., the parties reached a settlement through conciliation, which led to discontinuation of the arbitral proceedings.

If we compare these figures with population data for the two countries, we find that arbitration is used as often in Sweden as in Denmark. The distributions between cities and rural disttricts was also rather similar. I regard this fact, which emerged from a closer analysis of our data, to be of great importance, as earlier it was taken for granted that arbitration was used more in Sweden than in Denmark. Why was such a notion so widespread? Did it have something to do with the comparative use of litigation in civil cases? Since one of the main assumptions of our study was that commercial arbitration and litigation could be regarded as alternative types of conflict settlements, we tried to estimate the use of civil procedure in commercial cases. Unfortunately, legal statistics in Sweden and Denmark are differently kept; and there were problems of comparability. A close analysis allowed us, though, to draw the following conclusions: in the relevant period, the number of civil cases dealt with in court in Sweden decreased. Since the population was growing, this decrease was rather marked. This development might perhaps explain the previously mentioned notion which was especially widespread among lawyers. In Denmark, the situation was different. Here the absolute number of court cases increased, though the increase disappears if population growth is taken into account. In other words: there is a *decrease* in Sweden, but a rather *stable pattern* in Denmark.

Aubert has distinguished between *conflicts of interests* and *conflicts of values* (8). The type of situations we have been dealing with stems from, for example, lack of knowledge about how a certain type of new building material functions. Should the seller of the material or the builder be responsible and bear the burden? This is best regarded as a conflict of interest. Such conflicts, according to *Aubert*, imply compromise solutions. Indeed, compromises seem to be more common in connection with arbitration than with litigation (9).

B. Composition of the arbitration tribunals

No legal rules govern selection of arbitrators. A special procedure is recommended in the Swedish statute; Danish law has no equivalent. It is therefore interesting to see that a common pattern prevails in both countries. The tribunal consists of three persons. Each party chooses one arbitrator, and these two in their turn choose the third. In the United States the parties often choose arbitrators from a list put together by "neutral" organization, such as the American Arbitration Association. Neither in Germany nor in Scandinavia is there a general organization of this sort. The parties appoint persons whom they trust for one or another reason, or persons drawn from panels selected by trade organizations. The two arbitrators then in their turn choose the third, often a judge. The position of the parties is therefore stronger in arbitration than in litigation, where the parties cannot influence selection of the judge who will decide the case.

Judges both in Sweden and Denmark must meet rather strict qualifications which each arbitrator must possess. There is considerable discussion of the role of the arbitrator. Note the two following statements, drawn from interviews:

> "An arbitrator chosen by a party should act as his representative".
> and:
> "Arbitrators lean too much toward the side of the parties who have selected them".

The question is: should an arbitrator act as a party representative, or as an impartial judge. Obviously the expectations of the parties, and the arbitrator's concept of his role, can vary from individual to individual. This is especially true for arbitrators who are not legally trained; legally trained arbitrators have a common set of rules to refer to. But all in all, the influence of the parties is very strong in choosing the arbitrators. Probably this is one of the most important differences between arbitration and litigation. The parties here seem to want a rather mixed tribunal. The two arbitrators selected by the parties tend to be technically experts; they guarentee reasonable treatment of the technical aspects of the controversy. The third arbitrator is often legally trained; he can guarantee a certain legal correctness in the handling of the case.

C. The decision making process

The parties can in the main decide what kind of procedural rules they want to use. Arbitrators are not bound by many formalities. They have only, according to the Swedish Arbitration Act. to act as far as possible in accordance with the instructions of the parties, "and deal with the case in an impartial, practical, and speedy manner". This is probably also the rule according to Danish case law.

In the survey, we asked Swedish lawyers if, in handling arbitration cases, they made use of the general rules of the Swedish procedure law; and we asked the Danes if they used the rules regarding high court cases in first instance, from the corresponding act. A positive answer was very common in both groups. Answers clustered around the response alternatives "Quite often" and "Very often".

One Danish comment compared arbitration procudure with that of litigation as follows:

> "1) Procedure before arbitration tribunals is normally far more informal and less binding than court procedure, as set out in the procedure act.
> 2) The arbitrators are normally far more active in finding evidence and narrowing down the issues.
> 3) The arbitration tribunals divide procedures and production of evidence into convenient parts. Such a practice would be effective in court, but for procedural and psychological reasons it would be unthinkable in the Danish High Courts."

To conclude: according to the survey material, arbitrators often fall back on the existing procedural rules for the treatment of civil cases in court. This, however, happens more often in Sweden than in Denmark. It is furthermore fairly common in Sweden and in Denmark that the president of the arbitration tribunal, when opening the negotiations, "narrows down" the issues in the introductory stage of the proceedings. On this sole point the Swedish answers indicate less formality than the Danish ones. This is probably due to the fact that Swedish advocates are used to such a practice in court procedures. The material indicates that Swedes "Quite often" fall back on this practice, whereas the Danes do this "Quite often" or "Sometimes".

In the types of cases included in this study, the parties often appear with a counsellor. This is more common in Sweden than in Denmark. But both in Sweden and Denmark the members of tribunals give special assistance to a party not represented by counsel.

We found more formalism and legalism in the data gathered though Swedish advocates. For example, half of the Swedish arbitration cases in which our responding advocates have taken part make records, but only one third of the Danish ones. This may be due to the differences in recording practices in court; Swedish courts always use legally trained secretaries. Swedish lawyers may therefore take the detailed recording of conflict-settlements for granted, in comparison to their Danish colleagues.

What seems amazing is that so many cases do *not* use detailed recording. Arbitration cases are often of highly complicated technical character. It is difficult to understand how, for example, disputes over details in a major construction contract can be resolved without recording. But it may be that parties choose arbitration to avoid the need to present technically complicated material orally, which would be obligatory in litigation. The president of the arbitration tribunal often takes notes during the proceeding, to be used, if needed, as the basis for the award. Perhaps our respondents do not regard these notes as equivalent to official records.

To conclude: when we look at the procedural rules used in Sweden and Denmark in the arbitration process, we find a decision making system which has many similarities to litigation process. It has a legal flavor. There are, however, some interesting differences in the Swedish and Danish patterns, which may be explained by different legal traditions in the two countries.

D. The application of substantive law

Several Scandinavian authors have in recent years claimed that the courts have declined in importance (10). *Aubert* (1969 and 1972) has analyzed this development sociologically and historically; he suggests that other forms of conflict resolution are now more often used. This change may be connected with the diminshed importence of older religious and sexual norms. Conflicts regarding such norms could in the old peasant society be solved only by a strong third party, that is, a judge (11).

Furthermore, the center of gravity in conflict-resolution has shifted to an earlier stage in the decision making procedure. One reason is that the legal profession to a great extent prevents or resolves conflicts before they reach the stage where they must be submitted to court.

It is not only conflicts, which are increasingly settled by other means than by litigation; changes in the legal system evolve outside court to a greater extent than in the past. It has been pointed out by *Strömholm* that one can now also speak of the development of legal rules via arbitration; one of the reasons is that courts could not manage "to render to the business world a societal service in the form of quick, rational, and creative solutions to its problems" (12). The legal rules cannot keep up with the developments produced by new technology and economic complexity, the rapid proliferation of "new needs and new constellations of interest as a consequence" (13).

If the parties in developing their case, feel a need to use points other than legal ones, e.g. arguments based on common sense or social-scientific data, this may incline them to attempt to solve the conflict by arbitration rather than by litigation (14).

In our survey, several questions aimed to shed light on the matters sketched above. Among other things, we asked "whether arbitral tribunals are ever more inclined to decide the cases ex acquo et bono than are the law courts".

The study shows that in about 60 per cent of the cases which Swedish and Danish advocates have taken part in, they experienced an attitude of arbitration tribunals more liberal than in the courts. One interviewee described the development as follows:

> "Formerly one insisted on one's rights – nowadays one is more inclined to look at the issues from both sides and then perhaps to find a compromise. This leads to the use of equity – a decision ex aequo et bono becomes more frequent."

Some key Swedish interviewees also claimed that arbitration tribunals are less restricted than the courts. A judge says:

> "One follows the law as far as possible; provided that the judgment is interpreted correctly, it will be fair."

Some respondents, however, clearly expressed the view that a liberal interpretation is sometimes a danger. For instance it could lead to a speculative element in arbitration cases:

> " 'Equitable' aspects enter into an arbitration, when one starts to discuss the reasonableness of certain costs and the like."

We asked direct questions in our survey about the use of legal norms in arbitration cases. It turned out that significantly more Danish than Swedish advocates think that arbitration tribunals aim at the same strict application of the law as the courts.

But we also asked whether arbitration tribunals *should* decide cases with more regard to equity than the law courts, in order to avoid rigid decisions. The Danes felt more positively towards such a practice than their Swedish colleagues. In the "key-person" interviews we find some examples of explanations offered.

> "The agricultural associations recommend clauses of arbitration. ... This is because the farmers have been suspicious of the practices of the law courts, in cases of this special type. One had the feeling that the courts did not have the same understanding of what was right in relations between members as the associations (which furnished the arbitration tribunals with their members) did."

Finally we aked about the attitude of non-legally trained arbitrators toward the rules of law. It turned out that significantly more Swedish than Danish advocates said that non-legally trained arbitrators have a more liberal attitude than legally trained ones. As mixed tribunals are the most common type, this is an important finding. Among the comments on the question, we found a view expressed that nonlawyers sometimes behave more legalistically than lawyers – the following comment bears on the "legalism" of trained legal professionals:

> "I am of the opinion that the professional judge is also familiar with compromises. Sometimes it happens that the president (of the tribunal), if he is a lawyer, says that this is a question on which I find it difficult to give an opinion. Tell me what you think, and I will than formulate your views in such a way that it satisfies all claims of justice."

VI. Further Theoretical Perspectives

I have in this exposition tried to present some material from the Swedish-Danish study of commercial arbitration which could be used for furhter discussion of the following questions:

1. *The development of "private" dispute settelement institutions*, i.e. under what conditions will less formalized institutions emerge in an industrialized society for the settlement of commercial disputes (as an alternative to already existing legal ones) and;
2. *The development of "informal" rules*, i.e. under what conditions will less formalized rules of dispute settlement emerge in an industralized society for the settlement of commercial disputes (as an alternative to already existing formal rules).

These questions suggest – contrary to *Weber* and *Durkheim* – that the rising curve of formalization in the legal system brakes when the social system reaches a certain degree of technical sophistication. A need for a less formal system of conflict resolution then emerges. In this social context, the use of informal means of dispute settlement – including arbitration – becomes ever more important.

Summary

Der Beitrag gibt einen kurzen Überblick über einige Fragestellungen, welche in einer vergleichenden Studie über Schiedsgerichtsbarkeit in Handelssachen behan-

delt wurden, die seit dem Ende der 60er Jahre in Schweden und Dänemark durchgeführt wurde.
Thema ist der Einsatz von Schiedsgerichten bei Konflikten, die Bauverträge, Handelsverträge zwischen nationalen und ausländischen Parteien und Miet- und Pachtverträge betreffen. Schiedsgerichtsbarkeit wird als eine der möglichen Alternativen zum Rechtsstreit vor den staatlichen Gerichten betrachtet und daher die folgenden Annahmen diskutiert:

- Schiedsgerichtsbarkeit wird „gewählt", weil sie nicht öffentlich ist.
- Sie ist eine einfachere Methode der Konfliktsbereinigung.
- Sie ist weniger kostspielig als gerichtliche Prozeßführung.

Der Aufsatz untersucht nun, ob die folgenden Faktoren für die Wahl maßgebend waren.

- Art des Rechtsstreits
- Zusammensetzung des Schiedsgerichts
- Das Entscheidungsverfahren und die Rechtsanwendung bei den Gerichten bzw. den Schiedsgerichten.

Zum Schluß werden noch einige allgemeine theoretische Behauptungen über die Entwicklung derart „privater" Methoden der Konfliktsbereinigung aufgestellt, wie die Schiedsgerichtsbarkeit es im Gegensatz zum staatlichen Gerichtsverfahren darstellt.

Notes

1 The study has been conducted by Professor P.O. Bolding, University of Lund, Sweden, Professor Ole Lando and Associate Professor Britt-Mari Blegvad, both of Copenhagen School of Economics. The research is supported by the Tri-Centennial Fund of the Bank of Sweden and the Danish Social Science Research Council. For a more detailed account of the legal background, the methodological aspects as well as the process of problem formulation, see the first part of the research report: B-M Blegvad, P.O. Bolding, Ole Lando in cooperation with K. Gamst-Nielsen: Arbitration as a means of solving conflicts, New Social Science Monographs E6, Kobenhaven 1973.

2 H.A. Smith: "Commercial Arbitration at the American Arbitration Association", The Arbitration Journal 1., 1956, pp. 1–20. S. Mentshikoff: "Commercial Arbitration", Columbia Law Review, Vol. 61, 1961, pp. 846–869. S. Lazarus et al.: Resolving Business Disputes, New York, 1965, pp. 208. R.L. Bonn: "The Predictability of Nonlegalistic Adjudication", Law and Society Review, Vol. 6, No. 4, pp. 563–579. Ibidem: "Arbitration: An Alternative System for Handling Contract Related Disputes: Administrative Science Quarterly, June 1972, pp. 254–264. K. Kohler: Die moderne Praxis des Schiedsgerichtswesens in der Wirtschaft, Berlin, 1967, pp. 154.

3 For a further discussion of the legal basis of commercial arbitration in Sweden and Denmark, see B-M Blegvad, P.O. Bolding, and Ole Lando in cooperation with K. Gamst-Nielsen: op. cit., Chapter 2, Kobenhavn, 1973.

4 The Swedish and Danish legal systems have rather similar structures. The Swedish and Danish societies also have many traits in common. Hence, a comparison of arbitration in the two countries might be particularly meaningful.

5 For a further discussion of this process, see B-M Blegvad, P.O. Bolding, and Ole Lando in cooperation with K. Gamst-Nielsen: op. cit., Chapter 1, Kobenhavn, 1973.

6 See also V. Aubert (ed.): Sociology of Law, Penguin Modern Sociology Readings, 1969, introduction p. 11. T. Eckhoff: "Juss og Samfunnsforskning", in H. Hessler (ed.) Festskrift till Per Olof Elelöf, Uppsala, 1972, p. 208.

7 For a preliminary analysis of this question, see B-M. Blegvad, P.O. Bolding, Ole Lando in cooperation with K. Gamst-Nielsen: op. cit., 1973, p. 95–107.

8 Aubert: "Two Types of Conflict and of Conflict Resolution". The Journal of Conflict Resolution, Vol. VII, 1963, pp. 26–42.

9 See also Eckhoff: "The Mediator, the Judge, and the Administrator" in Blegvad (ed.): Contributions to the Sociology of Law, Copenhagen, 1966, pp. 148–173.

10 Aubert: "Law as a Way of Resolving Conflicts. The Case of a Small Industrialized Society", pp. 282–304 in Nader, L. (ed.): Law in Culture and Society, Aldine Publishing Company, 1969; and Rättssociologi, Stockholm, 1972, Chapter 6. P.O. Bolding: Juridik och Samhällsdebatt (Law and Debate in Society), Almquist & Wiksell, Uppsala, 1968. T. Eckhoff: op. cit., 1966, p. 163. Strömholm: "Rättsutveckling pa annat sätt än genom lagstiftning" in Proceedings of the 25th Conference of Nordic Jurists, Oslo, 1969.

11 V. Aubert: op. cit., 1969, p. 293, See also T. Eckhoff: op. cit., 1969, p. 163.

12 Strömholm: op. cit., 1969, pp 37 and 41.

13 Strömholm: op. cit., 1969, p. 41.

14 P.O. Bolding: op. cit., 1968, pp. 85–87.

Jeffrey Jowell

Judicial Decision-Making and Administrative Tasks

In Britain today, "courts" make only a tiny minority of all official decisions. Legal research is however almost exclusively concerned with the judicial process. The purpose of this paper is to discover what principles, if any, do or ought to govern the allocation of "judicial" and "administrative" decision-making. Why are some decisions "hived off" to administrative tribunals, commissions, inquiries, ministries, and so on? Why are others dealt with by the courts in the 'judicial' system? What are the relative merits of courts, commissions and computers as decision-makers?

The questions I am asking have significance for a number of reasons. First, is the obvious one, that any principles we discover may help in future allocation of decision-making functions. Second, perhaps light can be shed on judicial decision-making; to what extent can and must the ideal or model form be followed within the judicial system? Finally, to what extent is the judicial model appropriate for other official decision-making? In other words, to what extent can administration be 'judicialised'?

This last question has been discussed recently both in the United States and Britain. In the United States, Charles Reich and Kenneth Culp Davis have made influential contributions in their proposals for legal control of administration. Reich, in a series of articles (1)*, has traced the growth of government largesse, those increasingly frequent situations where individuals receive privileges from the state, and are therefore at the mercy and subject to the control of official discretion. In welfare law, for example, Reich favours granting to recipients firm "rights" or "entitlement", under criteria established in advance, and protected by full adjudicatory procedures. Joel Handler has commented eloquently on this subject (2).

Davis (3) admits that some discretion is "necessary discretion", though he does not attempt to analyse why discretion may be necessary – a subject that will be dealt with here. But Davis is concerned with the amount of "unnecessary" discretion, wielded at all levels of administration, which provides opportunity for administrators to depart from official policy. He suggests the use of precise rules, to "confine" discretion – set its boundaries and shave it down to that minimum compatible with effective exercise of the task to be performed – or to "structure" discretion – channel it to take cognizance of officially-sanctioned criteria. Davis also suggests that where possible descretion should be "checked" by persons other than the decision-maker, and "structured" in such a way as to be "open", that is, exposed to public scrutiny – open plans, open policy

* Notes on pages 203 ff.

statements, open rules, open findings, open reasons, open precedents; and fair, informal procedures.

In England, a similar debate is presently raging, particularly in connection with welfare 'rights' and the 'judicialisation' of land-use planning inquiries (4).

Why Legality?

Official conduct may be brought under legal control by various degrees of "legalisation" or "judicialisation". Although these terms are frequently used interchangeably (5), "legalisation" will refer here to the process of subjecting official decision to predetermined rules, and "judicialisation" will refer to the process of submitting official decision to adjudicative procedures.

The advocates of "legalisation" of the administrative process would thus wish to transform policies (broad statements of general objectives) into rules (authoritative general directions that contain relatively specific and concrete guides for decision). For example, the administration of a law containing the broad policy objective of preventing unsafe driving would be progressively "legalised" as all elements of "unsafe" driving were reduced to rules specifying, for example, maximum speed limits and one way streets.

The advocates of "judicialisation" of the administrative process wish to submit administrative decisions to procedures more or less analagous to the adjudicative procedures carried out in the courts of law, and accompanied by some or all of the features of these procedures. Lon Fuller's definition of adjudication embodies the ideal-typical form. Fuller defines adjudication as "as social process of decision which assures to the affected party a particular form of participation, that of presenting proofs and arguments for a decision in his favor" (6). It follows from this concept of adjudication that a series of consequences flow from the adjudicatory process and the ways in which the parties participate. The main consequence is the restraint that is associated with the judicial role. First, the proofs and arguments presented by the litigants ought to be presented to a decision-maker who is impartial, and has not made up his mind before either side has presented its case. The decision-maker should not hold private conferences with either party. Otherwise, the party excluded from the conference may not know to what issue he should direct his proofs and arguments. Both parties should have the opportunity to cross examine the other.

What then are the merits of legalisation and judicialisation, both of which subject official decision to the governance of rules? The traditional Anglo-American argument in favour of the "rule of law" is put forward by such writers as Hayek, Dicey and Dickinson (7). The argument is based on an concept of fairness ('like' cases should be treated 'alike', and no person should be held accountable *ex post facto*) and a political philosophy that views as unacceptable decision-making without direct accountability. However, no part of this argument (which Davis terms the 'extravagant version' of the rule of law) considers the content of rules, or the integrity of their administration other than that treatment be 'evenhanded'.

On the other hand there is little doubt that when decisions are guided by rules of law, there is a better chance of congruence between officially determined ends (where these can be determined) and official action. In particular, both legalisation and judicialisation can help eliminate arbitrary decisions which are defined here as decisions based upon improper criteria, and criteria that do not relate in any rational way to organisational ends (8).

For example, rules might specifically exclude as criteria for determining wether or not an applicant was "suitable" or "desirable" as a prospective tenant in public housing, factors such as the applicant's race, his previous membership in certain political organisations, his previous participation in tenant rent strikes, or his relationship to other tenants, or to an official.

Alternatively, rules could explicitly prescribe certain objective decision-making criteria, by implication excluding those that might be improper and irrelevant. Among these criteria might be a certain minimum income level, to be used to measure eligibility for welfare benefits: another might be seniority, as a criterion for worker benefits or promotion.

Perhaps the most obvious merit of judicialisation, from the perspective of the litigant, is evident in the definition we have adopted; adjudication guarantees participation to affected parties. This participation, and especially adversary participation, stimulates administrative integrity for the following reasons: First, the parties to the dispute are also in a sense involved in the decision-making process. Although they do not make the final decision, they are permitted to suggest justifications for a decision in their favour and to challenge each other's proofs and arguments. Since they are directly involved, they will have knowledge of the "particular facts" of a situation, and thus be well placed to advance the strongest case for their proposition.

Secondly, the decision-maker is normally under a duty to articulate a reasoned basis for his decision. Rules as such, as Lawrence Friedman has pointed out (9), are in a sense nonrational. Whatever the reasoning behind enactment of a rule, the rule itself appears to an affected party as a plain injunction, for example, not to exceed thirty miles per hour, or not to park fifteen feet from the corner. When an adjudicator has an obligation to expose his reasons, he may be less likely to use criteria that are improper, arbitrary, legalistic or that fail to achieve congruence between the effect of the decision and official objectives.

It should be stressed again that the adjudicative model we are discussing is an ideal characterisation. Reality will frequently fall short of the ideal. Some reasoned decisions are no more than *ex post facto* rationalisations of positions formulated in advance. In addition, the symbols surrounding the judicial format may be manipulated in order to reassure people that the 'rules of the game' have been followed, thereby obtaining their "quiescence" in the face of decisions which would otherwise be unacceptable (10).

Nevertheless, adjudication does contain some inherent forces that tend to give "formal and institutional expression to the influence of reasoned argument in human affairs" (11). The requirement that a decision be justified, and the justification be written and published, implies that the justification is open to public criticism on similar rational grounds. Thus adjudication, especially when accompanied by public reasoned decision, will provide an opportunity for scrutiny and thus for accountability of decision-makers to their clientele and to the public.

What strengthens this point is the *nature* of the justifications embodied in judicialised decisions. Such decisions must be justified by a general rule, standard, or principle. Ascriptive or particularistic criteria are illegitimate. The litigants will make their claims as members of a legally defined class, as particular instances of a generalised category. In consequence, an appeal to power, private interests, or political expediency will be inappropriate. The adjudicator will in turn be pressed to evaluate the relative merits of claims in the light of accepted techniques for determining their importance and weight, and by reference to authoritative guides, rather than his personal interest in the result or his personal predisposition towards the claimants.

The Functional Limits of Legality

Legality may be an ideal, yet there are limits to the kind of decision that can be controlled by rules and standards.

Rules

Rules are concrete general directions, in which legal consequences are appended to the happening or non-happening of an event or the occurrence of a situation (12). The enforcement of a rule (such as the maximum speed rule) requires the event or situation (the driver exceeding thirty miles per hour) to be determined factually.

It should not be assumed, however, that the application of rules can always be mechanical. A parking meter, for example, may simply register the end of a maximum time limit. But since rules are purposive devices (they are techniques to effectuate a broader policy) and because language is often uncertain in its application to situations that cannot be foreseen, the applier of a rule will frequently possess some degree of discretion to interpret its scope. In doing so he will go beyond the wording of the rule in order to discover and weigh controlling principles and policies. He will not be a passive "applier" but will himself be an agent in the rule's elaboration.

What are the limits of rule-governed conduct? The essential limit arises as a corollary of the fact that a rule is a general direction, applicable to a number of 'like' situations that may arise in the future. Although rules may contain exceptions, they are not primarily tailored to individual circumstances; they view the individual to whom the rule is applied as one of a class or category. The speed rule does not distinguish between a person exceeding the speed limit in the rush hour and the person performing the same act in the early hours of the morning. According to the letter of the rule, the speeder is a violater in both cases.

The corollary therefore of the impersonal nature of rules is that they are unsuited to the guidance of situations where the action to be controlled is non-recurring, and is unique in the sense that it is not likely to repeat itself. Where a rule is to be applied "without regard to persons" (in Weber's phrase), it is unsuited to personalised, individual application. Personalised application means unique, non-recurring handling, because so many variables are to be taken into account that practically speaking no two cases are the same.

For example, university places could be filled according to a rule that specifies admission on the basis of an applicant's past grades. This would allow a disinterested, objective, admission procedure. However, if qualities such as personality, leadership potential, or potential for future development were required it would be much harder to frame rules that specify these qualities in advance. Similarly, where a decision is required that takes into account the "whole man" (13), in order to determine suitability for political leadership, or to provide specific rehabilitative care; or where a remedy is required that can be applied rehabilitative care; or where a remedy is required that can be applied against the background of a person's history and life-situation, then an impersonal rule prescribing certain objective "impersonal" guides is not suitable. James Q. Wilson has described the impossibility of formulating rules to "guide" the police patrolman's discretion in a situation of order-maintenance. He points out that rules prescribing certain courses of action ("don't use a racial epithet", "don't hit a man except in self defence") are more useful in guiding possible conduct than rules that prescribe affirmative action. Nevertheless,

> no very useful – certainly no complete – set of instructions can be devised as to what the officer *should* do with, say, quarrelling lovers. Defining a policy in such matters is difficult, not because the police have not given much thought to the matters or because they do not know how they should be handled, but because so much depends on the particular circumstances of time, place, event, and personality. Psychiatrists do not use "how to do it" manuals, and they have the advantage of dealing with people at leisure, over protracted periods of time, and in periods of relative calm (14).

Standards

Standards are directives more general than rules. Their purpose is to specify policies without loss of flexibility in application. A *rule* will provide for a definite speed limit (say thirty miles per hour); a *standard* will provide that drivers must exercise "due care". Application of a standard thus requires, in addition to the finding of a fact in a particular situation (how fast was the vehicle going?), a qualitative appraisal of the fact, in terms of its probable consequences or moral justification (does that speed in those circumstances imply lack of "due care"?).

The feature of standards that distinguishes them from rules is that their application is flexible and susceptible to change over time. In 1955, for example, "average" and "prudent" university administrators probably had little difficulty in applying a standard that required "neat" dress in university lecture halls. Obviously, skirts for women, and collar and ties for men, were essential criteria of "neatness". Some years later, however, the standard could allow trousers for ladies, open collars for men, or indeed anything, if not nothing at all.

Are there limits to the use of standards in making decisions? One limit arises where it is not meaningful to refer to a general community consensus. In commercial law, for example, the requirements of "fairness" can be meaningfully elaborated by drawing on conceptions and evaluations shared by the community of traders (15). However, a community consensus is often absent, or opinion may be in a state of transition. In such cases the decision-maker, despite the legitimacy of his own role as an agent in the articulation of standards, may expose himself to justifiable criticism if he boldly declares a standard to exist. When behaviour that was formerly clearly labelled either as desirable and right, or as undesirable and wrong, becomes transformed into a matter of preference and taste, a standard cannot be meaningfully articulated. Standards depend for their meaningful application upon the existence of a community norm. Thus it might be impossible today to specify what constitutes "immoral" sexual conduct (does it include homosexual conduct between consenting adults?), or pornography, or "neatness". Where a standard is expressed in terms that specifically incorporate a question of individual taste, the difficulty of applying the standard is thrown into high relief. Thus, in one case, a judge was not able to enforce a covenant restricting the erection of "any building of unseemly description" (16). Architectural standards, in land use planning, which speak in aesthetic terms, pose similar problems.

As we have seen in connection with the limits of rules, a situation to which a general direction may be applied must be capable of categorisation in a class with other 'like' cases. Similarly, where standards are to be applied by comparing an instance in question with other like-situated instances, either those that are directly competitive (as in a license application) or those that exist in the community, one must be able to put instances to be compared into a similar class or category. Judges of an agricultural show, for example, would find it very hard to select in a meaningful way the best fruit, or the best animal. Pears must be judged against pears, pigs against pigs. At a sporting event, high jumpers cannot easily be compared with long jumpers, though they have obvious affinities compared with long distance runners. The standard of "due care" similarly, while in general laying down an objective test of conduct (17), does not allow a child to be judged by the standards applied to an adult.

Discretion and the Administrative Process

We have thus far discussed why legalisation and judicialisation may be considered, from the perspective of affected parties, desirable constraints upon official decision-making (subject to the limitation that rules and standards cannot effectively govern certain situations).

We began by examining ideal requirements of a "judicial" decision. However, we may approach the question from another perspective, asking what the requirements are for administrative decisions.

First, we must dispel the view, particularly prevalent in legal thought in the United States, that administration can be split into two functions, 'adjudication' and 'rulemaking'. It is clear that administrative bodies perform tasks other than those two. Some administrative bodies run housing projects, and others grant money. Some dispense rehabilitative services; others collect garbage, rents, taxes and intelligence. The following typology will attempt to classify the adminis trative process in a manner that more realistically reflects the variety of tasks that administrative decision-makers perform.

A. Discretion

Discretion here will refer to the room for decisional manoeuvre possessed by a decision-maker. Discretion is rarely absolute, and rarely absent. It is a matter of degree, and ranges along a continuum between high and low (18).

The decision-maker has a high degree of discretion when he is guided only by such vague standards as "public interest" and "fair and reasonable". Where his discretion is low, the decision-maker is limited by rules that do not allow much scope for interpretation (19).

THE ADMINISTRATIVE PROCESS

Low Discretion		*High Discretion*
	1. Dispute-Settlement Tasks	
Adjudication		Allocation Conciliation
	2. Managerial Tasks	
'Pure' Administration Administrative Service		Administrative Policy-Making
	3. Rule-Making Tasks	
Interpretation		Planning
Low Discretion		*High Discretion*

The legal techniques for controlling discretion include rules, which "legalise" decisions, and adjudication, which provides a forum for the "judicialisation" of decisions. For the moment, we might note that discretion may be constrained too by non-legal factors, such as the amount of available resources, time, professional norms, and the political pressures to which the decision-maker is (or perceives himself to be) subjected.

B. Tasks

It is suggested that administrative tasks can be classified in the following manner: Dispute-settlement, managerial and rule-making. This classification more accurately reflects what administrators do than the traditional adjudication-rule-making dichotomy.

1. Dispute-Settlement Tasks

Dispute-settlement refers to a task that requires a decision on the merits of two or more competing claims. The dispute-settlor may have to decide between the claims of an organization (e.g., a welfare department) and an individual (e.g. a welfare recipient). The dispute might be between two individuals – one complaining about the other's behavior (e.g., a complainant and a respondent before an antidiscrimination commission), or the dispute might involve two individuals competing for an independent item (e.g., two persons competing for allocation of a radio channel).

Dispute-settlement in which there is a low degree of discretion is, in Fuller's sense, adjudication in its ideal-typical form. The degree of discretion is low because the decision-maker is constrained by his obligation to justify the decision by reference to principles, rules or standards. This constraint in turn fosters procedures in which proofs and arguments are presented to an independent decision-maker.

It is wrong however, to view adjudication as the only method of dispute-settlement. Conciliation, for example, is another. Conciliation (as performed by antidiscrimination commissions, for example) is a process in which the decision-maker will attempt to reach a decision that is supported by the affected parties to the dispute. The task necessarily involves a high degree of discretion, both as to the terms to be arrived at and as to the process of arriving at a decision, during which time the conciliation officer has the power to propose concessions, adjustments and compromises to the parties involved. The procedural restraints necessary to adjudication are thus absent, since the decision-maker often meets with the parties in private, and has wide discretion to set flexible terms of settlement (20).

Similarly, those who perform allocative tasks (disbursing limited resources among competing alternatives) normally possess a high degree of discretion, for example, the power of the U.S. Federal Communications Commision to issue licenses for the frequencies on the radio spectrum, guided by the vague standard of "the public interest".

The broad discretion in such determinitations renders them unsuitable for adjudicative decision. Agencies performing allocative tasks may reduce their discretion by selecting narrow decision-making criteria, thus rendering the problem more suitable to decision by adjudication. For example, the "public interest" may be operationalised or factored into sub-goals or criteria, such as a "balanced program".

2. *Managerial tasks*

Managerial tasks are oriented toward social goals (21). There are two kinds of managerial tasks, placed at either end of the discretion continuum - 'pure' administration, and administrative policy-making. It would be an error to assume that there is a distinct dichotomy between "policy" on the one hand and "administration" on the other (22). Rather, 'pure' administration and administrative policy-making are functionally similar, but situated at opposite ends of the discretion continuum.

'Pure' administration (or, in Ernst Freund's words, "administrative service") (23) refers to the execution of largely routine service or regulatory tasks. It involves little choice about organisational objectives, but involves the strict "implementation" or "application" of policies already determined. As these tasks become less routine or mechanical, the discretion exercised in their performance increases and they move along the discretion continuum towards administrative policy-making, where the decision-maker will make a choice about organisational goals and the means to pursue them.

For example, where a traffic policeman follows instructions to allow traffic to pass along an intersection for two minutes from the East to West and then for three minutes from the North to South, he is performing a purely administrative task. So little discretion is needed for this task that an automated traffic light may be used in place of a person. Where the policeman has discretion to regulate traffic flow "as he sees fit" or "to maintain the free flow of traffic", he is exercising policy choices and performing a task unsuited to disposition by a traffic light. A welfare intake worker, routinely deciding eligibility on the basis of set qualifications (such as the age of sixty-five for Old Age Assistance) performs a purely administrative task. Where the caseworker makes decisions about a recipient's 'special need', the decision requires a policy-determination that involves a higher degree of discretion.

3. Rulemaking Tasks

An organisation performs a rulemaking task when it engages in a legislative process. The end product of the task will be a rule, order, regulation or plan. The process may be accompanied by various consultative techniques, to obtain the views or participation of affected parties.

Rulemaking performed according to a low degree of discretion is refered to as "interpretative". An agency makes interpretative rules when it "fills in the gaps" of relatively clear policy, rules or decisions, or specifies the means or procedures necessary for application of these policies, rules, or decisions.

Planning refers to the legislative task of devising a course of action that will effect an alteration in the public's state of affairs in accordance with the ends of an agency that is authorised to select those ends and the means for their attainment (24). The urban renewal agency performs a planning task that normally involves a wide degree of discretion as to the means to be employed to carry out its ends. Although we may not normally think of an urban renewal plan as a piece of legislation, the plan is in fact reduced to legislative form, and will consist of a pattern of interlocking rules specifying the proposed alterations in a given area. Planning differs from allocation to the extent that the task does not involve a specific dispute situation, but the designing of a course of action for the public as a whole. Once the plan in enacted, it remains to be implemented by a managerial process.

Implications of the typology

The essential implication of our typology is that the tasks on the left hand side (those to be performed with low discretion) are the most suited to control by law – to legalisation or judicialisation. The tasks on the right hand side are not capable of legal control, because they do not lend themselves to decision according to rule or standard, or because they are polycentric.

An important English example of a decision not readily capable of judicialisation was the planning decision of the Greater London Council that provided, in 1968, that the Covent Garden area of London (an area of great character and containing a variety of uses) should be virtually demolished and replaced by new development, including housing, schools and conference centres. A lengthy inquiry into the matter was conducted by an Inspector from the Department of the Environment. Many objections were heard during the course of the inquiry, which was conducted on the English judicial model. The Inspector's recommendation was accepted by the Minister, who, while approving some kind of comprehensive redevelopment, virtually scuttled the original plan by "listing" about two hundred buildings in the area, that is, in effect preventing their demolition.

The polycentric nature of the problem is highlighted by this example: One of the buildings "listed" by the Minister, was the famous, old, and beautiful Flower Market. The former plan had provided for demolition of this building, and erection of a conference centre in its place. Now where is the conference centre to go? Is it to be abandoned, or sited elsewhere? If it is to go elsewhere, what will it displace? And where will the displaced item go? If housing were displaced, what would happen to the inhabitants?

Clearly, then, the decision about one item (the Flower Market) is linked by chains of influence to many other decisions, necessitating readjustment of the entire scheme. The decision about a complex plan is not ideally suited to adjudicative decision-making, that allows proofs and arguments to be directed to questions that require a "yes-no", "either-or" answer. Apart from approving or rejecting the plan as a whole, the decision-maker has no way of avoiding polycentric issues; and this necessitates adjusting them 'out of court'.

It should be stressed that it is only the ideal-type of the "legal" decision which requires a decision by rules or standards and which must not be polycentric. Clearly *some* decision can be made about any question, and using any procedure. For example, the cooks in a college cafeteria could be required to submit their menu daily to a committee nominated by the faculty, and students and staff could argue for a against English pudding, Danish pastry or American apple pie. But as Fuller suggests, if reality veers too far from the ideal, the "integrity" of the system will be eroded, because the claimants, under the guise of the judicial format, will in effect be unable to find referents for their arguments, and will thus be joining issue in an "intellectual void".

The Enforcement of Laws Against Discrimination

Let me illustrate the implications of the typology through another example, this time drawn from the legal arrangements concerning the enforcement of laws against racial discrimination.

In England and America (at the state and federal level) laws have been passed outlawing discrimination on the grounds of race or religion. In both countries the machinery of enforcement involves conciliation procedures, carried out by administrative bodies. The criminal and civil remedies enforced through courts of law are not to be used, except as a last resort. In England the first draft of the 1965 Race Relations Bill did make race discrimination a criminal offence, but this was soon abandoned in favour of conciliation procedures (25).

I would like briefly to report on my own research into one American agency charged with enforcing these laws: The Massachusetts Commission Against Discrimination (MCAD). This Commission, first established in 1946, was modelled upon New York's similar law, introduced a year earlier. Initially the

MCAD was to enforce the law against discrimination in employment; later its jurisdiction was expanded to cover housing and other areas (26).

The Commission proceeds in the following way: After a complaint has been laid by a person alleging discrimination, one of the three Commissioners will have the matter investigated. A determination may be made that a "probable cause" of discrimination exists. Should the Commissioner find a lack of probable cause, the case is dismissed without further appeal. Upon a finding of probable cause, the Commissioner endeavours to eliminate the practice complained of by "conference, conciliation and persuasion". The Commission will draw up a conciliation agreement providing, for example, that the respondent write a letter of apology to the complainant; that he offer the next available job to the complainant, or to another black person, or that he advertise his jobs in future in black areas and newspapers. If the respondent, however, fails to agree to conciliation, the Commission holds a public hearing (over which all three Commissioners preside) where the discrimination must be proved. An order issued at a public hearing may be enforced through contempt proceedings in the courts.

In practice the public hearing is seldom resorted to, and the vast majority of cases are settled by conciliation. The individual Commissioners have wide discretion in this procedure. No guidelines have been established indicating either the permissible range or the content of conciliation agreements, or the variety of possible purpose (such as deterrence, rehabilitation of the respondent, general retribution, or providing a remedy to the complainant.

My own study of the outcome of cases before the Massechusetts Commission in 1965–70, showed that there could not be said to be a uniform Commission approach to conciliation. Each of the three Commissioners had his own pattern of conciliation agreements. Slicing the Commission open displayed three approaches, three patterns, three views of the purpose of the law, and of the appropriate role of the administrator.

Commissioner B's approach could, by contrast, be termed a "tort approach". Here a complainant is viewed as a plaintiff in a civil action, suing the defendant for a civil wrong (tort) in a manner that violated the defendant's duty of care towards the plaintiff. Commissioner B's view could be chacterised thus: "The primary object of the law is to vindicate the rights of individuals who have been the victims of unlawful discrimination. The function of the Commission is to adjudicate a dispute and protect the rights of the parties".

Commissioner C's approach was again different and will be referred to as the The function of the Commission is to persuade and educate members of the community to obey the law".

Commissioner B's approach could, by contrast, be termed a "tort approach". Here a complainant is viewed as a plaintiff in a civil action, suing the defendant for a civil wrong (tort) in a manner that violated the defendant's duty of care towards the plaintiff. Commissioner B's view could be chacterised thus: "Thus primary object of the law is to vindicate the rights of individuals who have been the victims of unlawful discrimination. The function of the Commission is to adjudicate a dispute and protect the rights of the parties".

Commissioner C's approach was again different and will be referred to as the "equal opportunity" approach, since the complaint is viewed largely as a lever to reduce discriminating practices, rather than to educate the respondent or to vindicate the strict legal rights of the complainant. This view could be characterised thus: "The primary object of the law is to equalise opportunities for blacks. The function of the Commission is to remove obstacles to equal opportunity by eliminating discrimination that faces the complainant (and blacks generally in the community)" (29).

Commissioner A's cases, reflecting the 'didactic' approach, showed the following features:

1. The complainant received the accommodation or employment which was the subject of his complaint in a relatively low percentage of cases (16 per cent as compared with 22 per cent and 45 per cent for Commissioners B and C respectively). This demonstrates a relative lack of concern for the rights of the individual complainant; in contrast to the "tort approach".

2. In a relatively high number of cases (three in every five) the respondent indicated his intention to comply with the law in the future, by writing the Commission a letter to that effect. This too indicates that Commissioner A is mainly concerned with eliciting from the respondent some commitment to non-discriminatory behavior in the future.

3. In only three of thirty-seven cases did the respondent agree to undertake affirmative action. In two of these, the action was merely to place the Commission's poster on view in the respondent's model home and rental agency. In the other complaint, the respondent agreed to place a poster on display and to inform the Commission of any future vacancies.

Thus Commissioner A, though anxious to press for some commitment from the respondent, is reluctant to urge more than a minimum *negative* undertaking, such as a statement not to discriminate. Such reluctance typifies the "didactic" approach, in which the Commissioner views as his function, educating respondents and encouraging or persuading them to obey the law.

4. There were relatively few specific findings of probable cause or lack of probable cause. This, above all, distinguishes the approach of Commissioner A from that of Commissioners B and C, and seems to be due to two reasons, each typifying the didactic approach. First, the Commissioner is anxious to obtain the goodwill of respondents. In the absence of blatant evidence of discrimination, Commissioner A is reluctant to put undue pressure on the respondents for fear of jeopardizing any goodwill that exists or might be induced on their part. Commissioner A believes that a finding of probable cause would "antagonize" the respondent. Second, Commissioner A sees himself less as an adjudicator of a dispute, than as a negotiator on behalf of the Commission. He is loathe to assign culpability at an early stage of the proceedings, for to do so, in his view, would imperil the satisfactory outcome of the case, either by stiffening respondents' resistance, or by placing an extra bargaining weapon in the hands of the complainant. The Commissioner stated that he specifically finds probable cause only in cases where "they (respondents) give me enough trouble". As he considers that his task is to obtain a commitment not to discriminate, rather than to make a determination of right, Commissioner A is likely to ignore the letter of the law in order to reach what he considers to be its goal. Once a complaint has been laid, therefore, he will consider a case "satisfactorily adjusted" upon an indication from the respondent of an intention not to discriminate in the future.

Commissioner B's cases, reflecting the 'tort' approach, showed the following features:

1. In only one case in three (compared with two in three for Commissioner A) was the case closed without requiring respondent to take any action. Whereas Commissioner A is anxious to obtain from the respondent some commitment not to discriminate, Commissioner B sees his primary function as that of adjudicating the dispute between the complainant and the respondent. He will thus close a case upon a finding of lack of probable cause, and will not concern himself with educating the respondent nor use the complaint in any way to further opportunities for blacks in the community. Similarly, on a finding of probable cause, Commissioner B will seek a remedy that is closely related to the terms of the original complaint and the vindication of the rights of the complainant.

Many cases brought before Commissioner B demonstrate his prime concern with the rights of the complainant, and an unwillingness to demand anything more of the respondent than action *towards the complainant*. The final disposition of one case, for example, reads: "Discrimination is clear and admitted. Respondent offered housing to complainant who declined it. Therefore this case is closed." No future compliance commitment was elicited from the respondent, even though respondent's discriminatory behavior was clear. In another case an owner of many apartments was not required to make any commitment to future compliance once his offer to the complainant was refused, even though the evidence of discrimination was blatant, the respondent having complained to the field representative of "the trouble the Niggers are causing". In employment cases, Commissioner B was on the whole unwilling either to request any action until he made a finding of lack of probable cause, or to make the terms of the conciliation wider than the terms of the complaint even in cases where the respondent's firm was virtually segregated and his recruitment so designed as to exclude black placement sources or areas.

2. In most cases, Commissioner B makes a specific finding relating to probable cause. Again, this is because Commisioner B regards his function rather like that of adjudicating an issue in tort, and is keen to make a clear determination of the rights of the parties.

3. In only two cases was affirmative action required of the respondent and in no case was there a commitment to future compliance, again showing that Commissioner B was primarily concerned with the immediate parties to the dispute.

Commissioner C's cases reflectet the "equal opportunity" approach: The complainant is regarded by Commissioner C as more or less like the plaintiff in a class action, representing the blacks in the community. Respondent will generally be required to take affirmative action not only towards the complainant, but also towards blacks in the community in general.

The main feature of Commissioner C's housing cases that distinguishes their results from those of Commissioners A and B's cases is the fact that in *every* case the respondent was asked to undertake in some way to assure compliance with the law in the future. The guarantee of future compliance differed from those sought by Commissioner A, however. Commissioner C virtually never obtained compliance letters from the respondent. Rather, he required affirmative action; and then checked whether respondent lived up to their promises.

Unlike Commissioner A, Commissioner C treats the rights of the complainant as also relevant; almost half the complainants before Commissioner C obtained the accommodation or employment which was the subject of the dispute (as compared with just over one in ten in Commissioner A's cases, and one in five in Commissioner B's cases). Unlike Commissioner B, however (who required respondent to take action only towards the complainant), Commissioner C would almost always try to obtain a wider undertaking. In one case, for example, although the complainant was not qualified for the job in question, the Commissioner required the respondent to manifest good faith by offering the next available job to a black.

How do we account for this divergence within the Commission? To a large extent it reflects the fact that the three Commissioners represented different stages in the Commission's history. The history of the Commission shows that it developed in stages, each stage corresponding to one of the three approaches we have discussed. The stages were obviously not clearly demarcated one from the other. Rather one approach became dominant (rather than unanimous) as it evolved from the previously dominant approach.

Stage 1: The Didactic Approach

The first stage of the Commission's history stretches from its inception in 1946 to approximately 1960. The approach in this stage owes much to the fact that the legislation had aroused strong opposition; the Commission was anxious to ensure its legitimacy (30).

Business and real estate interests opposed the law. The Massachusetts Bar Association also expressed opposition, fearing a "new Governmental Bureau with inquisitorial powers ... at a time when the public looks forward hopefully to less interference from government at the end of the war, and when Massachusetts needs to attract business to provide jobs for returning servicemen (31).

In response to statements such as these, the bill's draftsman was at pains to point out that the new commission's "chief job will be *neither administration nor enforcement as such, but education and conciliation*" (32).

The first Commission appointed by the Governor of Massachusetts with the advise and consent of the Senate, was likely to consist of individuals who appreciated the social and political factors surrounding the genesis of the law, and who would seek the support of those who opposed the bill most strongly – commerce and industry. An editorial advised on the choice of a Chairman and associate members: "Ardent crusaders might well be by-passed, for cool judgement, patience and tolerance and a spirit of inquiry and compromise are the requisites, not a zeal for quick reforms and for exemplary penalties" (33). The first Annual Report of the Commission echoed these sentiments, stating that "It has not chosen to conduct a punitive expedition in Massachusetts but has preferred to steer a conservative course of educating employers and workers alike as to their responsibilities and obligations under the Law" (34).

Mayhew's study corroborates the fact that the first stage of the Commission was "didactic". For this reason, employers did not see the Commission as a "serious threat or powerful force" (35). The Commission, during this stage, conceived of truly as an instrument of persuasion and education; it was also anxious to disprove the contention made by opponents of the law, that the Commission would provoke, not lessen, racial tension. A practical limitation on this last aim consisted in the fact that the same businessmen who had to be persuaded to cease political opposition to the law, confronted the Commission as respondents. Because the Commission's uppermost concern was to appease the opposition, respondents were mollified rather than restrained in their actions.

Stage 2: The Tort Approach

Up to about 1960, it appears that the commissioners adopted a uniform approach along the lines suggested as characterizing that of the "didactic" stage. From roughly after passage of an amendment prohibiting discrimination in 1959, some of the commissioners seem to have adopted a view that accords more closely with the "tort approach".

In contrast with the controversy surrounding passage of the 1946 Act, the 1959 bill (and others that expanded the Commission's remedies and jurisdiction) passed with unanimous and bipartisan support (36).

The change in the view of the law and of the Commission's function was no doubt influenced by changes in public attitudes and social conditions during the late 1950's and early 1960's. Fair housing groups sponsored complaints to the Commission and watched their progress through every stage of the Commission's procedure, often providing complainants with counsel to press for their rights. For the first time, therefore, pressure was brought to bear on the Commission from the complainant's side; at the same time pressure from the respondent's side had eased.

Mayhew's study bears out the suggestion that at this time some commissioners at least came to believe that the purpose of the law was to vindicate the rights of individual complainants, and that the function of the Commission was to enforce the rights of the parties. His survey shows that respondents in housing cases learned to be more aware of the force of the law and the power of the Commission (37). In contrsst to respondent employers, in the earlier years, respondents in housing cases found the Commission "ominous, threatening and very salient" (38). The vast majority of respondents interviewed by Mayhew saw the law as operating against their interests and were more likely to see the law as controlling their behaviour. Emphasis now shifted to vindication of the rights of the complainant, rather than appeasement of opponents of the law.

Stage 3: The Equal Opportunity Approach

The third stage of the Commission's development emerges from an analysis of the cases which were closed before Commissioner C. The Commission seemed to move into this stage in the late 1960's

As we have seen, this approach to enforcement sees a strong, affirmative purpose to the law. The goal is to remove barriers in the way of opportunities for blacks in the community. Individual cases that come to the Commission are regarded as levers, to be used to pry open and expose to scrutiny the respondent's whole range of operations. Where the respondent's recial patterns (in housing or jobs) show strong imbalances, with few blacks, this fact will be taken as circumstantial evidence of discrimination.

The equal opportunity approach demands 'affirmative action' from the respondent even if discrimination against the complainant is not demonstrated – for example, where the complainant is clearly unqualified for the job in question.
Thus the Commission may still exploit its access to the respondent's operations, require him to widen his sources of recruitment to include black placement sources or black newspapers, or to offer the next available job to a black or to lessen superflous qualifications that might indirectly discriminate against blacks because of their relatively lower educational status, or to train blacks for certain skilled jobs – even in cases where the Commission dismisses the complaint for want of probable cause, or when the respondent moots the case by yielding on the specific apartment or job.
The Commission's annual report for 1965 contained for the first time a policy statement on affirmative action:

> Aggressive affirmative action, as well as corrective action is a necessary ingredient in our rapidly changing times.
> ... Positive, affirmative actions by the leadership of business, labor, public education, social agencies – all the institutions of our communities and government are necessary to achieve ... constructive social change.
> We will attempt to improve the handling of individual complaints, intensify our own efforts in affirmative action and give leadership encouragement and expert assistance to any such efforts.

What conclusions can we draw from the divergence in caseoutcomes and goals, between the three commissioners, and over time? Should we see the divergences as problems to be solved? Ought we to insist that the procedures of the Commission be modelled more closely on those in courts of law? Ought we to insist that rules be enacted to specify the "correct" approach and the desired outcome? Ought we to insitute checks on individual discretion, in order to attain a uniform approach – over time, or at any one time? A reply to these questions can only be given when we know *why* the divergence occurred. The reason for differences in outcome among the three commissioners in 1965, is in a sense coincidental, as the three commissioners represented different stages in the Commission's history. Their divergences thus represented a cross section of the Commission's history, during which it had evolved from the didactic to the tort to the equal opportunity approach. Naturally the change from one stage to another was not clear-cut, and involved a process of accretion rather than distinct elaboration. Different approaches between all of the three commissioners was exceptional, although often at least one of the Commissioners retained the approach which was dominant at the time of his appointment (39).
Why did the MCAD change over time in this way? First an administrative body often is itself involved in the elaboration of "purpose", to be ascribed to the law that gave it birth. In this case, the purposes of that law were not clear; each of the three differing approaches was a logically acceptable reading of that purpose. Organisations such as the MCAD therefore cannot merely "mechanically" carry out their governing statute, as Weber's ideal-typical bureaucrat does; rather, such organisations may be created for the express purpose of flexible task-performance, exercising a high degree of discretion. For some tasks, machine-like impersonality and efficiency is welcome. In our society machines such as the parking meter and computer are usurping some of these. But other tasks are not

well suited to control by rules or standards. Decisions of welfare agencies about private need, and of urban renewal agencies about public need, are cases in point. The task of conciliation similarly requires a high degree of discretion. In other situations, even though the task might possibly lend itself to relatively precise legal definition, the lawmakers might pass a vague mandate on to the enforcing agency because they are unable to muster a majority in favour of a clearer standard. Legislative indefiniteness, in other words, may reflect a "political reason" (40). In still other situations, the legislature may grant a high degree of discretion to an agency for the specific purpose of achieving a flexible response to situations that cannot be perfectly anticipated (41).

It should be remembered that public agencies are often unable to assess with any degree of accuracy the effectiveness of their operations. In the absence of an objective, ascertainable or quantifiable criterion of 'success', such as profit margin, ratings, or productivity, organisations are frequently in the dark as to how well they are doing. James Q. Wilson points out, for example, that no police department can know how much crime and disorder a community would produce if the police functioned differently, or not at all (42).

How do antidiscrimination commissions evaluate the success of their operations: By the number of complaints they receive? By the amount of discrimination in the community? By the 'strategic' nature of the complaints? And what *is* a 'strategic' complaint? How can we know if discrimination is reduced? And how much of any reduction shall one attribute to the Commission's work? In welfare, too, goals are incapable of accurate measurement. How do we tell if an agency is bringing recipients to a level of 'self-support', or rehabilitating them?

Bureaucracies often respond to the problem of evaluating output by becoming "means oriented" – for example, judging the succes of law enforcement by the number of complaints filed, or judging the succes of traffic enforcement by the number of traffic tickets written (43). However, another way of measuring whether targets are being reached is to measure the voices raised in support of or against the proposition that the organisation is operating as it should.

The MCAD is therefore more than an elaborator of unclear standards. It does more than what organisation theorists refer to as the "factoring of goals into subgoals" (44). Peter Blau, for example, has described the "succession of goals" within agencies; once the agencies have been successful in accomplishing their original purposes, "irritating difficulties" may induce them to seek out or attain new organizational objectives (45). Blau thus argues that, contrary to some views (46) organizations do not necessarily resist change. They adapt to their environment, in order to ensure their survival and, implicitly, the survival of the goals they are charged with furthering. It is not haphazard, then, that case outcomes in the MCAD changed over time. Shifts in emphasis represented adaptations to the environment. The first stage reflected a response to strong opposition, at a time when little organized support from civil rights groups was forthcoming. In the mid-1950's, overt opposition to the Commission and the law abated, and pressure from representatives of complainants intensified. Perhaps the mode of enforcement in the first stage itself contributed to the abatement of opposition. In its third stage the MCAD seemed to find itself secure enough to act aggressively. In any event, how the MCAD acts can be attributed in large part to the way it evaluated its political options.

One conclusion that may be drawn from this account of the MCAD is that the lack of uniformity in administrative decision may well be quite functional. It may be possible to "legalize" or "judicialize" the MCAD's procedures, and to limit the divergences (over time and at any one time) by techniques that would minimize the scope of discretion. The advantage of rule-governed administration – such as evenhanded application and predictability – would then be achieved. The MCAD's flexibility, however, would be curtailed – perhaps at the expense of its capacity to adapt in order to survive and promote its objectives.

Conclusions

We began this paper by examining some of the strategic advantages of "law", such as evenhanded application, and congruence between objectives and outcomes. We saw the merits of adjudication as a method of institutionally guaranteed participation. However, legal techniques of decision also contain certain strategic defects. For example, rules, which are general directions, may easily catch within their ambit technical violators whose actions could not be said to contravene the objectives of the law. For example, a parking meter will not show understanding or mercy to a person who placed his coin in the slot one minute late, because he was helping an old lady across the street. Rigid adherence to rules is called legalism; and, because of its close affinity to arbitrariness (namely, lack of rational relationship to official ends), may cause dissatisfaction on the part of 'technical' violators.

The adversary nature of adjudication may also impose costs on society. As Joel Handler (47) has pointed out, it is distruptive to on-going relationships and not viable for those who depend on such realitonships. A welfare recipient who may not wish to prejudice her relationship with her caseworker, through litigation. Tenants may for similar reasons be reluctant to challenge their landlords. Tenant and welfare recipients are too dependent on discretionary power to sue and risk antogonising the holders of that power.

"Law", we argued, has certain functional limits. We developed a typology of the administrative process, and suggested that certain tasks require discretion for their effective exercise. Even tasks involving dispute-settlement need not be pursued in every case within the format of pure adjudication. This is because the adversary situation places the participants in what game theorists call a "zero-sum" situation. On side must win; the other must lose. The defendant is liable or not liable, guilty or not guilty. As we discussed in connection with urban planning decisions and anti-discrimination laws, matters that are suited to compromise, mediation and accommodation do not suit the structured adversary setting of adjudication. In addition, flexible adaptation to the political environment is often functional for the survival and effective enforcement of a law.

In England, in recent times, more and more tasks that would traditionally have been assigned to the courts, or subject to judicialisation, are being handed over for enforcement to administrative agencies that are relatively free from the restraint of the judicial format. Laws against discrimination are a case in point. Another is land-use planning, where future Inquiries (to be known as 'Examinations in Public') will even be conducted around a round table, so as to emphasise symbolically the non-adversary nature of the decision-making process, where the criteria for decision are not amenable to 'objective' rules (48).

In a sense the plea to legalise and judicialise involves a call for increasing the rights of individuals in an era of growing governmental intervention into social and economic life. But governmental action is diverse and complex. For those who wish to pursue official objectives in a manner that allows tasks to be adapted sensitively to political and other pressures, and for those who recognise that legalisation has defects (to the client, public and decision-maker) as well as merits, the virtues of the legal model will not be accepted in a wholesale, unquestioning manner.

At least in Britain, decision-making through judicial forms is increasingly viewed as inappropriate for many issues to which, in the past, it would have been unthinkingly adapted. More and more tasks will therefore be assigned to non-judicial bodies for resolution. Alternatively, courts may remold their own techniques to fit diverse situations in an more flexible way.

Summary

Welche Prinzipien führen dazu, daß Aufgaben der Entscheidungsfällung eher Gerichten zugewiesen werden als Verwaltungsbehörden, Kommissionen, Tribunalen usw.? Verrechtlichung und „Vergerichtlichung" des Entscheidungshandelns bringen bestimmte Vorteile mit sich: unparteiische Anwendung der Entscheidungsnormen und unparteiische Suche nach den maßgebenden Regeln und Präzedenzfällen. Es gibt jedoch bei denjenigen Problemen, die unter Heranziehung von Vorschriften und Regeln gelöst werden können, bestimmte funktionale Grenzen. Probleme nämlich, die eine auf die Sache oder die Person bezogene Lösung verlangen, oder Probleme, die vielschichtig sind, bedürfen zu ihrer Lösung in hohem Maße des Ermessens.

Der Beitrag versucht, eine Typologie von Verwaltungsverfahren zu geben, die dem Bedürfnis nach Ermessen bei verschiedenen Aufgabenstellungen Rechnung trägt und dabei die drei Gebiete der Streiterledigung, des Managements und der Regelaufstellung unterscheidet.

Diese Typologie wird erläutert am Beispiel der Durchsetzung von Gesetzen gegen Rassendiskriminierung in Massachusetts. Drei Stadien in der Durchsetzung des Rechts (Didaktik, unerlaubte Handlung und Gleichbehandlungsanspruch) bringen drei getrennte Möglichkeiten mit sich, sich dem Ziel des Gesetzes und dem Ziel derer, die es handhaben, zu nähern. Diese Stadien zeigen, daß die Anwendung von Ermessen für das Überleben eines Gesetzes oder einer Institution funktional sein kann. Allgemein gesehen werden komplexe Aufgaben und solche, die eine feinfühlige Anpassung an die politische Umgebung erfordern, nicht mit Hilfe des typischen gerichtlichen Entscheidungsprozesses bewältigt werden können.

Notes

1 C. Reich, The New Property, 73 Yale L.J. 733 (1964); Midnight Welfare Searches and the Social Security Act. 72 Yale L.J. 1347 (1963); Individual Rights and Social Welfare; The Emerging Issues, 74 Yale L.J. 1245 (1965); The Law of the Planned Society, 75 Yale L.J. 1227 (1966).

2 See e.g. J. Handler, Controlling Official Behavior in Welfare Administration, 54 Calif. L. Rev. 479 (1966).

3 K. Davis, Discretionary Justice (1969).

4 See J. Jowell, The Legal Control of Administrative Discretion, Public Law, Autumn 1973, p. 178.

5 E.g. by P. Nonet, Administrative Justice (1969); P. Selznick, Law, Society and Industrial Justice (1969).

6 L. Fuller, Collective Bargaining and the Arbitrator, Wis. L. Rev. 3 (1963). See also L. Fuller, The Forms and Limits of Adjudication (unpubl. paper); H. Hart and A. Sacks, The Legal Process at. 155 ff. (tent. ed., 1958).

7 F. Hayek, The Road to Serfdom (1944); A.V. Dicey, The Law of the Constitution (1885); J. Dickinson, Administrative Justice and the Supremacy of Law (1927).

8 Neither the terms 'improper' and 'irrational' are of course possible of objective determination. In my view the arbitrary decision must be both 'improper' and 'irrational'. See J. Jowell, op. cit. supra, at 186.

9 L. Friedman, On Legalistic Reasoning – A Footnote to Weber, Wis. L. Rev. 148 (1966): "A law appears normally as naked fiat, as plain and uncompromising as the Ten Commandments".

10 This point about "symbolic reassurance" is made by Murray Edelman in The Symbolic Uses of Politics (1964).

11 Fuller, The Forms and Limits of Adjudication, supra, at 13.

12 See H. Hart and A. Sacks, supra, at 155.

13 See Nonet's account of early stages in the history of the California Industrial Accident Commission, where a claimant was seen as a "whole man", in the context of his work record, to judge whether he possessed a "reliable character" and to provide for his problems, family adjustment, physical and mental health, etc. Nonet, Administrative Justice, at 250–60 (1969).

14 J.Q. Wilson, Varieties of Politice Behavior, at 65–66 (1968).

15 See Fuller, The Morality of Law, at 64 (1964).

16 Murray v. Dunn (1907), A.C., 283.

17 See F. James, The Qualities of the Reasonable Man in Negligence Cases, 16, Missouri L. Rev. 1 (1951).

18 K.C. Davis has recently defined discretion as follows: "A public officer has discretion whenever the effective limits on his power leave him free to make a choice among possible courses of action or inaction". K.C. Davis, Discretionary Justice, at 4 (1969). This difinition views discretion as a matter of degree, and not as an activity distinct from 'law-application', and accords with the view of discretion put forward here. Others who view discretion in this way are J. Griffith and H. Street, Principles of Administrative Law, chapter IV (1966); and G. Ganz, Allocation of Decision-Making Functions, Public L., Autumn and Winter 1972. Contra, see R. Dworkin, The Model of Rules, 35 U. of Chi. L. Rev. 14 (1967), who considers that a judge does not have discretion when he is bound to reach an understanding of what his orders or the rules require, and to act on that understanding.

19 It should be pointed out too that we are not referring here to the discretion of any given body (tribunal, ministry, etc.) but to discretion exercised at any point of time with respect to a particular task. For example, an organisation might start out with high discretion to perform a particular task and may then proceed to impose a limit upon its discretion by abiding by past decisions. Hart and Sacks refer to this as "discretion on a one-way ratchet". H. Hart and A. Sacks, The Legal Process, at 160–180 (Tent. ed. 1958).

20 This particular form of conciliation differs from the usual form of mediation, which is categorised here as a purely administrative function, where the mediator only supervises a negotiated settlement, and the parties themselves are authorised to set its terms. See T. Eckhoff, The Mediator, The Judge and the Administrator in Conflict-Resolution, 10 Acta Sociologica, p. 158 (1966).

21 The distinction between managerial and dispute-settlement tasks is similar to that adopted by Selznick between 'administration', the job of which is to "get the work of society done" and 'adjudication' the primary function of which is to "discover the legal coordinates of a particular situation". Selznick, supra, at 16.

22 See S. Simon, S. Smithburg and V. Thompson, Public Administration, at 428 (1950).

23 E. Freund, Administrative Powers over Persons and Property, ch. 1 (1928).
24 See M. Myerson and E. Banfield, Politics, Planning and the Public Interest, 312–14 (1955); and J.Q. Wilson, An Overview of Theories of Planned Change, in Morris, ed. Centrally Planned Change, at 13 (1964).
25 For a detailed study of the evolution and workings of the English Act see A. Lester and G. Bindman, Race and Law (1972).
26 For a legal-sociological study of the MCAD's early history, see L. Mayhew, Law and Equal Opportunity (1968).
27 D. Henderson, Conciliation and Japanese Law, at 4 (1965).
28 Id. at 5 (emphasis in original). See also J. Cohen, Chinese Mediation on the Eve of Modernization, 54 Calif. L. Rev. 1201, 1224–5 (1966).
29 Further details will appear in J. Jowell, Law and Bureaucracy (Dunellen Press, forthcoming). The number of cases reported is 82 (37 for Commissioner A, 24 for Commissioner B, 21 for Commissioner C). These were all the 1965 cases alleging discrimination in housing and employment.
30 Much of the early history of the Commission is well documented in L. Mayhew, supra.
31 30 Mass. L. Q. 11, (1945).
32 Memorandum by Charles P. Curtis, Jr., To the Legislative Commission on State Administration, op. cit. supra, at 2 (emphasis added). Similar arguments were employed to overcome opposition to proposed anti-discrimination legislation in England. E.g. "... much of the restance should disappear when it becomes generally understood that legislation doesn't mean that every act of discrimination will be treated as a ciminal offence – but that the law will simply be used as an ultimate sanction if the machinery of conciliation and persuasion does't work". The Observer, Sunday 23 April 1967, p. 12, col. 1. See generally, A. Lester and G. Bindman, supra.
33 Undated and unidentified editorial in the Henry L. Shuttuck Collection, Littauer Library, Harvard.
34 Commonwealth of Mass., Fair Employment Practices Commission, Annual Report, December 1946, p. 1.
35 Mayhew, supra, at 248.
36 Ibid. at 91–100.
37 Ibid. at 249.
38 Ibid.
39 Commissioner A was one of the original appointees to the Commission in 1946. By habit, or inclination, he had retained his old techniques and approach. Commissioner C had recently been appointed, and was pioneering a departure from the then-dominant approach of Commissioner B. The following year Commissioner B was replaced by a Commissioner following the "equal opportunity" approach.
40 W. Leys, Ethics and Administrative Descretion, 3 Pub. Admin. Rev., at 14 (1943).
41 See H.L.A. Hart on the two handicaps to advance regulation of human conduct – relative ignorance of fact, and relative indeterminancy of aim, H.L.A. Hart, The Concept of Law, at 125 (1969). See also H. Simon's discussion on the limits of human rationality in decision, H. Simon, Administrative Behavior, ch. V (1945), and the discussion of the "cognitive limits of rationality" in J. March and H. Simon, Organisations, ch. 6 (1958).
42 J.Q. Wilson, Varieties of Police Behavior, ch. 3 (1968). See also A. Downs, Inside Bureaucracy, ch. 3 (1967).
43 Ibid. at 86.
44 See V. Thompson, supra, at 14–18.
45 P. Blau, The Dynamics of Bureaucracy, at 241 (1955).
46 See e.g. R. Merton, Bureaucratic Structure and Personality, in R. Merton (ed.) Reader in Bureaucracy (1952). Nonet's study of California Industrial Accident Commission shows a change in Approach over the years. P. Nonet, Administrative Justice (1969). See also M. Bernstein, Regulating Business by Independent Commission (1955) for an account of the "life cycle" of federal regulatory commissions.
47 J. Handler, op. cit. supra.
48 For a fuller account see J. Jowell, op. cit. supra, 217–19 (1973).

Ernesto Ugo Savona

Civil Trial and Social Justice in Italy. A Sociological Analysis of Proceedings under Art. 28 of the Workers' Statute.*

Lately a sizeable literature about the civil trial has been developing in Italy(1)**. This literature abandons legal formalism, and takes much deeper account of the economic and social premises and consequences of norms and judicial process. Though long retarded by the conservatism of legal thought, there are now new perspectives on the civil trial. Now it is seen as a means to carry out principles of social policy embodied in substantive law. This is a reaction to the false view of judicial proceedings as value-neutral, which results *de facto* in favoritism toward economically stronger parties. The proceedings are to be reformed so as to bring about an equality that does not now exist, given the current state of social stratification. The need for protection of the weaker party is most evident in labor trials.

To focus debate upon these aspects of trials will hopefully bring about change in norms and in institutional arrangements. The reform of labor trials, now in force, represents a first (and long delayed) step towards the more difficult and general reform of the civil code.

It seems likely that reform legislation will ultimately pass, and new norms, more conducive to social justice, will be instituted. But mere enactment is no solution to the problem. Enforcement of the new norms will make or break them. This phase of legal change will be the longest and most delicate; numerous difficulties are sure to arise; resistance will be strong. The interests that have hampered and still hamper legislative reform of the code of civil procedure, will concentrate their strength at the point of application as well.

This paper is concerned with this problem of effectuating reform. It aims to provide some information about the relationship between the change in procedure norms, with the object of enhancing social justice, and actual realization of this goal. We begin with some references to the social disfunctions of the existing system, and their social consequences; describe the innovative aspects of the new labor provisions, and attempt to assess the effectiveness of these reforms, which beginning with labor trials, are ultimately to be introduced into civil trials in general.

We have chosen Art. 28 of the Workers' Statute as the center of gravity of our discussion. This provision has been in effect three years, and contains elements that can be treated, as it were, as hypotheses about reform of the Italian judicial system. Analysis of Art. 28 may serve, then, to evaluate the effectiveness of procedural reforms, both present and future. Finally, we will present some data drawn from

* This paper reports on the author's research in progress, on the effectiveness of Art. 28 of the Worker's Statute, financed by the Committee for National Research (C. N. R.) contract n. 72.00914.10.

** Notes on pages 215.

research in progress, dealing with three elements necessary for evaluation of judicial reform: the demand for justice, the supply, and the actual effectiveness of the measures taken.

1. Civil trials and expectations of justice.

We begin with some information on current court procedures. A useful frame of reference for analysis of the judicial system may be provided by the demand-supply model (2). This model does not fit the system of justice perfectly, drawn as it is from economic analysis. One must bear in mind the opposition of interests between the citizen on the demand side, and the judiciary on the supply side. Law and justice are matters of private initiative (in civil trials); this serves the interests of ruling economic forces. The conflict of interest between citizen and jurist shoud progressively decrease if the struggles of trade union and other political forces heighten the commitment of the judiciary to public service.

What we compare, then, is not purely supply and demand. We compare the functioning of civil trial with the expectations of justice of parties, specifically economically and socially weaker parties. This goal is social justice; it may be attained either by introducing new norms of civil procedure, by speeding up the mechanism of trials (thus reducing its costs) or finally by granting legal aid to the poor.

If we analyze the present functioning of trials in Italy, we can readily see that they are wholly incapable of meeting these expectations.

a) Length of trial

According to data for the period 1955–1967 (3) the average length of civil trials passing through three levels – first instance courts, courts of appeals, Supreme Court (Cassazione) – varied from 4 years and 6 months in 1955 to 7 years and 4 months in 1967 for lawsuits initiated in courts (tribunali); and from 4 years and 15 days in 1955 to 6 years and 10 months in 1967 for lawsuits initiated before single-judge courts (pretura). During this twelve year period average length of a civil trial increased about 60 %. These data are all the more relevant if we note the general decline in the number of civil lawsuits initiated in the period: from 585033 in 1955 to 493727 in 1967; from 1968 on, there was some tendency to increase – 1968 (447765), 1969 (471557); 1970 (502585); 1971 (495640) (4).

The consequences of these trends are further elucidated in the enclosed table of civil trials initiated, pending and completed with or without judgment in recent years. The data bear on the capacity of civil trial, as it presently exists, to fulfil the expectations of justice of Italian society.

Though the data of 1971 on lawsuits concluded with and without judgment are laking, the table shows that on the average 43.7 % of the cases at the trial instance went to judgment during this period; in the preceding five years, 1962-1966, the figure was 39 %. Lawsuits concluded without judgment were, respectively, on the average 56.29 % in the period 1968–1970, and 60 % in the period 1962–1966 (5). Of course, many factors enter into these failures to go to judgment. But the data surely indicate renunciation of the right to judicial decision, and therefore a

preference for litigation outside of the trial mechanism. In a general way, they point to a malfunctioning of the judiciary.
Parties that have greater economic capacity, of higher social classes and occupational strata can withstand lengthy trials better than the poor; the long trials can be used by those who see in delayed justice an indirect advantage (fulfilment of obligations can be postponed) or a way practically to force the weaker party to renounce his rights. That Italian justice favors the wealthier classes can be partially confirmed on the basis of an investigation (6) conducted upon 378 civil trials in 1962 with judgments in the Court of Appeal of Rome and the Supreme Court (Cassazione). Parties received differential treatment according to their occupational position. It was reported that "professionals, managers, and high officials conclude positively 62.5 % of the trials in which they are parties as against 60 % of officials, 55 % of small entrepreneurs, 40 % of clerks, and only 39.1 % of artisans, farmers, small tradesmen, workers, etc." (7) Research data show that the upper class obtains a favorable judgment in 58 % of its trials; the lower and working classes obtain a negative result in 60 % of their cases.

b) The costs of civil justice and the functioning of legal aid

Another element that contributes greatly to the malfunctioning of the judiciary is the high cost the parties must bear, either in the form of direct costs related to the trial (judicial documents, attorney fees, fees for experts) or indirectly in the form of earnings lost. This last increases proportionally with the length of the trial. Along with devices to speed up the work of the courts, some sort of effective instrument for the legal aid of poor persons is indispensable. This is especially true when we consider how necessary expensive legal counselling and technical services may be to a successful lawsuit. Legal aid has long since been introduced in a number of countries. The Italian law, passed in 1923, is wholly inadequate, especially compared with other modern nations. It is, of course, difficult to compare laws that are different in many ways; yet it is noteworthy that in England, legal aid (free for the parties but paid for by the State) in 1967 was granted in 25 % of civil trials before the High Court; in federal Germany legal aid is granted in 20 % of all civil trials; in France in about 30 % (8). In Italy the situation has gone progressively downhill. From 1952 to 1956 the average was 1.5 %; in 1960 it decreased to 1 %; in 1964 to 0.61 % and in 1965 to 0.54 %. If we consider the lower standard of living of our country, as against the other countries mentioned, it is perfectly clear that the present scheme of legal aid is completely useless and must therefore be wholly transformed.

3. The reform of labor trials

Labor law is a glaring example of the contradictions between progressive norms of substantive law, and procedural arrangements that handicap the party who is economically less strong.
Labor trial procedures are basically the same as those generally used in civil trials. In 1970, there were 43,992 labor trials as a whole (including cases about fringe benefits and agrarian litigations) that went to judgment at the trial level, and 8,702

Civil Trials Initiated, Pending and Completed with or without Sentence 1968–1971
(Absolute and percentage data)

Judical offices	Initiated (% on the total)				Completed with sentence (% on the total compl.)			Completed without senten ce (% the tot. compl.)			Total of completed (% on the total)				Pending at the beginning of the year (% on the total)				Total			
	1968	1969	1970	1971	1968	1969	1970	1968	1969	1970	1968	1969	1970	1971	1968	1969	1970	1971	1968	1969	1970	1971
First degree																						
Conciliation offices	66549	66070	54840	52422	29004	31017	26842	31593	37030	28932	60597	63872	55774	53666	60652	58816	56986	60675	187798	188758	167600	166763
Preture	210587	215148	229310	235560	89065	89720	89961	118733	116589	120067	207838	206309	210028	209482	305238	307987	316826	336108	723663	729444	756164	781150
Tribunals	168276	189753	217343	206963	76591	76602	78903	112669	106517	92241	189260	183119	171144	174644	447884	426100	433534	479733	805420	799772	604678	861340
Courts of Appeal	2353	586	1092	695	1892	368	788	362	338	372	2254	706	1160	583	1340	1439	1319	1251	5947	2731	3571	2529
Total	447765	471557	502585	495640	196552	197707	196494	263397	260474	241612	459949	454006	438106	438375	815114	795142	808665	877767	1722828	1719745	1532013	1811782
	(25,99)	(27,42)	(32,81)	(27,36)	(42,73)	(43,54)	(44,85)	(57,26)	(57,37)	(55,14)	(26,70)	(26,40)	(28,60)	(24,20)	(47,31)	(46,24)	(52,78)	(48,45)	(100)	(100)	(100)	(100)
Degree of Appeal and Supreme Court																						
Preture	393	350	470	444	240	200	266	171	108	232	411	308	498	463	950	932	974	946	1754	1590	1942	1853
Tribunals	9608	9395	10605	9659	7644	7076	7124	1444	1361	3561	9088	8437	10685	9702	18812	19332	20290	20210	37508	37164	41580	39571
Courts of Appeal	27749	28826	28379	28431	19249	21103	21542	4990	5019	4516	24239	26122	26058	24498	46031	49541	52245	54566	96019	104489	106682	107495
Total	37750	38571	39454	38534	27133	28379	28932	6605	6488	8309	33738	34867	37241	34663	65713	69805	73509	75522	135281	143243	150204	148919
	(27,90)	(26,93)	(26,27)	(25,88)							(24,98)	(24,34)	(24,79)	(23,28)	(48,63)	(48,73)	(48,94)	(50,71)	(100)	(100)	(100)	(100)
Supreme Court	4334	4673	4715	4896							4816	4684	3225	4370	11788	11306	11295	12785	20486	20663	19235	22051
	(21,16)	(22,62)	(24,51)	(22,20)							(23,51)	(22,67)	(16,77)	(19,82)	(57,54)	(54,72)	(58,72)	(57,98)	(100)	(100)	(100)	(100)
Total	489849	514801	546754	539070	341754	226086	225426	270002	266962	249921	498503	493557	478572	477408	892695	876253	893469	966274	1878595	1883651	1701452	1982452
	(26,08)	(27,33)	(32,13)	(27,19)							(26,54)	(26,20)	(28,13)	(24,08)	(47,52)	(46,52)	(52,51)	(48,74)	(100)	(100)	(100)	(100)

Elabozation of data of ISTAT

in the Courts of Appeal. This was respectively 22.39 % (trial level) and 30.08 % (Court of Appeal) of all civil trials. There were 20,412 cases about subordinate and autonomous labor – for which the demand for procedural reforms has been particularly strong – that went to judgment at the trial level (46.40 % of all labor cases and 10.39 % of all civil cases that went judgment at the trial level); 4,381 went to judgment in the Courts of Appeal (50.34 % of all labor cases and 15.14 % of all civil cases going to judgment at the appellate level) (9). It has not been possible to obtain data for labor trials that ended without final judgment in 1970. Earlier research, however, has shown that this figure should be more or less equivalent to that for civil trials in general (10).

Because of the strong demand in this area of law for social justice, it is understandable that a first step towards reform of the Italian judicial structure has been undertaken for labor cases. The recent labor procedure law (11) represents in fact an attempt at a broad reform of civil procedure. The principle of orality, the power of the judge to intervene at every phase of the trial, the creation of special labor judges, streamlining of procedures, and many other innovating elements all constitute steps toward the realization of the goals of social policy already expressed in the norms of the constitution.

Enforcement of this reform will not be easy. At the parliamentary level, resistance was strong, and hampered and delayed enactment. The same forces will appear once more when the law comes to be implemented, unless the judicial system is able to change its attitudes and structures.

The future course of events is, to be sure, unknown. But we can outline with sufficient clarity the probable level of effectiveness in the short run of the new form of labor trial. One partial way to do this is to analyze compliance with decisions of the single judge (pretore), deciding cases under Art. 28 of the Workers' Statute of 1970. The statute reads as follows: "In case the employer performs acts aimed at preventing or limiting the exercise of union liberties and activity and of the right of strike; upon request of the interested local organs of the National Union Association the judge of the place where the conduct complained of occurred, within two days following a hearing and the taking of summary information, should he believe the violation to exist, shall order the employer by a reasoned, immediately enforceable order, to stop the illegal behavior and to remove all its effects. . . ." This is a procedural norm that refers to a broad range of anti-union conduct. The employer's compliance with the judge's order is crucial; and experience with this compliance will suggest the probable future effectiveness of the new labor trial.

2. Data about the enforcement of Art. 28 of the Workers' Statute.

Art. 28 is the procedural norm meant to realize the political goal of the Workers' Statute. This goal is widely assumed to be the legitimation and support of union activity in factories, and, through this means, the effective protection of the working class. The norm is designed, in part, to guarantee swiftly and effectively the free exercise of any kind of union activity, and to eliminate any repressive intervention on the employer's part.

Three distinct parties are given roles by Art. 28: the union, the magistrate, the entrepreneur. The behavior of these parties determines the effectiveness, present and future, of the law. We define effectiveness to mean the actual advantage brought to the working class by the utilization of Art. 28. Research on this point is now in progress. The research seeks to verify a series of hypotheses about the relationship between trade-union power and the utilization of Art. 28, and consequently about capacity to enforce the magistrate's decisions. For this purpose, orders under Art. 28 pronounced by single judges (pretori) during the three years the law has been in effect are being analyzed. A survey in depth is planned in some Italian industrial areas where problems related to employers' anti-union conduct have arisen and frequently still arise.

We focus here upon a specific problem: actual compliance of the employer with what has been ruled by the judge. In other words, where the judge had ruled in favor of the trade-union ,ordering anti-union conduct to cease, we attempted to find out whether the employer actually modified his behavior as demanded by the judge's decision. The research reported on was confined to the city of Rome. Despite this limitation, the results are highly suggestive.

Out of a total of 201 suits, brought during the three years studied, it was possible to locate the order in 192. In 79 of those the judge ruled in favor of the union; in 70 he rejected the union's claim; 15 suits were concluded by agreement between the parties; in five, the judge partially accepted and partially rejected the union's claim; 18 lapsed for failure of the parties to appear; and 5 were voided.

The research design selected, initially, the cases in which the union prevailed, and where one or all three union confederations (12) acted as claimant. There were 62 such cases. Excluded were cases brought by openly reactionary unions, which tried to use the Statute to legitimize their presence in the factory (13).

Agriculture was represented in 1.3 % of the cases, industry in 28.3 %; the "tertiary" sector in 69.5 %. This dominance of the tertiary sector is understandable, because of the importance of trade and bureaucracy in Rome. The trade sector indeed produced the highest number of suits, 18 (29.2 %). Metal workers produced 6 (9.4 %) and construction workers only 2 (3.1 %). The last figure is significant. Construction is important in Rome, but unions are poorly represented in this sector.

Anti-union conduct appearing most frequently in the suits included: threats, harassments, violence, etc. (21.6 %); firing of union leaders (16.4 %); transferring of union leaders (12.2 %); denial of the right of assembly (9.4 %); collective anti-union firings (8.1 %); suspensions and collective reductions of working hours (6.6 %). As to the duration of proceedings (from the date suit was filed to the judge's order) they lasted less than ten days in 50 %; from 10 to 20 days in 21.4 %; from 20 to 30 days in 20 %; over a month in 8.2 %. The duration of these proceedings is particularly short when compared to average durations in civil cases, as we have noted.

On employer compliance, three variables were distinguished: (a) time of compliance, (b) mode of compliance, (c) increase of union power following the suit.

The data were collected either through the union that brought suit or through information gathered directly in the work setting where the subject of the suit arose. It was possible to gather almost complete data in 48 cases out of the 62. For the remaining 14 cases, it was not possible to obtain the necessary information, because the union had not organized in the plant and it proved difficult to approach other sources.

The data, on the whole paints a picture of some effectiveness. Though limited to a small part of the scope of Art. 28, the figures showing high immediate (77.4 %) and total (69.1 %) compliance, certainly suggest this. The increase of union power in

Times of compliance after sentence	
immediately	77.4 %
within 15 days	8.1 %
within 1 month	2.4 %
over 1 month	2.4 %
no compliance yet	8.1 %
compliance at first, followed by the same anti-union conduct	2.4 %
	100.8 %

Modes of compliance	
total	69.1 %
partial	12.1 %
only apparent compliance	10.1 %
no compliance	8.8 %
	100.1 %

Increase of union power in the work setting after the judge's order	
increase of membership in the union	46.3 %
no increase of membership in the union	44.2 %
decrease of union power	9.5 %
	100.0 %

Increase of bargaining power	
increase	60 %
no increase	30 %
decrease	10 %
	100 %

the work-setting where the anti-union conduct occurred (60 %) provides further corroboration, and demonstrates that the statutory goal of increasing and legitimizing the union's presence has at least partly succeeded. Of course, the data ignore the many other variables that may be important. Nor can we explain exactly why employers comply with the judge's decision.

Conclusion

The success of Art. 28 (confirmed also by national data not reported here) allows us to propose some generalizations or hypotheses.

First of all, it is necessary to point out the absolute interdependence of judicial procedures and social structure. The latter as a system of interrelated values and interests, affects the judicial system deeply; the social structure is highly stratified, and as a result the judicial system becomes formalized in such a way as to advance the political goals of the social structure as it is. Change within the social system is continuous – arising, more or less, out of processes of conflict, which transform the premises on which procedural norms are based. Despite these altered circumstances, however, procedural norms and practices do not change rapidly. They may continue thus to function according to earlier schemes, retarding the realization of new goals of social policy. Inertia reflects a lack of political determination. Conservative interests prevail; and considerably lessen the credibility of the judiciary for users and administrators.

Inevitably, then, individual judges take upon themselves the responsibility of filling in legislative "gaps," and arriving at new solutions. But this is by no means satisfactory. Fresh legislation is needed to change both substantive and procedural law. The experience under Art. 28 shows that new arrangements, here applying to labor-management problems, can have an immediate effect upon the social structure. Art. 28 has changed behavior and situations in a way that may have long-run impact. The worker's Statute and the new labor procedures are still only one example. They do not reflect the general situation but merely a trend. But they strengthen the belief that only within a new procedural system can principles of substantive law advancing social justice be truly and successfully carried out.

Zusammenfassung

In der laufenden Diskussion um die Rechtsreform in Italien weisen viele Juristen darauf hin, daß die Reform des materiellen Rechts im Interesse der sozialen Gerechtigkeit von einer entsprechenden Reform des Prozeßrechts begleitet werden muß.

Im Vergleich zum Strafrecht ist es im Zivilrecht – wo der Prozeß nur unter einem technischen Gesichtspunkt behandelt wird – viel schwieriger, dieses Postulat zu verwirklichen. Es hat sich jedoch gezeigt, daß eine anscheinend neutrale Rechtsauffassung nur konservativen Interessen und Ideologien dient.

Die Justiz ist ineffizient; die Prozesse dauern immer länger; die Parteien versuchen die Gerichte zu umgehen. Die Justiz ist deshalb mehr und mehr ein zur Erlangung der Gerechtigkeit unbrauchbares Instrument. Die ökonomisch und sozial schwache Partei ist benachteiligt. Forschungsergebnisse zeigen, daß im Zivilprozeß die Parteien auf Grund ihrer sozialen Stellung unterschiedlich behandelt werden. Diese Situation (von formaler Gleichheit und wirklicher Ungleichheit) ist noch offensichtlicher in arbeitsgerichtlichen Prozessen.

Wissenschaftler und Praktiker sind sich schon lange der Notwendigkeit einer Reform des Arbeitsprozesses und des Zivilprozesses ganz allgemein bewußt. Die kürzlich, nach einer starken Opposition, erfolgte Reform des Arbeitsprozesses zeigt erneut, daß das Arbeitsrecht ein fortschrittlicher Teil innerhalb des italienischen Zivilrechts darstellt. Man könnte deshalb die Hypothese aufstellen, daß Änderungen im Arbeitsprozeßrecht, wenn sie sich bewähren und effektiv werden, auf die ganze Breite des Zivilprozesses ausgedehnt werden können.

Das neue Arbeitsprozeßrecht zielt auf eine soziale Justiz ab. Es sieht Einzelrichter, schnelle Prozesse, niedrige Kosten, unentgeltliche Rechtsberatung und Klarheit der juristischen Fachsprache vor. Es ist zu hoffen, daß die Arbeit der Gerichte auch eine

Änderung in der Arbeitswelt bewirkt. Die Wirksamkeit in dieser Beziehung ist vom Erfolg der technischen Reformen abhängig.
Wird dieses Ziel erreicht werden? Als Anhaltspunkt kann man auf Art. 28 des Arbeitsgesetzes betreffend die richterliche Kontrolle gewerkschaftsfeindlicher Aktivitäten verweisen. In Rom wurden Fälle, die unter diesen Artikel fallen, untersucht. Es wurde überprüft, inwieweit sich der Arbeitgeber der Entscheidung des Richters fügt, wenn die Gewerkschaft obsiegt hat. Die Pilotstudie ergab, daß sich Arbeitgeber in hohem Maße der Entscheidung des Richters fügen. Das weist darauf hin, daß die neuen Verfahrensvorschriften eine Änderung im Verhalten der Arbeitgeber bewirken.

Notes

1 See M. Cappelletti, Processo e ideologie, Bologna 1969, and Giustizia e Società, Milano 1972; V. Denti, Processo civile e giustizia sociale, Milano 1971, which deal extensively with the relationship between social justice and judicial procedure.
2 G. De Rita, Le Trasformazioni qualitative della domanda di giustizia, paper presented at the "seconde giornate internazionali di sociologia del diritto", Varese September 1971, particulary part I, pp. 1–6.
3 M. Cappelletti, Giustizia e Società, Milano 1972 pp. 226–227.
4 See the Annuari di Statistica Guidiziaria, of ISTAT for the relative years.
5 CNR, Controversie di lavoro e previdenziali, Milano 1971 p. 24.
6 Castellano, Pace, Palomba, Raspini, L'efficienza della giustizia italiana, e i suoi aspetti economico-sociali, Bari 1970 pp. 245–264.
7 Castellano, Pace, Palomba, Raspini, L'efficienca della giustizia italiana, e i suoi aspetti economico-sociali, Bari 1970 p. 259.
8 For the data see M. Cappelletti, Giustizia e Società, Milano 1972, p. 230; see also V. Ferrari, The Problem of Legal Aid with Special Reference to Legislation, paper presented at the meeting of the I.S.A. Committee on Sociology of Law, Cambridge 1973 (mimeographed)
9 The data are taken from Compendio Statistico Italiano 1971 of ISTAT
10 CNR, Controversie del lavoro e previdenziali, p. 31.
11 Law n. 533 of the August 11th 1973.
12 The General Confederation of Labor (CGIL), Italian Confederation of Labor (CISL) and Italian Union of Labor (UIL) are each national in scope, cover all categories of workers, and are presently working towards fusion in a single united union.
13 Mainly CISNAL, which has a clearly fascist ideology.

V. Die Auswirkung gerichtlicher Verfahren auf die Gesellschaft

Joel F. Handler*

Social Reform Groups and the Legal System: Enforcement Problems

Social scientists have conflicting views about the efficacy of social reform groups in American political life. McCarthy and Zald think that changed structural conditions – the increase in affluence, the growth of student and professional populations, and the use of mass media – have contributed to a massive expansion of social reform groups during the last decade (1)**. Theodore Lowi agrees that there has been a rise in social reform activity, but he assigns a different reason; it is the decay and failure of existing institutions that has produced the new surge of reform activity in the United States (2). Lowi, and others, however, are pessimistic about the efficacy of reform activity, in bringing about meaningful social change (3). Mancur Olsen, Jr., argues that large social reform groups are inherently weak, unable to counter the political power of smaller, special interest groups (4).

Questions of efficacy ultimately reduce to an empirical question: to what extent can social reform groups mobilize and use resources effectively? During the past two decades, social reform groups have increasingly used the legal system, litigation in particular, as a resource. Lawyers have won some notable, widely publicized cases for reform groups. Ralph Nader, civil rights lawyers, environmentalists, and OEO legal services lawyers are often portrayed by the media as powerful forces of social change. This image has been enhanced by the political attacks of their opposition. Changes in the law seemed to accomplish the goals of social reform group and, in addition, to act as powerful symbolic rewards enabling social reform groups to attract outside resourses. If social reform groups can successfully use the legal system, it is possible that the new uses of the judicial branch of government may have revitalized the pluralist model of American society by providing an effective forum for those groups who cannot persuade the other branches of government to act on their behalf. On the other hand, perhaps the legal system, by responding too readily to the claims of reform

* A.B. Princeton University, 1954; J.D., Harvard University, 1957; Professor of Law, Wisconsin Law School; Institute Fellow, Institute for Research on Poverty, University of Wisconsin.
This paper was prepared for the Conference on the Sociology of Judicial Process, Center for Interdisciplinary Research, University of Bielefeld, Bielefeld, West Germany, September 24–28, 1973. The research was supported by the Institute for Research on Poverty, University of Wisconsin pursuant to the provisions of the Economic Opportunity Act of 1964. The conclusions are the sole responsibility of the author.
I wish to express my appreciation to Gloria W. Handler and Michael Nowakowski for their very valuable research assistance.

** Notes on pages 240 ff.

groups, is lending credence and legitimacy to demands that do not reflect genuine grievances or to social reform groups that lack the membership resources to take advantage of opportunities that the law has given them.

This paper will examine some theoretical problems in the use of the legal system by social reform groups. Of particular importance will be the problems in enforcing legal rules that represent legal gains for reform groups. A change in the law does not automatically produce change in society, though the publicity given to some legal victories of reform groups may create this impression. Indeed, social reform groups may have special difficulties in implementing their legal victories.

First, we will briefly trace how the legal system opened its doors to social reform groups, discussing some specific examples, selected to illustrate particular problems and issues. We will try to explain the experience of social reform groups with the legal system by referring to the behavioral theories of groups. The theoretical and empirical considerations may shed light on the efficacy of the legal system as a resource for social reform groups.

1. Opening up of the Legal System

Social reform groups have turned to litigation to accomplish their goals throughout American history (5), but courts have become increasingly hospitable to the demands of social reform groups in the last two decades. The activism of the United States Supreme Court under Chief Justice Earl Warren was one factor in this development (6). The Warren Court opened the doors of the federal judiciary to claims of minorities and oppressed groups. As the Court saw it, "... (U)nder the conditions of modern government, litigation may be the sole practicable avenue open to a minority to petition for redress of grievances" (7).

The starting point was *Brown v. Board of Education* (1954) (8). The case itself was confined to one field (school desegregation). But it stimulated litigation in countless other areas. *Brown* itself was the climax of a long struggle led by civil rights groups. This was a field where social reform groups were already active, and ready to seize the opportunity presented by the Court. The *Brown* decision, and the civil rights struggle of the 1950's, established a model for social reform activity through law.

The Warren Court quickly fashioned technical tools to carry out its program of aiding minorities, and protecting individual rights against all levels of government (9). To do so, however, it had to expand federal power at state expense. The court extended the reach of the federal Bill of Rights against the states. Schools, criminal justice administration, hospitals, welfare, apportionment, and voting, among others, had usually been treated as of exclusively "local" concern. Now they fell under the partial rule of federal courts. The Court viewed itself as the appropriate forum for groups that could not get a hearing from other branches of government. In *Baker v. Carr* (10) the voting apportionment cases, the Court eroded the "political question" doctrine. This meant that the Court was no longer afraid to meddle in legislative affairs – was willing, in fact, to draw the boundary lines of electoral districts, if need be (11).

To make federal courts more accessible, the Court radically changed some traditional barriers to use of the courts – doctrines of standing, jurisdiction, and the "case or controversy" doctrine. For example, it was once the rule that no plaintiff could come into court (have "standing") to assert the rights of third parties; yet the court allowed the National Association for the Advancement of Colored People to assert the constitutional rights of its members, who were otherwise too fearful or poor to press their claims (12). The court was also willing to undertake jobs and issue commands not usually thought of as strictly "judicial". The federal courts, from time to time, became virtual managers of school systems, when necessary to plan desegregation. The *Brown* decision itself declared segregated schools unconstitutional. The Constitution, said the Court, insisted on "equal protection" for all citizens. Segregation soon fell under the ban in buses, golf courses, bathhouses, courtrooms, voting, marriage, public accomodations, and housing. The revitalized concept of "equal protection" was, the Court held, especially potent to protect "fundamental interests". The Court was especially vigilant in protecting these interests (13). Laws which on their face did not discriminate, might still violate the equal protection clause, if they operate unequally and impaired a fundamental interest. For example, if a state allowed an appeal from a criminal conviction, then it had a duty to provide some way for the poor to prosecute appeals. Voting, free speech, education, marriage and procreation, interstate travel, and fair trials were all "fundamental", in the Court's view. Although the Court never spelled out why certain interests were fundamental and others were not, it seemed to stress interests which went to the ability of people to participate in the political process, and to live with minimal standards of social decency.

The Court also expanded the meaning of constitutional protections of liberty and property. "Property", for example, included a person's interest in his job, in public housing, in welfare benefits, in public education, and in the use of public facilities (14). Government benefits were of such importance to people, and allowed such control over their lives, that courts must keep government under the restraints of "due process". Some rights, indeed, were so important – the court called them "preferred freedoms" – that the state had a particularly hard burden to sustain, in justifying any restriction. "Preferred freedoms" included those which safeguarded the integrity of the democratic process: freedom of speech, association, assembly, and the press (15). As one commentator explained, "Economic interests are typically respresented in the legislative bodies – or able to obtain a hearing from them. Despised ideologies are not" (16). Freedom of religion, freedom to travel, and some aspects of the right to privacy, were also "preferred" (17). In short, under the Warren Court, the federal judiciary heard with a more sympathetic ear the claims of the deviant, and oppressed, and the unrepresented. The Court provided a sympathetic forum for those without representation elsewhere in the political system. For this reason, the federal judiciary became especially inviting to groups seeking social reform.

Lawsuits need lawyers. The invitation extended by the Warren Court could only be accepted if at least some lawyers moved away from traditional law practice into social reform work (18). Following the *Brown* decision in the civil rights movement, many young liberal lawyers took part. They worked on the many cases demanding desegregation. Meanwhile, blacks began their own massive peaceful protest. There was a great need for lawyers to defend sit-ins, freedom riders, and voter registration workers. Hundreds were drawn into the movement. For example, in 1964, 400 law students and young lawyers went to Mississippi to defend civil rights workers. Out of this experience grew the Law Students Civil Rights Research Council. The Council expanded legal assistance to blacks. The NAACP Legal Defense Fund grew to include a wide range of legal defense activities.

The idea that legal action, especially litigation, was an important strategy for social change was greatly stimulated by the "War on Poverty" of the Johnson administration. In the Office of Economic Opportunity, a Legal Services program began. Legal Services was a part of the Community Action Program (CAP), perhaps the most dramatic aspect of the War on Poverty. The basic idea of CAP was to organize (with government help) the community; they would then help themselves. The poor suffered under the existing system of law; legal service lawyers would help them help themselves. The federal government thus paid the bills for a growing number of energetic, young, activist lawyers. These lawyers did primarily "service" cases – handling routine, individual matters on a case-by-case basis. But under the leadership of Clinton Bamberger and Earl Johnson, the first two national directors of Legal Services, emphasis was placed on "law reform" or "impact litigation". This meant test case litigation, that would affect large numbers of people. Johnson's view coincided with the predispositions of many young lawyers in the most important offices in the country. These young men, in previous years, might have worked for large law firms or for the government. They expected and wanted the excitement of important cases fought through to the appellate level, changing the law. Of course, the overwhelming majority of the poverty lawyers continued to handle service cases. But the official position, the ideology of the times, favored test case litigation on behalf of social reform; and this was the work that won glory and public attention.

Middle-class social reform groups were similarly encouraged. Ralph Nader, a lawyer, was a key figure in the rise of the consumer movement. He constantly stressed the role of law and lawyers in the movement, and exhorted law students to work for his cause. One of his basic approaches was to protect the consumer by forcing administrative agencies to enforce existing law. Similar approaches were taken by environmentalists. Environmental protection statutes were passed at the federal and state levels and environmental groups worked to make the government enforce these (as well as other) laws. This is not to suggest that consumer and environmental groups did nothing but litigate. They continued to lobby and engage in political activity and public relations; but litigation rapidly evolved into an improtant part of their tactics.

Changes in the law of standing and of class actions were especially important to consumers and environmentalist organizations. In an influential case *(Scenic Hudson Preservation Committee v. Federal Power Commission)* (19), environmentalist groups protested against a hydroelectric project that would hurt the beauty of the Hudson River area. A Federal Court of Appeals held that the Commission must consider aesthetic and environmental factors in its decisions on power projects; also, the Commission must afford an opportunity to be heard to "those who by their activities and conduct exhibited a special interest" in the "aesthetic, conservational, and recreational aspects of power development". In another case, on licenses for television license renewals, the court ordered a federal agency to grant a hearing to "listeners" respresentatives. The plaintiff claimed to represent black listeners, who were discriminated against by the television station.

Other reform groups also used litigation. By the mid-1970's, there was litigation by groups interested in improving the conditions of the mentally ill, juvenile delinquents, prisoners, and retarded children. Practically all of these lawsuits were class actions; and the plaintiffs included not only individuals but also organizations or groups of interested people.

A "public interest bar" developed along with this rise in middle-class test case litigation. These lawyers represented many groups that could not buy good legal services at the market price. Public interest lawyers often worked in law firms supported by charitable foundations. A few were in private practice, holding themselves out as "public interest" lawyers. Such practitioners tried to restrict their intake of regular cases, working mostly for social reform groups. Other lawyers, in conventional law firms, did public interest law work as a contribution to public service. On the whole, the public interest bar was small; in 1974 there were no more than fifty lawyers in foundation-supported firms in the entire country. Yet many of their lawsuits were significant cases. For example, in one case plaintiffs prevented a powerful consortium of oil companies, the State of Alaska, and the U.S. Government from constructing an oil pipeline. It took an Act of Congress, after a two-year delay, to force construction to begin.

During the decades of the 1950's and 1960's, to be sure, legislatures as well as courts created new legal rights for the poor, minorities, environmentalists, and consumers. But the primary focus of this paper is on litigation. The problem we are examining is the reform potential of litigation. "Litigation" includes adjudication in the administrative process as well as in courts. Necessarily, too, we will look at the tactics of confrontation and bargaining that precede and influence litigation.

2. *The Uses of Litigation*

Litigation is only one of a number of strategies available to social reform groups. Quite often, litigation is used in conjunction with other tactics. Tactics change over time, as some succeed and some fail, and as changes take place within social reform groups and their environment (20). For purposes of analysis, we will discuss three types of litigation strategy: [1] litigation may be used *defensively*, where the group, its leaders, or its supporters are being sued or prosecuted; [2] litigation may be *subsidiary* to other strategies or goals of the organization; and [3] litigation may be used *affirmatively* to accomplish the primary objectives of the group. In practice, these are hardly neat categories. The lines between them frequently blur.

Defensive Litigation. When members of a social reform group are prosecuted criminally, to accept litigation, and fight in court, is only one of several options. Defendants can flee or go underground. If they choose to defend themselves in court, they have many choices about the manner, style, or goals of litigation to make.

Litigation can be used, first of all, purely for defensive purposes. This may occur where repression is vigorous and widespread, and the organization must fight for its life by any means available. The history of the Black Panther party can serve as an illustration. The Party adopted its "Off the Pig" strategy (21) in 1967, about a year after they had electrified militant young blacks by displaying guns, standing up to the police, and proclaiming a program of self-defense. Membership grew rapidly. In the light of urban unrest, outsiders took the Party very seriously. The media and law enforcement officers painted the Panthers as extremely dangerous, if not crazy, white-haters. The slogan "Off the Pig" could be interpreted as meaning "Destroy the Police". It was violent rhetoric, and the criminal justice system struck back to crush the Party. Within about a two year period, twenty-eight Panthers died, over 300 arrests were made as a result of hundreds of raids, and over eighty Panthers were jailed for weeks and months. In about 90 per cent of the cases, the charges were ultimately dropped after members made bail. High bail depleted Party funds. The Panthers spent over § 200,000 in bail-bond premiums. Charles Garry, the lawyer for the Party, claimed that "In these cases, the purpose has clearly been to intimidate, to frighten, to remove from operation the activities of the Panthers, and to hope that the hysteria against the Black Panther Party would produce convictions and imprisonments" (22). During this period, the Party fought for its very life. The main purpose of litigation was survival. The Party was seriously crippled, but it did manage to survive and begin rebuilding out of its base in Oakland, California. Defensive litigation was successful in freeing its principal spokesmen, Huey Newton and Bobby Seale.

The Panther episode was extreme. A social reform group is rarely so oppressed that it must litigate for sheer survival. Unions, for example, are often faced with court injunctions, arrests and jailings. They will struggle to free their organizers, and get them back into the field. But the unions will often seek to use arrests, jailings and court fights for publicity and sympathy, and to attract outside resources. Litigation used in this manner has more than one purpose.

Subsidiary Uses of Litigation. Occasionally, defendants will forego technical defenses or choose to remain in jail, for propaganda reasons. This is one example of the political uses to which litigation can be put. There are many forms of political trial. Here, we mean cases where the defendant deliberately eschews technical, legal defenses, using the trial as a forum for publicizing his cause (23). During the early days of the Black Panther Party, when Newton was trying to establish the rights of blacks to carry arms for self defense against the police (24), he was arrested and tried for the murder of a police officer. This was Newton's first trial as the leader of the Party, and he specifically told his lawyer, Charles Garry, "If there is a conflict between a move that will further the cause politically and one that will serve Huey Newton personally, pursue the political motive. Let no tinge of racism pass unchallenged for fear the challenge will offend a juror; let nothing discriminatory about the system go unexposed even should the exposure make defense more difficult" (25). The Panthers immediately launched a Free Huey campaign, which attracted support from white radicals. Newton himself used the trial to explain his background, the reasons for forming the Party, and what the Party stood for.

Although the political trial most often centers on a single defendant or a small number of defendants, it was used as a mass basis during the civil rights struggles. Direct action on a mass scale began when four black college students sat in at a Wollworth lunch counter in North Carolina in 1960. The idea spread throughout the South. The Student Nonviolent Coordination Committee (SNCC) was formed, emphasizing brotherhood, integration, and nonviolent mass action (26). When the first sit-in arrests were made, the groups used litigation defensively, to get members out of jail as quickly as possible. Then, in the face of repeated jailings throughout the South, SNCC adopted the "jail without bail" tactic. The students remained in jail to dramatize the repression, in the South, stimulate northern white sympathy, and, at the same time, lessen the problems of soaring legal and bail costs.

The National Welfare Rights Organization used pressure on administrative agencies to build and maintain an organization (27). This was civil, not criminal, litigation; but, as in other examples cited, the idea was to exercise legal rights, and then use litigation if and when the exercise of these rights was blocked. NWRO did not use litigation defensively to ward off attacks; rather, when rights were denied, the organization became the moving parties. The idea for the NWRO grew out of the experience of a store-front service agency in New York City, Mobilization For Youth. As poor people began to come into MFY for help, it was discovered that many people were eligible for welfare but not enrolled, or on welfare but not receiving what they were entitled to. The MFY staff rapidly became skilled in aggressive advocacy on behalf of their clients. At this time, under welfare, recipients were legally entitled to a variety of benefits in addition to their basic allowance. For example, it was New York City policy to allow an extra benefit of about § 150 per family of four for winter clothing. In fact, however, these extra benefits were rarely granted. Most recipients did not know about them; if they did know and requested the benefits, welfare caseworkers either refused the requests or gave less than the prescribed amounts.

The MFY handled a number of special grant request cases, then decided to bargain with the welfare department on behalf of groups of welfare recipients. At this time, there was a great deal of unrest in the urban ghettoes. The organization backed up its demands with mass picketings and demonstrations, and demands for administrative hearings as required by federal law. In the first confrontation, the New York City welfare department gave in. Shortly thereafter, hundreds of families received checks for winter clothing. Naturally, word spread rapidly. Within six months, thousands of welfare families joined the campaign for extra benefits. This was the start of the welfare rights organizations. At the height of the campaigns, NWRO workers would station themselves outside of welfare centers with check lists of various benefits that recipients were entitled to. When recipients came into the outer office, they were asked to check the items they had not received. Then, they went in to see the welfare caseworkers and demanded the items. If they were refused, the NWRO worker went back in with them to help them present their case. If the demand was still refused, requests for hearings were filed; lawyers were available for this purpose. These campaigns were backed up by marches, demonstrations, sit-ins, conventions, platforms, and lobbying. In New York City, at least, the campaigns were very effective. For example, in June 1967, special grants in New York City were about § 3 million; in June, one year later, they had reached § 13 million.

Although NWRO was interested in immediately increasing benefits for its members, and attracting new members, this was not its major goal. Its effort was part of a larger strategy to reform the welfare system. The strategy, developed by Professor Richard A. Cloward, a founder of MFY, and Francis Fox Piven, and adopted by NWRO, envisioned a massive drive to recruit all the eligible poor to demand the maximum benefits they were legally entitled to. This, it was hoped, would disrupt state and local welfare agencies, create a fiscal crisis, and force the Federal government to take over welfare and reform it.

Eventually, welfare agencies struck back in two ways. First, they eliminated special grants. At a stroke of the pen, NWRO was robbed of its principal organizing tool and its power to create a fiscal crisis. Welfare departments also resisted at administrative hearings, by delay, or simply by continuing to deny requests after hearings. Welfare organizations lacked the resources to pursue judicial remedies on a massive scale.

In the preceding examples, litigation or pressure on administrative hearings was used as an integral and continuous technique of the strategy of a social reform group. Quite often, however, litigation has a more limited ad hoc (although still important) use. In the Montgomery bus boycott (1955–56), the goal of Reverend Martin Luther King, Jr.'s organization was to induce the city council to repeal an ordinance which required segregation on buses (28). The boycott tactic had a number of advantages for blacks. It was not illegal; thus the leaders and participants could not be legally arrested. It avoided confrontation, which was important because any confrontation in the deep South at this time would have meant brutal repression. At the same time, the black leaders displayed moderation and self-discipline, helpful in attracting outside support. The disadvantage of the boycott was it did not put the city council under any real pressure to yield, until the revenue loss began to hurt. For a long time, then, there was a stalemate. The matter was finally resolved by a lawsuit in which the court declared the ordinance unconstitutional. The city lost, but it could save face by blaming the courts. The litigation allowed both sides to avoid escalating the conflict; leaders used litigation to sidetrack more militant members of the group.

In other situations, social reform groups will use litigation to *produce* conflict, or to hamper or delay some governmental process. For example, environmental groups will use litigation to gain time (i.e., to stop the bulldozer) to enable them to mobilize political or other resources. Litigation, then, has many uses besides the obvious ones of defense and the gaining of direct, concrete goals.

How successful are these tactics? If legal services are free or cheap, the social reform group risks few resources. But the legal proceedings can be long and drawn out. Proceedings are in the hands of leaders and lawyers. Mere members of the group may drift away from lack of activity and interest. The group can also become too dependent on lawyers. Many legal services lawyers who worked with minority and poverty groups stress the real dangers of cooptation by the lawyers. Then, there is always the possibility of losing the case, which may result in a loss of legitimacy for the group (29). Victories, too, can take their toll. Despite the fact that the Federal Government has lost practically all of the political trials of the past few years, and has not prevailed even in grand jury proceedings against radicals, these have been hard-fought, difficult legal battles. They have seriously depleted the resources of the radical left. At the present time, there is a real shortage of sympathetic lawyers (30).

Affirmative Litigation. Litigation is used affirmatively, when it is used to accomplish the substantive goals of a social reform group. At least four types of difficult enforcement problems can arise, even when the lawsuits win.

a) Enforcement involves massive lower-level official discretionar decisions

This is perhaps the most common and formidable hurdle that social reform groups face – when favorable court decisions and legislation are addressed to large numbers of lower-level officials and direct them to change their activities. If voluntary compliance is not forth-coming, social reform movements are usually incapable of countering the intransigence of lower-level officials.

Perhaps the best example is the school desegregation controversy. The basic decision in 1954, *Brown v. Board of Education*, was the culmination of many years of efforts by the NAACP to attack segregation in the courts. Its importance for black civil rights leaders could not be overestimated. They considered it "a visible sign ... that the white establishment and federal government were supporting the legal road to changing their subordinate position" (31). According to Louis Lomax, blacks were confident that victory for an integrated society had come. They felt that the white establishment of the South, while not in favor of integration, would insist on law and order, and not be bullied and cowed into submission by white trash, fanatics, and mobs. It was anticipated that local school boards would voluntarily obey the Supreme Court (32). The decision was viewed as of equal importance by the white opposition to desegregation. According to Anthony Lewis, "Any breakdown in school segregation necessarily endangered the perpetuation of the southern myth that the Negro is by nature culturally distinct and inferior. And there was the fear – surely felt deeply by many in the South, however others regarded it – that school integration was a step toward racial intermarriage" (33). Mississippi's Senator James Eastland said, "The people of the South will never accept this monstrous decision. I predict this decision will bring a century of litigation" (34). Desegregation began to occur almost immediately in the border areas of the country, and by 1956, several hundred school districts integrated voluntarily (35). Then the tide turned. The Southern Manifesto of 1956, signed by 101 U.S. Senators and Congressmen called the *Brown* decision a "clear abuse of judicial power". Southern states started their campaigns of massive resistance, and violent resistance movements spread rapidly throughout the South. Southern whites were a determined, substantial minority in the nation as a whole, and a militant majority in their home states. Opposition to *Brown* took two forms. Social and economic pressure, violence, and mob action would intimidate blacks and moderate whites. A massive legal battle would also be mounted. Every school district would litigate. Every other move toward desegregation would be resisted in court. The Southerners hoped that eventually public opinion would turn against the Court, and the decision either would be reversed or lapse for lack of enforcement. At this time, the North was relatively indifferent to civil rights and the Federal Government, under President Eisenhower, was equivocating in its support of the Supreme Court (36).

The legislative components of the massive resistance strategy took a variety of forms. Initially, laws provided for withdrawing state funds from any school district that adopted desegregation plans; closing such schools; repealing compulsory education laws; providing tuition grants for private schools, cutting off salaries of teachers in desegregated schools; and preventing school boards from borrowing from their usual commercial sources. As these laws were declared invalid, more subtle techniques were adopted, such as pupil placement laws. These laws – which aid not mention race – allowed local officials to assign pupils to schools on the basis of various criteria. In fact, the assignments were used to perpetuate desegregation. Black students who objected faced a maze of administrative hurdles, followed by difficult court battles. School boards also adopted plans assigning students to schools on the basis of geographic zones. Whether the lines of any particular plan were gerrymandered to preserve segregation presented questions difficult to litigate, especially if the blacks had the burden of proof. Where desegregation plans were adopted, school boards fought in court as long as possible (37).

By 1961, the U.S. Civil Rights Commission reported that desegregation was proceeding only when ordered by courts. Moreover, the cases were hard fought, long, and complicated. In the typical public school case, seven years would elapse between the start of the litigation and actual admission of black children to white schools (38). Charles Silberman reported that ten years after the *Brown* decision two of the four school districts in the original case had still not admitted a single black student. In ten states of the Deep South, less than six-tenths of one per cent of all black students were in desegregated schools (39). Writing in 1963, Louis Lomax reported that it took seven years of effort to get only seven per cent of the black children in the South into desegregated schools (40).

Segregation in public schools was not the only issue. The federal courts invalidated segregation laws for a variety of public facilities; the follow-up here too required litigation, if communities refused to comply voluntarily. The NAACP and other civil rights organizations did not have the resources to challenge this kind of massive resistance on a comprehensive basis. Even after years of struggle, some communities did not have a single desegregated facility, and in others, desegregation was minimal (e.g., a few lunch counters only). In Montgomery itself, after the boycott was over, white violence increased, juries refused to convict, and the city passed several new segregation ordinances. Martin Luther King's organization lacked the resources to challenge these laws (41). Silberman reports that seven years after the court ordered integration of the buses, most blacks "had returned to the old custom of riding in the back of the bus" (42).

By 1961, blacks had grown impatient and frustrated with the strategy of integration through court order. This approach was time consuming, costly, and seemed to produce little in the way of results. Attention then turned to non-violent, direct action techniques. The Student Non-violent Coordinating Commitee (SNCC), formed out of a nucleus of activist students, worked to desegregate facilities through direct action. They also began voter registration projects in the Deep South. The workers met with political harassment, violence, arrests, and slow-downs at registrars' offices. After the passage of the Civil Rights Act of 1964, SNCC tried to build a political organization outside of the regular Mississippi Democratic Party. But the Democratic party convention refused te seat SNCC's delegates. SNCC decided that national politics were unreliable and that blacks must organize their own local political base. But his too was difficult. A black-organized party in Lowndes County, Alabama, after a year and a half of dangerous grass roots political activity, failed to gain the 20 percent of the electorate needed for legal recognition – in a county that was 81 per cent black. Blacks were too intimidated by harrassment, violence, and other forms of pressure to register and vote for their own party. Other voter registration drives met with bitter resistance too. Blacks faced intransigent voting registrars, corrupt and brutal law-enforcement personell, and in many instances, prejudiced judges. Finally, SNCC turned northward and inward, toward a policy of black nationalism and separatism; non-violence as a strategy was abandoned.

During the next half decade, however, black registration in the South began to grow. The principal reason for this change was the Voting Rights Act of 1965. Under that law, federal registrars replaced Southern state and local officials whenever and wherever registration of blacks fell below a certain proportion of the population. In many areas of the country, federal registrars were appointed to register blacks and, in other places, state and local registrars realized that their strategy of intransigence would result in their replacement. The Voting Rights Act of 1965 was successful, then, not only because of a stiffening attitude on behalf of the federal government, but also because it eliminated as a stumbling block lower-level officials with power to make discretionary decisions.
The failures of desegregation and voter registration campaigns in the South, during the years 1956–1966, were dramatic, examples of the obstacles that social movement groups face in trying to implement legal rules in the face of lower-level officials who massively resist. The same problem is well-known in other areas of law. There is great difficulty in getting police officers to follow court rules which the police feel will shackle them in their work. Welfare caseworkers, public health personnel, building inspectors, child protection workers, housing officials, lower criminal and civil courts, probation officers, prison officials, and those who work in dozens of other federal, state and local regulatory agencies, are similarly hard to move. If lower-level officials feel strongly that a court-imposed rule is wrong, they can circumvent it in many ways. One major weapon is the fact that clients are often unaware of the rule; or afraid to seek enforcement. Fear is particularly important if the clients are subject to retaliation; in the examples given, clients are usually vulnerable because they have a more or less continuing relationship with the agency (43). Ignorance and fear can be overcome by a social reform organization capable of disseminating the necessary information, engaging in the necessary advocacy, and protecting those willing to stand up. With massive, pervasive regulatory programs like education, voting registration, police, welfare, or health, the lawlessness of front-line officials may be so widespread and so diffuse, that the task of ensuring compliance becomes insuperable.

b) Enforcement involves massive private discretionary decisions

A similar enforcement problem occurs where legal rules favorable to a group require compliance from large numbers of people in the private sector. If compliance is resisted, then government initiative is necessary. But government usually prefers to respond to pressure, rather than take the initiative. For example, where laws prohibit employment discrimination, it has long been recognized that private remedies are ineffective, and there are now government agencies with enforcement powers. However, with few exceptions private complainants must activate the agencies, and even if the agencies obtain favorable decisions, subsequent monitoring has to be used to make sure that the discriminator adheres to the order or the agreement. Employment discrimination is widespread and the victims, of course, are among the most powerless people in society. Social reform groups have attempted to fight cases and negotiate settlements on behalf of their membership or constituencies, but there are many employers, the constituency is poor, and it is difficult to maintain sufficient membership support. Recently, there has been some success in negotiating favorable agreements with a few large employers, partly due to the leverage of outside resources, particularly foundation-supported lawyers. The agreements are with very large employers (e.g., Bell Telephone of California, some large banks), and it is too early to tell whether organizations will be able to monitor agreements.

Gary Bellow, who worked with migrant labor, remarks as follows:

> "Rule" change, without a political base to support it, just doesn't produce any substantial result because rules are not self-executing; they require an enforcement mechanism. California has the best laws governing working conditions of farm laborers. ... (W)orkers are guaranteed toilets in the fields, clear, cool drinking water, covered with wiremesh to keep flies away, regular rest periods, and a number of other "protections". But when you drive into the San Joaquin Valley, you'll find there are no toilets in field after field, and that the drinking water is neither cold, nor clean, nor covered. If it's provided at all, the containers, will be rusty and decrepit. It doesn't matter that there's a law of the books. There's absolutely no enforcement mechanism. Enforcement decisions are dominated by a political structure that has no interest in prosecuting, disciplining or regulating the state's agricultural interests (44).

The current controversy over abortion reform is also of interest. Abortion is in demand among minorities and poor people; but it is also a middle-class issue. Vigorous reform groups, with middle-class members, have been active in the reform movement. The Supreme Court in 1973 invalidated most state laws restricting abortion. One would have predicted ready compliance with the law. In fact, one might even have expected profit-making abortion clinics to spring up around the country. So far, this has not happened. Although many more abortions are now performed, compared to before the court's decision, there is on the whole, massive resistance to the more liberal policy in many parts of the country.

In the 1960's, all states still prohibited abortion, except to save the mother's life (45). Through therapeutic abortion committees, hospitals restricted abortions by creating quota systems and charging high fees. Many public hospitals virtually eliminated abortions for the poor. Starting in the 1960's, a few doctors and individuals began to challenge these laws, performing abortions openly, and disseminating information. There were arrests and some convictions; a few lower courts declared some laws invalid. At about this time, reform group activity gathered strength. In part, this trend was stimulated by the notoriety of the criminal prosecutions and some of the successful litigation. In 1967, three states – Colorado, California, and North Carolina – passed the first liberalized laws; abortions could be performed to preserve the mother's life, or her physical and mental health; or in cases of rape, incest, or where there was reason to believe that the fetus might be defective. These laws had disappointing results. In Colorado, abortion fees were high, and nineteen out of twenty women seeking abortions were rejected. Hospitals imposed restrictions over and above the law.

In 1969 the abortion laws of California and the District of Columbia were declared unconstitutional. The medical profession generally ignored the decisions. In the District of Columbia, abortion committees were retained in the hospitals; they continued to reject most applicants. The public hospital – D.C. General – refused to take abortions. It took two additional court actions by abortion reformers before this hospital agreed to set up a special abortion unit. In Wisconsin, the federal court declared the state law unconstitutional, but had to issue orders preventing local law enforcement officials from subsequent prosecutions of two doctors. In the meantime, lawsuits were brought in other states.

In 1970, liberalized laws were passed in four other states, including New York. In New York, hospitals and the State Health Commissioner sought to restrict abortions to hospitals, which quickly developed long waiting lists and restrictive requirements. Many clinics and medical groups defied the Commissioner. In a further effort to restrict abortions, Governor Rockefeller banned Medicaid payments for abortions.

Then, in 1973, came the Supreme Court decision (46). The Court held that a state might not regulate abortions during the first three months of pregnancy, might regulate abortions in the second three months to protect the health of the mother, and in the last three months to protect the fetus and the mother. The Court gave no opinion on whether hospitals could be forced to perform abortions, if they chose not to.

The Supreme Court's decision had an immediate impact. Since abortions could now be performed regardless of existing state law, state legislatures began to act quickly. However, few states enacted laws implementing the decisions. Several re-enacted old laws or laws plainly unconstitutional, which produced further litigation. Others are seeking to establish the right of any individual or institution to refuse to provide abortion services. Many state legislatures have called on Congress for a constitutional amendment overruling the Court. On the administrative level, there continues to be discrimination against the poor. At the present time, the situation is in flux. In most areas of the country, abortions are still not available. Hospitals and doctors refuse to perform the service; some lower court decisions have upheld this right. There is active opposition to abortion, led by the Catholic Church, which continues to exert great pressure at the local and national level. The profit-making services have not grown as anticipated. Massive resistance continues.

c) Enforcement requires continuous inputs at key regulatory agencies

In the problems already examined, social reform groups may win a court decision, or a rule change from legislative or executive, but because decision-making authority for implementation is widely diffused, enforcement makes little headway. There are also enforcement problems when decision-making authority remains within a single agency. Regulation is a continuous process and a rule change is usually only one stage in the process. The political, social, and economic context remains the same; and the old forces or interests continue to exert efforts to cope with any new rules that social reform groups have been able to win through litigation or related legal process.

One theory behind recent litigation by environmental and consumer groups is that for a long time regulatory agencies have only listened to the industry point of view and have become "captives" of the forces they were meant to control. The new litigation had a procedural aim – to open up the decision-making process, so that environmentalist or consumer points of view could be expressed. Regulatory agencies would, then, be more likely to reach decisions in the "public interest". In *Scenic Hudson Preservation Committee v. Federal Power Commission*, the court held that the Federal Power Commission must take into account environmental and aesthetic considerations in decisions on the sites of power plants. It must grant those who have a special interest in these matters (i.e., environmental groups) an opportunity to be heard. But the court did not say which way the agency must decide on the merits, merely that the agency must take a look at various point of views. If it did this fairly, the agency was free to abide by its original position. And in fact, this was more or less the result in this particular case. The environmentalists presented their evidence to the agency; the agency considered the evidence, rejected much of it, and authorized the construction of the power plant, though with certain modifications.

Although the social reform group failed to win a complete victory in the *Scenic Hudson* case, it did win an important principle. This principle has been extended by the National Environmental Policy Act (NEPA) and by state legislation, to many areas of regulation that affect the environment. Regulatory agencies may not proceed without taking environmental factors into account. Under NEPA, federal agencies must prepare statements about the impact of proposed action on the environment. Many agencies at first claimed that NEPA did not apply to them. Others did not take the Act seriously and filed superficial impact statements. These agencies immediately ran into trouble. The environmentalists won many cases in court. Highways, urban renewal projects, and a great variety of projects that affected wilderness areas and conservation (e.g., dams, roads, exploitation of mineral and luber rights, etc.) were stopped, for failure to comply with NEPA. The most famous case involved the proposed construction of the Trans-Alaska Pipeline; social reform groups and a public interest law firm halted construction of the pipeline. These decisions came as great shocks to government and the business world. Environmental groups. and their public interest lawyers, were using litigation apparently to great advantage. The opposition began to cry that the environmentalists were zealots, they were going "too far", and that growth and development would be unnecessarily restricted.The initial decisions under NEPA were procedural only; there remained the problem of implementation. The first problem of implementation involved taking advantage of the opportunity to be heard. Many of the substantive issues in the environmental disputes are extraordinarily complex. The industry has the technical resources to back up its position. Such social reform groups as the Sierra Club, the Wilderness Society, and the Friends of the Earth, are membership organizations and rely for their experts mostly on voluntary contributions. They could not even finance the initial lawsuits without help from public interest law firms, financed by foundations. Some group members are engineers and scientists, who may donate a few evenings a week or a day or two on a weekend; but industry has many more experts on permanent call.

The need for a continuous input of information is well illustrated by the Trans-Alaskan Pipeline controversy. The litigation at first stopped construction completely. The Department of Inerior and the industry then took NEPA seriously, and drafted a comprehensive impact statement. Many design features of the pipeline and its construction were altered to lessen environmental damage and risks. Construction was finally authorized by an Act of Congress. The present construction plans are more sound from an environmental standpoint than the original plans, hence the environmentalists did have a substantial impact.

But whether or not this victory will prove hollow depends on how the construction actually proceeds. Throughout the whole controversy, the Department of Interior was unsympathetic to the environmentalists. Now, with the energy crisis, there should be enormous pressure to modify the impact statement to save costs and time. Unless the environmental groups are capable of persevering, even their partial victory will almost certainly evaporate.

The need for continuous struggle is not restricted to environmental problems. As a result of a petition from various consumer groups, including Ralph Nader, the Federal Trade Commission announced a new procedure whereby all major companies, on an industry basis, would provide the agency with documented support for claims made in their advertisements. The Commission started by asking substantiation from manufacturers of automobiles, electric razors, air conditioners, toothpaste, and head cold remedies. The problem now is to keep up with the flood of information that is pouring in (47). The agency has already fallen behind in its work. It will be up to consumer groups to make sure that the information leads to reform in advertising. But will these groups have the technical resources to do so (48)?

d) The strongly recalcitrant government defendant

The State of California's refusal to implement federal law requiring an increase in welfare benefits illustrates the fourth kind of enforcement problem (49).

Under the program of aid to families with dependent children, the California State Department of Social Welfare determined each recipient's minimum need by computing budgets containing allowances for housing, food, clothing, personal needs, recreation, and other needs. County departments of welfare calculated the amount of income the family had available. If the family's need exceeded its available income, then AFDC paid the difference between the family's income and its need standard, unless the difference would exceed a fixed maximum amount for a family of that size.

Congress then enacted legislation under which, by July 1, 1969, the states had the duty to increase their need standards and their maximum grants, to reflect changes in the cost of living. There was a long controversy over the precise meaning of this law, and particularly whether a state could avoid complying through various techniques.

But from the beginning, high officials in the California State Department unterstood that these techniques did not apply to California. They knew exactly what the new law meant and that they were required to raise the maximum grants in the state. Nevertheless, when the statute was passed by Congress, and despite the fact that the states were given 18 months to meet the requirements, California did nothing to implement the statute. The July 1st deadline passed, California did not comply, and the federal Department of Health, Education and Welfare did nothing to enforce the law. On August 6, 1969, a class action on behalf of all California AFDC recipients was commenced in the Federal District Court to require California to comply with the statute. California strenuously resisted the lawsuit and tried to delay the judicial decision. In the fall and spring of 1969 and 1970, HEW wrote letters of inquiry to California, about its non-compliance, but took no concrete action. The National Welfare Rights

Organization then filed suit against HEW to force it to take steps to make the states comply. Apparently in response to this lawsuit, HEW began proceedings against several states, including California. On August 25, 1970, 13 months after Congress had required compliance, HEW held a hearing on California's non-compliance. California then tried to convince the Federal Court to defer any action in the lawsuit, until HEW had had an opportunity to act. The Federal Court refused to do so.

In September 1970, the Federal Court ordered an immediate increase in the maximum grants, to conform to federal law. The HEW hearing examiner also issued a proposed decision, finding California in violation of federal law, and noting widespread malnutrition and suffering on the part of welfare children. Nevertheless, California continued to refuse to increase the grants. Instead on November 24, California submitted in Federal Court a proposal which would permit the state to avoid a real rise in grants; and at the same time, California appealed the federal court order to a higher court. Later, on January 8, 1971, HEW issued its final report, holding California in violation of federal law and ordering a termination of federal funds to California, effective April 1, 1971, unless the state complied. Immediately, the Governor of California conferred with Vice President Agnew and HEW Secretary Eliott Richardson. The following day, HEW withdrew its decision to termine the federal funds.

In March 1971, the California Supreme Court, in a unanimous decision, arising out of a state lawsuit, held that the state had authority to increase the maximum grants, to conform to federal law. The court also recognized a clear and continued violation of federal law by the state. Plaintiffs continued to press HEW to reissue its non-conformity decision; and they brought suit to force HEW to act. One week after the California Supreme Court removed any doubt about California's ability to comply with federal law, HEW issued its decision and ordered once more a termination of federal funds. Finally, faced with imminent termination of federal funds, the California State Department of Welfare raised its grants, effective July 1, 1971, 23 months after Congress had ordered the increase, and almost a year after HEW had notified California that a conformity hearing would be held.

Note that, in contrast to most of our other examples, here the violation of law was quite clear. The California officials had no doubt as to what the law required; there was no discretion even as to implementation. The relief sought was money payments. Implementation did not require massive lower-level discretionary decisions, or continuous inputs to an on-going administrative process, or the staffing of an administrative bureaucracy. All that the state had to do was re-calculate the standards, and re-program its check-writing machines. The effective date of the legislation was generous, and California could not seriously plead poverty. Despite all this, it took two years of expensive litigation, in five different forums, before the state finally capitulated.

3. Theories of Groups

Those who seek to maintain the status quo, as well as those who seek to alter the existing distribution of social, political, and economic power, make use of the legal system. Changes in legal rules alone do not bring about changes in the social order. Individuals, groups and organizations have to be induced to change their behavior. The extent to which social reform groups have been able to accomplish change by using the legal system varies greatly. Results can be very dramatic when litigation is used defensively. Small, weak, and despised groups have been able to thwart the combined power of the executive and legislative branches of government. When social reform groups use the legal system affirmatively, they often encounter insuperable problems of implementation, despite the enactment of new laws, the fashioning of new rights, the openness of the judiciary, and the availability of subsidized legal talent. Other groups in society, for example, trade associations, unions, and various special interest groups, seem to have more success. What are the characteristics of social reform groups that explain this result?

The traditional assumption about the behavior of social reform groups is that individuals with common interests will band together to further those common interests, since all members will be better off if the objectives of the group are achieved. Thus, group action is the product of rational, self-interested behavior by individuals. Mancur Olson, Jr., in *The Logic of Collective Action* (50), argues that this basic assumption is incorrect. In fact, says Olson, the opposite is the case. Rational, self-interested individuals will *not* act together to achieve common interests, unless they are coerced, or the group is quite small.

The key to Olson's analysis is the distinction, well known to economists, between collective goods and selective goods. A collective or public good is a good such that if any person in a group consumes it, it is not possible or practical to keep others in the group from consuming it as well. The defense provided by an army is a public good. Another is a public park. If an organization seeks to obtain higher wages for workers in a plant, or favorable legislation for an interest group, these are (for the members) collective goods. Note that members of the enjoying group can consume even though they have not paid or contributed anything to obtain that good. If a union negotiates for higher wages and better working conditions, all workers will get the benefit of the bargain, whether or not they are members of the union or contributed in any way to the union's success. Collective goods, then, involve the problem of the "free rider" – the person who consumes a good, without contributing toward a cost.

The basic purpose of an organization is to provide a generalized benefit – that is, a collective good – for all of its members. Under what circumstances, if any, will an individual join or contribute to an organization? Olson's hypothesis is that if the individual's efforts will not have an appreciable effect on the efforts of the organization, and, if at the same time, he will enjoy the benefits of the collective good that the organization provides, without any contribution on his part, then there is no incentive for him to contribute. On the other hand, if a person finds that his personal benefit from the collective good will exceed the cost of providing at least some amount of that good, then he will contribute to the organization. This latter situation is most likely to occur if the group is small, or if there is considerable inequality within the group, so that some members will receive a disproportionate share of the collective good (51). There is a basic difference then, between large and small groups. The larger the group, the less likely it will be able to further the common interests of its members. If the group is so large that an individual's contribution has no noticeable effect on the others' costs and benefits, then collective goods will not be provided without coercion, or some other special incentive (52). Large groups, too, will have high organization costs – that is, costs of communication among members, costs of bargaining, staffing, and maintaining the organization.

Three factors, then, act to prevent large groups from furthering common interests: [1] the benefit from the collective good to any one member will be small; [2] the larger the group, the less likely that some small subgroup would be willing to pay for the cost of the collective good; and [3] the larger the group, the higher the organizational costs. For large groups, then, rational members will act on behalf of the common interests only if there are separate and selective incentives; that is, if the organization treats contributors differently from non-contributors.

Large groups can be mobilized by leaders who receive selective incentives. Groups also become mobilized through social pressure; social status and acceptance are selective incentives since they distinguish among individuals. Moral incentives are also selective incentives for the same reason – they distinguish among those who contribute and those who do not. But social and moral incentives operate only in small or intermediate groups, not with large groups. Olson's conclusion, then, is that in the United States, most large organizations have had to develop special devices to solve their membership problem. Olson uses a number of examples to support his theory. A primary example, of course, are labor unions. Unions provide selective benefits – insurance, grievance procedures, seniority rights, social amenities, etc., but to maintain their membership they must rely on compulsion (e.g., the union shop), or on picket lines and violence. The members themselves rarely attend meetings, but are overwhelmingly in favor of compulsory membership and the obligation to pay considerable dues. Members obtain the benefits of union membership, whether they attend meetings or not.

Olson's argument cast some doubt on the interest group theory of politics. This theory seeks to explain political life in terms of the growth and competition of special interest groups. Groups have power more or less in proportion to their numbers. Generally speaking, larger, more general interests should tend to defeat smaller, narrower interests. As society increases in complexity, more groups or associations arise to fill peoples' needs. Equilibrium is reached at any given time because any "excessive" demands are curtailed by overlapping memberships (e.g., tariff lobbyists are also consumers) and the rise of counter pressure groups. But Olson's theory of group behavior suggests that smaller groups will frequently defeat much larger groups, since members of the small group have strong incentives to pay for the cost of collective goods. Hence, interests are not as neatly or equitably represented as the interest-group theorists assume.

But how, then, does one explain the activities of organized pressure groups in the United States? There are many large organizations, and they do exert great influence on government, the economy, and society. How are they able to achieve this power in the light of Olson's theory? Olson argues that large economic groups that lobby and campaign for collective goods are also organized for some other purpose; the lobbying activities, in fact, are by-products of their main activities. These organizations mobilize their membership through selective incentives or coercion. Labor unions, for example, only became powerful politically in the United States after they achieved compulsory membership. Many professional organizations have achieved guild status or provide selective incentives to join. The business community is made up of oligopolistic industries, each of which contains only a handful of firms; what appear to be large groups are really sets of small groups receiving selective benefits. In almost half of the important trade associations, a few members pay 50 per cent of the costs or more (53).

There is little hope, then, that the downtrodden and unrepresented – the migrant workers, consumers, taxpayers – will be able to organize effectively to achieve reform.

The sociologists, McCarthy and Zald, offer a theory of social reform groups which they claim, decreases the cogency of Olson's analysis (54). Traditional sociological theory of social reform groups, in the opinion of the authors, focused on the states of mind of the mass, the development of group consciousness about grievances, and the processes by which groups develop ideologies and social action (55). This theory has a certain validity, but fails to explain many features of the recent upsurge of reform groups. The authors ask, how do groups mobilize resources *beyond* their own membership? If they are able to do this, they can avoid the "free rider" dilemma.

The authors reject the common view that affluence explains reform group activity: that a large middle class with leisure will participate more in social and civil organizations (56). They claim that the affluent participate not with time but with money. But many occupations have great control over allocation of time; members can thus engage in group activities for specific social reforms. The authors point to the student and professional populations which become available as "transitory teams" for specific purposes at specified times at relatively low cost. Ad hoc committees can be formed to run newspaper ads, circulate petitions, organize protest marches, and raise funds. These cadres of sympathizers come together for the event and then maintain loose ties after the event is over.

Finally, the authors point to a dramatic change in the funding support for social reform groups. During the 1960's, churches, foundations, corporations, and individuals contributed heavily to social reform groups that were very different from prior beneficiaries. For example, foundation giving during the period 1963–1970, showed an increase in "social participation grants" (primarily for race relations, and urban and poverty problems) from § 3.7 million annually to § 54.9 million. During the latter half of the 1960's, the government also funded social reform groups; there were some direct grants (e.g., to the National Welfare Rights Organization), and much indirect support through Community Action Programs, some Model Cities programs, VISTA, and legal services.

The new sources of support brought about what the authors call "funded social movement organizations", which employ professional leadership and staff. Traditionally, charismatic leaders emerging from the aggrieved group, or intellectuals who identified with the groups, held leadership positions. Now, a professional full-time staff moves in and out of government, private agencies, foundations, or universities. The new funding has relieved the professional leadership from dependence on the membership for financial support.

The mass media have aided the leaders in raising funds and swelling membership rolls. Leaders use the media to attract members, to gather support for the organization's goals, and to influence elites. Thus, the size of the organization and its activity may depend more on the media than on the size of membership, the intensity of their support of the nature of the grievances. Many large organizations depend on members who mail in their contributions and have no other membership ties. In others, the leaders become full time actors, with much of their money coming from outside the group that the movement claims to represent. Despite the fact that actual membership may be small or even nonexistent, the leaders will claim that they "speak" for a particular constituency; in fact, they may make all the decisions with little or no participation. The authors claim that the growth of these funded social movements "deflects the *importance* of Olson's argument, since . . . individual citizen participation may be unimportant to movement vitality" (57).

Funding sources tend to be unstable. Certainly one could not expect establishment sources to fund radical social reform, to any significant extent. McCarthy and Zald call donors "contributing beneficiaries"; they participate in the group by paying for the collective good, but they do not consume the collective good. The task of the leaders is to induce these people to contribute. Potential donors have other choices and demands, and will only contribute so much. Because these donors do not experience the grievances that the members of the group feel, their commitment to the group is more tenuous. There is an uneasy relationship, therefore, between the leaders of the group and the contributing beneficiaries. The leaders are induced to serve and lead by the resources given by donors; the leaders receive selective benefits, as part of a privileged group within the larger group. On the other hand, the leaders are constrained by their reliance on outside support. Somehow, they have to convince contributing beneficiaries that their cause is worthy.

A social reform group may need to mobilize resources only once. More typically, mobilization is a continuous process, going through various stages, depending on conditions in the outside society. Quite often, effectiveness of a social reform group depends upon staying power, its ability to continue its efforts through the ups and downs of its political struggles. Michael Lipsky points out that groups made up of the relatively powerless will sometimes use protest tactics to enlist the resources of third parties since the groups often lack those resources upon which effective participation in the political process depends. Yet because of these deficiencies, the "target groups" can often placate protest groups with largely symbolic rewards (58).

McCarthy and Zald do not deal with the problem of staying power. Leaders of funded social reform groups may be able to dispense with a strong membership base, but for how long and for what purposes? Outside funding may give a group a start, then abandon it. The ready availability of outside money may actually hinder the growth of strongly organized social reform groups by stimulating the growth of ephemeral movements and groups.

4. Use of Law by Social Reform Groups

A social reform group wishing to use the legal system must first obtain access. We described earlier how groups "opened" up the legal system, particularly the federal judiciary, with the help of subsidized lawyers. Next, groups sought changes in the actual rules. A favorable decision from a court or administrative agency is a resource in and of itself; it lends legitimacy to the demands of the group. This, in turn, stimulates some voluntary compliance and helps the group to solicit additional resources. The Supreme Court's decision in *Brown v. Board of Education*, at the minimum, had this kind of effect for civil rights groups; there was immediate voluntary compliance in many border school districts, and the decision stimulated a vast amount of northern liberal support.

At this point in the mobilization process, social reform groups resemble McCarthy and Zald's "funded social movement organizations". The resources that enabled the groups to progress to the point of gaining changes in legal rule to their benefit were mostly outside resources: The legal system, subsidized lawyers, and the sources of the subsidy. To get to this point, may social reform groups did not have to rely on mass membership support.

Implementation or enforcement of the legal rule is a further stage. Sometimes, enforcement or implementation is practically automatic, and, thus, does not present a distinct problem. For example, the National Welfare Rights Organizations used litigation and the threat of litigation to obtain cash benefits for individuals; once agreement was reached, the money was promptly paid. When the criminal law is used defensively to ward off attacks on group members and free them from jail, enforcement is almost always automatic. Implementation may also come easily when the legal system is used to provide a collective good, subsidiary to other goals of the social reform group. For example, an environmental group may bring an action to stop the bulldozer, in order to gain time for negotiation, and mobilize additional outside resources. If the court decision grants a temporary injunction, there is usually no problem of enforcement. On the other hand, if negotiations drag on, the developers may seek modifications of the court order; or the order itself may allow development to proceed under specified conditions. When litigation begins to take on continuing charakter, with further participation by the parties, and requests for modifications and other changes, the problem of enforcement and staying power comes to the fore. Implementing court victories in the Alaska Pipeline case took continuous inputs from the litigants.

The implementation stage becomes most critical when the legal system is affirmatively asked to provide collective goods. Changes in desegregation laws, voter registration requirements, abortion laws, and welfare benefits are collective goods. The potential beneficiary class is large. According to Olson, it is not rational economically for any one member to contribute to the reform effort. The member's contribution will not affect the result, and the member will benefit in any event from collective goods obtained through the efforts of others. Frequently, the groups will fail at this stage through inability to muster resources sufficient to handle implementation.

The examples used in this paper cast serious doubt on the ability of social reform groups to achieve affirmative results through litigation. The most obvious problem may be lack of staying power. The "contributing beneficiaries" have a tenuous relationship with the group. They experience the grievances of the membership only vicariously, and there is competition from other organizations and interests for their attention and money. Contributing beneficiaries may not appreciate the problems of implementation; money may be forthcoming only in sudden bursts, at dramatic moments, such as a Supreme Court victory. Whatever the reason, existing sources of outside support may not be sufficient for the long, drawn-out, undramatic tasks of implementation.

At least in some situations, too, legal victories may not reach the real grievances of the members. Leaders become more responsive to the outside resources than to the membership. In some social reform groups, as McCarthy and Zald point out, it would be impossible for the leaders to find out what the membership wants; the membership base is small, amorphous, or transient. There is a danger that in the funded social movement organizations, leaders may manufacture issues to sell to contributing beneficiaries. The leaders, as a privileged group, receive selective benefits. Some scattered evidence suggests that social reform groups use subsidized legal talent to fight legal battles that are not of great salience to the members. For example, Louis Lomax claims that one of the reasons that the NAACP Legal Defense Fund had so much trouble getting southern blacks to join in school desegregation lawsuits was that for most blacks in the South, attending white schools had a low priority. They had much more pressing needs. Lomax charges that the NAACP top leadership and their lawyers were seriously out of touch with the wishes of the potential membership. Lomax feels that there is not much communication between the top leadership and the grass roots, in the NAACP.

Active members of a group may not put a high priority on litigation. The lawsuit may rest largely in the hands of the subsidized lawyers. Public interest lawyers like to take up class action test cases. The publicity is tempting; and the lawyers are practicing "real law" (e.g., appellate court litigation, intricate negotiations with high officials). Because the lawyers are subsidized, the costs to the group leadership are low. The members are not likely to be involved or even to contribute. Whether or not the goals of the litigation are salient to the members, the free rider problem may prevent effective mass support.

Obviously more theory and research is needed on the problem of the efficacy of social reform groups. The examples discussed do point up real problems. Experience casts come doubt on the McCarthy-Zahl theory of funded social movement organizations, if that theory implies that social reform groups, through the use of outside resources, are able to overcome the free rider problem and become effective in the political process. Outside resources have made groups more effective than previously. To this extent, the free rider problem is lessened. Access to litigation has somewhat increased the effectiveness of social reform groups. But these groups cannot avoid the facts of political process by relying on the courts.

Summary

In den letzten beiden Jahrzehnten nahm die Inanspruchnahme des Prozeßweges durch sozialpolitisch engagierte Reformgruppen stark zu. Dies wurde durch das Entgegenkommen der Gerichte gegenüber den Forderungen derartiger Gruppen und durch die Tatsache gefördert, daß sich junge und aktive Rechtsanwälte zur Verfügung stellten, die finanziell unterstützt wurden. Der Beitrag untersucht die Inanspruchnahme des Rechtssystems durch Gesellschaftsreformer und die Probleme, die diese haben, Rechtsänderungen durchzusetzen. Diskutiert werden drei Typen von Prozeßstrategien:

1. Verteidigungsstrategie, falls die Gruppe, ihre Führer oder ihre Mitglieder verfolgt werden.

2. Hilfsstrategie, falls der Prozeß zugunsten anderer Strategien geführt wird.
3. Durchsetzungsstrategie, falls die primären Ziele der Gruppe erreicht werden sollen.

Die meisten Probleme treten nun bei der Durchsetzungsstrategie auf. Vier Typen von Durchsetzungsproblemen werden analysiert:

1. Die Durchsetzung bedingt eine große Zahl von amtlichen Ermessensentscheidungen auf unterer Ebene.
2. Die Durchsetzung bedingt eine große Zahl privater Ermessensentscheidungen.
3. Die Durchsetzung bedingt fortwährende Anstöße bei entscheidend wichtigen Überwachungsbehörden.
4. Die Durchsetzung wird von einer mächtigen und widerspenstigen Regierungsstelle behindert.

Der Beitrag erklärt zum Abschluß die empirischen Ergebnisse mit Hilfe neuerer Verhaltenstheorien über sozial engagierte Reformgruppen.

Notes

1 John D. McCarthy and Mayer N. Zald, The Trend of Social Movements in America: Professionalization and Resource Mobilization (1973).
2 Theodore J. Lowi, The Politics of Disorder (1971).
3 See William E. Connolly (ed.), The Bias of Pluralism (1969).
4 Mancur Olson, Jr., The Logic of Collective Action – Public Goods and the Theory of Groups (1965).
5 Clement Vose, Constitutional Change (1972).
6 See Robert McCloskey, The Modern Supreme Court (1972), P. 345.
7 NAACP v. Button, 371 U.S. 415 (1963).
8 347 U.S. 483 (1954).
9 See McCloskey, supra, pp. 338–341.
10 369 U.S. 186 (1962).
11 See McCloskey, supra, p. 342; Powell v. McCormack, 395 U.S. 486 (1969).
12 NAACP v. Alabama, 357 U.S. 449 (1958); see Griswold v. Connecticut, 381 U.S. 479 (1965) (doctor has standing to assert constitutional rights of patients); Dombrowski v. Pfister, 380 U.S. 479 (1965). See Edgar Cahn, Law in the Consumer Perspective, 112 U. Pa. L. Rev. 1 (1963).
13 See Harper v. Virginia Board of Elections, 383 U.S. 663, 667. See also Reynolds v. Sims, 377 U.S. 533 (1964).
14 See Greene v. McElroy, 360 U.S. 474 (1959); Thorpe v. Housing Authority of Durham, 393 U.S. 268 (1969); Shelton v. Tucker, 364 U.S. 479 (1960); Goldberg v. Kelly, 397 U.S. 254 (1970).
15 See, e.g., Edwards v. South Carolina, 372 U.S. 229 (1963); NAACP v. Alabama, 357 U.S. 449 (1958); N.Y. Times v. Sullivan, 376 U.S. 254 (1964).
16 Laurent B. Frantz, The First Amendment in the Balance, 71 Yale L.J. 1424 (1962).
17 See, e.g., Engel v. Vitale, 370 U.S. 421 (1962); Sherbert v. Verner, 374 U.S. 398 (1963).
18 See Morlis James, The People's Lawyers (1973), Introduction; Philip C. Kazanjian, Preparing for the Law: A Look at the New Breed, 17 Student Law Journal, No. 7 (April 1972); Wendy Moonan & Tom Goldstein, "The New Lawyer" in The New Professinals (1972); Peter Vanderwicken, "The Angry Young Lawyers", Fortune, September, 1971.
19 354 F. 2d 608 (2d Cir. 1965).
20 For a discussion of the tactics, including litigation, used by social reform groups in one community, see Kenneth E. McNeil, Citizens as Brokers: Cooptation in an Urban Setting (unpublished Ph.D. dissertation, 1973, Vanderbilt University).
21 Data on the Black Panther Party was obtained from the following sources: Robert

L. Allen, Black Awakening in Capitalist America (1970); The Black Panther, Intercommunal News Service, Black Panther Party; Sara Blackburn, White Justice (1971); Eldridge Cleaver, Post-Prison Writings and Speeches (1969); Phillip S. Foner, The Black Panther Speaks (1970); Lockwood Lee, Conversations with Eldridge Cleaver (1970); Reginald Major, The Panther Is a Black Cat (1971); Gene Marine, The Black Panthers (1969); Huey P. Newton, To Die For The People (1972); Revolutionary Suicide (1973); Bobby Seale, Seize the Time (1968); Jerome Skolnick, The Politics of Protest (1969); U.S. Congress, Committee on Internal Security, Black Panther Party Hearings (1970).

22 Foner, supra, p. 258.

23 See Otto Kirchheimer, Political Justice (1961); Theodore L. Becker (ed.), Political Trials (1971), XI–XVI; there are many examples of this kind of political trial. Kirchheimer says that according to Lenin, "The supreme rule of a political defense is propagation of the doctrine rather than the fate of the individual defendent". Ibid., p. 245.

24 The Panthers first became prominent when they displayed their guns openly, announced a policy of self-denfense against the police, and began citizen patrols to observe police tactics and advise blacks of their rights. Their first confrontation with the police came when Newton, Seale, and some other members walked out of Party headquarters carrying guns. A policemen confronted them and demanded to know what they were doing with their guns. Newton refused to answer; the law, he felt, required only that a citizen give his name and address to an officer. Other police came and started harassing the crowd of blacks who had gathered to watch. Newton told the people that a citizen had the right to stay and observe an officer carrying out his duty as long as the citizen stayed a reasonable distance away and did not interfere. After further threats, Newton warned the police that if they tried to take away his gun or shoot at him, he would shoot back. The police then gave in and left. The impact of this confrontation on the black community was electrifying. They had seen, as one Panther biographer said, "Something they had never seen before: black men, proud and dignified, daring to meet the white policemen on equal terma and face him down". This initial confrontation brought in dozens of applications for membership. With more members, the Panthers increased their patrols of the police and began their program of advising the black community of their rights and offering free legal aid. During this initial period. the Panthers spent a great deal of time disseminating knowledge of legal rights (mostly in the criminal law area), the right of self-defense, and the promise that the Party would be available for protection. These were benefits to Party members, their friends and supporters in the black community because victimization, oppression, and arbitrary action by law enforcement people were among the most serious problems that blacks encountered. The Party grew rapidly during this period, and chapters were established in many major cities throughout the country.

25 Marine, supra, p. 43.

26 On SNCC, see the following: Stokely Carmichael and Charles Hamilton, Black Power (1967); Stokely Carmichael, "Who Is Qualified? " New Republic, Jan. 8, 1966, p. 21; Coben and Hale, The New Student Left: An Anthology (1966); Harry Edwards, Black Students (1970); James Forman, The Making of Black Revolutionaries (1972); Joanne Grant, Black Protest (1968); Anthony Lewis, Portrait of a Decade – The Second American Revolution (1964); Jerome Skolnick, The Politics of Protest (1969); Arthur I. Waskow, From Race Riot to Sit-In (1966); Howard Zinn, SNCC – The New Abolitionists (1964).

27 The data on the National Welfare Rights Organization are from the following sources: Frances Fox Piven and Richard H. Cloward, Regulating the Poor (1971); Cloward & Piven, A Strategy to End Poverty, The Nation, May 2, 1966; Cloward & Elwan, Advocacy in the Ghetto, Transaction, December 1966; NOW' National Welfare Rights Bulletin, Feb. 9, 1968; Robert Nelson gathered much data from newspaper accounts in New York City, Boston, and Newark as well as personal interviews with welfare rights leaders and legal services Lawyers. There is a vast literature in legal periodicals dealing with welfare rights.

28 For a discussion of the Montgomery bus boycott, see Anthony Oberschall, Social Conflict and Social Movements (1973), pp. 126–27; 267–68.

29 McNeil, supra, note 21, makes these points in his case study.

30 In most instances, the defendants cannot afford legal fees and the lawyers work at subsistence wages. These lawyers are not supported by foundations or by government.

The cases are demanding and the defense lawyers are short-handed; in many instances, the lawyer's private practice withers away.

31 Oberschall, supra, p. 206.

32 Louis E. Lomax, The Negro Revolt (1971), pp. 83–86.

33 Anthony Lewis and the New York Times, Portrait of a Decade (1964), p. 5.

34 Quoted in Lomax, supra, p. 85.

35 Lewis, supra, c. 3.

36 See Alexander M. Bickel, The Least Dangerous Branch (1962), pp. 255–66.

37 U.S. Civil Rights Commission, 1963 Staff Report, Public Education, December 1963, pp. 1–57.

38 U.S. Civil Rights Commission, Education, Vol. II, 1961, p. 177–78.

39 Charles E. Silberman, Crisis in Black and White (1964), p. 289.

40 Lomax, supra, note 32, p. 125.

41 Oberschall, supra note 28, p. 223.

42 Silberman, supra note 39, p. 142.

43 This problem is discussed at length in Joel F. Handler, Controlling Official Behavior in Welfare Administration, 54 California Law Review 479 (1966) and The Coercive Social Worker (1973), chs. 1, 7.

44 The New Public Interest Lawyers, 79 Yale Law Journal 1056, 1069–79 (1970).

45 The materials on the abortion controversy are from the following sources, among others: Lawrence Lader, Abortion (1966); Abortion II – Making the Revolution (1973); Daniel Callahan, Abortion: Law, Choice and Morality (1970); Bea Blair, "Abortion: Can We Lose Our Right to Choose?" MS. Oct. 1973, pp. 92–95; Jimmy Kimmey, "How Abortion Laws Happen", MS., April 1973, pp. 118–20; materials prepared for Workshop on Abortion and Reproduction Control, Center for Law and Social Policy, Washington, D.C., June 9, 1973. In addition, information was obtained from interviews with lawyers active in the abortion controversy.

46 Roe v. Wade, 410 U.S. 113 (1973).

47 See Richard Leone, Public Interest Advocacy and the Regulatory Process, The Annals, Vol. 400 (March 1972), pp. 46–47, 52.

48 Another example of the policing problem concerns maritime oil pollution. On behalf of three environmental organizations, a public interest law firm filed a lawsuit to enjoin the Secretary of Commerce and the Maritime Subsidy Board from awarding construction subsidies for oil tankers; petitioners charged failure to comply with NEPA. Shipyards, ship purchasers, ship building and operating unions, and the shipbuilders' trade association intervened. A settlement was quickly reached, which provided that the Government would provide a comprehensive environmental impact statement that would cover the following matters: the tanker construction program as a whole, tankers presently under construction, present and future pollution abatement specifications, oil pollution effects of tankers, alternatives to the tanker construction program, alternative mixes of oil carrying vessels and their relative environmental effects, alternative design and equipment requirements for oil carrying vessels, such as double bottoms and fully segregated ballast systems, alternative energy strategies such as reducing the demand for oil, and the environmental impact of the deep water port development which would be necessary to accommodate supertankers. The settlement was signed on January 8; the draft impact statement was due to be released on February 19; all interested parties would then have 15 days to submit comments; another draft statement would be released on March 15, with public hearings on May 1, and final comments due on May 15.

The settlement was considered an important victory for the environmentalists and the Government seemed genuinely cooperative. The immediate problem, though, was whether the environmentalists could take advantage of the opportunity they had won. There were enormous financial stakes involved. The industry had no difficulty in marshalling its experts. The environmental groups, on the other hand, had a very difficult time. They needed experts willing to devote substantial blocks of time on short notice, if the groups were going to have any sort of effect on the impact statement. Furthermore, the impact statement would function as a kind of blueprint for construction of future vessels and ports. There are always changes in construction plans as technical and economic contingencies materialize. Changes to meet environmental considerations are costly; as construction proceeds, the industry will seek modifications of the original impact statement. The environmentalists will have to be ready to consider proposed construction changes from their perspective and be prepared to press their point of view with the government agency. Otherwise, in time, the agency will again fall captive to the industry, which will usually be the agency's primary source of information.

49 This account is taken from Peter E. Sitkin, Welfare Law: Narrowing the Gap Between Congressional Policy and Local Practice, in Studies in Public Welfare, Paper No. 5 (Part 2), Issues in Welfare Administration: Intergovernmental Relationships, U.S. Joint Economic Committee, Subcommittee on Fiscal Policy (U.S. Government Printing Office, Washington 1973), p. 36; see also Robert L. Rabin, Implementation of the Cost-of-Living-Adjustment for AFDC Recipients: A Case Study in Welfare Administration, 118 U. of Pa. L. Rev. 1143 (1970); Rosado v. Wyman, 397 U.S. 397 (1970).

50 Mancur Olson, Jr., The Logic of Collective Action – Public Goods and the Theory of Groups (1965).

51 Even for small groups, Olson argues that collective goods will not be supplied at an optimal level, because the members of the group will not provide enough of the good to satisfy their common interests. This happens because the individual member who pays for a collective good gets only part of the benefit and will therefore discontinue paying before the optimal amount of the good is reached for all of the members. And, the larger the group, the more likely it is that the optimal amount will not be reached.

52 The only exception, he would argue, is where there are very unequal degrees of interest in the group; under those circumstances, collective goods may be provided.

53 Olson stresses throughout that his subject is economic organizations. He thinks that his theory would apply as long as rational individuals are interested in common goals. He does not think the theory is useful in describing religious or philanthropic groups, nor does he think the theory useful with groups "with a low degree of rationality – that is, working for lost causes".

54 John D. McCarthy and Mayer N. Zald, The Trend of Social Movements in America: Professionalization and Resource Mobilization (1973).

55 See, e.g., Stanley Milgram and Hans Toch, "Collective Behavior: Crowds and Social Movements", in Handbook of Social Psychology, Vol. 4, p. 590. See also Neil Smelser, Theory of Collective Behavior (1962). For a critical survey of research on social reform groups, see Jack M. Weller and E.L. Quarantelli, Neglected Characteristics of Collective Behavior, 79 Journal of Sociology, No. 3, p. 665 (1973).

56 McCarthy and Zald argue that survey data do not show that with the increasing size of the middle class social and political involvement or participation by the middle class increases correspondingly. Nor does increased leisure time lead to greater participation. People in higher status occupations tend to work longer hours. In addition, the increase in per capita income without a corresponding increase in leisure time, means that there is a tendency to spend money on what the authors call "high-yield" leisure time activities rather than "low-yield" activities. Social reform activities are low-yield; they therefore predict a declining allocation of time to these activities.

57 McCarthy and Zald, supra, p. 22, n. 14.

58 Michael Lipsky, Protest As a Political Resource, 62 American Political Science Review 1144 (1968); see also, Murray Edelman, Symbolic Uses of Politics (1964).

Marc Galanter

The Distribution of Advantages in the Litigation Process

In this paper, I shall put forward some conjectures about the way in which the basic features of the process of litigation (in a legal system like that of the United States) create and limit the possiblities of using that system as a means of redistributive (i.e., equalizing) change. We shall take litigation in the broadest sense of the presentation of claims to be decided by courts (or court-like agencies) and the whole penumbra of threats, feints, etc., surrounding such presentation.

For purpose of this analysis, let us think of the legal system as comprised of these elements:

A body of authoritative normative learning – for short, RULES.

A set of institutional facilities within which the normative learning is applied to specific cases – for short, COURTS.

A body of persons with specialized skill in the above – for short, LAWYERS.

Persons or groups with claims they might make to the courts in reference to the rules, etc. – for short, PARTIES.

Let us also make the following assumptions about the society and the legal system

- wealth and power are widely but unevenly distributed in the society. There are units with different amounts of wealth and power. Such units are constantly in competitive or partially competitive relationships, in which they have opposing interests.
- this society has a legal system in which a wide range of disputes and conflicts are settled by court-like agencies which purport to apply pre-existing general norms impartially (i.e., unaffected by the identity of the parties).
- the rules and the procedures of these institutions are complex; wherever possible disputing units employ specialized intermediaries in dealing with them.
- the rules applied by the courts are in part worked out in the process of adjudication. Courts articulate interstitial rules, apply old rules to new situations, and elaborate ways in which different rules are combined). There is a living tradition of such rule-work and a system of communication such that the outcomes in some of the adjudicated cases affect the outcome in certain future adjudicated cases.
- resources on the institutional side are insufficient for timely full-dress adjudication in every case, so that parties are permitted or even encouraged to forego bringing cases, or to "settle" cases – i.e., bargain to a mutually acceptable outcome.
- there are several levels of legal agencies; "higher" agencies announce (make,

interpret) rules, with other "lower" agencies assigned the responsibility of enforcing (implementing, apllying) these rules. (Although there is some overlap of function in both theory and practice, I shall treat them as distinct and refer to them as "peak" and "field level" agencies.)

– not all the rules propounded by "peak" agencies are effective at the "field level" – due to imperfections in communication, shortages of resources, skill, understanding, commitment, etc. (Effectiveness at the field level will be rererred to as "penetration".) (1)*

I. A Typology of Parties

Most analyses of the legal system start with the rules, and work down through institutional facilities to see what effect the rules have on the parties. I would like to reverse that procedure and look through the other end of the telescope. Let's think about the different kinds of parties and the effect these differences might have on the way the system works.

Actors (persons, groups, companies) differ in resources, and in exposure to the law. Some actors utilize the courts (in the broad sense) to make (or defend) claims on many occasions; others do so only rarely. We might divide our actors into those claimants who have only occasional recourse to the courts (one-shotters or OS), and repeat players (RP) who are engaged in many similar litigations over time (2). The spouse in a divorce case, the auto-injury claimant, the criminal accused are OS's; the insurance company, the prosecutor, the finance company are RP's. obviously this is an oversimplification – there are intermediate cases (e.g., the professional criminal). Persons who get in a situation only once are "pure" OS's (the auto accident victim); there are also those who are in a continuing series of transactions (welfare clients or taxpayers) but whose situation is such, or their resources are such, that they will have only a single crack at litigation, if any. (The taxpayer may protest his taxes or be charged with fraud; the welfare client may sue or be sued about benefit claims.) The categories are ends of a continuum, rather than sharp dichotomies. Typically, the RP is a larger unit and the stakes in any given case are smaller (relative to total worth). OS's are usually smaller units. The stakes in the case may be high relative to the OS's total worth (e.g., the injury victim, criminal accused, etc.). Sometimes the OS suffers from the opposite problem: his claims may be so small and unmanageable that the cost of enforcing them outruns any promise of benefit (e.g., the shortweighted consumer or the holder of performing rights) (3).

Let us refine our notion of the RP into an "ideal type" if you will – a unit which has had and anticipates repeated litigation, which has low stakes in the outcome of any one case, and which has the resources to pursue its long-run interests. This does not include every real-world repeat player – e.g., that most common repeat player, the alcoholic derelict, enjoys few of the advantages that may accrue to the RP (see below). His resources are too few to bargain in the short run or take heed of the long run (4). An OS is a unit whose claims are too large (relative to his size) or too small (relative to the cost of remedies) to be managed routinely and rationally.

* Notes on pages 259 ff.

We would expect an RP to play the litigation game differently from an OS. Let us consider some of his advantages:

1. RP's, having done it before, have advance intelligence; they are able to structure the next transaction, build a record, etc. It is the RP who writes the form contract, requires the security deposit, etc.
2. RP's develop expertise, can employ specialists, enjoy economies of scale and have low start-up costs for any case (5).
3. RP's have opportunities to develop facilitative informal relations with institutional incumbents (6).
4. The RP must establish and maintain credibility as a combatant. His interest in his "bargaining reputation" serves as a resource; it is easy for him to establish "commitment" to his bargaining positions. With no bargaining reputation to maintain, the OS has more difficulty in convincing the other party of the strength of his commitment to a bargaining position (7).
5. RP's can play the odds. The larger the matter at issue looms for OS, the more likely he is to adopt a minimax strategy (i.e., minimize the probability of maximum loss). Assuming that the stakes are relatively smaller for RP's, they can adopt strategies calculated to maximize gain over a long series of cases, even where this involves the risk of maximum loss (8) in some cases (9).
6. RP's can play for rules as well as immediate gains. First, it pays an RP to expend resources in influencing the making of the relevant rules by lobbying, etc. (10) (and his accumulated expertise enables him to do this persuasively).
7. RP's can also play for rules in litigation itself, whereas an OS is unlikely to. That is, there is a difference in what they regard as a favorable outcome. Because his stakes in the immediate outcome are high and because by definition OS is unconcerned with the outcome of similar litigation in the future, OS will have little interest in that element of the outcome which might influence the disposition of the decision-maker next time around. For the RP, on the other hand, any result is worthwhile, if it will favorably influence the outcomes of future cases. The larger the stake for any player and the lower the probability of repeat play, the less likely that he will be concerned with the rules which govern future cases of this kind. Consider, two parents contesting the custody of their only child, the prizefighter vs. the IRS for tax arrears, the convict facing the death penalty. On the other hand, the player with small stakes in the present case and the prospect of a series of similar cases may be more interested in the state of the law (e.g., the IRS, the adoption agency; the prosecutor).

   Thus, if we analyze the outcomes of a case into a tangible component and a rule component (11), we may expect that in the immediate case OS will attempt to maximize tangible gain. But if RP is interested in maximizing his tangible gain in a whole series of cases, he may be willing to trade off tangible gain in any one case for rule gain (or to minimize rule loss) (12). We assumed that the institutional facilities for litigation were overloaded and settlements were prevalent. We would then expect RP's to "settle" cases where they expected unfavorable rule outcomes (13). Since they expect to litigate again, RP's can select to adjudicate (or appeal) those cases which they regard as most likely to produce favorable rules (14). On the other hand, OS's should be willing to trade off the possibility of making "good law" for tangible gain. Thus, we would expect the body of "precedent" cases – i.e., cases capable of influencing the outcome of future cases – to be relatively skewed toward those favorable to RP (15).

Of course it is not suggested that the strategic configuration of the parties is the sole or major determinant of rule-development. Rule-development is shaped by other factors as well – a relatively autonomous learned tradition, the impingement of intellectual currents from outside, the preferences and prudences of the decision-makers. But courts are passive, and these factors operate only when the process is triggered by parties. The point here is merely to note the superior opportunities of the RP to trigger promising cases, and prevent the triggering of unpromising ones. This point does not rule out the possibility that a course of rule-development may favor OS's (though, as indicated below, OS's will often fail to get the benefit of favorable new rules).

In stipulating that RP's can play for rules, I do not mean to imply that RP's pursue rule-gain as such. If we recall that not all rules penetrate (i.e., become effectively applied at the field level) we come to some additional advantages of RP's.

8. RP's by virtue of experience and expertise, are more likely to be able to discern which rules are likely to "penetrate" and which are likely to remain merely symbolic commitments. RP's may be able to concentrate their resources on rule changes that are likely to make a tangible difference – that is, they can trade off symbolic defeats for tangible gains.
9. Since penetration depends in part on the resources of the parties (i.e., knowledge, attentiveness, expert services, money), RP's are more likely to be able to invest the matching resources necessary to secure the penetration of rules favorable to them.

It is not suggested that RP's are to be equated with "haves" (in terms of power, wealth and status) or OS's with "have-nots". They overlap, but there are obvious exceptions. RP's may be "have nots" (e.g., alcoholic derelicts) or may act as champions of "have-nots" (as government does from time to time); OS's such as criminal defendants may be wealthy, etc. What this analysis does is to define a position of advantage in the configuration of contending parties and indicate how those with other advantages tend to occupy this position of advantage and to have their other advantages reinforced and augmented thereby (16). This position of advantage is one of the ways in which a legal system formally neutral as between "haves" and "have-nots" may perpetuate and amplify the advantages of the former (17).

We may think of litigation as typically involving various combinations of OS's and RP's. We can then construct a table, such as Table 1, illustrating the combinations with well-known if only approximate American examples. (We ignore for the moment the fact that the terms OS and RP represent ends of a continuum, rather than a dichotomous pair.)

On the basis of our incomplete and unsystematic examples, let us conjecture a bit about the content of these boxes:

Box I: OS vs. OS

The most common examples in this category are divorces, related proceedings (custody, support), and insanity hearings. Most divorces (over 90 per cent) are

Tab. 1: A Taxonomy of Litigation by Strategic Configuration of Parties

		Initiator, Claimant	
		One-Shotter	Repeat Player
Defendant	One-Shotter	Parent v. Parent (Custody) Spouse v. Spouse (divorce) Family v. Family-Member (Insanity Commitment) Family v. Family (Inheritance) Neighbor v. Neighbor Partner v. Partner OS vs. OS I	Prosecutor v. Accused Finance Co. v. Debtor Landlord v. Tenant I.R.S. v. Taxpayer Condemnor v. Property Owner RP vs. OS II
	Repeat Player	Welfare Client v. Agency Auto Dealer v. Manufacturer Injury Victim v. Insurance Company Tenant v. Landlord Bankrupt Consumer v. Creditors Defamed v. Publisher OS vs. RP III	Union v. Company Movie Distributor v. Censorship Board Developer v. Suburban Municipality Purchaser v. Supplier Regulatory Agency v. Firms of Regulated Industry RP vs. RP IV

uncontested (18). A large portion of these are really psuedo-litigation – i.e., a settlement is worked out between the parties, and ratified in the guise of adjudication. When we get real litigation in Box I, it is often between parties who have some intimate tie with one another, fighting over some unsharable good, often with overtones of "spite" and "irrationality". Courts are resorted to where an ongoing relationship is ruptured; they have little to do with routine patterns of activity. The law is invoked *ad hoc* and instrumentally by the parties. There may be a strong interest in vindication, but neither party is likely to have much interest in the long-term state of the law (e.g., rules about custody or nuisance). There are few appeals, few test cases, little expenditure of resources on rule-development. Legal doctrine is likely to remain remote from everyday practice and from popular attitudes (19).

Box II: RP vs. OS

The great bulk of litigation is of this type – indeed every really common kind except personal injury cases, insanity hearings, and divorces. The law is used for routine processing of claims by parties for whom the making of such claims is a regular business activity (20). Often the "cases" here are in the form of stereotyped mass process; the particular case does not get the individual attention of a full-dress trial and adjudication. Even greater numbers of potential cases are settled "informally", with settlement keyed to possible litigation outcomes (discounted by risk, cost, delay).

The state of the law is of interest to the RP, though not to the OS defendants. Insofar as the law is favorable to the RP it is "followed" closely in practice (21) (subject to discount for RP's transaction costs) (22). Creditors, police, draft boards, and other RP's build transactions to fit the rules (23). Rules that favor OS's are less likely to be applied, since OS's do not ordinarily plan the underlying transaction. Or they may be less meticulously observed in the field, since OS's are unlikely to be as ready or able as RP's to invest in insuring penetration of the rules to the level of actual practice (24).

Box III: OS vs. RP

The cases in this category occur infrequently except for personal injury cases. These are (in the United States) distinctive, in that the contingent fee finances access to lawyers and courts (25). In auto injury cases, litigation is routinized; settlements are closely geared to possible litigation outcomes. Outside the personal injury area, litigation of this third type is not routine. It usually represents the attempt of some OS to invoke outside help, to bring some leverage to bear on an organization with which he has had dealings but is now at the point of "divorce" (for example, the holder of a cancelled franchise) (26). The OS claimant generally has little interest in the state of the law; the RP defendant, however, is greatly interested.

Box IV: RP vs. RP

Let us consider the general case first and then several special cases. We might expect that there would be little litigation in Box IV, because, to the extent that two RP's play with each other repeatedly (27), the expectation of continued mutually beneficial interaction would give rise to informal bilateral controls (28). This seems borne out by studies of the behavior of businessmen (29), and in labor relations. Official agencies are invoked by unions trying to get established and by management trying to prevent them from getting established, and only rarely in dealings between bargaining partners (30). Units with mutually beneficial relations do not adjust their differences in courts. Where they rely on third parties in dispute-resolution, it is likely to take a form (e.g., arbitration, domestic tribunal) detached from official sanctions and applying domestic rather than official rules.

However, there are several special cases. First, there are those RP's who seek not furtherance of tangible interests, but vindication of ideological positions – e.g., the organizations which sponsor litigation on seperation of church and state (31). Where RP's are contending about value differences (i.e., who is right) rather than interest conflicts (i.e., who gets what) there is less tendency to settle, and less basis for developing a private system of dispute settlement (32).

Second, government is a special kind of RP. Informal controls work because there is a potential sanction behind them: withdrawal and refusal to continue beneficial relations (33). Withdrawal of future beneficial relations is sometimes not possible as a tactic in dealing with government. This limits the possibility of using informal controls. Informal relations do develop between regulatory agencies and regulated firms; and the regulated may have other sanctions than withdrawal which they can apply – political opposition, for one. But the more inclusive the unit of government, the less effective the withdrawal sanction and the greater the likelihood that a party will try to invoke outside help by litigation, even while sustaining the ongoing relationship. This applies also to monopolies – i.e., units which share the government's relative immunity to withdrawal sanctions (34). RP's in monopolistic relationships will occasionally invoke formal controls to show prowess, and to give credibility to threats. Thus we would expect litigation by and against government to be more frequent than in other RP vs. RP situations.

A somewhat different kind of case is that in which plaintiff and defendant are RP's, but do not deal with each other repeatedly – e.g., two insurance companies. This is unlike the monopoly and government case, where the parties were so inextricably bound together that informal controls were unavailing; here they are not sufficiently bound to each other to give informal controls their bite, i.e., there is nothing to withdraw from! The large one-time deal that falls through, the marginal enterprise – these are staple sources of litigation.

We might also expect that where there is litigation in the RP vs. RP situation, there would be heavy expenditure on rule-development; many appeals; rapid and elaborate development of the doctrinal law. Since the parties can invest to secure implementation of favorable rules, we would expect practice to be closely articulated to the resulting rules.

On the basis of these preliminary guesses, we can sketch a general profile of litigation and the factors associated with it. The great bulk of litigation is found in Boxes II (mostly) and III (much less); most is mass routine processing of disputes between parties who are strangers (i.e., not in mutually beneficial continuing relations) or divorced (35) and between whom there is a disparity in size. One party is a bureaucratically organized "professional" (i.e., doing it for a living) who enjoys strategic advantages. Informal controls between the parties are tenuous or ineffective; their relationship is likely to be established and defined by official rules; in litigation, these rules are discounted by transaction costs and manipulated selectively to the advantage of the parties. On the other hand, in Boxes I and IV, we have more infrequent but more individualized litigation between parties of the same general magnitude, among whom there are or were continuing and multiplex relationships, with attendant informal controls. Litigation appears when the relationship loses its future value; when its "monopolistic" character deprives informal controls of sufficient leverage, and the parties invoke outside allies to modify it; when the parties seek to vindicate conflicting values.

II. Lawyers

What happens when we introduce lawyers? Lawyers are themselves RP's. Does their presence equalize the parties, dispelling the advantage of the RP client? Or does the existence of lawyers amplify the advantage of the RP client? We might assume that the RP's (who tend to be larger units) can buy legal services more steadily, in larger quantities, in bulk (and by retainer) and at higher rates. They would thus get services of better quality. They would also have better information about lawyers (especially where there are restrictions on information about legal services) (36). Not only would the RP get more talent to begin with, but he would on the whole get greater continuity, better recordkeeping, more anticipatory or preventive work, more experience and specialized skill in pertinent areas. One might expect that just how much the legal services factor would accentuate the RP advantage would be related to the way in which the profession was organized. The more members of the profession were identified with their clients (i.e., the less they were held aloof from clients by their loyalty to courts or to an autonomous guild) the more the imbalance would be accentuated (37). The more close and enduring the lawyer-client relationship, the more the primary loyalty of lawyers is to clients rather than to courts or guild, the more telling the advantages of accumulated expertise and guidance in overall strategy (38).

What about the specialization of the bar? Might we not expect the existence of specialization to offset RP advantages by providing OS with a specialist who in pursuit of his own career goals would be interested in outcomes that would be advantageous to a whole class of OS's. Does the specialist become the functional equivalent of the RP? We may divide specialists into [1] those specialized by field of law (patent, divorce, etc.) [2] those specialized by the kind of party represented (e.g., house counsel) and [3] those specialized by both field of law and "side" or party (personal injury plaintiff, criminal defense, labor, etc.). Divorce lawyers do not specialize in husbands or wives (39), nor real-estate lawyers in buyers or sellers. But labor lawyers and tax lawyers and stockholders-derivative-suit lawyers do specialize not only in the field of law but in representing one side. Such specialists may represent RP's or OS's. Table 2 provides some well-known examples of different kinds of specialists:

Tab. 2: A Typology of Legal Specialists

		Lawyer	
RP	Specialized by Party	Specialized by Field and Party	Specialized by Field
Client	"House Counsel" or General Counsel for Bank, Insurance Co. etc. Corporation Counsel for Government Unit	Prosecutor Personal Injury Defendant Staff Counsel for NAACP Tax Labor/Management Collections	Patent
OS	"Poverty Lawyers" Legal Aid	Criminal Defense Personal Injury Plaintiff	Bankruptcy Divorce

Most specializations cater to the needs of particular kinds of RP's. Those specialists who service OS's have some distinctive features:

First, they tend to make up the "lower echelons" of the legal profession. Compared to the lawyers who provide services to RP's, lawyers in these specialties tend to be drawn from lower socio-economic origins, to have attended local, proprietary or part-time law schools, to practice alone rather than in large firms, and to possess low prestige within the profession 40). (Of course, the correlation is far from perfect – some lawyers who represent OS's do not have these characteristics and some representing RP's do, but on the whole there are large differences between the two types.)

Second, specialists who service OS's tend to have problems of mobilizing a clientele (because of the low state of information among OS's) and "ethical" barriers imposed by the profession – forbidding solicitation, referral fees, advances to clients, etc. (41) – make their situation more difficult.

Third, the episodic and isolated nature of the relationship with particular OS clients tends to elicit a stereotyped and uncreative brand of legal services. Carlin and Howard observe that:

> The quality of service rendered poorer clients is ... affected by the non-repeating character of the matters they typically bring to lawyers (such as divorce, criminal, personal injury): this combined with the small fees encourages a mass processing of cases. As a result, only a limited amount of time and interest is usually expended on any one case – there is little or no incentive to treat it except as an isolated piece of legal business. Moreover, there is ordinarily not desire to go much beyond the case as the client presents it, and such cases are only accepted when there is a clear-cut cause of action; i.e., when they fit into convenient legal categories and promise a fairly certain return (42).

Fourth, while they are themselves RP's, these specialists have problems in developing optimizing strategies. What might be good strategy for an insurance company lawyer or prosecutor – trading off some cases for gains on others – is branded as unethical when done by a criminal defense or personal injury plaintiff lawyer, i.e., it is not permissible for him to play his series of OS's as if they constituted a single RP (43) (which is not to say it is not done).

Conversely, the demands of routine and orderly handling of a whole series of OS's may constrain him from maximizing advantage for any individual OS. Rosenthal (44) shows that "for all but the largest (personal injury) claims an attorney loses money by thoroughly preparing a case and not settling it early". The lawyer who services OS's has a transient clientele. His permanent "client", then, is the forum, the opposite party, or the intermediary who supplies clients. For example, the criminal defense lawyer is quite dependent in his work on the cooperation of the court community (45). Similarly, Carlin notes among metropolitan individual practitioners whose clientele consists of OS's, a shifting of loyalty from the client to those who act as business intermediaries:

> In the case of those lawyers specializing in personal injury, local tax, collections, criminal, and to some extent divorce work, the relationship with the client ... is generally mediated by a broker or business supplier who may be either another lawyer or a layman. In these fields of practice the lawyer is principally concerned with pleasing the broker or of winning his approval, more so than he is with satisfying the individual client. The source of business generally counts for more than the client, especially where the client is unlikely to return or to send in other clients. The client is then expendable: he can be

exploited to the full. Under these conditions, when a lawyer receives a client ... he has not so much gained a client as a piece of business, and his attitude is often that of handling a particular piece of merchandise or of developing a volume of a certain kind of merchandise (46).

The existence of a specialized bar on the OS side should overcome the gap in expertise, allow some economies of scale, provide for bargaining commitment and personal familiarity. But this falls short of overcoming the fundamental strategic advantages of RP's – their capacity to structure the transaction, play the odds, and influence rule-development and enforcement policy.

Specialized lawyers may, by virtue of their identification with parties, become lobbyists, moral entrepreneurs, proponents of reforms on their behalf. But lawyers have a conflicting interest in preserving complexity and mystique so that a client cannot approach an area of law without the help of a lawyer (47). Lawyers should not be expected to be proponents of reforms which are optimum from the point of view of the clients taken alone. Rather, we would expect them to seek to optimize the clients' position without diminishing that of lawyers. Therefore, specialized lawyers have an interest in a framework which keeps recovery (or whatever) problematic at the same time that they favor changes which improve their clients' position within this framework. (Consider the lobbying efforts of personal injury plaintiffs and defense lawyers.) Considerations of interest are likely to be fused with ideological commitments: the lawyers' preference for complex and finely-tuned bodies of rules, for adversary proceedings, for individualized case-by-case decision-making (48). Just as the culture of the client population affects strategic position, so does the professional culture of the lawyers.

III. Institutional Facilities

We see then that the strategic advantages of the RP may be augmented by advantages in the distribution of legal services. Both are related to the advantages conferred by the basic features of the institutional facilities for the handling of claims: passivity and overload.

These institutions are passive, first, in the sense that they are reactive – they must be mobilized by the claimant – which gives the advantage to the claimant with information, ability to surmount cost barriers, and skill to navigate restrictive procedural requirements (49). They are passive in the further sense that once in the door the burden is on each party to proceed with his case. The presiding official acts as umpire, while the development of the case, collection of evidence and presentation of proof are left to the initiative and resources of the parties (50). Parties are treated as if they were equally endowed with economic resources, investigative opportunities and legal skills (51). Where, as is usually the case, they are not, the broader the delegation to the parties, the greater the advantage conferred on the wealthier, more experienced and better organized party (52).

The advantages conferred by institutional passivity are accentuated by the chronic overload which typically characterizes these institutions (53). Typically there are far more claims than there are institutional resources for full dress adjudication of each.

In several ways overload creates pressures on claimants to settle rather than to adjudicate:

a) by causing delay (thereby discounting the value of recovery);
b) by raising costs (of keeping the case alive);
c) by influencing institutional incumbents to place a high value on clearing dockets, discouraging full-dress adjudication in favor of bargaining, stereotyping and routine processing (54);
d) by influencing the forum to adopt restrictive rules to discourage litigation (55).

Thus, overload increases the cost and risk of adjudicating and shields existing rules from challenge, diminishing opportunities for rule-change. This tends to favor the beneficiaries of existing rules.

Second, by increasing the difficulty of challenging going practice, overload also benefits those who reap advantage from the neglect (or systematic violation) of rules which favor their adversaries.

Third, overload tends to protect the possessor – the party who has the money or goods – against the claimant (56). For the most part, this amounts to favoring RP's over OS's, since RP's typically can structure transactions to put themselves in the possessor position (57).

Finally, the overload situation means that there are more commitments in the formal system than there are resources to honor them – more rights and rules "on the books" than can be vindicated or enforced. There are, then, questions of priorities in the allocation of resources. We would expect judges, police, administrators and other managers of limited institutional facilities to be responsive to the more organized, attentive and influential of their constituents (58). Again, these tend to be RP's.

Thus, overloaded and passive institutional facilities provide a setting in which RP advantages in strategic position and legal services can have full play (59).

IV. Rules

We assume here that rules tend to favor older, culturally dominant interests. This should not imply that the rules are explicitly designed to favor these interests (60), but rather that those groups which have become dominant have successfully adapted their operations to fit existing rules (61). To the extent that rules are evenhanded or favor the "have-nots", the limited resources for their implementation will be allocated, I have argued, so as to give greater effect to those rules which protect and promote the tangible interests of organized and influential groups. Furthermore, the requirements of due process, with its barriers or protections against precipitate action, naturally tend to protect possessors or holders against claimants (62). Finally, the rules are sufficiently complex (63) and problematic (or capable of being problematic if sufficient resources are expended to make them so) that differences in the quantity and quality of legal services will affect capacity to derive advantage from the rules (64).

Thus, we arrive at Table 3 which summarizes why the "haves" tend to come out ahead. It points to layers of advantages enjoyed by different (but largely overlapping) classes of "haves" – advantages which interlock, reinforcing and shielding one another.

Tab. 3: Why the "Haves" Tend to Come out Ahead

Element	Advantages	Enjoyed by
Parties	– ability to structure transaction	
	– specialized expertise economies of scale	
	– long-term strategy	– repeat players (large,
	– ability to play for rules	professional*)
	– bargaining credibility	
	– ability to invest in penetration	
Legal services	– skill, specialization continuity	– organized professional* wealthy
Institutional facilities	– passivity	– wealthy, experienced, – organized
	– cost and delay barriers	– holders, possessors
		– beneficiaries of existing rules
	– favorable priorities	– organized, attentive
Rules	– favorable rules	– older, culturally dominant
	– due process barriers	– holders, possessors

*in the simple sense of "doing it for a living"

V. Conclusion: Implications for Reform and the Role of Lawyers

We have discussed the way in which the architecture of the legal system tends to confer interlocking advantages on overlapping groups whom we have called the "haves". To what extent might reforms of the legal system dispel these advantages?

Our categorization of four layers of advantage (Table 3) suggests a typology of strategies for "reform" (taken here to mean equalization – i.e., conferring relative advantage on those who did not enjoy it before). We then come to four types of equalizing reform:

1. rule-change
2. increase in supply of institutional facilities
3. improvement of legal services in quantity and quality
4. improvement of strategic position of have-not parties

Reformers will have limited resources to deploy and they will always be faced with the necessity of choosing which uses of those resources are most productive of equalizing change. What does our analysis suggest about strategies and priorities?

Our analysis suggests that change at the level of substantive rules is not likely in itself to be determinative of redistributive outcomes. Rule change is in itself likely to have little effect because the system is so constructed that changes in the rules can be filtered out unless accompanied by changes at other levels. In a setting of overloaded institutional facilities, inadequate costly legal services, and unorganized parties, beneficiaries may lack the resources to secure implementation; or an RP may re-structure the transaction to escape the thrust of the new rule (65). Favorable rules are not necessarily (and possibly not typically) in short supply to have-nots; certainly less so than any of the other resources needed to play the litigation game (66). Programs of equalizing reform which focus on rule-change can be readily absorbed without any change in power relations. The system has the capacity to change a great deal at the level of rules without corresponding changes in everyday patterns of practice (67) or distribution of tangible advantages (68). Indeed rule-change may become a symbolic substitute for redistribution of advantages (69).

The low potency of substantive rule-change is especially the case with rule-changes procured from courts. Courts are relatively insulated from retaliation by antagonistic interests, and may therefore more easily propound new rules which depart from prevailing power relations. But such rules require great inputs of resources to secure effective implementation. And courts have less capacity than other rule-makers to create institutional facilities and re-allocate resources to secure implementation of new rules. Litigation then is unlikely to shape decisively the distribution of power in society. It may serve to secure or solidify symbolic commitments. It is vital tactically in securing temporary advantage or protection, providing leverage for organization and articulation of interests and conferring (or withholding) the mantle of legitimacy (70). The more divided the other holders of power, the greater the redistributive potential of this symbolic/tactical role (71).

Our analysis suggests that breaking the interlocked advantages of the "haves" requires attention not only to the level of rules, but also to institutional facilities, legal services and organization of parties. It suggests that litigating and lobbying have to be complemented by interest organizing, provision of services and invention of new forms of institutional facilities (72).

The thrust of our analysis is that changes at the level of parties are most likely to generate changes at other levels. If rules are the most abundant resource for reformers, parties capable of pursuing long-range strategies are the rarest. The presence of such parties can generate effective demand for high grade legal services – continuous, expert, and oriented to the long-run – and pressure for institutional reforms and favorable rules. This suggests that among the various kinds of reform, we can assign a high priority, as a fulcrum for further change, to new arrangements which relate directly to the strategic position of the parties, by facilitating organization, increasing the supply of legal services (where these in turn provide a focus for articulating and organizing common interests) and increasing the costs of opponents – e.g., authorization of class action suits, awards of attorneys fees and costs, awards of provisional remedies. The intensity

of the opposition to class action legislation and autonomous reform-oriented legal services (73) (e.g., California Rural Legal Assistance) indicates that the "haves" themselves estimate the strategic impact of such changes as high (74).
The contribution of the lawyer to redistributive social change, then, depends upon the organization and culture of the legal profession. We have surmised that court-produced substantive rule change is unlikely in itself to be a determinative element in producing tangible redistribution of benefits. The leverage provided by litigation depends on its strategic combination with inputs at other levels. The question then is whether the organization of the profession permits lawyers to develop and employ skills at these other levels. The more that lawyers view themselves exclusively as courtroom advocates, the less their willingness to undertake new tasks and form enduring alliances with clients and operate in forums other than courts, the less they are likely to serve as agents of redistributive change. Paradoxically, those bodies of legal professionals who have the most potentiality to become (or more likely have room for) agents of change, are precisely those who are best at accentuating the advantages of the haves. These professionals have a less strict definition of what activities are proper to the profession. They are most apt to be "captured" by recurrent clients, and are therefore most closely identified with clients and their "causes" (75).

Summary

Auf der Grundlage früherer Forschungsergebnisse analysiert dieser Beitrag das offizielle System des Prozesses auf vier Ebenen: Normen, Gerichte, Rechtsanwälte und Parteien. Es wird versucht zu zeigen, daß die Struktur dieses Systems ineinandergreifende und sich verstärkende Vorteile für diejenigen bringt, die man abkürzend die „Besitzenden" nennen kann.

- Auf der Ebene der Parteien: Vorteile der strategischen Position haben diejenigen, die wiederholt vor Gericht ziehen.
- Auf der Ebene der Rechtsberatung: Vorteile in bezug auf Tüchtigkeit, Spezialkenntnisse und Kontinuität haben solche Parteien, die beruflich angesehen und wohlhabend sind.
- Auf der Ebene der Rechtseinrichtungen: Passivität bringt Vorteile für organisierte und erfahrene Parteien, Kostenschranken bringen Vorteile für „Besitzende" und die Nutznießer überholter Normen; günstige Rechtspositionen kommen nur den Organisierten und Aufmerksamen zugute.
- Auf der Ebene der Normen: ältere und kulturell dominierende Interessen werden begünstigt, rechtsstaatliche Schranken kommen den „Besitzenden" zugute.

Der Beitrag schließt mit einer Diskussion der daraus folgenden Voraussetzungen für Strategien zur Bewirkung sozialen Wandels mit Hilfe des Rechtssystems. Es wird die These vertreten, daß die Vorteile der „Besitzenden" es unwahrscheinlich machen, daß Veränderungen der Normen allein eine Neuverteilung bewirken können und daß Veränderungen in der Organisation der Parteien (und Veränderungen der Rechtsberatung, die diese Organisation erleichtern) die weitaus wirkungsvollsten Ansatzpunkte sozialen Wandels sind.

Notes

1 Cf. Friedman (1969:43) who defines penetration as "the number of actors and spheres of action that a particular rule ... actually reaches".

2 The discussion here focuses on litigation, but I believe an analogous analysis might be applied to the regulatory and rule-making phases of the legal process. OS's and RP's may be found in regulatory and legislative as well as adjudicative settings. For an interesting example of this distinction in the regulatory arena, see Lobenthal's (1970:20 ff.) description of the regulation of parking near a pier, contrasting the "permanent" shipping company and longshoreman interests with the OS pier visitors, showing how regulation gravitates to the accommodation of the former. This is, of course, akin to the "capture by the regulated" that attends (or afflicts) a variety of administrative agencies. See, e.g., Bernstein (1955); Edelman (1967).

3 See Finklestein (1954:284–86).

4 On the "processing" of these parties and their limited strategic options, see Foote (1956); Spradley (1970:Chap. 6).

5 An intriguing example of an RP reaping advantage from a combination of large scale operations and knowledgeability is provided by Skolnick's (1966:174 ff.) account of professional burglars' ability to trade clearances for leniency.

6 See, e.g., Jacob's (1969:100) description of creditor colonization of small claims courts. The opportunity for regular participants to establish relations of trust and reciprocity with courts is not confined to these lowly precincts. See Scigliano (1971:183–84) on relation of the Solicitor General and the United States Supreme Court.

7 See Ross (1970:156 ff.); Schelling (1963:22 ff., 41). An offsetting advantage enjoyed by some OS's deserves mention. Since he does not anticipate continued dealings with his opponent, an OS can do his damnedest without fear of reprisal next time around or on other issues. (The advantages of those who enjoy the luxury of singlemindedness are evidenced by some notorious examples in the legislative arena – e.g., the success of prohibitionists and of the gun lobby.) Thus there may be a bargaining advantage to the OS who (a) has resources to damage his opponent; (b) is convincingly able to threaten to use them. An OS can burn up his capital, but he has to convince the other side he is really likely to do so. Thus an image of irrationality may be a bargaining advantage. See Ross (1970:170 n.); Schelling (1963:170 n.). An OS may be able to sustain such an image in a way that an RP cannot. But cf. Leff (1970 a:18) on the role of "spite" in collections and the externalization to specialists of "irrational" vengeance.

8 I.e., not the whole of RP's worth, but the whole matter at issue in a single claim.

9 Cf. the overpayment of small claims and underpayment of large claims in automobile injury cases. Franklin, Chanin and Mark (1961); Conard, et al. (1964). If small claim overpayment can be thought of as the product of the transaction costs of the defendants (and, as Ross [1970:207] shows, organizational pressures to close cases), the large claim underpayment represents the discount for delay and risk on the part the claimant. (Conard, et al. 1964:197–99.)

10 Olson's analysis (1965:36 ff., 127) suggests that their relatively small number should enhance the capacity of RP's for coordinated action to further common interests.

11 This can be done only where institutions are simultaneously engaged in rule-making and dispute-settling. The rule-making function, however, need not be avowed; all that is required is that the outcome in Case 1 influence the outcome in Case 2 in a way that RP can predict.

12 This is not to imply that rule loss or gain is the main determinant of settlement policy. First, the RP must litigate selectively. He can't fight every case. Second, rules are themselves the subject of dispute relatively rarely. Only a small fraction of litigation involves some disagreement between the parties as to what the rules are or ought to be. Dibble (1970).

In addition, the very scale that bestows on RP's strategic advantages in settlement policy exposes them to deviations from their goals. Most RP's are organizations and operate though individual incumbents of particular roles (house counsel, claims adjuster, assistant prosecutor) who are subject to pressures which may lead them to deviate from the optimization of institutional goals. Thus Ross (1970:220–21) notes that insurance companies litigate large cases where, although settlement would be 'rational' from the overall viewpoint of the company, it would create unacceptable career risks to incumbents. Newman (1966:72) makes a similar observation about prosecutors' offices. He finds that even where the probability of conviction is slim "in cases involving a serious offense which has received a good deal of publicity . . . a prosecutor may prefer to try the case and have the charge reduction or acquittal decision made by the judge or jury".

13 The assumption here is that "settlement" does not have precedent value. Insofar as claimants or their lawyers form a community which shares such information, this factor is diminished – as it is, e.g., in automobile injury litigation where, I am told, settlements have a kind of precedent value.

14 Thus the Solicitor General sanctions appeal to the Supreme Court in one-tenth of the appealable defeats of the Government, while its opponents appeal nearly half of their appealable defeats. Scigliano points out that the Government is more selective because:

> In the first place, lower-court defeats usually mean much less to the United States than they do to other parties. In the second place, the government has, as private litigants do not, an independent source of restraint upon the desire to litigate further (1971:169).

Appellants tend to be winners in the Supreme Court – about two-thirds of cases are decided in their favor. The United States government, wins about 70 % of the appeals it brings.

> What sets the government apart from other litigants is that it wins a much higher percentage of cases in which it is the appellee (56 % in 1964–66). (1971:178)

Scigliano assigns as reasons for the government's success in the Supreme Court not only the "government's agreement with the court on doctrinal position" but the "expertise of the Solicitor General's Office" and "the credit which the Solicitor General has developed with the Court" (1971:182).

15 Macaulay (1966:99–101) in his study of relations between the automobile manufacturers and their dealers recounts that the manufacturers:

> . . . had an interest in having the (Good Faith Act) construed to provide standards for their field men's conduct. Moreover they had resources to devote to the battle. The amount of money involved might be major to a canceled dealer, but few, if any cases involved a risk of significant liability to the manufacturers even if the dealer won. Thus the manufacturers could afford to fight as long as necessary to get favorable interpretations to set guidelines for the future. While dealers' attorneys might have to work on a contingent fee, the manufacturers already had their own large and competent legal staffs and could afford to hire trial and appellate specialists. . . . an attorney on a contingent fee can afford to invest only so much time in a particular case. Since the manufacturers were interested in guidelines for the future, they could afford to invest, for example, § 40,000 worth of attorneys' time in a case they could have settled for § 10,000. Moreover, there was the factor of experience. A dealer's attorney usually started without any background in arguing a case under the Good Faith Act. On the other hand, a manufacturer's legal staff became expert in arguing such a case as it faced a series of these suits. It could polish its basic brief in case after case and even influence the company's business practices – such as record keeping – so that it would be ready for any suit.
>
> . . . While individual dealers decide whether or not to file a complaint, the manufacturer, as any fairly wealthy defendant facing a series of related cases, could control the kinds of cases coming before the courts in which the Good Faith Act could be construed. It could defend and bring appeals in those cases where the facts are unfavorable to the dealer, and it could settle any where the facts favor the dealer. Since individual dealers were more interested in money than establishing precedents . . . the manufacturers in this way were free to control the cases the court would see. The net effect . . . was to prompt a sequence of cases favorable to the manufacturers.

16 Of course, even within the constraints of their strategic position, parties may fare better or worse according to their several capacities to mobilize and utilize legal resources. Nonet (1969:Chap. IV) refers to this as "legal competence" – i.e., the capacity for optimal use of the legal process to pursue one's interests, a capacity which includes information, access, judgment, psychic readiness, etc.

An interesting example of the effects of such competence is provided by Rosenthal (1970:Chap. 2) who notes the superior results obtained by "active" personal injury plaintiffs. ("Active" clients are defined as those who express special wants to their attorneys, make follow-up demands for attention, marshall information to aid the lawyer, seek quality medical attention, seek a second legal opinion, and bargain about the fee.) He finds such "active" clients drawn disproportionately from those of higher social status (which presumably provides both the confidence and experience to conduct themselves in this active manner).

The thrust of the argument here is that the distribution of capacity to use the law beneficially cannot be attributed solely or primarily to personal characteristics of parties. The personal qualities that make up competence are themselves systematically related to social structure, to systems of stratification, and to the degree of specialization of the parties. Nonet makes competence a central concept, and treats organization as one means of enhancing competence; I prefer to view personal competence as operating in a marginal way only, within the framework of social structure and of the parties' relations to each other. This reversal permits us to account for systematic differences in competence of parties, and for the differences in the structure of opportunities which face various kinds of parties when personal competence is held constant.

17 The tendency for formal equality to be compatible with domination has been noted by Weber (1954:188–91) and Ehrlich (1936:238), who remarked that "The more the rich and the poor are dealt with according to the same legal propositions, the more the advantage of the rich is increased".

18 For descriptions of divorce litigation, see Virtue (1956), O'Gorman (1963).

19 For an estimate of the discrepancy between the law and popular attitudes in a "Box I" area, see Cohn, Robson and Bates (1958).

20 We lack good quantitative data on the identity and character of litigants. Our speculations fit the findings of Wanner (1972), who collected data on 7900 civil cases (excluding marital) in three cities in the United States. He found that business and governmental units were plaintiffs in about 2/3 of all cases; and that they won more, settled less and lost less than individual plaintiffs. Individuals, on the other hand, were defendants in almost 2/3 of all cases; they won less and lost more than did government or business units. A similar preponderance of business and governmental plaintiffs and individual defendants was reported by Pagter, et al. (1964), in their study of a metropolitan California small claims court: individuals made up just over a third of the plaintiffs and over 85 % of defendants. A later survey of four small-town California small claims courts (Moulton 1969:1660) found that only 16 % of plaintiffs were individuals – but over 93 % of defendants.

21 The analysis here postulates logical formal rationality in the adjudicator – i.e., that judges apply rules routinely and relentlessly to RP's and OS's alike. In the event, litigation often involves some admixture of individuation, Kadi-justice, fireside equities, sentimentality in favor of the "little guy".

22 Cf. Friedman (1967:806) on the zone of "reciprocal immunities" between, e.g., landlord and tenant, afforded by the cost of enforcing their rights. The foregoing suggests that these immunities may be reciprocal, but they are not necessarily symmetrical. That is, they may differ in magnitude according to the strategic position of the parties. Cf. Vaughan's (1968:210) description of the "differential dependence" between landlord and low-income tenant. He regards this as reflecting the greater immediacy and constancy of the tenant's need for housing, the landlord's "exercise of privilege in the most elemental routines of the relationship", greater knowledge, and the fact that the landlord, unlike the tenant, does not have all his eggs in one basket (i.e., he is, in our terms, an RP).

> Whereas each tenant is dependent upon one landlord, the landlord typically diffuses his dependency among many tenants. As a result, the owner can rather easily retain an independent position in each relationship.

A similar asymmetry typically attends relations between employer and employee, franchiser and frachisee, insurer and insured, etc.

23 See note 61 below. Cf. Skolnick's (1966:212 ff.) description of police adjustment to the exclusionary rule.

24 Similarly, even OS's who have procured favorable judgments may experience difficulty at the execution stage. Even where the stakes loom large for the OS, OS's may be too small to enlist unsubsidized professional help in implementation. A recent survey of consumers who 'won' in New York City's Small Claims Court found that almost a third were unable to collect. Marshalls either flatly refused to accept such judgments for collection or

"conveyed an impression that, even if they did take a small claims case, they would regard it as an annoyance and would not put much work into it". New York Times, 19 Sept. 1971.

25 Perhaps high volume litigation in Box III is particularly susceptible to transformation into relatively unproblematic administrative processing when RP's discover that such processing is to their advantage, and the transformation to administrative process may produce gains (or at least no losses) to OS's as well as RP's. Cf. the shift from tort to workmen's compensation in the industrial accident area (Friedman and Ladinsky [1967]) and the contemporary shift to no-fault plans in the automobile injury area.

26 Summers (1960:252) reports that

> more than 3/4 of the reported cases in which individuals have sought legal protection of their rights under a collective agreement have arisen out of disciplinary discharge.

The association of litigation with 'divorce' is clear in Macaulay (1963, 1969) and other discussions of commercial dealings (Bonn 1972 b:573 ff.). Consumer bankruptcy, another of the more numerous species of litigation in Box III, might be thought of as representing the attempt of the OS to effectuate a "divorce".

27 E.g., Babcock (1969:53–54) observes that what gives the suburb its greatest leverage on any one issue is the fact that the builder will be in constant contact with the regulatory powers of the suburb on various issues.

28 The anticipated beneficial relations need not be with the identical party but may be with other parties with whom that party is in communication. RP's are more likely to participate in a network of communication which cheaply and rapidly disseminates information about the behavior of others in regard to claims and to have an interest and capacity for acquiring and storing that information. Thus RP's can cheaply and effectively affect the business reputation of their adversaries and thus their future relations with relevant others. Leff (1970 a; 26 ff.); Macaulay (1963:64)

29 ... why is contract doctrine not central to business exchanges? Briefly put, private, between-the-parties sanctions usually exist, work and do not involve the costs of using contract law either in litigation or as a ploy in negotiations. ... most importantly, there are relatively few one-shot, but significant, deals. A businessman usually cares about his reputation. He wants to do business again with the man he is dealing with and with others. Friedman and Macaulay (1967:805).

30 Aspin (1966:2) reports that 70 to 75 % of complaints to the National Labor Relations Board about unfair labor practices of companies arise under the single section of the governing statute [8 (a) (3)] which makes it an unfair labor practice for employers to interfere with union organizing.

31 In his description of the organizational participants in church-state litigation, Morgan (1968:chap. 2) points out the difference in approach between value-committed "separationist purists" and their interest-committed "public schoolmen" allies. The latter tend to visualize the game as non-zero-sum and can conceive of advantages in alliances with their parochial-school adversaries (1968:58 n).

32 Cf. Aubert's (1963:27 ff.) distinction between conflicts of interest and conflicts of value.

33 This analysis is illuminated by Hirschman's distinction between two modes of remedial action by customers or members disappointed with the performance of organizations: (1) exit (i.e. withdrawal of custom or membership); (2) and voice ("attempts at changing the practices and policies and outputs of the firm from which one buys or the organization to which one belongs") (1970:30). Hirschman attempts to discern the conditions under which each will be employed and will be effective in restoring performance. He suggests that the role of voice increases as the opportunities for exit decline, but that the possibility of exit increases the effectiveness of the voice mechanism (1970:34, 83). Our analysis suggests that it is useful to distinguish those instances of voice which are "internal" – i.e., confined to expressions made to the other party and those which are external – i.e., seek the intervention of third parties. This corresponds roughly to the distinction between two-party and three-party dispute settlement. We might then restate the assertion, to suggest that internal voice is effective where there is a plausible threat of sanction (including exit and external voice).

34 The potency of the monopolistic character of ties in promoting resort to third parties is suggested by the estimate that in the Soviet Union approximately one million contract disputes were arbitrated annually in the early 1960's. (Loeber, 1965: 128, 133,) Cf.

Scott's (1965:63–64) suggestion that restricted mobility (defined in terms of job change) is associated with the presence of formal appeal systems in business organizations.

35 I.e., the relationship may never have existed, it may have "failed" in that it is no longer mutually beneficial, or the parties may be "divorced". It appears that, in the American setting at any rate, litigation is not only incompatible with the maintainance of continuing relationships, but also with their subsequent restoration. On the rarity of successful reinstatement of employees ordered reinstated by the NLRB, see Aspin (1966). Bonn (1972 a:262) finds this pattern even among users of arbitration, which is supposedly less lethal to continuing relations than litigation. He found that in 78 cases of arbitration in textiles, "business relations were resumed in only fourteen".

36 As it happens, the information barriers vary in their restrictiveness. The American Bar Association's Code of Professional Responsibility

> permits advertising directed at corporations, banks, insurance companies, and those who work in the upper echelons of such institutions ... (while proscribing) most forms of dissemination of information which would reach people of 'moderate means' and apprise them of their legal rights and how they can find competent and affordable legal assistance to vindicate those rights (Burnley 1973:77).

On the disparate effect of these restrictions, cf. note 41.

37 The tension between the lawyer's loyalties to the legal system and to his client has been celebrated by Parsons (1954:381 ff.) and Horsky (1952:chap. 3). But note how this same deflection of loyalty from the client is deplored by Blumberg (1967) and others. The difference in evaluation seems to depend on whether the opposing pull is to the autonomous legal tradition, as Parsons (1954) and Horsky (1952) have it, or to the maintenance of mutually beneficial interaction with a particular local institution whose workings embody some admixture of the "higher law" with parochial understandings, institutional maintenance needs, etc.

38 Although this is not the place to elaborate it, let me sketch the model that underlies this assertion. Let us visualize a series of scales along which legal professions might be ranged:

	A	B
1. Basis of Recruitment	Restricted	Wide
2. Barriers to Entry	High	Low
3. Division of Labor		
a. Coordination	Low	High
b. Specialization	Low	High
4. Range of Services and Functions	Narrow	Wide
5. Enduring Relationships to Client	Low	High
6. Range of Institutional Settings	Narrow	Wide
7. Identification with Clients	Low	High
8. Identification with Authorites	High	Low
9. Guild Control	Tight	Loose
10. Ideology	Legalistic	Problem-solving

It is suggested that the characterisitcs at the A and B ends of the scale tend to go together, so that we can think of the A and B clusters as means of describing types of bodies of legal professionals – e.g., the American legal profession (Hurst 1950; Horsky 1952: Pt. V.; Carlin 1962, 1966; Handler 1967; Smigel 1969) would be more of a type B profession, compared to British barristers (Abel-Smith and Stevens 1967) and French avocats (Le Paulle 1950); Indian lawyers (Galanter 1968–69) would be intermediate between these two. Some characteristics of Type B professions tend to accentuate or amplify the strategic advantages of RP parties; though the conservative function of the British bar warns us not to overemphasize this point.

39 Which is not to deny the possibility that such "side" specializations might emerge. One can imagine "women's liberation" divorce lawyers – and anti alimony ones – devoted to rule-development that would favor one set of OS's.

40 On stratification within the American legal profession, see Ladinsky (1963); Lortie (1959); Carlin (1966) but cf. Handler (1967).

41 See Reichstein (1965); Northwestern University Law Review (1953). On the differential impact of the "Canons of Ethics" on large law firms and those lawyers who represent OS's, see Carlin (1966); Shuchman (1968); Christianson (1970:136).

42 Carlin and Howard (1965:385).

43 Ross (1970:82) observes the possibility of conflict between client and

> the negligence specialist, who negotiates on a repeated basis with the same insurance companies. (H)is goal of maximizing the return from any given case may conflict with the goal of maximizing returns from the total series of cases he represents.

For a catalog of other potential conflicts in the relationship between specialists and OS clients, see O'Connell (1971:46–47).

44 Rosenthal (1970:172).

45 Blumberg (1967); Skolnick (1967). On the interdependence of prosecutor and public defender, see Sudnow (1965:265,273).

46 Carlin (1962:161–62). On the "stranger" relationship between accident victim client and lawyer, see Hunting and Neuwirth (1962:109).

47 Cf. Consumer Council (1970:19). In connection with the lawyer's attachment to (or at least appreciation of) the problematic character of the law, consider the following legend, carried at the end of a public service column presented by the Illinois State Bar Association and run in a neighborhood newspaper:

> No person should ever apply or interpret any law without consulting his attorney. Even a slight difference in the facts may change the result under the law (Woodlawn Booster, July 31, 1963).

Where claims become insufficiently problematic they may drop out of the legal sphere entirely (e.g., social security). In high-volume and repetitive tasks, which admit of economies of scale and can be rendered relatively unproblematic, lawyers may be replaced by entrepeneurs – title companies, bank trust departments – serving OS's on a mass basis (or even serving RP's, for example, collection agencies). Cf. Johnstone and Hopson (1967:158 ff.).

48 Stumpf, et al. (1971:60) suggest that professional responses to OEO legal services programs require explanation on ideological ("the highly individualized, case-by-case approach ... as a prime article of faith") as well as pecuniary grounds. On the components of legalism as an ideology; see Shklar (1964:1–19). Of course this professional culture is not uniform but contains various subcultures. Brill's (1973) observations of OEO poverty lawyers suggest that crucial aspects of professional ideology (e.g., the emphasis on courts, rules and adjudication) are equally pronounced among lawyers who seek far-reaching change through the law.

49 Black (1973:141) observes the departures from the passive or "reactive" stance of legal institutions tend to be skewed along class lines:

> ... governments disproportionately adopt proactive systems of legal mobilization when a social control problem primarily involves the bottom of the social-class system. ... The common forms of legal misconduct in which upper status citizens indulge, such as breach of contract and warranty, civil negligence, and various forms of trust violation and corruption, are usually left to the gentler hand of a reactive mobilization process.

50 Homberger (1970:31–31). For a description of more "active" courts see Kaplan, et al. (1956:1221 ff.); Homberger (1970). Our description is of courts of the relatively passive variety typical of "common law" systems, but should not be taken as implying that "civil law" systems are ordinarily or typically different in practice. Cf. Merryman (1969:124). The far end of a scale of institutional "activism" might be represented by institutions like the Soviet Procuracy (Berman, 1963; 238 ff.).

51 Cf. Homberger (1971:641).

52 A further set of institutional limitations should be mentioned here: limitations on the scope of matters that courts hear; the kind of relief that they can give; and in their capacity for systematic enforcement.

53 On the limited supply of institutional facilities, consider Saari's (1967) estimate that in the early 1960's total governmental expenditures in the United States for civil and criminal justice ran about 4–5 billion dollars annually. (Of this, about 60 % went for police and prosecution, about 20 % for corrections, and 20 % for courts.) This amounted to about 2.5 % of the direct expenditures of American governments. In 1965–66 expenditures for the judiciary represented 1/17 of 1 % of the total federal budget; 6/10 of 1 % of state budgets; something less than 6 % of county and 3 % of city budgets.

54 The substitution of bargaining for adjudication need not be regarded as reflecting institutional deficiency. It has been frequently praised as wise and necessary.

> It is elementary, historically and statistically, that systems of courts – the number of judges, prosecutors and courtrooms – have been based on the premise that approximately 90 per cent of all (criminal) defendants will plead guilty, leaving only 10 per cent, more or less, to be tried. . . . The consequences of what might seem on its face a small percentage change in the rate of guilty pleas can be tremendous. . . . in Washington, D.C. . . . the guilty plea rate dropped to 65 per cent . . . (T)welve judges out of fifteen in active service were assigned to the criminal calendar and could barely keep up. . . . (T)o have this occur in the National Capital, which ought to be a model for the nation and show place for the world, was little short of disaster (Burger, 1970:931).

55 On institutional means of coping with overload, see Friedman (1967:798 ff.).

56 In the criminal process, too, the "possessor" has great advantages. There is a higher likelihood that those detained before trial will be convicted, and their sentences will be more severe; see Rankin (1964) and Wald (1964). Engle (1971) finds that among those convicted, pre-trial status explains more of the variation in sentencing severity than any of 23 other factors tested.

57 See Leff (1970 a:22) on the tendency of RP creditors to put themselves in the possessor position, shifting the costs of "due process" to the OS debtor. There are, however, instances where OS's may use overload to advantage – e.g., the accused out on bail may benefit from delay. Cf. Engle's (1971) observation of the "weakening effect of time on the prosecutor's position". Rioters or rent-strikers may threaten to demand jury trials – but the effectiveness of this tactic depends on coordination among OS's resulting in a change of scale.

58 E.g., the court studied by Zeisel, et al. (1959:7) "had chosen to concentrate all of its delay in the personal injury jury calendar and to keep its other law calendars up to date, granting blanket preferment to all commercial cases . . . and to all non-jury personal injury cases". [Recovery in the latter was about 20 % lower than jury awards in comparable cases (1959:119).]

59 This analysis has not made separate mention of corruption – i.e., the sale by incumbents of system outcomes divergent from those prescribed by authoritative norms. Insofar as such activities are analytically distinguishable from favorable priorities and "benign neglect" it should be noted that the organized, professional and wealthy are better able to make use of corrupt institutions, especially on a large scale. This, then, would be yet another layer of advantage to some classes of "haves".

60 This is sometimes the case – consider, e.g., the rules of landlord and tenant. Ohlhausen (1936) suggests that rules as to the availability of provisional remedies display a pronounced pattern of favoring claims of types likely to be brought by the "well to do" over claims of types brought by the impecunious.

61 E.g., Shuchman (1971:761–62) points out how in consumer bankruptcies:

> Consumer creditors have adjusted their practices so that sufficient proof will be conveniently available for most consumer loans to be excepted from discharge under section 17 a(2). They have made wide use of renewals, resetting, and new loans to pay off old loans, with the result that the consumers' entire debt will often be nondischargeable. Section 17 a(2) constitutes, in effect, an enabling act – a skeletal outline that the consumer creditor can fill in to create nondischargable debts – that operated to defeat the consumer's right to the benefits of a discharge in bankruptcy.

Similarly, Shuchman (1969) shows how RP auto-dealers and financial institutions have developed patterns for resale of repossessed automobiles that meet statutory resale requirements but which permit subsequent profitable second sale and in addition produce substantial deficiency claims.

62 For some examples of possessor-defendants exploiting the full panoply of procedural devices to raise the cost to claimants, see Schrag (1969); Macaulay (1966:98). Large (1972) shows how the doctrines of standing, jurisdiction and other procedural hurdles, effectively obstruct application of favorable substantive law in environmental litigation. Facing these rules in serial array, the environmentalists win many skirmishes but few battles.

63 Cf. the observation of Tullock (1971:48–49) that complexity and detail – the "maze" quality of legal rules – in itself confers advantages on "people of above average

intelligence, with literary and scholarly interests" – and by extension on those who can develop expertise or employ professional assistance.

64 For an example of the potency of a combination of complexity and expertise in frustrating recovery, see Laufer (1970). Or course, the advantage may derive not from the outcome, but from the complexity, expense and uncertainty of the litigation process itself. Borkin (1950) shows how, in a setting of economic competition among units of disparate size and resources, patent litigation may be used as a tactic of economic struggle.

65 Leff (1970 b); Rothwax (1969:143); cf. Grossman (1970).

66 Targets of demands for reform often argue that reform cannot come until the rules are changed. Frequently the rules are already adequate, in principle. Lipsky (1970:94–96), discussing the rent-strike movement, shows how housing officials claimed that implementation of rent-strikers' demands required new legislation, when they already had the needed power.

67 Dolbeare and Hammond (1971:151) observe in discussing implementation of decisions banning prayers in public schools, that "images of change abound while the status quo, in terms of the reality of people's lives, endures".

68 See, e.g., Lipsky (1970:chap. 4, 5).

69 See Edelman (1967:40).

70 On litigation as an organizational tool, see the examples given in Yale Law Journal (1970:1089–88).

71 Dahl (1958:294).

72 Cf. Cahn and Cahn's (1970:1016 ff.) delineation of the "four principle areas where the investment of ... resources would yield critically needed changes: The creation (and legitimation) of new justice-dispensing institutions, the expansion of the legal manpower supply ... the development of a new body of procedural and substantive rights, and the development of forms of group representation as a means of enfranchisement", and the rich catalog of examples under each heading.

73 It is clear e.g. that what Agnew (1972:930) finds objectionable is the redistributive thrust of the legal services program:

> ... the legal services program has gone way beyond the idea of a governmentally funded program to make legal remedies available to the indigent ... We are dealing, in large part, with a systematic effort to redistribute societal advantages and disadvantages, penalties and rewards, rights and resources.

74 Summed up neatly by the head of OEO programs in California, who, defending Governor Reagan's veto of the California Rural Legal Assistance program, said:

> What we've created in CRLA is an economic leverage equal to that of a large corporation. Clearly that should not be.

Quoted at Stumpf, et al. (1971:65).

75 Cf. Note 38 above. Legal professions closer to "Type B" will accentuate the advantages of the 'haves'; but they will also be most capable of producing redistributive change.

References Cited

Abel-Smith, Brian and Robert Stevens, 1967, Lawyers and the Courts: A Sociological Study of the English Legal System, 1750–1965. Cambridge, Harvard University press.

Agnew, Spiro 1972, What's Wrong with the Legal Services Program. A.B.A. Journal 58:930-32.

Aspin, Leslie, 1966, A Study of Reinstatement Under the National Labor Relations Act. Unpublished dissertation, Mass. Institute of Technology.

Aubert, Vilhelm, 1963, Competition and Dissensus: Two Types of Conflict Resolution. Journal of Conflict Resolution 7:26–42.

Babcock, Richard S., 1969, The Zoning Game: Municipal Practices and Policies. Madison, University of Wisconsin Press.

Berman, Harold J., 1963, Justice in the U.S.S.R.: An Interpretation of Soviet Law. Revised Ed., Englarged. New York: Vintage Books.

Bernstein, Marver H., 1955, Regulating Business by Independent Commission. Princeton, Princeton Univ. Press.
Black, Donald J., 1973, The Mobilization of Law. Journal of Legal Studies 2:125–49.
Blumberg, Abraham, 1967, The Practice of Law as a Confidence Game. Law and Society Review 1:15–40.
Bonn, Robert L., 1972 a, Arbitration: An Alternative System for Handling Contract Related Disputes. Administrative Sciences Quarterly 17:254–64.
–, 1972 b, The Predictability of Nonlegalistic Adjudication. Law and Society Review 6:563–78.
Borkin, Joseph, 1950, The Patent Infringement Suit – Ordeal by Trial University of Chicago Law Review 17:634–52.
Brill, Harry 1973, The Uses and Abuses of Legal Assistance. The Public Interest No. 31: 38–55 (Spring).
Burger, Warren, 1970, The State of the Judiciary – 1970. American Bar Association Journal. 56:929–34.
Burnley, James H. IV, 1973, Comment, Solicitation by the Second Oldest Profession: Attorneys and Advertising. Harvard Civil Rights and Civil Liberties Law Review 8:77–103.

Cahn, Edgar S. and Jean Camper Cahn, 1970, Power to the People or the Profession? – The Public Interest in Public Interest Law. Yale Law Journal 79:1005–48.
Carlin, Jerome E.,
1962, Lawyers on their Own: A Study of Individual Practitioners in Chicago. New Brunswick, Rutgers University Press.
–, 1966, Lawyer's Ethics: A Survey of the New York City Bar. New York, Russell Sage Foundation.
Carlin, Jerome E. and Jan Howard, 1965, Legal Representation and Class Justice. UCLA Law Review 12:381–437.
Christianson, Barlow F., 1970, Lawyers for People of Moderate Means: some problems of availability of legal services. Chicago: American Bar Foundation.
Cohen, Julius, Reginald A.H. Robson, and Alan Bates, 1958, Parental Authority: The Community and the Law. New Brunswick: Rutgers University Press.
Conard, Alfred F., James N. Morgan, Robert W. Pratt, Jr., Charles F. Voltz, and Robert L. Bombaugh, 1964, Automobile Accident Costs and Payments: Studies in the Economics of Injury Reparation. Ann Arbor, Univ. of Michigan Press.
Consumer Council, 1970, Justice Out of Reach: A Case for Small Claims Courts. London: Her Majesty's Stationery Office.

Dahl, Robert A., 1958, Decision-making in a Democracy: The Supreme Court as a National Policy-maker. Journal of Public Law 6:279–95.
Dibble, Vernon K., 1970, What is, and What Ought to Be: A Comparison of Certain Formal Characteristics of the Ideological and Legal Styles of Thought: Second Draft, Feb. 1970.
Dolbeare, Kenneth M., and Phillip E. Hammond, 1971, The School. Local Practice. Chicago, University of Chicago Press.

Edelman, Murray, 1967, The Symbolic Uses of Politics. Urbana, University of Illinois Press.
Ehrlich, Eugen, 1936, Fundamental Principles of the Sociology of Law. New York: Russell and Russell Publishers.
Engle, C. Donald, 1971, Criminal Justice in the City. Doctoral Dissertation, Temple University.

Finklestein, Herman, 1954, The Composer and the Public Interest – Regulation of Performing Rights Societies. Law and Contemporary Problems 19: 275–93.
Foote, Caleb, 1956, Vagrancy-type Law and Its Administration. University of Pennsylvania Law Review 104:603–50.
Franklin, Marc, Robert H. Chanin, and Irving Mark, 1961, Accidents, Money and the Law. A Study of the Economics of Personal Injury Litigation. Columbia Law Review 61:1–39.
Friedman, Lawrence M., 1967, Legal Rules and the Process of Social Change. Stanford Law Review 19:786–840.
–, 1969, Legal Culture and Social Development. Law and Society Review 4:29–44.

Friedman, Lawrence M. and Jack Ladinsky, 1967, Social Change and the Law of Industrial Accidents. Columbia Law Review 67:50–82.

–, *and Stewart Macaulay,* 1967, Contract Law and Contract Teaching: Past, Present, and Future. Wisconsin Law Review 1967:805–21.

Galanter, Marc, 1968–69, Introduction: The Study of the Indian Legal Profession. Law and Society Review 3:201–17.

Grossman, Joel, 1970, The Supreme Court and Social Change: A Preliminary Inquiry. American Behavioral Scientist 13:535–51.

Handler, Joel, 1967, The Lawyer and His Community: The Practicing Bar in a Middlesized City. Madison, University of Wisconsin Press.

Hirschman, Albert O., 1970, Exit, Voice, and Loyalty: Responses to Decline in Firms, Organizations and States. Cambridge, Harvard University Press.

Homberger, Adolf, 1970, Functions of Orality in Austrian and Americal Civil Procedure Buffalo Law Review 20:9–39.

–, 1971, State Class Actions and the Federal Rule.,*Columbia Law Review 71:609–59.*

Horsky, Charles, 1952, The Washington Lawyer. Boston, Little, Brown Co.

Hunting, Roger Bryant and Gloria S. Neuwirth, 1962, Who Sues in New York City? A Study of Automobile Accident Claims. New York, Columbia Univ. Press.

Hurst, James Willard, 1950, The Growth of American Law: The Law Makers. Boston: Little, Brown and Company.

Jacob, Herbert, 1969, Debtors in Court: The Consumption of Government Services. Chicago, Rand McNally.

Johnstone, Quintin and Dan Hopson, Jr., 1967, Lawyers and Their Work: An Analysis of the Legal Profession in the United States and England. Indianapolis: Bobbs Merrill Co.

Kaplan, Benjamin, von Mehren, Arthur T., Schaefer, Rudolf, 1958, Phases of German Civil Procedure. Harvard Law Review 71:1193–1268, 1443–72.

La Fave, Wayne R., 1965, Arrest: The Decision to Take a Suspect into Custody. Boston, Little, Brown Company.

Ladinsky, Jack, 1963, Careers of Lawyers, Law Practice and Legal Institutions. American Sociological Review 28:47–54.

Laufer, Joseph, 1970, Embattled Victims of the Uninsured: In Court with New York's MVAIC, 1959–69. Buffalo Law Review 19:471:513.

Le Paulle, Pierre George, 1950, Law Practice in France. Columbia Law Review 50:945–58.

Leff, Arthur A., 1970 a, Injury, Ignorance, and Spite – The Dynamics of Coercive Collection. Yale Law Journal 80:1–46.

–, 1970 b, Unconscionability and the Crowd-Consumers and the Common-Law Tradition. University of Pittsburgh Law Review 31:349–358.

Lipsky, Michael, 1970, Protest in City Politics: Rent Strikes, Housing, and the Power of the Poor. Chicago, Rand McNally and Company.

Lobenthal, Joseph S., Jr., 1970, Power and Put-On: The Law in America. New York, Outerbridge and Dienstfrey.

Loeber, Dietrich A., 1965, Plan and Contract Performance in Soviet Law. in (W. La Fave, ed.) Law in the Soviet Society. pp. 128–79. Urbana: Univ. of Ill. Press.

Lortie, Dan C., 1959, Laymen to Lawmen: Law School, Careers, and Professional Socialization. Harvard Educational Review 29:352–69.

Macaulay, Stewart, 1963, Non-Contractual Relations in Business. A Preliminary Study. American Sociological Review 28:55–67.

–, 1966, Law and the Balance of Power: The Automobile Manufacturers and their Dealers. New York, Russell Sage Foundation.

MacCallum, Spencer, 1967, Dispute Settlement in an American Supermarket. in Paul Bohannon (ed.) Law and Warfare, Garden City, N.Y.: Natural History Press for American Museum of Natural History. 291–99.

Merryman, John Henry, 1969, The Civil Law Tradition: An Introduction to the Legal Systems of Western Europe and Latin America. Stanford, California: Stanford University Press.

Morgan, Richard S., 1968, The Politics of Religious Conflict: Church and State in America. New York, Pegasus.
Moulton, Beatrice A., 1969, The Persecution and Intimidation of the Low-Income Litigant as Performed by the Small Claims Court in California. Stanford Law Review 21:1657–84.

Newman, Donald J., 1966, Conviction: The Determination of Guilt or Innocence Without Trial. Boston, Little, Brown & Co.
Nonet, Philippe, 1969, Administrative Justice: Advocacy and Change in a Government Agency. New York: Russell Sage Foundation.
Northwestern University Law Review, 1953, "Settlement of Personal Injury Cases in the Chicago Area". 47:895–914.

O'Connell, Jeffrey, 1971, The Injury Industry and the Remedy of No-Fault Insurance. Commerce Clearing House.
O'Gorman, Hubert, 1963, Lawyers and Matrimonial Cases: A Study of Informal Pressures in Private Professional Practice. New York, Free Press.
Ohlhausen, George C., 1936, Rich and Poor in Civil Procedure. Science and Society 11:275–309.
Olson, Mancur, Jr., 1965, The Logic of Collective Action: Public Goods and the Theory of Groups. Cambridge: Harvard University Press.

Pagter, C.R., R. McCloskey and M. Reinis, 1964, The California Small Claims Court. California Law Review 52:876–898.
Parsons, Talcott, 1954, A Sociologist Looks At The Legal Profession: in Essays in Sociological Theory. New York, Free Press, pp. 370–388.

Rankin, Anne, 1964, The Effect of Pretrial Detention. N.Y.U. Law Review 39:641–55.
Reichstein, Kenneth J., 1965, Ambulance Chasing: A Case Study of Deviation Within the Legal Profession. Social Problems 3:3–17.
Rosenthal, Douglas E., 1970, Client Participation in Professional Decision: the Lawyer-Client Relationship in Personal Injury Cases. Yale University Doctoral Dissertation.
Ross, H. Laurence, 1970, Settled Out of Court: The Social Process of Insurance Claims Adjustment. Chicago, Aldine.
Rothwax, Harold J., 1969, The Law as an Instrument of Social Change in Justice and the Law in the Mobilization for Youth Experience. (Harold H. Weissman, Editor) New York, New York Association Press.

Saari, David J., 1967, Open Doors to Justice – An Overview of Financing Justice in America. Journal of the American Judicature Society 50:296–302.
Salisbury, Robert H., 1969, An Exchange Theory of Interest Groups. Midwest Journal of Political Science 13:1–32.
Schelling, Thomas C., 1963, The Strategy of Conflict. New York, Oxford Univ. Press.
Schrag, Philip G., 1969, Bleak House 1968: A Report on Consumer Test Litigation. New York University Law Review 44:115–58.
Scigliano, Robert, 1971, The Supreme Court and the Presidency. New York, Free Press.
Scott, William G., 1964, The Management of Conflict: Appeal Systems in Organizations. Homewood, Ill.: Irwin/Dorsey.
Shklar, Judith N., 1964, Legalism. Cambridge, Massachusetts, Harvard University Press.
Shuchman, Philip, 1968, Ethics and Legal Ethics: The Property of the Canons as a Group Moral Code. George Washington Law Review. 37:244–69.
–, 1969, Profit on Default: an archival study of automobile repossession and resale. Stanford Law Review. 22:20–66.
–, 1971, The Fraud Exception in Consumer Bankruptcy. Stanford Law Review. 23:735–73.
Skolnick, Jerome, 1966, Justice Without Trial: Law Enforcement in a Democratic Society. New York, John Wiley.
–, 1967, Social Control in the Adversary Process. Journal of Conflict Resolution 11:52–70.
Smigel, Erwin O., 1969, The Wall Street Lawyer: Professional Organization Man? Blooming ton. Indiana University Press.
Spradley, James P., 1970, You Owe Yourself a Drunk: An Ethnography of Urban Nomads. Boston: Little, Brown and Company.

Stumpf, Harry P., Henry P. Schroerluke and Forrest D. Dill, 1971, The Legal Profession and Legal Services: Explorations in Local Bar Politics. Law and Society Review 6:47–67.

Sudnow, David, 1965, Normal Crimes: Sociological Features of the Penal Code in a Public Defender Office. Social Problems 12:255–74.

Summers, Clyde, 1960, Individual Rights in Collective Agreements: A Preliminary Analysis. Buffalo Law Review 9:239–54.

Tullock, Gordon, 1971, Logic of the Law. New York. Basic Books, Inc.

Vaughan, Ted R., 1968, The Landlord-Tenant Relationship in a Low-Income Area. Social Problems 16:208–18.

Virtue, Maxine Boord, 1956, Family Cases in Court: A Group of Four Court Studies Dealing with Judicial Administration. Durham, Duke University Press.

Wald, Patricia, 1964, Foreward: Pretrial Detention and Ultimate Freedom. N.Y.U. Law Review 31:631–40.

Wanner, Craig P., 1972, The Public Ordering of Private Relations: Winning Civil Disputes in Urban Trial Courts. Paper Prepared for Delivery at the 1972 Annual Meeting of the American Political Science Association.

Weber, Max, 1954, Max Weber on Law in Economy and Society. Max Rheinstein, ed. Cambridge: Harvard University Press.

Yale Law Journal, 1970, The New Public Interest Lawyers. Yale Law Journal 79:1069–1152.

Zeisel, Hans, Harry Kalven, Jr., and Bernard Buchholz, 1959, Delay in the Court. Boston, Little Brown Company.

Philip Lewis*

Defamation: Reputation and Encounter

In all societies there is a continuing flow of information (1)**, and within this flow there is constant evaluation of individuals (2). There are many ways of looking at the flow of information. In this paper I propose to concentrate on the concerns that societies may have that the available information and evaluation correspond with reasonable accuracy (3) to facts about individuals, including, where relevant, their potentialities, and the corresponding interests that individuals may have both in the accuracy or fairness of such information and evaluation, and, where appropriate, in control of the flow of information about the individuals' private affairs. I am not dealing with the question of whether in any society such an accurate correspondence exists, or individuals do have such a control, but only with the values and institutions which express such concerns and interests.

In English the concept of 'reputation' covers at least part of this area; it connotes what is thought and spoken of a person, and not what he is (4), though sometimes his reputation may be regarded as a good guide to what he is. People may value their reputations, but the word has no reference to the idea that a person's alignment to the world or his feelings may be spoiled by an insult or affront. Concepts of honour, self-respect or shame are not my concern (5).

Particular features of a legal system may be seen as intended to affect or participate in the flow of information and evaluation about individuals. Most obviously, both the criminal and the civil law may give public authorities, such as the police, or private citizens directly affected, the power to take court proceedings against a person who has passed on information or evaluation in a particular context (6), and the knowledge that this power exists and may be used may either directly deter such acts or may give rise to or reinforce social norms restricting them. Again, a legal framework may more or less directly facilitate control by a supervisory body of standards of publication in defined areas; for instance supervisory bodies in British broadcasting are given some direct powers to control what is broadcast, whereas private bodies such as the Press Council (7) and indeed, the leadership of social clubs which can or could influence what is published or said by laying down rules about information flow, or punishing

* Fellow, All Soul's College, Oxford. I should like to thank Lawrence Friedman, Stanton Wheeler and other participants in the meeting at Bielefeld, and William Twining and other members of the Warwick Law Faculty, for their helpful comments on an earlier draft. I should particularly like to express my indebtedness to the discussion by Haviland (see note 17) of the problems of understanding gossip.

** Notes on pages 283 f.

"defamation", are strengthened by the surrounding culture, and by the law's tolerance of their activities (8). A legal system also provides structures for the support of valuable commercial reputations. The law of trade-marks facilitates the use of brand-names, and these may acquire reputations separate from those of the manufacturer of the branded goods (though to his advantage). Laws providing for the professional qualification of doctors or stringent inquiry into the background of the owners of public-houses may enhance the reputations of those who are successful in achieving licensing. Laws providing for the conviction and sentencing of criminals (particularly where no restraint is imposed on newspaper publication of the details) add injury to reputation to the more official punishments (9). We should also bear in mind provisions of law which facilitate the expression of adverse opinions, such as prohibitions against duels or the horsewhipping of editors.

It is probably not possible to study fully the values and institutions which express a concern for reputation, or even their legal aspects, without having some general idea of the nature of the flow of information about reputation in a society, and its major social determinants. Legal institutions, for instance, will be based on and will formulate judgments about the social facts of information flow. The social reality that lies behind the law is, in large part, beyond the scope of this paper. One might also want to know what is the actual contribution made by the law to that social reality, whether one is interested in policy questions or in descriptions of the law in society or in the assumptions made by legal institutions about their social effects or roles. This contribution, however, is not easy to examine. For instance, the law may have a deterrent effect on behavior; but it is not easy to go beyond theory and say something about the actual extent of that deterrence. One can look at particular examples, or case-studies, of situations where the flow of information has been halted by a lawyer's advice that there was danger of legal proceedings, or by an actual threat of proceedings. One can more generally try to compare the flow of information in countries with different laws, but social norms may be so different as to make a comparison meaningless (10).

It is thus very difficult to study the part that the law plays in the flow of information. What is easier is to look more directly at some of the legal institutions which express a concern for reputation, the assumptions underlying them, the use to which they are put and the processes of using them. It may turn out, as has been suggested, that much in legal institutions does affect reputation; in particular societies, for instance, people will regard their reputation as at risk in any litigation in which they are concerned (11), and the desire to protect a reputation or the value of a reputation may be recognised as relevant in many areas of law (12). Nevertheless, some legal institutions are more exclusively concerned with reputation, and it is one of those that I now discuss.

If an English lawyer is asked how reputation is protected by the law he will answer that it is by reason of the tort, the actionable wrong, of defamation. There are two forms of this, libel (written, broadcast or in a play) and slander, which is oral; basically the rules are the same, but where slander is complained of, plaintiffs must prove special circumstances or specific damage in order to recover. The tort is committed by the publication to a third party of a defamatory statement, one which will 'tend to lower' the party complaining of it 'in the eyes of right-thinking persons generally', that is, to make others think worse of him. The plaintiff does not have to prove the statement false. It is not legally relevant, except as to damages, whether the statement was made carelessly or intentionally, or whether anyone believed the statement true, or, except sometimes in slander, that the plaintiff suffered damage from it. In a civil action the truth of the statement is a complete defence, whether or not publication of the matter was for the public benefit, and whether or not the plaintiff had a legitimate interest in keeping the matter secret. Broadly speaking, if the defendant was reporting what was said in Parliament or in a court or in certain kinds of meeting open to the public, he is not liable for a fair report of what was said, although it is usually no defence that one has repeated the defamatory statement of another. To repeat a rumour, for instance, is as bad as to originate it, and sometimes worse, if one adds an appearance of respectabilitiy to it. The defendant is also protected without having to prove the words true if he published them because it was his duty to, or if he was "privileged", that is, if he had an interest in publishing the words to someone who had an interest in hearing them. Thus, an employer's reference on the merits of a former employee, or communications between directors of a company on the company's business cannot be sued on unless the defendant has used the occasion for some wrongful purpose, to damage the interests, say, of his former employee in revenge for his leaving. Finally, some words are regarded as comments and not statements of fact, such as criticism of a politician's conduct or of an artistic production; these are not actionable if they represent the writer's real opinion.

Defamation actions are usually tried by a judge sitting with a jury; the jury will decide questions of fact, the meaning of the words, whether they are defamatory, their truth or otherwise, questions as to the state of mind of the defendant, and the amount of the damages, if any. The judge provides a general check on any tendency of the jury to go to extremes. He will decide, where appropriate, whether there was a duty or interest of the kind the defendant asserts, or whether conduct of the plaintiff was open to comment by the defendant.

Libel, but not slander, is also a crime: with perhaps some exceptions for trivial cases, criminal proceedings can be brought for any libel, though the leave of a judge is needed to prosecute a newspaper. Up to at least 1900, and perhaps later, prosecutions brought by the person defamed were common. Up to 1888, the defendant could not give evidence in a criminal case, and truth was not by itself a defence in a criminal case, unless publication was also found by the jury to have been for the public benefit.

Defamation actions are interesting for a number of reasons. The possibility of an action undoubtedly has a deterrent effect on defamatory publications in England (13). Knowledge of high awards of damages against newspapers is widespread, more so than that of cases in which juries have found against plaintiffs or given them only nominal damages. However, as has been said, to assess the nature and extent of this deterrent effect is extremely difficult. A wide range of questions can arise in defamation cases. There may be a dispute as to whether the words complained of are defamatory. The jury will have to consider whether they ascribe to the plaintiff conduct knowledge of which would have lowered him in the estimation of right-thinking people. Thus, in effect, they have to set a standard by which they can judge not actual behaviour, but the behaviour of which the plaintiff has been accused, but which *ex hypothesi* he has not committed. In deciding whether the defendant has misused an occasion which would otherwise have been privileged they may have to consider the general propriety of his conduct. Perhaps most interestingly, if the plaintiff succeeds, they may weigh up the whole conduct of both plaintiff and defendant in context – the words complained of, their publication and the way the parties conducted the proceedings. The jury need give only nominal damages (often, in times past, a farthing), if they think that the action, though technically justified, should not have been brought.

The least then that one can get from a study of defamation actions is unusual light on attitudes toward a wide range of subjects. Thus in one case in 1879 (14) a chief of police attempted to avoid a scandal about a clergyman by getting him to resign. The then Lord Chief Justice criticised the chief of police quite severely, for acting as a *censor morum:* we get some flavour of life in an English country area, and also the way in which this life struck a lawyer in London.

But the range of questions which may need decision also makes defamation actions unusually flexible as forms of dispute. The legal process sometimes forces parties to a dispute to change the nature of the dispute, in order to get it settled by the courts; but in defamation actions the original dispute often comes to court unaltered. The fact that the legal category gives this flexibility probably justifies picking it as a category for sociological examination.

The materials used here as background, practically speaking, are drawn from newspaper sources. They come from two periods of one year each – November 1878 to October 1879, and October 1967 to September 1968. The first was chosen because it was the period in which a Parliamentary Committee heard evidence on the working of the law as it affected newspapers, resulting in the only legislative change in a 60 year time span. The dates correspond with those covered in the annual volume of Judicial Statistics. Cases for the second period came from a press cutting service.

The 1879 cases are drawn entirely from *The Times,* which printed an extensive law report each day. *The Times* often refers to a court as trying cases "of no public interest", but it is not clear what that means. Cases were tried in London or in the provinces ("on Assize" or "on circuit"): coverage of the latter (except for murder cases) was less good. We are told by the Judicial Statistics that during 1879 124 libel and slander cases were tried in London or entered for trial on circuit. Of these *The Times* reports 42–46 (depending on how one classifies). The largest category are libel cases in London, in which 23 out of 38 are reported, whereas only 1–3 slander cases in London out of 19 are reported. Surprisingly enough 13–14 out of 47 slander cases on circuit are reported. Some reports are only a line or so, but most set out the facts of the case in summary form, as well as the result. The great majority of cases reported were decided by a jury, but frequently the parties settled, and allowed a verdict to be entered for the plaintiff, as the shape of the case became clear. Some of the cases have very full reports, extending over a period of days, with detailed reports of evidence and cross examination, speeches of counsel and summing-up by the judge. The age was not leisured: courts sat far longer hours than they do now, and got through cases much more quickly.

There were also, we know from tables in the Judicial Statistics, about 15 cases sent down to lower courts to be tried, but *The Times* has no reference to them. We have no easy way of knowing how many cases were started by writ, and ended after an apology. *The Times* records one or two, as well as a few in which the proceedings before trial raised an interesting point.

The biggest change between 1879 and 1968 is in criminal proceedings. Libel is not listed separately in the Criminal Judicial Statistics for 1879, but there were at least 40 prosecutions, all privately instituted, mentioned in *The Times.* There were no criminal prosecutions for libel in 1968, although it is said that 14 cases were known to the police, and 11 cleared up.

The 1968 cuttings came from the whole English press and one would expect them to cover proceedings in the provinces more adequately. Unfortunately, the current Civil Judicial Statistics does not classify cases by their causes of action, so it is not possible to test the adequacy of the reporting. The cuttings mention about 106 cases. 15 of these are decisions by a judge or jury, and 7 by the Court of Appeal. 58 of them are settlements: in practically all of them an agreed statement of the way in which the plaintiff has been injured and the defendant's apology is made before a judge who has approved the statement, a form of settlement which barely existed in 1879 or indeed for many years afterwards. The remaining reports mainly refer to the beginning of litigation by the issue of a writ. It may pay people who are in a controversy to issue a writ and announce the fact to the Press, as a particularly emphatic form of denial. If the practice existed in 1879, *The Times* hardly opened its columns to it.

The comparison between the two periods turned out less fruitful than one hoped. There seem to be fewer cases in 1968, and the change to agreed statements from litigated cases suggests that litigation has become more of a last resort, perhaps because of length and expense. There seem in 1968 to be more actions concerning politicians (who hardly appear at all in 1879), and more actions against national newspapers. In the earlier period it seems that it was more common to answer newspaper criticism by publishing a letter in reply. On the other hand, clergymen seemed to figure more in actions in 1879. Clergymen had greater social importance then, and there was greater interest in matters of religion and ritual.

On the whole, such comparisons of forms and litigants seem to yield little. There might be some point in classification not by profession but by position in the social structure, but that is a difficult concept to define. It seems more profitable to ask what the actions are about. The subject matter of a defamation action in one sense is words, in another the legal questions which the court will have to decide. But the question, what a defamation action was about, can be approached also from the point of view of its social significance. One aspect of this will be the parties' purpose in suing and defending, and in adopting particular styles of suing and defending. The questions which have to be legally decided *may* be incidental to these purposes, although, as we have seen, they range widely, and thus may fall in well with the party's purposes. Often, a person against whom an authoritative finding has been made by an investigating body, sues in defamation a third person, who repeats the allegation that the plaintiff is guilty; the plaintiff now gets in effect a determination of innocence from the court, which he can use to improve his position.

Basically then, each action may be regarded as part of a process, purposefully begun and carried on; we should only begin categorising cases when we have some idea of these underlying processes. While some cases are simple, others are more complicated. The case in which the painter Whistler recovered only a farthing damages (said by the Times to be a more damaging verdict than if he had lost) against the critic Ruskin, who criticized his impudence in producing what Ruskin regarded as half-finished work, cannot be understood without a knowledge of the social position and aesthetic views of each, and the place that each held in current movements in art. One cannot simply classify the case along with others in which authors sued over criticisms of their books and plays.

In looking at legal cases, we are not confined to the concepts of the law or to such theories as we may formulate while analysing them; we can see what sociological theory has to offer and how it needs to be modified to accomodate the special situation of formalised norms and authoritative determinations (15). Two sets of theory are offered which may be of help: theories of status and theories about gossip. The first set deals, very relevantly, with role-performance and its evaluation; but the second set may be more helpful, since it concentrates on social acts, information passing and evaluation of the kind with which defamation actions are also concerned. In addition, study of norms *about* gossip, and when it is permissible, might help us to understand norms about defamation, though this subject is not dealt with here.

One substantial caveat must be entered: we are concerned to a large extent with complex societies. In these, a man's reputation may be created and destroyed without the participation of people who have directly interacted with him: but theories of gossip have on the whole been concerned with less complex societies, in which there may be quite a lot of knowledge about the person gossiped about. In this respect, however, London in 1879 seems not as distant from such societies as one might imagine.

A recent article (16) summarizes anthropological study of gossiping as having seemingly coalesced about two general positions: the functionalist, which concentrates on explicating the latent functions of gossip in various social units, and the transactionalist stance, which stresses how particular persons tactically utilise gossip for purposes of impression or information management to further their rather explicit aims. The transactionalist account seems to offer most to the understanding of the materials we have; the functionalist accounts are useful rather as bases for speculation.

I would pick out three strands in the functionalist approach. One is that the ability to gossip in a society is closely related to the ability to understand it (17). Since ability to gossip requires and is known to require an understanding of the society, to be allowed to gossip is to be accepted as part of a group in that society, and to gossip is to take part in the group and to accept one's position as a member of it (18). The second strand is closely related: to gossip is to share in the activity of applying evaluative standards to the conduct of society members. The continued shared existence of such standards in necessary to keep societies together. Gluckman (19) expounds this view from previous studies: he relies particulary on Colson's work on the Makah Indians (20), a group on the fringes of American society, to some extent existing as a group only for the purpose of exercising their rights to tribal lands. Makah standards of pure birth and ancient lineage could only be applied in gossip, since those standards did not relate to current activities which could be sanctioned in any other way. Some of Gluckman's argument reads like Lord Devlin's defence of the need to enforce shared moral standards, in order to keep society together (21): counter-arguments would read very much like Hart's careful description of the facts which would need to be proved if this "disintegration hypothesis" were to be made good (22). The third strand is perhaps more in the tradition of sociology: gossip as a means of social control. The transmission of information, through gossip, makes it possible to evaluate and to sanction effectively activity which is contrary to shared norms. Individuals know that their acts will be judged, and refrain accordingly: they are punished if they do not.

A few points here are indirectly relevant to the study of defamation. We might speculate that if we accept the functionalist point, that maintenance of shared evaluative standards is necessary to keep society together, then one might also require some mechanism to restrain the emergence of competing and divisive standards. To some extent defamatory talk may be regarded not only as misstatement (which might be functionally irrelevant, as it was with the Makah, who always contradicted each other on fact) but also as an application of interpretative or evaluative standards which are not generally shared. If, then, the functionalist thesis were correct, one might expect the law to treat such deviant standards severely. The English rule that honest comment is not actionable goes against this, but I would not rule out the possibility of finding traces of it. Let me, however, use an example which is admittedly extreme the other way. Heppenstall (23) refers to an incident in an Austrian village where a school teacher (an outsider) established social relationships with pupils and ex-pupils, a most unusual proceeding. Gossip spread, unrestrained by any necessity to respect the feelings of his supporters, for he had none. Quite false stories were spread about, and parents of other children laid a formal complaint about him: he then laid "an official complaint against them for defamation of character. This was successful and the business officially closed." But he was still as ostracised as ever. In this case, the "deviant" attitudes were locally predominant, and legal action was a resort to an outside authority. This suggests caution in speaking of defamation actions as enforcing prevailing standards. We must ask: prevailing where and for whom? We may suspect that in our materials London standards may not be the same as provincial ones and that cases differ; some may be like the Austrian one, some may involve enforcement of dominant standards against a deviant, and most involve an authoritative determination favouring one of two sets of competing standards or a compromise between them.

Theories which see gossip as a means of social control, encouraging and enforcing adherence to shared social norms, also do not go very far to explain the phenomenon of defamation law. Intuitively one is inclined to say that gossip works as social control only if people know that their conduct will be correctly interpreted and evaluated; if it is not we shall have a society which in effect punishes the innocent. People go to great lengths to avoid actions or situations which can be misinterpreted; it does not seem inevitable that the existence of shared norms leads to a situation in which misinformation or misevaluation itself becomes subject to sanction. One nineteenth century writer on the law of defamation in England expresses the view that society needs conduct to be correctly judged, so as to encourage desired activity and discourage others (26). Apparently, this line of thought was not pursued by others; while there may be truth in it in some circumstances, the underlying theory needs much elaboration before it can be applied to the law of defamation.

I turn then to transactionalist theories (27). In these theories the emphasis is on the way individuals in a society use gossip as a means of manipulating the information available to others and the impressions which others have of them and people with whose position they are concerned. This position is not necessarily inconsistent with functionalism (28). The application of widely shared standards in gossip may help to keep societies together, precisely to the extent that people are led to gossip by motives of selfinterest. What does seem less consistent with a functionalist account is that much gossip involves, if not the formation, at least the clarification of norms and their application to new circumstances (29). Once one admits this account of some gossip as a quasi-legislative process, then consideration of the motives for engaging in it may cast light on processes of norm formation as a result of individual or group interests. Descriptions of competing interpretations of behavior emanating from hostile factions are found in the literature and gossip begins to seem more than merely the application of existing standards.

Taking part in gossip in village communities may well be a "political" act (30). It is certainly sometimes a valuable strategy. There are costs and benefits in different ways of passing on information. A person who passes on information as a rumour does not commit himself to a judgment of its truth or falsehood. His standing as an authority is not increased or lessened, whether it turns out to be true or false. He has risked nothing. But he does risk something if he says: "I know as a fact that..." and commits himself to an adverse moral judgment. He may be more respected if it turns out to be true, and he can get others to agree with his judgment: if not, he may be labeled a "trouble-maker" (31).

This approach catches at least some of the flavour of defamation proceedings. Someone has said something reflecting on another, and the question may be whether he can show what he said to be true or get others to agree with his interpretation or evaluation. Defendant for his part may try to show that he behaved well, in that he was fulfilling a duty or expressing his honest opinion.

Handelman (32) allows us to see gossip transactions from a different viewpoint. He is concerned to enlarge on what he regards as an insight by Goffman, that norms and roles existing in the wider social structure are not necessarily reproduced in encounters, which may have their own rules, directed at ensuring the viability of the encounter rather than the application of social norms to particular circumstances. He points out that the quality of information and its significance to those who receive it vary according to the kind of encounter. He describes one kind as the "oscillating" encounter, in which the parties are competing to impose their own definitions of the way the encounter is to be conducted, what "rules of irrelevance", in Goffman's language, should be adopted, and what roles the participants should fill. He describes face-to-face encounters in a workshop, pointing out that such "oscillating" encounters can be expected when someone is gossiped about to his face, and the participants are trying to enlist the support of bystanders. I would suggest that actions for defamation can profitably be looked at in this way. The "oscillations" which Handelman describes may occur in some form in any interaction where the parties have different aims. The parties try to define transactions in terms of past role performances of one or both, invoking the authority of each as a reliable passer of information, and asserting of themselves that they are persons whose definition of the transaction may safely be accepted. Reputation and reliability are at issue, as they are in a defamation action, and analysis of transactions of this kind may thus be expected to be particularly relevant. In defamation cases, unlike the workshop situation, the court is actually (or potentially in a settlement situation) present as an extremely influential bystander and ultimate arbiter; also, many of the norms to which reference is made are laid down more formally than in the workshop, still, the situations have many points of resemblance.

Handelman gives only one example of an "oscillating" encounter, in which comments on role performance and reliability play a principal part. One would like to see a study of a range of transactions, showing that they took this particular "oscillating" form because past role performance and reliability were relevant. As it is, I can only give some examples of defamation proceedings and suggest that the presence of those features provides motivation which give a plausible explanation of the form the proceedings took. The cases also illustrate Goffman's point that encounters are not merely to be understood as the application of social norms.

The process is clearest when one has a full report of a reported case. In particular, the questions asked by counsel when cross-examining witnesses on the other side, especially the opposing party, show very clearly the attempts that are being made to impose a definition on the original transaction which gave rise to the statement complained of, and on the legal proceedings as well, Let me give three examples.

Two from 1879 concern clergymen. In the first (33) the plaintiffs owned a popular Protestant paper campaigning against the so-called evils of the confessional. The paper described some of these "evils". The defendant, a clergyman with no particular sympathy for the confessional, attacked plaintiffs' paper for its content, and the plaintiffs sued. Both their counsel and a juryman cross-examined the defendant with a view to showing that he sympathised with confession or belonged to a society which did so, so that his original attack was suspect. They failed to show this, but moderate damages were given against him, and his language criticised as excessively strong.

In the other case from 1879 (34) both sides' motives were suspect. The plaintiff, a clergyman who had celebrated mass and kept a nunnery (both unpopular activities) refused to bury an unbaptised child in consecrated ground or to allow a Nonconformist clergyman to do so. The Nonconformist wrote an account of the unpleasant scene in the defendant's newspaper, in scathing terms. Both in the article and at the subsequent trial the plaintiff was accused of misusing his powers in the service of his doctrine, while in counsel's speeches and cross-examination the defendant was accused of taking part in a put-up job, intended to draw attention to the need for legislation then pending on the burial of nonconformists. Had the latter charge been made good, the plaintiff would not have seemed so heartless, and the subsequent article would have been discredited. However, neither party was successful in its attacks on the good faith of the other, and plaintiff recovered nominal damages and his costs in spite of his unpopular position. Here the formal trial procedures seem to have isolated, as the question for decision, whether the original article was a fair account of what happened. The parties failed in their attempts to impose their own definitions on the situation.

In the case in 1968 (35) the plaintiff had been a Member of Parliament. During a visit to Russia in 1961, while he was a widower, he had a short affair. Later, when he had remarried, photographs of him and a woman in a Moscow bedroom were circulated anonymously. He claimed that this was an attempt by a Russian intelligence organization to discredit him because he had been drawing attention to the security risk presented by Russian diplomatic staff in England. There was controversy in his constituency as to whether he should be readopted as a candidate, in which the defendant opposed him. He was readopted, but lost in the ensuing General Election. The defendant was alleged to have said some time later that the affair had really taken place during his second marriage, thus amounting to adultery; a further implication was that plaintiff had lied about the date of the affair. At the trial, the jury found (with some hesitation) that the defendant had made the defamatory statements, and they awarded damages.

The case is an odd one. The plaintiff said in court that he brought the action to nail the rumour of his adultery (his wife had in fact founded divorce proceedings on it); the defendant's attack had shocked him. The defendant sought to show that the plaintiff had brought the publicity on himself. The issue the jury had to decide was whether or not the defendant had spoken the words. There was a conflict of evidence, and a suggestion that either the plaintiff's witness or the defendant was lying. But the plaintiff in fact saw the case in wider terms. He was quoted as saying that the great significance of the case was that it was the last round of his truggle with a Russian intelligence organisation: he hoped they would "take note that British justice can, although rather belatedly, catch up with their effort to cause damage by misuse of our free institutions" (36). The form of the encounter was not only affected by prior events (37), but justified as part of a larger controversy.

In these cases the focus of the action was on the ways in which parties chose to define the situation. Sometimes legal doctrines provide incentives to define the situation in such a way as to put the other party into some adversely labelled category. Thus in 1968, when a theatrical producer alleged that 4 of his leading actors in a successful play had given notice simultaneously as the result of a plot by their agents and other producers who wanted the theatre for a play of their own, he failed to show any plot. To bring the case within a rule allowing punitive damages against someone who deliberately set out to profit from wrongdoing, counsel for one of the plaintiffs set out to show that the defendant had made this allegation in order to get publicity for the play. The attempt failed conclusively, and may have backfired, as damages awarded by the jury were very moderate (38).

On the other hand, where the case has been settled, as were most of the 1968 cases, unless one has access to lawyer's files or the discussions of counsel, one has to infer the process from the form of the settlement. What one has is a final statement which represents the most that the parties can get each other to agree to. The plaintiff will want a creditable account of himself and an account of how the original statement was made which will rob it of credibility; the defendant will want to show both that his original statement was excusable and that his later conduct in giving redress has been good. The plaintiff will also want to be able to say that his costs have been paid, and would like to receive and be able to say he had received substantial damages. The further the defendant goes on these lines the more he shows himself in the wrong unless he wants the reputation of giving adequate redress. As a compromise, the plaintiff may say that he is not interested in damages, only in clearing his name.

In spite of the agreed nature of the final settlement, there are occasionally statements in open court from which it is possible to reconstruct the likely course of the negotiation. The absence of any payment of costs or damages by the defendant may indicate that the plaintiff has virtually failed; and sometimes the defendant may apologise for or regret something which is plainly not the plaintiff's main concern. Private Eye, the English satirical weekly, is unusual in practically never explaining how the matter complained of came to be published and merely regretting its publication; they do not disavow what Goffman has described as the "virtual offence" (39), what everyone concerned in a remedial interchange must usually be careful to avoid confirming. In apologies for defamation, this would be that the defamatory words were published intentionally, with full knowledge of the kind of person the plaintiff was and of his position, thus affirming that he was indeed the kind of person of whom such things could be said.

Settlements in these cases are bargains struck between the parties; but they can also be seen as encounters; the court's reactions replace the role of bystanders who can be enlisted to support one stand or another. We can infer that there must have been some "oscillation". But in some cases the reaction may be so predictable that the encounter becomes onesided. When a pop group, to launch a new record, sent out postcards suggesting that the then Prime Minister was having an affair with his secretary, (the affair had been rumoured) there can have been little oscillation in the encounter: it must have been the kind Handelman labels as oppositional (40). With the aid of the court, the plaintiff and his advisers clearly had the upper hand; the defendants could do nothing to improve their position except apologise and thank the plaintiff for his generosity. The "extremely generous" terms were that the defendants should pay £ 2,000 costs and give all the profits of the record to charity (41). The manager of the group later said that it was worth it in publicity (an argument also used by a defeated publisher in 1879), but that was a reaction far away from the encounter.

On the whole then, the best immediate prospects for research on the social meaning of defamation cases comes from the transactional analysis of encounters, arising out of processes with meaning for the participants. Through such analysis, we shall be able to see what is important in the subject for its bearing on the sociology of law, and what features of the encounter are affected by the court setting and the authoritative norms.

Summary

Im Sozialleben finden wir eine Flut von Informationen, die sich auf einzelne Menschen beziehen. Es besteht nun sowohl ein soziales wie auch ein individuelles Interesse daran, daß diese Informationen innerhalb vernünftiger Grenzen mit denen ihnen zugrunde liegenden Tatsachen übereinstimmen. Verschiedene rechtliche Institutionen beeinflussen den Informationsfluß in direkter oder versteckter Weise. Für den vorliegenden Beitrag sind hauptsächlich diejenigen Rechtseinrichtungen und -werte von Bedeutung, die im Hinblick auf die oben erwähnten Interessen bestehen.

Ein englischer Jurist nun würde meinen, daß die wichtigste dieser maßgebenden Institutionen die Klage wegen Verleumdung ist. Bei Verleumdungsklagen können nämlich eine Fülle von Fragen bezüglich der Rechtmäßigkeit verschiedener

Verhaltensweisen entstehen und das Geschworenengericht, das Tatfragen entscheidet, kann durch sein Urteil über Schadensersatzleistung eine generelle Ansicht über das Verhalten von Kläger und Beklagten ausdrücken. Die Verfahrensvorschriften sind so flexibel, daß der ursprüngliche Streit fast unverändert vor Gericht gelangen kann und auch keine Notwendigkeit besteht, ihn so zu modifizieren, daß er in juristische Kategorien paßt.

Der vorliegende Beitrag nun diskutiert die Anwendbarkeit von soziologischen und anthropologischen Theorien bei der Analyse von Verleumdungsprozessen, wobei er sich auf englische Zeitungsberichte von 1879 und 1968 stützt. Dabei wird davon ausgegangen, daß ein Vergleich lediglich der verschiedenen Menschentypen, die zu diesen beiden Zeitpunkten in Verleumdungsprozesse verwickelt waren, nicht hilfreich ist, und daß – sollte ein Vergleich angestellt werden – jeder Fall als Teil eines sozialen Prozesses gesehen werden sollte; denn Gerichtsverfahren sollten nicht ohne ihren Kontex betrachtet werden.

Theorien über Klatsch dagegen können sehr hilfreich sein. Daher wurde ihre Bedeutung in Einzelheiten untersucht. Funktionelle Beschreibungen von Klatsch zeigen, wie die Teilnahme am Klatsch vom Teilnehmer ein Verständnis für die Gesellschaft erfordert und die Zugehörigkeit zu dieser anzeigen kann. Die Anwendung gemeinsam anerkannter Wertungsgrundlagen hält die Gesellschaft zusammen und wirkt als eine Art sozialer Kontrolle, die das Aufkommen abweichenden Verhaltens hindert. Diese funktionellen Theorien scheinen jedoch wenig hilfreich zu sein für das Verständnis von Verleumdungsprozessen, wo sich widersprechende Wertungsgrundlagen im Streit sind.

Handlungsbetonte Theorien betonen den Nutzen von Klatsch als Mittel, den Informationsfluß anderen gegenüber zu manipulieren und neue soziale Normen zu schaffen. Zuweilen ist die Glaubwürdigkeit des Klatsches in Gefahr, wenn sich nämlich jemand einem Urteil unterworfen hat, das seine eigene Glaubwürdigkeit überprüft, und wenn der Klatsch dann widerlegt wird. Dies gleicht der Situation in Verleumdungsprozessen, wo der Angeklagte der die Wahrheit dessen, was er gesagt hat, zu beweisen versucht.

Eine der handlungsbetonten Theorien, diejenige von Handelman, gibt eine Beschreibung von Klatsch, der in Konfrontationen zwischen einzelnen wiedergegeben wird. Einige solcher Konfrontationen nun „oszillieren", weil die Parteien versuchen, ihre persönliche Darstellung über das Thema dieser Konfrontation in den Vordergrund zu schieben mit dem Ziel, ihr eigenes früheres Rollenverhalten und ihre gegenwärtige Glaubwürdigkeit ins beste Licht zu rücken und die der anderen Partei in ein möglichst schlechtes. Andere solcher Konfrontationen sind „oppositionell", einseitig, indem nur eine Partei die Situation definiert. Es wird die Auffassung vertreten, daß diese Analyse für Verleumdungsprozesse sehr gut geeignet ist, denn diese beschäftigen sich auch mit vergangener Rollenerfüllung und gegenwärtiger Glaubwürdigkeit, und es wird durch Beleg mit veröffentlichten Gerichtsentscheidungen aufgezeigt, daß sie entweder „oszillieren", weil die Parteien versuchen, sich selbst und ihre Gegner zu kategorisieren, oder daß sie „oppositionell" sind, wenn Recht und Verdienst sich alle auf einer Seite befinden. Das Gericht und die Entscheidungsnormen können folglich als Beiwerk gesehen werden, das die Parteien versuchen, während der Konfrontation für die eine oder andere Seite zu gewinnen.

Notes

1 In this discussion "information" is used without any connotation of truth. There may be conflicting information as well as conflicting evaluations.
2 Even in simple societies there will be prevalent stereotypes about members of groups and the incumbents of roles („fathers are always cruel", "judges are wise"); in more complex societies there will also be information and evaluation about associations.
3 Some might wish to deny the reality of facts about an individual independent of information about him: there might be no such thing as an account of him and his behavior which was separate from interpretations passing current as information. For the purposes of this discussion it is sufficient that the distinction is made in societies with which we are concerned.
4 There are other concepts of reputation. For instance, where it is being considered as an interest of an individual which may be affected by some wrongful act, it may be defined as the attitudes that others have towards him, such as esteem, good-will and confidence: Spencer-Bower, Actionable Defamation (2nd ed. 1923), p. 3; or as the likelihood that others will act in a way advantageous to him: Bentham, Principles of Morals and Legislation (Bowring ed.), vol. 1, p. 99.
5 Such feelings may, however, be part of the motivation for bringing defamation actions, with which this paper is mainly concerned.
6 Such powers are given in English law most directly by the law of defamation, which is discussed in the text. For the patchwork of provisions protecting privacy see the Report of the Younger Committee on Privacy, Cmnd. 5012 (1972), Appendix I. The laws of other countries are outlined in Appendix J.
7 Press Councils are being set up in a number of countries; they provide a mechanism of control, without the taint of state censorship.
8 In a number of English cases in the nineteenth century clubs expelled members who had defamed others; and these actions were upheld in the courts.
9 See Schwartz and Skolnick: Two Studies in Legal Stigma, 10 Social Problems 133 (1962); Martin and Webster: Social Consequences of Conviction, c. III.
10 If one compares the coverage of public affairs in the newspapers of the U.S.A. (where the law of defamation is much weaker) with that in newspapers in England (where the law is comparatively strict), one can see great differences. But these seem not the effect of differences in the laws, but rather the cause, or at least are associated with values which are the cause of the difference.
11 Victorian England was one such society; Torstein Eckhoff suggests that rural Norway is another.
12 Finlay v. Kwik Hoo Tong [1929] 1 K.B. 400.
13 People connected with the Press often complain of this. Riesman thought that the readiness of English juries to give high damages against Left and Right impartially in the 1930's had restrained extremist propaganda: (1942) 42 Columbia L.R. 1117 ff.
14 Chamberlaine v. Barnwell, The Times, 20 February – 5 March 1879.
15 This type of approach is outlined in the Preface to Problems and Prospects of Socio-Legal Research, ed. Floud, Lewis and Stuart (1972).
16 Handelman: Gossip in Encounters, Man (N.S.) 8, 210–227 (1973).
17 Gluckman: Gossip and scandal, Curr. Anthrop. 4, 307–316 (1963); Haviland, Gossip, gossips and gossiping in Zinacantan, unpublished Ph.D. thesis, Harvard, Human Relations.
18 Gluckman, loc. cit.
19 Gluckman, loc. cit.
20 Colson, The Makah Indians (1953).
21 Devlin, The Enforcement of Morals (1965).
22 Hart, Social Solidarity and the Enforcement of Morality, 35 U. Chicago L.R. 1 (1967).
23 Reputation, criticism and information in an Austrian village in Gifts and Poison (ed. Bailey 1971) pp. 164–165.
24 Compare this with the point Handelman takes from Goffman (in the text to note 32).
25 Particularly in the contributions to Gifts and Poison.
26 Starkie, Treatise on the Law of Slander and Libel, 2nd ed. (1830), pp. xvi ff.
27 The principal exponent of these is Paine: What is gossip about? Man (N.S.) 2, 278–285; Gossip and Transaction, Man (N.S.) 3, 305–308. They are applied by the contributors to Gifts and Poison and, most helpfully, by Handelman (see note 16).

28 Gluckman, Psychological, sociological and anthropological explanations of witchcraft and gossip, Man (N.S.) 3, 20–34; articles by Paine cited in note 27.
29 Haviland, loc. cit. (see note 17).
30 See note 23.
31 Gifts and Poison, pp. 284–290.
32 See note 16.
33 Collingridge v. Ahier, The Times, 8 – 23 April 1879. Papers of this kind are described in Best, Popular Protestantism in Victorian Britain, in Ideas and Institutions of Victorian Britain, ed. Robson (1967).
34 Drury v. Wilson, The Times, 8–12 March 1879.
35 Courtney v. Constantine, The Times and Daily Telegraph, 19–21 March 1968. The plaintiff described the background in Courtney, Sailor in a Russian Frame (1970).
36 The Times, 21 March 1968.
37 As it was in the encounter described by Handelman, loc. cit. (see note 16), pp. 218 ff.
38 A.T.V. v. Littler [1968] 1 W.L.R. 607; The Times and other newspapers, 13 February – 6 March 1968.
39 Goffman, Relations in Public (Penguin ed. 1972), p. 139.
40 Loc. cit. (see note 16), pp. 221–223.
41 Wilson v. The Move, The Times and other newspapers, 12 October 1967.

VI. Die Rollen im Gerichtsverfahren

Maria Borucka-Arctowa

Citizen Participation in the Administration of Justice: Research and Policy in Poland

Citizen (that is, public) participation in the administration of justice is a fundamental principle of the policy towards the development of socialist judicial systems. The socialist societies stress the concept of a "social element" juxtaposted between professional jurists and the public – that is, persons or organizations, with no special professional qualifications, who play a role in the administration of justice outside their regular job, and without remuneration, except for expenses and lost earnings. The principle has been carried into effect differently in various systems and times. It flows from a mere general political and constitutional principle: citizens must increasingly participate in the governing power of the state. Thus, the political goal of the "citizens' participation" principle is the democratization of power, the growth of self-government in the community, and the educating and reshaping of citizens to perform public functions – in the administration of justice, among others.

The principle of "citizens' participation" is meant also to further the performance of the judiciary in their proper social role. The aims here – in brief – are to bring law closer to life, to bring courts of law closer to the community, overcoming the alienation of the court from society as a whole, or its social groups. This particular aim should be achieved when the court penetrates into as wide circles of society as possible, intervening socially where necessary to carry out policy and law; it should be buttressed by the court's authority, by the citizen's trust in decisions issued by the court, and finally by the citizen's easy access to the court.

To bring courts closer to the community, and improve their effectivenss, repressive means of coercion are to be supplemented by social pressure. These "social means" can be considered educational measures; however, the means of coercion currently applied also pay a great deal of attention to educational effects. The point is to put emphasis not so much upon coercion as upon persuasion, and upon mobilizing opinion in the neighborhood, intitutionalizing social sanction, which is usually diffuse and – as a result – less effective. Mobilization of social pressure is clearly related to the principle of citizen participation in the administration of justice.

To carry out the principle of citizen participation in the administration of justice, and expand the citizen role, is a difficult job. A number of difficulties and objections have to be surmounted.

The principle of "citizens' participation" is less readily accepted in the administration of justice than in some other aspects of government (1)*. The reasons for this are complex. Traditionally, "democracy" has meant representative

* Notes on pages 298 f.

bodies. To extend the "citizens' participation" principle to the administration of justice is a breach of tradition; it conflicts with the usual stereotype of the court, and gives rise, moreover, to constitutional and legal problems.

Legal theoreticians have much discussed the exact boundaries of the constitutional rule that justice shall be administered by the courts (2). The discussion has centered on such issues as the conditions under which extra-judicial administration of justice is admissible, and what these institutions (sometimes defined as "quasi-judicial") should be like. There is conflict here between the technocratic urge toward efficiency in operation, and the "socialization" of the courts. From the technocratic standpoint, citizen participation in the modern world is an obstacle to efficiency, especially in the light of the more and more difficult problems that courts have to solve.

These technocratic arguments lead us to ask whether the price which one has to pay for the principle of citizen participation in the administration of justice is not too high. To answer this question, one must look beyond the administration of justice to larger social questions, seeking some principle for measuring the right proportion between professional and social elements, and their functional relationship to each other. One recalls that in many countries nowadays there is talk of the "decline of judicature", and the need to reform the courts, to free them from bureaucratization, excessive formality, and solemnity, all of which put barriers between court and citizen, making him feel alien to this institution. These criticisms refer to the traditional courts, which are purely "professional", or admit only a limited degree of "social" participation. Can the courts be fundamentally transformed by introducing changes within traditional judicial forms, i.e., changes in the training and social background of judges, simplification of judicial procedure, at least in some parts of the law; or are these measures to be considered inadequate, since they will not eliminate certain professional habits which will inevitably deform judicial behavior, if not leavened by participation of the social element?

Adoption of the principle of citizen participation by no means ends the process of forming a new type of judiciary. Experience both in Poland and in other socialist countries indicates that particular solutions to the underlying problem wil vary. If we compare the premises on which the new institutions have been founded, with their actual operation, we see a need to look for ways to mold institutions to the needs of actual situations. The point is to ensure real influence on the administration of justice, not the "make-believe" influence of so many institutions of this type (3).

It is not easy to foster expanding participation of citizens in the administration of justice; there are many distorting factors. The general level of legal culture is an important variable. The selection of social (lay) judges is sometimes not careful enough. On the other hand, jurists tend to distrust the opinions and judgments of the "social element". The common citizen, with his stereotypes and traditional views, also tends toward this attitude.

In Poland some of these new institutions were introduced experimentally, limited in area, time, and scope and subsequently extended throughout the country. Thanks to this technique and to empirical reserarch on the operation of citizen participation, we have been able to compare aims with accomplishment, to analyze tentativly the reasons for successes and failures, and to assess the effect of citizen participation on the work of the court.

Social participation in the administration of justice may take two forms:
(a) co-participation in the administration of justice by the courts,
(b) autonomous conflict resolution, by institutions composed exclusively of the "social element."

The first of these finds its chief expression in the lay judge, with decision-making power equal to his professional colleagues on a panel of judges. It also manifests itself in participation of representatives of social organizations in judicial process. The institution of the lay judge is especially noteworthy because it is common, and it takes the form of a mixed social and professional panel, which makes it possible to study variations in decisions, and measuring the differential outputs of lay and professional judges. Indeed, use of lay judges in Poland was the object of extensive empiric reserarch, completed serveral years ago (4). The study showed marked and interesting results on the effect of lay judges on the work of the courts.

Over twenty years have elapsed since lay judges were introduced into courts of first instance. At first they served two years terms, then three; they have numbered 50,000. They participated in nearly fifty per cent of the criminal cases, and a great many civil ones as well. That so many "laymen" have passed through the system of justice is highly relevant to the dissemination of legal culture in the community. But the effect of lay judges also extends to those who come in contact with them. This cultural aspect of the institution of lay judges is not terribly controversial. Differences of opinion do occur, however, on the question, do lay judges influence the administration of justice – the decision-taking process itself, and the function of the court – and how?

The inquiry undertaken by the Institute of Legal Sciences at the Polish Academy of Sciences aimed to answer this question. The investigation was confined to court decisions in criminal cases, and was carried out in five provinces and major provincial towns in Poland. Various research methods were used, i.e., questionnaires, interviews, participant observation, analysis of court records, and analysis of statistical data about the social composition of lay-judge teams during the different terms of office, as well as their demographic structure. The inquiry was extended to prosecutors and counsels (advocates). The inquiry was carried out by a special team of jurists and sociologists. The sessions of the team were also attended by judges and officials of the Ministry of Justice (5).

Contrary to what had been expected, it proved far from easy to define what we might call the "statutory model" of the institution of lay judges. The legal norms were comparatively few, and quite terse. Both Art. 49 of the Polish Constitution and Art. 7 of the Law of the Common Courts emphasize as a general rule (with some exceptions) the collegiate composition of the courts, with lay and professional participation. Art. 2 of the Lay Judges Act stipulates equal rights and duties for lay and professional judges; they are to have equal decisionmaking power, in fact-finding, establishment of guilt and in sentencing. Lay judges are judges with full rights; they are independent actors; but they cannot preside over trials and court hearings. Practice shows that this need not, but may lead to supremacy of professional judges. On the other hand, in every panel of judges, there are two lay judges and one professional judge. This makes it possible for the lay judges to outvote the professional judge. Either type of judge is entitled to bring in a *votum separatum.*

The principle of a mixed social-and-professional panel presupposes *some* division of roles; but it would be an oversimplification to see the system as one in which the professional judge contributes professional knowledge, and the lay judge practical experience. In fact, professional judges can be and often are active in social affairs; and a lay judge may be well acquainted with law. This last is particularly possible in Poland, where legal regulations do not exclude legally-trained persons from the ranks of potential lay judges. Rather, the lay judge institution is conceived as a means of preventing, or counter-balancing, a certain tendency toward the routine, a professional deformation inevitable in the performance of various professional functions, to which the judge is subject as well. A lay judge transmits values and opinions current of members of the public, assesses on his own the strength of the evidence, the circumstances under which the offense was commited, the situation of the accused, and the nature of the penalty. The idea is to force confrontation between the approach of the professional judge – always in danger of lapsing into professional routine – and the "fresh" view of the lay judge.

Data obtained through research on lay judges have shown that they fully realize and accept their functions as "social judges"; their opinions on their functions as "full-rights judges" are less clear. They interpret the function of a "social judge" as the introduction of public values and opinions into the administration of justice, as a means of social control. In replies to questionnaires, a large majority (80 per cent of the overall replies) expressed the opinion that the presence of a lay judge on the panel of judges improves the conformity of court verdicts to public opinion. The answer put special stress on that aspect of a lay judge's function which makes his very presence, his participation at the trial, a kind of social control. The main point is the effect of the lay judge on the panel, quite apart from his effect on the case. This is some sort of "latent function" which, incidentally, affects not only the judge himself, but other parties to the proceedings as well.

Lay judges perceive to a certain extent that different roles on the panel are "mutually complementary" and that the social and professional correct each other. 72 percent of the respondents felt that lay judges served a function in counteracting the tendency of statutory law to ignore the realities of life. The respondents explain the differences between the views of lay and professional judges, by pointing out that a professional judge can more easily grasp legal problems, and has greater knowledge of the administration of justice; but he pays excessive attention to the prosecutor's view, and does not take into due account the future fate of the accused.

Lay judges are much less clear about their function as "full-rights judges." A fair number of lay judges just beginning their activities, have not real views about their rights, or else fail to answer this question. When asked whetherthe lay judge actually exerts any influence on the judgment, hardly 30 per cent of respondents answer "yes, decidely"; 55 per cent say "yes, somewhat". Lay judges with some experience state that the lay judge does not enjoy much prestige among professional jurists. One can note, incidentally, a certain inconsistency in the answers supplied by lay judges. When they speak about their relations with professional judges, they point out many cases where the professional judge treated them in a supercilious way, arbitrarily imposed his own view, or settled the case practically on his own; at the same time only an insignificant number (5 per cent) complain of "difficulties in co-operating" with the professional judge.

This leads us to suppose that some respondents do not see domineering or supercilious behavior as a transgression by professionals on the function or rights of lay judges.

The professional judges were quite critical of lay judges this must be largely attributed to experience with particular lay judges. It has a bearing, however, on their estimate of the institution as a whole. The most frequent objection advanced by professional judges is that lay judges are unable to take an impartial view and grasp the case as an integral whole, that they tend to be biased. On the other hand, there were few imputations of ill-will, carelessness, or neglect of their duties. On the positive side, professional judges cited that they could draw on practical experience of the lay judges. And the very presence of a lay judge promotes the feeling that the verdict conforms to public opinion. Judges pointed out that even where lay judges lack an opinion on the case, or fail to add anything substantial to the judge's observations, the very fact that the arguments have to be clearly summed up in front of lay judges, that all doubtful points have to be carefully considered, promotes a more mature mode of making decisions.

Prosecutors and counsels characteristically look at the lay judge through a screen of stereotypes. For instance, the opinion prevails that lay judges at the trival are above all inclined to yield to emotional arguments, while research shows that they most often follow the arguments advanced by court experts, less often those expounded by the prosecutor, and least often by counsel for the defense. And, even though the prevailing opinion among professional jurists is that lay judges for the most part do not take any interest in the case, yet 75 per cent of respondents state that in their speeches at the trial they try to use those arguments which would be most convincing to the lay judges. This seems to corroborate our previous conclusion that, despite its shortcomings, the lay judge system affects, by its very presence, the behavior of the parties at the trial, inducing them to take greater account of arguments of "social" character.

Most jurists feel that lay judges tend to reduce the penalty, taking more account of extenuating circumstances. Our research does show some tendency to reduce punishment; this, however, varies greatly, depending on the type of offense. Thus, the tendency to reduce punishment is very marked for petty offenses of economic character. On the other hand, lay judges view hooliganism, pugnatciy, violence causing bodily injury, large scale theft of socialized property and offences against private property in a sterner light than do professional judges.

That the severity or leniency of lay judges varies with the offense indicates that lay judges act according to their own hierarchy of values, which does not always correspond to that of the professional judges. Awareness of these divergences often underlie the opinions expressend by professional judges about the conduct of the lay judges on the panel.

Now let us compare the results of the opinion survey with the results of participant observation at trials and court sessions.

Lay judges take much more interest in the trial than appears from views expressed by jurists. About 30 per cent of the lay judges actively intervene in the course of the trial by asking questions. It should be borne in mind, however, that a lay judge will intervene actively only when the professional judge does not take due account of circumstances which the lay judge feels are essential to the case, or when the questions the lay judge poses may help to elucidate the case. A lay judge who carefully watches the case and evolves his own view, which he will subsequently advance during court deliberations, is also "active".

On the most vital issue – whether the lay judges influence those pre-verdict deliberations – four types of deliberation can be distinguished:

Type I (21 per cent of observed deliberations): The professional judge incontestably predominates during the deliberation, and arbitrarily decides the issues, taking no account of the opinion, and even the presence, of lay judges.

Type II (31 per cent): again, the judge predominates during deliberation, but there are some formal elements of discussion; lay judges show some activity, though this does not affect the professional judge's preconceived attitude toward the case.

Type III (8 per cent): the professional judge tries to involve the lay judges, but they do not respond; this inaction compels the judge to express his own view and to make the decision on his own.

Type IV (40 per cent): lay judges express their opinions before listening to those of the professional judge, that is, without any suggestion on his part; this leads to a real discussion, in which the views of the various members of the panel confront each other.

These results undermine the stereotype that the participation of lay judges in criminal cases is a makebelieve. Even though their influence is still too limited, in 40 per cent of cases lay judges press their own views, and appear to exert substantial influence on the verdict. In many of the remaining cases, we cannot exclude the important latent function – that quite apart from actual activity of individual lay judges at the trial, their very presence shapes the behavior of the judge and other participants.

Professional and lay judges do hold different views about appropriate levels of punishments; they rarely dispute the fact of guilt. It is probably in regard to punishment that the influence of the lay judge is most keenly felt. They represent attitudes widespread among the public, stressing personal traits and circumstances of the offender; more than the professional judges, they tend to act on the basis of regard for special prevention of future misconduct of the offender, rather than with strict regard for general directives of current penal policy. Their attitudes may well contribute toward the individualization of punishment.

It should be noted, moreover, that analysis of records for cases in which there was a *votum separatum* shows that in 42 per cent of those cases a higher court approved the view of the lay judge, in the direction of leniency in punishment.

A lay judge will fulfill his function to a marked degree when there is proper division of labor between his role and that of the professional. The actual influence of the lay judge upon decision-making depends on particular relationships within the panel. The attitude of the professional judge toward the lay judge is highly relevant. On the other hand, the lay judge must be intelligent, experienced and dedicated, in order for adequate cooperation to take place.

The social element in the administration of justice is also enhanced when representatives of social organizations are admitted as co-partners in civil and criminal proceedings. Social organizations are authorized to bring lawsuits, to enter pending proceedings on behalf of a party, to express opinions about proceedings, or to appoint legal representatives to act on their behalf. The new code of penal procedure has extended the role of social organizations by introducing the concept of the social representative (Art. 81), acting for and promoting group interests.* It also extends the role of social probation. Moreover, social organizations may take part in executive proceedings, acting as tutelar authorities in civil cases and court custodians in criminal ones.

It is too early to tell what effect these new provisions will actually have. The necessary research has not yet been undertaken. Jurists generally believe that the wide use of social organizations in court proceedings will promote civil rights and further democratize judicial proceedings.

Much more controversial, and not yet adequately investigated, in the second, form of citizen participation in the administration of justice: social courts composed exclusively of public participants, with full authority over certain types of case. Such courts, made up of men and women chosen by local citizens, work within narrow, familiar settings – a factory, a block of flats, a neighborhood. Such courts may either have the right to use coercive measures (arbitration committees), or in some cases, "social" measures alone, emphasizing educational aspects of the proceedings (workers' courts, social reconciliation committees).

Arbitration committees were introduced throughout Poland in 1954 after a three-year experimental period. They were formed after search for new forms of conflict resolution, under the labor laws. Half of the members of these committees are designated by the Workers' Board (the trade union organization at the factory), half by the management of the plant. The Central Board of Trade Unions exercises general supervision over the committees, and also acts as a kind of court of appeals.

The arbitration committees act much like ordinary courts. Apart from conciliatory functions, committees are entitled to settle conflicts, and can enforce their decisions coercively. Only employees can bring cases; management has no such right. (It may bring cases to court.)

Arbitration committees were introduced in order to bring institutions which settle controversies under the labor laws closer to the place of employment and to take into account circumstances specific to a particular occupation, as well as the sense of justice of the workers in a particular collective. Cases would be heard in the presence of the parties and of other employees. This public would take an interest in the matter, and spread information about the decision; this would help disseminate knowledge of major labor regulations among the workers. The committee's activities are also a form of social control, and exert a certain pressure on managerial decisions.

Analysis of the work of these committees, which have been active for nearly ten years, permits some assessment of their work. In 1970, there were in Poland over 8,000 arbitration committees; they heard nearly 27,000 cases; 75 per cent of these were settled in the employee's favor. The number of cases examined by the respective committees varies greatly. White-collar employees made proportionately greater use of these committees than blue-collar workers.

A team at the Institute of Legal Sciences of the Polish Academy of Sciences, charged with researching legal consciousness among citizens, carried out investiga-

* The social representative is admitted as a participant in penal proceedings when the social organization which he represents demonstrates that the case concerns of social interest which the organization is statutorily charged with protecting. The social representative will not be an adherent of either prosecutor or defendant, but should act as an objective protector of the social interest he is charged with protecting.

tions in ten large industrial plants, including the work of arbitration committees (7). These activities vary greatly from one plant to another. Personnel is a critical variable. Where the committee is drawn mostly from administrative staff of the plant, the committee tends to fail as a forum in which employees' rights are vindicated. These committees decide, in the main, against the employee. This leads to a sharp decrease in the number of cases.

Some committees work intensively at conciliation, intervening in cases even before a formal claim is brought, and frequently settling matters at this stage. Intervention of this type is not recorded in the files of the committee. Management is often reluctant to admit that conflicts exist; management will in such event try to satisfy the employees' demands or even use some form of pressure. When workers bring few cases, it may mean they have little awareness of their rights; sometimes, however, lack of confidence in the arbitration committees is the reason. One must also remember that other institutions – for example, the Workers' Board – also have the duty to intervene in labor conflicts. In general, though the research disclosed some deficiencies in the work of particular committees, it also uncovered examples of great effectiveness. For example, in one of the plants studied, the committee had become a key factor in settling conflicts within the factory.

Intensive discussion of possible amendments to the labor regulations has produced some suggestions *de lege ferenda.* The arbitration committees should be made more independent of plant management; their decisions should not be hamstrung by the requirement of unanimity; the scope and range of their cases should be extended; the employee should be able to choose between bringing his case before the committee or before a court (if, for example, the committee does not enjoy the employee's confidence), or at any rate might bring his case to court as a form of appeal (8).

But even if these suggestions were fully carried out, thus improving the procedure and organization of the committees, problems would remain. A certain atmosphere tends to obstruct the work of these committees: an atmosphere produced by management's reluctant, distrustful attitude toward public participation, its prerogatives, and the control it is allowed to exert over professional matters. A more thorough analysis is needed, of the sense of conflict of interest between management on the one hand and the employees on the other, who must function in the double role of workers and co-managers of the plant.

I should like to refer here briefly to the role of the legal adviser employed in the plant. In principle, his job is to advise both management and the employees; in fact, he defends the interests of management, inordinately at times, thus often complicating and hampering the work of the committee. Employees do not think well of these legal advisers; workers suggest that the Workers' Board employ a solicitor to give legal advice independently of the plant's legal adviser.

The lively discussions among jurists, including judges, about modes of settling labor conflicts, has made the problems and solutions in that field of law more salient. This is bound to exert at least some influence on the way the ordinary courts handle protective labor cases, on the style of courts proceedings, and on some attitudes within the bureaucracy toward the subject.

The social courts – either workers' courts or social reconciliation committees – are established at the instance of employees of a plant, or inhabitants in a given neighborhood or block of flats, under a law of 1965, after an experimental period. These courts are purely social, and are optional. They investigate minor transgressions committed by employees or by local inhabitants. Their main objective is not to lift the burden of minor lawsuits off the regular courts, nor to shorten the proceedings, but rather to act directly on the local community as a preventive and an educational body.

Research conducted during the experimental period (9) showed that traditional coercive measures used by courts were ineffective in small cases with low penalties, protracted procedures, and difficult methods of prooftaking. The social courts have at their disposal only persuasive measures, based on the court's moral authority. The court is made up of friends. co-workers, neighbors; it invokes public opinion, the moral sense of the community. The social courts have recourse mainly to educational sanctions. Thus, the court may decree that an offender should offer a public apology to an injured party, or compensate damage he had caused; or he might be publicly reprimanded, or directed to do nonpaid work for the public welfare, or directed to pay for some public purpose a sum of money not exceeding 300 zlotys, and not surpassing 10 per cent of his monthly pay. But performance cannot be coerced, except by the pressure of public opinion.

There is striking agreement, buttressed by research, about the effect of these social courts. The defendants resent not so much the sanctions as the trial itself, the compulsion of facing their acquaintances, people they meet professionally and privately. The very idea of social courts assumes that no man can be indifferent to the opinion of those around him.

The workers' social courts have proved somewhat disappointing as educative institutions. Here too research reveals great differences among courts at various work settings. This confirms the preliminary hypothesis that good relations with the social surroundings, a stable work-force, and support from professionals are prerequisites to effective operation. To be effective, too, management and political and social organizations active in the plant must recognize tham as legitimate instruments for solving conflicts (10).

Investigations, carried out during the experimental period, and also within the last year, have shown that in many places, workers who have transgressed in one way or another and who are thus liable to proceedings before a workers' court, do everything in their power, usually successfully, to avoid the court. They apply to the Workers' Board, or to the management, promising to mend their ways. This tends to confirm the notion that people are concerned with public opinion. Thus, the Workers' Court may exert influence as an agent of social control even when no trial takes place, through its threat of mobilizing social opinion.

Whay do interviewed workers make a rather pessimistic appraisal of the efficacy of these courts? One must recall that temporary or transient workers make the most trouble within a plant. But this mean that they are less likely to respond to the feelings and attitudes of the permanent workers.

Workers' courts formed on the initiative of employees have not increased in number in recent years; nor has the case-load of existing courts gone up. In 1970 there were in all 1080 courts, and they heard 3,382 cases, mostly concerning petty offenses aginst social and individual property, violations of labor regulations (coming to work drunk, disorderly conduct at work, etc.), neglect of family duties, improper conduct toward co-workers, defamation.

Some courts are entirely "dead", or act at irregular intervals only; others have acquired a store of experience, enjoy great authority, and perform the functions assigned to them successfully.

Social courts, then, need further insight, further search for solutions. The contrast between courts belies over-optimistic expectations, on the one hand, and, on the other hand, excessively pressimistic views, suggesting that these courts should be abolished altogether.

Interviews with workers, active in organizations and judicial institutions within their place of employment (11), suggest some means of improvement. Some recommend a single body, to combine arbitration committees and a reformed workers' court; trade unions should employ their own lawyers who would help these institutions, as well as offer legal advice to workers. In the opinion of activist workers, this would enhance the effectiveness of the committees and social courts, raise their prestige among workers, and help disseminate knowledge of law and a positive attitude toward law among employees.

The social reconciliation committees active in settlements, blocks of flats, and so on, have evolved quite differently. The committees are numerous and busy, which testifies to a strong social demand, and satisfaction with the output. In 1972 there were 6,447 committees – 40 per cent in towns and 60 per cent in the country. They handled in all 72,042 cases, approximately in the same proportions; of these, 45,452 (62 per cent) were settled by agreement. More than half of the cases had been brought on the citizens' motion, the rest were transferred by courts of law, the prosecutor's office, militia and the administrative collegia, social organizations (10 per cent), or were initiated by committees themselves (ca. 10 per cent). It would be desirable to study in greater detail how durable the settlements were. Fragmentary investigations, carried out in different regions of Poland, seem to indicate that the settlements are durable, and faithfully observed, in the majority of instances.

Taking into account the time and effort wasted by quarreling neighbors, the social consequences of disturbances of the peace, family conflicts and misunderstandings, these committees with their high effectiveness, must be regarded as a great success. It should be remembered, too, that controversies of this kind took up much time in courts, whereby the parties involved lost still more time and money; what is more, the ordinary courts were far less effective in reaching settlements.

In previous sections of this paper, I have discussed various forms of citizen participation in the administration of justice, describing the legal norms and principles on which these institutions have been based. We have explored causes of their successes and failures. The influence of the social element on the administration of justice is a particularly relevent topic; but it is hard to investigate. There is danger that the participatory element of these institutions may become a kind of "make-believe" – established for political reasons, but without conditions necessary for proper functioning, and without opportunity to carry out their goals.

Research suggests that (in addition to organizational and legal variables) the relationship of professionals to the public participants, the qualifications of the participants, the type of neighborhood or context, all play a part in determining effectiveness.

As we have noted, research on the effectiveness of these institutions is difficult to carry out. There are formal or technical obstacles – debates are secret; the panels are small, hence participant observation is almost impossible; yet ordinary obervation affects the behavior of those observed. The effectiveness of these institutions is especially hard to measure because so much of it is latent. The overt behavior of these institutions, constrained by their structure and by the general principles of law, is manifest in the output of the members of these bodies. But above and beyond this is their latent influence – high relevant to the "style" of court work as well as to its impact upon the community.

Thus, as we observed, the very presence of public members on a panel of judges will affect the behavior of the professional judges, and the behavior of other parties to the proceedings; social policy arguments will receive consideration along with purely legal ones; verdicts will conform better to public opinion. Arbitration committees thus affect the behavior and attitudes of management. Workers' courts affect workers who might transgress. At least some workers will want to avoid falling a foul of these courts. They will voluntarily change their ways, or compensate for damages caused; thus the very existence of the court has an educational, rehabilitative effect.

Legal institutions which include social participation produce important side-effects. These are not always favorable. A newly-established institution occasionally produces conflicts between management and the work-force. This may arise out of mistakes committed by arbitration committees, pressure of management, employee dissatisfaction with their representatives within the institution, or misconceived ideas about labor regulations. When there is reluctance to use a social court, pressure grows for establishment of still other agencies to settle disputes; or there may be a partial return to the traditional courts. Such a return enhances the court's prestige, but also produces new expectation: that the professional courts carry into effect what had been inadequately performed by social courts.

The most pronounced, and broadest, positive effect of citizen participation in the administration of justice is in the area of *social control.* Values and attitudes of the public are imported into the administration of justice, preventing or counterbalancing the threat of legalism and the distortions of the professionals, adapting judicial decisions to public opinion, activating the local citizenry and invoking persuasion and prevention along with coercive measures.

Closely linked is the *educational function,* prominent in the work of social courts. In ordinary courts, when lay judges take part in criminal cases, they cause greater account to be taken of special prevention and resocialization.

The educational function is particularly important for every form of tribunal dealing with labor law. It is, in general, for the sake of the educational function that representatives of social organizations have been allowed to take part in judicial proceedings.

In *dispute-settlement*, citizen participation shifts emphasis to conciliation. Arbitration committees emphasize the *protective function.* the committee sits in the worker's own plant; it uses simplified procedure, it is accessible to the workers. But, as we have seen, these committees sometimes suffer distortions; when all members are laymen, it is particularly important to guard against conditions which may impair the protective function.

Another impoartant function is *dissemination of legal culture.* Public participation performs this function among those taking part in the administration of justice, and among others in the surroundings. Information about law, and legal values, are transmitted. In courts that sit in places of employment, employees attend trials, and in this way they learn about legal process. But this merely accentuates the importance of finding the proper method of training lay judges and other public participants.

In a socialist society committed to social planning, transformation of social structure, industrialization, and urbanization, the question, how citizen participation affects the work of courts as instruments for carrying out planned social change through law, is of vital interest.

New values and patterns of behavior are realized through the application of law as well as by enactment of norms. What part will social elements play in this process? They may express and promote progressive trends; or, on the other hand, they may transmit attitudes of certain groups and localities that resist innovation. Research on lay judges has disclosed differences in value systems and priorities of lay and professional judges, with regard to some protected goods. Can one a well notice differences in readiness to accept new models and values, and receptivity, to planned changes instituted by means of the law? A complete answer to this question would require fresh research.

Indeed, the call for more research on the effect of citizen participation is a major theme of this paper – research which would explore the phenomena in the widest context, and would carefully analyze the functions, old and new, performed by the institutions.

The factors that determine the functions of the institutiones discussed seem to be closely-related with the changes in economic and social structure. We have noted the importance, first of all, of organization and institutional imperatives. The state has mandated extension of citizen participation in the administration of justice, and has directed formation of new types of courts. These directives in turn follow from constitutional principles, and from policy on the development of judicial systems with a socialist state. The directives, in the broad sense, serve political aims, but these are connected with policy toward the judicial systems and its role in society.

Another causal factor is the field of law the institution works in. The functions performed by courts in labor law, criminal law, and family law are different from each other. As new branches of law develop or modernize, new types of social relation fall under legal regulation; emphasis shifts from certain functions of the courts to others. The social background of lay and professional judges, and the values determined by this background, are a third factor. A fourth is the general level of legal culture in the society, knowledge of the law and readiness to have recourse to law when one's rights are transgressed upon, and readiness to react, too, against transgression upon other persons' rights. These factors determine what type of "clientele" will use various courts, and what kind of cases and actions will be brought to them.

Summary

Die Teilnahme von Staatsbürgern an der Rechtspflege ist ein fundamentales Prinzip der sozialistischen Gerichtsbarkeit. Dieses Prinzip ist mit bestimmten politischen Zielvorstellungen verknüpft. Zu ihnen gehört die Absicht, das Recht dem Leben näher zu bringen und die Entfremdung der Gerichte von der Gesellschaft als ganzer oder von bestimmten sozialen Gruppen zu überwinden.

Aufgabe dieses Beitrages und vorangegangener Untersuchungen war, die normativen (legislatorischen) Lösungen einer Teilnahme von Staatsbürgern an der Rechtspflege auf ihre Wirkung in der Praxis hin zu überprüfen und den Einfluß der Beteiligung auf die Tätigkeit der Gerichte festzustellen.

Die Anerkennung des Prinzips der Bürgerbeteiligung bedeutet keineswegs, daß die Arbeiten an neuen Verfahrensmodellen für die Gerichtsbarkeit zum Stillstand gekommen seien. Auf dem Wege zu neuen Formen sind manche Rückschläge und Schwierigkeiten zu überwinden. Eine Periode von Experimenten und empirischer Forschung hat uns jedoch gewisse Kenntnisse der Bedingungen gebracht, unter denen die betreffenden Institutionen ihre Aufgaben ausüben, und die Gefahr des Abgleitends in bloße Vermutungen gebannt.

Die Teilnahme des „gesellschaftlichen Elementes" an der Rechtspflege kann die folgenden Formen annehmen:

a) Mitbeteiligung an der Rechtspflege auf der Grundlage einer Gleichberechtigung mit den Berufsrichtern (das hat seinen Ausdruck in der Institution der Laienrichter gefunden).
b) Autonome Konfliktbereinigung (mit Schwerpunkt auf Schlichtungstätigkeit) durch Institutionen, die allein aus dem „gesellschaftlichen Element" zusammengesetzt sind. Diese Form, die Anlaß zu größeren Kontroversen gibt, befindet sich noch im Stadium der Erprobung und des Experiments.

Forschungsergebnisse deuten darauf hin, daß es notwendig ist, die folgenden Probleme näher zu betrachten: Die Beziehungen zwischen Berufs- und Laienrichtern, Herkunft, Ausbildung und Fähigkeit der Teilnehmer aus der Öffentlichkeit und (im Hinblick auf Gesellschaftsgerichte) den sozialen Kontext, in welchem sie arbeiten.

Bürgerbeteiligung erhöht die soziale Kontrolle, erzieht die Öffentlichkeit und verbreitet Rechtskultur. Bei der Konfliktbereinigung wird durch die Teilnahme von Bürgern, speziell bei Gesellschaftsgerichten, großer Wert auf die Aussöhung gelegt. Die Schutzfunktion ist bedeutend in Schiedskommissionen von Fabriken (leichter Zugang zum Gericht, vereinfachtes Verfahren); diese Art von Gericht läuft aber Gefahr, Unabhängigkeit und Unparteilichkeit zu verlieren.

Besonders interessant – gerade in einer sozialistischen Gesellschaft – ist das Maß, in welchem die Teilnahme von Staatsbürgern Einfluß auf die Funktion des Gerichtes als Mittler gesetzlich geplanten sozialen Wandels hat. Die hier geschilderte Untersuchung ist recht vielsagend, jedoch sind zu dieser Frage noch weitere Abklärungen nötig.

Notes

1 A. Turska, Czynnik Społeczny i zawodowy w wymiarze sprawiedliwości (Social and Professional Partnership in the Administration of Justice), Warszawa 1971, p. 51.

2 S. Włodyka, Granice konstytucyjnej zasady sadowego wymiaru sprawiedliwości (The Limits of the Constitutional Principle of the Judicial Administration of Justice) publication in honor of K. Stepko, Warszawa 1967.

3 M. Borucka-Arctowa and M. Rybicki, Wymiar sprawiedliwości w krajach socjalistycznych (The Administration of Justice in Socialist Countries), Report from the Conference held at Pecs, "Panstwo i Prawo" 1971, No. 2.

4 Results of research on lay-judges can be found in: M. Borucka-Arctowa, L. Kubicki, A. Turska, and S. Zawadszki, Udział ławnikow w postępowanju karnymn (Lay Judges' Participation in Criminal Proceedings) Warszawa 1970. See also M. Borucka-Arctowa, Die Funktion der Laienrichter in der Polnischen Gerichtsbarkeit, Schriftenreihe des Institutes der Soziologie an der Universität Graz, 1970.

5 Particulars about the members of the team, the stages of research, and the methods and techniques used are to be found in chapter I of the work, Udział ławnikow ... and in the article cited above.

6 M. Hasiec, Wyniki funkcjonowania zakładowych komisji rozjemczych na terenie Łubelszczyzny (Results of the Activites of Arbitration Committees at the Works in the Lublin Region), "Panstwo i Prawo" 1960, Nos. 4–5.

7 Świadomość prawna robotników (The Workers' Legal Consciousness) edited by M. Borucka-Arctowa, Wrocław 1974, Chapters III and IV.

8 Some of these suggestions and some quite new solutions are considered in the draft labor law code prepared and discussed in 1974.

9 E. Modlinski, O społecznych sadach robotniczych (About Workers' Social Courts), "Panstwo i Prawo" 1962, No. 1; A. Podgórecki, Eksperyment w socjologii prawa (An Experiment in the Sociology of Law), "Panstwo i Prawo" 1962, No. 1 J. Górski, Doświadczenia i perspektywy sądów robothiczych w Polsce (Workers' Courts: Experience and Future Perspectives in Poland 1960–1965), Warszawa 1967.

10 J. Górski, op. cit., pp. 82, 182.

11 Świadomosc prawna robotników, Ch. III (The Workers' Legal Consciousness, q.v.).

Zdenek Krystufek

The Function of the Lay Judge in Czechoslovakia

After the Communist Party assumed power in Czechoslovakia in 1948, the ruling ideologists believed sociology to have been absorbed in and replaced by Marxist-Leninism. Although sociology had a long tradition in Czechoslovakia, its revival occurred later there than in some other Soviet satellite countries. In the late 1950's, as Hungary and Poland were about to resume sociological investigations, the Czechoslovakian Communist Party explicitly declared itself the exclusive source of social knowledge, and the acquisition of social information needed by the Party bureaucracy was considered an internal matter. A reversal of the official position took place in the 1960's, symbolized by the creation of a Sociological Institute of the Czechoslovak Academy of Sciences and the reintroduction of the study of sociology into Czechoslovakian universites. However, the Institute was short-lived. It was abolished shortly after the Soviet military intervention in Czechoslovakia in August 1968.

The first sociological project in the field of law in Czechoslovakia after 1948 was initiated by the author and sponsored by the Czechoslovakian Academy of Sciences in 1963. The research was suspended when the author was studying aboard and another scholar who was given responsibility for the project eventually withdrew. Although incomplete, this research did offer results of both theoretical interest and practical significance (1)*.

The research topic was the effectiveness of the work of the lay judges (judges who fulfilled judicial duties in addition to their regular occupations).

Among the changes made in the judicial structure of Czechoslovakia after the coup d'etat of 1948, was the abolition of the single-judge courts and the jury. The jurisdiction of the regular courts was transferred to a "senate" consisting of both professional and lay judges. Criminal investigation, formerly performed by and inquisitor judge, was removed from the judicial sphere and delegated to the Ministry of Interior and to the Procuratura (Office of the Prosecutor) (2).

In the newly structured judicial system, the senate of a trial court consisted of two lay judges and one professional judge; three lay judges and two professional judges comprised the senate of the courts of appeal; and the senate of the Supreme Court consisted of two lay judges and three professional judges. Later, there were several reorganizations of the system. As of now, the senate of courts of first instance remains as it was; the senate of the courts of appeal consists of two lay judges and three professional judges; and the Supreme Court consists entirely of professional judges.

A professional judge always presides over a senate. In all other respects, the

* Notes on page 306.

professional and lay judges have equivalent duties and rights. Both deliberate on questions of fact as well as conclusions of law. In criminal matters both determine guilt and punishment.

The ideological purpose of this arrangement was "to bring the judiciary closer to the people." It was argued that the typical professional judge gradually loses interest in the social context of the many routine cases that come before him. Karl Bergbohm's view, that a practicing judge ceases to be interested in "justice" and cares only about "the law," was acknowledged to be correct. However, the state did not accept Bergbohm's conclusion that this situation was right and proper. The proposed solution was the creation of lay judges, to whom judicial decision-making should be fresh and therefore not stereotyped.

In practice it soon became clear that lay judges did not meet the theoretical expectations. Of course, countries under Soviet influence, expecially insofar as they follow Soviet patterns, do not allow mere practical failure to impair ideology. But the institution of the lay judge not only failed to fulfil its theoretical purpose, it also represented a financial burden, a particularly critical fact in the early 1960's, when Czechoslovakia was in the grips of economic crisis.

Any social research in Czechoslovakia must be submitted for approval to the Communist Party. Economic reasons were undoubtedly the main factor inducing decision-makers inside the Communist Party to authorize inquiry into the effectiveness of the lay judge. Characteristically, permission was given with the explicit condition that it be called social, not sociological research.

The first objectives of the project were to establish a suitable forum for empirical investigation of legal matters, and to determine whether in fact such investigation is feasible in a monolithic political system. If feasible, then the established forum could initiate and carry out empirical research about law on a broader scale. Results of such empirical research might be important in Czechoslovakia, not only to verify controversial working hypotheses, but also to make it possible to expose facts which otherwise could not be disclosed, because they were incompatible with official ideology.

Since the focus of the project was on ascertaining the political and methodological possibilities of social inquiry, the resource base was limited to a sample, embracing only the city of Prague and a single court jurisdiction. Two practical factors contributed to this restriction. First, a fifteen-year-long hiatus in teaching and application of sociology considerably narrowed the availability of qualified experts. Secondly, the research was unsubsidized and depended on voluntary cooperation by individual members of the research team.

This team was formed with the idea in mind of eventually moving into larger empirical inquiries into legal problems. The team, headed by the author, included a sociologist who had acquired his professional skill before sociology became taboo in Czechoslovakia; a specialist in legal logic; a social psychologist; a lawyer specializing in data processing and jurimetrics; an economist specializing in statistics; civil law and criminal law judges; two practicing attorneys; a representative of the "procuratura" (Office of the Prosecutor); several faculty members of the Charles University School of Law and the Institute of State and Law of the Czechoslovakian Academy of Sciences; and a representative of the Ministry of Justice specializing in the legislative process (who became a Deputy Minister of Justice in the Dubček period in 1968) (3). Thus the ministry was continually informed of the work in progress, and could make use of research findings even if not published.

The research method: Czechoslovakian courts deliberate in closed sessions; minority or dissenting opinions, if any, do not appear in the decision. Therefore, the research could examine only external data on conditions of work of lay judges, and their observable behavior.

The data included information on the assignment of lay judges to individual cases; the frequency of their appearances in court; the regularity of their participation in particular cases; the costs of the system. In addition, information was gathered on the behavior of the lay judge in court. The pertinent information here could only be provided by participants – in the first place by the lay judges themselves; next by other regular participants in the court proceedings, i.e., professional judges, attorneys, and public prosecutors; and finally by the litigants.

Preliminary informal interviews with some lay judges and other participants in court proceedings were followed up by questionnaires sent to a representative sample of each group. These were to be anonymously answered. Finally, a sample of litigants was formally interviewed on their experiences with lay judges.

The research did not address the question of lay judge recruitment. When the lay judge system was instituted, the law provided for nomination of lay judges by various state organs. A later version of the law spoke about the "election" of lay judges by a state organ or electorate without, however, stipulating any means of choosing between eligible candidates.

Regardless of the law, it remains a fact that the actual selection of lay judges, like the selection of any other "people's representatives" in a Soviet-type political regime, was made by the apparatus of the Communist Party. Any investigation into the procedure and principles internally applied by the Communist Party went beyond the scope of the research team.

The preparatory work was centered on depicting problems and devising methodologies. Preliminary research had already revealed some interesting findings.

1. It was revealed that the Ministry of Justice, which administered the judiciary, knew only the number of lay judges and some aspects of their background (e.g., age and Communist Party membership). It had no records of the frequency of their court appearances nor even any general rules for assigning lay judges to individual cases.

2. The professional judge (Chairman of the Senate) normally had full discretion in selecting, for an individual case, anyone from an extensive list of lay judges assigned to his senate. Hence he was apt to select those whom he approved of or preferred.

Moreover, the Chairman of the Senate was requested to evaluate all lay judges assigned to his senate and thereby partially controlled whether they were re-selected for the next "electoral" term. Thus the chairman not only influenced what lay judges would serve in his senate, he also could force them to comply with his wishes if they wished to be re-selected.

If the Communist Party was interested in treating a case specially, the Party bureaucracy could set up a senate composed of both professional and lay judges of its own choice. This was formally carried out by the Chairman of the Court, who is always a member of and subordinate to the Communist Party.

3. The most curious fact uncovered by the preliminary research was that at different phases of a trial different lay judges might appear. This occurred most often in private law cases which required several continuances. Chairmen of the

senates simplified their work by assigning the same lay judge to participate in all hearings and decisions of a court on a particular day, without considering his role in previous stages of the docketed cases.

It is true that the lay judge had access to court records, and could familiarize himself with the history of any case in which he was to participate. However, he seldom took this opportunity, and typically joined the senate completely unprepared.

4. The effectiveness of the participation of the lay judge in court depended on the type of case:

a) In criminal cases, which were usually concentrated into one hearing or at least one court sitting, the same lay judge participated in all hearings and the decision-making for each case. Informal interviews revealed that in these cases, lay judges generally formed and expressed their own opinion.

b) Complicated private law cases, particularly divorces and other family law matters, often require several hearings at different sittings. In the course of these trials, lay judges were rotated. They usually expressed no opinion whatsoever during court proceedings. There is reason to believe that they were equally nonactive in the decisionmaking as well.

c) Some private law cases of technical character (e.g., tort or contractual liability for damages) were often concentrated into one hearing; but their legal or technical complexity generally precluded the lay judge from any active participation.

However, there was an important exception of this pattern. If by chance one of the lay judges was personally acquainted with a technical aspect of the case, he was inclined to demonstrate his knowledge. The rest of the senate, if unfamiliar with the technical problem, tended then to rely on his opinion, even though it was often based only on personal experience and was perhaps inappposite to the case in question. Thus this lay judge became an "expert" – possibly one who presented an erroneous opinion. The effect of this was especially debilitating if he gave his opinion only after the court withdrew for deliberation. The trial parties would then be unaware of this testimony, and have no chance to rebut it.

5. It was also surprising to find that the cost of the system of lay judges has never been estimated. The author of the original draft of the statute on lay judges revealed in an informal interview that neither the legislature nor the Communist Party had been concerned with the financial question.

The courts reimbursed only the actual expenses (4). Loss of earnings was paid by the courts only to self-employed persons, but these were naturally very exceptional in the Czechoslovakian economic system. Wage-earners were allowed paid absences from work. The costs to the state economy of this system were never evaluated.

During the first stage of the actual research, questionnaires were distributed to a sample of attorneys from two Offices of Legal Advice (about thirty attorneys). The results proved disappointing. Even the anonymity of the answers did not relieve the respondents from political anxiety. The responses conformed completely to official doctrine of the time, which proclaimed the lay judge as an indisputably positive feature of the "socialist judiciary." The information gained from the questionnaires differed substantially from that given to the author by the same respondents during informal discussions.

It was evident that political questions could not be addressed objectively in

Czechoslovakia in the early 1960's. Nevertheless, it was also clear that even under such conditions, sociological inquiry might contribute useful knowledge and stimulation. The limited findings of the preliminary research were sufficient to provide for a more realistic understanding of the function of lay judges.
When the Dubček regime, in 1968, temporarily permitted a critical view of the Czechoslovakian judiciary, a reform of the lay judge system, in accordance with the findings of this research, then five years old, was prepared. The Action Program of the Ministry of Justice, in the spring of 1968, read as follows:
"The participation of lay judges in proceedings and decision-making, in courts of first instance, should be restricted if the lay judge cannot help in the ascertainment of facts; and if the application of his common sense, his life experience, and his general knowledge cannot usefully contribute to a factually correct decision of the case. For example, the participation of the lay judge should be omitted in the following matters: the increase (decrease) of child support; the calculation of compensatory damages; deliberations on strictly legal problems (e.g., statutes of limitations); property litigation concerning values under, for instance, 1,000 Czechoslovak crowns; and criminal cases that cannot result in a sentence exceeding, for instance, one or two years of imprisionment. The principle of the multiple panel (senate) also will be abandoned in many instances . . .
There arises also the problem of assigning the lay judge to individual cases. It should be considered whether the current direct influence of the chairman of the senate upon the assignment of a lay judge to an individual case does not affect the opinion of the senate."
After the Soviet invasion of Czechoslovakia in August 1968, hostile attitudes toward ideas of the Dubček era also affected the intended revision of the judiciary. In the final outcome, the only improvements carried out were those which had immediate economic significance. Law No. 56/1969 Sb. partially reestablished the jurisdiction of a single judge in courts of first instance, and limited the number of days on which the lay judge could be assigned to a court. In all other respects, the institution of the lay judge remained as before, with all its deficiencies.

Summary

Nachdem im Jahre 1948 die kommunistische Partei in der Tschechoslowakei die Macht übernommen hatte, wurden im Rahmen einer Justizreform die Institutionen des Einzelrichters und des Schwurgerichts abgeschafft. Alle Gerichte entscheiden in Zukunft nur in Senaten, die aus Berufs- und Laienrichtern zusammengesetzt waren. Jeder Richter war dabei gleichermaßen berechtigt, an der Entscheidung sowohl über Tat- wie über Rechtsfragen, über Schuld wie über Strafe mitzuwirken.
Der Verfasser dieses Beitrages hat im Jahre 1963 in der Tschechoslowakischen Akademie der Wissenschaften eine soziologische Untersuchung begonnen, die die Effektivität der Funktion der Laienrichter überprüfen sollte. Da nach 1948 jede

soziologische Aktivität in der Tschechoslowakei unterbunden wurde, sollte diese erste Untersuchung auf dem Gebiete des Rechtes gleichzeitig feststellen, ob eine empirische Gesellschaftsforschung im monolitischen politischen System überhaupt möglich ist.

Obwohl die Antwort auf die zweite Frage unbefriedigend ausfiel und die Forschungsarbeit unbeendet blieb, hat sie doch einige interessante Ergebnisse gebracht. Es wurde z.B. festgestellt, daß die Auswahl der Laienrichter für einzelne Gerichtssitzungen im wesentlichen dem Senatsvorsitzenden, der immer ein Berufsrichter war, überlassen wurde. Dieser konnte sich die Laienrichter so aussuchen, wie es seinem Interesse entsprach oder wie es ihm bequem war. Die merkwürdige Folge dessen war, daß er meistens Laienrichter für je einen Gerichtstag einberief ohne Rücksicht darauf, ob sie auch in den vorhergehenden Stadien der behandelten Fälle teilgenommen hatten. Das hat sich in dem Verhalten der Laienrichter niedergeschlagen, die in der Regel nur aktiv wurden, wenn sie dem ganzen Prozeß beiwohnten. Dementsprechend war die Teilnahme der Laienrichter in Kriminalsachen, die in einer Gerichtssitzung erledigt wurden, größer als in komplizierten Zivilsachen, wobei es jedoch sehr erhebliche Ausnahmen gab.

Während der vorübergehenden innenpolitischen Entspannung im Jahre 1968 hat das Justizministerium einen Reformplan vorgelegt, der unter anderem, die Nachteile der Funktion der Laienrichter beseitigen sollte. Dieser Entwurf wurde aber nach der bewaffneten sowjetischen Intervention nur in sehr beschränktem Ausmaße realisiert.

Notes

1 The author unfortunately has no access to original materials and this belated report can therefore be based only on his memory.
2 The Law on Popularization of the Judiciary, No. 319/1948 Sb.
3 The author was also a member of a commission established in the Dubček period within the Ministry of Justice to provide a reorganization plan for the judiciary.
4 In Prague, where these expenses were nothing but the cost of public transportation, they were often not even claimed.

b) Sachverständige

Jutta Limbach

Die rechtliche Erheblichkeit gesellschaftlicher Unwissenheit

Das Phänomen der Unwissenheit beschäftigt die Jurisprudenz in zunehmendem Maße. Der traditionsreiche Grundsatz „Ignorantia juris nocet" ist inzwischen seiner Selbstverständlichkeit beraubt und zum Problem geworden. Der Titel der Schrift von Mayer-Maly „Rechtskenntnis und Gesetzesflut" (1)* indiziert bereits ein Verhältnis von umgekehrter Proportionalität. Die Unwissenheit des Bürgers im Recht, die es als Faktum zu konstatieren gilt, erscheint als Folge parlamentarischer Überproduktion. Die Frage nach dem Warum der Gesetzesinflation wird zumeist mit dem Hinweis auf die zunehmende Verflochtenheit und Mannigfaltigkeit des gesellschaftlichen Lebens beantwortet, die immer mehr Konfliktmöglichkeiten und damit auch mehr Entscheidungsprobleme hervorbringt.
Trotz der Einsicht, daß die überschaubaren idyllischen Daseinsformen unwiderbringlich dahin sind, sieht Mayer-Maly die letzte Chance in der Selbstzucht des Gesetzgebers. Er plädiert für eine enzyklopädische Jurisprudenz, „die auf das Recht als Ganzes sieht" (2). In dem Zusammenhang, in dem sich Mayer-Maly weniger der Analyse der Rechtswirklichkeit als der Suche nach Auswegen widmet, begegnet uns eine überraschende Feststellung:

> „Die gegenwärtige Gesetzesinflation stellt sich zu einem guten Teil überhaupt nur als eine Reaktion auf die Verkümmerung der Privatautonomie dar" (3).

Nicht das Gesetz, sondern der Richterspruch und der Vertrag seien die geeigneten Instrumente, um in unserer so komplexen Welt zu differenzieren. Schon die Sachnähe der Kontrahenten spreche zugunsten der Privatautonomie. Mißtraue man der Vertragsfreiheit im Hinblick auf die wirtschaftliche Schwäche der Kontrahenten, so erkaufe man diese Sicherung um einen zu hohen Preis: „um den der Hilflosigkeit gegenüber dem undurchschaubar gewordenen Recht" (4).
Dieser Satz läßt sich in die Behauptung umkehren, daß das Orientierungsvermögen der Bürger in dem Maße wachse, in dem sich der Gesetzgeber auf das Grundlegende beschränke und das Differenzieren und Spezialisieren des Rechts im Hinblick auf bestimmte Situationen den autonomen Individuen überlasse.

I. Das gesellschaftliche Wissen im Bereich der Privatautonomie

Wir wissen aber alle nur zu gut, daß derjenige, der im Reich der Vertragsfreiheit den informierten Bürger sucht, alsbald einem anderen Dickicht von Regeln

* Anmerkungen auf den Seiten 317 ff.

begegnet: den Allgemeinen Geschäftsbedingungen. An Hand dieses Erzeugnisses der Kautelarjurisprudenz soll versucht werden, der Kategorie der Unwissenheit im Vertragswesen auf die Spur zu kommen.

1. Die Definition des gesellschaftlichen Wissens

Was ist mit der Kategorie des „gesellschaftlichen Wissens“ gemeint?

> Der Begriff „*gesellschaftliches Wissen*“ soll die allgemeine Kenntnis darüber bezeichnen, welches Verhalten die Gesellschaft in typischen Situationen erwartet und fordert und mit welchen mutmaßlichen Reaktionen und Sanktionen bei einem von dem Verhaltensmodell abweichenden Handeln zu rechnen ist (5).

Diese Definition ist gewissermaßen das Exzerpt aus einer Reihe von Entscheidungen des Bundesgerichtshofs, denen die Rücksichtnahme auf die Unwissenheit einer Personengruppe gemeinsam ist. Es handelt sich dabei überwiegend um richterliche Verweisungen darauf, daß den Angehörigen einer Gruppe ein Rechtsinhalt unbekannt und es ihnen daher unmöglich ist, die Folgen ihres Handelns vorauszusehen und sich an den mutmaßlichen Wirkungen zu orientieren.

Nur ein Beispielsfall aus der Rechtsprechung des Bundesgerichtshofs in Zivilsachen soll als Illustration des Gemeinten dienen: Ein Haftpflichtversicherer hat geltend gemacht, von der Pflicht zur Leistung befreit zu sein, weil der versicherte Kraftfahrer eine ihn nach den Versicherungsbedingungen treffende Obliegenheit vorsätzlich verletzt hat. Die Obliegenheit nämlich, „alles zu tun, was zur Aufklärung des Tatbestandes dienlich sein kann“. Die Einsicht, daß der „Masse der Versicherten“ die Regelung in jenen Vorschriften im einzelnen nicht geläufig sei (6), hat den Bundesgerichtshof veranlaßt, eine *Hinweispflicht* des Versicherers zu statuieren. Es sei „weithin unbekannt“, so ausdrücklich das Gericht, „daß der Versicherungsnehmer durch bewußt unrichtige oder unvollständige Angaben über einen Verkehrsunfall den Versicherungsschutz selbst dann gänzlich verlieren kann, wenn ihm nicht nur eine betrügerische Absicht fehlt, sondern sein Verhalten für den Versicherer auch keine nachteiligen Folgen hat“. Mit dieser Unwissenheit der Versicherten und der damit verbundenen Gefahr mangelhafter Auskünfte über den Unfall müsse der Versicherer rechnen. – Der Bundesgerichtshof läßt sich also von der Erkenntnis leiten, daß es den Versicherten nicht möglich ist, ihr Handeln auf das Tun und Lassen des Versicherers abzustimmen; denn sie sind nicht ausreichend darüber unterrichtet, welche Reaktionen oder Sanktionen sie hervorrufen, wenn sie von dem geforderten Verhaltensmuster abweichen.

Das Adjektiv „gesellschaftlich“, „sozial“, das dem Begriff Wissen beigefügt ist, versteht sich im Rahmen der hier aufgeworfenen Frage von selbst; denn es geht darum zu wissen, woran man sich in seinem Verhältnis zu anderen Rechtsgenossen und in dem Verkehr mit ihnen zu halten hat (7).

Das der Kategorie „Wissen“ überdies vorangestellte Adjektiv „kollektiv“ soll hier schlicht den Gegensatz von „individuell“ ausdrücken und eine Verhaltensweise kennzeichnen, die von vielen Mitgliedern der Gesamtgesellschaft oder einer ihrer Gruppen in einer bestimmten sozialen Situation beobachtet wird (8). Die Aufmerksamkeit gilt nicht dem individuellen Informationsstand – etwa der Prozeßparteien –, sondern dem kollektiven Wissen der Rechtsgenossen. Auf diese Weise soll einer „Einzelfallgerechtigkeit“ aus dem Wege gegangen werden. Gewiß kann auch einer auf den Einzelfall abstellenden Billigkeitsentscheidung paradigmatische Wirkung für die Zukunft zukommen. Man hat jedoch eher die Chance, dem Wechselverhältnis von Gesellschaft und Rechtssprechung auf die Spur zu kommen, wenn man sein Augenmerk auf kollektive Denk- und Verhaltensweisen richtet, d.h. auf soziale Erscheinungen, die hinsichtlich ihrer gesellschaftlichen Tragweite auf einer entsprechenden Ebene liegen.

2. Die Behandlung des Wissensproblems durch den Bundesgerichtshof

Das zur Illustration der Definition angeführte Urteil des Bundesgerichtshofs darf nicht ohne weiteres verallgemeinert werden. Das Gericht folgt nicht dem Satz, daß die Unkenntnis von Allgemeinen Geschäftsbedingungen von der Verantwortung befreit. Als Grundsatz hält das Gericht vielmehr den Gegen-Satz hoch. Der Standpunkt des sorgfältigen Hausvaters dient nach wie vor als Maßstab dafür, was von einem Rechtsgenossen in einer bestimmten sozialen Situation erwartet werden darf. Und das, obgleich die Soziologie des Verbraucherverhaltens lehrt, „daß gerade in der Sphäre des Konsums das angesonnene rationale Verhalten zum unwahrscheinlichen Grenzfall wird“ (9). Der Satz, daß man sich um das, was man unterschreibt, zu kümmern hat, wenn man Rechtsnachteile vermeiden will (10), ist heute in den Wind gesprochen. Flume, der sicher nicht verdächtigt wird, Rechtstatsachen überzubetonen, hebt in seiner Rechtsgeschäftslehre als „das Charakteristikum dieser Vereinbarung“ (der Allgemeinen Geschäftsbedingungen) hervor, „daß nach den Gepflogenheiten des Verkehrs der eine Vertragspartner die Geltung der Geschäftsbedingungen verlangt und der andere sich dem fügt, ohne von dem Inhalt der Bedingungen sonderlich Notiz zu nehmen“ (11).
Der Bundesgerichtshof hat denn auch das Ignorieren der Ignoranz der Verbraucher nicht durchgehalten. In seiner Rechtsprechung zum finanzierten Abzahlungskauf, bei dem das Abzahlungsgeschäft in zwei selbständige Verträge, nämlich einen Kaufvertrag mit dem Verkäufer und einen Darlehensvertrag mit einem Kreditinstitut aufgespalten ist, hat sich der Bundesgerichtshof dem Phänomen der allgemeinen Unerfahrenheit nicht verschließen können.
Das Gericht hatte die Rechtsfrage zu entscheiden, inwieweit der Käufer bei einem solchen Ratenkauf trotz der rechtlichen Selbständigkeit der Verträge dem Darlehensgeber Einwendungen aus dem Kaufvertrag entgegenhalten darf. In den Streitfällen hatte der Ratenkäufer anläßlich des Ratenkaufs ein Formular unterschrieben, das neben dem Darlehensantrag, den Vordruck eines Bestellscheins oder Kaufvertrags sowie eine Bestätigung über den Empfang der Waren enthielt. Auf der Rückseite des Formulars waren die Verkaufs- und Darlehensbedingungen abgedruckt. Diese enthielten u.a. die Klausel, daß der Käufer Mängelrügen und sonstige Rechte aus dem Kaufvertrag nur gegenüber dem Verkäufer geltend machen darf und diese den Darlehensvertrag, vornehmlich die Pflicht, das Darlehen in den vereinbarten Raten zurückzuzahlen, nicht berührt. Die mit dieser Klausel ausgedrückte rechtliche Selbständigkeit der beiden Verträge ist in den Urteilen des BGH zwar stets als rechtlicher Tatbestand anerkannt worden (12). In der Mehrzahl der Streitfälle jedoch hat der Bundesgerichtshof die dieser textlich formulierten Rechtlage entsprechenden rechtlichen Folgerungen mit Rücksicht auf das „Schutzbedürfnis des vielfach geschäftlich und rechtlich unerfahrenen Ratenkäufers“ (13) nicht gezogen (14).

3. Der „Werdegang" der Rechtsprechung

Die Feinfühligkeit des Bundesgerichtshofs für die Unwissenheit und Unerfahrenheit der Verbraucher stellte sich allerdings nicht schlagartig ein. Zunächst erschien ihm die Unkenntnis als Ausdruck des subjektiven Unvermögens einiger Verbraucher im Vergleich zu anderen. Das besondere Schutzbedürfnis der Leute mit kleinem Einkommen, die selbst die Anschaffung von Hausrat nur mittels Ratenzahlungen möglich machen können, hat offenbar die Rücksichtnahme auf das beschränkte juristische Begriffsvermögen des „Durchschnitts-Käufers" inspiriert. So ist in den Urteilen von „Personen dieser Käuferschicht" (15) oder von dem Käuferkreis die Rede, der „schon seiner sozialen Stellung nach häufig nicht imstande sei, zwischen dem Kaufgeschäft einerseits und dem Darlehensvertrag andererseits klar zu unterscheiden (16). In einer anderen Entscheidung wird die Tatsache, daß die Käufer im Zeitpunkt des Geschäftsabschlusses „in ärmlichen Verhältnissen" (17) lebten, als ein im Sachverhalt mitteilenswerter Umstand erachtet. Doch alsbald keimte bei dem BGH der Verdacht, daß es dem Normalverbraucher auch kaum mehr gelingen kann, die in den Allgemeinen Geschäftsbedingungen fixierten Denkinhalte geistig zu vollziehen. Zwei weitere Streitfälle, in denen ein Arzt medizinische Geräte (18) und ein Gastwirt drei echte Perserteppiche (19) gekauft hatten, nahm der Bundesgerichtshof zum Anlaß, ganz allgemein die Unfähigkeit des gewöhnlich rechtlich ungeschulten Ratenkäufers zu berücksichtigen, die von der Kautelarjurisprudenz formulierten Texte, insbesondere die Vertragsvordrucke und Allgemeinen Geschäftsbedingungen, zu begreifen und die sich aus ihnen ergebenden rechtlichen Folgen vorauszusehen. Das Schutzbedürfnis des Käufers und Darlehensnehmers bestehe ohne Rücksicht auf den Bildungsstand, die Geschäftserfahrung und den Kaufgegenstand, sofern der Käufer nicht als Kaufmann im Handelsregister eingetragen sei.

> „Denn die Formularverträge ... müssen so ausgestaltet sein, daß „jedermann" sie verstehen, ihren rechtlich wesentlichen Inhalt aufnehmen und das (erst durch Einschaltung des Finanzierungsinstituts entstehende) Risiko erfassen kann" (20).

Die Klausel in den Allgemeinen Geschäftsbedinungen

> „Mängelrügen und sonstige Rechte aus dem Kaufvertrag kann der Käufer nur gegenüber dem Verkäufer geltend machen und berühren nicht den Darlehensvertrag mit der Bank und die Verpflichtung, das Darlehen in den vereinbarten Raten an die Bank zurückzuzahlen"

sei jedenfalls nicht geeignet, einem Käufer und Darlehensnehmer eindeutig und unmißverständlich die für ihn schwer begreifliche Folge klar zu machen, daß er auch zahlen soll, wenn er die Ware nicht erhält.

Diese sich erst nach und nach einstellende Einsicht in die Allgemeinheit des Problems ist ein weiteres Indiz für die heute sehr strapazierte These von der schichtspezifischen Urteilsweise unserer Richter.

Die *Sensibilität* der Richter für *gesellschaftliche Bedürfnisse* nimmt in dem Maße zu, als der in Rede stehende soziale Konflikt in die Interessensphäre der eigenen Gesellschaftsschicht hineinreicht.

Als ein anderer Beleg für dieses schichtbezogene Einfühlungsvermögen der Richter kann noch die Entscheidung des Bundesgerichtshofs herangezogen werden, laut der Rechtsanwälte das Berechnen der einfachen Fristen ihrem geschulten Personal überlassen dürfen (21). Hier öffnete sich der Bundesgerichtshof dem Argument der Anwälte, daß die juristische Arbeit in den letzten Jahren erheblich schwieriger geworden sei, – daß man der von der Legislative und Judikatur produzierten Stoffülle nur in wenigen Fällen durch Spezialisierung auf ein Rechtsgebiet Herr werden könne.

II. Die unterschiedliche Reichweite des Wissensproblems

Hinsichtlich der Unerfahrenheit und Verständnislosigkeit der Verbraucher gegenüber den Klauselwerken der Kautelarjurisprudenz kann man verschiedene Erscheinungsformen der Unwissenheit feststellen, was ihren Grund, d.h. ihre Ursache und zugleich ihre Tragweite angeht. Je nachdem, ob es sich um eine Frage der Willigkeit oder der Fähigkeit oder der Möglichkeit handelt, lassen sich drei Varianten der Unwissenheit unterscheiden:

1. Ist der Rechtsuchende ohne Einfluß äußerer Umstände schlicht nicht *willig,* etwas zur Kenntnis zu nehmen, so ist die Unwissenheit eine rein individuelle Angelegenheit. Im Falle solcher Nachlässigkeit setzt sich der Rechtsgenosse dem Vorwurf unzureichender Sorgfalt aus. Hier wird gemäß § 276 BGB judiziert. Dieser Fall soll uns nicht kümmern.

2. Ist jedoch die Unwilligkeit, Geschriebenes zur Kenntnis zu nehmen, darauf zurückzuführen, daß das Verständnisvermögen der geschäftlich unerfahrenen und rechtlich ungeschulten Käufer mit den „rechtlich bis ins letzte ausgeklügelten" und textlich überladenen Geschäftsbedingungen und Formularen erheblich überfordert wird (22), so ist die *Fähigkeit,* und zwar die Verständnisfähigkeit betroffen. Hier ist der Befund der Verbrauchersoziologie aufzubieten, daß der Einsatz geistiger Mittel mit der ständig zunehmenden Komplexität der Marktsituation nicht Schritt halten konnte (23). Soweit die Frage des Verständnisvermögens in Rede steht, ist eine unterschiedliche Betroffenheit der Bürger je nach Bildungsniveau und Erfahrung denkbar. Diese Art der Unwissenheit erscheint grundsätzlich als behebbar; indem man z.B. den Verfassern von Geschäftsbedingungen auferlegt, die Allgemeinen Geschäftsbedingungen gemeinverständlich abzufassen und lesbar zu gestalten. Hier hat die vom Bundesgerichtshof statuierte Aufklärungspflicht der Banken und Finanzierungsinstitute ihren Gefechtsstand.

3. Bei der zweiten Variante von Unwissenheit kann man noch davon sprechen, daß den Verbrauchern der Einblick in die Begleitumstände des Kaufs *nur subjektiv* verwehrt ist. Zwar sind die Geschäftsbedingungen schwer begreiflich, aber grundsätzlich ist ihr Inhalt bestimmbar. Bei der dritten Variante, die wir zur Frage der *Möglichkeit* in Bezug gesetzt haben, ist der Transparenzmangel dem Kaufgeschehen selbst inhärent. Hier kann die Passivität der Verbraucher nicht mit den formalen Qualitäten des Textes erklärt werden. Die Gleichgültigkeit der Käufer ist nicht allein auf seinen mitunter jedes Interesse im Keim erstickenden Umfang zurückzuführen. Sie muß auch als ein Zeichen der Resignation angesichts des Unvermögens der Verbraucher verstanden werden, die Geschäftsbedingungen abzuändern oder ihnen auszuweichen (24). Die Situation ist mit dem Aphorismus von Stanislaw Lec bloßgelegt: „Wo alle einstimmig singen, ist der Text ohne Bedeutung". Hier ist die Unwissenheit mehr Symptom wirtschaftlicher Ohnmacht als Ursache der Hilflosigkeit der Verbraucher.

Die unter 2 und 3 unterschiedenen Varianten stehen zueinander nicht im Verhältnis des Entweder-Oder. Sie lassen sich in der Wirklichkeit nicht säuberlich scheiden, sondern überlappen einander.

III. Die Ignoranz der „fatalistischen" Variante der Unwissenheit

1. Die Partnerschaftsstrategie

Der Bundesgerichtshof läßt das, was praktisch miteinander verwoben ist, auch in der Theorie ungeschieden. Er nimmt vornehmlich die zweite Art der Unwissenheit zur Kenntnis, die auf die geistigen Fähigkeiten bezogen ist. Abhilfe soll der Partner, d.h. das Finanzierungsinstitut schaffen, indem es in verständlicher Sprache auf das Risiko des finanzierten Abzahlungskaufs hinweist.
Die weitere Frage nach einem möglichen Zusammenhang zwischen allgemeiner Unwissenheit und der eingeschränkten Kompetenz der Verbraucher wird nicht gestellt. Die Partnerschaftsstrategie des BGH, die darauf gerichtet ist, dem Verbraucher Aufklärung zuteil werden zu lassen, erscheint angesichts der damit eröffneten Alternative „Unterwerfung oder Konsumverzicht" als ein Herumdoktern an Symptomen. Der punktuell gewarnte Rechtsgenosse wird dem Bundesgerichtshof die Fürsorge danken, — seine Wiedergeburt als autonomer Bürger, der an der vertraglichen Willensbildung aktiv teilhat, bleibt ihm vorbehalten. Das liegt allerdings auch außerhalb der Möglichkeit der Gerichte.
Die Partnerschaftsstrategie des Bundesgerichtshofs hat sich nicht in dem Ziel erschöpft, den Verbraucher in die Lage zu versetzten, im Zustand des Aufgeklärtseins entweder das Geschäft zu dem ihm diktierten Allgemeinen Geschäftsbedingungen abzuschließen oder angesichts des damit verbundenen Risikos davon Abstand zu nehmen. Der BGH hat in den im 47. Band abgedruckten Entscheidungen — über die Begründung der Informationspflicht hinaus — mit verschiedenen dogmatischen Konstruktionen versucht, dem Schutzbedürfnis der Ratenkäufer gerecht zu werden. Die Absicht des Bundesgerichtshofs war offensichtlich eine rechtspolitische (25), sein Ziel die Korrektur eines neuen Geschäftstyps (26).
Die rechtspolitische Absicht des Bundesgerichtshofs ergibt sich vorzugsweise aus der dem Abzahlungsgesetz hinsichtlich des Kreises der Normadressaten und des Vertragsgegenstandes nachgebildeten abstrakten Formulierung des Tatbestandes der Aufklärungspflicht. Der Leitsatz des Urteils (27) lautet:

> „Beim finanzierten Abzahlungskauf besteht die Aufklärungspflicht der Bank, insbesondere die Pflicht zur deutlichen Warnung, eine Empfangsbestätigung nicht vor Erhalt der Ware zu erteilen, nicht nur gegenüber geschäftlich unerfahrenen Käufern und beim Kauf von Haushaltsgegenständen, sondern allgemein gegenüber „Jedermann" und beim Abzahlungskauf von beweglichen Sachen jeder Art, soweit der Schutzgedanke des Abzahlungsgesetzes reicht".

2. Die „apokryphe Technik des Lernens" in der Rechtsprechung

Die Unwissenheit der Verbraucher, die mehr Symptom denn Grund ihrer wirtschaftlichen Hilflosigkeit ist, war der Beweggrund für die zugunsten der Verbraucher gefällten Urteile. Bei der Rechtfertigung des Urteils zieht sich der Bundesgerichtshof aber stets auf dogmatische Argumentationsinstanzen zurück, und sei es notfalls auf die recht allgemeinen Vorstellungen von unzulässiger Rechtsausübung. Die Fragwürdigkeit der rechtgeschäftlichen Entscheidungsfreiheit (28) wird in den Urteilsgründen nicht diskutiert, obwohl der Bundesgerichtshof mit der Ansammlung von 8 Streitfällen eine gewisse Basis dafür hatte, dem

behaupteten Mißverhältnis von ökonomischer und juristischer Gleichheit nachzuspüren.
Die Frage, warum die Käufer allgemein nicht einmal den Versuch einer Lektüre (29) machen, führt über die Beschaffenheit des Textes nicht hinaus. Wenn auch das übliche Verhalten der Rechtsgenossen nicht den Maßstab für die Frage bilden kann, was von ihnen gefordert werden darf, so gibt es doch einen Anhaltspunkt dafür, was möglich ist. Kollektive soziale Verhaltensweisen geben nicht nur Auskunft über irgendwelche Neuerungen im gesellschaftlichen Zusammenleben und Zusammenwirken. Sie können auch gewandelte Bedürfnisse im negativen Sinne anzeigen. Sie können den Richter darauf aufmerksam machen, daß die Rechtsgenossen oder eine Gruppe von ihnen dem „Leistungsanspruch" eines Standards nicht mehr gerecht zu werden vermögen. D.h., daß sie die „Last der Konformität" nicht mehr zu ertragen vermögen (30).
Zweifel, ob das mangelnde Verständnisvermögen oder die wirtschaftliche Inkompetenz für die mangelnde Lektüre der Allgemeinen Geschäftsbedingungen ursächlich sind, waren gewiß am Platze. Hier sei, was die sogenannte Verbrauchersouveränität angeht, nur auf den jüngsten Bericht des Bundeskartellamtes verwiesen (31). „Im System der Sozialen Marktwirtschaft", so wird dort ausgeführt, „nimmt der Verbraucher eine zentrale Stellung ein. Unter den Voraussetzungen des marktwirtschaftlichen Modells steuern die Konsumenten durch die Art der Verwendung ihrer Einkommen die Produktion; . . ." „Die Wirklichkeit sieht anders aus: Auf den meisten Konsumgütermärkten befinden sich die Anbieter in einer überlegenen Position gegenüber dem Verbraucher: sie sind die aktiven, die Verbraucher nur die reaktiven Tauschpartner. An Stelle von Konsumenten herrscht vielfach Produzentensouveränität".
Aber so weit wollte sich der Bundesgerichtshof nicht – mit Hilfe einer soziologischen Analyse etwa – vorwagen. Gewiß darf der Richter das Recht nur innerhalb der Grenzen neu begreifen, die ihm der anhängige Rechtsstreit setzt. Die 8 anhängigen Musterprozesse hatten aber dem Bundesgerichtshof eine gewisse Plattform gegeben, die Fragen anzugehen, die Wieacker (32) als die Hauptfragen des Privatrechts der Gegenwart herausstellt, nämlich die nach den Bedingungen der Privatautonomie und nach der materialen Vertragsgerechtigkeit. Der Bundesgerichtshof verzichtet auf das Grundsätzliche, um sich sogleich an die juristische Kleinarbeit zu machen. Die Vertragsfreiheit wird nicht problematisiert.
Schlußfolgerung: Die Gerichte sind nicht Stifter neuer Konzepte. Sie orientieren sich am konventionellen, dem hergebrachten Wissen. Und sollten ehemals brauchbare Prinzipien allmählich den Charakter von Postulaten annehmen, so werden die Gerichte eher versuchen, diesen eine „neue" Seite abzugewinnen, als von ihnen Abschied zu nehmen. Empfindliche Einbrüche in das Prinzip versuchen die Gerichte durch „fürsorgerische" und in der Dogmatik ansiedelbare Korrekturen an dem Prinzip zu kompensieren.
Luhmann kennzeichnet diese Form der Rechtsänderung teffend als „apokryphe Techniken des Lernens, Adaptierens und Modifizierens, die mit der formalen Identität von Normen zu vereinbaren sind" (33).
Diese Taktik des behutsamen Lernens hat Robert Fischer als richterliche Selbstzucht herausgestellt. Das begrenzte Leistungsvermögen der Richter und das Gebot der Kontinuität rechtfertigen diese Arbeitsweise. Zum einen können die Richter, die „am Fall" bleiben müssen, die Bedeutung und Tragweite nicht beurteilen, die ihre Entscheidungen für eine sich anbahnende Rechtsentwicklung haben. Zum

anderen hat gerade die höchstrichterliche Rechtsprechung darauf zu achten, daß sie im Interesse der Rechtssicherheit und Rechtsklarheit an ihre Rechtsprechung in Zukunft selbst gebunden ist (34).

IV. Die Rechtssicherheit als Motivation richterlicher Aktivität

Der zum Schluß angeführte Aspekt der Rechtssicherheit verdient noch einige Aufmerksamkeit. Denn dieses Prinzip scheint nicht nur als Ursache richterlicher Zurückhaltung, sondern gleichermaßen als Antriebskraft richterlicher Aktivität wirksam zu sein.

Man gewinnt Anhaltspunkte für die These, wenn man einmal der Frage nachgeht, warum der Bundesgerichtshof die Geltung Allgemeiner Geschäftsbedingungen nicht rigoroser eingeschränkt hat. Welche Folgen hätte es gezeitigt, wenn das Gericht dem Lösungsvorschlag von Huhn (35) gefolgt wäre:

> Danach soll der Käufer, der trotz des Bewußtseins, die wirtschaftliche Tragweite nicht zu überschauen, die Allgemeinen Geschäftsbedingungen unterschreibt, lediglich beweisen müssen, daß er die Bedingungen nicht gelesen, ihnen folglich getraut, d.h. eine *gerechte Interessenwertung* durch die Bedingungen erwartet hat. Der Unternehmer dagegen kann geltend machen und beweisen, daß die Unterschrift des Kunden ein Ausdruck seiner Gleichgültigkeit über den Inhalt der Allgemeinen Geschäftsbedingungen war.

Eine empfindliche Verunsicherung der Unternehmer wäre die Folge. Wie soll es ihnen gelingen, Gleichgültigkeit von Resignation zu scheiden und diesen inneren Sachverhalt dem Gericht zu beweisen? Götz (36) trifft wohl mit seiner Vermutung ins Schwarze, daß die Rechtsprechung die Irrtumsanfechtung aus dem Grunde unterbunden habe, „um den Ablauf des Wirtschaftsverkehrs nicht zu beeinträchtigen". Selbst die Gerichte können sich die heutigen Massengeschäfte ohne Allgemeine Geschäftsbedingungen wohl nicht mehr vorstellen. Hier sei auf eine frühe Einsicht von Robert Fischer (37) verwiesen, wonach das Streben nach einer Rationalisierung des modernen Vertragswesens durch Allgemeine Geschäftsbedingungen gewissermaßen zwangsläufig dazu führe, daß diese Bedingungen in der Praxis den Charakter unabdingbarer Vertragsbestimmungen erhalten. „Denn nur wenn sie in der tatsächlichen Handhabung nicht abgedungen werden, können sie die Funktionen erfüllen, die ihnen in der modernen Wirtschaft bei der Rationalisierung des Vertragswesens zugewiesen sind". Gewiß ist das nur eine Illustration und kein Beleg dafür, daß der Sinn der Richter für eine funktionale Betrachtungsweise rechtlicher Erscheinungen durchaus empfänglich ist.

Unwissenheit, die Vermutung drängt sich auf, ist hier im gewissen Sinne „*Eufunktional*" (38), d.h. ein positives Element im Ablauf der modernen Vertragspraxis, die den Massenkonsum zu bewältigen hat. Wenn sie das Getriebe des modernen Wirtschaftsverkehrs auch nicht gerade ölt, so bewahrt es ihn doch vor Störungen. Ein Erfolg, der sich alsbald einstellen würde, wenn die Verbraucher nicht nur vereinzelt darangingen, das ihnen in den Formularverträgen und Allgemeinen Geschäftsbedingungen Dargebotene in Frage zu stellen. Fallen diese Rationalisierungsmittel fort, so werden die Unternehmer argumentieren, wäre ein Kosten- und damit ein Preisauftrieb die unausweichliche Folge. In diesem Zusammenhang sei auch auf die Erkenntnis der Verbrauchersoziologie hingewiesen, daß die aufs Bequeme zielenden Methoden und die wachsende Unpersön-

lichkeit des Marktes, die vielfach den Einsatz geistiger Mittel durch den Konsumenten erübrigt, gerade von den unteren Bevölkerungsschichten als Wohltat empfunden wird (39).
Louis Schneider hat sich in einem Aufsatz in der American Sociological Review mit der Rolle der Kategorie der Ignoranz in der soziologischen Theorie beschäftigt. Er hat u.a. untersucht, unter welchen Umständen Unwissenheit ein positives Element sein kann. Er stellt neben mehreren den Satz auf, daß Unwissenheit „eufunktional" sei in Fällen, in denen Wissen das Offenbaren von Informationen bedeutet, die einfach schmerzlich sind und keine anderen bedeutsamen Konsequenzen, d.h. keinen Nutzen für den Unwissenden mit sich bringen.

> "Ignorance is eufunctional in cases or conditions in which knowledge would mean the revealing of information that would be directly and simply painful to have and no other significant consequences would occur" (40).

Schneider hat hierbei vornehmlich den Fall im Auge, daß Eltern von der unheilbaren Krankheit ihres Kindes erfahren. Gewiß erscheint es übertrieben, wenn hier eine Parallele gesehen wird. Aber, was gewinnt der Käufer, der das ausgeklügelte Vertragswerk begreift? Er wird sich alsbald seiner geringen Autonomie im Rechtsverkehr bewußt werden. Eine Einsicht, die den Feinfühligen vielleicht demoralisiert. Die Information kann leicht zu einer völlig indifferenten Haltung der Rechtsgenossen führen. Ein Ergebnis, daß alle die mißbilligen werden, die sich von Verantwortungsbewußtsein und Rechgsgesinnung der Bürger einen wohltätigen Einfluß auf das Rechtsgeschehen versprechen. Nur setzt Verantwortung die Möglichkeit voraus, auf das Geschehen Einfluß nehmen zu können, für dessen Folgen man einstehen soll. Spätestens hier offenbart sich der zirkelschlußartige Charakter des Wissensproblems.
Die Rechtsprechung zum finanzierten Abzahlungskauf liefert noch einige direkte Anhaltspunkte für die These, daß die Gefährdung der Rechtssicherheit richterliche Aktivitäten herausfordern kann. Dadurch, daß zu diesem Problemkreis acht Sachen an zwei Tagen gemeinsam verhandelt worden sind, sollte – laut einer Äußerung des Vorsitzenden des zuständigen Senats (41) – „die rechtliche Durchdringung des komplexen Gebildes des ‚finanzierten Abzahlungsgeschäfts' über den Einzelfall hinaus zu einer gewissen Gesamtschau versucht werden". Zwar ist das Gericht dem von einem Vertreter einer Gruppe von Teilzahlungsbanken geäußerten Wunsch, möglichst umfassend alle Fragen dieses Rechtsgebiets zu entscheiden, bewußt nicht gefolgt (42). Das Argument dieses Interessenvertreters: „Die Ungeklärtheit vieler Rechtsfragen des finanzierten Abzahlungsgeschäfts und die hieraus sich ergebende Unsicherheit machen eine sachgerechte Kalkulation für die Abzahlungsbanken fast unmöglich", ist ein beredtes Zeugnis dafür, welchen Rang das Bedürfnis nach Rechtssicherheit vor allen anderen Prinzipien unseres Rechts, selbst vor dem der Privatautonomie für die beteiligten Wirtschaftskreise einnimmt. Hat auch der III. Zivilsenat nicht dem Ansinnen entsprochen, mehr zu entscheiden, als der Einzelfall erfordert, so hat sich doch der Vorsitzende des Senats „dem berechtigten Verlangen der Abzahlungsbanken nach Beseitigung der ihre Kalkulation erschwerenden Unsicherheiten" nicht ganz verschlossen. In einem Aufsatz hat er es unternommen, die einzeln nebeneinanderstehenden Urteile in den Gesamtzusammenhang des finanzierten Abzahlungsgeschäfts zu stellen, „aus dem heraus sich vielleicht Anhaltspunkte ergeben, später auch andere auftauchende Rechtsfragen zu beantworten".

Nach alledem läßt sich die Hypothese wagen, daß sich die Gerichte in ihrem Entscheidungsverhalten eher durch eine drohende Beeinträchtigung der Rechtssicherheit als durch das Gewahrwerden eines sozialen Mißstands im Rechtsleben motivieren lassen.
Oder auf unser Wissensproblem bezogen: Unwissenheit der Rechtsgenossen fordert erst dann die Rücksichtnahme richterlicher Instanzen heraus, wenn sie ein Ausmaß annimmt, daß sie das Selbstverständnis des Partners und dessen Zuversicht verunsichern, daß das Gericht entsprechend seiner Erwartung judizieren werde.

V. Das Aufleben der Privatautonomie als Chance für eine enzyklopädische Jurisprudenz

Mayer-Maly deutete die Gesetzesinflation als Reaktion auf die Verkümmerung der Privatautonomie. Von einem Wiederaufblühen dieser versprach er sich Muße für den Gesetzgeber und damit Besinnung auf die Grundlagen des Rechts. Doch die Erfahrung lehrt, daß das Spezialisieren und Differenzieren auf der Ebene der Privatautonomie entsprechende Folgen zeitigt, und daß die gepriesene Sachnähe ein recht einseitiger Vorzug sein kann. Die Unwissenheit wird nur auf eine andere Ebene verlagert. Hier mögen ihr durchaus wohltätige Wirkungen beizumessen sein. Daß aber auch eine auf den ersten Blick nützliche Unwissenheit dem Rechtsbewußtsein auf die Dauer abträglich sein kann, liegt auf der Hand. Denn die Rechtsgesinnung, an der Mayer-Maly und Manfred Rehbinder aus gutem Grunde so sehr gelegen ist, gründet sich nicht allein auf die Gebrauchstüchtigkeit, sondern auch auf die inhaltliche Beschaffenheit rechtlicher Regelungen.
Daß ein gleichgerichteter Appell zur Selbstzucht an die Adresse der Kautelarjurisprudenz Gehör finden wird, ist kaum zu erwarten. Vielleicht wäre ein erzieherischer Effekt erzielt worden, wenn der Bundesgerichtshof nicht nur die Kaufleute, sondern auch die Juristen aus dem Kreis der schutzbedürftigen Bürger ausgeschieden hätte? – Zieht sich der Gesetzgeber in die Gefilde einer enzyklopädischen Jurisprudenz zurück, so wird das Vertragswesen gewiß blühen, wenn nicht wuchern. Aber wettmachen muß diese Askese des Gesetzgebers die Rechtsprechung. Denn an ihr ist es dann, das Dickicht von differenzierenden und spezialisierenden Klauseln auf der Suche nach der Vertragsgerechtigkeit zu durchforsten.
Doch die Erfahrung lehrt, daß die Gerichte die Untätigkeit des Gesetzgebers nicht zu kompensieren vermögen. Das Kostenrisiko, der Zeitaufwand, die geschäftliche und rechtliche Unerfahrenheit der Rechtsgenossen und der gläubige Respekt vor dem geschriebenen Wort führen dazu, daß nur ein winziger Ausschnitt der beanstandenswerten Fälle vor den Gerichten verhandelt wird. Bei den wenigen Fällen „geglückter" richterlicher Inhaltskontrolle Allgemeiner Geschäftsbedingungen ist überdies die paradigmatische Wirkung auf das Wirtschaftsleben weitgehend ausgeblieben (43). Die „mangelhafte Rückwirkung der BGH-Rechtsprechung in der Rechtswirklichkeit" (Rehbinder) hat gerade zu einem immer heftiger werdenden Plädoyer für eine gesetzliche Regelung des Rechts der Allgemeinen Geschäftsbedingungen geführt (44). Auch die Hoffnung auf die Rechtsprechung trügt also und weist nur einmal mehr auf das eigentliche Problem hin, auf das wirtschaftliche Ungleichgewicht der Marktteilnehmer.

Summary

The text concerns itself with the scope of the concepts of "social ignorance" in the law, particularly in case law. "Social knowledge" refers to general knowledge about that behavior which society expects and demands in various type-situations, and with reactions and sanctions one must reckon with when conduct deviates from model behavior. The low level of knowledge of law, so obvious in modern society, is not primarily to be ascribed to the sheer volume of legal rules and doctrines, but rather to the multiplicity and impenetrability of market behavior, and the economic powerlessness of the ordinary consumer. The author illustrates the problem with analysis of cases in the *Bundesgerichtshof* on installment sales, in which the court has attempted to take "social ignorance" into account.

The author shows, by means of this case-law, that that "social ignorance", which can be completely functional, only evokes the attention of courts, when it reaches a magnitude such that it impairs the party's understanding, and his confidence that the court will rule in accordance with his expectations.

Anmerkungen

1 Theo Mayer-Maly, Rechtskenntnis und Gesetzesflut, Salzburg 1969.

2 A.a.O., S. 81 f. und 85.

3 A.a.O., S. 82.

4 S. Anm. 2.

5 Diese Definition umfaßt ihrem Wortlaut nach einen weiteren Sachverhalt aus dem Bereich der Kraftfahrzeugversicherung. Im Zusammenhang mit der Frage nämlich, ob der versicherte Kraftfahrer die ihn nach § 7 I Nr. 2 S. 2 AKB treffende Obliegenheit vorsätzlich verletzt hat, wird ebenfalls darauf abgestellt, ob es den Kraftfahrern heute allgemein bekannt sei, im Versicherungsfall zur Aufklärung des Versicherers verpflichtet zu sein (OLG Düsseldorf, NJW 1969, 1390, 1391). Der Rückgriff auf die allgemeine Kenntnis von der Regel dient hier aber nicht der Antwort auf die Rechtsfrage, wie etwa der Begriff des Vorsatzes zu bestimmen sei. Mit dem Hinweis wird vielmehr die Beweisfrage zu beantworten versucht, ob die individuelle Prozeßpartei in Kenntnis der sie treffenden Obliegenheit gehandelt habe. Die reine Tatsächlichkeit vorsätzlichen Handelns steht in Frage und das allgemeine Wissen soll das individuelle Wissen indizieren, das wegen der mangelnden Anschaulichkeit des inneren Geschehens nicht direkt bewiesen werden kann. Richterliche Bezugnahmen auf den gesellschaftlichen Erfahrungsstand innerhalb der Tatfrage sollen hier unberücksichtigt bleiben. Hier gilt die Aufmerksamkeit den richterlichen Hinweisen auf soziale Geschehensweisen und Einstellungen, die unmittelbar Gegenstand der rechtlichen Würdigung sind.

6 S. Anm. 9.

7 Vgl. Theodor Geiger, Vorstudien zu einer Soziologie des Rechts, 1964, S. 102, laut dem in der Orientierungssicherheit die soziale Funktion eines jeden Ordnungsgefüges besteht.

8 Der Begriff ist hier im Geigerschen Sinne gebraucht (Anm. 7, S. 93, 95) und impliziert keinen Bezug zu einer Theorie kollektiven Verhaltens.

9 Wiswede, Soziologie des Verbraucherverhaltens, Stuttgart 1972, S. 5.

10 RGZ 134, 25, 31 und BGH NJW 1951, 705; BGHZ 33, 293.

11 „So ist es jedenfalls in der Regel, wenn sich ein Privater auf einen Vertragsschluß zu Allgemeinen Geschäftsbedingungen einläßt". So Flume, Das Rechtsgeschäft, Berlin u.a. 1965, S. 610.

12 So ausdrücklich in BGHZ 20, 36, 51; 33, 293, 295; 47, 217, 219 und 47, 224, 227.

13 So die Formulierung in BGHZ 33, 193, 195.

14 So hat er die §§ 5 und 6 des Abzahlungsgesetzes entsprechend angewandt und demgemäß den Anspruch auf Darlehensrückzahlung verneint, wenn der Darlehensgeber die Kaufsache an sich genommen hatte (BGHZ 3, 257, 259); BGH LM Nr. 2 zu § 6 AbzG). Mit dem Argument, daß der Verkäufer nicht Dritter im Sinne des § 123 Abs. 2 Satz 1 BGB gewesen sei, hat der Bundesgerichtshof das Recht des von dem Verkäufer arglistig getäuschten Käufers anerkannt, den Darlehensvertrag anzufechten (BGHZ 20, 36; 33, 302; 47, 224). Er hat unter bestimmten Voraussetzungen gegenüber dem Darlehensanspruch auch den mit Mängeln der Kaufsache begründeten oder den auf die Nichtigkeit des Kaufvertrags gestützten Einwand des Käufer zugelassen (BGHZ 22, 90; 47, 233). Schließlich hat der Bundesgerichtshof eine Aufklärungspflicht des Finanzierungsinstituts gegenüber dem geschäftlich unerfahrenen Käufer begründet, deren Verletzung dieses zugunsten des Käufers zum Schadensersatz verpflichtet (BGHZ 33, 293; 47, 217).

15 BGHZ 22, 90, 99.

16 BGHZ 20, 36, 41.

17 BGHZ 33, 293.

18 BGHZ 33, 303.

19 BGHZ 47, 217/18.

20 BGHZ 47, 217, 222.

21 BGHZ 43, 148, 153.

22 BGHZ 33, 295, 297.

23 Wiswede, a.a.O., S. 235 und S. 212: „. . . daß nämlich Individuen geringere Sorgfalt und Umsicht beim Kauf an den Tag legen, je ärmer sie sind. Je geringer das Einkommen ist, desto geringer ist der Einsatz geistiger Mittel“.

24 Wenn v. Brunn (in: Die formularmäßigen Vertragsbedingungen der deutschen Wirtschaft, 2. Aufl., 1956, S. 7) feststellt, daß bei der Masse der Verbraucher „ein großes Vertrauen gegenüber allem Gedruckten“ bestehe, sie sich der eigenen geschäftlichen Unerfahrenheit und rechtlichen Unkenntnis meist bewußt sei und sich darauf verlasse, „daß bei dem Verfasser gedruckter Bedingungen diese Mängel nicht vorhanden“ seien, so hält er ein Wunschbild für die Wirklichkeit. Diese Sichtweise erklärt wohl seine berufliche Position als Geschäftsführer des Verbandes der Automobilindustrie und der dadurch bedingten Parteilichkeit für die Belange der sich Allgemeiner Geschäftsbedingungen bedienenden Unternehmer. Vgl. hierzu vor allem R. Fischer, in: BB 1957, 482, 483 und Huhn, a.a.O., S. 197–198.

25 So vor allem Esser, in: Das Verhältnis von Kaufvertrag und Darlehensvertrag beim B-Geschäft des finanzierten Teilzahlungsgeschäfts, S. 87/88 und Thomas Raiser, in: RabelsZJG 33 (1969), S. 457, 471.

26 Vgl. Larenz, Schuld R II, S. 97, der hier zu Recht von einer richterlichen Korrektur eindeutiger vertraglicher Vereinbarungen spricht.

27 BGHZ 47, 217.

28 Vgl. hierzu die Schrift von Manfred Wolf, Entscheidungsfreiheit und vertraglicher Interessenausgleich, Tübingen 1970, S. 101 ff.

29 Vgl. Huhn, in: Emmerich u.a., Grundlagen des Vertrags- und Schuldrechts, 1972, S. 197.

30 Auf dieses Konformitätsproblem hat Spittler in seiner Arbeit „Norm und Sanktion“, Olten und Freiburg 1967, S. 30, aufmerksam gemacht. Er weist darauf hin, daß soziales Verhalten immer Leistungen impliziere, denen der Betroffene auszuweichen versucht, falls sie ihm unerträglich werden.

31 Bundestags-Drucksache, 7/986, S. 110.

32 Privatrechtsgeschichte der Neuzeit, 2. Aufl., 1967, S. 617.

33 So Luhmann, Rechtssoziologie, Bd II, 1973, S. 237: „Im übrigen ist richterliche Innovation selbst gegen das Gesetz möglich – aber doch vergleichsweise selten und daran gebunden, daß eine Zeitlang mit falschen Argumenten gearbeitet wird, bis die Neuerung eingeführt ist und als altes Recht dargestellt werden kann“.

34 Robert Fischer, Zur Methode revisionsrichterlicher Rechtsprechung auf dem Gebiet des Gesellschaftsrechts, in: Recht und Rechtsleben in der sozialen Demokratie, Festgabe für Otto Kunze, S. 95 ff., 98–100, 101.

35 Anm. 29, S. 199.

36 Götz, Zum Schweigen im rechtsgeschäftlichen Verkehr, 1968, S. 131.

37 Die Allgemeinen Geschäfts- und Lieferungsbedingungen, in: BB, 1957, 481, 482.

38 Vgl. Louis Schneider, The Role of the Category of Ignorance in Sociological Theory, in: American Sociological Review, Bd. 27, 1962, S. 492 ff., S. 503.

39 Wiswede, a.a.O.

40 S. Anm. 38, S. 504.

41 Pagendarm, Das finanzierte Abzahlungsgeschäft, in: WM IV, 1967, 434.

42 S. Anm. 41.

43 Vgl. hierzu insbesondere Manfred Rehbinder, Allgemeine Geschäftsbedingungen, in: Kritik 5, Recht im sozialen Rechtsstaat, S. 107 ff., 113–118.

44 Vgl. hierzu jüngstens Eith, Zum Schutzbedürfnis gegenüber Allgemeinen Geschäftsbedingungen, in NJW 1974, Nr. 1/2, S. 16 ff., 17, und Manfred Wolf, Vorschläge für eine gesetzliche Regelung der Allgemeinen Geschäftsbedingungen, in: JZ 1974, Nr. 2, S. 41, insbes. 44.

Helmut Pieper

Sachverständigengutachten und Urteilsfindung im Zivilprozeß – Vorbericht über eine empirische Untersuchung –

A.

I. Ausgangspunkte

Die im gerichtlichen Erkenntnisverfahren regelmäßig erforderliche Aufbereitung („Zurichtung") des entscheidungsrelevanten Tatsachenstoffes (1)* setzt oft spezielle Kenntnisse und Erfahrungen auf außerrechtlichen Gebieten voraus, so vor allem bei komplexen Sachverhalten und schwierigen Fragen naturwissenschaftlicher Art im Bereich von Technik und Medizin, aber etwa auch bei Problemen einer Bewertung oder Schätzung. Verfügen die – nur juristisch ausgebildeten – Richter nicht hinreichend über solche Kenntnisse und Erfahrungen, so benötigen sie die Hilfe von Sachverständigen (2). Diesen erwächst damit die Möglichkeit einer wesentlichen Einflußnahme auf die jeweilige „Wahrheitskonstruktion" und damit auf den Entscheidungsinhalt. Sachverständigengutachten können dabei – was namentlich einige spektakuläre Strafprozesse auch der Öffentlichkeit bewußt gemacht haben – eine für das betreffende Verfahren „entscheidende" Bedeutung erlangen. Das führt zu der Frage nach der Funktion des Sachverständigen in dem zur gerichtlichen Entscheidung führenden Erkenntnisprozeß. Diese Ausgangsfrage des hier vorzustellenden Forschungsvorhaben stellt sich unter verschiedenen Aspekten, und zwar – was nachfolgend nur skizziert werden soll – vor allem unter einem normativen, einem methodischen und einem faktischen Aspekt.

1. Die Mitwirkung von Sachverständigen im Prozeß ist zunächst von der konkreten Ausgestaltung durch das geltende Recht her zu sehen (normativer Aspekt). Die einzelnen Rechtsordnungen haben die Mitwirkung von Sachverständigen in unterschiedlicher Weise konzipiert (3). Das deutsche Prozeßrecht hat das – schriftliche bzw. mündliche – Sachverständigengutachten als Beweismittel geregelt und eng an den Zeugenbeweis angelehnt (4). Allerdings werden Sachverständige – anders als die Zeugen – nicht nur zwecks Feststellung streitiger Tatsachen zugezogen. Vielmehr besteht ihre Aufgabe auch und vor allem in der Mitteilung von Erfahrungswissen und meist auch in dessen Verknüpfung mit konkreten Tatsachen (5).
   Gerade hierbei aber handelt es sich um eine Aufgabe, die eigentlich dem Richter selbst obliegen würde, wenn er über das erforderliche Fachwissen verfügte. Der Sachverständige wird also nicht nur als Helfer bei der Aufbereitung des Tatsachenstoffes eingeschaltet, sondern übt damit insoweit, genau genommen, selbst richterliche Tätigkeit aus (6). Das wird besonders deutlich,

* Anmerkungen auf den Seiten 339 ff.

wenn es sich um die Vermittlung und Anwendung gesicherter wissenschaftlicher Erfahrungssätze handelt: Es ist heute anerkannt, daß diese auch die Rechtsprechung binden (7). Das aber bedeutet nichts anderes, als daß insoweit der sog. Grundsatz der freien richterlichen Beweiswürdigung (§ 286 ZPO; § 261 StPO) eingeschränkt ist. Die Funktionsbereiche von Richter und Sachverständigen überschneiden sich auch dann, wenn – vor allem bei Blankettnormen (Fahrlässigkeit, Zurechnungs- bzw. Deliktsfähigkeit) – die Grenze zwischen Erfahrungssätzen und den rechtlichen Obersätzen flüssig ist (8).

Auch wenn sich hiernach die Funktionen nicht scharf voneinander trennen lassen, so heißt das nach deutschem Recht keineswegs, daß die Sachverständigen – wenigstens soweit sie auf der „Ebene" richterlicher Beurteilung tätig werden – den gesetzlichen, die rechtsprechende Gewalt ausübenden Richtern (Art. 92 GG) zugerechnet werden (9). Gleichwohl kann nicht übersehen werden, daß der Sachverständige gegenüber den anderen „Beweismitteln" und insbes. dem Zeugen im Verhältnis zum Richter eine Sonderstellung einnimmt. Diese kommt nicht nur in der oft verwendeten Bezeichnung als „Richtergehilfe" (10) zum Ausdruck, sondern ist schon durch den Gesetzgeber selbst anerkannt worden, indem er anordnete, daß der Sachverständige aus denselben Gründen wie ein Richter abgelehnt werden kann (§ 406 Abs. 1 i.V.m. § 42 ZPO; § 74 i.V.m. § 24 StPO). Im übrigen aber wird diese Sonderstellung nicht weiter ausgeformt, sondern durch die beweisrechtliche Konzeption des geltenden Rechts eher verschleiert.

2. Die spezifische Aufgabenverteilung zwischen Richtern und Sachverständigen, die der gesetzlichen Konzeption zugrunde liegt, steht offenbar im Zusammenhang mit dem überkommenen Rechtsanwendungsmodell (methodischer Aspekt). Entsprechend der Stellung, die das Gesetz dem Sachverständigen zugewiesen hat, sehen Rechtslehre und Praxis dessen Aufgabe allein darin, daß er dem Richter – durch die Vermittlung von Fakten- und Erfahrungswissen – bei der Vorbereitung der Entscheidung „behilflich" ist, nicht aber auch in einer Beteiligung an der eigentlichen Entscheidung selbst. Diese Betrachtungsweise entspricht dem traditionellen Erklärungsmodell der Rechtsanwendung als der Subsumtion gegebener Tatsachen unter – freilich interpretierbare – Rechtsnormen (11). Dabei kann das Sachverständigengutachten praktisch nur der Tatsachenseite zugerechnet werden, sodaß es als bloßes Hilfsmittel bei der entscheidungsvorbereitenden Sachverhaltsfeststellung erscheint.

   Das Subsumtionsmodell hat durch die neuere Methodenlehre Korrekturen erfahren (12). Diese erlauben nicht nur eine theoretische Erklärung der aufgetretenen Schwierigkeiten bei der Interaktion zwischen Richtern und Sachverständigen, sondern können – empirische Belegbarkeit vorausgesetzt – Ausgangspunkt von Reformüberlegungen auch für den Sachverständigenbeweis werden. Insoweit läßt sich eine Aussage erst am Schluß der geplanten Untersuchung treffen.

   An dieser Stelle muß unter Verzicht auf eine detaillierte Methodendiskussion der Hinweis genügen, daß die Feststellung des entscheidungsrelevanten Sachverhalts nicht vollständig von den normativen Möglichkeiten seiner rechtlichen Bewältigung getrennt werden kann. Die Tatsachenarbeit des Richters ist also nicht ohne Vorgriff auf rechtliche Überlegungen und damit auf kognitive Teile der eigentlichen Entscheidung möglich (13). Die Trennung zwischen Tat- und Rechtsfrage kann in der herkömmlichen Reinheit nicht aufrecht erhalten bleiben. Bezieht man die Mitwirkung von Sachverständigen in diese relativierte Sicht von der Rechtsanwendung ein, so wird deutlich, daß der Sachverständige kaum für eine Entscheidung „brauchbare" Gutachten abgeben kann, wenn er nicht die normativen Aspekte des konkreten Falles mitbeachtet. Anderenfalls können sich, besonders bei komplizierten Sachverhalten, infolge eines Auseinanderfallens der Perspektive des Richters einerseits und des Sachverständigen andererseits Inkongruenzen ergeben, die vermutlich eine der wesentlichen Ursachen für die häufig beschworenen Kommunikationschwierigkeiten zwischen Richtern und Sachverständigen sind.

3. Die Stellung und Funktion des Sachverständigen im Prozeßgeschehen läßt sich schließlich nur dann adäquat erfassen, wenn auch die Faktoren einbezogen werden, die mit den konkreten Gegenständen und Bedingungen der Sachverständigentätigkeit selbst zusammenhängen (faktischer Aspekt).
   a) Infolge der wissenschaftlich-technischen, der wirtschaftlichen und sozialen Entwicklung haben sich in den letzten Jahrzehnten die verschiedenen Lebens- und Wissensbereiche zunehmend kompliziert (14). Zugleich mit einem starken Anschwellen des Wissenstoffes haben sich Fachsprachen herausgebildet und demgemäß weitgehende Spezialisierungen ergeben. Entsprechend sind die Richter, wenn es auf außerrechtliche Kenntnisse und Erfahrungen ankommt, häufig auf das Gutachten von Sachverständigen angewiesen.
   b) Die Abhängigkeit von den Sachverständigen wird noch dadurch verstärkt, daß die Richter selbst vorwiegend Experten für Rechtsfragen sind. Das hat seinen Grund auch darin, daß die bisherige Ausbildung – wie die Reformdiskussion im Hinblick auf eine stärkere Praxisintegration zeigt – fast ausschließlich die Arbeit mit der Norm in den Vordergrund gestellt hat. Ein wissenschaftlich-kritisches Training für die Deskription von Fakten und für die Rekonstruktion von Sachverhalten fehlt bisher weitgehend, was auch damit zusammenhängen dürfte, daß die Arbeit am Sachverhalt nicht so sehr als Bestandteil richterlicher Tätigkeit angesehen wird. Dies alles fällt umsomehr ins Gewicht, als die Auseinandersetzung mit spezifisch juristischen Fragen nur einen sehr begrenzten Teil der richterlichen Tätigkeit ausmacht.

Verknüpft man die vorstehenden angedeuteten Ausgangspositionen, so ergeben sich folgende Feststellungen: Die Richter, denen die Rechtsordnung die Entscheidungsgewalt übertragen hat, sind in vielen Fällen hinsichtlich des relevanten Fachwissens nur partiell kompetent. Wegen der oft komplizierten Materie – und vielfach auch einfach aus Mangel an Zeit zur Einarbeitung – sind sie oft nicht in der Lage, den Erfahrungs- und Sachkundevorsprung der Sachverständigen so weit aufzuholen, daß sie den Gutachteninhalt in vollem Umfang verstehen und überprüfen können. Dann aber wird die Entscheidung über Sachverhaltsfragen und damit auch über den Prozeß insgesamt letztlich durch die Sachverständigen als die zu „Hilfe" gerufenen Personen mit entsprechender fachlicher Kompetenz getroffen. In gleichem Maße erweist sich auch der Grundsatz der freien richterlichen Beweiswürdigung als zusätzlich eingeschränkt.

Schon das bisher Gesagte erlaubt zumindest die Hypothese, daß offenbar zahlreiche Prozesse faktisch durch Sachverständige entschieden werden und nicht durch die an sich dazu berufenen „gesetzlichen Richter". Zwischen dem noch heute maßgebenden normativen Bild, nämlich der gesetzlichen Konzeption des Sachverständigengutachtens als eines von mehreren Beweismitteln, und der Realität der Mitwirkung von Sachverständigen im Prozeß besteht mithin eine auffallende Diskrepanz. Die verschiedenen Gründe für dieses Phänomen, vor allem also das oft nicht zu beseitigende Gefälle von Wissen, Informationen und Erfahrungen, sind zugleich Ursache für vielfältige sonstige Schwierigkeiten der Interaktion und der Kommunikation zwischen Richtern und Sachverständigen. Nicht von ungefähr ist deshalb, wenn auch vor allem im Zusammenhang mit Fehlurteilen im Strafprozeß, von einer Krise des Sachverständigenbeweises gesprochen worden (15).

II. Anlaß und Verlauf des empirischen Vorhabens

1. Schwierigkeiten der dargestellten Art ergeben sich auch im Zivilprozeß. Dies wird nicht nur durch veröffentlichte Gerichtsentscheidungen und sonstige Informationen über einzelne Prozesse belegt, sondern entspricht insbesondere auch der Erfahrung der Industrie- und Handelskammern, denen die in § 36 GewO vorgesehene öffentliche Bestellung und Vereidigung von Personen obliegt, die als Sachverständige gewerbsmäßig tätig sind oder tätig werden wollen (16). Die Kammern sind deshalb zusammen mit ihrer zentralen Organisation, dem Deutschen Industrie- und Handelstag (DIHT), seit langem bemüht, bessere Voraussetzungen für die Tätigkeit von Sachverständigen und für ihr Zusammenwirken auch mit den Gerichten zu schaffen.
   Hinweise insbesondere von seiten der Industrie- und Handelskammer zu Köln auf zahlreiche offene Fragen (17) führten zunächst zu einer Bestandsaufnahme der veröffentlichten Judikatur und des vorhandenen Schrifttums (18). Schon in diesem Stadium wurde deutlich, daß sich für viele der auftretenden Probleme eine nähere Bestimmung und Klärung allein mit den herkömmlichen Mitteln der Dogmatik nicht erreichen läßt. Abgesehen von der grundsätzlichen Frage nach der Stellung des Sachverständigen im Prozeß gilt dies z.B. einmal für die Bedingungen und die Bedeutung der immer wieder beklagten Verständigungsschwierigkeiten und zum anderen für die Möglichkeiten einer Abhilfe sowie in Betracht kommende Alternativen, so etwa für die Berechtigung der Forderung, dem Sachverständigen einen Platz auf der Richterbank zuzuweisen, oder die Möglichkeiten einer Spezialisierung. Daraus ergab sich die Notwendigkeit einer Erschließung des zugänglichen empirischen Materials, also einer möglichst umfassenden Rechtstatsachenforschung.
   Soweit die Justiz und die bei ihr laufenden Verfahren bereits Gegenstand der Analyse vermittels Einsatzes von Methoden empirischer Sozialforschung gewesen sind, haben von den beteiligten Personen bisher die Richter das hauptsächliche Interesse gefunden (19). Dagegen stand im Bereich der Normen über die Tätigkeit von Sachverständigen und insbesondere über den Sachverständigenbeweis rechtstatsächliches Material bisher nur in sehr begrenztem Maße zur Verfügung. So ließen sich nicht einmal verläßliche Aussagen darüber treffen, welche quantitative Bedeutung der Sachverständigenbeweis hat. Deshalb ist es z.B. nicht mehr als eine Behauptung, wenn gesagt wird, in mehr als der Hälfte aller Zivilprozesse liege der Entscheidung ein Sachverständigengutachten zugrunde, und ebenso ist es nicht mehr als eine Vermutung, wenn man hört, die Anzahl der Prozesse mit Sachverständigenbeweis steige an. Teilweise geklärt ist lediglich durch die Untersuchung von Baumgärtel mit Mitarbei-

tern (20) die Frage, welcher Zusammenhang zwischen der Einschaltung von Sachverständigen und der Prozeßdauer besteht. Aber auch in dieser Hinsicht ist noch manches offengeblieben. Völlig ungeklärt jedoch ist wieder die fundamentale Frage, in welchen Fällen und in welchem Maß die Richter ein Gutachten inhaltlich nachvollziehen und überprüfen können und welche Bedeutung dies für die spezifische Funktion des Sachverständigen im Prozeß, für das Prinzip der freien Beweiswürdigung durch die Richter sowie für die jeweilige Entscheidung hat.

2. Aus diesen Gründen begann das unter Leitung des Verfassers stehende Seminar für Rechtswissenschaft der Technischen Universität Hannover im Jahre 1970 mit einer empirischen Untersuchung, die den Sachverständigenbeweis im Zivilprozeß als zentralen Gegenstand hat. Da nur beschränkte personelle und finanzielle Mittel zur Verfügung standen, mußte sich die Untersuchung im ersten Stadium verhältnismäßig enge Grenzen setzen. Die Vorüberlegungen in methodischer Hinsicht führten zu dem Entschluß, mit einer Umfrage bei Richtern zu beginnen, die Erfahrungen in Zivilsachen haben. Ausschlaggebend hierfür war die Überlegung, daß sich über eine Richterbefragung am leichtesten der Zugang zu dem Problemkreis auch des Sachverständigenbeweises finden läßt, aber zugleich auch die Notwendigkeit, die Einschätzung durch die Richter als die Träger der zentralen Rolle im Rechtsfindungsprozeß zu erfahren.
Aufgrund einer größeren Zahl von Arbeitshypothesen wurde ein Fragebogen von 20 teils geschlossenen und teils offenen Fragen entwickelt (21). Dieser wurde in einer ersten Stufe an 330 Richter mit Erfahrungen in Zivilsachen versandt, und zwar vor allem an Richter bei Landgerichten des Landes Niedersachsen, beim Oberlandesgericht Celle und außerdem – um ein Gebiet hinzuzunehmen, dessen Infrastruktur durch Industrie und Wirtschaft geprägt ist, – beim Landgericht Frankfurt/Main. Von etwa 330 versandten Fragebögen sind 142 ausgefüllt zurückgelangt, von denen jedoch nur 110 voll verwertbar waren. Die Ergebnisse dieser Untersuchungsphase wurden in einem längeren Zwischenbericht niedergelegt, von dessen Veröffentlichung allerdings abgesehen wurde (22). Da im Bundesgebiet als Zielgruppe etwa 6000 bis 7000 Richter in Betracht kamen, wäre bei einer Stichprobengröße von 3–4 % der Grundgesamtheit ein Rücklauf von etwa 180 bis 200 verwertbaren Fragebögen erforderlich gewesen (23). Deshalb wurden in einer zweiten Phase alle Land- und Oberlandesgerichte des Landes Nordrhein-Westfalen in die Untersuchung einbezogen. Es konnte erwartet werden, daß allein aus diesem Gebiet mehr als 180 verwertbare Fragebögen zu erhalten waren. Da dies jedoch nicht sicher war, mußte eine Vergleichbarkeit mit den in der ersten Phase ausgefüllten Fragebögen sichergestellt werden. Deshalb wurde dasselbe Fragebogenmuster verwendet, obwohl sich inzwischen gezeigt hatte, daß einige Fragen teilweise mißverstanden wurden und den Antwortkategorien teilweise die genügende Trennschärfe fehlte. Der Fragebogen wurde in der zweiten Phase an über 500 Richter gesandt, die nach Mitteilung der verschiedenen Präsidenten Erfahrungen in Zivilsachen hatten. Hiervon sind 269 Fragebögen – also über 50 % – zurückgelangt. Im gleichen Zeitraum wurden zusätzlich Fragebögen auch an die Mitglieder der damals etwa 35 Zivilkammern gesandt, die im Bundesgebiet nach dem „Stuttgarter Modell" arbeiten, also die sogen. Hauptverhandlung in Zivilsachen praktizieren (24). Für die Einbeziehung dieser Kammern in die Untersuchung war die Erwägung maßgebend, daß das durch sie geübte Verfahren in einigen wesentlichen Punkten

von der üblichen Praxis auch des Sachverständigenbeweises abweicht. 51 der bei solchen Kammern tätigen Richter haben verwertbare Fragebögen zurückgesandt, welche z.T. die zusammengefaßten Angaben mehrerer Kammermitglieder enthielten.

3. Bei den folgenden Ausführungen soll, da eine Veröffentlichung bisher nicht erfolgen konnte, die Darstellung verschiedener Ergebnisse der Umfrageaktion im Vordergrund stehen. Es braucht wohl kaum der Vorbehalt hinzugefügt zu werden, daß die durch die Befragung ermittelten Erkenntnisse noch nicht endgültig sein können. Da sich die Untersuchung bisher fast ausschließlich auf die Angaben von Richtern gestützt hat, muß auch mit der Möglichkeit, ja Wahrscheinlichkeit von Fehlerquellen subjektiver Art gerechnet werden. Die gegenwärtig in Vorbereitung befindliche Fortsetzung der Untersuchung (25) wird insofern auch eine Überprüfung der bisherigen Ergebnisse zum Ziel haben.

B.

Zu einigen Ergebnissen der Richterbefragung

I. Die Häufigkeit der Zuziehung von Sachverständigen

Da die Justizstatistiken in dieser Hinsicht keine Angaben enthalten, haben wir vorweg zu ermitteln versucht, wie es sich mit der Bedeutung des Sachverständigenbeweises in quantitativer Hinsicht verhält. Wir haben uns hier wie auch bei anderen Fragen mit geschätzten Zahlen begnügt, dürfen jedoch annehmen, daß diese einigermaßen zuverlässig sind. Eine Gegenkontrolle wurde nämlich vor allem dadurch ermöglicht, daß ein Teil der Richter sich die Mühe gemacht hat, die Akten bestimmter Zeiträume auszuzählen, wobei sich Werte ergeben haben, welche sich von den geschätzten Zahlen nicht stark entfernen. Aus diesem Bereich seien nachstehend wenigstens einige Informationen wiedergegeben.

1. Schon über den *durchschnittlichen Anteil* der Zivilsachen, in denen Beweis durch Sachverständige erhoben wird, gehen die Meinungen auseinander. Die manchmal zu findende Ansicht, daß bereits in mehr als der Hälfte aller gerichtlichen Verfahren Sachverständigengutachten eingeholt würden (26), ist durch die Antworten auf eine entsprechende Frage (27) nicht bestätigt worden. Die überwiegende Anzahl der Richter (70 % in Niedersachsen; mehr als 85 % in Nordrhein-Westfalen) hat vielmehr angegeben, daß bei ihnen der Anteil der Verfahren mit Sachverständigenbeweis unter 20 % liege. Die Einzelauswertung für Nordrhein-Westfalen ergab einen Mittelwert von ca. 14 % der Verfahren mit Sachverständigenbeweis. Um etwa 2 % niedriger lagen die Angaben der Richter, welche ihre Akten aus der letzten Zeit vor der Befragung ausgezählt haben, was sich aber mit Besonderheiten der Geschäftsverteilung erklären läßt. Auch bei den Hauptverhandlungskammern ergab sich für die auf Schätzungen und Zählungen beruhenden Angaben ein Mittelwert von ca. 13 %, wobei allerdings die Einzelnennungen wiederum zwischen 3 % und 30 % schwankten (28).
   Hiernach ist zwar der Anteil von Verfahren mit Sachverständigenbeweis nicht so hoch, wie bisher vielfach angenommen wurde. Jedoch bezieht sich diese Feststellung nur auf die Zahl der Verfahren insgesamt. Die einzelnen Verfahren können sich nun aber im Grad der rechtlichen und tatsächlichen Schwierigkeiten und vor allem im Umfang des Streitstoffes erheblich voneinander unterscheiden. Deshalb ist mit den ermittelten Werten noch nichts Endgültiges

über den Anteil der Prozesse mit Sachverständigenbeweis an der gesamten Spruchtätigkeit der Gerichte und damit auch über das Ausmaß, in dem Sachverständige Einfluß auf den Entscheidungsinhalt nehmen können, ausgesagt. In dieser Hinsicht bedarf es noch weiterer Feststellungen.

2. Da sich ein verhältnismäßig niedriger Anteil der Verfahren mit Sachverständigenbeweis ergeben hat, war von besonderem Interesse zu erfahren, ob in der letzten Zeit eine *Zunahme* solcher Verfahren festgestellt wurde (29). Vielfach wird aus der wissenschaftlich-technischen Entwicklung und der wachsenden Kompliziertheit der Verhältnisse im sozialen, wirtschaftlichen und technischen Bereich ohne weiteres geschlossen, daß sich der Anteil der Verfahren mit Sachverständigenbeweis entsprechend erhöht habe und weiter erhöhe. Während sich Sachverständige oft in diesem Sinn äußern, wird eine solche Annahme durch das Ergebnis der Umfrage zwar noch nicht generell widerlegt, aber auch nicht bestätigt. Mehr als die Hälfte, in Nordrhein-Westfalen sogar zwei Drittel aller Richter, haben angegeben, daß der Anteil der Verfahren mit Sachverständigenbeweis sich in den letzten Jahren nicht verändert habe, sondern konstant geblieben sei. Diese Angaben werden vor allem auch im Hinblick auf die verschiedenen Prozeßgegenstände und den Schwierigkeitsgrad der einzelnen Fälle noch überprüft werden müssen.

   Ein anderes Bild haben die Antworten der Richter ergeben, die Hauptverhandlungskammern angehören. Zwei Drittel von ihnen hat die Auffassung ausgesprochen, daß die Verfahren mit Sachverständigenbeweis in der letzten Zeit zugenommen haben. Auch diese Divergenz bedarf noch der Klärung. Es liegt die Vermutung nahe, daß ein Zusammenhang mit der besonderen Arbeitsweise dieser Kammern besteht. Denn zu ihr gehört die Übung, daß ein Sachverständiger bereits oft von Amts wegen zu der entsprechend vorbereiteten mündlichen Verhandlung zugezogen wird, was dazu führen dürfte, daß es öfter als im konventionellen Verfahren zu einem Sachverständigenbeweis kommt (30).

3. Von Interesse war weiterhin, wie sich die gerichtlichen Sachverständigengutachten auf die verschiedenen Sachgebiete verteilen (31). Es ergab sich, daß allein drei Sachgebiete nahezu 85 % der Verfahren mit Sachverständigenbeweis ausmachen, wobei den Hauptanteil mit fast 50 % das Bau- und Architektenwesen einnimmt, gefolgt von medizinischen Gutachten mit etwa 20 % und von Gutachten in Straßenverkehrs- und Kraftfahrzeugschadensangelegenheiten mit etwa 15 %. Daß der Anteil der letztgenannten Angelegenheiten nicht höher liegt, hat etwas überrascht und wird u.a. damit zu erklären sein, daß unter Mitwirkung der Versicherungen ein großer Teil von Verkehrsunfallfolgen außergerichtlich abgewickelt wird (32). Zwischen den einzelnen Landgerichtsbezirken haben sich in dieser Hinsicht übrigens erhebliche Unterschiede ergeben. Unabhängig davon kann jedoch schon heute als feststehend gelten, daß sich der größte Teil der Sachverständigengutachten auf den technischen Bereich – Bau-, Kraftfahrzeug- und Verkehrsangelegenheiten – und auf medizinische Sachverhalte bezieht.

II. *Die Zuziehung von Sachverständigen im Rahmen des einzelnen Verfahrens*

1. Die Einholung eines Sachverständigengutachtens hängt – anders als beim Zeugenbeweis – nicht von einer entsprechenden Initiative und insbesondere

nicht von dem Antrag einer Partei ab (§ 144 ZPO). Deshalb – und damit auch zwecks Klärung der Rolle des Sachverständigen allgemein – haben wir um Angabe darüber gebeten (33), wie groß der Anteil der Verfahren mit Sachverständigenbeweis war, in welchen ein Gutachten auf *Antrag* einer Partei oder *von Amts wegen* eingeholt worden ist. Hierzu hat in Niedersachsen, Frankfurt/Main und Nordrhein-Westfalen der größte Teil der Richter – nämlich über 90 % – angegeben, daß in 50 bis 90 % aller Fälle die Zuziehung von Sachverständigen auf Antrag erfolgt sei, wobei zwei Drittel dieses Kreises von Richtern sogar meinten, ein Sachverständigengutachten werde in weniger als 10 % der Fälle ohne Vorliegen eines Antrags eingeholt. Nur 5 % – in Niedersachsen sogar nur 3,6 % – der Richter haben angegeben, daß in mehr als der Hälfte der Fälle die Beauftragung von Sachverständigen ohne Antrag erfolgt sei. Anders stellt sich – erwartungsgemäß – das Bild dar, soweit es sich um Angehörige von Hauptverhandlungskammern handelt. Mehr als die Hälfte von ihnen hat angegeben, daß die Zuziehung eines Sachverständigen ohne Antrag in 10 bis 50 % der Fälle, also in weitergehendem Maße erfolge. Eine noch stärkere Abweichung zwischen den Hauptverhandlungskammern und den sonstigen Zivilkammern bzw. -senaten ergab sich übrigens bei einer Zusatzfrage (34), welche sich auf die Anwendung von § 272 b Abs. 2 Nr. 5 ZPO bezog, also auf die Möglichkeit der Beauftragung eines Sachverständigen bereits vor der ersten mündlichen Verhandlung. Während in Niedersachsen, Frankfurt/Main und Nordrhein-Westfalen etwa 75 % der Richter diese Möglichkeit nie praktiziert haben, hat etwa der gleiche Anteil der Angehörigen von Hauptverhandlungskammern angegeben, daß von der genannten Vorschrift in mehr als 90 % der Verfahren Gebrauch gemacht werde, wobei über 40 % der Richter sogar die Zahl von 100 % genannt haben.

Nun wird sicher dann, wenn es auf spezielle Fragen außerrechtlicher Art ankommt, oft die Einholung eines Sachverständigengutachtens auch beantragt oder doch angeregt worden sein (35). Gleichwohl zeigt sich nach dem bisherigen Ergebnis der Umfrage außerhalb der Hauptverhandlungskammern die Tendenz, daß Gutachten ohne entsprechenden Antrag und vor allem ohne vorherige mündliche Verhandlung nur selten eingeholt werden, und auch dann – und zwar ohne eine entsprechende gesetzliche Anordnung – im allgemeinen nur gegen Kostenvorschuß (36). Den für diese Praxis maßgebenden Gründen wird noch nachzugehen sein. Möglicherweise wollen Richter das Fehlen der erforderlichen Sachkunde nicht von sich aus hervorheben, zumal die Einholung eines Sachverständigengutachtens den Prozeß im allgemeinen verlängert (37). Wahrscheinlich wollen sie auch dem möglichen Vorwurf der unterliegenden und nach geltendem Recht mit den Kosten des Gutachtens belasteten Partei begegnen, das eingeholte Gutachten sei nicht erforderlich gewesen. Außerdem will man vielleicht auch vermeiden, daß im Ergebnis die Staatskasse mit den Gutachterkosten belastet wird, falls die später unterliegende Partei nicht in der Lage ist, die Gerichtskosten und insbesondere die Kosten eines Sachverständigengutachtens zu tragen.

Die Übung, daß Gutachten i.d.R. nur auf Antrag gegen Kostenvorschuß eingeholt werden, erweist sich übrigens gerade unter dem Gesichtspunkt als besonders problematisch, daß durch die Einholung eines Gutachtens das Prozeßkostenrisiko der unterliegenden Partei (38) wesentlich erhöht wird. Es könnte durchaus sein, daß finanziell schwache Parteien eher von einem solchen

Antrag absehen werden, insofern also in ihrer Rechtsverfolgung behindert sind. Hierauf wird zurückzukommen sein.

2. Wird – auf Antrag oder von Amts wegen – die Einholung eines Sachverständigengutachtens angeordnet, kommt gleich die Frage ins Spiel, ob und in welchem Maße dadurch die *Dauer* des betreffenden Prozesses insgesamt beeinflußt wird.

   a) Als feststehend darf bereits heute gelten, daß die Einholung eines (schriftlichen) Sachverständigengutachtens die Erledigung des Verfahrens verzögert (39). Ebenso offenkundig ist aber, daß eine solche Prozeßverzögerung verschiedene Gründe haben kann, welche durchaus nicht notwendig beim Gutachter liegen. Um zu klären, wie sich die Problematik vom Richter her ausnimmt, haben wir auch die Frage gestellt, in welchem Verhältnis der Zeitaufwand für die Erstattung eines Gutachtens zu der *Schwierigkeit* und dem *Umfang* der Aufgabe gestanden habe (40). Die Antworten lassen ein gewisses Unbehagen der Richter erkennen. Nur 25 bis 30 % von ihnen halten die Dauer der Gutachtenerstattung – stets bezogen auf Schwierigkeitsgrad und Umfang der Aufgabe – für angemessen, und immerhin 11 bis 15 % der Richter halten die Zeit für die Gutachtenerstattung sogar für zu lang. Nicht ganz so negativ war das Ergebnis bei den Hauptverhandlungskammern, wo jeweils mehr als 40 % der Richter erklärt haben, daß die Gutachten in angemessener bzw. tragbarer Zeit erstattet worden seien. Hierin dürfte sich ausdrücken, daß diese Kammern einen besseren Weg der Kooperation mit den Sachverständigen gefunden haben. In die gleiche Richtung zielt, daß auch andere Richter es wiederholt für wünschenswert erklärt haben, daß die Sachverständigen schon in der Anfangsphase des Prozesses und möglichst bereits bei der Vorbereitung des Beweisbeschlusses zugezogen werden sollten.

   b) Ergänzend ist nach den *Gründen* gefragt worden, die insbesondere zu *Verzögerungen* der Gutachtenerstattung (und damit der Verfahrensbeendigung) geführt haben (41). Der weitaus größte Anteil der Richter aus allen Gebieten hat als Hauptursache für die verspätete Fertigstellung der Gutachten die Überlastung der Sachverständigen bezeichnet. Bei den Angehörigen der Hauptverhandlungskammern galt dies allerdings nur in etwa 36 % der Fälle gegenüber z.B. fast 90 % der Fälle in Nordrhein-Westfalen. Dies dürfte damit zusammenhängen, daß zum Stuttgarter Modell das Streben nach einer rechtzeitigen und evtl. telefonischen Abstimmung mit dem in Aussicht genommenen Sachverständigen und dessen Teilnahme an der ersten mündlichen Verhandlung und der Verzicht auf ein vorheriges – ausführliches – schriftliches Gutachten gehört.

   Von den Richtern aus Niedersachsen, Frankfurt/Main und Nordrhein-Westfalen ist der Hinweis auf eine Überlastung der Sachverständigen als Verzögerungsgrund allerdings mehrfach dahingehend eingeschränkt worden, daß lediglich die guten Sachverständigen überfordert seien, weil sie in besonders weitgehendem Maße Aufträge erhielten. Vielfach ist auch die Annahme geäußert worden, daß die Erledigung der Gutachtenaufträge nicht selten deshalb so lange dauere, weil die Sachverständigen die Erstattung gerichtlicher Gutachten zugunsten privater Aufträge zurückstellten. Diese Vermutung hängt damit zusammen, daß die Höhe der den Sachverständigen zufließenden Vergütungen bzw. das geltende Vergügungssystem vielfach als unbefriedigend und nicht sachgemäß empfunden wird. In der Tat steht unverkennbar für einen großen Teil gerade der hauptberuflich tätigen Sachverständigen die erheblich besser honorierte Gutachtertätigkeit in privatem Auftrag ganz eindeutig im Vordergrund (42). Angesichts der wiederholt festgestellten Tendenz höher qualifizierter Sachverständiger, gerichtliche Aufträge, die sie als unzureichend und vor allem nicht leistungsgerecht honoriert ansehen, verzögerlich zu behandeln oder abzulehnen, haben nicht wenige Richter vorgeschlagen, daß durch eine entsprechende gesetzliche Regelung die Vorrangigkeit der Erstattung gerichtlicher Gutachten angeordnet werden sollte. Dieses Mittel dürfte jedoch kaum geeignet sein, um der geschilderten Entwicklung zu begegnen. Aber auch durch eine einfache (weitere) Anhebung der Honorarsätze für die Sachverständigentätigkeit, die wiederholt angeregt wurde, oder durch die sich wohl anbietende Umstellung des Vergütungssystems auf das Leistungsprinzip allein wird man nicht Abhilfe schaffen können. Dies ergibt sich z.B. schon daraus, daß bei geringerem Streitwert die Verhältnismäßigkeit der Kosten noch mehr als bereits jetzt in Frage gestellt würde, was mit dem Sozialstaatsprinzip kaum vereinbar wäre (43). Vielmehr müßte die Erwägung hinzutreten, ob es sich weiter rechtfertigt, das Kostenrisiko für die Sachverständigentätigkeit allein den Parteien aufzuerlegen, was – wie schon bemerkt – vor allem die wirtschaftlich schwächeren Parteien benachteiligt (44).

III. Die Qualität erstatteter Gutachten

Angesichts der Bedeutung, die einem Gutachten für Verlauf und Ausgang des betreffenden Prozesses zukommt, wäre es wichtig, Informationen darüber zu erhalten, ob Gutachten nach Form, Inhalt und vor allem Verständlichkeit im Rahmen des Möglichen ihren Zweck erfüllen oder ob sich in diesen Hinsichten öfter Beanstandungen ergeben. Die Antworten auf verschiedene Fragen, die in diesem Sinn die Qualität der erstatteten Gutachten im Verhältnis zu den jeweils gestellten Beweisfragen zum Gegenstand hatten (45), vermitteln zumindest auf den ersten Blick den Eindruck, daß die Richter mit den eingeholten Gutachten im wesentlichen zurechtkommen und mit ihnen zufrieden sind. Diese Zufriedenheit ist jedoch nicht ohne Einschränkungen.

1. Auf eine allgemein gestellte Frage über das *qualitative Verhältnis* der Gutachten zum Beweisbeschluß (46) haben in beiden Phasen der Umfrage mehr als 90 % der Richter die Beantwortung der Beweisfragen für i.d.R. erschöpfend oder doch wenigstens ausreichend erklärt. Nur 1 bis 3 % der Richter haben angegeben, die Gutachten seien in der Mehrzahl der Fälle nicht ausreichend gewesen; bei den Hauptverhandlungskammern fehlt sogar jede negative Nennung. Dieses Ergebnis mag z.T. darauf zurückzuführen sein, daß nur die Antwortkategorien „erschöpfend" – „ausreichend" – „nicht ausreichend" vorgesehen waren und die Fragestellung auch im übrigen nicht hinreichend differenziert hat. Gleichwohl läßt sich sagen, daß die Beantwortung in einem gewissen Widerspruch etwa zu der Tatsache steht, daß die Mehrzahl der antwortenden Richter in anderem Zusammenhang auf eine entsprechende Frage hin mehr oder weniger ausführliche Vorschläge für eine rationellere

Gestaltung des Verfahrens oder auch für die Änderung entsprechender Vorschriften der ZPO gemacht hat (47).

Unter diesen Umständen drängt sich die Frage auf, ob es nicht möglicherweise so ist, daß die Richter die mit dem Sachverständigenbeweis verbundene Problematik nicht erkennen können oder nicht erkennen wollen. Neben einer gewissen — natürlich nicht nur bei Richtern zu findenden — Betriebsblindheit wäre immerhin denkbar, daß die Richter es nicht wahrhaben wollen, wenn verschiedentlich gesagt wird, daß sie mit Sachverständigengutachten oft überfordert seien und diese im Grunde ungeprüft übernähmen. Insofern steht die Frage nach der Qualität der Gutachten mittelbar mit derjenigen nach der Nachvollziehbarkeit des Gutachteninhalts durch die Richter in Zusammenhang (48).

2. Ein Hinweis darauf, daß die Richter möglicherweise die Problematik des Sachverständigenbeweises — bewußt oder unbewußt — herunterzuspielen suchen, läßt sich auch aus der Beantwortung einer zusätzlich gestellten Frage nach der Häufigkeit von *Nachtragsgutachten* entnehmen (49). Während gut die Hälfte der Richter angegeben hat, daß die Beweisfragen erschöpfend beantwortet würden, haben 5 % von ihnen angegeben, daß in 3 bis 30 % der Fälle Nachtragsgutachten eingeholt würden, und ein weiteres Drittel hat darüber hinaus mitgeteilt, Nachtragsgutachten seien in 20 bis 50 % aller Fälle erforderlich. Nachtragsgutachten werden aber ebenso wie weitere Gutachten eines anderen Sachverständigen bzw. Obergutachten i.d.R. dann eingeholt werden, wenn das Beweisthema als nicht ausreichend geklärt angesehen wird. Welche Gründe hierfür im einzelnen maßgebend sind und in welchem Maß sich etwa auswirkt, daß die Prozeßpartei, zu deren Ungunsten das Gutachten ausgefallen ist, dessen Richtigkeit in Frage gestellt hat, ist noch näher zu klären.

IV. Die Einwirkung der Gutachten auf den Entscheidungsinhalt

1. Die außerrechtlichen Fragen, von deren Beantwortung der Ausgang des Prozesses abhängen kann und für die Sachverständigengutachten eingeholt werden, können äußerst kompliziert und schwierig sein. Dann muß sich stets die Frage ergeben, ob bei den zur Entscheidung berufenen Richtern das für die jeweilige Spezialmaterie erforderliche *Beurteilungsvermögen* einschließlich der dazu notwendigen Erfahrungen vorhanden ist oder ob es ihnen wenigstens durch Sachverständigengutachten verschafft wird. Denn an sich könnte nur dann von einer ausreichenden inhaltlichen Überprüfung im Sinn des Prinzips der freien Beweiswürdigung (50) gesprochen werden. Daher war notwendigerweise auch die Frage zu stellen, wie oft die inhaltliche Überprüfung eines Gutachtens auf Schwierigkeiten gestoßen ist (51). Die hier angesprochene *Nachvollziehbarkeit* der Gutachten steht, wie schon angedeutet, in enger Wechselwirkung mit den Fragen nach der Qualität der Gutachten, wenn es hierbei auch nicht primär um Verständlichkeit des lege artis erstatteten Gutachtens an sich geht, sondern — um es einmal so auszudrücken — um das Verstehenkönnen auf seiten der Richter. Wohl schon wegen des erwähnten Zusammenhangs sind die Antworten hier ähnlich ausgefallen wie bei der Frage nach der (subjektiv) zufriedenstellenden Erledigung der Beweisthemen und einer weiteren Frage nach der Häufigkeit der Abweichungen vom Beweisbeschluß (52). In beiden Phasen der Untersuchung

haben jeweils nur 2 % der befragten Richter angegeben, daß die inhaltliche Überprüfung eines Gutachtens im Wege der freien Beweiswürdigung häufig auf Schwierigkeiten gestoßen sei. 77 bzw. 85 % der Richter haben dagegen mitgeteilt, daß sie bei dem Nachvollzug des Gutachteninhalts nur selten Schwierigkeiten gehabt hätten.

Sollten diese Angaben zutreffen, so würde der Sachverständigenbeweis auch hinsichtlich des Grundsatzes der freien Beweiswürdigung weitaus weniger Probleme bieten als vielfach angenommen wird. Dann wäre auch wohl – jedenfalls für den Zivilprozeß – das Schlagwort von der „Krise des Sachverständigenbeweises" widerlegt, und man könnte allenfalls sagen, daß es sich um eine Krise der Kunst der Beweisaufnahme insgesamt handele. Indessen wird man sich mit den vorstehend dargestellten Angaben kaum zufriedengeben dürfen. Es muß nämlich bezweifelt werden, ob die Richter bei komplizierten Fragen aus den verschiedensten Wissensgebieten stets oder auch nur in der Mehrzahl der Fälle in der Lage sind, dem Gedankengang eines Gutachtens in jeder Hinsicht zu folgen und die Richtigkeit der darin enthaltenen Schlüsse zu prüfen. Vielmehr spricht einiges dafür, daß sich die Überprüfung der Gutachten neben der Würdigung formaler Gesichtspunkte oft auf Seriositätsindizien wie etwa das Ansehen des Sachverständigen beschränkt (53). Die „Arbeitsteilung" zwischen Richtern und Sachverständigen hat sich möglicherweise seit langem in der Weise eingefahren, daß die mangelnde Beurteilungsmöglichkeit durch die Richter nicht mehr reflektiert wird und daß es deswegen an einem ausreichendem Problembewußtsein fehlt.

2. Nach dem Gesagten bedarf es näherer Untersuchung, inwieweit Richter in der Lage sind, den Erfahrungs- und Informationsvorsprung der Sachverständigen einzuholen und sich in hinreichend freier Beweiswürdigung ein eigenes Urteil zu bilden. Daß in dieser Hinsicht Skepsis geboten ist, findet eine Bestätigung wiederum in den Fragebögen selbst. Auf eine zusätzliche Frage, welche *Schwierigkeiten* bei Verfahren mit Sachverständigenbeweis vorwiegend aufgetreten seien (54), sind nämlich allein in Nordrhein-Westfalen bei einem Rücklauf von 269 verwertbaren Fragebögen 256 Nennungen erfolgt. Wenn es auch Mehrfachnennungen gab, kann doch insgesamt nicht verkannt werden, daß etwa die Hälfte aller Richter Ursachen für Schwierigkeiten beim Nachvollzug der Sachverständigengutachten angegeben hat, welche zunächst auf eine entsprechende Frage hin negiert worden waren. In Nordrhein-Westfalen sind es immerhin 66 Richter gewesen, die eingeräumt haben, daß ihr eigenes außerrechtliches Fachwissen nicht ausreiche, um Gutachten immer zu verstehen und nachzuvollziehen. 31 von ihnen haben als Ursache hierfür fachspezifische Ausdrucksweise der Sachverständigen und auch sonstige Gründe angegeben, die primär der „Sphäre" der Sachverständigen zuzurechnen sind, aber eher auf Unrichtigkeit bzw. Unvollständigkeit der Gutachten abstellen (z.B. mangelnde Kontrollmöglichkeiten; pauschale Behauptungen; fehlende Begründungen; unklare und widersprüchliche Ausdrucksweise; Gedankenfehler; nicht überzeugende Schlußfolgerungen; Verwendung nicht eindeutiger tatsächlicher Feststellungen). Der überwiegende Teil der Richter indessen sieht die Ursachen für aufgetretene Schwierigkeiten bei der Überprüfung des Gutachteninhalts nicht in den Gutachten selbst oder in der Person der Sachverständigen, sondern in der unzureichenden eigenen Beurteilungskompetenz. So ist wiederholt hervorgehoben worden, daß gerade auf dem Gebiet des Bau- und Architektenwesens auf unbekannte

Normen verwiesen werde, Gutachten mit komplizierten Fachausdrücken angereichert seien und insgesamt bei den Richtern zu viel Fachkenntnisse vorausgesetzt würden. Aufgrund der schwierigen physikalischen, chemischen oder sonstigen technischen Vorgänge auf diesem Gebiet können die Gutachten nach Meinung mancher Richter schlechterdings überhaupt nicht überprüft werden. Nichts anderes bedeutet es übrigens, wenn unlängst im Zusammenhang mit einem Prozeß, in welchem es auf komplizierte Bewertungsfragen ankam, der zuständige Richter gemäß Presseberichten geäußert hat, die Feststellungen der Gutachter seien eigentlich „injustiziabel" (55).

3. Die Gründe dafür, daß die inhaltliche Überprüfung der Gutachten jedenfalls nicht immer ohne weiteres möglich ist, sind – wie schon bemerkt – z.T. bei den Sachverständigen zu suchen. Soweit sich deshalb die von den Richtern erbetenen *Verbesserungsvorschläge* (56) mit der Person des Sachverständigen beschäftigen, werden vor allem schon bekannte Forderungen nach einer besseren Auswahl, Überwachung und rechtskundlichen Ausbildung wiederholt. Im Vordergrund der Antworten stehen jedoch Kommunikationsprobleme, welche mit dem Fehlen spezieller Erfahrungen und Kenntnisse über entscheidungsrelevante Fachprobleme zusammenhängen. Um in dieser Hinsicht möglichst Wandel zu schaffen, ist bekanntlich schon öfters angeregt worden, nach dem Vorbild etwa der Kammern für Handelssachen Spezialkammern und Spezialsenate zu schaffen. Eine *Spezialisierung* auch nach außerrechtlichen Kriterien findet sich bisher nur auf einzelnen Gebieten, und zwar vor allem bei den Gerichten höherer Instanzen. Für ihre Ausdehnung auch auf die Eingangsgerichte könnte u.a. sprechen, daß die betreffenden Richter sich mit einem bestimmten Sachgebiet besonders vertraut machen können, was der Zusammenarbeit mit den Sachverständigen zugute kommen müßte.

Wir haben versucht, die allgemeine Haltung der Richter auch zu diesem Problem zu ermitteln (57). Etwa 30 % von ihnen haben diese Frage unbeantwortet gelassen. In Ermangelung abweichender Anhaltspunkte wird davon auszugehen sein, daß sie entweder unentschieden sind oder der Bildung von Spezialkammern bzw. -senaten negativ gegenüberstehen. Von 216 Richtern, die in Nordrhein-Westfalen die Frage beantwortet haben, hat sich im übrigen fast die Hälfte gegen jede Spezialisierung ausgesprochen. Folgende hierfür angegebene Gründe seien erwähnt: Die Spezialisierung sei auf die Dauer unbefriedigend und unzumutbar; sie stempele den Richter zum „Fachidioten"; einseitig spezialisierte Richter seien für die Justiz nicht brauchbar; eine Spezialisierung sei auch nicht erforderlich, da der Richter sich einarbeiten könne (58).

Die andere Hälfte der Richter hat sich indessen grundsätzlich positiv zu der Einführung von Spezialkammern und -senaten geäußert und erwartet offenbar hiervon Vorteile für die Einbringung von außerrechtlichem Fachwissen in die betreffenden Prozesse und den Abbau von Kommunikationsschranken. Wer aber einer solchen Tendenz folgt, gibt auch dadurch zu erkennen, daß bisher mit dem Zusammenwirken von Richtern und Sachverständigen Schwierigkeiten verbunden waren, welche auf diesem Weg vielleicht behoben oder doch vermindert werden könnten.

Interessant ist allerdings ein Vergleich mit den Hauptverhandlungskammern. Bei ihnen haben sich weniger als 25 % der Richter für eine Spezialisierung ausgesprochen. Dies könnte den Schluß zulassen, daß zwischen der Zuziehung der Sachverständigen zur mündlichen Verhandlung und der Einstellung der Richter zur Bildung von Spezialkammern ein Zusammenhang besteht. Anders ausgedrückt kann man vielleicht sagen: Je häufiger und je rascher die Sachverständigen zur mündlichen Verhandlung zugezogen werden, um so weniger sehen die Richter eine Notwendigkeit für die Einrichtung von Spezialkammern oder -senaten. Allerdings ist auch nicht auszuschließen, daß sich bei dieser Beantwortung das Engagement für das praktizierte neue Verfahren ausgewirkt hat.

Nähere Aufschlüsse wird auch in diesen Hinsichten erst die weitere Untersuchung geben können. Schon jetzt läßt sich sagen, daß – wenn überhaupt – durchweg lediglich eine Spezialisierung für Bau- und Architektenwesen sowie zum anderen für Verkehrs- und Kraftfahrzeugsachen empfohlen wird, wobei es sich allerdings um den größten Anteil der Prozesse mit Sachverständigenbeweis handelt (59). Da Kammern und Senate dieser Art bei verschiedenen Landgerichten und vor allem Oberlandesgerichten bereits eingeführt sind, sollte es möglich sein, in absehbarer Zeit die dort gemachten Erfahrungen in die weitere Untersuchung einzubeziehen.

C.

Die Darstellung einiger Ergebnisse der ersten Phase unseres empirischen Vorhabens mußte fragmentarisch bleiben. Jedoch dürfte schon hierdurch deutlich geworden sein, daß noch viele Einzelfragen der weiteren Klärung bedürfen. Nachdem die Stiftung Volkswagenwerk ihre Förderung zugesagt hat, soll deshalb die empirische Untersuchung so bald wie möglich in erweitertem Rahmen forgesetzt werden, wobei eine ständige Zusammenarbeit insbesondere mit Soziologen beabsichtigt ist. Zum weiteren Verlauf des Projekts kann unter Weglassen von Einzelheiten schon jetzt gesagt werden:

1. Für den theoretischen Bezugsrahmen des Projekts kann auf Kategorien der Entscheidungstheorie zurückgegriffen werden (60). Gerade die Zuordnung zu verschiedenen Phasen, die sich weitgehend aufgrund des formellen Verfahrensprogramms innerhalb eines Prozesses und insbesondere bei der Zuziehung von Sachverständigen ergeben, gestattet hierbei eine Analyse der vielfältigen Problematik. Solche Phasen lassen sich, wenn allein der innerprozessuale Ablauf ins Auge gefaßt wird, etwa wie folgt unterscheiden:

   a) Entscheidung über die Einholung eines Sachverständigengutachtens
   b) Auswahl des mit der Erstattung zu beauftragenden Sachverständigen einschließlich des Einholens von Informationen über Personen, die für die Erstattung eines Gutachtens in Frage kommen
   c) Erteilung des Auftrags an den Sachverständigen und Formulierung des Beweisbeschlusses
   d) Vorbereitung und Erstattung des Gutachtens; Kooperation zwischen Gericht und Sachverständigem z.B. durch Erläuterung des Auftrags, Angabe von Anknüpfungstatsachen und sonstige Anleitung
   e) Mündliche Erläuterung und/oder Ergänzung des Gutachtens
   f) Verwertung des Gutachtens im Prozeß und Einwirkung auf den Entscheidungsinhalt.

2. Innerhalb des zu wählenden Bezugsrahmens sind – anhand des bisherigen Auswertungsergebnisses – die der Untersuchung zugrunde liegenden Hypothesen zu überprüfen, weiter zu entwickeln und schließlich erneut zu operationalisieren. Ebenso bedarf es einer weiteren Konkretisierung der Untersuchungsziele. Diese lassen sich – wobei auf die bisherigen Ausführungen Bezug genommen werden kann – einstweilen durch folgende Stichworte umschreiben:
   a) Bestimmung der dem Sachverständigen im Prozeß zufallenden Aufgaben und der durch ihn ausgeübten genauen Funktion; auch Überprüfung des Ausmaßes, in dem Sachverständige auf Prozeßablauf und Entscheidungsinhalt Einfluß nehmen. Die Schwerpunkte werden hierbei bei der Entscheidung über die Zuziehung und bei der Frage des Einflusses auf den Entscheidungsinhalt liegen müssen.
   b) Feststellung informeller Einflüsse und die Art ihrer Einwirkung auf das Entscheidungsprogramm. Inwiefern sich solche Einflüsse feststellen lassen, steht allerdings dahin.
   c) Klärung der Gründe, die im einzelnen für Verständigungsschwierigkeiten maßgebend sein können, und Prüfung der Möglichkeiten eines Abbaues solcher Schwierigkeiten.
   d) Mögliche Folgerungen für eine verbesserte Zusammenarbeit der professionell oder nur gelegentlich am Erkenntnisprozeß Beteiligten, insbesondere der Richter, Anwälte und Sachverständigen. Hierher gehört auch die Frage, welche Anforderungen an die Ausbildung gestellt werden müssen und welche Konsequenzen sich für eine Weiterbildung ergeben.
   e) Untersuchung der Frage, ob durch zusätzliche Spezialisierung (Bildung von Spezialkammern und -senaten) oder durch die zusätzliche Einbeziehung von Nichtjuristen in das Erkenntnisverfahren (Modell: Kammern für Handelssachen) Verbesserungen möglich sind.
   f) Untersuchung der Frage, welches Gewicht die Diskrepanz zwischen gesetzlicher Konzeption der Mitwirkung von Sachverständigen und tatsächlicher Funktionsverteilung hat und welche Veränderungen demgemäß für die heutige Praxis bzw. das geltende Recht zu fordern sind.
3. Was die künftigen Untersuchungsmethoden angeht, kommen standardisierte Fragebögen nicht mehr in Betracht, weil dadurch z.B. genügend differenzierte Angaben über die Qualität von Gutachten oder den dem Richter verbliebenen Spielraum nicht erlangt werden können. Im Mittelpunkt des Vorhabens wird vielmehr die Auswertung von gerichtlichen Akten insbesondere über Verfahren mit Sachverständigenbeweis stehen müssen. Mit dieser Erhebungstechnik sind allerdings weitere Methoden zu kombinieren. Nachdem bisher die richterliche Sicht bestimmend war, muß nunmehr auch ermittelt werden, wie sich die gesamte Interaktionsproblematik auch in den Augen der anderen beteiligten Personen ausnimmt. Zu der Aktenauswertung sollen daher Interviews nicht nur mit den Richtern, sondern auch mit Parteien, Parteivertretern und vor allem mit den Sachverständigen selbst treten.
   Die Kriterien der für die Aktenauswertung zu ziehenden Stichprobe sind noch festzulegen. Einiges spricht dafür, daß zum Untersuchungsgegenstand nicht Akten gemacht werden, die schon längere Zeit abgelegt worden sind, sondern solche über erst kürzlich abgeschlossene oder gar noch laufende Verfahren. Nur dann nämlich werden – insbesondere durch entsprechende Befragungen –

zusätzliche Informationen von genügender Verläßlichkeit zu erlangen sein. Dies aber erscheint notwendig, da die Gerichtsakten das Resultat vielfältiger Selektionsmechanismen sind und deshalb kein vollständiges Bild des Verfahrensablaufs vermitteln. Auch aus diesem Grund ist die Aktenauswertung durch Interviews mit den am Verfahren beteiligten bzw. beteiligt gewesenen Richtern, Parteien, Rechtsanwälten und Sachverständigen zu ergänzen. Um eine weitgehende Objektivierung zu erreichen, werden unter Umständen noch weitere Methoden wie z.B. teilnehmende Beobachtungen anzuwenden sein.

Fragebogen zum Sachverständigenbeweis
(Zivilprozeß)

Bemerkungen zur Ausfüllung:
Bitte jeweils Zutreffendes ankreuzen oder unterstreichen. Zahlenangaben in Prozent- oder absoluten Zahlen machen; möglichst beides. Bei absoluten Zahlen Bezugsgröße angeben. Geschätzte Zahlen durch Zusatz von „g." kennzeichnen. Bei sonstigen Antworten genügen Stichworte. Ergänzende Bemerkungen und die Mitteilung von sonstigen Beobachtungen wären jedoch sehr erwünscht. Bei Frage 20 ist hierfür besonders Raum vorgesehen; im übrigen bitte evtl. besondere Blätter verwenden.

1. In welchem Gerichtszweig (Gerichtsbarkeit, Instanz) sind Sie tätig? ....
2. Fungieren Sie als
   Vorsitzender einer Kammer – eines Senats? ☐
   Beisitzer einer Kammer – eines Senats? ☐
   Einzelrichter (Amtsgericht)? ☐
3. Wieviel Jahre sind Sie bisher als Richter tätig gewesen? ....
   Davon in Zivilsachen? ....
4. Wie groß war in letzter Zeit (im Zeitraum ....) in Ihrem(r) Dezernat – Kammer – Senat der durchschnittliche Anteil der Zivilsachen, in denen Beweis durch Sachverständige erhoben worden ist? ☐ %
5. Wie verteilten sich die von Ihnen eingeholten Sachverständigengutachten in der letzten Zeit – im Jahr 1969 – im Zeitraum .... auf die einzelnen Sachgebiete?
   Bau- und Architektenwesen? ☐ %
   Medizin (einschl. Blutgruppengutachten, erbbiologische und psychiatrische Gutachten)? ☐ %
   Straßenverkehrs- und Kraftfahrzeugwesen? ☐ %
   Buchprüfung? ☐ %
   sonstige Sachgebiete (bitte evtl. im einzelnen angeben)?
6. Hat sich der Anteil der Verfahren mit Sachverständigenbeweis in den letzten Jahren erhöht? ja ☐ nein ☐
   Besondere Beobachtungen hierzu? ....
   ....

7. Wie groß war der Anteil der Verfahren mit Sachverständigenbeweis, in welchen die Einholung eines Gutachtens (Anordnung einer Begutachtung) erfolgte auf Antrag einer Partei? [%]
von Amts wegen? [%]

In wievielen dieser Fälle wurde eine Begutachtung (zunächst) ohne Beweisbeschluß nach § 272 b II Nr. 5 ZPO angeordnet? [%]

8. In welchem Umfang wählten Sie die Sachverständigen aus auf Grund
veröffentlichter Verzeichnisse? [%]
Auskunft der Industrie- und Handelskammer? [%]
Auskunft anderer Institutionen (z.B. Handwerkskammer)? [%]
Benennung durch Parteien? [%]
sonstiger Informationen? [%]

Besondere Bemerkungen hierzu? ....

....

9. Wie wurden die gestellten Beweisfragen in der Regel beantwortet?
erschöpfend [ ]
ausreichend [ ]
nicht ausreichend [ ]

Wie groß ist der Anteil der Verfahren mit Sachverständigenbeweis, in welchen die Einholung eines Nachtragsgutachtens notwendig wurde? [%]

10. Auf welchen Sachgebieten haben sich hinsichtlich der Beantwortung der Beweisfragen öfters Beanstandungen ergeben?

....

....

11. Wie häufig kommt es vor, daß Sachverständige das Beweisthema in einem vom Wortlaut abweichenden Sinn interpretieren?
oft [ ]
mittel [ ]
selten [ ]

In welchen Fällen insbesondere? ....

....

12. Wie häufig kommt es vor, daß die Sachverständigen versuchen, Rechtsfragen (mit-) zu entscheiden?
oft [ ]
mittel [ ]
selten [ ]

In welchen Fällen insbesondere? ....

....

13. Wie häufig haben sich hinsichtlich der Pflicht zur *persönlichen* Erstattung des Gutachtens (Einschaltung von Hilfskräften) Beanstandungen ergeben?
oft [ ]
mittel [ ]
selten [ ]

Welcher Art waren diese Beanstandungen? ....

....

....

14. In welchem Verhältnis stand der Zeitaufwand für die Erstattung des Gutachtens im Verhältnis zu der Schwierigkeit und dem Umfang der Aufgabe?
angemessen [ ]
tragbar [ ]
unangemessen [ ]

Welche Gründe haben insbesondere zu Verzögerungen der Gutachtenerstattung (und damit der Verfahrensbeendigung) geführt?

....

15. Wie groß war der Anteil der Verfahren mit Sachverständigenbeweis, in denen
der Sachverständige zur mündlichen Verhandlung zugezogen wurde? | | % |
das persönliche Erscheinen des Sachverständigen zwecks mündlicher Erläuterung eines schriftlichen Gutachtens angeordnet wurde? | | % |

16. Wie groß war der Anteil der Verfahren mit Sachverständigenbeweis, in denen eine Begutachtung durch einen weiteren Sachverständigen („Obergutachter") angeordnet wurde? | | % |

17. Wie oft stieß die inhaltliche Überprüfung (Nachvollziehbarkeit) eines Gutachtens im Wege der freien Beweiswürdigung auf Schwierigkeiten?
häufig ☐
mittel ☐
selten ☐
Aus welchen Gründen? ....
....
Auf welchen Sachgebieten ergaben sich solche Schwierigkeiten besonders häufig? Gründe hierfür? ....
....
....

18. Wie groß war der Anteil der Verfahren mit Sachverständigenbeweis, in denen die gerichtliche Entscheidung von dem Ergebnis eines Sachverständigengutachtens abgewichen ist? | | % |
Wie groß war der Anteil dieser Fälle, in welchen die abweichende Entscheidung ergangen ist
in Übereinstimmung mit – einem – weiteren Gutachten? | | % |
ohne Einholung eines weiteren Gutachtens? | | % |

19. Würden Sie sich dafür aussprechen, daß die Entscheidung auf besonderen Sachgebieten (z.B. Bausachen) einzelnen Kammern – Senaten – übertragen wird?
Wenn ja: Für welche Sachgebiete? ....
....

20. Welche sonstigen *Beobachtungen* haben Sie im Zusammenwirken mit Sachverständigen gemacht? Welche *Vorschläge* für eine rationellere Gestaltung des Verfahrens oder auch für die Änderung entsprechender Vorschriften der ZPO möchten Sie machten?

Name, Anschrift ....
....

Falls Sie den Fragebogen ohne Nennung des Namens abzugeben wünschen, bitte möglichst noch folgende Angabe machen: Befindet sich ihr Gericht in einer
Großstadt (über 100.000 Einw.)? ☐
Mittelstadt (30.000 – 100.000 Einw.)? ☐
Kleinstadt (bis 30.000 Einw.)? ☐

Summary

The "conversion" of factual material, during judicial proceedings, often presupposes special cognitions and experiences of an extra-legal sort. These are not available, or not sufficiently available, to professional judges, who are solely educated in legal materials. Thus the use of experts becomes necessary; and these often gain a decisive influence on the decision. The evidence of experts, according to German law, is simply one means of proof among others. But their specific task is to draw conclusions out of empirical propositons by virtue of their special competence. This means that the experts enter the functional domain of the judge and in a sense exercise judicial functions. Practically speaking, decision-making competence may be shifted entirely to the experts, especially when the case depends on empirical propositions, and the judge cannot close the gap between his own competence and the advantages of the experts.

Interaction between judge and experts creates many problems. This is not merely a matter of the difficulties of grasping expert evidence, but the problem of specifying the proper role of the expert at the trial. Traditional legal techniques cannot answer this question. It requires investigation of the actual situation. The author and co-workers have planned research into the role of experts, beginning with a questionnaire addressed to over 800 judges. The following are some provisional results: The percentage of trials that use experts has apparently not increased in recent years. Judges rarely call an expert except when a party demands one. Judges feel that difficulties in working with the experts and in evaluating his evidence rarely occur. Judges almost uniformly reject the idea of expanding the principle of participation of lay judges ("experts on the bench"). However, the idea that panels of judges might specialize in extra-legal areas seems to be gaining a hearing.

The study, within a framework oriented toward decision theory, will continue with an analysis of trials still in process or recently closed. We will try to investigate the whole interaction problem, as it appears in the eyes of participants. We shall interview not only judges but also parties, party representatives, and above all experts themselves. We attach particular importance to the question, whether we can establish to which degree there are informal influences on decisions. When the project is completed we shall address ourselves to the question of the need for procedural and substantial reform.

Anmerkungen

1 Dieser Vorgang steht in enger Wechselwirkung mit der sich parallel vollziehenden Zurichtung der Normseite, wie die neuere Methodenlehre in Abkehr vom herkömmlichen Subsumtionsmodell gezeigt hat. S. unten S. 340 zu Fn. 11 u. 12.

2 Eines entsprechenden Antrages der Parteien bedarf es nicht. Das Gericht entscheidet über die Zuziehung nach pflichtgemäßem Ermessen. S. dazu Stein-Jonas-Schumann/Leipold, Kommentar zur ZPO, 19. Aufl. 1972, Vorbem. zu § 402 III 2 mit Nachw.

3 Vgl. dazu die Berichte in L'expertise dans les principeaux systèmes juridiques d'Europe, Travaux et Recherches de l'Institut de droit comparé de Paris, Vol. XXXII, Paris 1969.

4 Im einzelnen hierzu Pieper, Richter und Sachverständiger im Zivilprozeßrecht, ZZP, Bd. 84 (1971) S. 3 ff., 30 ff. mit Nachw.; s. auch R. Bruns, Zur Systematik der gesetzlichen Beweisarten im Zivilprozeß, JZ 1957 S. 489.

5 S. dazu z.B. Rosenberg-Schwab, Zivilprozeßrecht, 11. Aufl. 1974, S. 648 (§ 124 I); auch Jessnitzer, Der gerichtliche Sachverständige, 4. Aufl. 1973, S. 1 ff. und Pieper a.a.O. S. 8 ff.

6 Vgl. dazu Pieper a.a.O. S. 30 f., 39 mit Nachw. und neuerdings etwa auch Kruchen, Der gerichtliche Sachverständige als Organ der Zivilrechtspflege, Diss. Frankfurt 1973, S. 39 ff., 65 f., 139 f., 170. – Rechtsprechung und Lehre gehen weiter von zwei grundsätzlich getrennten Funktionsbereichen aus, obwohl anerkannt wird, daß solche Überschneidungen bestehen und die Richter bei schwierigen Fragen zu einer Überprüfung des Gutachtens nicht in der Lage sind. Vgl. Stein-Jonas-Schumann/Leipold Vorbem. III 1 zu § 402; Helmuth Mayer, Der Sachverständige im Strafprozeß, Festschrift für Edmund Mezger, 1954, S. 476; Jessnitzer a.a.O. S. 53.

7 So ausdrücklich BGHSt 21, 157 (159) und BGH NJW 1971, 1997 zu II 3; s. auch BGHZ 12, 22 (25). Vgl. hierzu auch Pieper a.a.O. S. 28 f. und Kruchen a.a.O. S. 58 f.

8 S. dazu Esser, Vorverständnis und Methodenwahl in der Rechtsfindung, 1970, S. 57 und das in Fn. 21 angeführte Schrifttum. Vgl. z.B. auch Rosenberg-Schwab a.a.O. S. 600 (§ 116 II 1).

9 Eine Konsequenz hiervon ist, daß der Staat zwar für Amtspflichtverletzungen von Richtern grundsätzlich in Anspruch genommen werden kann (Art. 34 GG; § 839 BGB), nach ganz herrschender Auffassung jedoch nicht für fehlerhafte Sachverständigengutachten, auf denen gerichtliche Entscheidungen beruhen. So z.B. BGHZ 59, 310 (313); vgl. dazu Friederichs, DRiZ 1973, 113 ff.; Arndt, DRiZ 1973, 272 f.; J. Blomeyer, Schadensersatzansprüche des im Prozeß Unterlegenen wegen Fehlverhaltens Dritter, 1972, S. 118 ff. und ZRP 1974, 217.

10 Dieser Kennzeichnung bedienten sich schon die Motive zur ZPO; s. Hahn, Die gesamten Materialien zur Civilprozeßordnung, 1. Abt., 1880, S. 316. Vgl. dazu Pieper a.a.O. S. 4 f., 30 ff. und Kruchen a.a.O. S. 46. Jessnitzer a.a.O. S. 48 ff., 54 setzt sich nachdrücklich dafür ein, daß von einem „Helfer des Richters" gesprochen wird.

11 Näheres dazu bei Enneccerus-Nipperdey, Allg. Teil des Bürgerlichen Rechts, 15. Aufl. 1959, S. 311 ff. (§ 51 I).

12 Vgl. dazu Esser, Vorverständnis und Methodenwahl in der Rechtsfindung, 1970, S. 27 ff., 50 ff.; s. auch Larenz, Methodenlehre der Rechtswissenschaft, 2. Aufl. 1969, S. 233 ff.; Kriele, Theorie und Rechtsgewinnung, 1967, S. 162 ff.

13 Vgl. hierzu Esser a.a.O., S. 50 ff. (52) u. passim.

14 Dies ist übrigens kein neues Phänomen. Schon früher wurde beobachtet oder besser beklagt, daß die wissenschaftlich-technische Entwicklung dem Bildungsstand der Juristen um einige Jahrzehnte voraus sei. Vgl. z.B. Eugen Ehrlich: „Was kann geschehen, um bei der Ausbildung (vor oder nach Abschluß des Universitätsstudium) das Verständnis des Juristen für psychologische, wirtschaftliche und soziologische Fragen in erhöhtem Maße zu fordern" in: Verhandlungen des 31. Deutschen Juristentages, Band II, Berlin 1912, S. 200 ff. (212 f.). – In neuerer Zeit zu diesem Phänomen z.B. J. Blomeyer, ZRP 1970, S. 153 ff.; vgl. auch Steindorff, Repräsentanten- und Gehilfenversagen und Qualitätsregelungen in der Industrie, AcP Bd. 170 S. 127 mit Fn. 52.

15 Vgl. Gerchow, über die Tätigkeit des Sachverständigen vor Gericht und über die sogenannte Krise des Sachverständigenbeweises, in: Jahrbuch der Johann Wolfgang Goethe-Universität Frankfurt, 1966, S. 11 ff.

16 Näheres dazu z.B. bei Niessen in: Wellmann, Der Sachverständige in der Praxis, 2. Aufl. 1968, S. 103 ff.; Bremer, Der Sachverständige, 2. Aufl. 1973, S. 79 ff.

17 Ausgangspunkt dieser Initiative war die Frage, welche Möglichkeiten einer Aus- und Weiterbildung von Sachverständigen hinsichtlich der an ein Gutachten zu stellenden Anforderungen und auch der Kenntnisse rechtlicher Grundlagen bestünden. Die Herren Hauptgeschäftsführer Rehker und Rechtsanwalt Carl R. Wellmann haben auch in der Folgezeit wertvolle Anregungen gegeben.

18 Ergebnis dieser Bestandsaufnahme war ein Referat, das Verf. im April 1970 bei der Tagung der Deutschen Zivilprozeßrechtslehre in Wien gehalten hat. Es ist in ergänzter Fassung als Aufsatz erschienen in ZZP Bd. 84, S. 1–40 (s. oben Fn. 4). Gegenstand der Tagung war zugleich die entsprechende Problematik in der Sozial- und Strafgerichtsbarkeit. Vgl. Friederichs, Richter und Sachverständiger aus der Sicht der Sozialgerichtsbarkeit, ZZP Bd. 83, S. 394 ff.

19 Aus der umfangreichen Literatur seien z.B. genannt: Feest, Die Bundesrichter, Herkunft, Karriere und Auswahl der juristischen Elite, in Wolfgang Zapf (Herausg.) Beiträge zur

Analyse der deutschen Oberschicht, 2. Aufl. 1965, S. 95–113; Zwingmann, Zur Soziologie des Richters in der Bundesrepublik Deutschland, 1966; Kaupen, Die Hüter von Recht und Ordnung, Die soziale Herkunft, Erziehung und Ausbildung der deutschen Juristen, 2. Aufl. 1971; Lautmann, Justiz – die stille Gewalt, Teilnehmende Beobachtung und entscheidungssoziologische Analyse 1972; W. Richter, Zur Bedeutung der Herkunft des Richters für die Entscheidung, 1973.

20 S. dazu Baumgärtel-Mes, Rechtstatsachen zur Dauer des Zivilprozesses (1. Instanz), 2. Aufl. 1972, S. 209 ff., 268; Baumgärtel-Hohmann, Rechtstatsachen zur Dauer des Zivilprozesses (2. Instanz), 1972, S. 128 ff., 210; vgl. auch Baumgärtel, JZ 1971, S. 446 zu III 5.

21 S. den Text des Fragebogens im Anhang.

22 Zur Situation des Sachverständigenwesens in der Bundesrepublik Deutschland. Ein Zwischenbericht von Helmut Pieper unter Mitarbeit von Jörg Wolff, Hannover 1971.

23 Zur Anzahl der in der Bundesrepublik Deutschland tätigen Richter insgesamt s. Handbuch der Justiz, 11. Jahrg. Hamburg 1972.

24 Vgl. die Darstellung von Bender in DRiZ 1968, S. 163; 1969 S. 105 sowie ZRP 1969, S. 58. S. dazu auch Baumann-Fezer, Beschleunigung des Zivilprozesses, Recht und Staat, Nr. 390/391, 1970, S. 16, 39 f., 41 f.

25 Näheres hierzu s. unten Teil C.

26 So z.B. Sven Henckel im Leitartikel der Hannoverschen Allgemeinen Zeitung vom 21.11.1969.

27 S. den Fragebogen, Frage 4.

28 Zu einem ähnlichen Ergebnis sind auch Baumgärtel-Mes a.a.O. (Fn. 20) S. 209 f. gelangt. Danach betrug der Anteil der Verfahren mit Sachverständigenbeweis in allen streitig abgewickelten landgerichtlichen Prozessen 13,1 %, wovon 11,8 % auf schriftliche Gutachten entfielen.

29 S. Frage 6 des Fragebogens.

30 Zur Arbeitsweise der Hauptverhandlungskammern vgl. z.B. Bender, DRiZ 1969, S. 105 f.

31 S. Frage 5 des Fragebogens.

32 Auch die Einrichtung von Schiedsstellen des Kraftfahrzeughandwerks könnte hier eine gewisse Bedeutung erlangen.

33 Frage 7 1. Teil des Fragebogens.

34 Frage 7 2. Teil des Fragebogens.

35 Einiges spricht insbes. dafür, daß Anwälte beim Auftreten von Schwierigkeiten tatsächlicher – und auch rechtlicher – Art gern Zuflucht zu einem Antrag auf Sachverständigenbeweis nehmen. Das ist noch näher zu überprüfen.

36 S. dazu Pieper a.a.O. (Fn. 4) S. 38.

37 Näheres hierzu unten zu 2.

38 Zum Problem der Kosten als Hemmnis für die Inanspruchnahme gerichtlicher Hilfe überhaupt: Erika Bokelmann, Rechtswegsperre durch Prozeßkosten, ZRP 1973, S. 164 ff. mit umfassenden Nachweisen, besonders aus der neueren Literatur. Vgl. insbes. noch Fechner, Kostenrisiko und Rechtswegsperre – steht der Rechtsweg offen? JZ 1969, S.,349 ff.; Däubler, Bürger ohne Rechtsschutz – Kostenrisiko und Grundgesetz, BB 1969, S. 545 ff.

39 S. oben S. 324 f. mit Fn. 20.

40 Frage 14 1. Teil des Fragebogens.

41 Frage 14 2. Teil des Fragebogens.

42 So liegt z.B. im Bezirk der Industrie- u. Handelskammer Hannover-Hildesheim der mittlere Anteil der Gutachten, welche die Sachverständigen im gerichtlichen Auftrag erstatten, nur bei etwa 15–25 % ihrer gesamten Tätigkeit.

43 S. im einzelnen Bokelmann a.a.O. (Fn. 38) m. weiteren Nachw.

44 Eine Lösung erscheint um so dringlicher, als nicht unwahrscheinlich ist, daß Anträge auf Sachverständigenbeweis wegen des Kostenrisikos entweder nicht gestellt werden oder es zu einem Gutachten deswegen nicht kommt, weil die Einholung von einem Auslagenvorschuß abhängig gemacht wird, den die betreffende Partei nicht zahlen kann.

45 S. dazu die Fragen 9–12 des Fragebogens.

46 Frage 9 1. Teil des Fragebogens.

47 Es handelt sich hierbei vor allem um die zahlreichen Antworten auf die Frage 20, die offen formuliert war.

48 Hierauf wird unter IV. zurückzukommen sein.

49 Frage 9 2. Teil des Fragebogens.
50 S. dazu oben S. 322 (Fn. 7).
51 Frage 17 des Fragebogens.
52 Frage 11 des Fragebogens.
53 Bezeichnend z.B. BHGZ 12, 41 (47): bei der „freien richterlichen Würdigung" eines Sachverständigengutachtens komme „in erster Linie auch die Vertrauenswürdigkeit des Gutachters in Betracht". S. auch Pieper a.a.O. (Fn. 4) S. 28 mit Fn. 125.
54 Frage 17 2. Teil des Fragebogens.
55 Hannoversche Allgemeine Zeitung vom 14.12.1972, S. 5, („Neues Gutachten im Ilseder-Hütte-Streit" und dazu die Glosse „Unjustitiabel").
56 Frage 20 des Fragebogens.
57 Frage 19 des Fragebogens.
58 Mit ähnlichen Gründen hatte sich in Niedersachsen und Frankfurt/Main ein noch etwas größerer Anteil gegen eine Spezialisierung ausgesprochen.
59 S. oben zu B I 3.
60 Insofern, nicht allerdings hinsichtlich der gewählten Erhebungstechnik, kann das von Lautmann durchgeführte Vorhaben als Beispiel dienen; s. dazu den Bericht „Justiz – die stille Gewalt", 1972, s. 14 ff.

VII. Probleme der Forschung und Rechtsreform

Peter Arens

Das Problem des Musterprozesses

1. Abgrenzung von anderen Verfahren

Der Begriff „Musterprozeß" wird in der deutschen ZPO nicht gebraucht. Man versteht heute darunter einen Rechtsstreit, dem die Parteien oder Dritte eine über die Beurteilung der konkreten Klage hinausgehende Bedeutung zumessen. Dies kann, muß aber nicht auf einer besonderen Abrede beruhen. Meistens handelt es sich dabei um eine Gruppe von rechtlich oder tatsächlich mehr oder weniger gleichgelagerten Fällen, von denen aus Gründen der Kostenersparnis zunächst nur ein einzelner Fall dem Gericht zur Entscheidung unterbreitet wird. Man gebraucht insoweit auch den Ausdruck „Modellprozeß". Streng genommen gehört hierhin auch der sehr häufig vorkommende Fall der Teilklage, weil auch die daraufhin ergehende Entscheidung in gewisser Weise Modellcharakter hat. Diese Fälle der Teilklage haben jedoch die Besonderheit, daß die Parteien des Rechtsstreits auch die Parteien des von der Klage (noch) nicht erfaßten Teiles der Streitsache sind. Die sich daraus ergebenden Unterschiede zu den anderen Fällen sind so schwerwiegend, daß man die Teilklage nicht im Zusammenhang mit dem Musterprozeß erörtert. Es soll deshalb im folgenden von der Teilklage nicht mehr die Rede sein.

2. Unzureichende Behandlung des Musterprozesses in der Literatur

Trotz des Fehlens einer gesetzlichen Regelung hat der Musterprozeß eine nicht unbeträchtliche Bedeutung erlangt. Dies gilt sicher nicht nur für den Zivilprozeß, sondern auch für die anderen Verfahrensarten, also etwa den Arbeitsgerichtsprozeß, das Verwaltungsstreitverfahren, aber auch die Sozial- und die Finanzgerichtsbarkeit. Die Wissenschaft hat dieser von der Rechtspraxis entwickelten Institution verhältnismäßig wenig Beachtung geschenkt. Die wenigen Untersuchungen (1)*, die es zu diesem Thema gibt, haben sich zudem auf dogmatische Fragen konzentriert, wie etwa die, ob der Kläger auch dann noch ein streitiges Urteil verlangen kann, wenn der Beklagte ein Anerkenntnis i.S. des § 307 ZPO abgibt (2) (oder umgekehrt der Kläger verzichtet, § 306 ZPO (3)), oder ob die Parteien durch Vereinbarungen die Rechtskraft der im Musterprozeß ergehenden Entscheidung auf andere Streitkomplexe erstrecken können (4). Auch ist erörtert worden, ob die Klagemöglichkeit für diese anderen Streitkomplexe für die Dauer des Musterprozesses ausgeschlossen werden kann (5). Damit wurde die Frage nach

* Anmerkungen auf der Seite 355.

dem Musterprozeß weitgehend zur Frage nach der Problematik des Streitgegenstandes und der materiellen Rechtskraft – eine der meist diskutierten Streitfragen des Verfahrensrechts.

3. *Gründe für eine rechtstatsächliche Untersuchung des Musterprozesses*

Es erhebt sich der Verdacht, der durch unsere Untersuchung dann bestätigt worden ist, daß damit die wissenschaftliche Untersuchung an den eigentlichen Fragen, an den Problemen der Praxis vorbeigeht, wenn sie es ablehnt, nach den sozialen Ausgestaltungen des Musterprozesses zu fragen (6). Es lag deshalb nahe, durch eine rechtstatsächliche Untersuchung festzustellen, in welchem Umfang Musterpozesse auf dem Gebiet des Zivilprozesses vorkommen, wo die dort auftauchenden Probleme liegen und wo deshalb auch eine sinnvolle dogmatische Untersuchung anzusetzen hat.

Eine solche Übertragung der Methoden der empirischen Soziologie auf die Betrachtung des Prozeßrechts ist in Deutschland zwar noch verhältnismäßig neu, aber nichts ungewöhnliches mehr, seit Baumgärtel und Mes ebenso wie schon vorher eine Gruppe Freiburger Soziologen Prozeßakten ausgewertet haben, um die Ursachen zu langer Prozeßdauer festzustellen. Diese Untersuchungen sind im Zusammenhang mit der umstrittenen Beschleunigungsnovelle der Bundesregierung erfolgt.

Es könnte schon hier die Frage gestellt werden, warum eine solche Untersuchung auf das Gebiet des Zivilprozesses beschränkt worden ist. Aus sachlichen Gründen rechtfertigt sich diese Beschränkung nicht, ganz im Gegenteil besteht Grund zu der Vermutung, daß eine Untersuchung aller oben genannten Gerichtszweige und auch der Vergleich der bei den einzelnen Verfahren erzielten Resultate zu aufschlußreichen Ergebnissen führen könnte.

Der Grund für diese Beschränkung liegt in den engen Möglichkeiten eines normal ausgestatteten Lehrstuhls für eines der klassischen Fächer (bürgerliches und Zivilprozeßrecht). Rechtstatsächliche Untersuchungen größeren Stils setzen einen Apparat voraus, der einem Lehrstuhl der bezeichneten Art heute nicht (mehr) zur Verfügung steht. Ich mußte mich deshalb darauf beschränken, die Untersuchung nur der im Zivilprozeß vorkommenden Musterprozesse einem Doktoranden zu übertragen, der unter meiner Anleitung und Aufsicht diese Erhebung durchgeführt hat (7).

4. *Erläuterung der bei der Untersuchung angewendeten Methode*

Die erste Frage, die sich für die rechtstatsächliche Erfassung des Musterprozesses erhob, war die nach der dabei anzuwendenden Methode. Auch ihre Beantwortung mußte sich an den beschränkten Möglichkeiten orientieren, auf die ich oben hingewiesen habe. Damit schied eine umfangreiche mündliche Befragung aus Kostengründen aus, weil sie wegen der Streuung der Adressaten zahlreiche Reisen und möglicherweise zusätzliches Personal erfordert hätte, das diese Befragung durchzuführen gehabt hätte. Am einfachsten und billigsten wäre eine Auswertung der amtlichen Zählkartenstatistik gewesen. Dies erschien jedoch nicht erfolgversprechend, weil in den Zählkarten Angaben über die Parteien und die Bedeutung des Verfahrens nicht erfaßt werden. Eine Aktenauswertung, wie sie den ersten Untersuchungen von Baumgärtel und Mes (8) und der Freiburger Forschungsgruppe Empirische Rechtssoziologie zugrunde liegt (9), kam nicht in Frage, weil die erfaßbaren Stichproben zu klein gewesen wären (den genannten Untersuchungen lagen nur 286 bzw. 120 Akten zugrunde). Die große Untersuchung von Baumgärtel und Mes (10) konnte eine weit höhere Zahl von Akten auswerten (1367 amts- und 1998 landgerichtliche Akten (11). Diese Untersuchung konnte dann auch nur in Teamarbeit von Juristen, Mathematikern und Statistikern erfolgen. Die Auswertung erfolgte unter Benutzung der IBM der Gesellschaft für Mathematik und Datenverarbeitung (12). Solche Hilfsmittel stehen einem normalen Lehrstuhl oder Institut heute nicht ohne weiteres zur Verfügung.

Angesichts der vorhandenen Möglichkeiten blieb also nur der Weg einer schriftlichen Befragung an Hand eines standardisierten Fragebogens. Um die bekannten Nachteile der Postwurfbefragung zu vermeiden (große Ausfallziffern infolge fehlender Motivation der Befragten), wurde dem Fragebogen ein Begleitschreiben beigefügt, in dem Hintergrund und Ziele der Befragung erläutert wurden. Die weitere mit Postwurfbefragungen verbundene Schwierigkeit, daß sie nämlich für komplexe Sachverhalte – und um einen solchen handelt es sich bei dem Musterprozeß ohne Zweifel – nur beschränkt tauglich ist, wurde hier dadurch gemildert, daß es sich bei dem Kreis der Adressaten zum größten Teil um eine am Forschungsergebnis interessierte, fachkundige und in den Kategorien der Befragung denkgewohnte Gruppe handelte.

Der nächste Schritt betraf die Auswahl der Adressaten. Ausgehend von der Breitenwirkung der Musterprozesse konnten wir annehmen, daß der einzelne Privatmann gegen einen anderen einzelnen Privatmann nur ausnahmsweise einen Musterprozeß führen wird. Liegt einmal ein Fall vor, in dem es um gleichgelagerte Rechtsbeziehungen zwischen verschiedenen Privatleuten geht, so wird ein darüber geführter Prozeß nur dadurch zum Musterprozeß, daß irgendein Verband oder eine andere Organisation die Interessen dieses Einzelnen vertritt. Diese Überlegung führte uns dazu, Unternehmen der Wirtschaft und ihre Verbände anzuschreiben, also Banken und Sparkassen, Versicherungen, Industrie- und Handelsunternehmen und jeweils deren Verbände. Hinzu kamen die Sozialpartner, Berufsverbände sowie sonstige Schutz- und Interessenverbände. Bei der Auswahl im einzelnen entschieden wir uns für solche Adressaten, von denen nicht nur die Führung von Musterprozessen erwartet werden konnte, sondern überhaupt eine Zivilprozeßtätigkeit von einigem Umfang.

Von einer Befragung der Gerichte haben wir aus verschiedenen Gründen abgesehen. Einmal führen die Parteien einen Prozeß als Musterprozeß unabhängig vom Willen des Gerichts, sie sind in keiner Weise verpflichtet, dies dem Gericht gegenüber zu erkennen zu geben, und man kann davon ausgehen, daß sie dies vor allem in der unteren Instanz auch häufig nicht tun. Das Gericht könnte auch keinerlei Konsequenzen aus einer solchen Unterrichtung ziehen. Hinzu kommt eine weitere Überlegung. Man kann für die deutschen Verhältnisse wohl davon ausgehen, daß die Justitiare der Verbände, Banken, Industrieunternehmen usw. in der Regel höher qualifizierte Juristen sind als die Richter jedenfalls der unteren und mittleren Instanzen. Und der Erfolg einer Befragung dieser Art hängt ja nicht zuletzt von der Qualifikation der Befragten ab.

5. Ergebnisse der Untersuchung

Insgesamt wurden 102 Adressaten angeschrieben. Begonnen wurde die Aktion im Dezember 1970. Die Befragung bezog sich auf die letzten fünf dem Befragungsjahr vorangehenden Kalenderjahre, in der Absicht, möglicherweise vorhandene Entwicklungstendenzen sichtbar zu machen. Von den 102 verschickten Fragebogen wurden 63 beantwortet, also rund 62 %, ein keinesfalls schlechtes Ergebnis. Bei den 39 Nichtantwortenden handelte es sich um kleine Verbände und um Angehörige der Gruppen, die, wie die Auswertung der eingegangenen Antworten ergab, keine Musterprozesse führten. Man wird also wohl den größeren Teil der Nichtantwortenden zu den Fehlanzeige meldenden Adressaten rechnen können. Dies waren von den 63, die geantwortet hatten, immerhin 42. Es blieben von den 102 angeschriebenen Unternehmen und Verbänden also nur 21, die tatsächlich zivilprozessuale Musterprozesse führen, davon aber nur fünf, bei denen es im Jahresdurchschnitt mehr als drei waren.
Da die Frage sich auch auf die Zahl der überhaupt geführten Zivilprozesse bezog, wurden insgesamt rund 6.000 Prozesse erfaßt, davon waren 350 Musterprozesse. Es wäre wohl verfehlt, daraus den Schluß zu ziehen, die Befragung habe die Annahme nicht bestätigt, daß der Musterprozeß im Zivilprozeß erhebliche wirtschaftliche und soziale Bedeutung habe. Er hat diese Bedeutung, aber freilich nur in einem bestimmten Bereich. Dies hat die Befragung ergeben: die Musterprozeßtätigkeit konzentriert sich bei bestimmten Gruppen der Adressaten und in bestimmten Rechtsgebieten.
Auf die Parteien bezogene Schwerpunkte ergaben sich auf folgenden Gebieten:
Versicherungsunternehmen; Schutzverbände; Berufsverbände der freien Berufe;
nach dem Rechtsgebiet des Streitgegenstandes:
im gewerblichen Rechtsschutz (vor allem im Bereich von UWG und Urheberrecht); im Versicherungsrecht; im Haftpflichtrecht (vor allem im Recht der Unfallhaftpflicht); im Recht der Staatshaftung und schließlich im Dienst- und Werksvertragsrecht.

6. Überprüfung der durch die Befragung erzielten Ergebnisse durch eine Analyse der in der amtlichen Sammlung des Bundesgerichtshofs veröffentlichten Entscheidungen

Das durch die Befragung erzielte Ergebnis wurde durch eine Analyse der in der amtlichen Sammlung des Bundesgerichtshofs veröffentlichten Entscheidungen ergänzt und zugleich kontrolliert. Dabei wurden Entscheidungen aus den Rechtsgebieten von vornherein ausgeschieden, die auch von der Befragung nicht erfaßt worden waren, weil sie nicht zivilrechtlicher Natur waren.
Es wurden dann die Urteile der Jahre 1968, 1969 und 1970, insgesamt 250 von 344 abgedruckten Entscheidungen daraufhin untersucht, ob die dort getroffene Entscheidung über eine bestimmte Rechtsfrage geeignet war, weitere Sachverhalte zu beeinflussen. Dies entsprach dem auch bei der Befragung verwendeten Kriterium der Breitenwirkung. Die so qualifizierten Urteile wurden als Musterurteile angesehen. Dies schien auch deshalb als gerechtfertigt, weil Musterprozesse in aller Regel mit dem Ziel einer höchstrichterlichen Entscheidung angestrengt werden. Auch werden die für die amtliche Sammlung bestimmten Entscheidungen

danach ausgewählt, ob sie für die Zukunft und für einen größeren Personenkreis von Bedeutung sind.
Diese Untersuchung der veröffentlichten Entscheidungen des Bundesgerichtshofs hat das Umfragungsergebnis bestätigt; die Prozesse lagen auf den Rechtsgebieten, die oben aufgeführt sind. Hinzu kommen zwei weitere Rechtsgebiete, auf denen deutliche Schwerpunkte festzustellen waren, nämlich das Verfahrensrecht und das Kaufrecht. Dabei kann für die Fragen des Musterprozesses das Verfahrensrecht wohl außer Betracht bleiben, weil diese Rechtsfragen gewissermaßen zufällig auftauchen, die Parteien jedenfalls keine Prozesse führen, um prozeßrechtliche Fragen klären zu lassen. Es bleibt also dabei, daß die durch die Befragung als Schwerpunkte der Musterprozeßtätigkeit ermittelten Rechtsgebiete nur durch das Kaufrecht ergänzt worden sind.

7. *Ergänzung durch Einzelinterviews*

Die Umfrage und die Auswertung der amtlichen Sammlung des Bundesgerichtshofs sind ergänzt worden durch insgesamt zwanzig mündliche und schriftliche Einzelinterviews mit Justitiaren, Geschäftsführern und Rechtsanwälten von Unternehmen und Verbänden. Dabei ging es vor allem um zwei Fragen. Einmal um die Breitenwirkung der Musterprozesse, also darum, wie viele Verfahren durch einen Musterprozeß miterledigt und auf diese Weise unnötig werden. Sodann um die Gründe, die zu der aufgezeigten Schwerpunktbildung hinsichtlich der Parteien und der Rechtsnatur des Streitgegenstandes geführt haben.

8. *Beispiele für die Breitenwirkung von Musterprozessen*

Genaue Angaben über die Breitenwirkung erwiesen sich nur für bestimmte Einzelfälle als möglich. Eine generelle Aussage scheiterte schon daran, daß sich die Musterprozesse im allgemeinen erst in der Zukunft auswirken. Aufgrund einer Anzahl mitgeteilter Fälle war aber eine Aussage möglich über die Breitenwirkung einzelner Prozesse.

Einzelbeispiele mit erfaßbarer Breitenwirkung

Mitgeteilt von der Siemens-AG und von der Verwertungsgesellschaft „Wort":
Eine Urheberrechtsgesellschaft klagt gegen dasjenige Unternehmen, das die größte Werksbücherei der Bundesrepublik unterhält. In dem Verfahren soll geklärt werden, ob Werksbüchereien verpflichtet sind, für die von ihnen zur Ausleihe benützten Werke eine Urheberrechtsvergütung zu leisten.
Die Entscheidung beträfe alle Werksbüchereien der Bundesrepublik, das sind einschließlich 100 sehr kleiner Büchereien insgesamt 426.
Mitgeteilt von der Siemens-AG:
Ein Vermieter klagt gegen eine Industriefirma auf Zustimmung zu einer Mieterhöhung für Werkswohnungen. Da es sich um 64 gleichgelagerte Fälle handelt, wird vereinbart, einen Fall gerichtlich klären zu lassen, und in den anderen Fällen nach diesem ergangenen Urteil zu verfahren.

Mitentschieden wurden also 63 weitere, gleichgelagerte Fälle.
Mitgeteilt vom Verein zur Wahrung des lauteren Wettbewerbs:
Ein Verein nach § 13 UWG klagt gegen eine Handelsorganisation auf Unterlassung folgender Werbung: „Wenn Sie unsere Geschäftsräume bis 18.29 Uhr betreten haben, können Sie in Ruhe einkaufen und werden beliebig lange bedient“. Wäre diese Werbung für zulässig erklärt worden, so wären nahezu alle der insgesamt 400.000 Einzelhändler in der BRD gezwungen gewesen, diese Werbung und die damit verbundene Geschäftspraxis nachzuvollziehen.
Mitgeteilt von der Neckermann KG a.A.:
Eine Herstellerfirma klagt gegen ein Versandhausunternehmen, in Zukunft die Bezeichnung „Tosca“ nicht mehr als Unterscheidungsmerkmal im Versandkatalog zu benützen, da dies eine warenzeichenrechtliche Verwendung sei.
Betroffen sind alle deutschen Versandhausunternehmen, die mit namentlichen Artikelbezeichnungen arbeiten, da kaum noch irgendeine Bezeichnung nicht als Warenzeichen registriert ist. Insbesondere betroffen sind die vier größten Unternehmen der Branche. Allein im Katalog des größten Versandhauses sind auch heute noch ca. 300–400 derartige Artikelbezeichnungen enthalten.
Mitgeteilt von der Hessischen Landesbank-Girozentrale:
Ein Bausparer klagt gegen seine Bausparkasse, weil diese ihm, wie in einem Teil des Bauspargewerbes üblich, für die Bearbeitung seines Prämienantrags DM 2,– berechnet hat. Betroffen wären ca. 5 Millionen Prämienanträge pro Jahr. Streitwert pro Antrag: DM 2,–. Wirtschaftliche Bedeutung des Gesamtkomplexes ca. 10 Millionen DM pro Jahr.
Mitgeteilt von der Arbeitsgemeinschaft der Berufsvertretungen Deutscher Apotheken (ABDA) (vgl. Pharmazeutische Zeitung 1970, S. 1925 und 1971, S. 309):
Ein Apothekerverein klagt gegen eine Ersatzkasse, weil diese zu Unrecht den Abschlag nach § 376 RVO von ihren Leistungen einbehalten habe.
Betroffen wären 1.600 Krankenkassen und 11.000 Apotheken. Streitwert des anhängig gewesenen Verfahrens: DM 25.000,–. Wirtschaftliche Gesamtbedeutung: ca. 130 Millionen DM.
BGHZ 52, S. 194 ff.:
Die Hinterbliebenen mehrerer bei dem Absturz eines Charterflugzeugs ums Leben gekommener Passagiere klagen gegen den Charterunternehmer auf Zahlung des Schadens, der durch den Tod des Ernährers entstanden ist und noch entstehen wird. Mitentscheiden werden die Ansprüche von insgesamt 74 Opfern.
Diese Fälle zeigen, daß bei vielen Musterprozessen eine erhebliche Diskrepanz besteht zwischen dem Streitwert, der nach deutschem Recht für die Berechnung der Kosten maßgebend ist, und der wirtschaftlichen Bedeutung der de facto mitentschiedenen Fragen. Darauf wird noch zurückzukommen sein.

9. Gründe für die Schwerpunktbildung nach Rechtsgebieten und Parteien

Über die Gründe für die Schwerpunktbildung nach Rechtsgebieten und Parteien hat sich folgendes ergeben. Zunächst für die Rechtsgebiete: Staatshaftungsprozesse werden angesichts der Bindung der Verwaltung an das Gesetz im allgemeinen nur dann nötig, wenn die Rechtslage unklar ist. Da sich die Verwaltung dabei grundsätzlich an das durch ein Urteil weiter entwickelte Recht hält, sind hier viele Urteile Musterurteile. Im Dienst- und Werksvertragsrecht spielten besonders die Streitigkeiten im Bauwesen eine große Rolle. Die Baurechtswissenschaft befindet sich in einem unbefriedigenden Zustand (13), auch werden hier eine Vielzahl von Mittel- und Kleinfirmen tätig, die angesichts des Booms in diesem Gewerbe nicht immer sorgfältig arbeiten. Im Recht der unerlaubten Handlungen und im Haftpflichtrecht wirkt sich die Zunahme des Straßenverkehrs aus: dreiviertel aller Haftpflichtsachen der Versicherungen kommen aus dem Straßenverkehrsrecht. Im gewerblichen Rechtsschutz sind wegen der Vorschrift des § 13 UWG sehr viele Verbände an der Prozeßtätigkeit beteiligt, die die für ein Musterverfahren nötige Größe haben. Außerdem ist hier wegen der schnellen Änderung der tatsächlichen und rechtlichen Verhältnisse, auf die das Wettbewerbsrecht schnell zu reagieren hat, die Rechtsunsicherheit besonders groß. Aus dem Gebrauch vom Recht der einstweiligen Verfügung, die hier besonders häufig sind, ergeben sich noch besondere Probleme, auf die ich noch zurückkommen werde. Im Urheberrecht hat sich seit dem Inkrafttreten des jetzt geltenden Gesetzes vom 9. September 1965 die Musterprozeßtätigkeit stark vermindert. Die hier tätig werdenden Verbände bevorzugen zur Klärung von Grundsatzfragen Schiedsverfahren mit anschließenden Tarifvereinbarungen (14). Diese Praxis könnte sich wieder ändern, wenn durch Musterprozesse Einfluß auf den Gesetzgeber bei der Novellierung genommen werden soll.

Bei der Frage nach der Schwerpunktbildung nach Parteien ergaben sich sowohl Gründe für wie gegen eine Musterprozeßtätigkeit. Kleine und mittlere Unternehmen, kleinere, finanzschwache Verbände und die meisten Privatpersonen können aus finanziellen Gründen keine Musterprozesse führen, die doch meistens auf eine höchstrichterliche Entscheidung zusteuern und einen entsprechenden Kostenaufwand voraussetzen. Daneben gibt es Unternehmen und Verbände, deren Tätigkeit sich dem strengen Recht mehr oder weniger entzieht. Dies gilt etwa für Rückversicherungsunternehmen, deren Geschäftsbeziehungen international verflochten sind, weitgehend auf ungeschriebenem Recht beruhen und deren vertragliche Vereinbarungen sich überwiegend an den praktischen Bedürfnissen orientieren (15). Große Unternehmen, vor allem auch Großbanken, vermeiden den Prozeß wiederum aus anderen Gründen. Einmal scheuen sie die öffentliche Austragung von Streitigkeiten, zum anderen stehen ihnen andere, für sie günstigere Mittel zur Konfliktbereinigung zur Verfügung. So können sie bei außergerichtlichen Vergleichen ihr wirtschaftliches Gewicht und die Qualität ihrer Rechtsabteilung besser zur Geltung bringen als im normalen Zivilprozeß. Da sie außerdem an schnellen Entscheidungen interessiert sind, ziehen sie meistens die Vereinbarung von Schiedsgerichtsverfahren (§§ 1025 ff. ZPO) vor. Dies gilt auch für die Gruppe der großen Verbände, die außerdem kraft ihres Gewichtes und den hinter ihnen stehenden Wählerstimmen die Möglichkeit haben, auf den Gesetzgeber Einfluß zu nehmen, um die Regelung bestimmter grundsätzlicher Rechtsfragen in ihrem Sinne zu erreichen.

Dieser Gruppe stehen die Parteien gegenüber, die nach dem Ergebnis der Befragung Musterprozesse führen. Hier sind wegen des Umfangs der Prozeßtätigkeit die Versicherungsunternehmen an erster Stelle zu nennen. Diese müssen in den Haftpflichtsachen prozessieren, weil sie über § 3 Pflichtversicherungsgesetz Partei im Prozeß ihres schadenstiftenden Versicherungsnehmers sind. Häufig kommt es dabei auf die Entscheidung von grundsätzlichen Fragen an, so daß der Prozeß dann mit dem Ziel eines Musterurteils weitergeführt wird. Bei Deckungsprozessen lassen sich die Versicherer verklagen, wenn sie befürchten, daß sonst ein Einbruch in eine gesicherte Praxis erzielt werde. Daraus werden dann häufig Musterprozesse, die bis zu einer höchstrichterlichen Entscheidung weitergehen (16). Berufsverbände freier Berufe und andere Schutzverbände, die nicht das Gewicht und damit die oben angedeuteten Möglichkeiten der außergerichtlichen Einflußnahmen haben, klären Grundsatzfragen häufig durch Musterprozesse. Dies wird dadurch begünstigt, daß sie die Mindestgröße und finanzielle Stärke haben, die dafür erforderlich ist. Bei mittleren Industrieunternehmen und großen Handelsunternehmen sind diese Voraussetzungen ebenfalls gegeben. Musterprozesse kommen bei diesen Gruppen dann auch vor, wenn auch nicht sehr häufig; dies geht auf die lange Dauer der Prozesse zurück.

10. Gründe für die Vermeidung von Musterprozessen

Die Befragung hat ergeben, daß ein Teil der Parteien, für die der Musterprozeß an sich als Mittel zur Klärung rechtlicher Grundsatzfragen in Betracht käme, sich statt dessen anderer Hilfsmittel bedienen, die, da sie im außergerichtlichen Rahmen liegen, die Gefahr mit sich bringen, daß die betreffenden Lebensverhältnisse nach anderen Prinzipien als denen der geltenden Rechtsordnung geregelt werden. Es liegt deshalb nahe, nach Wegen zu suchen, auf denen der Musterprozeß vor den Zivilgerichten für die Parteien attraktiver gemacht werden kann.
Der zunächst ins Auge springende Mangel unserer Zivilprozesse wirkt sich auch bei den Musterprozessen aus: die lange Dauer eines Verfahrens, das durch alle Instanzen bis zu einer höchstrichterlichen Entscheidung des Bundesgerichtshofs geht. Hierzu läßt sich in diesem Rahmen nichts auf die besonderen Eigenarten des Musterprozesses Gemünztes sagen; die Möglichkeit, den Gang des zivilgerichtlichen Verfahrens zu beschleunigen, wird seit Jahren in viel größerem Rahmen diskutiert. Dies gilt sowohl für Versuche, auf der Basis des geltenden Rechts Abhilfe zu schaffen (Stuttgarter Modell) als auch für Bestrebungen des Gesetzgebers (Beschleunigungsnovelle).
Neben diesem allgemeinen Problem der Prozeßdauer gibt es bei den Musterprozessen aber noch Besonderheiten. Dies betrifft zunächst eine Auswirkung der Dauer eines Musterprozesses: infolgedessen können sich die tatsächlichen und rechtlichen Verhältnisse, für die das Musterurteil ebenfalls streitklärend wirken soll, so ändern, daß das Urteil diese Aufgabe eben nicht mehr erfüllen kann, vor allem dann, wenn die nicht mit der Klage geltend gemachten Ansprüche inzwischen verjährt sind.
Aus dem Umstand, daß der Musterprozeß de iure nur ein auf der Entscheidung des rechtshängigen Streitgegenstandes gerichtetes Verfahren ist, ergeben sich zwei weitere möglicherweise negative Folgen. Einmal die, daß das Gericht nicht immer gezwungen ist, die Rechtsfrage, um deren Entscheidung es den Parteien geht, zu beantworten. Es kann vielmehr den häufig einfacheren und kürzeren Weg einschlagen und den Fall aufgrund bestimmter, nur hierfür geltender Besonderheiten entscheiden.
Das andere Problem ergibt sich daraus, daß im deutschen Zivilprozeßrecht die Zulässigkeit von Rechtsmitteln, von einer Ausnahme abgesehen (§ 546 II ZPO), von festen Streit- bzw. Beschwerdewerten abhängig ist (§§ 511a, 546 ZPO); gegen Berufungsurteile der Landgerichte gibt es überhaupt kein Rechtsmittel mehr (§ 545 I ZPO). Diese Regelung, die der wirtschaftlichen Bedeutung eines Muster-

prozesses nicht gerecht wird, führt in vielen Fällen dazu, daß eine höchstrichterliche Entscheidung nicht erlangt werden kann.
Wie schon erwähnt, wirkt sich dies besonders im Wettbewerbsprozeß aus, der meistens im Verfahren der einstweiligen Verfügung geführt wird. Dieses Verfahren endet mit der Berufung (§ 545 II ZPO); die Revision ist nur möglich, wenn das Verfahren zur Hauptsache geführt wird. Dies wiederum ist wegen der Verfahrensdauer wenig sinnvoll und geschieht auch selten. In weiten Bereichen ist hier das Verfahren der einstweiligen Verfügung an die Stelle des ordentlichen Zivilprozesses getreten. Die Folge dieses Rechtszustandes im Wettbewerbsprozeß ist eine beträchtliche Rechtszersplitterung und damit Rechtsunsicherheit; überregional anbietende Teilnehmer am Wettbewerb müssen ihre Maßnahmen nach den verschiedenen Oberlandesgerichtsbezirken verändern.
Und schließlich muß die fehlende Präjudizialität des Musterurteils bedacht werden: rechtlich bindet dieses für die nicht entschiedenen Parallelfälle weder das Gericht noch die Parteien, wenn man von den wenigen Fällen der Rechtskrafterstreckung einmal absieht (17). Von erheblichem Gewicht ist aber doch die Autorität eines höchstrichterlichen Urteils. So haben Abmachungen von Verbänden nach § 13 UWG zu 80 % Erfolg, wenn sie sich auf ein Urteil des Bundesgerichtshofs stützen können (18).

11. Möglichkeiten zur Erleichterung von Musterprozessen

a) Nach geltendem Recht

Bereits das geltende Recht beiet bestimmte Möglichkeiten, bei den aufgezählten Problemgruppen zu helfen. Sie setzen allerdings eine vertragliche Einigung der Parteien sowohl des rechtshängigen Verfahrens als auch des Parallelverfahrens voraus. Damit sind zugleich die Grenzen dieser Abhilfemöglichkeiten aufgezeigt, weil diese Einigung häufig nicht möglich ist. Immerhin kann dieser Vertrag folgendes zum Inhalt haben: Zunächst die Abrede der Sprungrevision, § 566 a ZPO. Diese ist dann sinnvoll, wenn der Sachverhalt im wesentlichen unstreitig ist, eine zweite Tatsacheninstanz also nicht erforderlich ist. Hier kommt man dann schneller zu einer höchstrichterlichen Entscheidung. Auf den Instanzenzug kann auch durch eine Zuständigkeitsvereinbarung (§§ 38 ff. ZPO) Einfluß genommen werden, allerdings nur in beschränktem Umfange. Ist auf diesem Weg die Berufung zum Oberlandesgericht ermöglicht worden, besteht Aussicht, auch die Zulassung der Revision zu erreichen, weil es bei den Musterprozessen um Rechtssachen von grundsätzlicher Bedeutung geht (§ 546 II ZPO). Eine ähnliche Wirkung wie die Vereinbarung über die Zuständigkeit kann auch eine Vereinbarung über den Streitwert haben. Dieser wird zwar vom Gericht festgesetzt (§ 3 ZPO), das dabei auch an einen übereinstimmenden Parteivertrag nicht gebunden ist. In der Praxis wird es sich aber an diese Angaben im allgemeinen jedenfalls bei Übereinstimmung halten.
Um eine Entscheidung nach den Umständen des Einzelfalles unter Offenlassung der eigentlichen Streitfrage zu vermeiden, wird versucht, nur typisch gelagerte Sachverhalte zum Gegenstand eines Musterprozesses zu machen, die möglichst keine Besonderheiten aufweisen und deshalb zur Konzentrierung auf die streitige Frage zwingen (19). Bei manchen Verbänden bestehen für die Auswahl der für

einen Musterprozeß geeigneten Sachverhalte besondere Sachverständigenausschüsse, die nach diesen Kriterien auswählen (20). Im übrigen wird man dem Gericht nicht die Möglichkeit nehmen können – auch de lege ferenda nicht – einen Prozeß auf dem schnellsten, einfachsten und billigsten Weg zu beenden. Ein Verfahren zur Entscheidung abstrakter Rechtsfragen kennt unsere Zivilprozeßordnung nicht.
Auch über die Erstreckung der Bindungswirkung auf die nicht vom Gericht entscheidenen Fälle können in gewissem Umfang Vereinbarungen getroffen werden. Eine vertragliche Erstreckung der Rechtskraft dürfte zwar nicht möglich sein. Die materielle Rechtskraft ergibt sich aus dem hoheitlichen Charakter des Richterspruchs, sie ist deshalb nicht disponibel (21). Für zulässig zu erachten ist aber die Vereinbarung, daß die Parteien die Parallelsachverhalte dem Musterurteil entsprechend umgestalten sollen. Hier verpflichten sich die Parteien hinsichtlich ihres eigenen Verhaltens, darin liegt keine Verfügung über hoheitliche Rechte (22). Auch hinsichtlich des Eintritts der Verjährung kann man wirksame Vereinbarungen treffen. Zwar nicht mit unmittelbarer Wirkung: verjährungserschwerende Verträge sind nach § 225 BGB grundsätzlich nichtig. Dies gilt nach h.M. auch für den prozessualen Vertrag, die Einrede der Verjährung nicht im Prozeß geltend zu machen (23). Mittelbar kommt man hier aber doch zur Verlängerung der Verjährungsfrist: die Rechtsprechung hat anerkannt, daß die Berufung auf den Eintritt der Verjährung nach § 242 BGB treuwidrig und damit unzulässig ist, wenn der Gläubiger im Vertrauen auf den Verzicht des Schuldners auf die Verjährungseinrede den Anspruch nicht rechtzeitig klageweise geltend gemacht hat (24). Einfacher und ebenso wirksam ist die Vereinbarung oder die Umdeutung einer mit anderem Wortlaut getroffenen Vereinbarung dahin, daß der Gläubiger den Anspruch wegen der Dauer des Musterprozesses nicht geltend macht, diesen also stundet. Damit tritt dann eine Hemmung der Verjährung nach § 202 I BGB ein.

b) de lege ferenda

Wenn auch nach geltendem Recht durchaus Möglichkeiten bestehen, den Musterprozeß effektiver zu gestalten, so bleibt gleichwohl manches zu wünschen übrig. Dies wirft die Frage nach einer Lösung de lege ferenda auf. Was die Prozeßdauer im allgemeinen betrifft, so muß hier auf die allgemeine Diskussion verwiesen werden. Skepsis scheint hier geboten, was wirksame Abhilfe betrifft (25).
Die Einführung des sog. dreistufigen Gerichtsaufbaus, also die Abschaffung der doppelten Eingangsstufe bei Amtsgericht und Landgericht und ihre Ersetzung durch ein einheitliches Eingangsgericht, die seit einiger Zeit im Gespräch ist (26), würde die Aussichten erhöhen, für jeden Musterprozeß den vollen Instanzenzug zu haben, jedenfalls dann, wenn zugleich die Streitwertrevision durch die Grundsatzrevision ersetzt werden würde (27). Man wird davon ausgehen können, daß bei Musterprozessen im allgemeinen eine grundsätzliche Bedeutung der Rechtssache vorliegen würde. Hier würde die Grundsatzrevision, der ich sonst eher skeptisch gegenüberstehe, sicher einen Fortschritt bedeuten. Eine Erleichterung für die Zulässgikeit der Revision bei Musterprozessen könnte im übrigen auch bei Beibehaltung des jetzigen gemischten Systems der Streitwert- und Grundsatzrevision erreicht werden, wenn man bei der Berechnung des Beschwerdewertes die

wirtschaftliche Bedeutung der Musterklage, die ja in aller Regel weit höher ist als der Streitwert, berücksichtigen würde. Freilich dürfte man diesen höheren Wert nur bei der Zulässigkeit der Rechtsmittel, nicht bei der Kostenfrage berücksichtigen, weil sonst die Kostenersparnis, die den Musterprozeß veranlaßt hat, entfallen würde.

Eine Abhilfe sollte der Gesetzgeber für die Rechtszersplitterung beim Wettbewerbsprozeß schaffen. Dabei scheint es wenig sinnvoll, auf die Möglichkeit der allgemeinen Verfahrensbeschleunigung zu verweisen, die dann das Hauptverfahren attraktiver machen und damit über die Revision zur Rechtsvereinheitlichung führen könnte. Man wird realistischerweise davon ausgehen müssen, daß der Wettbewerbsprozeß auch in absehbarer Zukunft eben nicht im ordentlichen Prozeß, sondern im Verfahren der einstweiligen Verfügung geführt werden wird. Hier nun eine besondere Revisionsmöglichkeit für dieses Verfahren zu schaffen, würde wohl zu einer nicht vertretbaren, zusätzlichen Belastung des ohnehin überlasteten Bundesgerichtshofs führen. Zweckmäßiger und durchaus ausreichend wäre es dagegen, wie schon in § 120 III GVG für den Strafprozeß und in Art. III Abs. 1 des 3. Mietrechtsänderungsgesetzes von 1968 vorgesehen, eine Vorlagepflicht des Oberlandesgerichts an den Bundesgerichtshof einzuführen, wenn das Oberlandesgericht in einer bestimmten Frage von der Entscheidung eines anderen Oberlandesgerichts abweichen will. Auf diese Weise könnte eine Vereinheitlichung der Rechtsprechung in diesem Bereich erzielt werden, ohne daß es zu einer allzu großen Belastung der Revisionsinstanz käme.

Summary

Scholarly research into the problem of "test cases" in Germany, have so far confined themselves to technical, doctrinal questions. The author has undertaken direction, however, of an empirical investigation, which has broken new ground. Questionnaire data has revealed that this type of process in mainly used by insurance companies, professional associations, and chiefly in such fields as protection of trade rights, insurance law, liability for accidents, and labor contracts. These results were checked against an analysis of the published opinions of the federal courts for the years 1968 to 1970.

It turns out, that some parties, for whom clarification of basic questions of law through a "test case" should be appropriate, choose extrajudicial paths. This poses the danger that these areas of life will be regulated by principles other than those of the legal order. To encourage "test cases", a general shortening of the length of process is suggested. A special problem in German law arises from the fact that legal remedies are often dependent on the monetary value of the complaint. Here the "test case", since it always concerns a fundamental legal question, deserves special regulation.

Anmerkungen

1 Vor allem: Kempf, Zur Problematik des Musterprozesses, ZZP 73 (1960) S. 387 ff.
2 BGHZ 10, 333 = JZ 1954, S. 242 mit Anm. Bötticher.
3 BGHZ 49, 213 = JZ 1968, S. 797 mit Anm. Bötticher.
4 Kempf, a.a.O.
5 Kempf, a.a.O.
6 So aber ausdrücklich Kempf, a.a.O. S. 345.
7 Inzwischen als Dissertation gedruckt: Wolfram Haug, Die Problematik des Musterprozesses, unter Einbeziehung von Ergebnissen der Rechtstatsachenforschung. Freiburger Dissertation, 1973.
8 JZ 1971, 441 ff.; Anw Bl. 1970, 333.
9 Blankenburg, Erhard; Blankenburg, Viola; Erlbruch, Volker; Feest, Christa: Die Dauer von Zivilprozessen in erster Instanz vor dem Landgericht, Freiburg 1970.
10 Baumgärtel und Mes, Rechtstatsachen zur Dauer des Zivilprozesses (erste Instanz), Köln, Berlin, Bonn, München 1971.
11 A.a.O. S. 129.
12 Baumgärtel-Mes, a.a.O. (Anm. 10), S. V f.
13 Mitteilung des Bundes deutscher Architekten (BDA) vom 18.12.1970.
14 Mitteilung der GEMA vom 7.12.1970.
15 Auskunft der Münchner Rückversicherungs-Gesellschaft vom 9.12.1970.
16 Mitteilung der Allianz-Versicherungs-Aktiengesellschaft vom 11.2.1971.
17 Dazu Rosenberg-Schwab, Zivilprozeßrecht, 10. Aufl., München 1969, § 157 II und III, S. 814 ff.
18 Auskunft der Zentrale zur Bekämpfung des unlauteren Wettbewerbs e.V.
19 Mitteilung der Hauptgemeinschaft des Deutschen Einzelhandels vom 18.1.1971.
20 Mitteilung des Vereins Deutscher Maschinenbau-Anstalten (VDMA) vom 22.1.1971.
21 Stein-Jonas-Schumann-Leipold, Kommentar zur ZPO, 19. Aufl., Tübingen 1969, § 325 I 4; BGH LM § 125 BGB Nr. 29; Kempf, a.a.O. (Anm. 1), S. 371.
22 Kempf, a.a.O. (Anm. 1), S. 374.
23 BGH VersR 1960, 515 (517); 1962, 809 (810).
24 BGH VersR 1960, 515 (517).
25 Vgl. etwa Henke, Judicia perpetua oder: Warum Prozesse so lange dauern. ZZP 83 (1970), S. 125 ff.
26 Dazu Schier, ZRP 1970, 157.
27 Dazu Holtgrave, Zur Reform des Zivilprozeßrechts, ZZP 86 (1973), S. 1 ff. (14 ff.).

Franz von Benda-Beckmann

Das rechtliche Verfahren in der Rechtsethnologie: Versuch zu einem interkulturell anwendbaren Bezugsrahmen

Das rechtliche Verfahren, die Behandlung des 'trouble case' steht seit der Veröffentlichung von "The Cheyenne Way" durch Llewellyn und Hoebel (1)* im theoretischen und methodologischen Mittelpunkt der ethnologischen Rechtsbetrachtung. Soweit Rechtsethnologie heute empirisch betrieben wird, ist sie vorwiegend eine Analyse von rechtlichen Verfahren, die auf teilnehmender Beobachtung oder dem Studium von Gerichtsakten beruht.
Die Kriterien, die im rechtethnologischen theoretischen Verständnis bestimmte soziale Handlungsabläufe zu ‚rechtlichen' machen, dürfen freilich nicht in der Art westlich dogmatisch-juristischer verstanden werden. Nach diesen nämlich hätten viele der von der Rechtsethnologie untersuchten Gesellschaften weder ‚rechtliche Prozesse' noch ein ‚Recht'. Dies mag auch erklären, daß bei der Suche der Rechtsethnologen nach der Inhaltsbestimmung der Begriffe ‚rechtlich' und ‚Recht' ein wesentlicher Faktor stets das Bemühen war, allen Gesellschaften Recht und rechtliche Verfahren zuzugestehen – um so Recht zu einem Konzept interkultureller Verwendbarkeit zu machen (2). Es hat sich jedoch in der rechtsethnologischen Literatur keine Definition des Rechts durchsetzen können, was wohl darauf zurückzuführen ist, daß die gegebenen Definitionen, gemessen an dem ihnen beigelegten Anspruch diachroner und interkultureller Verwendbarkeit, unvollkommen blieben.
Es soll hier jedoch nicht eingehend erörtert werden, wie und zu welchen Zwecken die case-method in all ihren Spielarten (3) in der Rechtsethnologie verwendet wurde. Es mag lediglich erwähnt werden, daß es den Wissenchaftlern zunächst darum ging, über Fälle das Recht zu finden, sei es, daß soziale Normen durch das rechtliche Verfahren ihren rechtlichen Charakter erst erhielten (4), sei es, daß Recht als Abstraktion der in einem rechtlichen Verfahren ergangenen Entscheidungen verstanden wurde (5). Die Analyse der rechtlichen Verfahren als selbständiger sozialer Handlungsabläufe kam über diesem Telos meist zu kurz und wurde erst seit den bahnbrechenden Arbeiten von Gluckmann und Bohannan der eigentliche Gegenstand von Beschreibung und Analyse (6).
Im folgenden möchte ich die dem Konzept ‚rechtliches Verfahren' gemeinhin zugeordneten sozialen Phänomene analysieren. Ziel dieser Analyse ist es nicht, eine neue Variante des ‚rechtlichen' zu definieren. Vielmehr möchte ich versuchen, über meine Beschreibung dieser sozialen Handlungsabläufe zu einem Konzept zu kommen, das einen Teil des "comparative analytical system" (CAS) bilden könnte, in der Art, wie uns dies als späte Geburt der sog. Gluckman – Bohannan Kontroverse präsentiert wurde (7).

* Anmerkungen auf den Seiten 373 ff.

Dies hat nur Sinn vor dem Hintergrund eines bestimmten theoretischen Vorverständnisses vom Recht, welches ich hier kurz skizzieren möchte (8):
Die ethnologische Rechtsbetrachtung zielt nicht auf die Definition eines Rechts, das in allen Gesellschaften gegenwärtig ist. Ebensowenig sucht die empirische Rechtsethnologie nach dieser inhaltlich genau vordefinierten Institution Recht. Wenn das Wort Recht überhaupt verwendet wird, so steht es in vager Weise für einen Teilbereich des gesamtgesellschaftlichen Lebens, in welchem bestimmte Elemente von Bedeutung sind, Verhalten und Ideen. Etwas spezifizierter ausgedrückt: bestimmte Verhaltensregelmäßigkeiten wie u.a. auch die noch näher zu beschreibenden rechtlichen Verfahren, sowie die sich hierauf beziehenden, hierfür vorgesehenen und hierbei entstehenden Ideen, normativen wie wertindifferenten Inhalts. Statt nun diese Elemente oder Teile derselben in einer Definition zu kombinieren, geht es darum, sie miteinander und mit anderen Elementen und Faktoren in Beziehung zu setzen und die dabei entstehenden Relationen und Korrelationen zu deuten.
Diese Charakterisierung des rechtlichen Bereichs ist reichlich oberflächlich; die ihn ausfüllende Wirklichkeit ist in fast allen Gesellschaften wesentlich komplexer. Diese Komplexität liegt zunächst innerhalb dieses Bereichs: In den meisten Gesellschaften gibt es unterschiedliche Formen der Behandlung von trouble cases, die sich dem Grad der Formalisierung und der sozialen Bedeutung nach unterscheiden. Und auch der Bereich der Ideen, vor allem der normativen Ideen, ist keinesfalls einheitlich, sondern in den meisten Gesellschaften ideologisch vordifferenziert. Die Komplexität liegt ferner außerhalb dieses Bereichs: der hier als rechtlich bezeichnete Bereich ist kein in sich geschlossenes System, sondern nur ein nach einem bestimmten Schwerpunkt gekennzeichneter Teilbereich des gesamtgesellschaftlichen Lebens, der wiederum mit anderen, ebenso vage bestimmten Teilbereichen, etwa der Wirtschaft etc., in einem Verhältnis wechselseitiger Beeinflussung steht. Auch für die Elemente des rechtlichen Bereichs (wie für jeden Bereich menschlichen Zusammenlebens) ist ein Verhältnis dauernder gegenseitiger Beeinflussung anzunehmen; die in ihnen verkörperten sozialen Phänomene beruhen auf einer „strukturellen Gesamtverursachung", die Geiger (9) wie folgt beschrieben hat: „Wenn zwei oder mehrere Einzelfaktoren innerhalb eines Systems in gewisser Weise kovariant sind, mag es sein, daß eine unabhängige Variable, genannt Ursache, nicht zu entdecken ist. Es läßt sich nur der innerkonnektive Verlauf der einzelnen Veränderungen im System beschreiben und quantifizieren".
Danach kann man davon ausgehen, daß beispielsweise die Tätigkeit bei der Behandlung von trouble cases (die Entscheidungstätigkeit in rechtlichen Verfahren) sowohl die Verhaltensweisen wie auch die normativen Ideen in einer Gesellschaft beeinflußt, daß andererseits die Verhaltensweisen die normativen Ideen und die Entscheidungstätigkeit beeinflussen (10) und daß schließlich die normativen Ideen die Entscheidungstätigkeit und die Verhaltensweisen beeinflussen (11). Im eigenen Erkenntnisprozeß spiegelt sich dies so wieder, wie es von Gluckman treffend gekennzeichnet wurde (12): "We are caught in a circle in which law, it is true, can only be understood through cases — but cases can be understood only through law, and both have to be set in the matrix of social process".
Innerhalb dieses rechtlichen Bereichs kann man im Grunde jedes Element mit der gleichen Berechtigung zum Mittel- und Bezugspunkt machen. Legalismus, Be-

haviourismus und Rechtsrealismus haben dies auf ihre Weise getan. Jede dieser Denkrichtungen kann auch durchaus einen Realitätsbezug für sich in Anspruch nehmen, denn schließlich sind die Elemente, auf die sie sich beziehen, in jeder Gesellschaft tatsächlich vorhanden. Der Unterschied liegt nur in den Relevanzkriterien, dort, wo der konkrete Bezugspunkt gesucht wird und welche Bedeutung ihm zugemessen wird. Dies ist jedoch weder ein theoretisches Problem noch ein methodologisches, sondern nur ein Unterschied im Erkenntnisinteresse.

Die erkenntnistheoretische Ausgangsbasis jedoch, daß es sich bei der Beschreibung, Definition und Analyse des Rechts um analytische Spiele, Beschreibungs- und Deutungsversuche innerhalb eines Korrelationsmodells mit jeweils künstlich fixiertem Mittelpunkt handelt, wurde fast immer dadurch verschleiert, daß es nicht dabei blieb, eines dieser Elemente in den Mittelpunkt zu rücken, sondern daß dies Element oder eine bestimmte Kombination von Elementen zu „Recht" erklärt wurde – und hier unterscheiden sich dogmatische Rechtswissenschaftler in keiner Weise von dogmatischen Sozialwissenschaftlern.

Der Unterschied zwischen Erkenntnistheorie, Erkenntnisinteresse und Methodologie sollte klarer gesehen werden. Und es ist wohl das unrühmliche Verdienst der sog. methodologischen Trias, daß durch sie dieser Unterschied weiterhin verwischt wird, obgleich gerade sie ihrer inneren Logik nach ein theoretisches Vorverständnis in dem hier skizzierten Sinn voraussetzt (13).

In der Praxis hat das dazu geführt, daß Erkenntnistheorie aus Methodologie deduziert wurde (14) und daß die Dogmatik durch die Hintertür der Methodologie wieder in die ehtnologische Rechtsbetrachtung hineinschleicht, obgleich sie dort seit der Erkenntnis, daß jede Auseinandersetzung nur darum gehen kann, was Recht sein soll und nicht darum, was Recht ist, nichts mehr zu suchen hat (15).

Eine absolut gültige, objektiv richtige Fixierung der rechtlichen Elemente gibt es nicht. Methoden und ihre theoretische Aufbereitung werden stets durch die eigenen gesellschaftlichen Verhältnisse und die dort herrschenden wissenschaftlichen Denkmuster bestimmt. Diese sind weder falsch noch richtig, ihr Wert kann nur an ihrer inneren logischen Konsistenz und ihrer relativen methodologischen Sinnhaftigkeit gemessen werden, die sich wiederum an dem eigenen oder einem vorgegebenen Erkenntnisinteresse orientiert. Da sich Erkenntnisinteresse und methodologische Sinnhaftigkeit weitgehend an den in einer Gesellschaft beobachteten oder erwarteten sozialen Phänomene orientieren, werden verständlicherweise auch unterschiedliche Methoden in unterschiedlichen Gesellschaften von unterschiedlichem Wert sein.

In einer Gesellschaft mit einem sehr umfassenden und differenzierten System von kodifizierten normativen Ideen ist es durchaus sinnvoll, als Bezugspunkt für die Betrachtung des rechtlichen Bereichs in den Mittelpunkt der Betrachtung jene kodifizierten Sätze zu stellen, die Recht sein sollen nach dem Willen derjenigen, die in der Gesellschaft das Privileg haben zu bestimmen, was Recht sein soll und diese dann mit der Entscheidungstätigkeit der Gerichte und/oder dem Verhalten der Bevölkerung in Beziehung zu setzen, um so auf klassisch juristisch-soziologische Weise über die funktionale Analyse des schriftlichen Idealrechts zu der ‚Rechtswirklichkeit' zu kommen.

Ebenso deutlich ist, daß sich dieser Ansatz für die Gesellschaften, die den Untersuchungsbereich der traditionellen Rechtsethnologie bilden, nicht besonders gut eignet, da es dort keine Kodifikationen gibt. Hier liegt es nahe – wie es auch heute üblich ist – die Behandlung des trouble case in den Mittelpunkt zu rücken, und sie mit den in einer Gesellschaft beobachteten Verhaltensweisen und normativen Ideen in Beziehung zu setzen. Und hierbei dürfte es gleichermaßen interessant sein, diese normativen Ideen zu erfragen, aus Verhaltensweisen zu inferieren oder aus den Entscheidungen früherer Konfliktsbehandlungsverfahren zu abstrahieren (16).

Von den zunächst anzustellenden erkenntistheoretischen Überlegungen kann und sollte man die methodologischen jedoch trennen. Deshalb scheint es auch absurd, einen der Beobachtungs- und Deutungsausschnitte theoretisch (Pospisil) oder methodologisch (Abel) zu dogmatisieren und zu ‚Recht' zu erklären (17). Um der Gefahr eines Mißverständnisses vorzubeugen: hiermit soll nichts gegen die ad-hoc Inhaltszuschreibung für Arbeitsbegriffe für die Untersuchung des Rechts einer Gesellschaft gesagt werden. Diese sind unumgänglich und ermöglichen erst Verstehen, wenn die einmal gewählten Begriffsinhalte konsequent verwendet werden (18). Absurd wird dies erst, wenn mit dem Begriffsinhalt das „Recht an sich" beschrieben und diesem Konzept ein 'cross-cultural analytical value' (19) beigegeben wird. Die Selektivität, die Definitionen des Rechts bei den vielen unterschiedlichen semantischen Implikationen des Wortes automatisch gewinnen, bedarf noch einer besseren Begründung als sie uns bisher gegeben wurde (20). So hat Holleman kürzlich eindrücklich auf die Bedeutung hingewiesen, die in manchen Gesellschaften den 'trouble-less cases' und den Prozessen der 'preventieve rechtszorg' zukommt (21), und zwar nicht nur allgemein in dem Rahmen des hier vage umrissenen rechtlichen Bereichs, sondern gerade für den Bereich effektiver sozialer Kontrolle, der Schaffung von normativen Ideen, des Entstehens von Präzendenzfällen etc., gerade also für jene Kriterien, die für die selektiven dogmatischen Rechtsdefinitionen für relevant erklärt werden (22). Versteht man die Rechtsethnologie auch als sozialwissenschaftliche vergleichende Betrachtungsweise des rechtlichen Bereichs, so sollte man nicht durch selektive Definitionen, die zu einer Selektivität in der Methodologie animieren, seine eigene wissenschaftliche Arbeitsweise sterilisieren.

Für die sozialwissenschaftliche Betrachtungsweise des rechtlichen Bereichs auf der Basis des hier skizzierten Vorverständnisses liegt noch keine ausgearbeitete Theorie oder Methodologie und auch kein diesen entsprechender Begriffsapparat vor, obgleich das Bedürfnis danach immer wieder betont wird (23). Die Zukunft hierfür wird in der Erarbeitung von Korrelationsmodellen für beschreibende und analytische Zwecke liegen sowie in der Aufstellung von Funktionshypothesen, die die Basis für diachrone und interkulturelle Vergleiche bilden könnten. In das Repertoire der analytischen Spiele, die angestellt werden müssen, um das ‚Recht' zu erfassen, werden soviel Methodenvarianten aufgenommen werden müssen, wie man Teilelemente des rechtlichen Bereichs bei der Untersuchung zum Bezugspunkt macht.

Von den vielen Elementen, die im Rahmen des rechtlichen Bereichs von Bedeutung sind, möchte ich nun diejenigen sozialen Handlungsabläufe, die meist trouble cases, conflict resolution, dispute settlement, rechtliche Prozesse, genannt werden, analysieren. Dies mit dem Ziel und in der Hoffnung, daß die daraus resultierende Beschreibung im Sinne eines CAS als Bezugsrahmen für interkulturelle Vergleiche dienen könnte. Daß diese Beschreibung zunächst sehr weit und allgemein sein muß, und weiterer Differenzierung und Typologisierung bedarf, versteht sich von selbst, wenn man bedenkt, was sie umfassen soll. Dennoch muß man, wenn man nicht bei dem direkten Vergleich mit ethnozentrisch verdinglichten Konzepten stehenbleiben will, auch hier den ersten Schritt vor dem zweiten tun – man muß angeben, was man differenziert und wovon man eine Typologie aufstellt.

Bei diesem ersten Schritt müssen zunächst jene ‚rechtlichen Verfahren' ihrer ihnen meist beigelegten funktionalen und normativen Attribute entkleidet werden. Hiermit meine ich Worte wie dispute settlement, conflict resolution, social control, rechtliches Verfahren. Sie implizieren, daß Streitigkeiten beigelegt, Konflikte gelöst werden etc. – wir wissen jedoch, daß dies zwar oft, sicher jedoch nicht immer der Fall ist. Es soll nun hiermit keinesfalls der Untersuchungsbereich der Rechtsethnologie eingeschränkt werden. Vielmehr geht es darum, für eines der analytischen Spiele bei der Untersuchung des rechtlichen Bereichs einen Bezugspunkt – die noch näher zu beschreibende Behandlung von trouble cases – festzulegen, und ihn dann mit bestimmten Variablen in Beziehung zu setzen (24). Eine Reihe dieser Variablen würde dann durch die genannten funktionalen oder normativen Attribute gebildet. Die Funktionen des ‚rechtlichen Verfahrens' stellen sich dann in der Untersuchung als die jeweilige Höhe von nach bestimmten Funktionshypothesen (settlement, resolution, rechtlich, control) ausgewählten Korrelationen dar (25).

Der bisher beste Ansatz zur Beschreibung der als rechtlich im weitesten Sinne interessierenden sozialen Handlungsabläufe stammt von Bohannan, der sie als 'counteraction' bezeichnet (26). Diese folgen Vorfällen, die als Normbruch apostrophiert werden können – ihr Resultat ist eine Berichtigung (correction), die in der Wiederherstellung der Norm (re-establishment of norm) oder in einer Vergeltung für ihren Bruch (retribution) liegt. Bohannan kommt daher zu folgender Kette von sozialen Akten, die die rechtlichen Prozesse schlechthin kennzeichnen:

Breach of Norm ⟶ counteraction ⟶ correction

Diese allgemeine Beschreibung ergänzt Bohannan durch die unterschiedlichen modalen Formen, in welchen sie im Tiv-Rechtsleben institutionalisiert ist:

Courts:
Breach of norm ⟶ jir(court) ⟶ restoration of norm or substitute for norm

Self-right enforcement:
Breach of norm ⟶ action of self-help ⟶ retribution or restoration

Moot:
Omens(including illness and death) ⟶ jir (moot) ⟶ ritual reparation

und schließlich:
Sin ⟶ ritual ⟶ restoration of norm

Dieser Beschreibung ist mit Recht entgegengehalten worden, sie sei für vergleichende Zwecke zu allgemein (27). Dem wäre hinzuzufügen, daß Bohannan trotz seiner Abscheu vor der Übersetzung sozialer Phänomene in traditionellen Gesellschaften in die ethnozentrischen juristischen Begriffe der westlichen Welt bei der Beschreibung dessen, was die counteraction auslöst, wie bei der Beschreibung der ihr folgenden Ergebnisse gerade auf diese Begriffe zurückfällt. Ein

weiterer Grund, aus dem sich sein Schema nicht für ein CAS eignet (28), ist, daß er bei der Differenzierung der counteraction-Prozesse von den Typen des Tiv-Folk-System ausgegangen ist.
Den Ansatz, die Beschreibung dieser Prozesse als Kette von sozialen Akten, möchte ich übernehmen. Mit der obigen Kritik sind zugleich die Anforderungen erhoben, die eine solche Beschreibung als CAS erfüllen müßte: Der Begriff der counteraction sollte weiter präzisiert werden (a), es sollte, möglichst ohne Rückfall in ethnozentrische Kategorien, deutlich gemacht werden, worauf diese Prozesse erfolgen (b), und zur Differenzierung dieser Prozesse sollte auf Prinzipien zurückgegriffen werden, die diese analytisch strukturieren (c).
Unter Berücksichtigung dieser Punkte möchte ich diese Prozesse „formalisierte Reaktionsweisen auf Sachverhaltsbilder, die einen Konflikt zum Inhalt haben" nennen und diese Wortwahl im folgenden erläutern:

1. Sachverhaltsbilder, die einen Konflikt zum Inhalt haben

Ich möchte die Charaterisierung dessen, worauf die counteractions, die formalisierten Reaktionsweisen (fRW) folgen, mit dem Gebrauch des Wortes Sachverhaltsbild (SB) beginnen. Damit soll die, keineswegs neue, Erkenntnis betont werden, daß bei allen Reaktionsprozessen, sei dies ein gerichtlicher Prozeß oder ein Fall von legal self-redress, auf ein Vorstellungsbild, ein SB, reagiert wird; daß stets über ein SB geurteilt wird. Die inhaltlichen Bezugspunkte, die diese SB formen, können unterschiedlichster Art sein. Im Grunde liegt immer ein Bild von einem Zustand vor, welcher durch unterschiedliche Dominanten geprägt wird, beispielsweise Handlungen, Meinungen, vermutete oder geäußerte Auffassungen über einen vergangenen, gegenwärtigen oder zukünftigen Zustand. Diese SB werden gebildet durch individuelle Perzeption, Kausalitätshypothesen, Zurechnungs- und Wahrscheinlichkeitshypothesen etc.
Dieser Umstand scheint mir deshalb so betonenswert, da die meisten ethnologischen und soziologischen Normtheorien von sozialen Normen und Verhaltensregelmäßigkeiten ausgehen. Diese implizieren, daß über Verhalten, besonders über von Verhaltensregelmäßigkeiten abweichendes Verhalten geurteilt, auf dieses reagiert werde: dies meist in der guten Absicht, zu einer realitätsbezogenen Rechtsbetrachtung zu kommen. Die Betonung des Verhaltensaspekts ist jedoch irreführend: Reagiert, geurteilt wird stets auf ein SB. Dieses bezieht sich zwar oft, aber längst nicht immer auf Verhalten. Und selbst wenn es das tut, muß dies mit unseren Vorstellungen von Verhalten (nach unseren Kausalitätshypothesen) nicht immer viel zu tun haben.
Dies gilt für rechtliche Prozesse in unserer Gesellschaft genauso wie für solche in traditionellen Gesellschaften. Jedem, der einmal den Tatbestand eines modernen Urteils gelesen hat, wird das schnell klar sein. Besonders deutlich ist es bei den Reaktionsweisen, die auf das SP ‚Verdacht' folgen, sei dies die Einleitung eines Ermittlungsverfahrens oder ein Indizienurteil.
Um ein Beispiel aus einer traditionellen Gesellschaft zu geben: Bei manchen afrikanischen Stämmen, z.B. den Cewa in Zentralafrika, herrscht die Vorstellung, daß Unglück durch die Übertretung bestimmter Verhaltensvorschriften verursacht werde. Ein häufiger Fall ist das Stereotyp, daß der Tod einer Frau während der Schwangerschaft oder im Kindbett auf einen Ehebruch ihres Mannes zurückzu-

führen ist. Der Mann muß den Verwandten seiner Frau in einem solchen Falle Schadensersatz leisten (29). Legt man unsere Kausalitätsvorstellungen zugrunde, so hat dies mit einem tatsächlichen Verhalten des Mannes nichts zu tun. Das Beispiel macht deutlich, daß die Normtheorie, wenn sie es erfassen will, notgedrungen in die Kategorien Verhalten (Tötung der Frau durch/und Ehebruch) – Beweis (Tod der Frau) – Wertung – Sanktion zurückfallen muß, in die Kategorien Tat- und Rechtsfrage (30).

Dies soll nicht heißen, daß rechtswissenschaftliche Kategorien für die sozialwissenschaftliche Betrachtung des rechtlichen Bereichs unbrauchbar seien; aber gerade der geschilderte Fall macht deutlich, daß es sehr fragwürdig ist, innerhalb dieser Kategorien den theoretischen und begrifflichen Ansatzpunkt zu suchen (31).

Dies gilt auch gegenüber Bohannan, wenn er meint, die counteractions erfolgten auf etwas, was man als Normbruch apostrophieren könne. Schließlich starten viele Reaktionsweisen, auch bei uns viele gerichtliche Prozesse damit, daß jemand schlicht sauer ist, und wenn es ihm auch gelingen mag, das als Normbruch zu rationalisieren, so ist damit noch lange kein analytisches Konzept geschaffen. Und auch wenn man Normbruch zum analytischen Konzept gestaltet (nach welcher Normtheorie auch immer), so kann man schlecht sagen, der Prozeß habe auf einen Normbruch erfolgt, wenn im Laufe des Prozesses festgestellt wird, daß kein Normbruch vorgelegen habe.

Können wir die SB, denen die Reaktionsweise folgt, nicht als Normbruch bezeichnen, so bleibt doch weiterhin die Frage und das Bedürfnis nach einer weiteren formell-inhaltlichen Konkretisierung der SB.

Hier bietet sich der Bezug auf den Begriff Konflikt an, der in der Literatur auch meist in diesem Zusammenhang verwendet wird. Freilich ginge es hier dann nicht um Reaktionsweisen auf Konflikte, sondern um Reaktionsweisen auf SB, die einen Konflikt zum Inhalt haben.

In der sozialwissenschaftlichen Rechtsbetrachtung wird Konflikt meist zur Charakterisierung der Nichtübereinstimmung von Interessen oder Wertungen zweier Parteien (alter und ego (32)) und des Widerstreits derselben als Interaktion zwischen den beiden Parteien verwendet (33). Der Konflikt, die Nichtübereinstimmung, hat zwei Pole. Und so wird Konflikt auch weithin synonym gebraucht mit dem Begriff Streitigkeit (dispute) (34). Die Idealtypen der Konfliktsbehandlung gehen dann auch meistens von den Fällen aus, in denen die Pole, zwischen denen die Nichtübereinstimmung besteht, zugleich die an der Behandlung des Konflikts beteiligten Parteien sind, erfolge dieser Prozeß zwischen den beiden Parteien allein oder werde er vor einer oder durch eine dritte Partei durchgeführt (35).

Keinesfalls soll in Abrede gestellt werden, daß die meisten sozialen Handlungsabläufe, um die es hier geht, und für die ein CAS gefunden werden soll, dieser Art sind. Es liegt auch nahe, es bei dieser Charakterisierung zu belassen. Vergegenwärtigen wir uns jedoch den Sinn des CAS, so können wir uns hiermit nicht zufrieden geben. Denn das CAS soll ja gerade nicht den Regelfall zum Bezugspunkt machen, sondern soll einen Bezugspunkt darstellen, vor welchem eine bestimmte Kategorie von Fällen erst als Regelfall erkannt werden kann. Und mehr als Regelfälle sind die erwähnten nicht. Folgende Ausführungen mögen das näher illustrieren:

X hat einen Streit mit Y wegen einer Forderung. Da Y nicht zahlen will, verklagt ihn X vor einem (gegenwärtigen deutschen) Gericht. Y reagiert nicht, läßt sich im Prozeß auch nicht vertreten. Es ergeht ein (Versäumnis-)Urteil gegen ihn, auf das er ebenfalls nicht reagiert.

Hier liegt eine Streitigkeit, ein Konflikt zwischen Y und X vor. Im gerichtlichen Verfahren jedoch, der Reaktionsweise, die diesem Konflikt folgt, war einer der Konfliktspole nicht aktiv beteiligt. Seine Beteiligung wird durch das deutsche Folk-System (ZPO) fingiert, d.h. es wird davon ausgegangen, daß er die Behauptungen des X anerkennt. Dies ist jedoch ein Spezifikum des deutschen Folk-Systems, das die Nichtbeteiligung des Y an dem sozialen Handlungsablauf ‚gerichtliches Verfahren' nicht ersetzen kann. Schon dieses Beispiel führt zu folgenden Fragen, die das Verhältnis zwischen Konflikt und der darauf folgenden Reaktionsweise erhellen:

1. Hat das SB, auf das mittels der fRW reagiert wird, einen zweipoligen Konflikt zum Inhalt?
2. Wird es von einer oder zwei (mehreren) Parteien in die RW eingeführt?
3. Sind die das SB in die fRW einführenden Parteien die Pole des Konflikts?
4. Kommt es während der fRW zur Interaktion zwischen den Polen der Nichtübereinstimmung?

Am obigen Beispiel sieht man, daß die Zweipoligkeit des Konflikts durchaus zu vereinbaren ist mit der einseitigen Einführung des SB in den Prozeß und der Beteiligung nur eines Poles an der fRW.

Im folgenden Fall, bei den Eskimos, scheint dies schon fraglich (36): „P. hatte drei Menschen umgebracht, den Ehemann einer Frau, die P. ihm weggenommen hatte, sowie zwei andere Männer, die den Tod des Ehemannes rächen wollten. Die Einheimischen wollten P. nach diesen Gewalttaten loswerden, trauten sich jedoch nicht an ihn heran. Als der Häuptling des Akudmirmiut von diesen Vorkommnissen hörte, begab er sich nach Süden und fragte jedermann, ob P. getötet werden solle. Alle stimmten dafür. Also ging er mit P. auf die Jagd und schoß ihn in den Rücken".

Etwas später heißt es: „Ähnliche Gebräuche gibt es bei allen Eskimos ... Dabei ist von Bedeutung, daß derjenige, der die Tötung durchführt, im voraus die Billigung der Gemeinschaft erlangt. Hat er diese Billigung erlangt, dann kann keine Blutrache an ihm verübt werden, denn seine Tat gilt nicht als Mord. Sie ist die Vollstreckung eines Urteils, das im Namen des Volkes gesprochen wurde, und damit trägt das Volk auch die Verantwortung dafür".

Ein Konflikt, eine Streitigkeit, lag vor: zwichen P. und den von ihm getöteten Männern. An der Reaktionsweise, dem Urteilsprozeß der Gemeinschaft, war jedoch keiner der jeweiligen beiden Pole beteiligt. Auslöser für die fRW ‚Urteilsprozeß' war die Evaluation des SB „P. hat drei Menschen getötet" seitens der Gemeinschaft. Die für den Konflikt essentielle Nichtübereinstimmung entstand auf nur einer Seite, einem Pol, der Gemeinschaft, durch die Konfrontation eines SB mit einem Wertungsmaßstab. Mit einem zweipoligen Konflikt, mit einer Streitigkeit hat das nicht viel zu tun.

Allerdings ist der Zusammenhang mit dem zweipoligen Konflikt im Eskimo-Beispiel noch gegeben: das SB, daß die Nichtübereinstimmung auf der Seite der Gesellschaft hervorrief, hatte einen zweipoligen Konflikt zum Inhalt.

Aber auch diese Sachlage kann nicht für alle Prozesse des "conflict management" angenommen werden: Die SB zum Beispiel, „zwei erwachsene Männer haben intimen Umgang miteinander" oder „zwei nicht verheiratete Menschen haben geschlechtlichen Verkehr im Hause ihrer Eltern mit deren Billigung" enthalten für die an diesem Verhalten beteiligten Personen keine Konfliktelemente. Dennoch haben diese SB Gerichtsverfahren ausgelöst, die wir ohne weiteres als fRW

betrachten. Auslöser dieser fRW ist die Evaluation der SB durch die Staatsanwaltschaft; die Konfrontation des SB mit einem Wertungsmaßstab, den in diesem Fall das Gesetz bietet.
Das Individuum (oder eine Gruppe von Individuen) kann natürlich differenziert werten – es mag ein SB als „moralisch noch vertretbar", „rechtlich jedoch zu beanstanden" oder vice versa empfinden, die Evaluation kann gegenüber dem eigenen Gefühl und/oder anderen differenzierten Wertungsmaßstäben erfolgen.
Will man auch diese SB, denen fRW folgen, als Konflikt bezeichnen, muß man neben dem zweipoligen Konflikt auch von einem einpoligen ausgehen: eine Reaktion auslösende Nichtübereinstimmung, die durch die Konfrontation eines SB mit einem Wertungsmaßstab im weitesten Sinne entsteht.
Diese Reaktion kann zur Interaktion mit einem anderen führen: in diesem Falle liegt dann ein zweipoliger Konflikt vor, dem wiederum eine fRW folgen kann. Die Reaktion kann aber auch direkt in eine fRW führen, in der es zur Interaktion zwischen zwei Polen kommen kann, aber nicht muß. So schließen Reaktion und Interaktion einander nicht aus, können jedoch nicht gleichgesetzt werden.
Für beide Arten von Konflikt gilt, daß wir sie letztlich erst aus der Reaktion erkennen können, denn inhaltlich objektive und interkulturell gleichermaßen gültige Kriterien für den Konfliktscharakter eines SB gibt es nicht (37). Für beide Arten von Konflikten gilt weiter, daß jeder, der nicht einer der Pole ist, nie sicher davon ausgehen kann, daß die nach außen präsentierte Evaluation, sei diese verbalisiert oder aus dem reaktiven Verhalten inferiert, der tatsächlich vorgenommenen „echten" Evaluation entspricht. Hier sind wir jedoch an einer Erkenntnisgrenze angelangt, die wir als Rechtsethnologen in der Regel nur mit Spekulation überbrücken können, und welche die Psychoanalyse weiter durchdringen mag. Bei der Bestimmung des CAS braucht uns dieser Umstand jedoch nicht zu bekümmern, denn auch die Frage nach den „echten" Evaluationen und Konflikten wird stets von dem ausgehen müssen, was hier als SB, die einen Konflikt zum Inhalt haben (KSB), beschrieben wurde.

2. Formalisierte Reaktionsweisen

Bei der Beschreibung von fRW können und sollen natürlich nicht alle Reaktionshandlungen auf KSB erfaßt werden. Mit der Formulierung „formalisierte Reaktionsweisen" sollen aus dem Spektrum denkbarer Reaktionshandlungen bestimmte Reaktionsverhaltensformen herausgefiltert werden, die in der Regel mehr umfassen werden als nur eine Reaktionshandlung.
FRW sind ein Verhaltensausschnitt, der nach bestimmten Kriterien begrenzt und nach anderen Kriterien inhaltlich charakterisiert werden muß. Dabei muß man von vornherein von einer, zumindest potentiellen Multiplizität und Multidimensionalität von RW ausgehen: auf dasselbe SB können mehrere RW nebeneinander oder nacheinander erfolgen.
So mögen auf das SB: „Ein bekannter Arzt hat bei einem Verkehrsunfall einen Passanten schwer verletzt", folgende unterschiedlichen Formen von Reaktionsverhalten folgen:
- die Staatsanwaltschaft betreibt ein Untersuchungsverfahren, verzichtet jedoch nach dessen Abschluß auf die Erhebung der Anklage;
- der Verletzte erzwingt ein Strafverfahren, in welchem der Arzt verurteilt wird;

– Arzt und Opfer einigen sich vergleichsweise über die Zahlung von Schadenersatz;
– die Ärztekammer leitet ein standesrechtliches Verfahren ein;
– alle, die von dem Unfall gehört haben, meiden fortan die Praxis des Arztes.

Oder, auf das SB: „ein Afrikaner meint, von einem anderen eine Schuld eintreiben zu dürfen, der andere will jedoch nicht zahlen"
– greift der Afrikaner zur Selbsthilfe;
– da diese nichts fruchtet, wird ein Vermittler in den Streit einbezogen, dem es gelingt, den anderen zur Zahlung eines Teiles der Schuld zu bewegen;
– alle, die das SB kennen, überhäufen den Zahlungsunwilligen mit Spott und nennen ihn fortan ‚den Geizhals'.

Die beiden Beispiele zeigen weiterhin, daß Reaktionsweisen unterschiedlichster Art auf ein KSB folgen können. Die Charakterisierung der RW kann daher nur die umfassende Beschreibung der Gemeinsamkeiten der unterschiedlichen modalen Formen von RW sein, muß also von vornherein im Zusammenhang mit den analytischen Prinzipien gesehen werden, welche die fRW strukturell differenzieren.

Der Beginn der RW ist dadurch festgelegt, daß sie auf ein KSB folgt. Das bedeutet: der(die) von einem KSB ausgelöste(n) Verhaltensimpuls(e) bestimmter Zielrichtung (38), bestimmter finaler Ausrichtung, führt als Verhalten direkt in die RW – bzw. eine ihrer modaler Formen. Für die Zielverwirklichung wird eine bestimmte Verhaltensform gewählt.

Konstitutiv für jene Verhaltensformen, die ich fRW nennen möchte, sind folgende Merkmale:

In dem nun folgenden Verhaltensausschnitt wird das SB und der(die) von ihm ausgelösten Verhaltensimpuls(e) finaler Ausrichtung einem Abstimmungsprozeß unterzogen mit der Folge, daß das auf diesen Abstimmungsprozeß folgende Verhalten auf das Ergebnis des Abstimmungsprozesses rückbezogen wird.

Wesentlich ist dabei, daß es zu einer Abstimmung der Verhaltensimpulse, der claims, kommt. Meist wird dem eine Abstimmung des SB nach dem tatsächlichen Inhalt oder der Wertung des SB vorausgehen, jedoch nicht notwendigerweise, da über tatsächlichen Inhalt und/oder Wertung u.U. keine Nichtübereinstimmung besteht (39).

Sein Ende findet dieser Abstimmungsprozeß in einer ‚Schlußfeststellung' – das Wort steht als Sammelbegriff für alle den Abstimmungsprozeß beendenden Erscheinungsformen wie Urteil, Befehl, Kompromiß, Ratschlag, Entschluß etc. Diese Schlußfeststellung bildet einen, und vielleicht den einzigen Fixpunkt der fRW. Es stellt sich die Frage, ob er zugleich der Endpunkt sein soll. Die Antwort auf diese Frage liegt in einem Kompromiß oder einer Wertung verschiedener Interessen des Wissenschaftlers, seinem Erkenntnisinteresse, seinem Interesse an der analytischen Begrenzung eines ihm wesentlich erscheinenden Verhaltensausschnitts und seinen voraussichtlichen Erkenntnismöglichkeiten. Diese können bei den einzelnen modalen Formen von fRW durchaus unterschiedlich sein.

Ich meine, daß die ersten beiden Punkte dafür sprechen, die RW über die im Abstimmungsprozeß getroffene Schlußfeststellung hinaus auf das dieser folgende Verhalten zu beziehen; und den Abstimmungsprozeß als einen durch die Schlußfeststellung analytisch begrenzten Teilbereich der RW anzusehen. Im Falle eines Gerichtsprozesses mag uns der Abstimmungsprozeß als Untersuchungsbereich genügen. Der Übergang von der reinen Fall-Analyse zur 'situational analysis' und

zum 'extended case' (40) zeigen aber deutlich eine allgemeine Ausweitung des Erkenntnisinteresses zum follow-up, zur Einbeziehung des auf den Abstimmungsprozeß folgenden Verhaltens. Wählt man als Ausgangspunkt seiner Überlegungen reaktives Verhalten, so ist der Abstimmungsprozeß im Grunde auch nur der Transformator für die von dem KSB ausgehenden final ausgerichteten Verhaltensimpulse: das ursprünglich gewollte reaktive Verhalten, bezogen auf die Evaluation des SB, wird ersetzt durch Verhalten, welches nunmehr auf die im Abstimmungsprozeß getroffene Schlußfeststellung rückbezogen wird. Bei manchen dieser als fRW einzuordnenden sozialen Handlungsabläufe wird auch dem ‚transformierten' Verhalten das Hauptinteresse gelten, bei dem Eskimo-Beispiel z.B. die tatsächliche Tötung des P.; bei einem Fall von legal self-redress steht das Handeln im Vordergrund vor der Entschlußfassung.
Mit dem Kriterium ‚formalisiert' soll eine weitere Eingrenzung der RW genannten Verhaltensausschnitte erreicht werden. Formalisiert steht für unterschiedliche Formen von Gleichförmigkeit, in erster Linie für abstrakt gleichförmig. Diese Gleichförmigkeit wird durch ein abstraktes Muster vorgegeben; wenn diese Form der RW gewählt wird, wird auf dieses abstrakte Muster reflektiert. Die Quelle dieser Gleichförmigkeit kann unterschiedlich sein: Gesetz oder Tradition; sie kann außerordentlich differenziert sein wie ein Prozeßgesetz in Deutschland oder kaum differenziert wie die Vorstellung: Wenn es einen Streit gibt, dann gehen die Leute zu X, um ihn beizulegen. Sie kann sich in unterschiedlicher Intensität auf die beiden Teilbereiche der RW beziehen, den Abstimmungsprozeß wie im gerichtlichen Verfahren oder auf die der Schlußfeststellung folgenden Handlungsmuster wie bei Formen der Selbsthilfe.
In diesem Sinne deckt sich formalisiert weitgehend mit dem Folk-System einer Gesellschaft. Immer dort, wo ein Folk-System für eine RW vorliegt, liegt auch eine fRW vor. Hiermit ist jedoch nicht gesagt, daß Folk-System und fRW identisch seien: Das Folk-System ist lediglich der Indikator für das Vorliegen einer fRW — eine Kongruenz zwischen Folk-System, das ideologischer Art ist, und dem sozialen Handlungsablauf fRW kann natürlich nicht angenommen werden (41). Der Wert der fRW als CAS liegt ja gerade darin, daß vor seinem Hintergrund Folk-Systeme beschrieben, analysiert und verglichen werden können. Als formalisiert würde ich weiter Gleichförmigkeit durch die Regelmäßigkeit eines bestimmten Reaktionsverhaltens bezeichnen. Wird dieses bewußt reflektiert, liegt eine Form von abstrakter Gleichförmigkeit vor. Doch gilt das nicht vice versa: abstrakt gleichförmige Reaktionsverhaltensformen sind auch dann fRW, wenn sie nicht regelmäßig ausgeübt werden (42).

3. Differenzierung der formalisierten Reaktionsweisen

Es wurde schon gesagt, daß sich die fRW nicht unabhängig von ihren einzelnen modalen Formen sehen lassen können. In der rechtsethnologischen Literatur finden wir auf die Frage, wie die hier fRW genannten sozialen Handlungsabläufe zu differenzieren und zu klassifizieren seien, meist die Antwort in einer Reihe von Idealtypen, nämlich:

- die einseitige Form: Blutrache, legal self-redress,
- die zweiseitige: Verhandlungen zwischen zwei Parteien, justice without courts, und

– die dreiseitige: die Verhandlung von zwei Parteien vor einer dritten Partei, third party decision, pro tanto official etc. (43). Dieser Anreihung von Idealtypen liegt in der Regel, bewußt oder unbewußt, eine genetische, evolutionäre Vorstellung von der Entwicklung des Rechtslebens zugrunde, nach der man von Recht erst sprechen kann, wenn es in einer Gesellschaft die letzte Stufe von Konfliktsbehandlung gibt. Strukturelle Prinzipien, nach denen sich die fRW analytisch differenzieren ließen, werden durch diese Beispiele jedoch nicht bereitgestellt oder versinnbildlicht, im Gegenteil, sie werden eher durch sie verwischt.

Die Angabe der an einer RW, besonders am Abstimmungsprozeß, beteiligten Seiten sagt nämlich nichts über die Zahl der an ihr beteiligten Parteien (am Abstimmungsprozeß formalisiert beteiligten Konfliktspole) aus, ebensowenig darüber, ob eine Institution (formalisierte Nicht-Partei) an ihm beteiligt ist. Die Angabe der Beteiligung einer Institution wiederum sagt ebenfalls nichts über die Zahl der an einer RW beteiligten Seiten oder Parteien aus. Die Differenzierung nach den an einer fRW beteiligten Seiten ist daher ungenau.

Es müssen vielmehr zwei Fragen, und zwar zusammen, gestellt werden, um eine analytische Strukturierung zu ermöglichen:

1. wieviele Parteien sind am Abstimmungsprozeß beteiligt?
2. ist eine Institution am Abstimmungsprozeß beteiligt?

Erst die Antwort auf beide Fragen ergibt die Anzahl der an einer RW beteiligten Seiten, nämlich Parteien ± Institution. Im Schema drückt die Horizontale das strukturelle Prinzip: Institution (I.) in einer Gesellschaft vorhanden/nicht vorhanden, und wenn vorhanden, an der RW beteiligt oder nicht? aus, während die Vertikale das Prinzip: wieviel Parteien sind an der fRW beteiligt? ausdrückt.

	I. nicht vorhanden	I. vorhanden	
		nicht beteiligt	beteiligt
1 Partei	1	1	2
2 Parteien	2	2	3
(3 Parteien)	(3	3	4)

Zu der Beteiligung der Parteien:

Eine Partei kann ein Individuum sein wie eine Gruppe von Individuen. Sie sind als Partei anzusprechen, wenn sie im Rahmen der RW einen der Pole des in der RW einer Abstimmung unterzogenen KSB und einen gemeinsam durch das KSB ausgelösten Verhaltensimpuls (claim) verkörpern. An einer fRW können ein, zwei oder mehr Parteien in dieser Form beteiligt sein.

Charakteristisch für die Beteiligung nur einer Partei ist es, daß, in der Regel auf Grund eines einpoligen KSB, nur der final ausgerichtete Verhaltensimpuls einer Partei abgestimmt wird, ohne daß es während des Abstimmungsprozesses zu einer formalisierten Verhaltenskoordination mit einer anderen Partei, z.B. demjenigen, gegen den sich dieser Verhaltensimpuls richtet, käme, sei dies, daß der andere nicht an dem Abstimmungsprozeß teilnehmen will, sei es, daß er gar nichts davon weiß (Eskimo-Beispiel, die meisten Formen der Selbsthilfe und der Blutrache).

Zwei (oder mehr) Parteien sind an einer RW beteiligt, wenn es während des Abstimmungsprozesses formalisiert zu einer Verhaltenskoordination zwischen ihnen kommt.

Als Institution im obigen Sinne ist eine individualisierbare Person(engruppe) zu verstehen, die in einer Gesellschaft formalisiert als Nicht-Partei an fRW beteiligt sein kann bzw. es ist (44). Wann eine fRW institutionell ist, wird im Einzelfall nicht immer leicht zu sagen sein, und es wird viele Grenzfälle geben, die sich nicht eindeutig einordnen lassen. Mit Bezug auf ethnographische Literatur würde ich die Grenze ansiedeln bei dem Tiv jir – at home – (45): institutionelle fRW, und den Ndendeuli-Moots (46): nicht-institutionell.

Im Verhältnis fRW und besonders institutionelle fRW zu Öffentlichkeit und Gesellschaft, steht Gesellschaft für alle Personen innerhalb einer nach bestimmten Gesichtspunkten festgelegten Grenze. Wo und nach welchen Gesichtspunkten diese Grenze gezogen wird, ist prinzipiell willkürlich. In der Regel sind es sozio-strukturelle Größen, die sich auf territoriale oder ethnische Bezugspunkte beziehen. Diese sozio-strukturellen Größen sind für Beschreibung und Analyse der fRW die primär festzulegenden Variablen (47).

Öffentlichkeit steht im Grunde für alle, die von dem SB im Einzelfall Kenntnis erlangt haben, wobei mit ‚alle' alle Personen oder nach bestimmten einschränkenden Kriterien ausgewählte Personengruppen innerhalb der Gesellschaft sind. Diese Öffentlichkeit ist potentiell allgegenwärtig, alle Formen von Reaktionsverhalten spielen sich in ihr oder vor ihr ab. Auch geht von ihr immer ein potentieller sozialer Druck aus. Dieser kann derart formalisiert sein, daß man ihn als fRW einer Partei ansprechen müßte. Ist er es nicht, so liegt eben keine fRW, sondern nur unformalisiertes Reaktionsverhalten einzelner oder vieler zur Öffentlichkeit gehörender Personen vor (48).

4. *Weitere Differenzierung der formalisierten Reaktionsweisen*

Die beiden Prinzipien „Parteien ± Institution" genügen zur ersten groben Strukturierung der fRW. Sie wurden hier nur an Hand des Abstimmungsprozesses verdeutlicht und müssen konsequenterweise auch auf den zweiten Teilbereich der fRW, auf das dem Abstimmungsprozeß folgende Verhalten ausgedehnt werden. Hierbei ist allerdings zu bedenken, daß Bezugspunkt nunmehr die Schlußfeststellung des Abstimmungsprozesses mit den transformierten Verhaltensimpulsen ist, und nicht mehr das in die fRW hineinführende SB und die von ihm ausgehenden Reaktionsimpulse.

Abgesehen davon drängen sich natürlich auch innerhalb der modalen Formen von fRW weitere Differenzierungen auf, vor allem wohl auf dem horizontalen Ast des Schemas, der institutionellen Beteiligung. Diesem Problem sind jedoch schon viele rechtsethnologische und – soziologische Überlegungen gewidmet (49), es soll darum hier nicht weiter aufgegriffen werden. Weitere Klarheit wird erreicht, wenn man die Vertikale, die an der fRW beteiligten Parteien, differenziert, wodurch insbesondere der Status der Institution in traditionellen Gesellschaften weiter erhellt wird. Denn in Gesellschaften, in denen politische Macht kaum oder gar nicht differenziert ist, kann und wird es vorkommen, daß die Institution, die an fRW beteiligt ist, die einzige Institution, das einzige Organ der Gesellschaft (d.h. innerhalb der sozio-strukturell bestimmten Grenze) ist. Es kann daher häufig geschehen, daß diese Institution selbst eine der an der fRW beteiligten Parteien ist – in Gesellschaften mit funktionell differenzierter politischer Macht werden das meist andere Organe der Gesellschaft sein.

Durch die Differenzierung der Vertikalen kann nun der Tatsache Rechnung getragen werden, daß die Institution nicht nur auf der Horizontalen erscheinen muß, sondern auch auf der Vertikalen erscheinen kann (50). Im folgenden Schema ist auf der Vertikalen: I. die I. der Horizontalen, O. eine Institution, ein Organ der Gesellschaft, welches nicht funktional identisch mit I. ist, und P. Private, Parteien, die weder I. noch O. sind.

		I. nicht vorhanden	I. vorhanden nicht beteiligt	beteiligt
	I.	–	–	1
1 Partei	O.	–	1	2
	P.	1	1	2
	P.+P.	2	2	3
	P.+O.	–	2	3
2 Parteien	P.+I.	–	–	2
	O.+O.	–	2	3
	O.+I.	–	–	2

5. Formalisierte Reaktionsweisen oder rechtliche Verfahren?

In der bisherigen Betrachtung wurden die ‚reinen' Elemente formalisierte Reaktionsweisen auf Sachverhaltsbilder, die einen Konflikt zum Inhalt haben, und (normative) Ideen zugrunde gelegt, um einen für interkulturelle und diachrone Vergleiche verwendbaren Bezugsrahmen für „rechtliche" Verfahren zu beschreiben.

Diese Konzepte mögen zu bescheiden wirken und sich deshalb unvorteilhaft von dem Begriffsapparat der Rechts- und Sozialwissenschaft abheben. Es ist nicht die Absicht dieses Beitrags, die in der Wissenschaft gängigen Definitionen des ‚rechtlichen' auf ihre Tauglichkeit zur weiteren Qualifizierung der fRW zu untersuchen.

Abschließend möchte ich lediglich diese Bescheidenheit in der Gegenüberstellung mit zwei Kriterien rechtfertigen, denen in der Rechtsethnologie und –soziologie eine große Bedeutung bei der weiten Qualifizierung der hier fRW genannten sozialen Handlungsabläufe zukommt, den Kriterien Legitimität und soziale Effektivität. Hierbei wird sich, wie ich meine, zeigen, daß auch diese Kriterien nur Variablen sein sollten, die mit den fRW in Beziehung gesetzt werden können und sollen, mit ihnen jedoch keine feste Verbindung in der Form einer Definition eingehen sollten.

Eine den meisten Definitionen des ‚rechtlichen' drohende Tautologie führt uns in das Problem hinein: Rechtlich sind die normativen Ideen, die in rechtlichen Verfahren angewendet werden – Verfahren sind rechtlich, wenn in ihnen rechtliche Ideen angewendet werden. Will man diese Tautologie vermeiden, so muß man entweder die Ideen unabhängig vom Verfahren oder das Verfahren unabhängig von den in ihm angewendeten Ideen qualifizieren.

Die Qualifizierung von normativen Ideen als rechtlich ohne Bezug auf soziale Prozesse soll hier nicht weiter untersucht werden. Sie sind stets ideologischer Art und werden in der Sozialwissenschaft kaum noch gewagt.

Man ist daher auf die weitere Qualifizierung der Verfahren angewiesen, und zwar unabhängig von der Art der Ideen, die in ihnen zur Verwendung kommen. Die

Kriterien Legitimität und soziale Effektivität (zumindest potentielle Effektivität) sollen in den meisten Definitionen diese Qualifizierung leisten (51).

Legitimität

Der für Legitimität gewählte Bezug ist in der Regel normativer Art, gebunden an die ad-hoc Zustimmung der jeweils höchsten politischen Autorität, an innere Wertvorstellungen der Gesellschaftsmitglieder oder an ein für legitim erklärtes abstraktes Formalisierungsmuster (52). In diesem Sinne ist die Unterscheidung: legitim – nicht legitim nichts anderes als die Dichotomie: Recht – Unrecht oder rechtmäßig – unrechtmäßig. Da diese Wertzumessung zu verschiedenen Zeiten und in verschiedenen Gesellschaften unterschiedlich ist, kann sie keine interkulturell gültige Qualifizierung leisten.
Es stellt sich nur die Frage, ob die jeweilige Legitimität der fRW konstant gesetzt werden soll. Hier kommt man jedoch schnell zu dem Ergebnis, daß dann sehr viele Formen von Reaktionsverhalten ausgeschieden werden müßten, die wir zu unserem Untersuchungsbereich zählen und die auch trotz fehlender Legitimität rechtlich genannt werden (53).
Legitimität kann jedoch auch nicht-normativ als soziale Größe bestimmt werden, in das rein Faktische abgedrängt werden (54). Die Legitimität einer fRW bestünde dann in der Tatsache ihrer Zugelassenheit, ihrer Existenz. Begreift man aber unter dem ‚Faktischen' lediglich die Existenz, so sind wir im Grunde bei der Beschreibung der fRW. Durch die Verwendung des Begriffs Legitimität würde also keine weitere Qualifizierung geleistet; die Verwendung des Begriffs in diesem Sinne würde hier nur Verwirrung stiften.
Eine weitere Qualifizierung im Bereich des Bestehenden wird versucht durch das Kriterium der *sozialen Effektivität* (55). Was soziale Effektivität im Einzelfall bedeuten soll, läßt sich nur vor einem oder mehreren Bezugsrahmen bestimmen. Als Bezugsrahmen kommen in erster Linie die Zweckbestimmungen der fRW in Betracht. Soziale Effektivität steht dann für die Höhe der Korrelation zwischen der Zweckbestimmung und dem erreichten Zweck. Diese Zweckbestimmungen der fRW sind jedoch keine objektive, interkulturell gleiche Größe. Entweder sind sie gesellschaftliche und gesellschaftsgebundene Zweckzuweisungen, die zu den abstrakten Formalisierungsmustern der Folk-Systeme gehören. Oder sie sind das Ergebnis der Interpretation empirischer Daten oder auf andere Weise gewonnene analytische Konstrukte des Untersuchenden. Zudem wird soziale Effektivität innerhalb der modalen Formen der fRW auf die beiden Teilbereiche der fRW in unterschiedlicher Weise bezogen:
Beim einparteiigen Reaktionsverhalten ist die soziale Effektivität nahezu gleichbedeutend mit der Existenz der fRW: die innere Absicht, auf ein KSB einer bestimmten finalen Ausrichtung entsprechend zu handeln, konstituiert noch keine fRW (56). Dagegen stehen bei der institutionellen fRW die Zweckbestimmungen der abstrakten Formalisierungsmuster im Vordergrund, die in der Regel allein auf den Abstimmungsprozeß bezogen werden. Hier wird soziale Effektivität am Ende des Abstimmungsprozesses gemessen und nicht nach der Effektivität des Abstimmungsprozesses selbst gefragt. Hier reicht es, wenn ein Urteil gefällt wird, wenn normabweichendes Verhalten sanktioniert wird, und damit die Zweckbestimmung erreicht wird, die in der westlichen Rechtsbetrachtung so im Vordergrund steht

und der man einen gewissen Scheuklappencharakter nicht absprechen kann (57): Ob nun ein Urteilsspruch tatsächlich befolgt wird, ob andere mit dem Verfahren verbundene Zweckbestimmungen erreicht werden, gehört nun auf einmal nicht mehr zu den essentials der für das rechtliche wesentlichen sozialen Effektivität (58).

Soziale Effektivität kommt daher als die fRW weiter qualifzierendes Merkmal nicht in Frage. Im vorne angedeuteten Korrelationsmodell würde sie durch eine Reihe von analytischen Spielen ersetzt, z.B. Verhältnis der final ausgerichteten Verhaltensimpulse zu a) der im Abstimmungsprozeß getroffenen Schlußfeststellung und b) zu dem dieser folgenden Verhalten; das Verhältnis Schlußfeststellung zu dem ihr folgenden Verhalten; alle drei bisher genannten Elemente zu bestimmten normativen Ideen, Schlußfeststellung und ihr folgendes Verhalten zu den einzelnen Zweckbestimmungen etc.

Abschließend stellt sich nur noch die Frage, ob es sinnvoll ist, *eine* Zweckbestimmung der fRW konstant zu setzen, sei dies eine durch ein Folk-System vorgegebene oder auf dem „Reflexionsüberschuß des Betrachters" (59) beruhende Zweckbestimmung (Funktion). Dies scheint jedoch aus zwei Gründen nicht sinnvoll:

1. Funktionen wie Zweckbestimmungen treten uns als Ideen, als Funktionshypothesen entgegen. Ohne Bezug auf wahrnehmbare Wirklichkeit haben sie rein ideologischen Charakter und eignen sich wegen ihrer Beliebigkeit nicht zur Qualifikation der fRW (60).
2. Geben sie andererseits den Wirlichkeitszusammenhang der Funktionshypothese oder der Zweckbestimmung wieder, so haben wir die, von Gesellschaft zu Gesellschaft unterschiedliche, Höhe der Korrelation zwischen Funktionshypothese/Zweckbestimmung und den ihr entsprechenden empirischen Daten vor uns. Diese eignet sich wegen ihrer Unterschiedlichkeit ebenfalls nicht zur weiteren Qualifizierung.

Es zeigt sich deutlich, daß man gerade für die funktionale Analyse einen ‚reinen', seiner funktionalen Attribute entkleideten Bezugspunkt benötigt. Die Zweckbestimmungen und Funktionen der fRW erscheinen daher in dem eingangs angedeuteten Korrelationsmodell nicht als Konstanten, sondern als Variablen, die mit dem konstanten Bezugspunkt in Beziehung gesetzt werden. Für den Bereich der „rechtlichen Verfahren" meine ich diesen Bezugspunkt mit der Formulierung: formalisierte Reaktionsweisen auf Sachverhaltsbilder, die einen Konflikt zum Inhalt haben, hinreichend klar beschrieben zu haben.

Summary

Legal anthropology has more and more become a comparative sociology of law, focussing its attention on non-western countries – in order not to be confined to historical analysis of the tribal legal systems of socalled primitive people. How trouble cases are handled is the core of theoretical and methodological thinking; thus legal anthropology today is essentially a comparative sociology of legal process. However, adequate frames of reference for cross-cultural comparative description and analysis are still lacking.

In this paper it is argued that both description and analysis should be analytical games to be carried out within a correlation-model. This model would be formed by the basic elements of the *legal* field: products of thought and behaviour. These elements, or rather their parts would then be related to each other and to other variables taken from different folk-systems and from theoretical models. All of these elements should be reduced to analytical points of reference, which together would form the comparative analytical system which could be used for cross-cultural comparative research.

In this paper, an attempt is made to find an analytical point or reference for one of those behavioural elements, namely those social processes which go by the name of legal process, dispute settlement, conflict resolution, etc. The common denominator seems to be *formalized ways of reactive behaviour to situation-image about conflict.* This formulation is universal and can serve as comparative frame of reference.

The formulation can be further differentiated according to: 1) how many parties (and what sort of parties) participate, and 2) whether an institution (defined as a 'formalized non-party') participates in this process.

Though further differentiation is necessary in order to reach the goal of a comprehensive model for this point of reference, no further attributes, functional or normative, should be added to the basic frame of reference, because otherwise the aim of cross-cultural applicability cannot be upheld.

The formulation and analysis of this important basic 'legal' element might be a starting-point for a new theoretical and methodological approach to law in legal anthropology. It should be followed by elaborating analytical frames of reference for other elements of the legal fields and by formulating hypotheses which would form the bases for empirical research.

Anmerkungen

1 K.N. Llewellyn/E.A. Hoebel: The Cheyenne Way: Conflict and Case Law in Primitive Jurisprudence. University of Oklahoma Press, 1941.

2 Wie z.B. bei L. Pospisil: Anthropology of Law. New York 1971. Eine Logik, der man sich verschließen sollte. Schließlich beruht der Wert eines interkulturellen Konzepts nicht darin, daß auf die Frage, ob die dem Konzept zugeordneten sozialen Phänomene vorhanden sind, für jede Gesellschaft eine positive Antwort kommt; sondern darauf, daß es in unterschiedlichen Gesellschaften gleichartige soziale Phänomene erfassen kann. Treffend hierzu Fallers: "The anthropological study of law has, I think, suffered form a reluctance to recognize that some societies make little, if any, use of law, as if this would somehow be a matter for reproach". L. Fallers: Law without Precedent, Chicago-London 1969, S. 11.
Für einen Überblick über die begriffstheoretischen Streitigkeiten s. L. Nader: The Anthropological Study of Law, in: L. Nader(ed): The Ethnography of Law, American Anthropologist, Special Publication, vol. 67, no. 6, S. 3 ff.

3 Es gibt, wie Twining zu Recht bemerkt, mehrere Formen von case-method: ob man Gerichtsakten studiert, Prozesse beobachtet oder Interviews durchführt, ist schließlich nicht dasselbe, s. W. Twining: Law and Anthropology: A Case Study in Inter-Disciplinary Collaboration, in: Festschrift Hoebel, Law and Society Rlevlew, vol. 7, no. 4, S. 561 ff., 565.

4 Wie z.B. bei E.A. Hoebel: The Law of Primitive Man, Cambridge, Mass., 1954.

5 Wie z.B. bei Pospisil: a.a.O.

6 M. Gluckman: The Judicial Process among the Barotse of Northern Rhodesia. Manchester 1955 (1967); P. Bohannan: Justice and Judgement among the Tiv. London 1957.

7 L. Nader: Introduction, in: L. Nader(ed): Law in Culture and Society, Chicago 1969, S. 4.

8 Dieses Vorverständnis ist hauptsächlich durch die Schriften Llewellyns und Gluckmans beeinflußt. Die erste Fassung dieses Beitrags lag bereits vor der Veröffentlichung der Festschrift Hoebel, a.a.O., vor. Die in den Beiträgen von Gluckman und Holleman geäußerten Gedanken entsprechen weitgehend meiner Sichtweise und haben mich bei der Überarbeitung dieses Beitrags angeregt, s. M. Gluckman: Limitations of the Case-Method in the Study of Tribal Law, und J.F. Holleman: Trouble-Cases and Trouble-Less Cases in the Study of Customary Law and Legal Reform, in Festschrift Hoebel, S. 611 ff. und S. 585 ff.

9 Th. Geiger: Vorstudien zu einer Soziologie des Rechts. Neuwied 1964, S. 170 f.

10 In etwa die Jellinek'sche ‚normative Kraft des Faktischen'.

11 In etwa ‚die faktische Kraft des Normativen', s. E.E. Hirsch: Das Recht im sozialen Ordnungsgefüge. Berlin 1966, S. 255.

12 Gluckman in Festschrift Hoebel S. 622.

13 Twining, a.a.O. S. 570, verdeutlicht dies an Hand von Llewellyns und Hoebels Denkweise.

14 Typisch hierfür Hoebels Darstellung der sog. ideologischen und beschreibenden Methode im 3. Kapitel von "The Law of Primitive Man", S. 29 ff.

15 Gluckman: in Festschrift Hoebel, hat dies am Beispiel von Abels methodologischem Ansatz sehr klar gezeigt, vgl. R.L. Abel: Customary Law of Wrongs in Kenya: An Essay in Research Method, 17 American Journal of Comparative Law, (1969), S. 573 ff. S. auch die Kritik von Holleman in Festschrift Hoebel: a.a.O.

16 Vgl. Gluckman in: Festschrift Hoebel S. 624.

17 Es geht hier, wie auch Gluckman gegenüber Abel bemerkt, nicht um eine Kritik der tatsächlich geleisteten Arbeit, sondern um die daraus gezogenen Schlüsse, s. Gluckman: Festschrift Hoebel, S. 634.

18 Das beste Beispiel immer noch Gluckmans Judicial Process.

19 Pospisil: a.a.O., S. 23.

20 Pospisils sieben Gründe für den Wert der casuistic method leuchten bei der Betrachtung des Papua-Rechts durchaus ein – übertragen auf unser Rechtssystem muten sie jedoch eher parodistisch an, s. Pospisil: a.a.O., s. 34 f.

21 Holleman: a.a.O., S. 594.

22 Der holländische Rechtstheoretiker B. ter Haar schloß sie daher auch neben den Entscheidungen in trouble cases in seine Definition des Rechts ein, s. u.a. B. ter Haar: Het adatprivaatrecht van Nederlandsch-Indie in wetenschap, praktijk en onderwijs. Rede Batavia 1937.

23 S. vor allem die Beiträge zum Thema „Vergleichende Studien" in L. Nader(ed): Law and Culture in Society a.a.O.; S.F. Moore: Introduction, S. 337 ff.; M. Gluckman: Concepts in the comparative Study of Tribal Law, S. 349 ff.; P. Bohannan: Ethnography and Comparison in Legal Anthropology, S. 401 ff.

24 Diese Variablen können dann bei anderen analytischen Spielen ihrerseits zum Bezugspunkt gemacht werden.

25 Hierzu s. u. S. 227 ff.

26 Bohannan: Justice and Judgement, S. 211.

27 L. Nader: The Anthropological Study of Law, a.a.O., S. 22.

28 Dies war allerdings auch nicht Bohannans Absicht.

29 W. Rangeley: Notes on Cewa Tribal Law, in: Nyasaland Journal vol. 1, no. 2, S. 1 ff. Diese Vorstellung wurde als rechtlich von englischen Kolonialrichtern akzeptiert, s. F. v. Benda-Beckmann: Rechtspluralismus in Malawi, Ifo-Institut für Wirtschaftsforschung. Afrika-Studien No. 56, München 1970, S. 52 f.

30 Dies wird sehr deutlich bei Geiger: a.a.O., S. 233 ff., 238.

31 So auch V. Aubert nach L. Nader in: Introduction, S. 4, in: L. Nader(ed) Law in Culture and Society.

32 V. Aubert: Law as a Way of Resolving Conflicts: The Case of a Small Industrialized Society, in: L. Nader(ed): Law in Culture and Society, S. 282 ff., bes. 283.

33 V. Aubert: Competition and Dissensus: Two Types of Conflict Resolution, in: The Journal of Conflict Resolution 7 (1963), S. 26 ff.; T. Eckhoff: Die Rolle des Vermittelnden, des Richtenden und des Anordnenden bei der Lösung von Konflikten, in:

E.E. Hirsch und M. Rehbinder (Hrsg.): Studien und Materialien zur Rechtssoziologie. Köln und Opladen 1967, S. 243 ff. Die weitere Differenzierung von Konflikten, s. Aubert und Eckhoff a.a.O., sowie deren Implikationen für die Art ihrer Behandlung kann hier dahinstehen.

34 Eckhoff: a.a.O., S. 243.

35 P.H. Gulliver: Case Studies of Law in Non-Western Societies: Introduction, in: L. Nader(ed): Law in Culture and Society, S. 11 ff., S. 17.

36 E.A. Hoebel: Das Recht der Naturvölker. Olten und Freiburg 1968, S. 114 f., nach F. Boas: The Central Eskimos, Bureau of American Ethnology, Annual Report 6, 1888, S. 399 ff., S. 668.

37 Natürlich gibt es analytische, vorgegebene, die sich jedoch nicht immer mit dem Konflikt als sozialem Phänomen decken werden. Auch die sog. Universals kann man kaum dazu zählen. Denn sie sind nur normative Destillate, die ihren eigentlichen Erkenntniswert erst dann erhalten, wenn man weiß, wie die den Universals zugrunde liegenden SB in jeder Gesellschaft konstruiert werden.

38 Der claim im Sinne Llewellyn und Hoebels, s. Llewellyn/Hoebel: a.a.O., S. 273 ff.

39 Abstimmung von Inhalt und Wertung können, wie politische Prozesse zeigen, auch nachträglich der Abstimmung der claims angepaßt werden. Auch ist es denkbar, daß alle Abstimmungselemente automatisch gekoppelt sind, wie z.B. beim Giftordal: es soll das SB nach der tatsächlichen Seite hin aufklären, behält die dem Aufklärungsziel ex- oder implizit beigegebene Wertung bei (etwa: ob ein bestrafenswerter Mord geschehen sei?), legt durch seine Wirkung die aus der Aufklärung zu ziehenden Handlungskonsequenzen fest und vollzieht diese zugleich in seiner Wirkung.

40 S. J. van Velsen: The Extended-Case Method and Situational Analysis, in: A.L. Epstein(ed): The Craft of Social Anthropology, London 1967, S. 129 ff.; s. auch A.L. Epstein: The Case Method in the Field of Law, a.a.O., S. 205 ff.

41 Gluckman veranschaulicht dies an Hand eines Bohannan-Falles, wo er das Folk-System der Tiv „ein Abstimmungsprozeß ist erst richtig beendet, wenn beide Parteien mit der Schlußfeststellung einverstanden sind" mit den von Bohannan beschriebenen sozialen Handlungsabläufen vergleicht, s. M. Gluckman: Politics, Law and Ritual, Oxford 1971, S. 185. Zu der allgemeinen Problematik s. P.E. de Josselin de Jong: The Participants' View of their Culture, in: D.G. Jungmans/P.W.C. Gutkind: Anthropologists in the Field, Assen 1967, S. 89 ff.

42 Die fRW werden bei Vergleichen meist den Vergleichsgegenstand begrenzen, bei der Untersuchung einer Gesellschaft jedoch nicht notwendigerweise den Untersuchungsbereich ausschließlich markieren. Hier interessiert im Grunde jeder ‚interessante' Einzelfall.

43 S. Gulliver: a.a.O.

44 Der Gebrauch des Wortes ‚institutionell' entspricht also in etwa dem englischen 'institutional' – nicht jedoch dem 'institutionalised', was wiederum weitgehend dem hier verwendeten ‚formalisiert' entspricht. Die Ndendeuli-Moots sind so sicherlich ‚institutionalisiert' (im Sinne von formalisiert), jedoch nicht ‚institutionell' in dem Sinn, daß eine Institution i.S. einer Nicht-Partei an dem Prozeß teilnimmt. Umgekehrt kann ein Prozeß institutionell sein, ohne notwendigerweise auch institutionalisiert i.S. von formalisiert zu sein. Da es sich hier um den Bezug auf unterschiedliche soziale Phänomene handelt, scheint mir der hier gewählte Sprachgebrauch gegenüber dem eindimensionalen Gebrauch von ‚institutionalisiert' von Vorteil.

45 S. Bohannan: Justice and Judgement among the Tiv, S. 160 ff.

46 S. Gulliver: Dispute Settlement without Courts: The Ndendeuli of Southern Tanzania, in L. Nader(ed) Law in Culture and Society, S. 24 ff. Auf Individuen bezogen könnte die Grenze liegen zwischen dem monkalun bei den Ifugao: institutionell, und den Ndendeuli-Notablen: nicht-institutionell, s. R.F. Barton: Ifugao Law, University of California Publications in American Archaeology and Ethnology, vol. 15, 1919, und Gulliver: a.a.O.

47 Zu den unterschiedlichen sozio-strukturellen Größen s. R.A. LeVine: Anthropology and the Study of Conflict, in: Journal of Conflict Resolution 5 (1961), S. 3 ff., S. 4. Die Bedeutung der sozio-strukturellen Variablen zeigt sich deutlich bei der Beschreibung der unterschiedlichen 'zones' bei den Ifugao, wo innerhalb unterschiedlicher territorialer Bereiche unterschiedliche fRW auf dieselben KSB zu folgen pflegen, s. R.F. Barton: Ifugao Law, a.a.O., ders.: The Kalinga, Chicago 1949, S. 138 ff. Vgl. auch Hoebel: The Law of Primitive Man: a.a.O., S. 121. Ähnlich, wenn auch nicht in zones ausgedrückt, bei den Nuer im Sudan, s. E.E.Evans-Pritchard: The Nuer. London 1940, S. 156 ff. Die

Konzeption der 'legal levels' bei Pospisil dagegen erscheint zu dogmatisch, weil sie eine bestimmte Kombination, nämlich fRW und 'functional subgroup' konstant setzt, s. Pospisil: a.a.O., S. 107.

48 Nicht hierzu gehört der soziale Druck, der das Individuum zu einem bestimmten Verhalten bewegt, sei dies allgemeines oder formalisiertes Reaktionsverhalten. Soweit dies nicht in den RW erfaßt ist, handelt es sich um die Erwartungen des Einzelnen von formalisiertem oder unformalisiertem Reaktionsverhalten ‚der anderen'. Dies ist im rechtlichen Bereich ebenfalls von Bedeutung, gehört jedoch nicht in den Bereich der modalen Formen von fRW, sondern in den Bereich der Ideen, die Verhalten wie Reaktionsverhalten beeinflussen.

49 S. z.B. Eckhoff: a.a.O.

50 Das Schema geht davon aus, daß es in einer Gesellschaft, in der es keine I. gibt, auch keine O. gibt.

51 Explizit liegt der Schwerpunkt meist auf der sozialen Effektivität, zu deren Garantie die Möglichkeit der Zwangsausübung verlangt wird. S. Llewellyn/Hoebel: a.a.O., S. 287: "Law has teeth for the case of breach or trouble". Aber auch 'functional realists' wie Hoebel und Pospisil, die Recht als soziales Phänomen nicht-normativ definieren wollen, kommen ohne das Kriterium der Legitimität nicht aus, vgl. Hoebel: The Law of Primitive Man: a.a.O., S. 27: "The essential of legal coercion are general social acceptance of the application of physical power . . . by a privileged party, for a legitimate cause, in a legitimate way, and a legitimate time". Ders. in R.F. Barton: The Kalinga, a.a.O., Introduction, S. 3: If the kin group of the original killer customarily *accepts* the action of the avengers as *just*, and stays its hands from further counterkilling, then we have legal law. Auch Pospisil für den Bereich einparteiigen Reaktionsverhaltens, a.a.O. S. 9: When a counterkilling is *accepted* by the overall political authority as a *just* punishment . . . the sanctioned reprisal constitutes a case of legal self-redress that is true law.

52 Hoebel, Pospisil, a.a.O. FN 51.

53 Legitimität kann natürlich auch immer nur innerhalb einer bestimmten sozio-strukturellen Größe gesehen werden. Davon wird es auch abhängen, ob z.B. die in der Kolonialzeit und auch heute noch nicht als rechtlich anerkannten fRW in traditionellen Gesellschaften legitim oder nicht legitim sind.

54 N. Luhmann: Legitimation durch Verfahren. Neuwied 1969, S. 27.

55 Hier wird in der Regel die Betrachtung auf die Effektivität von, meist normativen, Ideen beschränkt, die durch ihre Effektivität zu Normen werden. Die Untersuchung der Beziehung: normative Idee-Verwendung in der fRW nimmt in der Betrachtung des rechtlichen Bereichs sicher einen hervorragenden Platz ein. Sie kann jedoch nicht dazu beitragen, eine weitere nicht-tautologische Qualifizierung der fRW zu erreichen.

56 Z.B. Pospisil: a.a.O., S. 89: "I suggest that the effectiveness of social control is the only important qualification of a legal sanction".

57 Es geht hier meist, s. FN 55, um Effektivität, die an der Zweckbestimmung von Ideen gemessen wird. Da als Zweckbestimmung der (aller) rechtlichen Ideen verstanden wird: befolgt zu werden oder bei Nichtbefolgung im rechtlichen Verfahren sanktioniert zu werden, läßt sich ein in sich logisches und scheinbar umfassendes Modell aufbauen, wie z.B. bei Geiger. Die Einseitigkeit dieses Denkens, sowie die Untauglichkeit zur weiteren Qualifizierung der fRW wurden schon betont.

58 So z.B. Pospisil in reichlich inkonsequenter Weise (vgl. FN 56): a.a.O., S. 83, 91. Sanction ist auf einmal nur noch "the judge's (authority's) decision about how the conflict should be resolved" (S. 83).

59 H. Schelsky: Systemfunktionaler, anthropologischer und personalfunktionaler Ansatz der Rechtssoziologie, in: R.Lautmann/W.Maihofer/H.Schelsky (Hrsg): Die Funktion des Rechts in der modernen Gesellschaft, Jahrbuch für Rechtstheorie und Rechtssoziologie Band 1, Gütersloh 1970, S. 37 ff., S. 44.

60 Die Dogmatisierung einer Funktion des Rechts oder des rechtlichen Verfahrens scheint daher aus dieser Sichtweise unsinnig, s. z.B. Luhmanns Erklärung der Funktion der kongruenten Generalisierung von normativen Verhaltenserwartungen zur Hauptfunktion und zum Grundproblem des Rechts, N. Luhmann: Rechtssoziologie, 2 Bände, Hamburg 1972, S. 105 ff. S. hierzu F.v. Benda-Beckmann: Norm und Recht in Niklas Luhmanns Rechtssoziologie: Kritische Anmerkungen aus der Sicht der Rechtsethnologie, in: ARSP 2/1974, S. 275 ff.

Rolf Bender und Christoph Strecker

Zugangsbarrieren zur Justiz

Unser Beitrag befaßt sich mit einer Untersuchung, die das Institut für Rechtstatsachenforschung Stuttgart e.V. (1)* im Auftrag des Justizministeriums der Bundesrepublik Deutschland zur Zeit durchführt. Bevor wir zu den einzelnen Arbeitshypothesen kommen, wollen wir versuchen, unser Forschungsvorhaben in den Bezugsrahmen einer idealtypischen Beschreibung der staatlichen Justiz zu stellen, sowie einige Theorien „mittlerer Reichweite" zum gerichtlichen Verfahren diskutieren.

A. Eine idealtypische Beschreibung der Funktion der Justiz

I. Wenn hier eine idealtypische Beschreibung der Justiz versucht wird, so fühlen wir uns in diesem Unternehmen bestärkt durch eine Reihe von Referaten, die auf der Arbeitstagung in Bielefeld vom 24.–28.9.1973 gehalten wurden und in diesem Band wiedergegeben sind. Bei allen Unterschieden in der Thematik dieser Referate läßt sich vielleicht doch eine – mehr oder weniger – gemeinsame Überzeugung der Referenten feststellen: Die Gerichte, jedenfalls der westlichen Welt, sind im Umbruch begriffen.

Die herkömmliche Auffassung von der Funktion der Gerichte weist diesen – und damit auch den Richtern – die Aufgabe zu, den Rechtsfrieden zu bewahren, die Konflikte zwischen den Rechtsgenossen zu beenden, sei es durch Schlichtung, sei es durch Entscheidung; zwischen Rechtsgenossen, die als „Gleiche" vom Recht und den Richtern behandelt werden.

Diese herkömmliche Bedeutung der Gerichte ist im Rückgang begriffen. Die Konfliktsbereinigung unter (wirklich) Gleichen kann durch andere Prozeduren und Institutionen (Einigungsstellen, Konfliktskommissionen, Schiedsgerichte, Ordnungsämter) effizienter bewältigt werden als durch den schwerfälligen Justizapparat. So wurde z.B. aus Italien berichtet, daß dort ca. 90 % der Baustreitigkeiten durch Schiedsgerichte erledigt werden. Die ständige Zunahme von gerichtlichen Verfahren in Deutschland bedeutet nicht, daß die Bundesrepublik aus diesem internationalen Trend etwa ausscherte. Die Gerichtsverfahren nehmen lange nicht in dem Verhältnis zu, das nach der Vermehrung der Bevölkerung, ihrer progressiven Verstädterung und der zunehmenden Komplexität der gegenseitigen Beziehungen zu erwarten gewesen wäre (2).

In verschiedenen Referaten dieser Arbeitstagung wurde der Nachweis erbracht, daß die dogmatische Fiktion, im Prozeß stünden sich „prinzipiell Gleiche"

* Anmerkungen auf den Seiten 390 ff.

gegenüber, in der Realität keine Grundlage hat. Es wurde aufgezeigt, daß und aus welchen Gründen bestimmte Parteien entscheidende Vorteile haben, andere erheblich benachteiligt sind, wenn sie vor Gericht agieren. Insitutionen, die häufig vor Gericht auftreten (z.B. Versicherungsgesellschaften, Kaufhauskonzerne u.a.), für die also das Agieren vor Gericht eine professionelle Routineangelegenheit wird, tun sich aus vielen Gründen leichter (man denke nur an ihre Rechtsabteilungen, ihre Verbindungen zu spezialisierten Rechtsanwälten, an den Ausgleich des Prozeßkostenrisikos durch die Vielzahl der zu führenden Prozesse) als Parteien, für die die Führung eines Prozesses eine einmalige Angelegenheit ist. Für „Einmalprozessierer" aus der Mittelschicht ist das Prozeßrisiko viel zu hoch, weil sie einerseits keinen Anspruch auf Bewilligung des Armenrechts haben, andererseits die hohen Prozeßkosten ohne wesentliche Beeinträchtigung ihres Lebensstandards nicht tragen können. Angehörigen aus der Unterschicht wird vielfach nicht nur durch die mangelhafte Ausgestaltung des Armenrechts, sondern mehr noch aus anderen Gründen, insbesondere wegen mangelnder Kenntnis des Rechts, ihrer Rechte und der Institutionen der Zugang zu den Gerichten versperrt. Haben sie schließlich diese „Zugangsbarrieren" überwunden, so sehen sie sich bei Gericht durch Sprach- und andere Kommunikationsbarrieren daran gehindert, ihre Rechte zweckentsprechend zu verfolgen.

II. Als Ausweg aus dieser Situation wurde die „Organisationsstrategie" vorgeschlagen, im Sinne der Devise „Beklagt euch nicht, organisiert euch!". Diese Strategie kann sicher in vielen Fällen helfen, die ökonomische Ungleichheit der Parteien aufzuwiegen, die Realität der gesetzlichen Fiktion von der Gleichheit aller Prozeßparteien anzunähern. Wo es für den Einzelnen sich nicht lohnt, wegen – im einzelnen – geringfügiger Benachteiligung die Gerichte anzurufen, kann sich ein solcher Musterprozeß für die Organisation (z.B. einen Verbraucherverband) sehr wohl auszahlen, wenn das Ergebnis allen ihren Mitgliedern zugute kommt. Solche Organisationen werden häufiger prozessieren und deshalb auch in dieser Hinsicht mit ihren prozeßgwohnten Gegnern gleichziehen. Damit gestaltet sich auch für sie das sowieso schon auf die Mitglieder gestreute Prozeßrisiko kalkulierbar.
Freilich würde die Verwirklichung der Organisationsstrategie am Rückgang der Bedeutung der Gerichte nichts ändern; sind die Schwachen durch Organisation zu annähernd Gleichstarken geworden, so bieten sich auch für sie geeignetere und effizientere Konfliktsbewältigungsstrategien an als der gerichtliche Prozeß. Das wäre freilich nicht weiter schlimm. Niemand – als allenfalls die Richter, auf die es in diesem Zusammenhang nicht ankommen kann – hat ein Interesse daran, den Gerichten eine Bestandsgarantie zu gewährleisten, wenn ansonsten alles in Ordnung geht. Indessen regten auf der Tagung sich mit Recht erhebliche Zweifel, ob sich wirklich alle berechtigten Interessen von Individuen und Randgruppen in dieser Weise organisieren lassen. Auch tauchte die besorgte Frage auf, wer in dieser schönen, neuen und gut durchorganisierten Welt die Mitglieder gegen die Organisationen schützt, die zur „Verbürokratisierung" neigen.

III. Mit dieser Frage verband sich ein anderer Gedankengang, der sich aus einer allgemeinen Tendenz in der westlichen Welt ergibt: Gleichzeitig mit dem unaufhaltsamen Rückgang der traditionellen Bedeutung der Gerichte in der ganzen westlichen Welt droht der dritten Gewalt eine unmittelbare Gefahr aus der immer enger werdenden „unheiligen Allianz“ zwischen der ersten und zweiten Gewalt. Die erste Gewalt ist durch ihre enge Verflechtung mit der zweiten Gewalt zunehmend immer weniger in der Lage, diese zu kontrollieren. Diese Allianz könnte zu einer gefährlichen Schwächung der dritten Gewalt führen und ist schon zu einer akuten und drohenden Gefahr für die "balance of powers" geworden. Die Trennung und das Gleichgewicht der Gewalten aber ist die Grundlage der Freiheit. Sowohl die erste als auch die zweite Gewalt sind in der Demokratie notwendigerweise der Macht der jeweiligen Mehrheit ausgeliefert. Die freiheitliche Demokratie hat aber von ihrer Idee her nicht nur die Macht der jeweiligen Mehrheit auf ihre Fahnen geschrieben, sondern auch den Schutz der Minderheiten und die Freiheit des Individuums. Wer aber soll diese Güter schützen, wenn nicht eine starke dritte Gewalt, eine Gewalt, die unabhängig ist von den jeweiligen Mehrheitsverhältnissen, von der Gunst der Wähler, von momentanen Strömungen der öffentlichen Meinung? Hier ist den Gerichten eine neue Aufgabe zugewachsen. Nicht mehr die Bewahrung des Rechtsfriedens, die Konfliktbewältigung unter (fiktiv) Gleichen wird immer mehr zur zentralen Aufgabe der Gerichte; sondern der Schutz der Minderheiten, der Schwachen, der Freiheit des Individuums gegen übermächtige Organisationen wird im Mittelpunkt der Tätigkeit der Gerichte stehen (3). Diese Analyse und Prognose hat entgegen den ersten Anschein keinen klassenkämpferischen, noch nicht einmal einen schichtspezifischen Bezug. Sicher werden stimmlose Randgruppen, Ohnmächtige und Unterdrückte eher in der Unterschicht zu finden sein als in der Mittel- und Oberschicht. Doch gibt es davon so viele Ausnahmen, man denke nur an die Zeugen Jehovas, die Kriegsdienstverweigerer u.a., daß man nicht sagen kann, hier wachse den Gerichten eine Aufgabe mit schichtspezifischer Prägung zu – nur eben mit dem gegenteiligen Vorzeichen als jener schichtspezifischen Bevorzugung, die die Soziologen den Gerichten bislang vorgehalten haben. Hinzu kommt noch ein Weiteres: Die neue zentrale Funktion der Gerichte stellt primär nicht auf den Schutz der absolut Stimmlosen und Schwachen ab, sondern auf die in der konkreten Konfliktsituation jeweils Schwächeren. Gegenüber dem Computergiganten IBM können sehr große und mächtige Firmen um so viel schwächer sein, daß sie einen Konflikt mit dem Giganten eben nicht durch Verhandlung und Arbitrage angemessen zu lösen vermögen, sondern durchaus auf die Hilfe der Gerichte angewiesen sind, wie die Prozesse der jüngsten Zeit in U.S.A. zeigen. Auch durchaus mächtige und stimmgewaltige Gruppen können mit ihren berechtigten Interessen bei der Legislative und Exekutive kein Gehör finden, weil diese dem Druck noch größerer und stärkerer Gruppen unterliegen. Zum Gericht aber haben alle Interessen Zugang, gerade auch dann, wenn sie bei den anderen Gewalten Niederlagen erlitten haben (4). Von ihrer Organisation, ihren Trägern und ihrer legitimen Macht her gesehen ist keine Institution in ähnlicher Weise in der Lage, diese Aufgabe zu erfüllen, den Schutz des in der konkreten Konfliktsituation Schwächeren zu gewährleisten, wie die Gerichte. Es erscheint deshalb vertretbar, diese Aufgabe zum Gegenstand einer idealtypischen Beschreibung der Funktion der Gerichte zu machen.

IV. Ist man bereit, diese Beschreibung der veränderten Funktion der Gerichte zu akzeptieren, so ließe sich daraus eine Reihe normativer Postulate ableiten; eine neue Standortbestimmung der Gerichte und damit der Richter wäre dann erforderlich. Im Mittelpunkt der Betrachtung dürfte dann nicht mehr die rechtliche Gleichheit der Prozeßparteien stehen, die davon abstrahiert, welche realen Durchsetzungschancen und Ressourcen ihnen zur Verfügung stehen. Es wird zunehmend Aufgabe der Richter werden, im Sinne einer ausgleichenden Gerechtigkeit ihr Augenmerk von der formalen Gleichheit weg und hin zu einer materialen Gleichheit zu wenden. Die Richter, in ihrer herkömmlichen Berufstradition verfangen, tun sich gewiß schwer, sich von der gesetzlichen Fiktion zu lösen, daß die vor Gericht agierenden Parteien gleich seien, gehört(e) es doch zu den höchsten Richtertugenden, „ohne Ansehen der Person" Recht zu sprechen. Um aber wirklich „ohne Ansehen der Person" entscheiden zu können, werden die Richter die Personen ansehen müssen, die vor ihrem Richterstuhl Recht suchen. Die Richter müssen die Gleichheit der realen Verwirklichungschancen aller berechtigten Interessen in ihr Blickfeld bekommen. Aus neutralen Nichtaktivisten müssen die Richter zu „liberalen Aktivisten" (Joel Großmann) werden. Mit dieser neuen Leitidee werden die bisherigen Vorwürfe vieler Sozialwissenschaftler gegen „Opas Justiz" keineswegs obsolet, im Gegenteil, sie gewinnen eine ganz neue Dimension, freilich auch eine völlig andere Perspektive: Es geht nicht mehr bloß darum, einen von der Mittelschicht für die Mittelschicht eingerichteten Dienstleistungsbetrieb auch für die Unterschicht zu öffnen. Es geht vielmehr darum, einen Damm aufzubauen gegen die übermächtige Koalition der Legislative mit der Exekutive, die die Machtinteressen der jeweiligen Mehrheit repräsentiert; es geht darum, den Schwächeren, Minderheiten, Randgruppen und isolierten, stimmlosen Individuen mit ihren legitimen Interessen zu ihrem Recht zu verhelfen. In diesem Zusammenhang freilich ist es von zentraler Bedeutung, inwieweit es gelingt, die Zugangs- und Kommunikationsbarrieren zur Justiz auch für die Schwächsten in der Gesellschaft abzubauen, eine in etwa gleiche reale Rechtsverwirklichungschance zu gewährleisten auch unter solchen Parteien, zwischen denen hinsichtlich Prozeßroutine, Unterstützung durch starke Interessengruppen und hinsichtlich der ökonomischen Ressourcen Abgründe klaffen (5).

B. Einige Theorien „mittlerer Reichweite" zum Verhältnis Bürger und „Staatsapparat".

I. Im Hinblick auf die diskutierte Beschreibung der Funktion der Justiz gewinnen einige häufig unter dem Thema „Klassenjustiz" diskutierte Theorien zur Ungleichheit von Chancen neuartige Aktulalität auch für die Juristen, die diesen Theorien bisher weitgehend ablehnend gegenüberstanden, weil sie dahinter den Umsturz witterten.

Diese häufig emotionsgeladene Ablehnung der Theorien zur „Klassenjustiz" ist freilich auf eine Begriffsverwirrung zurückzuführen, für die nicht allein die insoweit häufig wenig problemorientierten Juristen verantwortlich gemacht werden können, zu der vielmehr auch etliche Soziologen beigetragen haben. Meist wird nämlich nicht deutlich zwischen dem „staatstheoretischen" und dem „verhaltenstheoretischen" Erklärungsansatz unterschieden, die beide unter dem Begriff Klassenjustiz thematisiert zu werden pflegen. Der staatstheoretische Erklärungsansatz von Klassenjustiz stammt aus der marxistischen Rechtstheorie. Diese hat die Kernbestandteile des historischen Materialismus, die Lehre von Basis und Überbau, zur Grundlage ihrer Auffassung von staatlicher Justiz gemacht, daß

heißt, daß das Recht und die Gerichte lediglich den „Überbau" der ökonomischen Basis, der bestehenden Produktionsverhältnisse, bilden. Da die Bundesrepublik Deutschland sich in der Phase des Kapitalismus befindet und daher notwendig in zwei Klassen gespalten ist, die Kapitalistenklasse, die über die Produktionsmittel verfügt, und die Arbeiterklasse, die von dieser Verfügungsgewalt ausgeschlossen ist, ist alles Recht notwendig Klassenrecht und die Justiz notwendig Klassenjustiz – ein Subsystem, das (neben anderen) die Ausbeutung der Klasse der Werktätigen durch die Kapitalistenklasse zugleich sichert und verschleiert (6). Dieser staatstheoretische Erklärungsansatz dürfte für die rigide Ablehnung verantwortlich sein, mit welcher unterschiedslos alles zurückgewiesen wird, was unter dem „Reizwort" Klassenjustiz firmiert. Es ist wohl auch verständlich, daß sich die Richter nicht in den Rang einer dienenden Zwischenklasse versetzt wissen wollen, die die Macht der Ausbeuter stabilisiert.
Der verhaltenstheoretische Erklärungsansatz, den man – zwecks Unterscheidung vom staatstheoretischen Ansatz – besser nicht unter dem Begriff „Klassenjustiz" (7), sondern richtiger unter dem Begriff „schichtspezifische Justiz" problematisieren sollte, läßt sich unschwer auf Theorien zurückführen, die in allgemeinerer Formulierung als Theorien über die Ungleichheit von Chancen längst auch in den „bürgerlichen" Sozialwissenschaften allgemein akzeptiert worden sind.

II. Wir wollen diese in den Sozialwissenschaften (die keinen Bundesgerichtshof über sich haben) nicht verbindlich festgelegten Theorien über Zugangsbarrieren zum Staatsapparat hier wie folgt formulieren:

1. Sprachbarriere
Zwischen der Unterschicht und der Mittelschicht besteht eine „Sprachbarriere". Die verschiedenen sozialen Schichten haben verschiedene Sprachen. Die elaborierte Sprache der Mittelschicht, insbesondere in ihrer speziellen Ausprägung als „Behördendeutsch", wird von den Angehörigen der Unterschicht häufig nicht verstanden, erst recht fehlt der Unterschicht die Fähigkeit, ihre Anliegen in dieser Sprache vorzutragen. Die Sprache der Unterschicht ist ihrerseits wenig geeignet, Motive, Empfindungen und Absichten in einer Form zu artikulieren, die von der Mittelschicht verstanden würde.

2. Spezielle Kommunikationsbarriere
Zwischen der Unterschicht und der Mittelschicht besteht eine über die bloße „Sprachbarriere" hinausreichende „Kommunikationsbarriere".
Innerhalb der beiden Schichten gelten verschiedene Wertpräferenzen (auch wenn – insbesondere von der oberen Unterschicht – teilweise mittelschichtspezifische Wertpräferenzen übernommen werden – so z.B. die mittelschichtspezifische Leistungsmotivation). Bestimmte äußerlich gleichgeartete Handlungsweisen haben innerhalb der beiden Schichten verschiedene Bedeutungen. Auch die Bewußtseinslage ist häufig eine verschiedene.

3. Professionalisierung der öffentlichen Hand
Durch die am optimalen ökonomischen Nutzen orientierte Spezialisierung der verschiedenen für die Gesellschaft notwendigen Tätigkeiten und die damit verbundene Professionalisierung der nicht vorwiegend handarbeitenden Berufe

kommt es zu einer Abkapselung der einzelnen Professionen sowohl untereinander als auch zur Gesellschaft, die zu einer zusätzlichen immer weitergehenden Entfremdung des Menschen von seiner sozialen Umwelt führt.

4. Bürokratisierung der öffentlichen Hand
Die ständig zunehmende Bürokratisierung des Staatsapparates zu einem anonymen Gebilde kafkaesken Zuschnitts liefert das Individuum umso mehr einer unendlichen Hilfslosigkeit aus, als es im modernen Staat zunehmend staatlichen Eingriffen ausgesetzt und auf die Leistungen der staatlichen Verwaltungen angewiesen ist.

5. Allgemeine Kommunikationsbarrieren
Die (unter sich „verwandten") grundlegenden Theorien Nr. 3 und 4 über Zugangsbarrieren zum Staatsapparat führen zu Kommunikationsschwierigkeiten, die im Prinzip die Bürger aller Schichten treffen. Diese allgemeinen Kommunikationsschwierigkeiten werden umso eher überwunden, als die Geschäftsgewandtheit, insbesondere die Übung im schriftlichen Verkehr und im Umgang mit Behörden zunimmt; diese Fähigkeiten aber sind schichtspezifisch unterschiedlich verteilt zum Nachteil der Unterschicht.

6. Schichtspezifische Benachteiligung der Unterschicht
Die Sprach- und die spezielle Kommunikationsbarriere (Theorien 1 und 2) führen zu einer zusätzlichen schichtspezifischen Benachteiligung der Unterschicht, weil die maßgebenden Stellen des professionalisierten Staatsapparats von Angehörigen der Mittelschicht besetzt sind (8) (9).
Diese Theorien (die wir hier eigenständig formuliert haben) wurden in anderen Wissenschaftsbereichen – allgemeine Soziologie, Organisationssoziologie, Soziolinguistik – entwickelt und scheinen sich zu bewähren. Es erscheint wichtig, empirisch zu überprüfen, ob diese Theorien über Zugangsbarrieren (10) auch unter den spezifischen Randbedingungen der Justiz Geltung haben. Sollten sie sich auch im Bereich der Justiz nicht falsifizieren lassen, so müßte auf Abhilfe gesonnen werden, wenn man unseren oben unternommenen Versuch einer idealtypischen Beschreibung der Justiz akzeptiert.

C. Einige Arbeitshypothesen zur Untersuchung „Zugangsbarrieren zur Justiz"

I. Anlaß für unsere Untersuchung war die in einem Verkehrsstrafreferat gemachte Beobachtung, daß ausländische Arbeiter im Verhältnis zu ihrem Anteil an der Gesamtzahl der Angeklagten auffällig selten Einspruch gegen Strafbefehle einlegen. Es ist nicht zu vermuten, daß Strafbefehle gegen Ausländer „gerechter" sind also solche gegen deutsche Beschuldigte. Vielmehr lieg die Annahme nahe, daß unsere Beobachtung darauf hinweist, daß ausländische Arbeiter besonders wenig in der Lage sind, sich sachgerecht zur Wehr zu setzen.
Es liegt nahe, diese Vermutung zu den dargestellten Theorien in Beziehung zu setzen. Ähnliche Unterschiede müßten sich, wenn die Theorien auch für das Gerichtsverfahren gelten, auch für deutsche Beschuldigte verschiedener Schichtzugehörigkeit ergeben (wenn auch vielleicht in geringerem Maße).

Vergleichbare Beobachtungen müßten sich auch im Zivilrecht beim Mahnverfahren machen lassen.

II. An den Theorien zur „schichtspezifischen Justiz“ ist schon immer bemängelt worden, daß sie – jedenfalls, soweit sie die Bundesrepublik Deutschland betreffen – lediglich Hypothesen seien, für die bisher jeder wissenschaftlich akzeptierbare empirische Beleg fehle. Inzwischen gibt es freilich auch in der Bundesrepublik einige empirische Untersuchungen (11).
Das Dilemma, in dem sich die analytische Soziologie befindet, wenn sie die Hypothesen zur schichtspezifischen Justiz verifizieren will, liegt, wie Rottleuthner (12) zutreffend ausgeführt hat, an der Unvergleichbarkeit der verschiedenen Fälle, dem juristischen Argument der „Einmaligkeit des Einzelfalles“. Opp und Peukert haben mit ihrer Methode der „fiktiven Fälle“ versucht, dieses Argument zu entkräften. Ihnen wurde entgegengehalten, daß sich derartige „Laborexperimente“ nicht auf die Wirklichkeit übertragen ließen. Wir glauben, diesem Argument auf anderem Wege ausweichen zu können. Einmal ist unser Ansatz breiter. Uns geht es ja in erster Linie darum, Zugangsbarrieren zur Justiz aufzudecken. Sollten sich aber dabei schichtspezifische Unterschiede ergeben, bevor also noch die Einmaligkeit des Einzelfalles überhaupt zum Tragen kommt, so wäre damit auch das Argument weitgehend ausgeräumt, daß die Fälle, die wir vergleichen, nicht vergleichbar seien. Entsprechend unserem Untersuchungsziel werden wir uns in erster Linie mit Zahlungs-, Vollstreckungs- und Strafbefehlen befassen, erst in zweiter Linie mit der Verwerfung von Einsprüchen durch Versäumnisurteile und nur ergänzend mit streitigen Entscheidungen.
Eine gewisse Einseitigkeit freilich läßt sich bei der Operationalisierung wie wir sie vorhaben, nicht vermeiden. Wir werden nur die Bürger erfassen können, die sich in der Verteidigung befinden, Leute, gegen die ein Zahlungs-, Vollstreckungs- oder Strafbefehl ergangen ist. Wer eigentlich Grund hätte, angriffsweise die Dienste der Justiz in Anspruch zu nehmen, der potentielle Kläger im Zivilprozeß, der Privatkläger oder Anzeigeerstatter im Strafprozeß, den erfassen wir nicht. Daraus folgt zwangsläufig, daß dann, wenn wir etwa keine Zugangsbarrieren feststellen könnten, das ganze Problem noch nicht ausgestanden wäre, weil unsere Aussagen nur für die „Verteidigung“ Gültigkeit hätten. Sollten sich aber auf der von uns untersuchten Seite Zugangsbarrieren feststellen lassen, so wird sich mit Grund sagen lassen, daß diese auf der Angriffsseite eher größer als geringer sein werden.
Eine erste Sichtung des Untersuchungsfeldes hat bereits ergeben, daß unsere ursprüngliche Absicht, uns nur mit den Bürgern zu befassen, die überhaupt nicht reagieren, wenn ihnen ein Vollstreckungs- oder Zahlungsbefehl ins Haus geschickt wird, wenig sinnvoll wäre. Eine offenbar sehr große Zahl von Betroffenen erhebt zwar noch ordnungsgemäß Einspruch oder Widerspruch und begründet ihn auch, verfolgt aber dann ihre Rechtssache nicht weiter, so daß vor Eintritt in das streitige Verfahren Versäumnisurteil gegen sie ergeht. Es scheint also so zu sein, daß die Überwindung der eigentlichen Zugangsbarriere noch nicht bedeutet, daß auch die weiteren innerhalb des Verfahrens selbst liegenden „Barrieren“ überwunden werden. Wir werden also 3 Hauptgruppen zu bilden haben:

1. Solche Bürger, die überhaupt keinen Zugang zum Gericht finden.
2. Solche, die zwar den Zugang finden, aber das Verfahren nicht bis zur streitigen Verhandlung durchstehen.

3. Solche, die das Verfahren bis zum Vergleich oder streitigen Urteil durchhalten (Kontrollgruppe).

III. Der Plan, unsere Hypothesen über Zugangsbarrieren zur Justiz in einer Untersuchung empirisch zu überprüfen, stieß beim Bundesjustizministerium auf Interesse. Dem Bundesjustizministerium kommt es vor allem auch auf empirische Daten über die Auswirkungen der 1969 erfolgten Einführung des § 6 a AbzG an. Nach dieser Vorschrift besteht bei Abzahlungsgeschäften ein ausschließlicher Gerichtsstand am Wohnsitz des Schuldners, das Mahnverfahren indessen kann am Domizil des Klägers durchgeführt werden. Das Bundesjustizministerium ist an einer Erfolgskontrolle hinsichtlich dieser Vorschrift besonders interessiert, weil erwogen wird, eine entsprechende Vorschrift für alle Rechtsgeschäfte des täglichen Lebens einzuführen.

a) Die erste Phase unserer Untersuchung besteht aus der Analyse von Mahn- und Strafbefehlsakten, wobei die Einspruchshäufigkeit verschiedener Gruppen von Schuldnern bzw. Beschuldigten festgestellt und verglichen werden soll.
Hierbei erwarten wir Daten zur Überprüfung unter anderem folgender Hypothesen:
1. Je höher der Status (Bildungsstand und/oder geschäftliche Erfahrung) des Angegriffenen, desto größer ist seine Chance, sich zur Wehr zu setzen.
Soweit nicht andere Faktoren interessieren, müßte die Einspruchshäufigkeit bei Geschäftsleuten und Akademikern am höchsten, bei ausländischen Arbeitern am niedrigsten sein.
Für die Richtigkeit dieser Hypothese spricht die eingangs geschilderte Beobachtung: Eine Sichtung des Prozeßkalenders des erwähnten Verkehrsreferats am Amtsgericht Stuttgart ergibt, daß in diesem Referat etwa 40 % der in Strafbefehlsverfahren Beschuldigten Ausländer sind. Ihr Anteil an den nach Einspruch durchgeführten Hauptverhandlungen beträgt jedoch höchstens 20 %.
Bei einer ersten kursorischen Sichtung von Strafbefehlsakten im Hinblick auf die genannte Hypothese haben wir 3 Gruppen von Beschuldigen gebildet (13):
I. Ungelernte Berufe (Arbeiter, Kraftfahrer u.ä.).
II. Gelernte Berufe (Facharbeiter, Handwerker, einfache Angestellte u.ä.).
III. Qualifizierte Berufe (gehobene Angestellte und Beamte, freie Berufe, selbständige Unternehmer u.ä.).
Es scheint sich ein Trend dahin anzudeuten, daß die Gruppe II die höchste Einspruchshäufigkeit aufweist (ca. 40 %), gefolgt von der Gruppe III (ca. 25 %) und der Gruppe I (ca. 15 %).
Hierbei ist allerdings zu berücksichtigen, daß die letztere Gruppe zu etwa 2/3 aus Ausländern zu bestehen scheint. Was für Werte sich ergeben werden, wenn man nur die deutschen Beschuldigten berücksichtigt, läßt sich erst bei größeren Zahlen übersehen.
Die gegenüber der Gruppe II geringere Einspruchshäufigkeit der Gruppe III kann der Hypothese widersprechen. Sie kann aber auch auf einer realistischeren Einschätzung der Chancen beruhen. Möglicherweise legen Angehörige der Gruppe III in aussichtslosen Fällen seltener Einspruch ein als Angehörige der Gruppe II. Das wird im Laufe der Untersuchung zu überprüfen sein.
Denkbar ist auch, daß Angehörige der Gruppe III (im wesentlichen Oberschicht und obere Mittelschicht) bereits im Ermittlungsverfahren zu einer effektiveren

Verteidigung in der Lage sind als Angehörige niedriger rangierender Schichten. Vielleicht hält bereits die Erwartung eines entschlosseneren Widerstandes die Staatsanwaltschaft gelegentlich in zweifelhaften Fällen von einem Strafbefehlsantrag ab. Vielleicht spielt die Schichtzugehörigkeit auch bereits bei der rechtlichen und tatsächlichen Beurteilung eines Vorganges durch die Polizei eine Rolle (14). All dies könnte dazu führen, daß gegen Angehörige der Oberschicht und oberen Mittelschicht ergehende Strafbefehle in größerem Umfange der tatsächlichen Rechtslage entsprechen als solche gegen Angehörige der unteren Mittelschicht und der Unterschicht (15).

2. Je größer die Entfernung des Schuldnerwohnsitzes vom Gerichtsort, desto geringer seine Chance, sich erfolgreich zur Wehr zu setzen.

Eine erste kursorische Sichtung von Strafakten gibt noch keinen Hinweis, daß sich diese Hypothese im Strafverfahren bestätigen wird. Einsprüche werden in den seltensten Fällen mündlich zu Protokoll der Geschäftsstelle, in aller Regel schriftlich eingelegt. Für einen per Post eingelegten Einspruch aber spielt die Entfernung keine Rolle. Andererseits zieht der Einspruch eine Hauptverhandlung nach sich, zu der eine Anreise zum Gerichtsort erforderlich ist. Vielleicht ist bereits diese Aussicht geeignet, manchen Beschuldigten von einem Einspruch abzuhalten. Vermutlich spielen in diesem Zusammenhang weitere bisher nicht erfaßte Faktoren eine Rolle, die sich möglicherweise erst im Laufe der Untersuchungen herausstellen und eine differenziertere Formulierung der Hypothese erfordern.

Diese zweite Hypothese liegt auch dem 1969 eingeführten neuen § 6 a des Abzahlungsgesetzes zugrunde (siehe oben Seite 384).

Nach dem Ergebnis unserer ersten Sichtung des Untersuchungsfeldes scheint die Vorschrift weitgehend ihren Zweck zu verfehlen. Diese Zweckverfehlung freilich hätte vorausgesehen werden können, wenn man vor Erlaß des Gesetzes einen Test durchgeführt hätte. Im Mahnverfahren – das gerade in Abzahlungsgeschäften weitaus den meisten Rechtsstreitigkeiten vorausgeht – unterläßt der Gläubiger verständlicherweise einen Hinweis darauf, daß es sich hier um ein Abzahlungsgeschäft handelt; ja, man hat darüber hinaus den Eindruck, der Zahlungsbefehl werde bewußt so abgefaßt, daß der Charakter eines Abzahlungsgeschäftes daraus gar nicht ersichtlich werden kann. Im Widerspruchsschreiben des Schuldners wird aber in aller Regel der Gesichtspunkt, daß es sich um ein Abzahlungsgeschäft handelt, ebenfalls nicht erwähnt (16).

Unter diesen Umständen wundert es kaum mehr, daß bei der Mahnabteilung eines großen Gerichts, das jährlich ca. 150.000 Mahnverfahren bearbeitet, sich niemand erinnert, daß seit 1969, also in den 4 Jahren, seit § 6 a AbzG in Kraft ist, jemals eine Verweisung des Rechtsstreits an das Wohnsitzgericht vorgekommen wäre (!). Ein klassischeres Beispiel für die Ineffizienz eines am grünen Tisch ausgeheckten Gesetzes läßt sich kaum mehr denken. Hier wird auch besonders deutlich, wie schlecht es um die Erfolgskontrolle erlassener Gesetze in der Bundesrepublik bestellt ist. Offenbar hat bis heute noch niemand bemerkt, daß die Schuldnerschutzvorschrift des § 6 a AbzG in der Praxis kaum eine Wirkung hat.

Wir haben uns zunächst gefragt, ob etwa die amtliche Belehrung für dieses Fiasko verantwortlich gemacht werden kann. An dieser Belehrung (17) zeigt sich wohl

besonders deutlich das Dilemma aller amtlichen Belehrungen im Justizsektor. Man ist aufs Äußerste bemüht, dem rechtsunkundigen Bürger zu helfen, will aber andererseits peinlich korrekt und vollständig bleiben. Dadurch wird die Belehrung so umfangreich, daß sie letztlich unverständlich werden muß und deshalb dem Bürger keine wirkliche Hilfe sein kann (vgl. dazu inbes. Seite 387 ff.). Die Industrie tut sich da mit ihren Rechtsbelehrungen wesentlich leichter (18).
Die im Gesetz vorgesehene Verweisung des Rechtsstreites durch den Rechtspfleger der Mahnabteilung findet also in der Praxis nicht statt. Die Akte wird nach Eingang der 2. Prozeßgebühr an die Gerichtsabteilung des Wohnsitzgerichts des Gläubigers abgegeben. Auch die Richter scheinen dann, wenn sich in der Rechtssache ein Versäumnisurteil abzeichnet, wenig Neigung zu zeigen, vom Gläubiger den Nachweis zu verlangen, daß es sich um keine Abzahlungssache handelt – es sei denn, der Gläubiger sei dem Richter als „notorischer Abzahlungsgläubiger" bekannt. Das Gesetz enthält insoweit auch keine klare Handlungsanweisung; ja es ist noch nicht einmal klargestellt, ob der Richter im Ernstfall vom Gläubiger hier einen Negativnachweis – daß nämlich kein Abzahlungsgeschäft vorliegt – verlangen kann.
Deshalb scheint der Schuldnerschutz nach § 6a Abzahlungsgesetz in der Praxis wenig wirksam zu sein; gerade im wichtigsten Fall, der Säumnis des Schuldners, scheint auch in Abzahlungssachen am schuldnerfernen Gericht in der Regel ein Versäumnisurteil zu ergehen. Anscheinend geschieht also in der Praxis genau das, was das Gesetz verhindern wollte.
Erst wenn der Prozeß streitig wird, dann verweisen die Richter in der Regel den Rechtsstreit an das Wohnsitzgericht des Schuldners. Ob das freilich ein Vorteil für den Schuldner im Sinne des Gesetzes ist, muß in Frage gestellt werden. Es hat den Anschein, daß auch die notorisch „faulen" Gläubiger, die selten einmal einen streitigen Prozeß gewinnen, nicht darauf verzichten, den Gerichtsstand am Ort ihrer Niederlassung zu vereinbaren. Das spricht dafür, daß sich wenige Schuldner dagegen wehren, wenn solche „faulen" Forderungen zu Vollstreckungsbefehlen werden. Wenn aber die wenigen streitigen Sachen an das Wohnsitzgericht des Schuldners verwiesen werden, wo der Gläubiger nicht als „faul" bekannt ist, wird dann die Erfolgsquote der „faulen" Gläubiger nicht steigen statt fallen (19)?

3. Je persönlichkeitsferner eine Zustellung erfolgt(Minimum: Aushändigung an Adressaten; Maximum: Niederlegung bei der Post), desto geringer die Wahrscheinlichkeit, daß der Adressat darauf reagiert.

In der Praxis ist häufig zu beobachten, daß Schuldner, Beschuldigte usw. geltend machen, von einer Zustellung keine Kenntnis erhalten zu haben. Es setzt einen gewissen Grad von Initiative und Schriftgewandtheit (s.u.) voraus, die hieraus entstehenden Rechtsnachteile wieder auszugleichen (20).

4. Je geringer der Rechtsbeistand, desto geringer die Chance einer erfolgreichen Durchsetzung von Rechten bei Gericht.

Ob – und in welchem Ausmaße – die Einschaltung von Rechtsanwälten sich positiv auf den Ausgang eines Verfahrens auswirkt, läßt sich auf Grund der bisherigen Sichtung des Untersuchungsfeldes noch nicht überblicken. Feststellen läßt sich einstweilen nur, daß die Häufigkeit der Einschaltung von Rechtsanwälten mit der Höhe des sozialen Status der Schuldner und Beschuldigten zunimmt — d.h. die sozialen Schichten, die ohnehin nach unserer ersten Hypothese die größte Chance einer erfolgreichen Rechtsdurchsetzung haben, sind auch im größten Umfang anwaltlich vertreten.

b) Weitere Hypothesen sollen in einer anschließenden Phase der Untersuchung überprüft werden:

5. Je verständlicher und umfassender die Information über die rechtlichen Möglichkeiten, desto größer die Wahrscheinlichkeit, daß diese genutzt werden.

Die vorgedruckten Rechtsmittelbelehrungen auf Strafbefehlen sind relativ langatmig und schwer verständlich formuliert (21). Es muß mit der Möglichkeit gerechnet werden, daß mancher in geschäftlichen Dingen und im Schriftverkehr ungewandte Adressat sie nicht versteht und es deshalb unterläßt, die in der Belehrung genannten Rechtsmittel einzulegen.
Wir beabsichtigen eine experimentelle Überprüfung dieser Hypothese: In einigen Strafreferaten sollen den Strafbefehlen kürzere und verständlicher gefaßte Rechtsmittelbelehrungen (22) beigefügt werden. Falls unsere Hypothese zutrifft, wäre eine Zunahme der Einsprüche in diesen Referaten gegenüber anderen Referaten zu erwarten, in denen weiterhin die bisherigen Rechtsmittelbelehrungen erteilt werden.
Zweifelhaft scheint es, ob die Möglichkeit der Wiedereinsetzung in den vorigen Stand bei unverschuldetem Versäumen der Einspruchsfrist von einer Woche allgemein bekannt ist. In den üblichen Rechtsmittelbelehrungen wird auf diese Möglichkeit nicht hingewiesen. Wir wollen in einigen Referaten Rechtsmittelbelehrungen erteilen lassen, in denen auf die Möglichkeit der Wiedereinsetzung in den vorigen Stand hingewiesen wird (23). Wir vermuten, daß — wenigsten bei den im Schriftverkehr weniger gewandten Adressaten — die Zahl der Einsprüche mit Wiedereinsetzungsgesuch zunehmen wird.

6. Mangelnde Übung im Schriftverkehr ist auch nach verständlicher und vollständiger Rechtsmittelbelehrung ein Hindernis bei der Wahrnehmung von Rechten.

In einigen Zivil- und Strafreferaten sollen den Rechtsmittelbelehrungen vorgedruckte Einspruchsschreiben nebst Wiedereinsetzungsgesuch beigefügt werden. Möglicherweise wird hierdurch — wenigstens bei den weniger gebildeten oder geschäftsgewandten Adressaten — die Zahl der Einsprüche und Wiedereinsetzungsgesuche steigen.

c) Neben diesen objektiven, durch Aktenanalyse und Experiment meßbaren Variablen spielen allerdings vermutlich auch weitere Faktoren eine Rolle, die im Motivationsbereich zu suchen und allenfalls im Interview zu erschließen sind. Denkbar wäre etwa, daß bestimmte Gruppen von Schuldnern oder Beschuldigten

zwar in der Lage sind, sich zu wehren, dies aber trotzdem auch in objektiv aussichtsreicher Lage nicht tun, weil sie den Gegner für zu stark oder sich für zu schwach halten, kein Vertrauen zur Justiz haben oder umgekehrt in besonderer Autoritätsgläubigkeit auch einen unrichtigen Beschluß als richterliche Entscheidung hinzunehmen bereit sind.
Aufschlüsse hierüber erwarten wir von der dritten Phase der Untersuchung, in der wir Interviews durchführen werden mit einer Auswahl von Schuldnern und Beschuldigten, die gegen Zahlungs- und Strafbefehle keinen Einspruch eingelegt haben. In die Interviews werden wir auch solche Betroffene einbeziehen, die zwar ordnungsgemäß Widerspruch gegen einen Zahlungsbefehl eingelegt, ihre Rechtssache dann aber nicht weiter verfolgt haben, so daß vor Eintritt in das streitige Verfahren Versäumnisurteil erging. Hierdurch erhoffen wir näheren Aufschluß darüber, welche „Barrieren" innerhalb des Verfahrens hinter den eigentlichen, von diesen Betroffenen schon überwundenen „Zugangsbarrieren" liegen.

D. Organisationsfragen in der Justiz

Die Ergebnisse unserer Untersuchung versprechen, auch wichtige Informationen zu ergeben über die derzeit im Mittelpunkt der Diskussion um eine Justizreform in der Bundesrepublik stehenden Organisationsfragen.

I. Sollte es im Rahmen einer „wirklichen" (24) Justizreform gelingen, die oben diskutierten Probleme zu lösen, nämlich

1. im Rahmen der zivilen Rechtsschutzgewährung die Zugangsbarrieren zu beseitigen, die alle Bürger, insbesondere aber die Unterschicht daran hindern, ihr Recht (überhaupt – oder jedenfalls im Rahmen eines justizförmigen Verfahrens) zu suchen und zu finden,
2. im Rahmen der Strafgerichtsbarkeit den Schwerpunkt der Verfolgungsintensität von den traditionellen Vermögensdelikten auf den weit sozialschädlicheren (freilich auch wesentlich arbeitsaufwendigeren) Bereich zu verlagern, den man gemeinhin unter „Wirtschaftskriminalität" versteht,

so käme auf die Justiz der Bundesrepublik eine Arbeitslast zu, von der wir uns heute noch kaum eine Vorstellung machen. Der derzeit vorhandene Rechtsstab würde unter dieser Arbeitslast voraussichtlich zusammenbrechen. Andererseits besteht keine reale Chance, den Rechtsstab so auszuweiten, wie es zur Bewältigung dieses Vielfachen der heutigen Arbeitslast unter Beibehaltung des derzeitigen Organisations- und Verfahrenssystems notwendig wäre.
Auf die öffentliche Hand kommt eine solche Vielzahl von sich ausweitenden alten und umfangreichen neuen Aufgaben zu, daß sie es sich nicht leisten kann, der Justiz die für eine solche Vermehrung des Rechtsstabs erforderliche Priorität einzuräumen.
Wollen wir bei der Justizreform nicht in denselben Fehler verfallen wie bei der Bildungsreform, daß nämlich die Folgen einer Veränderung an der Basis für das Gesamtsystem nicht rechtzeitig bedacht worden sind, so müssen wir durch gleichzeitige Reform der Organisation und des Verfahrens dafür sorgen, daß die zu erwartende Arbeitslawine im wesentlichen mittels eines Rechtsstabes herkömmlichen Umfangs bewältigt werden kann. Man kann schließlich keinen „numerus clausus" (25) für Straf- und Zivilprozesse einführen.

II. Als Möglichkeiten für eine durchgreifende Rationalisierung des gerichtlichen Verfahrens sollen hier zwei Wege diskutiert werden:

1. eine drastische Beschränkung des Instanzenzugs,
2. eine generelle Vereinfachung des erstinstanzlichen Verfahrens dadurch, daß dieses als ein mehr summarisches Verfahren ausgestaltet wird, das mit einem vorläufigen Rechtsentscheid endet, der – wenn er nicht angegriffen wird – zum endgültigen wird.

Gegen die Lösung zu Ziffer 1 spricht – abgesehen davon, daß es sehr fragwürdig ist, ob sie politisch durchführbar wäre –,

a) daß das Abschneiden des Instanzenzuges eine Perfektionierung der ersten Instanz bedingte, die den Rationalisierungseffekt weitgehend zunichte machte (26),
b) daß das Abschneiden des Instanzenzuges – trotz Perfektionierung der ersten Instanz – die Richtigkeitsgewähr der endgültigen Entscheidung erheblich beeinträchtigte (27).

III. Es erscheint daher sinnvoll, sich mit der Lösung Ziffer 2, der Einführung einer summarisch ausgestalteten ersten Instanz, näher zu befassen.

Bei dieser Lösung tauchen unter dem Gesichtspunkt des Gerechtigkeitsgebots (29) zwei grundsätzliche Probleme auf, nämlich: Es sollte erreicht werden,

1. daß möglichst viele derjenigen vorläufigen Rechtsentscheide (mit welchen die 1. summarische Instanz endete) mit Rechtsmitteln angegriffen werden, die nicht der „wirklichen Rechtslage" entsprechen;
2. daß möglichst wenige derjenigen vorläufigen Rechtsentscheidungen angegriffen werden, die der „wirklichen Rechtslage" entsprechen.

Nur wenn diese beiden Ziele – möglichst alle „falschen" und möglichst nur die „falschen" Entscheidungen 1. Instanz einer Überprüfung zuzuführen – gleichermaßen in etwa erreicht werden können, tritt der angestrebte Rationalisierungseffekt ein und ist diese Lösung rechtspolitisch verantwortbar.

Da in unserer Untersuchung die (bereits vorhandenen) „Prototypen summarischer Verfahren", der Vollstreckungs- und der Strafbefehl, im Zentrum unseres Interesses stehen, erwarten wir wichtige Aufschlüsse darüber, ob und gegebenenfalls in welcher Form summarische Verfahren in größerem Umfange als bisher eingeführt werden sollten.

Das Prinzip einer Rationalisierung der Justiz durch Erlaß erstinstanzlicher Entscheidungen auf Grund summarischer Prüfung müßte auch dann scheitern, wenn in zu vielen Fällen solche Entscheidungen angegriffen würden, obwohl sie zu Recht ergangen sind. Einen Hinweis darauf, daß eine solche Tendenz besteht (wenn auch vermutlich nicht gerade die Unterschicht dafür verantwortlich sein dürfte), gibt die ständig steigende Zahl von Berufungen in Zivilsachen gegen die gleichzeitig zahlenmäßig stagnierenden Urteile der Amtsgerichte. Auch hier läßt sich vermutlich durch eine emprische Untersuchung nachweisen, welche Gründe für die wachsende Rechtsmittelflut verantwortlich sind und wie sie ausgeräumt werden können, etwa, indem die von unserem Intitut durchgeführten Leitstudien (30) durch eine entsprechende Hauptuntersuchung ergänzt werden, ein Vorhaben, mit dem das Institut für Rechtstatsachenforschung Stuttgart inzwischen begonnen hat.

Summary

Our contribution concerns the theoretical framework and preliminary impressions coming out of a design for investigating barriers to access to justice.
The conflict-resolution role of courts has declined, at least as far as concerns parties equal legally and economically. Such parties frequently resolve their conflicts through other means (arbitration, negotiations), more efficiently than through use of the ponderous system of justice.
But justice is a necessity for weaker parties seeking to effectuate their rights against a more powerful one. Juridical effectuation is all the more important in the light of the strength of the government, which, in a democracy, is necessarily in the hand of the current majority, which may threaten the rights of minorities and the freedom of individuals. Only the courts stand independent of the favor of the electorate and temporary tides of public opinion, and hence are in a position to protect the weaker party, in such areas as integration of races, protection of the environment, protection of the consumer, and so on.
Between the lower class and the middle class is a considerable "language barrier". Different social strata have different manners of speech. Middle class speech and bureaucratic jargon are often not understood by those who belong to the lower class, which also lacks the ability to put forward claims in appropriate speech. Classes also differ in value preferences, consciousness and the meaning ascribed to certain courses of conduct. In the modern world, too, there is a high degree of specialization and professionalization; individual professions are compartmentalized not only from each other, but also from society. This is an addtitional source of the alienation of the person from his social environment. Continually increasing bureaucratization of government adds to the feeling of helplessness, the more so since in the modern state the state increasingly intervenes, so that individuals are greatly exposed to state activities.
General communication difficulties are more easily overcome by those with business skill, practice in written communication and contact with officials; these abilities however are differentially distributed, to the disadvantage of the lower class. Moreover, authoritative postition of the professionalized state apparatus are occupied by people who belong to the middle class.
The following are working hypotheses: the further away from the forum the residence of the debtor (and the closer the residence of the creditor); the more impersonal the mode of serving (maximum: deposit in the post office); the lower the status (educational and occupational experience) of the debtor (maximum: foreign workers) (and the higher the status of the creditor); the lower the level of legal counsel for the debtor, and the better for the creditor; the less information on rights in concrete and understandable (free legal advice, for example); the less practiced the debtor in business transactions in writing – the less the changes of the debtor to defend himself successfully.

Anmerkungen

1 Das Institut ist hervorgegangen aus einer Arbeitsgruppe aus praktizierenden Justizjuristen und Sozialwissenschaftlern. Ziel des Instituts ist neben anderem – im Sinne von

F.K. Beutel –, die Rechtstatsachenforschung nutzbar zu machen für eine rationalere Gesetzgebung und insbesondere die „technologische Lücke" zu füllen, die klafft zwischen dem „wirklichen Gesetzgeber", den „gelernten Juristen" der Ministerialbürokratie, und den verschiedenen sozialwissenschaftlichen Disziplinen, jenen Disziplinen, die einen entscheidenden Beitrag zur Schaffung einer Gesetzgebungslehre zu leisten vermöchten, deren Erkenntnisse und Methoden aber von den „gelernten Juristen" nicht beachtet werden. Hier taucht ein „Übersetzungsproblem" in mehrfacher Hinsicht auf. Sozialwissenschaftler in der Bundesrepublik Deutschland pflegen sich in der Regel so auszudrücken, als hätten sie es darauf angelegt, daß sie außerhalb des engen Kreises ihrer Fachgenossen nicht verstanden werden sollen, so als wünschten sie geradezu, daß ihre Werke in den Bibliotheken sozialwissenschaftlicher Seminare verstaubten. Zudem fürchten sie offenbar, bei allzu großer Praxisnähe, etwa zur Justiz, könnten die Sozialwissenschaften sozusagen zu Hilfswissenschaften der Justiz degradiert und mißbraucht werden. Praktizierende Juristen hingegen sind mangels hinreichender Kenntnisse sozialwissenschaftlicher Terminologien, Theorien und Methoden in der Regel weder willens noch imstande, mit den Sozialwissenschaftlern hinreichend zu kommunizieren. In der Regel können sie weder ihre Probleme so formulieren, daß sie von den Sozialwissenschaftlern verstanden werden, noch sind sie hinreichend sensibilisiert dafür, zu erkennen, welche Probleme sie eigentlich haben müßten. Die Sozialwissenschaftler wiederum, selbst wenn sie bereit wären, sich als „Hilfswissenschaftler mißbrauchen" zu lassen, fehlt in der Regel die „Insiderkenntnis" von den Problemen, Anforderungen und Möglichkeiten der Praxis.

2 Das Ausweichen auf andere Institutionen ist als Trend im Ansatz auch in der Bundesrepublik schon zu erkennen. Man denke etwa an die Einigungsstellen, die zur Regelung von Streitigkeiten über Kraftfahrzeugreparaturen eingerichtet wurden, an das neue Betriebsverfassungsgesetz, das eine Reihe von Streitigkeiten nicht den Arbeitsgerichten, sondern besonderen Einigungsstellen zuweist.

3 Diese Tendenz eines Bedeutungswandels der Gerichte ist nicht etwa auf die Zivilgerichtsbarkeit beschränkt. Die Übertragung großer Teile des Verkehrsrechts auf die Ämter für öffentliche Ordnung, die Bestrebungen, die Masse der kleineren Eigentumsdelikte in das Recht der Ordnungswidrigkeiten abzudrängen und der Versuch der Justiz, schwerpunktmäßig die weit sozialschädlicheren (und zu Lasten der Schwachen gehenden) Wirtschaftsdelikte in den Griff zu bekommen, deutet in diese Richtung.

4 So wurde von den Forschern aus den U.S.A. auf die Entwicklung der dortigen Rechtsprechung im Laufe der letzten fünfzig Jahre hingewiesen: Während früher, insbesondere noch zu Zeiten von Roosevelts "New Deal" die Gerichte als Bremse wirkten gegen die Innovationen zum Schutze der Schwachen, die von der Legislative und Exekutive ausgingen, sind die Gerichte heute bemüht – wiederum gegen Gesetzgebung und Verwaltung –, die Rassenintegration, die Legalisierung der Abtreibung, den Umweltschutz, den Verbraucherschutz u.a. durchzusetzen (vgl. insbes.: Andreas Heldrich, Höchstrichterliche Rechtsprechung (US Supreme Court) als Triebfeder sozialen Wandels, in: Effektivität des Rechts im Jahrbuch für Rechtssoziologie und Rechtstheorie Bd. 3, 1972 S. 305 ff.).

5 Sollte die hier analysierte Funktion der Gerichte als künftige zentrale Aufgabe der Richter akzeptiert werden, so hätte das vielfältige Folgen für das Verfahren.
So müßte die „Parteimaxime" im Zivilprozeß neu überdacht werden. Die Parteimaxime geht von der Fiktion aus, jede Partei habe die gleichen Möglichkeiten, diejenigen Fakten, Beweismittel usw. „beizubringen", die am ehesten geeignet sind, zu ihrem Prozeßsieg beizutragen. Ist dieser „Selbstregulierungsmechanismus" einmal als Fiktion erkannt, so gewinnt die gerichtliche Aufklärungspflicht einen ganz neuen Stellenwert.
Ein ähnliches Problem ergibt sich bei der Amtsermittlung des Staatsanwalts und des Strafrichters zu Gunsten des Beschuldigten. Je weniger der Beschuldigte in der Lage ist, seinerseits zu seiner Entlastung dienende Umstände vorzutragen oder Beweismittel beizubringen, desto intensiver muß die Prüfung sein, ob nicht von Amts wegen in dieser Richtung ermittelt werden muß.
Weiter wird man sich überlegen müssen, ob nicht auch im deutschen Recht ein der "class action" vergleichbares Rechtsinstitut geschaffen werden sollte, mit dessen Hilfe einzelne die Rechte ihrer ganzen Gruppe vor Gericht verfechten können, bzw. die "public interest action", vgl. dazu Scheer in JZ 1973, S. 709.

6 Vgl. dazu Klaus Röhl „Das Dilemma der Rechtstatsachenforschung" (Band 2 der Schriftenreihe des Instituts für Rechtstatsachenforschung Stuttgart e.V. „Reform der Justizreform") Tübingen 1972, S. 67 ff.

7 Vielleicht hängt die irreführende Begriffsprägung „Klassenjustiz" für das, was mit schichtspezifischer Justiz gemeint ist, damit zusammen, daß Karl Liebknecht einige Aspekte der schichtspezifischen Justiz in Deutschland erstmals problematisiert hat, freilich unter dem Namen „Klassenjustiz", vgl. „Rechtsstaat und Klassenjustiz" 1907 in „Gesammelte Reden und Schriften, Band 2, Neudruck Berlin 1960, und „Gegen die preußische Klassenjustiz" 1910, a.a.O., Bd. 3.

8 Die Spezifizierung der hier allgemein für den gesamten Staatsapparat formulierten Theorien auf die Justiz ist so naheliegend, daß sie hier wohl nicht explizit dargestellt zu werden braucht.

9 Die hier formulierte 6. Theorie hat keinerlei Verwandtschaft mit der bekannten Theorie „bürgerlicher" Rechtssoziologen, die „Klassenjustiz" folge notwendig aus der schichtspezifischen Rekrutierung der Justiz und der darin implizierten Forderung, den Richternachwuchs dem Schichtmodell der gesamten Bevölkerung adäquat zu rekrutieren. Wir neigen vielmehr zu der Annahme, daß der Aufsteiger aus der Unterschicht der Wertpräferenzen, Vorurteile usw. der Schicht, in die er aufgestiegen ist, rigider postulieren und internalisieren wird als der „geborene" Mittelschichtler. Einen Ansatzpunkt zur (teilweisen) Beseitigung der Benachteiligung der Unterschicht sehen wir deshalb eher in einer vielschichtiger angelegten Sozialisierung des Richternachwuchses auf der Universität, im Referendariat und in der Richterfortbildung. Vgl. dazu: Walter Richter, Zur Bedeutung der Herkunft des Richters für die Entscheidungsfindung, Berlin 1973, insbes. S. 47 ff.

10 Die außerordentlich wichtige Zugangsbarriere „Gerichtskosten" ist aus unserem Forschungsprojekt – und dementsprechend auch aus unseren Hypothesen – ausgeklammert. Mit diesem Problem befaßt sich der Beitrag von Manfred Rehbinder in diesem Band.

11 Z.B. Karl Dieter Opp und Rüdiger Peukert, Ideologie und Fakten in der Rechtsprechung, Köln und Opladen 1971, und Dorothea Peters, Richter im Dienst der Macht, Stuttgart 1973 Kurt F. Schumann/Gerd Winter, Zur Analyse der Hautpverhandlung im Strafprozeß in: Jürgen Friedrich (Hrsg.), Teilnehmende Beobachtung abweichenden Verhaltens, Stuttgart 1973.

12 Hubert Rottleuthner, Richterliches Handeln, Berlin 1973, S. 180 ff.

13 Hierbei handelt es sich nur um eine vorläufige Klassifizierung. Im Laufe der Untersuchung soll eine differenziertere Skala nach Berufen und evtl. sonstigen Merkmalen aufgestellt werden.

14 Anlaß zu dieser Annahme bietet: Johannes Feest, Die Situation des Verdachts, in Johannes Feest/Rüdiger Lautmann (Hrsg.), Die Polizei, Opladen 1971.

15 Näheres hierüber ist von den Ergebnissen einer gegenwärtig von Erhard Blankenburg und anderen durchgeführten Untersuchung „Der Staatsanwalt im Prozeß sozialer Kontrolle" zu erwarten (vgl. Kriminologisches Journal H. 3/1973, S. 181 ff.)

16 Die Auswertung von ca. 3.500 Mahnverfahren durch die beim Justizministerium Baden-Württemberg gebildete „Arbeitsgruppe Automatisation des Mahnverfahrens" ergab ca. 2 pro mille aller Fälle, in welchem aus dem Zahlungsbefehl oder Widerspruch ersichtlich war, daß es sich um ein Abzahlungsgeschäft handelte. In ca. 3 % der Fälle ergab sich immerhin ein „Verdacht" auf ein Abzahlungsgeschäft.

17 Auszug aus dem amtlichen Text (Gesamtlänge mehr als doppelter Umfang):
„Bei einem Kauf auf Teilzahlung darf, wenn der Empfänger der Ware nicht als Kaufmann in das Handelsregister eingetragen ist, der Gerichtsstand nur für das Mahnverfahren sowie für den Fall vereinbart werden, daß der Käufer nach Vertragsschluß seinen Wohnsitz oder gewöhnlichen Aufenthaltsort aus dem Geltungsbereich des Abzahlungsgesetzes verlegt oder daß sein Wohnsitz oder gewöhnlicher Aufenthaltsort im Zeitpunkt der Klageerhebung nicht bekannt ist. Sonst ist ausschließlich das Gericht zuständig in dessen Bezirk der Käufer zur Zeit der Klageerhebung seinen Wohnsitz oder gewöhnlichen Aufenthaltsort hat. Im Falle des Widerspruchs gegen den Zahlungsbefehl oder des Einspruchs gegen den Vollstreckungsbefehl verweist das Gericht von Amts wegen den Rechtsstreit ohne mündliche Verhandlung an das für den Wohnsitz oder gewöhnlichen Aufenthaltsort des Schuldners zuständige Gericht, sofern nicht der Schuldner beantragt, von der Verweisung abzusehen. Geben Sie daher, wenn Sie Widerspruch erheben sollten, an, ob die mit dem Zahlungsbefehl geltend gemachte Forderung aus einem Kauf auf Teilzahlung herrührt, ob sie ein in das Handelsregister eingetragener Kaufmann sind oder nicht und ob Sie den Antrag stellen, von der Verweisung an das für Ihren Wohnsitz oder gewöhnlichen Aufenthaltsort zuständige Gericht abzusehen.

18 Auszug aus einer Rechtsbelehrung eines „notorischen Abzahlungsverkäufers“:
In Anbetracht unserer berechtigten Forderung und der ganz eindeutigen Rechtslage empfehlen wir Ihnen dringend, in Ihrem eigenen Interesse gegen den Zahlungsbefehl keinen Widerspruch zu erheben. Es wäre sonst – und zwar ausschließlich auf Ihre Kosten – die Hinzuziehung eines Anwalts aus unmittelbarer Nähe Ihres Wohnsitzes erforderlich! Aus dem gleichen Grund, also nur darum, um Ihnen ganz erhebliche zusätzliche Kosten zu ersparen, möchten wir Ihnen nahelegen, bei dem für das Mahnverfahren zuständigen Amtsgericht Stuttgart unter Angabe des Aktenzeichens den Antrag zu stellen, von der Verweisung des Rechtsstreits an das Amtsgericht Ihres Wohnsitzes abzusehen.

19 Was freilich die Versäumnisurteile anlangt, spricht viel dafür, daß die Entfernung des Schuldnerwohnsitzes vom Gerichtsort von erheblicher Bedeutung ist:
Aus den Erhebungen der Arbeitsgruppe „Automatisation des Mahnverfahrens“ (vgl. Anm. 16) ergibt sich, daß im Amtsgerichtsbezirk ansässige Schuldner mit 24 % an allen Einsprüchen und Widersprüchen beteiligt sind, an den Versäumnisurteilen aber nur mit 15 %. Die außerhalb Baden-Württembergs ansässigen Schuldner sind an allen Einsprüchen und Widersprüchen mit 47 %, an den Versäumnisurteilen aber mit 58 % beteiligt.

20 Die Ergebnisse der Arbeitsgruppe „Automatisiation des Mahnverfahrens“ erlauben in dieser Hinsicht keine eindeutige Interpretation. Immerhin sind die Niederlegungen bei der Post bei den Zahlungsbefehlen nur mit 18 % beteiligt, bei den Einsprüchen gegen den Vollstreckungsbefehl aber mit 41 %. Es darf wohl vermutet werden, daß es sich bei diesen 41 % überwiegend um Personen handelt, die vom Zahlungsbefehl keine Kenntnis erlangt haben – infolge Niederlegung bei der Post –, wohl aber vom Vollstreckungsbefehl, weil dieser nicht wiederum niedergelegt, sondern unmittelbar zugestellt wurde.

21 Die auf der Rückseite der in Baden-Württemberg zur Zeit verwendeten Strafbefehle aufgedruckte Rechtsmittelbelehrung hat folgenden Wortlaut:
Dieser Strafbefehl wird vollstreckbar, wenn der Beschuldigte nicht binnen einer Woche nach der Zustellung schriftlich oder bei der Geschäftsstelle des Amtsgerichts zur Niederschrift Einspruch erhebt. Bei Einspruch findet Hauptverhandlung statt. Der Einspruch muß binnen einer Woche nach Zustellung beim Amtsgericht eingehen; es genügt also nicht, wenn der schriftliche Einspruch innerhalb dieser Frist zur Post gegeben wird. Die Zustellung ist auch dann wirksam, wenn der Strafbefehl in der Wohnung des Beschuldigten, an einen zu der Familie gehörenden erwachsenen Hausgenossen oder an eine in der Familie dienende erwachsende Person oder an den in demselben Hause wohnenden Hauswirt oder Vermieter übergeben oder am Ort der Zustellung bei der Postanstalt unter schriftlicher Benachrichtigung des Beschuldigten niedergelegt wird.
Die Einspruchsfrist beginnt in diesen Fällen also nicht erst mit der Aushändigung des Strafbefehls an den Beschuldigten.

22 Wir wollen die Belehrung etwa wie folgt fassen:
Wenn Sie die Strafe für ungerechtfertigt oder für zu hoch halten, können Sie Einspruch einlegen. Dann wird in einer Gerichtsverhandlung über die erhobenen Vorwürfe entschieden.
Der Einspruch muß binnen einer Woche beim Gericht (nicht erst im Briefkasten!) sein. Die Wochenfrist beginnt mit der Übergabe des Strafbefehls an die Person, die den Strafbefehl vom Postbeamten erhalten hat oder mit der Niederlegung bei der Post. Der Beginn der Frist ist auf dem Briefumschlag vermerkt (Zugestellt am . . .).

23 Etwa so: Wenn Sie die Einspruchsfrist ohne Ihre Schuld versäumt haben, gehen Sie sofort zum nächsten Amtsgericht und lassen sich dort beraten, ob Ihnen nicht trotzdem geholfen werden kann.

24 Die bisherigen Ansätze zu einer „Großen Justizreform“ in der Bundesrepublik Deutschland erschöpfen sich in rein technologischen Erwägungeb über eine verbesserte Effizienz des Justizapparates als solchen (wobei hier unerörtert bleiben soll, daß auch dieser rein „technokratische“ Ansatz auf – teilweise ideologisch gefärbte – Spekulationen und nicht auf wissenschaftlich überprüften Fakten aufbaut). Irgendwelche Ansätze, die wirklichen Probleme der Justiz auch nur versuchsweise anzugehen, etwa die Zugangs- Sprach- und Kommunikationsbarrieren zu beseitigen, fehlen bisher völlig.

25 Als man im Rahmen der Bildungsreform in der Bundesrepublik Deutschland die Zugangssperren (teilweise) abbaute, die die Unterschicht am Besuch weiterführender Schulen hinderte, hat man versäumt, die Folgen sprunghaft steigender Abiturientenzahlen mitzubedenken, und muß deshalb heute den Zugang zum Studium mittels eines Numerus clausus kanalisieren.

26 Nach unserer – hier nicht näher zu verifizierenden – These verursacht ein Abschneiden des Instanzenzuges notwendig eine Perfektionierung der ersten Instanz auch dann, wenn eine solche im Gesetz nicht vorgesehen ist. Einen empirischen Anhaltspunkt für diese These bietet die unerträglich lange Dauer von erstinstanzlichen Verfahren vor der großen Strafkammer in der Bundesrepublik, gegen deren Entscheidung nur ein beschränktes Rechtsmittel – die Revision – zulässig ist.

27 Nach unserer – hier ebenfalls nicht näher zu verifizierenden – These hat eine Entscheidung eine größere Richtigkeitsgewähr, wenn – bei insgesamt betrachtet gleichem Arbeitsaufwand – zwei Instanzen tätig werden. Die Notwendigkeit, beim Abschluß der ersten Instanz eine Entscheidung zu erlassen und die Auseinandersetzung mit dieser Entscheidung in der zweiten Instanz gewährleistet ein größeres Maß von Fehlereliminierung als ein gründlicheres Erstinstanzliches Verfahren.

29 Dieses Werturteil kann im Rahmen dieses Beitrags nicht näher diskutiert werden.

30 Wax, Bender, Schade, Die Berufungsgründe in Zivilsachen aus der Sicht der Richter, sowie E. und V. Blankenburg, H. Morasch, Der lange Weg in die Berufung, beide in Rolf Bender, Tatsachenforschung in der Justiz, Tübingen 1972.

Manfred Rehbinder

Die Kosten der Rechtsverfolgung als Zugangsbarriere der Rechtspflege

Mißstände und Reformbestrebungen in der Bundesrepublik Deutschland

Seit dem Ende der 60er Jahre mehren sich in der BRD die kritischen Stimmen (1)*, die darauf aufmerksam machen, daß das verfassungsmäßig verbriefte Recht auf Rechtsschutz für jedermann (2) in einigen Bereichen leerläuft, weil die Kosten der Rechtsverfolgung die Durchsetzung der materiellen Rechtsposition mit Hilfe der Rechtspflege unbillig erschweren, wenn nicht gar verhindern. Allzu lange hatte sich die zivilprozeßrechtliche Literatur damit begnügt, die sozialen Probleme, die mit den Kosten der Rechtsverfolgung verknüpft sind, mit einer mehr oder weniger unkritischen Darstellung des Instituts des Armenrechts zur Seite zu schieben. Als dann durch die Gutachtertätigkeit von Erich Fechner im „Feldmühlefall" (3) das Problem kleinerer Aktionäre in das Blickfeld rückte, die an sich nicht arm waren, aber gegen ein mächtiges Wirtschaftsunternehmen mit einem großen Streitwert antreten mußten, wurde das Kostenrisiko in Fechners Seminar für Rechtsphilosophie und Rechtstatsachenforschung aus rechtssoziologischer Sicht näher untersucht, wodurch die gegenwärtige Diskussion in Gang kam. Fritz Baur war der erste anerkannte Zivilprozeßrechtler, der das Thema aufgriff und eine versicherungsrechtliche Lösung vorschlug. Nunmehr ist die Problematik sogar in eine weit verbreitete systematische Darstellung des Zivilprozeßrechts gewandert (4). Im Bundesministerium der Justiz bestehen Pläne, das Armenrecht trotz der Forderung der Bundesländer nach Erhöhung ihrer Einnahmen aus der Rechtspflege durch eine allgemeine Regelung über die Herabsetzung des Streitwerts im Rahmen der Reform des Zivilprozesses zu ergänzen (s. unter V.).

Das Institut des Armenrechts war bereits in der deutschen Zivilprozeßordnung (ZPO) von 1879 enthalten. Lange vor den entsprechenden sozialstaatlichen Regelungen anderer Länder war hier das Deutsche Reich ähnlich wie bei der Sozialversicherung für Arbeitnehmer mit einer für die damalige Zeit respektablen „sozialen Tat" (5) vorangegangen, die zudem noch in der Folgezeit durch die Gewährung eines Honoraranspruchs des Anwalts der armen Partei gegen den Staat sowie durch die Erstreckung des Armenrechtsanspruchs auf Parteien kraft Amtes und (stark eingeschränkt) auf juristische Personen ausgebaut wurde. Von daher ist es verständlich, daß sich die Prozeßrechtsliteratur bis in die Gegenwart mit einer Darstellung des positiven Rechts begnügte und allenfalls in Teilfragen Kritik übte. Wie sehr Deutschland durch sein Institut des Armenrechts ursprünglich sozialpolitisch führend war, zeigt deutlich der Kampf von Karl N. Llewellyn um entsprechende gesellschaftliche Selbsthilfemaßnahmen noch nach dem Zweiten Weltkrieg durch Übernahme der Leitung der Legal Aid Society in den USA (6).

* Anmerkungen auf den Seiten 411 ff.

Fehlender Blick über die Grenzen ließ dann aber übersehen, daß schon seit einiger Zeit kein Anlaß mehr war, sich auf Lorbeeren auszuruhen, daß vielmehr Länder wie Frankreich, Schweden, England oder Italien (7) nicht nur ihren Rückstand an Sozialstaatlichkeit in diesem Punkte aufgeholt haben, sondern darüber hinaus neue Wege gegangen sind, die jetzt das einst so fortschrittliche Armenrecht deutlich als rückständig ausweisen. Worum geht es im einzelnen und was ist zu tun?

I. Rechtswegsperre trotz Armenrecht

Justiz ist nach der Zuständigkeitsverteilung des Grundgesetzes Sache der Länder (das Bundesverfassungsgericht und die Bundesgerichte ausgenommen, vgl. Art. 92 GG). Grund genug, daß keine Bundesjustizstatistik herausgegeben wird. Die alte Reichsjustizstatistik wiederaufleben zu lassen, würde sicher einen bedauerlichen Mangel an bundesstaatlicher Gesinnung offenbaren. So wird es daher wohl noch einige Zeit dauern, bis wir wissen, wieviele Gerichtsverfahren unseres sozialen Rechtsstaats unter Inanspruchnahme des Armenrechts begonnen werden. Bis dahin müssen wir mit Schätzungen vorlieb nehmen. Folgen wir einem kompetenten Autor, so liegt der Durchschnitt bei knapp 10 % der Verfahren (8). In 10 % der Fälle ist also zunächst im summarischen Verfahren darüber zu entscheiden, ob die beabsichtigte Rechtsverfolgung oder Rechtsverteidigung eine hinreichende Aussicht auf Erfolg bietet und nicht mutwillig erscheint und ob die Partei außerstande ist, ohne Beeinträchtigung des für sie und ihre Familie notwendigen Unterhalts die Kosten des Prozesses zu bestreiten. Diese in § 114 Abs. 1 ZPO für den Zivilprozeß aufgestellten Voraussetzungen gelten auch für andere Verfahren wie das verwaltungsgerichtliche Verfahren (§ 166 Abs. 1 VwGO), das finanzgerichtliche Verfahren (§ 142 Abs. 1 FinGO), das Klageerzwingungsverfahren (§ 172 Abs. 3 StPO), das Privatklageverfahren (§ 379 Abs. 3 StPO), für das Verfahren vor dem Bundessozialgericht (§ 167 SGG) (9) sowie sinngemäß für das arbeitsgerichtliche Verfahren (§ 11 a ArbGG). Sind die Voraussetzungen erfüllt, hat die betreffende Partei einen Rechtsanspruch auf Bewilligung des Armenrechts. Die Unzulänglichkeiten dieser Regelung liegen einmal in den Voraussetzungen des Rechtsanspruchs und zum anderen in der Ausgestaltung des Armenrechts selbst.

1. Anspruchsvoraussetzungen des Armenrechts

a) Da das Verfahren der unbemittelten Partei zunächst zu Lasten des Steuerzahlers geführt werden soll, muß nach § 114 Abs. 1 ZPO vorab geprüft werden, ob eine hinreichende Erfolgsaussicht besteht und ob die betreffende Partei nicht „mutwillig" handelt, das heißt ob ein Dritter nicht unter diesen Umständen bei verständiger Würdigung der Lage von einem Gerichtsverfahren absehen würde. Schon hier kommt es zu einer Benachteiligung der „armen" gegenüber einer „reichen" Partei. Denn die Frage der Erfolgsaussicht wird im Armenrechtsverfahren, das lediglich vorweg über die Bewilligung des Armenrechts entscheiden soll, notwendig nur summarisch geprüft, das heißt ohne Vertiefung in rechtlicher und tatsächlicher Hinsicht (§ 118 a ZPO). Auch wenn dabei in der Praxis meist großzügig verfahren wird, wird hier durch die summarische Art der Vorprüfung der Unbemittelte in seiner Rechtsverfolgung beschränkt (10). Jedes Gerichtsverfahren bringt – je nach Qualität der Richter und nach Unklarheit der Sach- und Rechtslage – eine mehr oder weniger hohe Wahrscheinlichkeitsquote der „Unrichtigkeit" (11) mit sich. Die Belastung nur der unbemittelten Partei mit einem solchen Vorverfahren bedeutet also ihr gegenüber eine Erschwerung der Rechtsverfolgung. Sollte sie ferner nach sachlich ungerechtfertigter Ablehnung ihres Antrages auf Armenrechtsbewilligung auf eigene Kosten das Verfahren durchführen, besteht zudem die Gefahr, daß diejenigen Richter, die ihr das Armenrecht wegen mangelnder Erfolgsaussicht verweigert haben, in dem nun folgenden Verfahren befangen sind, da sie ihre Entscheidung über das Armenrecht nunmehr „verteidigen" wollen (12).

Hinzu kommt, daß sich gerade bei schwieriger Sach- und Rechtslage der Schwerpunkt des Prozesses häufig ins Armenrechtsverfahren verlagert, wo die eigentliche Entscheidung vorweggenommen wird (13). Die unbemittelte Partei muß sich daher bereits für das Armenrechtsverfahren einen Anwalt nehmen, was ihr im Falle der Ablehnung der Armenrechtsbewilligung – worauf Däubler hinweist (14) – nicht unbeträchtliche Kosten verursacht.

b) Noch größere Mißstände zeigen sich bei der zweiten Anspruchsvoraussetzung für die Gewährung des Armenrechts, nämlich bei der Armut. Wann im konkreten Fall der „notwendige Unterhalt" im Sinne des § 114 Abs. 1 ZPO gesichert ist, ist nicht klar. Man kann sich am „notdürftigen Unterhalt" der §§ 850 b ZPO, 1611 BGB, am pfändungsfreien Betrag nach § 850 C ZPO oder am „standesgemäßen", das heißt am angemessenen Unterhalt des § 1610 BGB orientieren. In der Praxis geht man meist von dem ziffernmäßig festgelegten und berechenbaren pfändungsfreien Einkommen aus und rundet es großzügig nach oben ab, bleibt jedoch – „weil Staatsgelder im Spiele sind" – unter dem angemessenen Unterhalt (15). Wer um sein Recht kämpfen will, soll sich also einschränken müssen.

Ob es allerdings in einem sozialen Rechtsstaat zulässig sein sollte, die Rechtsdurchsetzung notfalls von einer Einschränkung des angemessenen Lebensunterhalts abhängig zu machen, das konnte als rechtspolitisches Problem nur solange offenbleiben, als man meinte, daß davon nur wenige betroffen würden. In jüngerer Zeit scheint man nun aber auf breiter Basis zu realisieren, daß auch andere als nur Unbemittelte Prozesse mit geringem oder mittlerem Streitwert bei wirtschaftlicher Betrachtung und genügender Aufklärung gar nicht führen können, sollten ihre Aussichten nicht völlig eindeutig sein. Nach einer von Fritz Baur veröffentlichten Zusammenstellung betragen z.B. die Gerichts- und Anwaltsgebühren ohne Auslagen (z.B. für Zeugen und Sachverständige) in zwei Instanzen

bei einem Streitwert von DM 200,–	DM 336,–
bei einem Streitwert von DM 1.500,–	DM 1.675,–
bei einem Streitwert von DM 10.000,–	DM 5.368,–.

Bei Inanspruchnahme von drei Instanzen sind die Gerichts- und Anwaltsgebühren bei einem Streitwert von DM 10.000,– fast genauso hoch, nämlich DM 9.112,– (16). Man braucht also gar nicht arm zu sein, um bei den gegenwärtigen Kostenregelungen von der gerichtlichen Geltendmachung seiner Rechte absehen zu müssen. Wenn diese Situation noch nicht weithin bekannt ist, so nur deshalb, weil die meisten mit der naiven Anschauung vor die Gerichte ziehen, im Recht zu sein und deshalb keine Kosten tragen zu müssen. Über ihr wahres Risiko werden sie meistens erst aufgeklärt, wenn es zu spät ist, nämlich wenn der Richter auf einen Vergleich drängt.

2. Ausgestaltung des Armenrechts

Hat eine Partei die Hürde der Anspruchsvoraussetzungen für die Bewilligung des Armenrechts genommen, bedeutet das noch lange nicht, daß nunmehr für sie das Kostenrisiko entfällt. Zunächst einmal bezieht sich das Armenrecht nur auf die Gerichtskosten und gewisse Auslagen sowie (in Prozessen mit Anwaltszwang) auf die Gebühren des beigeordneten Anwalts (vgl. §§ 115–116b ZPO). Der Gegner ist also nicht gehindert, im Falle seines Obsiegens die ihm entstandenen Kosten (Anwalt und Auslagen) von der armen Partei sofort zurückzuholen (17). Ferner und vor allem bedeutet die Gewährung des Armenrechts nur eine „einstweilige", keinesfalls die endgültige Befreiung von Gerichtskosten, Auslagen und den Gebühren des beigeordneten Anwalts. Der Staat hat die betreffenden Beträge, sollte die unbemittelte Partei unterliegen, also nur gestundet. Sobald die arme Partei „ohne Beeinträchtigung des für sie und ihre Familie notwendigen Unterhalts dazu imstande ist", die Kosten zu tragen, ergeht der sogenannte Nachzahlungsbeschluß (§ 125 ZPO). Schließlich kann ein Nachzahlungsbeschluß die arme Partei auch im Falle des Obsiegens treffen, nämlich dann, wenn die Beitreibung der Kosten beim Gegner erfolglos geblieben ist.

Das Gesamturteil über diese Regelung des geltenden Rechts ist daher eindeutig negativ. Mit den Worten eines so ausgewogenen Beurteilers wie Fritz Baur: „Unter dem Gesichtspunkt einer wirksamen Realisierung des Justizgewährungsanspruchs wie auch unter dem des gleichen Zugangs aller zum Gericht ist dieses Ergebnis alles andere als befriedigend" (18).

II. Nulltarif in der Justiz?

Allein die Tatsache, daß der armen Partei die Gerichtskosten nicht erlassen, sondern nur gestundet werden, zeigt die grundsätzliche Einstellung der Rechtsordnung zu unserem Problem sehr deutlich. Es ist die Auffassung des Liberalismus, daß der einzelne seinen (im Interesse der Rechtsordnung sogar erwünschten) „Kampf ums Recht" (19) auf eigenes Risiko zu führen hat. Solange man im Rechtsstreit in erster Linie die Durchsetzung individueller Rechte mit Hilfe des Staates sieht, mag man im Gang zum Gericht die Inanspruchnahme einer staatlichen Sonderleistung sehen, die bezahlt werden muß. Sieht man aber die Situation so, daß ein Rechtsstaat nicht nur individuelle Rechte zusprechen, sondern auch ihre Realisierung garantieren muß, weil er gleichzeitig die Selbsthilfe verbietet, dann ist der Justizgewährungsanspruch kein Anspruch auf eine Sonderleistung. Das hat man früher auch durchaus gesehen. So drückte Julius von Kirchmann in seinem berühmten Vortrag über die Wertlosigkeit der Jurisprudenz als Wissenschaft im Jahre 1848 seine Verwunderung über einen Staat aus, „der die Verwirklichung des Rechts zu seiner höchsten Aufgabe macht und doch die Handhabung desselben im einzelnen mit schwerem Gelde sich bezahlen läßt"(20). Die gerichtliche Austragung von Streitigkeiten ist stets zugleich von sozialem Nutzen, weil sonst sozialschädliche Formen der Auseinandersetzung gesucht werden. Wird überdies durch einen Prozeß eine unklare Rechtslage durch Rechtsfortbildung der Gerichte beseitigt, dann erlangt dieser soziale Nutzen eindeutig rechtserhebliche Bedeutung. Der einzelne, der hier auf eigene Kosten Rechtsklarheit erstritten hat, hat seine Kosten zugleich im Interesse der Allgemeinheit aufgewandt. Er hat Versäumnisse des Gesetzgebers ausgeglichen und damit dem Staat gegenüber eine Geschäftsführung ohne Auftrag getätigt. Zuweilen findet sich in den Materialien unvollständiger Gesetze die Bemerkung, Einzelheiten der Rechtslage zu bestimmen bliebe den Gerichten überlassen. Darin liegt bei näherem Zusehen sogar ein ausdrücklicher Auftrag des Staates an den einzelnen, bei Auftauchen der jeweiligen Fragen eine Rechtsklärung herbeizuführen. Es widerspricht daher grundlegenden Rechtsprinzipien, läßt man ihn die Kosten der Rechtsfortbildung allein tragen.

Aber auch in solchen Prozessen, die nicht der Rechtsfortbildung durch Beseitigung von Rechtsunklarheit dienen, ist die jetzige Kostenregelung in weiten Teilen ungerecht, ja sogar verfassungswidrig, weil sie gegen den Gleichheitsgrundsatz und das Sozialstaatsprinzip verstößt (21). Zwar hat das Bundesverfassungsgericht entschieden, der allgemeine Gleichheitsgrundsatz zusammen mit dem Sozialstaatsprinzip gebiete lediglich, die prozessuale Stellung von Bemittelten und Unbemittelten „weitgehend anzugleichen" und die Rechtsverfolgung des Unbemittelten „nicht unverhältnismäßig" zu erschweren (22). Wenn aber bei einem Streitwert von DM 10.000,– die Kosten der Rechtsverfolgung in drei Instanzen den Streitwert aufzehren, dann steht bei realistischer Betrachtung der Rechtsweg bei wirklich zweifelhafter Sach- und Rechtslage nur demjenigen offen, für den ökonomische Erwägungen keine Rolle spielen. Sicher soll man die praktische Bedeutung des Sozialstaatsprinzips als geltenden Verfassungsrechtssatz nicht überschätzen. Er bietet wohl nur eine Mindestgarantie. Immerhin ist er aber eine wichtige Leitlinie für die Rechtspolitik. Deshalb ist unabhängig von positivrechtlichen Erwägungen über Geschäftsführung und Sozialstaatswidrigkeit zu fragen, ob nicht hier in der Kostenfrage eine sozialstaatsgerechte Lösung möglich ist und wie sie im einzelnen auszusehen hätte.

Der radikalste Weg wäre sicher die Einführung eines Nulltarifs in der Justiz, nämlich die Kostenlosigkeit sämtlicher Verfahren. Dabei müßten konsequenterweise nicht nur die Gerichtskosten und notwendigen Auslagen, sondern auch die Anwaltskosten entfallen. Den Weg des Sozialgerichtsgesetzes, das in den unteren Instanzen einfach den Anwaltszwang abgeschafft hat und lediglich im Revisionsverfahren die Beiordnung eines Armenanwalts vorsieht (§ 167 SGG), wird man nämlich nicht gehen können. Denn gerade bei rechtlich und tatsächlich schwierigen Fällen gehört die Mitwirkung des Rechtsanwalts zur Garantie eines effektiven Rechtsschutzes (23). Die Anwälte müßten also ihre Gebühren vom Staat bekommen. Das braucht nicht zu einer Verbeamtung der Anwaltschaft zu führen wie unter Friedrich dem Großen, wie ja auch der Kassenarzt nicht verbeamtet ist (24). Die Gefahr des Mißbrauchs der Kostenfreiheit durch Querulanten, die ohnehin nicht allzu groß sein dürfte (25), könnte nach dem Vorschlag von Däubler (26) durch Einführung einer Prozeßstrafe entsprechend § 34 Abs. 4 BVerfGG gebannt werden.

Der entscheidende Einwand gegen die Einführung eines Nulltarifs in der Justiz ist daher allein das Finanzproblem. Alle bisherigen Stellungnahmen sind sich darin einig, daß die Finanzmisere des Staates die Forderung nach einem Nulltarif, so überzeugend sie in der Theorie sei, wegen politischer Undurchführbarkeit in den Bereich der Utopie verweist (27). Allerdings ist bisher kein genauerer Nachweis geführt worden, daß in der Tat die Kostenfrage eine Einführung des Nulltarifs verbiete. Ohnehin werden ja heute schon die Kosten der Rechtspflege überwiegend aus Steuermitteln finanziert. Nach einer Aufstellung aus dem Jahre 1965 (28) ergibt sich eine Kostendeckung

– bei den ordentlichen Gerichten zu 45,01 %;
– bei den Sozialgerichten zu 6,79 %;
– bei den Verwaltungsgerichten zu 12,40 %;
– bei den Arbeitsgerichten zu 9,19 % und
– bei den Finanzgerichten zu 4,34 %.

Man müßte vor allem auch einmal die Ersparnisse an Arbeitsaufwand errechnen, die bei Richtern und Kostenbeamten im Falle der Einführung des Nulltarifs möglich wären (29). In den USA und in Schweden werden jedenfalls kaum noch Gerichtsgebühren erhoben.

Aber selbst wenn der Nulltarif finanziell tragbar wäre, erscheint es wenig wahrscheinlich, daß er in absehbarer Zukunft eingeführt würde. Die überaus große Fülle kostenträchtiger Reformprojekte, die gegenwärtig auf allen Gebieten zur Diskussion stehen, dürfte dazu führen, daß die Prioritäten anders gesetzt werden. Eine mit Kosten verbundene Justizreform wäre in unserem Punkte auch gar nicht so populär, wie die Juristen glauben möchten. Einmal, weil nur die wenigsten Menschen mit den Gerichten zu tun gehabt haben und hoffen dürfen, daß dies so bleibt. Zum zweiten, weil sie annehmen, daß das Recht gewiß ist, so daß es ihnen als gerecht erscheint, wenn der Verlierer die Kosten tragen muß. Und schließlich, weil es weithin als unabänderlich hingenommen wird, daß die Rechtsverfolgung wie die meisten Dinge im Leben eben Geld kostet. Deshalb wird es zunächst darauf ankommen, mittlere Lösungen zu finden, die vom Staat weniger Geld erfordern.

III. Kostenfreiheit für besondere Prozeßarten?

Als eine solche mittlere Lösung ist von Eike Schmidt vorgeschlagen worden, „für bestimmte, existentiell wichtige Prozesse dem sozial Schwächeren kostenlosen Rechtsschutz von Staats wegen zu ermöglichen“, und zwar denkt er an solche Verfahrensarten, in denen erfahrungsgemäß besonders viele Armenrechtsgesuche eingereicht werden, z.B. Miet- und Unterhaltsstreitigkeiten, Scheidungsverfahren oder Arbeitsstreitigkeiten (30). Dabei möchte er die Nachteile der jetzigen Regelung des Sozialgerichtsverfahrens vermeiden. Zunächst einmal soll nur der sozial Schwächere von den Kosten befreit sein, während im Sozialgerichtsverfahren z.B. auch der Kassenarzt sein Honorar unentgeltlich einklagen kann (31). Allerdings sagt Schmidt uns nicht, wer als „sozial schwächer“ einzustufen sein soll. Es müßte vor allem klargestellt werden, inwieweit sich diese Klassifizierung von der Armut im Sinne des geltenden Armenrechts unterscheidet. Weiter sieht Schmidt im Gegensatz zum Sozialgerichtsverfahren die Befugnis vor, sich durch einen Anwalt eigener Wahl vertreten zu lassen, sofern auch die Gegenseite anwaltliche Unterstützung genießt. Würde man nämlich, was von anderer Seite vorgeschlagen wurde (32), den Anwaltszwang in weiten Bereichen aufheben, würde die bessere Rechtsberatung zu einem Privileg der Reichen werden und rechtlich Unerfahrene würden benachteiligt (33). Der Anwalt soll ferner nach den Vorstellungen von Schmidt entgegen der Regelung für Armenrechtsanwälte in § 123 BRAGO die normalen Gebühren aus der Staatskasse erhalten, damit die gegenwärtige negative Selektion bei der Anwaltschaft hinsichtlich der Vertretung im Armenrecht vermieden wird.

Der Nachteil dieses Vorschlags liegt – abgesehen von der Schwierigkeit einer

Festlegung, wer „sozial schwächer" ist – in der Beschränkung auf bestimmte Verfahrensarten. Schutzbedürftigkeit liegt z.B. auch häufig bei Abzahlungsstreitigkeiten vor und Streitigkeiten aus Allgemeinen Geschäftsbedingungen (34). Grund für die Forderung nach Kostenbefreiung ist ja nicht die Verfahrensart, sondern die wirtschaftliche Schwäche. Die Beschränkung auf bestimmte Verfahrensarten ist daher geeignet, immer wieder zu Unbilligkeiten zu führen. Das legt nahe, die Lösung eher in einer Erweiterung des Armenrechts in allen Prozeßarten zu sehen.

IV. Erweiterung des Armenrechts?

Zunächst wären beim Institut des Armenrechts diejenigen Beschränkungen aufzuheben, die allem Anschein nach verfassungswidrig sind. Das wäre einmal § 114 Abs. 2 ZPO, der die Gewährung des Armenrechts an Ausländer davon abhängig macht, ob die Gegenseitigkeit mit deren Heimatstaat verbürgt ist. Da die Verfassung den Zugang zu den Gerichten nicht nur Deutschen, sondern jedermann eröffnet, muß diese Schranke fallen (35). Sie verstößt zudem noch gegen Art. 6, Abs. 1 der Menschenrechtskonvention (36). Sodann ist § 114 Abs. 4 ZPO aufzuheben, der die Gewährung des Armenrechts an juristische Personen von der gesetzlichen Voraussetzung abhängig macht, daß „die Unterlassung der Rechtsverfolgung oder Rechtsverteidigung allgemeinen Interessen zuwiderlaufen würde". Damit wird nämlich das Armenrecht für kleinere juristische Personen praktisch ausgeschlossen, obwohl Art. 19 Abs. 3 GG eine Benachteiligung juristischer Personen gegenüber natürlichen Personen verbietet (37).
Im übrigen wäre eine Verbesserung des Armenrechts in mehreren Punkten möglich. So wäre der Begriff der Armut zu präzisieren. Dazu existieren zwei Vorschläge. Däubler möchte festgelegt sehen, daß der „notwendige Unterhalt" identisch sei mit dem angemessenen Unterhalt im Sinne des § 1610 BGB (38). Noch weiter geht Eike Schmidt. Er schlägt eine Verdoppelung der Sätze des pfändungsfreien Betrages vor (39). Dies hätte neben der großzügigeren Bemessung noch den Vorteil, daß damit zahlenmäßig festgelegte Grenzen gegeben sein würden. Weiter schlägt Schmidt vor, die Prüfung der Erfolgsaussicht fallen zu lassen. Die von ihm mitgeteilte Statistik von Baden-Württemberg – so begründet er dies – ergäbe kaum eine Ablehnung aus diesem Grunde. Auch würde das Verfahren der Armenrechtsbewilligung dadurch vereinfacht (40). Das Argument mit der Statistik ist allerdings solange nicht stichhaltig, als man nicht weiß, ob nicht die Anwälte oder die Rechtsantragsstellen von vornherein verhindern, daß Anträge in aussichtslosen Fällen überhaupt gestellt werden. Es könnte sein, daß die Anspruchsvoraussetzung der hinreichenden Erfolgsaussicht durchaus eine beachtliche Sperrwirkung ausübt. Ohne vorherige Rechtstatsachenforschung wäre hier also eine Reform aus Kostengesichtspunkten nicht zu empfehlen.
Schmidt empfiehlt als drittes die Einführung der Möglichkeit freier Wahl des Prozeßbevollmächtigten. In der Tat liegt hier ein Mißstand vor, der besonders bei der Bestellung des Pflichtverteidigers im Strafprozeß in Erscheinung tritt, die nach dem Gesetz durch das Gericht vorgenommen wird. Der betreffende Anwalt wird in der Regel darauf bedacht sein, auch für die Zukunft von dem betreffenden Gericht als Pflichtverteidiger bestellt zu werden. Er gerät so unwillkürlich in einen Rollenkonflikt, der häufig zu Lasten des Angeklagten gelöst wird (41). Schließlich ist nicht recht einzusehen, warum nicht auch die Kosten des

gegnerischen Anwalts gestundet werden (42). Entweder die Partei ist arm; dann kann man ihr eine Zahlung nicht zumuten. Oder sie ist es eben nicht. Die Gerichtsbarkeit eines Sozialstaats sollte jedenfalls so ausgestattet sein, daß keine unzumutbaren Forderungen auf den Rechtsuchenden zukommen. Hier dürfte allerdings ebenfalls die Reform an den finanziellen Belastungen scheitern, die bei Zahlung der vollen Anwaltsgebühren an den gegnerischen Anwalt auf die Staatskasse zukommen würden. Ob es darüber hinaus notwendig ist, den Armenanwälten die vollen Gebühren zukommen zu lassen, soll unter VIII erörtert werden. Würde man ihnen, wie Däubler vorschlägt (43), auch die außerprozessualen Beratungsgebühren als Anspruch gegen die Staatskasse zusprechen, so ist die Gefahr nicht von der Hand zu weisen, daß wir kassenarztähnliche Praxen bekommen, die ohne Grund aufgesucht werden. Hier scheint mir der Weg kommunaler Rechtsberatungsstellen der richtige zu sein, wie sie heute schon weithin mit Unterstützung der Anwaltschaft bestehen, Polikliniken vergleichbar, die billiger arbeiten können als Privatpraxen.
Allerdings wird das Institut des Armenrechts auch in großzügigerer Ausgestaltung immer in der öffentlichen Meinung die Vorstellung einer „Arme-Leute-Institution" behalten, die von Unbemittelten, die „bessere Tage gesehen haben", nicht gern in Anspruch genommen wird. Man wird es also mit einer Reform dieses Instituts allein nicht bewenden lassen können. Es sei denn, es werden alle Gerichts- und Anwaltsgebühren nicht mehr nach starren Sätzen, sondern stets nach den individuellen Einkommensverhältnissen gestaffelt, wobei Restbeträge zu einer Mindestgebühr vom Staat übernommen werden. Will man dies wegen der unvorhersehbaren Kosten nicht, muß man immer mit starren und niedrigen Ansätzen arbeiten (44). Damit aber hilft man denjenigen Bevölkerungskreisen nicht, die bei der heutigen Ausgestaltung der Kosten- und Gebührenstaffeln ebenfalls hart getroffen sind, nämlich der unteren Mittelschicht (45). Um hier individuell je nach den Vermögensverhältnissen des Betroffenen und der Bedeutung des Rechtsstreits vorgehen zu können, hilft nur der Weg, die bisher schon ausnahmsweise vorgesehene Möglichkeit des Gerichts, den Streitwert herabzusetzen, weiter auszubauen.

V. Generelle Möglichkeit der Streitwertherabsetzung durch die Gerichte?

Um der wirtschaftlich schwächeren Partei gegenüber einem wirtschaftlich starken Gegner helfen zu können, ist bisher schon durch Spezialvorschriften auf einzelnen Gebieten für die Gerichte die Möglichkeit eröffnet worden, einen niedrigeren als den wirklichen Streitwert auf Antrag einer Partei entsprechend deren Einkommens- und Vermögenslage festzusetzen. Insbesondere sollte hier dem Mißbrauch großer Unternehmen gesteuert werden, durch hohe Streitwerte ihren Gegnern von vornherein den Mut zu einem Prozeß zu nehmen. Wir finden solche Regelungen in den §§ 247 Abs. 2 AktG, 53 PatG, 17a GebrMG, 31a WZG und 23 a UWG. Obwohl mit der Herabsetzung des Streitwertes die Auslagen nicht erfaßt sind, die etwa als Gutachterkosten erheblich sein können, ist mehrfach vorgeschlagen worden, diese Sonderregelungen zu verallgemeinern (46). Im Jahre 1970 hatte das Bundesministerium der Justiz in einem Vorentwurf für ein neues Gerichtskostengesetz eine entsprechende Vorschrift vorgesehen. Da die Landesjustizverwaltungen jedoch eine zu starke Belastung der Gerichte durch Herabsetzungsgesuche befürchteten, wurde diese Bestimmung in den endgültigen Regierungsentwurf zur Änderung des Gerichtskostengesetzes (47) nicht aufgenommen. Obwohl die Länder seit Jahren eine Erhöhung ihrer Einnahmen aus der Rechtspflege fordern, soll die Frage der Streitwertherabsetzung im Rahmen der Reform der Zivilprozeßordnung erneut aufgegriffen werden. Die Formulierung, die das BMJ für das Gerichtskostengesetz erarbeitet hatte, lehnt sich eng an die Armenrechtsregelung an. Sie lautet:

> Herabsetzung des Streitwerts
>
> (1) Würde die wirtschaftliche Lage eines Prozeßbeteiligten durch die Belastung mit Prozeßkosten nach dem vollen Streitwert erheblich gefährdet, so setzt das Gericht auf Antrag des Prozeßbeteiligten einen seiner wirtschaftlichen Lage angepaßten Teil des Streitwerts fest, der nicht weniger als x DM betragen darf.
>
> (2) Der Prozeßbeteiligte, zu dessen Gunsten ein Teilstreitwert festgesetzt ist, hat Gerichts- und Rechtsanwaltsgebühren nur nach dem Teilstreitwert zu entrichten und zu erstatten. Von anderen Prozeßbeteiligten zu entrichtende und zu erstattende Gebühren bestimmen sich nach dem für sie geltenden Streitwert. Soweit die außergerichtlichen Kosten den anderen Prozeßbeteiligten auferlegt oder von ihnen übernommen werden, kann der Rechtsanwalt des begünstigten Prozeßbeteiligten seine Gebühren von den anderen Prozeßbeteiligten nach den für diesen geltenden Streitwerten beitreiben.
>
> (3) Der Antrag auf Festsetzung eines Teilstreitwertes kann durch Erklärung zu Protokoll der Geschäftsstelle oder schriftlich ohne Mitwirkung eines Rechtsanwalts gestellt werden. Die zu seiner Begründung angeführten Tatsachen sind glaubhaft zu machen. Besteht der Wert des Streitgegenstandes in einer bestimmten Geldsumme oder ergibt er sich aus früheren Anträgen, so ist der Antrag innerhalb eines Monats nach dem Beginn der Verhandlung zur Hauptsache zu stellen, sonst innerhalb eines Monats nach Verkündung oder Zustellung des Beschlusses über die Streitwertfestsetzung. Später ist er nur innerhalb eines Monats nach Erhöhung des angenommenen oder festgesetzten Streitwerts zulässig. Vor der Entscheidung über den Antrag sind die zum Antrag auf Wertfestsetzung Berechtigten zu hören. Die Entscheidung ergeht für jeden Rechtszug gesondert durch Beschluß.
>
> (4) Gegen den Beschluß findet die Beschwerde nach Maßgabe des § 4 Abs. 4, 5 statt.

Die Möglichkeit, in allen Prozessen eine Korrektur der Streitwerte nach unten vornehmen zu können, läßt jedoch eines außer acht. Hier werden nämlich nicht nur die Staatskasse, sondern auch die Einnahmen der Anwälte betroffen. Wenn es um große Streitwerte im gewerblichen Rechtsschutz oder im Aktienrecht geht, mag man vielleicht eine Herabsetzung der Gebühren für gerechtfertigt halten. Will man aber die Öffnung des Rechtswegs auch bei kleineren und mittleren Streitwerten sicherstellen, und darum geht es doch in erster Linie, dann kann man dies nicht ohne weiteres auf dem Rücken der Anwälte tun. Diese müssen als Freiberufler angemessene Verdienstchancen behalten. Anwälte jedenfalls, die vorwiegend eine Klientel aus den unteren und mittleren Einkommenschichten haben, gehören kaum zu den Spitzenverdienern. Bevor eine Regelung auf ihre Kosten getroffen wird, müssen genauere Untersuchungen über die zu erwartetenden Einkommensverluste erfolgen. Unbefangene Beurteiler schätzen jedenfalls die Situation so ein, daß diese Verluste ohne Ausgleichsleistungen durch den Staat nicht tragbar seien (48). Im übrigen ist es mißlich, die Entscheidung über die Streitwertherabsetzung als Billigkeitsentscheidung auszugestalten; denn mit Sicherheit wird es dann zu unterschiedlichem Vorgehen der Gerichte und damit zu unerfreulichen Rechtsungleichheiten kommen. Das legt den Gedanken nahe, es bei den jetzigen Streitwerten zu belassen, aber die Kosten anders zu verteilen.

VI. Verteilung der Kosten nach anderen Kriterien als dem Ausgang des Prozesses?

1. Kostenfreiheit bei Unklarheit der Rechtslage

So hat man vorgeschlagen, bei einer echten Unklarheit der Rechtslage die Gerichts- und Anwaltskosten vom Staat tragen zu lassen, da der Staat zur Rechtsklarheit verpflichtet sei. Da unklare Rechtslagen oft zugleich mit unklaren Sachlagen verknüpft sind, sollte dem Gericht ferner die Möglichkeit gegeben sein, je nach Verursachung der unklaren Sachlage und ihrer Bedeutung für den Umfang von Arbeitsaufwand und Kosten eine Billigkeitsentscheidung zu treffen. Eine solche Möglichkeit sei bereits für bestimmte Verfahren vor dem Bundespatentgericht in § 36 q PatG vorgesehen (vgl. auch §§ 10 GebrMG, 13 WZG). Revisionen, die vom Oberlandesgericht wegen grundsätzlicher Bedeutung nach § 546 Abs. 2 ZPO zugelassen wurden, seien aber auf jeden Fall für beide Parteien von Kosten zu befreien (49).

Dieser Vorschlag ist an sich einleuchtend, da bei Unklarheit der Einzelne den Prozeß zugleich in Geschäftsführung für die Allgemeinheit führt. Nur ist dem entgegengehalten worden, daß bei der Beurteilung der Frage, wann Rechtsunklarheit gegeben sei, nicht die Sicht des Juristen, sondern die Sicht des Laien ausschlaggebend sein müßte, und für den Laien seien heutzutage fast alle Rechtsfragen unklar, insbesondere für Unbemittelte, die meist zugleich Ungebildete seien (50). Hier wird jedoch übersehen, daß der Grund für die Kostenbefreiung die Nützlichkeit des Prozesses für die Allgemeinheit ist und daß der Laie kaum einen Prozeß beginnt, ohne von einem Anwalt oder von der Rechtsantragsstelle – wenn auch oberflächlich – beraten zu sein. Es könnte unter dem Gesichtspunkt der allgemeinen Rechtsunklarheit für den Laien wohl nur um die außerprozessualen Beratungskosten gehen, über die bereits gesprochen wurde. Daher ist die vorgeschlagene Kostenbefreiung nach Maßgabe der Rechtsunklarheit durchaus ein gangbarer Weg, der auch gegenüber dem allgemeinen Nulltarif billiger sein würde. Doch steht selbst bei dieser Lösung zu erwarten, daß die dadurch dem Staat entstehenden Kosten größer sind als politisch tragbar.

2. Kostenbefreiung je nach Instanzgewinn

Ein zusätzlicher Vorschlag ist der, bei Prozessen in mehreren Instanzen die Kosten je nach Instanzgewinn zu verteilen. Denn wenn die Gerichte sich bei ihrer Urteilsbildung korrigieren, das heißt in mehreren Instanzen widersprechende Urteile fällen würden, so fiele das – so meint man – nicht in den Verantwortungsbereich der Prozeßparteien. Entgegen § 91 Abs. 1 ZPO wären demnach von der im Endergebnis unterlegenen Partei nicht die Kosten des gesamten Verfahrens, sondern nur die Kosten der ersten Instanz zu tragen. Ein ohne Erfolg eingelegtes Rechtsmittel müsse dagegen weiterhin nach § 97 ZPO derjenigen Partei zu Last fallen, die es eingelegt hat (51).

Dieser Vorschlag ist ebenfalls sehr einleuchtend, sieht man einmal von der Kostenfrage ab. Er wirkt aber nur in Kombination mit der Kostenfreiheit für unklare Rechtslagen. Denn selbst wenn es nur um die Kosten einer Instanz geht, bliebe bei alleiniger Abhängigmachung der Kosten vom Erfolg die Kalkulation des Risikos ex ante weiterhin zu unsicher. Ferner besteht die Gefahr, daß die Urteile der Obergerichte von Kostenerwägungen bestimmt werden, ähnlich wie die Strafgerichte sich bei der Strafzumessung an der Länge der erlittenen Untersuchungshaft zu orientieren pflegen.

3. Belastung mit den eigenen außergerichtlichen Kosten trotz Prozeßerfolg

Man hat daher erwogen, die Belastung mit den eigenen außergerichtlichen Kosten, wenigstens mit den Kosten des eigenen Anwalts, vom Prozeßerfolg unabhängig zu machen, so daß sie auch im Falle eines Obsiegens erfolgen würde (52). Dies entspricht, wie die rechtsvergleichenden Hinweise von Bokelmann zeigen, der Situation in den USA, die seit je keine Erstattung der Kosten des gegnerischen Anwalts kennen, und entspricht ferner der 1958 in Frankreich neu eingeführten Regelung. In England, das die Kostentragung zunächst am Prozeßerfolg ausgerichtet hatte, hat seit dem Judicature Act von 1925 der Richter freie Hand. Umgekehrt verlief die Entwicklung in Schweden, wo 1948 die Kostenerstattung bei Unterliegen neu eingeführt wurde (53).

Die Belastung mit den eigenen außergerichtlichen Kosten trotz Obsiegens vor Gericht widerspricht jedoch der in Deutschland „tief eingewurzelten Rechtsüberzeugung, daß die unterlegene Partei die siegreiche auch von deren Kosten freistellen müsse“ (54). Wenn die Rechtsordnung dem Einzelnen ein Recht zuspricht, so spricht sie es ihm ganz zu und nicht abzüglich der Kosten einer eventuellen gerichtlichen Durchsetzung. Wer immer ihm sein Recht zu Unrecht streitig macht, muß die dadurch anfallenden Kosten als Schaden ersetzen. Diese Ersatzpflicht ist unabhängig vom Verschulden, ist also eine objektivierte Erfolgshaftung (55). Ein solches Denken geht allerdings von der naiven Vorstellung aus, es gäbe in Rechtsfragen eine „richtige“ Entscheidung, die von vornherein feststeht. Diese Vorstellung mag in der Öffentlichkeit durch die Art bestärkt werden, wie in Deutschland Gerichtsentscheidungen begründet werden. Abweichende Meinungen innerhalb des Richterkollegiums werden nämlich nicht mitgeteilt, und die Klippen der Entscheidung vermögen nur die Fachleute zwischen den Zeilen zu lesen. Erst in neuerer Zeit wird davon in den Entscheidungen des Bundesverfassungsgerichts eine Ausnahme gemacht. Wäre das Maß der Rechtsunsicherheit im gerichtlichen Entscheidungsprozeß weiteren Bevölkerungskreisen bewußt, würde man auch eher einsehen, daß gerichtliche Entscheidungen in der Regel im Interesse und zum Nutzen beider Parteien sind, da nur auf diesem Wege – außergerichtliche Einigung ausgenommen – der Streit über die unklare Sach- oder Rechtslage beendet werden kann. Hat der Unterlegene also den Rechtsstreit nicht „mutwillig“ oder in einer „offenbar aussichtslosen“ Situation geführt, ist es nicht billig, ihn für alle Kosten der Beseitigung der unklaren Sach- oder Rechtslage allein aufkommen zu lassen. Die Strafe dafür, daß er sich in der Beurteilung des Streitfalles verschätzt hat, wäre dann – so meint man in den USA (56) – allzu hart.

In der Tat spricht einiges dafür, den Unterlegenen nicht die außergerichtlichen Kosten des Gegners tragen zu lassen. Nur folgt daraus nicht schlüssig, daß damit diese Kosten vom Gegner selbst zu tragen seien, jedenfalls dann nicht, wenn die Rechtsunklarheit zu Lasten des Staates geht. Auch wird nicht jeder, der an einem unklaren Rechtsverhältnis beteiligt ist, mit einem Prozeß überzogen, so daß jeweils nur einige Bürger zu Kosten gezwungen werden können, die sie von selbst nicht aufgewandt haben würden. Es wäre daher zu untersuchen, wie es in Frankreich gelungen ist, eine den USA entsprechende Regelung durchzusetzen. In Deutschland – so scheint es jedenfalls (57) – wäre dies ohne besondere Öffentlichkeitsarbeit nicht möglich. Das wäre nur anders, wenn für die Kosten des Obsiegenden nicht er selbst, sondern eine Rechtsschutzversicherung eintreten würde.

VII. Obligatorische Rechtsschutzversicherung?

Der wichtigste Vorschlag, der bisher zur Verhinderung von Rechtswegbarrieren durch die Kostenregelung gemacht worden ist, ist in der Tat die Einführung einer Pflichtversicherung. Der ungeheure soziale Erfolg der obligatorischen Krankenverversicherung oder der obligatorischen Kraftfahrzeugversicherung, die beide in den meisten Kulturstaaten Probleme beseitigt haben, die anders nicht zu lösen gewesen wären, legt eine „versicherungsrechtliche Lösung" auch unseres Problems nahe. Die Vorsorge für mögliche, aber keineswegs sichere finanzielle Belastungen, die Schicksalsschlägen vergleichbar eintreten können, ist gerade bei geringeren Einkommen am zweckmäßigsten durch Versicherungen möglich. Daß die Kosten der Rechtsverfolgung ohne Schwierigkeiten versicherbar sind, zeigt deutlich der Aufschwung der privaten Rechtsschutzversicherung. Die gegenwärtig 10 als Rechtsschutzversicherung tätigen Gesellschaften haben in der Zeit von 1965–1970 ihr Prämieneinkommen verdoppelt, das um 400 Mio DM im Jahr liegt. Die Schadensquote im Jahre 1968 betrug dabei rund 45 % (58).
Es war der Prozessualist Fritz Baur, der nun nachdrücklich die Einführung einer obligatorischen Rechtsschutzversicherung zur Diskussion gestellt hat (59). Nach seinen Vorstellungen müßte eine Versicherungspflicht statuiert werden, der – wie bei der Sozialversicherungspflicht – durch Eintritt in eine öffentlich-rechtliche Pflichtversicherung oder durch Abschluß eines privaten Rechtsschutzversicherungsvertrages zu genügen ist. Demgegenüber hat der Versicherungsrechtler Karl Sieg sich für eine Obliegenheit zur Versicherungsnahme bei privaten Rechtsschutzversicherern eingesetzt. Durch öffentliche Aufklärungsarbeit sei auf die soziale Funktion der Rechtsschutzversicherung hinzuweisen. Wer gleichwohl keine private Rechtsschutzversicherung eingehe, müsse in Kauf nehmen, daß man ihm das Armenrecht versage, soweit er in seinem Falle hätte versichert sein könne. Denn in Anbetracht der Obliegenheit seien dann an die Bewilligung des Armenrechts schärfere Anforderungen zu stellen (60). Da seinerzeit das Problem der Sozialversicherung nicht mit Hilfe der privaten Versicherungswirtschaft, die schließlich verdienen will und soll, sondern mit Hilfe öffentlich-rechtlicher Träger der Sozialversicherung gelöst wurde, wird es sehr darauf ankommen, die Argumente zu prüfen, die gegen eine öffentlich-rechtliche Lösung vorgebracht werden. Denn anders noch als bei der Frage der Vorsorge für Krankheit ist es eine eminent staatliche Aufgabe, den Rechtsweg offenzuhalten. Auch die Finanzierung der Straßen ist ja nicht Aufgabe erwerbswirtschaftlicher privater Straßenträgergesellschaften.
Zunächst wird von Sieg eingewandt, eine öffentlich-rechtliche Lösung wie bei der gesetzlichen Krankenversicherung sei nur für die Personenversicherung geeignet. Generalisierend bemessener Bedarf und typisierte Sachverhalte seien die Voraussetzungen, unter denen die Sozialversicherung ihre Aufgaben bewältigen könne,

nicht aber das diffizile, höchst individuelle Geschäft der Rechtsschutzversicherung. Auch würde sich die Anwaltschaft energisch dagegen sträuben, wenn es neben dem Kassenarzt auch einen „Kassenanwalt" geben sollte. Beide Argumente sind jedoch in dieser kurz begründeten Form nicht überzeugend. Es mag sein, daß der Einzelne öfter krank wird als daß er zum Gericht muß. Warum die Versicherung des Rechtsschutzrisikos jedoch so diffizil sein soll wie die von Sieg vergleichsweise herangezogene Versicherung politisch riskanter Kreditgeschäfte im Außenhandel oder gar die Versicherung der Beine von Marlene Dietrich, vermag ich angesichts der zur Verfügung stehenden, wenn auch nicht zusammenfassend publizierten Gerichtsstatistiken nicht einzusehen. Hier müßten jedenfalls unabhängige Versicherungsfachleute um genauere Angaben gebeten werden. Im übrigen will Baur die Versicherungspflicht auf die durchschnittlichen Kosten eines in drei Instanzen geführten Zivilprozesses mit einem Streitwert von etwa DM 20.000,– begrenzen. Wenn die Anwaltschaft befürchten sollte, daß Teile ihres Berufsstandes zum Kassenarzt herabsinken, so sollte uns das nicht beeindrucken. Zum einen geht es den Kassenärzten gar nicht so schlecht, wie damit wohl behauptet werden soll. Zum zweiten gibt es einen gewissen negativen Typ von Kassenarzt unter der Anwaltschaft schon heute. Und schließlich hat niemand einen Anspruch darauf, an unsozialen Verhältnissen zu verdienen. Auch sieht der Vorschlag von Baur ausdrücklich die freie Wahl des Anwalts vor, der über die Erfolgsaussicht des Verfahrens und damit über die Zahlungspflicht der Versicherung selbständig entscheiden können soll. Politisch gesehen würde ein Widerstand der Anwaltschaft – trotz der „Diktatur der Anwälte" in unseren Parlamenten – nicht unbedingt dazu führen, daß der Plan einer Pflichtversicherung aufgegeben werden müßte. Denn auch die gegenwärtigen Möglichkeiten für eine Streitwertherabsetzung sind gegen den entschiedenen Widerstand der Anwälte durchgesetzt worden.
Nun sind gegen die Vorstellungen von Baur eine Reihe anderer Einwände erhoben worden. Eike Schmidt hat die Jahresprämie für das Prozeßkostenrisiko eines Streitwertes von DM 20.000,– bei drei Instanzen auf DM 100,– geschätzt und diese Summe für die Bezieher kleinerer Einkommen für untragbar erklärt (61). Dem hat Bokelmann unter der Voraussetzung widersprochen, daß die Prämie entgegen den Vorstellungen von Baur nicht für alle gleich hoch, sondern je nach dem Einkommen gestaffelt wird (62). Schmidt bezweifelt ohne Begründung die technische Möglichkeit einer Staffelung der Versicherungsprämien, angesichts unserer gegenwärtigen Sozialversicherungsbeiträge jedoch wohl zu Unrecht. Würde eine Staffelung nicht vorgenommen, dann müßten – worauf Bokelmann zu Recht hinweist (63) – die Einkommenschwachen die Prozesse besser gestellter Bürger mitfinanzieren, da die Inanspruchnahme der Gerichte nicht für alle Bürger gleich nahe liegt (64). Das insbesondere deshalb, weil schwerpunktmäßig nur besser gestellte Parteien mit höherwertigen Wirtschaftsgütern in Berührung kommen. Um hier einen sozialen Ausgleich dahin zu erreichen, daß die Bessergestellten den Schutz Einkommenschwacher mitfinanzieren, muß die Einkommensgrenze für den Wegfall der Versicherungspflicht sehr hoch liegen. Am besten wäre sie an die Sozialversicherungspflicht gekoppelt, um ihre Einhaltung überwachen zu können. Um Querulanten abzuhalten und die Belastung der Justiz mit Bagatellsachen zu verhindern, könnte man wie bei der Krankenversicherung oder der Kraftfahrzeugversicherung mit einem Bonus oder Malus arbeiten. Das wäre zwar aufwendig (65), aber für die Experimentierphase einer versicherungsrechtlichen Lösung durchaus empfehlenswert (66). Ferner wäre zu erwägen, den Versiche-

rungsschutz zunächst auf einige Lebensbereiche zu beschränken (67). Streitigkeiten aus Kraftfahrzeugunfällen sind ja in einigen Bereichen schon gedeckt. Wenn dagegen vorgebracht wird, daß ein Nebeneinander der öffentlich-rechtlichen Pflichtversicherung mit privaten Rechtsschutzversicherungen die Prozeßtätigkeit erhöhen und die Rechtsfremdheit der Bevölkerung vergrößern würde, weil Versicherungsgesellschaften untereinander gerne prozessieren und weil fremdfinanzierte Prozesse das Interesse der Parteien an einer Verfahrensbeteiligung herabsetzen (68), so sind diese Argumente nicht unbedingt überzeugend. Versicherungsgesellschaften wissen meist, daß es wirtschaftlicher ist, sich zu einigen, und führen deshalb nach Möglichkeit nur Musterprozesse über Rechtsfragen. Daran aber besteht ein öffentliches Interesse. Und der Rechtsfremdheit der Bevölkerung kann besser durch andere Maßnahmen begegnet werden als durch Beteiligung an Verfahren in eigener Sache (69).

Der entscheidende Einwand gegen das verwaltungsmäßig ungeheuer aufwendige Unternehmen einer Pflichtversicherung scheint mir daher ein anderer zu sein. Im Prinzip müßte in die Lastenumverteilung einer gestaffelten „Sozialversicherung" des Prozeßkostenrisikos jedermann einbezogen werden. Wenn nämlich die Justiz ohnehin schon zum allergrößten Teil auf Staatskosten erfolgt, dann nehmen die (wenigen) Reichen bei ihren Prozessen Einrichtungen in Anspruch, die von den Steuergeldern der (mehrheitlich) weniger Reichen unterhalten werden. Bejaht man aber das Prinzip, daß jedermann für den freien Zugang zu den Gerichten soll aufkommen müssen, dann ist nicht einzusehen, warum man alle Staatsbürger in eine Pflichtversicherung einbezieht, anstatt ohne den ganzen Verwaltungsaufwand einfach eine progressiv gestaffelte Steuererhöhung für die Zwecke der Rechtspflege vorzunehmen (70). Damit aber wären wir wieder beim Nulltarif für die Justiz angelangt, der wegen der damit verbundenen Steuererhöhung politisch nicht durchsetzbar erscheint.

VIII. Vorschlag für ein Experiment mit einem Ensemble von Randkorrekturen

Wollen wir also eine Reform, die politisch machbar ist, weil sie wenig Geld kostet, dann müssen wir auf tiefgreifende Lösungen verzichten und versuchen, in einem ersten Schritt mit einer Kombination kleinerer Korrekturen der gegenwärtigen Regelung auszukommen. Da die finanziellen Auswirkungen selbst kleinerer Änderungen angesichts des fehlenden Rechtstatsachenmaterials kaum hinreichend vorhersehbar sind, müßte jede solche Änderungen den Charakter eines Experiments haben (71), was dadurch zum Ausdruck gebracht werden könnte, daß eine Reformgesetzgebung in ihrer Geltung zeitlich begrenzt würde.

1. Reformmaßnahmen unter Belastung des Staatshaushalts

Ausgangspunkt der Reformdiskussion waren die Beschwerden, daß den Minderbemittelten gegenwärtig nicht ausreichend geholfen wird und daß auch der Mittelschicht die jetzige Kostenregelung nicht zumutbar ist. Das legt nahe, vorsichtig an zwei Punkten anzusetzen, nämlich beim Armenrecht und bei der Kostenregelung in Revisionssachen.

Eine Erweiterung des Armenrechts hätte den Begriff der Armut zu präzisieren

und zu Gunsten der Unbemittelten zu erweitern. Hier sollte man es mit dem Vorschlag von Eike Schmidt versuchen, die Sätze des pfändungsfreien Betrages zu verdoppeln. Wenn nämlich jemand mit Aussicht auf Erfolg gekämpft hat und unterlegen ist, dann sollte er sich nicht so stark einschränken müssen wie jemand, dessen Gläubiger hinter ihm her sind. Die Kosten des gegnerischen Anwalts kommen ohnehin auf ihn zu. Bei der Erstattungspflicht der Kosten des gegnerischen Anwalts sollte man es in einer ersten Reformphase zunächst belassen, weil hier die Mehrausgaben des Staates erheblich sein könnten. Dagegen müßte man bei dieser Gelegenheit die Regelungen von § 114 Abs. 2 und 4 ZPO (Armenrecht für Ausländer nur bei Gegenseitigkeit und für juristische Personen nur bei allgemeinem Interesse) wegen Verfassungswidrigkeit aufheben und die freie Wahl des Prozessbevollmächtigten einführen. Letzteres würde den Anwälten vielleicht erleichtern, mit der großzügigen Armutsgrenze einverstanden zu sein. Je mehr Prozesse im Armenrecht geführt werden können, desto größer ist der Einkommensverlust der Anwälte, die als Armenanwälte nach § 123 BRAGO nur einen geringeren Satz als die normalen Gebühren aus der Staatskasse erhalten. Diesen Einkommensverlust durch Einführung der Erstattung der vollen Gebühren abzuschaffen, kann gegenwärtig nur ein Fernziel sein. In einem sozialen Rechtsstaat muß es auch erlaubt sein, von einem Berufsstand einen Beitrag zur Lösung sozialer Probleme zu verlangen. Würde der Staat überhaupt nichts zahlen, würden sicher die meisten Prozesse, die jetzt im Armenrecht geführt werden, der Anwaltschaft als Einkommensquelle gänzlich verlorengehen.
Die zweite Richtung, in die ein Reformexperiment gehen müßte, wäre die Kostenregelung. Hier wäre ein erster Schritt, diejenigen Prozesse, die eindeutig zugleich im Interesse der Allgemeinheit geführt werden, weil sie eine unklare Rechtslage beseitigen, von Gerichtskosten freizustellen. Das wären Revisionen, die wegen grundsätzlicher Bedeutung von den Oberlandesgerichten zugelassen werden. Eine Stellungnahme zur Frage der grundsätzlichen Bedeutung einer eventuellen Revision sollte in allen revisiblen Fällen von Amts wegen erfolgen. Das wäre auch ohne größere zusätzliche Arbeitsbelastung möglich. Da die Parteien eines solchen Rechtsstreits an der Klärung der betreffenden Rechtsfrage zugleich ein eigenes Interesse haben, kann es zunächst dabei bleiben, daß sie die außergerichtlichen Kosten, insbesondere die Anwaltsgebühren weiterhin selbst zu tragen haben.

2. *Reformmaßnahmen durch Organisation gesellschaftlicher Selbsthilfe*

Mit diesen Maßnahmen, die zusätzliche Belastungen des Staatshaushalts zur Folge haben, könnte es zunächst bis zur Prüfung ihrer finanziellen Auswirkungen in der Praxis sein Bewenden haben. Bokelmann hat darüber hinaus von einer neuen Entwicklung in Schweden berichtet, wo jetzt die Anwaltsgebühren nach dem Einkommen gestaffelt werden, wobei den Anwälten die Differenz zur vollen Gebühr bei der Vertretung von Minderbemittelten vom Staat gezahlt wird (72). Anstelle der Zahlungen aus der Staatskasse hat sie die Gründung eines Ausgleichsfonds durch die Anwaltschaft vorgeschlagen, über den Zahlungen zu Gunsten derjenigen Anwälte zu erfolgen hätten, die überwiegend Prozesse mit kleineren Streitwerten übernehmen (73). Ich halte es jedoch für berufspolitisch unerfreulich, die Anwaltschaft wieder zur Zunft zu machen (mit einem Anspruch auf „bürgerliche Nahrung") und den Verwaltungsaufwand einer Ausgleichskasse heraufzubeschwören. Die freie Advokatur sollte auch frei im Verhältnis zu ihren eigenen Berufskollegen bleiben. Sie hat Anspruch darauf, kostendeckend zu arbeiten und braucht sich nicht subventionieren zu lassen. Das schließt kommunale Rechtsberatungsstellen für Minderbemittelte nicht aus. Da Prozesse mit kleinerem Streitwert erfahrungsgemäß kaum weniger Arbeit mit sich bringen, kommt auch die von Bokelmann vorgeschlagene Änderung der Gebührenstaffel bei geringen Streitwerten (74) nicht in Betracht. Gesellschaftliche Selbsthilfemaßnahmen sollten nicht durch die Anwaltschaft getragen werden müssen. Man hat ja auch nicht verlangt, daß die Krankenversorgung zu sozialen Preisen durch die Ärzteschaft organisiert wird. Hier müssen vielmehr die unmittelbar Betroffenen aktiviert werden.

Es empfiehlt sich zu diesem Zweck, die Öffentlichkeit vermehrt darüber aufzuklären, daß sie sich vor den Kosten einer Rechtsverfolgung durch Eintritt in Interessenverbände und durch Abschluß privater Rechtsschutzversicherungen schützen kann. Ferner muß dafür geworben werden, daß Interessenverbände wie Mieterverbände, Hausbesitzerverbände, Gewerkschaften, Arbeitgeberverbände oder die Vielzahl der Hobbyvereine (Sportvereine, Gesangvereine, Tierzüchtervereine, Sammlervereine usw.) verstärkt die Unterstützung ihrer Mitglieder in relevanten Rechtsstreitigkeiten zu ihrer Aufgabe machen (75). Hier läßt sich durchaus vieles verbessern, zumal diese Verbände in der Regel ohnehin Anwälte unter ihren Mitgliedern haben. Allerdings führt die Entscheidung über die Gewährung von Rechtsschutz auch zur Machtausübung gegenüber dem Einzelnen. Um hier den Einzelnen von Verbandsherrschaft unabhängig zu machen, muß auch die Möglichkeit der Einzelversicherung in privaten Rechtsschutzversicherungen aktiviert werden, jedoch auf freiwilliger Basis. Erst in dem Maße, wie schrittweise unter Belastung der Staatskasse der Nulltarif eingeführt wird, kann die Sicherung gegen die Rechtsverfolgungskosten entfallen. Bis dahin muß aber etwas geschehen, sollen nicht faktisch rechtsfreie Räume (76) entstehen, die sich meist zum Nachteil des sozial Schwachen auswirken. Der Weg von der formalen zur materiellen Rechtsgleichheit darf jedenfalls nicht an den mangelnden Staatsfinanzen scheitern.

Summary

Arrangements for the poor in the procedural norms of the Federal Republic of Germany consist of reduction of costs, provided that the case, in the opinion of the judge, has enough of an outlook for success. If so, the lawyer for the poor person has a claim against the state for an honorarium, which is less than the customary fee. The lawyer for the other party, however, must be paid by the poor client if he loses his case. These regulations do not provide enough relief for indigent parties, and provide no benefits for persons of middle and higher income, even though these litigants are often in no way responsible for the legal uncertainty of outcomes at law, and must assume financial burdens which, in disputes over smaller items, have no relationship to the economic value of the case.

The ideal solution is to introduce the principle of costless justice. This is currently not practical, politically or financially. The essay discusses other reform proposals – mandatory legal insurance, for example, and the plan of the federal Ministry of Justice, to give courts the right to set a low figure for the amount in controversy (the figure which is the basis on which costs and lawyers' fees are computed). The foreseeable disadvantages of these and other solutions are discussed; it is proposed that the ideal of costless justice be approached through small steps, that is, small marginal reforms.

Anmerkungen

1 Erich Fechner: Kostenrisiko und Rechtswegsperre, in: JZ 1969, S. 349–354; Wolfgang Däubler: Bürger ohne Rechtsschutz?, in: BB 1969, S. 545–551; Klaus F. Röhl: Zur Reform des Armenrechts, in: ZRP 1970, S. 274–275; Uwe Seetzen: Prozeßkosten und sozialer Rechtsstaat, in: ZRP 1971, S. 35–38; Egon Schneider, in: JurA 1971, S. 57–112 (104 ff.); Fritz Baur: Armenrecht und Rechtsschutzversicherung, in: JZ 1972, S. 75–78 (geringfügig verändert unter demselben Titel in Studi in memoria di Carlo Furno, 1973, S. 91–101), Eike Schmidt: Der Arme und sein Recht, in: JZ 1972, S. 679–682; Erika Bokelmann: „Rechtswegsperre" durch Prozeßkosten, in: ZRP 1973, S. 164–171. Frühere Kritik bereits bei Hiendl, NJW 1960, 1749; Tribian, DRiZ 1962, 416; Schumann, Anwaltsbl. 1963, 73; Koebel, NJW 1964, 392 und 1967, 535. Nach Abschluß des Manuskripts erschien die Stellungnahme von K. Redeker, in: NJW 1973, S. 1153–1162 (1159 f.) sowie H. Kollhosser: Der Arme und sein Recht, in VersR. 1974, S. 829–838; H.-M. Pawlowski: Zur Funktion der Prozeßkosten, in JZ 1975, S. 197–202, und G. Baumgärtel: Chancengleichheit vor Gericht, in JZ 1975, S. 425–430.

2 Der sog. Justizgewährungsanspruch ergibt sich für Prozesse gegen den Staat als Hoheitsträger aus Art. 19 Abs. 4 GG. Für die anderen Prozesse wird er zum Teil aus Art. 103 Abs. 1 GG, zum Teil aus Art. 6 Abs. 1 MRK oder aus dem Rechtsstaatsprinzip hergeleitet, vgl. Däubler (FN. 1), S. 550 mit Nachweisen.

3 E. Fechner/Peter Schneider: Verfassungswidrigkeit und Rechtsmißbrauch im Aktienrecht, 1960, S. 59 f.

4 Lent/Jauernig: Zivilprozeßrecht, 16. Aufl., 1972, S. 281.

5 So zu recht Baur (Anm. 1), S. 75.

6 Vgl. M. Rehbinder: Karl N. Llewellyn als Rechtssoziologe, in: Kölner Zeitschrift für Soziologie und Sozialpsychologie 18 (1966), S. 532–556 (533).

7 Vgl. R.M. Jackson: The Machinery of Justice in England, 6. ed. Cambridge 1972, S. 435–454; Ginsburg/Bruzelius: Civil Procedure in Sweden, The Hague 1965, S. 367 ff.; Ekelöf: Das schwedische Untergerichtsverfahren, 1968; Herzog: Civil Procedure in France, The Hague 1967, S. 542 ff.; Stein: Compendium van het burgerlijk procesrecht, Deventer 1968, S. 34 ff.; Vecchione: Spese Giudiziale, in Novissimo Digesto Italiano 17, Turin 1970, S. 1120–1143; Mauro Cappelletti: Giustizia e societa, Milano 1972.

8 So Baur (FN. 1), S. 75; siehe auch die Statistik für Baden-Württemberg bei Eike Schmidt (FN. 1), S. 680. Die Prognos AG (Europäisches Zentrum für Angewandte Wirtschaftsforschung, Basel) hat eine Auswertung der amtlichen Zählkartenstatistik von 1971 vorgenommen. Wie mir ihr Mitarbeiter Dr. Erhard Blankenburg freundlicherweise mitgeteilt hat, ergibt sich danach bei den Zivilprozessen vor den Amtsgerichten ein Anteil von 6,17 % und bei den erstinstanzlichen Zivilprozessen vor den Landgerichten ein Anteil von 12,23 %, bei dem Armenrecht beantragt wurde. Der erhöhte Anteil beim Landgericht läßt sich im wesentlichen auf Ehescheidungsverfahren zurückführen.

9 Über die Regelung im sozialgerichtlichen Verfahren vor den Sozialgerichten und Landessozialgerichten vgl. unter II.

10 So Baur (FN. 1), S. 76.

11 Will man überhaupt davon ausgehen, daß es in unklaren Rechtsfragen eine „richtige" Entscheidung gibt.

12 Darauf hat zu recht Baur (FN. 1), S. 76, Anm. 8, aufmerksam gemacht.

13 Vgl. Tribian (FN. 1), S. 416.

14 FN. 1, S. 546.
15 Vgl. Däubler (FN. 1), S. 546 mit Nachweisen.
16 Vgl. Baur (FN. 1), S. 76.
17 Kann die arme Partei nicht zahlen, hat der Sieger den Prozeß auf eigene Kosten geführt. Die Armenrechtsbewilligung bringt also auch ein Kostenrisiko für den Gegner, so Röhl (FN. 1).
18 Baur (FN. 1), S. 77.
19 Die klassische Darstellung dieser Sicht findet sich bei Rudolph von Jhering: Der Kampf ums Recht, 4. Aufl., 1874, (Nachdruck Darmstadt 1965).
20 Von Kirchmann: Die Wertlosigkeit der Jurisprudenz als Wissenschaft (1848), Nachdruck, Darmstadt 1966, S. 8. Auf diese Äußerung hat in unserem Zusammenhang Eike Schmidt (FN. 1), S. 679, aufmerksam gemacht. Vgl. zum folgenden auch Seetzen (FN. 1), S. 36.
21 So besonders Däubler (FN. 1), S. 549 ff.; Bokelmann (FN. 1), S. 165.
22 BVerfGE 22, 83–90 (86).
23 So zu recht Baur (FN. 1), S. 77.
24 Vgl. Bokelmann (FN. 1), S. 167.
25 Nach Baur (S. 76) sprechen die Erfahrungen der Rechtsschutzversicherungen und nach Eike Schmidt (S. 680) sprechen die Armenrechtsstatistiken gegen umfangreiches querulatorisches Prozessieren. Vgl. aber die Nachweise gegenteiliger Behauptungen bei Bokelmann (S. 164, Anm. 2).
26 FN. 1, S. 549. Sie würde allerdings dort nichts nützen, wo vom Querulanten nichts zu holen ist.
27 Däubler (FN. 1), S. 549; E. Schneider (FN. 1), S. 111 f.; Baur (FN. 1), S. 77; E. Schmidt (FN. 1), S. 680; Bokelmann (FN. 1), S. 165; Karl Sieg: Moderne Aspekte der Rechtsschutzversicherung, in: BB 1972, S. 1377–1380 (1379).
28 Vgl. die Mitteilungen im Anwaltsblatt 1971, S. 78. Die hohe Kostendeckung bei der ordentlichen Gerichtsbarkeit beruht sicher auf den Einnahmen aus der freiwilligen Gerichtsbarkeit.
29 So richtig Bokelmann (FN. 1), S. 166, Anm. 31.
30 Schmidt (FN 1), S. 681 f.
31 Das wird in AnwBL. 1971, S. 78 bemängelt.
32 E. Schneider (FN. 1), S. 111; Sauer in DRiZ 1970, S. 293–295.
33 E. Blankenburg/V. Blankenburg/H. Morasch: Der lange Weg in die Berufung, in: Rolf Bender: Tatsachenforschung in der Justiz, 1972, S. 81–104 (83, 87); Bokelmann (FN. 1), S. 165. So auch schon W. Kisch: Die soziale Bedeutung des Zivilprozesses, in Judicium 1 (1928/29), S. 1–37 (21).
34 So zu recht Bokelmann (FN. 1), S. 165.
35 Ebenso Maunz-Dürig, GG. Art. 103 Rd. Nr. 77.
36 Vgl. Däubler (FN. 1), S. 551, mit Nachweisen.
37 Vgl. Däubler, ebd.
38 Ebd. Den „angemessenen" anstelle des „notdürftigen" Unterhalts will auch der Reformentwurf zur Neuordnung des Armenrechts in Österreich gesichert sehen. Statt Armenrecht soll es in Zukunft „Verfahrenshilfe" heißen. Für höhere Einkommen soll ferner die Möglichkeit einer Teil-Verfahrenshilfe (z.B. bezüglich der Sachverständigengebühren) geschaffen werden.
39 Schmidt (FN. 1), S. 682. Ein darüberliegender Einkommensbetrag müßte dann ratenweise eingezogen werden können.
40 Ebd.
41 Dazu Ephard Wüstmann: Rolle und Rollenkonflikt im Recht, 1972, S. 184.
42 So zu recht die Forderung von Bokelmann (FN. 1), S. 165.
43 FN. 1, S. 551.
44 Vgl. Bokelmann (FN. 1), S. 165.
45 So zu recht Baur (FN. 1), S. 76.
46 Boy-Jürgen Andresen, Urteilsanmerkung in: JZ 1973, S. 519; ferner Däubler (FN. 1, S. 551), der diese Möglichkeit sogar im Wege verfassungskonformer Auslegung als geltendes Recht betrachtet, das es durchzusetzen gelte. Dagegen aber Erdsiek, NJW 1964, S. 912 f., und OLG Celle, NJW 1964, S. 1527.
47 Bundestagsdrucksache VI/2644.
48 So Baur (FN. 1), S. 77; Sieg (FN. 27), S. 1379; Eike Schmidt (FN. 1), S. 680; vgl. auch Bokelmann (FN. 1), S. 166, und Seetzen (FN. 1), S. 36. Bereits gegen die Einführung der

gegenwärtigen Sonderregelungen hatte der Deutsche Anwaltsverein scharfen Protest eingelegt, vgl. AnwBl. 1964, S. 168.

49 So Seetzen (FN. 1), S. 37.

50 So Eike Schmidt (FN. 1), S. 681.

51 So Seetzen (FN. 1), S. 36; AnwBl. 71, 78; Bokelmann (FN. 1), S. 166, Anm. 36.

52 So Ehrig in ZRP 1971, S. 252 f.; Hagen: Elemente einer allgemeinen Prozeßlehre, 1972, S. 68; Bokelmann (FN. 1), S. 170.

53 Vgl. die Nachweise bei Bokelmann, ebd.

54 So Sieg (FN. 27) ebd.; vgl. auch Bokelmann, ebd.

55 Vgl. Bokelmann (FN. 1), S. 168 f. mit Nachweisen über entsprechende Diskussionen im deutschen Schrifttum zu Beginn dieses Jahrhunderts.

56 Vgl. Karlen: Primar of Procedure, Ann Arbor 1962, S. 103.

57 Das muß auch Bokelmann (FN. 1 S. 170) zugestehen.

58 Siehe Baur (FN. 1), S. 77.

59 Ebd., S. 77 f.

60 Sieg (FN 27), ebd.

61 Schmidt (FN. 1), S. 681.

62 Bokelmann (FN.,1), S. 167.

63 Ebd.

64 Vgl. die Angaben bei Blankenburg u.a. (FN. 33), S. 82–87.

65 Vgl. Sieg, FN. 27.

66 So auch Baur (FN. 1), S. 78.

67 So Sieg (FN. 27), zweifelnd Baur (FN. 1), S. 77.

68 So Bokelmann (FN. 1), S. 167.

69 Vgl. dazu näher M. Rehbinder: Rechtskenntnis, Rechtsbewußtsein und Rechtsethos als Probleme der Rechtspolitik, in: Jahrbuch für Rechtssoziologie und Rechtstheorie 3 (1972), S. 25–46.

70 So richtig Bokelmann (FN. 1), S. 167.

71 Grundsätzlich zum Experimentcharakter von Gesetzgebung: Frederick K. Beutel: Experimentelle Rechtswissenschaft, 1971.

72 Bokelmann (FN. 1), S. 168.

73 Ebd., S. 171.

74 Ebd., S. 1968

75 So schon Kisch (FN. 33), S. 21.

76 Vgl. die Ausführungen von Lawrence Friedman über die "networks of reciprocal immunities" in: L. Friedmann/St. Macaulay: Law and the Behavioral Sciences, 1969, S. 499 f.

Gisela Zenz

„Kommunikation" als Untersuchungsgegenstand und Forschungsinstrument

*Zur Vorbereitung eines Forschungsprojekts über die vormundschaftsgerichtliche Entscheidungspraxis**

Problemstellung

Art. 6 Grundgesetz legt die Erziehung von Kindern grundsätzlich in die Hand der Eltern, der Familien. Dem Staat kommt nur ein „Wächteramt" zu: er hat die Ausübung der elterlichen Gewalt zu überwachen. Die Rechte und Pflichten, die sich daraus ergeben, nehmen neben den Jugendbehörden vor allem die Vormundschaftsgerichte wahr. Sie haben alle Maßnahmen zu ergreifen, die erforderlich sind, um Kinder vor Schäden zu bewahren, die ihnen aus schweren Unzulänglichkeiten der Erziehung, aus Konflikten der Eltern in Erziehungsfragen oder bei der Auflösung der Familie, z.B. durch die Scheidung der Eltern, erwachsen können. Im Extremfall kann den Eltern die elterliche Gewalt insgesamt entzogen werden. Die Vormundschaftsgerichte treffen damit Entscheidungen, die schwerwiegende und nachhaltige Folgen für das einzelne Kind und für die gesamte Familie haben können.

Es ist daher nicht verwunderlich, daß in den letzten Jahren als Folge allgemein wachsender Aufmerksamkeit für Erziehungsprobleme auch die vormundschaftsgerichtliche Praxis zum Gegenstand kritischer Diskussion wurde. Dabei konzentrierte sich die Kritik überwiegend auf die Auswirkungen bestimmter Entscheidungen, vor allem auf die Unzulänglichkeiten gerichtlich angeordneter Fürsorgeerziehung. Diese sind nun freilich vom Vormundschaftsrichter nicht in erster Linie zu verantworten und zu beeinflussen. Die Tatsache aber, daß sozialpolitische Versäumnisse den Vormundschaftsrichter wieder und wieder zwingen, ungeeignete Maßnahmen zu ergreifen bzw. von zwei Übeln das kleinere zu wählen, statt Kinder wirksam zu schützen, kann nicht ohne Einfluß auf die Entscheidungspraxis bleiben.

Rechtskritik allerdings muß weiter vordringen. Sie muß die Rechtsgrundlagen für vormundschaftsgerichtliche Entscheidungen zur Diskussion stellen, fragen, ob materielles und formelles Recht den gestellten Anforderungen entsprechen.

* Der Bericht bezieht sich auf ein Seminar, das 1972/73 am Frankfurter Sigmund-Freud-Institut unter Beteiligung von Psychoanalytikern, Juristen, Soziologen und Psychologen stattfand. Die dabei gesammelten Erfahrungen dienten der Vorbereitung eines Forschungsprojekts „Zur Integration sozialwissenschaftlicher Erkenntnisse und Methoden in den juristischen Entscheidungsprozeß – Entwicklung eines Modells für das Familienrecht", das gegenwärtig unter Leitung der Professoren L. Rosenkötter, S. Simitis und R.M. Vogel an der Universität Frankfurt/Main durchgeführt wird.

Materielles Recht

Das materielle Recht, wie es vor allem in den Bestimmungen des Bürgerlichen Gesetzbuches zur elterlichen Gewalt enthalten ist, befindet sich in einer Umbruchssituation. Die Vorstellungen von Kindeswohl und Elternrecht haben sich gewandelt, die Kriterien für „gute" und „schlechte" Erziehung sind unsicher geworden. Legitimation und Grenzen staatlicher Eingriffe zum Schutz des Kindes haben ihre Selbstverständlichkeit verloren. Die Reform des Rechts der elterlichen Gewalt ist wiederholt gefordert und neuerdings auch in Angriff genommen worden. Ein Regierungsentwurf liegt bereits vor. Die Rechte des Kindes in der Familie sollen verstärkt werden, das Verschulden der Erziehungsberechtigten soll nicht mehr Voraussetzung für gerichtliche Eingriffe zum Schutz des Kindes sein, Behörden und Gerichte sollen nicht erst dann eingreifen dürfen, wenn bereits schwerwiegende Schäden offenkundig sind. Wie auch immer die Reform ausfallen wird – es ist unwahrscheinlich, daß das Gesetz mehr als eine grobe Orientierung geben kann, die dem Richter wie bisher weiten Spielraum bei der Ausfüllung im Einzelfall läßt. Es ist sogar anzunehmen, daß dieser Spielraum eher größer als kleiner werden wird, da mit verschiedenen überholten gesetzlichen Entscheidungskriterien auch die letzten scheinbar festen Tatbestandsmerkmale aus dem Kindschaftsrecht verschwinden und das „Kindeswohl" vielfach zum einzigen benannten Maßstab wird, eine Generalklausel also, deren Anwendung im Einzelfall schon heute erhebliches Kopfzerbrechen macht.
Die Auffassungen darüber, was im allgemeinen dem Wohl des Kindes dient und was ihm schadet, haben sich nicht nur grundlegend geändert, sie gehen auch heute weiter auseinander denn je. Deshalb ist die Frage besonders dringlich geworden, in wieweit der Richter berechtigt sein soll, seine persönlichen Auffassungen oder auch obergerichtliche Vorstellungen vergangener Zeiten mit Hilfe staatlicher Sanktionsmacht durchzusetzen. Welche Kriterien und Maßstäbe aber legitime Verwendung finden können bei der Beurteilung des „Kindeswohls", darüber herrscht Unsicherheit. Die Rechtswissenschaft hat zur Klärung dieser Fragen wenig beigetragen. Kritische Analysen beschränkten sich zumeist auf einzelne Punkte oder Komplexe: auf das Verkehrsrecht des nichtsorgeberechtigten Elternteils etwa (§ 1634 BGB) oder auf Mündigkeitsprobleme (Stichwort Grundrechtsmündigkeit).

Verfahrensrecht

Das Verfahrensrecht für die Vormundschaftsgerichte ist in erster Linie im Gesetz über die Freiwillige Gerichtsbarkeit enthalten. Bemerkenswert ist auch hier der weite Spielraum, der dem Richter eingeräumt wird. Der Untersuchungsgrundsatz gibt ihm umfassende Ermittlungsbefugnisse, die nicht durch strenge Beweiserhebungs- und -verwertungsregeln eingeschränkt werden, wie sie etwa das Zivil- und Strafprozeßrecht beherrschen. Der Vormundschaftsrichter kann zu jedem ihm wichtig erscheinenden Punkt hören, wen er will und wann er es will: auch nach Abschluß eines Verfahrens kann er es jederzeit wieder aufrollen, wenn das Kindeswohl es erfordert. Er kann Sachverständige hören und Stellungnahmen und Berichte von Jugendbehörden anfordern. Im Vergleich zum Zivil- und Strafprozeß scheint auch für den Antragsteller, den Betroffenen, die Kommunikation mit dem

Richter wesentlich erleichtert: er kann seinen Antrag jederzeit ändern, neue Anregungen geben, neue Tatsachen vortragen. Es besteht kein Anwaltszwang in der ersten Instanz und die Gerichtsgebühren sind niedrig.
In einem gewissen Widerspruch hierzu scheint es zu stehen, daß gerade Vormundschaftsrichter über unzureichende Kontakte zu den Verfahrensbetroffenen und über unzureichende tatsächliche Entscheidungsgrundlagen klagen. Die ungenügende Aufklärung der Einzelfallsituation, vor allem der psychologischen und sozialen Hintergründe von Familienproblmen wird auch von Kritikern immer wieder beanstandet. Dazu paßt es, daß sich die Begründungen vormundschaftsgerichtlicher Entscheidungen oftmals wie eine Aufzählung gesetzlicher Tatbestandsmerkmale oder Lehrbuchfloskeln lesen, die in der allgemeinen Bemerkung gipfeln, daß die getroffene Entscheidung dem Wohl des Kindes am besten entspreche. Wo die Entscheidung generell als bloße Formalienkontrolle gehandhabt wird, verwendet man konsequenterweise Beschlußformulare.
Es ist erstaunlich, daß diese Situation bisher kaum zu Reformforderungen oder gar -bestrebungen Anlaß gegeben haben. Verfahrensreformen stehen zur Zeit nur im Zusammenhang mit der Scheidungsrechtsreform zur Debatte: Alle mit der Ehescheidung zusammenhängenden richterlichen Entscheidungen sollen künftig von demselben Gericht getroffen werden, das auch als „Familiengericht" bezeichnet wird. Diese Bestrebungen stehen vor allem im Zeichen der Prozeßökonomie und der Aufwandsersparnis für die Beteiligten. Mit der Familiengerichtsdiskussion vergangener Jahre, in der es um die Verbesserung der sachlichen Entscheidungskompetenz ging, haben sie wenig zu tun.
Zusammenfassend kann man sagen: Die Normen des materiellen ebenso wie des formellen Rechts räumen dem Vormundschaftsrichter erheblichen Spielraum für Ermittlung und Entscheidung ein. Seine Ausfüllung im Einzelfall ist mit der Veränderung der Auffassungen und realen Bedingungen von Erziehung problematisch geworden, der Rückgriff auf tradierte Maßstäbe und Beurteilungskriterien des Familienrechts überzeugt vielfach nicht mehr. Woher aber neue Kriterien, woher die Maßstäbe für Reformen nehmen?

Beiträge aus den Sozialwissenschaften

Für den aufgeklärten Juristen, sei er Richter oder Gesetzgeber, liegt es nahe, sich mit diesen Fragen an diejenigen Sozialwissenschaften zu wenden, die zur Problematisierung tradierter Vorstellungen von Erziehung in erster Linie beigetragen haben: Psychologie, Soziologie und Erziehungswissenschaft. Schon ein flüchtiger Blick zeigt, daß dort Einsichten und Methoden erarbeitet wurden, die auch für die gerichtlichen Bemühungen um das Kindeswohl von großer Bedeutung sind.
So hat z.B. die Soziologie schichtspezifische Determinanten von Familienerziehung nachgewiesen, die den Richter vor die Frage stellen, ob etwa „Kindeswohl" in verschiedenen Schichten auch Verschiedenes bedeuten mag. Devianztheorien formulieren Zusammenhänge zwischen Sozialisationsstörungen und Kriminalität, schlimmer noch: zwischen institutionellen Eingriffen in die Erziehung und „krimineller Karriere". Trägt also der Richter u.U. schon mit den ersten Aktenvermerken über die „Verwahrlosung" eines Fünfjährigen zu dessen gesellschaftlicher Stigmatisierung und devianter Entwicklung bei?
Psychoanalytiker betonen die vorrangige Bedeutung stabiler Objektbeziehungen,

d.h. verläßlicher Beziehungen zu den ersten Bezugspersonen, die nicht unbedingt mit den biologischen Eltern identisch sein müssen. Schädigt also der Richter vielleicht irreversibel das Kind, das er nach vierjähriger Erziehung durch die Großeltern oder Pflegeeltern an die Mutter zurückgibt, die sich erst jetzt selbst um ihr Kind kümmern will oder kann? Andere Ergebnisse verweisen auf pathogene Familienstrukturen als Auslöser neurotischer oder auch psychotischer Entwicklungen von Kindern. Dabei geht es häufig um Familien, die nach außen durchaus „intakt" sind und nach herkömmlichen Maßstäben in Rechtsprechung und Lehre ein Eingreifen des Richters nicht rechtfertigen. Muß der Richter hier untätig bleiben? Darf er es – im Hinblick auf das ihm anvertraute „Wächteramt"?

Schließlich verweisen pädagogische und psychotherapeutische Forschung nicht nur auf eine Vielfalt von Ursachen und Beeinflussungsmöglichkeiten von Erziehungsproblemen, die der Richter in dem ihm zur Verfügung stehenden Repertoire nicht findet, sondern sie zeigen ihm auch deutlich, wie schwierig die Ermittlung von „Wahrheit", die Wahrnehmung von Realität in diesem Bereich ist. Es wird unübersehbar, wie wichtig dafür Milieu und Methoden der Kommunikation sind, wie wichtig auch der persönliche Umgang mit beiden, ganz besonders wenn es sich um Kinder handelt. Diese Problematik ist dem Richter durchaus bekannt. Was kann er aber mit differenzierten neuen Ansätzen zu ihrer Bewältigung anfangen, für die er keine spezielle Ausbildung mitbringt, für die auch organisatorische Voraussetzungen fehlen? Soll er vielleicht nur noch im schriftlichen Verfahren entscheiden und die Ermittlungen im persönlichen Kontakt anderen Stellen überlassen, die dafür besser ausgerüstet sind, z.B. Sozialarbeitern?

Es scheint also, als ob der Blick über die Fachgrenzen hinaus dem Juristen mehr Fragen einbringt als Antworten. Der hier nur flüchtig skizzierte Eindruck wird sich auch bei näherem Zusehen nicht entscheidend ändern: Aus den einschlägigen Sozialwissenschaften sind wichtige Beiträge zu erwarten, aber es gibt keine auf Abruf verwendbaren Ergebnisse, aus denen der Richter die Orientierung für seine Entscheidung oder der Gesetzgeber objektive Kriterien für die Gesetzesformulierung herleiten könnte. Psychologie, Psychoanalyse, Soziologie und Erziehungswissenschaft haben ihre eigenen Problemansätze. Ihre Methoden und Erkenntnisse sind nicht auf die spezifischen Probleme der Vormundschaftsgerichtsbarkeit zugeschnitten.

Die unbekannte Praxis

Was sind aber „die spezifischen Probleme der Vormundschaftsgerichte"? Die publizierte Rechtsprechung gibt darüber keinen hinreichenden Aufschluß, einmal weil die Auswahl der Entscheidungen spezifisch juristisch-technischen Interessen folgt oder auch von Zufälligkeiten der Mitteilung abhängig ist, zum anderen aber wird ja beim Abdruck nur die Entscheidung selbst zugänglich gemacht, der Prozeß der Entscheidungsfindung ist daraus nicht zu erschließen. Gerade darüber wird man auch Kommentare und Lehrbücher vergebens befragen. Es ist unbekannt, welche juristischen Fallgruppen in der Praxis der Vormundschaftsgerichte am häufigsten vertreten sind, und welche den größten Aufwand verlangen. Es ist unbekannt, welche soziale und psychologische Problematik vorherrscht, und wie sie in juristische Kategorien umgesetzt wird – kurz: wie das von den Gerichten geschaffene Recht aussieht und welches seine bestimmenden Faktoren sind. Ebenso unbekannt ist der Ablauf des Rechtsschöpfungsprozesses selbst: Man weiß nicht, welchen Gebrauch der Richter von dem weiten Spielraum macht, den ihm das Verfahrensrecht einräumt, wie die Kommunikation im Verfahren tatsächlich aussieht – wer mit wem worüber spricht, woher Initiativen, Anregungen und Argumente kommen, welche Argumente sich durchsetzen und in welcher Form etwa Kinder am Verfahren beteiligt werden. Bilanz: Die Realität der vormundschaftsgerichtlichen Entscheidungspraxis, und d.h. ihre „spezifische Problematik" ist nicht bekannt. Ihre Erforschung ist erste Voraussetzung für weitere Reformdiskussionen. Diese Aufgabe steht daher im Mittelpunkt eines auf mehrere Jahre geplanten Forschungsprojekts, das gegenwärtig an der Frankfurter Universität mit Unterstützung der DFG durchgeführt wird.

Allgemeinere, methodische Ziele des Projekts

Die Zielsetzung des Projekts ist dabei letztlich nicht auf das Familienrecht beschränkt. Die Situation der Vormundschaftsgerichtsbarkeit kann ja als exemplarisch gelten für die juristische Entscheidungspraxis in manchen anderen Bereichen. Dies wird deutlich, wenn man die Ausgangsproblematik noch einmal etwas abstrakter formuliert: Die Rechtspraxis in einem spezifischen Bereich befindet sich in einer Umorientierungssituation. Die alten Maßstäbe und Begriffe sind fragwürdig geworden, neue Maßstäbe sind nicht allein aus juristischer Perspektive zu gewinnen. Beiträge aus anderen Sozialwissenschaften sind unentbehrlich, aber nicht so verfügbar, daß sie auf die spezifische juristische Problematik anwendbar wären. Diese selbst ist in ihrer realen Ausprägung nicht hinlänglich bekannt und kann deshalb auch theoretisch nicht präzise genug bestimmt werden – weder von der Rechtswissenschaft her noch von irgendeiner anderen wissenschaftlichen Theorie aus. Diese Situation fordert und ermöglicht einen Forschungsansatz, der bereits im Stadium der Problemformulierung interdisziplinäre Verständigung einschließt.
Es ist leicht zu sehen, daß eine solche Umschreibung nicht nur auf das Familienrecht bzw. die vormundschaftsgerichtliche Praxis zutrifft. Ein Problembewußtsein dieser Art beginnt sich aber gerade im Zivilrecht erst in den letzten Jahren herauszubilden und zu konkretisieren. Dagegen ist die parallele Situation im Strafrecht bzw. in der Kriminologie seit langem erkannt. Auch dort sind aber bis heute kaum Ansätze zur Integration interdisziplinärer Forschungen zu beobachten, vielmehr arbeiten Juristen, Soziologen und Psychologen durchweg getrennt und häufig genug auch gegeneinander im selben Problembereich. Es erscheint mithin ebenso dringlich wie schwierig, neue Wege zu eröffnen, Modellvorstellungen zu entwickeln und zu erproben, die eine Integration verschiedener sozialwissenschaftlicher Beiträge in Forschungs- und Entscheidungsprozesse ermöglichen. Das Frankfurter Projekt zielt daher auch darauf, am Beispiel des Familienrechts Erfahrungen mit Integrations- und Kooperationsmodellen zu sammeln, die über den spezifischen Bereich hinaus von Nutzen sein könnten. Methodischen Überlegungen kam somit von Anfang an besondere Bedeutung zu.

Die Entwicklung eines kommunikativen Arbeitsverfahrens

Die erste Aufgabe, vor die wir uns im Rahmen des Forschungsprojekts – oder besser: bei seiner Vorbereitung – gestellt sahen, bestand also darin, ein Verfahren zu entwickeln, das es ermöglicht,

a) eine erste Annäherung an die Realität vormundschaftsgerichtlicher Entscheidungspraxis sowohl aus jurstischer als auch aus soziologischer und psychologischer Perspektive vorzunehmen und
b) eine Verständigung über die jeweils fachspezifische Wahrnehmung und Beurteilung dieser Realität, (d.h. letztlich über Begriffe und Interessen) herbeizuführen und damit die Voraussetzungen für die Erarbeitung eines Forschungsansatzes zu schaffen, in dem Ziele, Problemstellung und Methoden in einen konsistenten und plausiblen Zusammenhang gebracht werden können.

Die Bewältigung dieser Aufgaben schien uns nur im Rahmen eines langfristigen Kommunikationsprozesses zwischen den verschiedenen Disziplinen vorstellbar und in möglichst direkter Konfrontation mit der konkreten vormundschaftsgerichtlichen Arbeit. Wir haben daher das eigentliche Forscherteam um interessierte Sozialwissenschaftler und Vertreter der juristischen Praxis erweitert und in dieser Arbeitsgruppe (1)* begonnen, Einzelfälle aus der Praxis an Hand von vollständigen Verfahrensakten zu untersuchen (2).

Die unmittelbare Beobachtung im Gerichtssaal zum Ausgangspunkt zu nehmen, erschien unzweckmäßig, weil sich nur ein kleiner Teil aller Verfahren und auch nur ein kleiner Teil jedes einzelnen Verfahrens in der mündlichen Verhandlung abspielt. Ergänzende Akten-Informationen wären uns für diese Fälle aber nicht zugänglich gewesen, weil es sich um laufende Verfahren handelte. Um dennoch nicht ausschließlich auf „papierne" Informationen angewiesen zu sein, haben wir jeweils Fälle ausgewählt, an denen mindestens ein Mitglied unserer Arbeitsgruppe selbst in irgendeiner Form real beteiligt war, sei es als Richter, als Anwalt, als sachverständiger Gutachter oder auch als „befreundeter Berater".

Die Diskussionen knüpften zunächst mehr oder weniger assoziativ an die Lektüre von Entscheidungen, Schriftsätzen, Briefen, Anhörungsprotokollen, Jugendamts- und Heimberichten und Sachverständigengutachten an. Stellungnahmen dazu, Bewertungen, Vermutungen über soziale und psychologische Hintergründe des Falles und über die Entstehung von Berichten, sowie Alternativvorschläge zu Entscheidungen gaben Anlaß zur Darstellung der unterschiedlichen Betrachtungsweisen in der Arbeitsgruppe, zu Fragen, Erklärungen und Auseinandersetzungen über den Stellenwert einzelner Aussagen. In Rollenspielen wurden Anhörungsgespräche simuliert, Kommunikationsverläufe – Herkunft, Selektion und Verarbeitung bestimmter Argumentationen – wurden schematisch nachgezeichnet; Sinn und Zweck jedes dieser Verfahren wurde ausgiebig diskutiert. Es ergab sich daraus ein kommunikativer Prozeß in der Arbeitsgruppe, in dem der Kommunikationsprozeß des jeweiligen gerichtlichen Verfahrens annäherungsweise nachvollzogen und gleichzeitig reflektiert wurde.

Nach nunmehr zwei Jahren sind die Beteiligten der Meinung, daß dieses Verfahren bei der Vorbereitung des Projekts wertvolle Dienste geleistet hat und auch im weiteren Verlauf des Projekts von Nutzen sein wird. Seine spezifischen Möglichkeiten, Begrenzungen und Schwierigkeiten lassen sich vielleicht am besten im Hinblick auf die verfolgten Ziele – interdisziplinäre Verständigung und Erfassung der gerichtlichen Entscheidungspraxis – sowie in Abgrenzung von anderen Forschungstechniken darstellen.

* Anmerkungen auf der Seite 426.

Der Beitrag des Verfahrens zur „interdisziplinären Verständigung“

Die Beiträge der einzelnen Disziplinen in der Arbeitsgruppe unterschieden sich deutlich voneinander. Das entspricht der Tatsache, daß Voraussetzungen und Erwartungen, die sich aus dem jeweiligen Wissens- und Erfahrungshintergrund ergaben, sehr verschieden waren. Für die beteiligten *Juristen* war die Fall-Diskussion an Hand von Gerichtsakten nichts Ungewöhnliches. Die Auflösung einzelner Situationen und Verläufe in ihre sozialen und psychologischen Elemente dagegen war ungewohnt, ebenso die Reflexion des eigenen rationalen oder irrationalen Umgangs mit dem Material. Der Beitrag der Juristen bestand zunächst vor allem darin, zu erklären, wo rechtliche Bindungen den Verfahrensablauf bestimmten, und wann juristische Auslegungs- oder Verfahrenstechniken ungenügend ausgenutzt oder in spezifischer Weise verwandt wurden. Fehlschlüsse, die Nichtjuristen leicht unterlaufen, wenn sie formaljuristisch bedingtes Richter- oder Anwaltsverhalten aus individuellen oder sozialen Determinanten zu erklären versuchen, konnten dadurch vermieden werden. Darüber hinaus repräsentierten die beteiligten Juristen natürlich auch in eigener Person eine ganze Reihe von Einstellungen und Reaktionsweisen, die als typisch gelten dürfen für Menschen, die eine juristische Ausbildung durchlaufen haben und in einer juristischen Berufspraxis stehen.

Für die beteiligten *Psychoanalytiker* war die Fall-Diskussion auf Grund ihrer klinischen Praxis ebenfalls eine gewohnte Arbeitsweise. Unser Versuch, einen historischen Kommunikationsprozeß nachzuvollziehen und uns gleichzeitig zum Zweck der Reflexion davon zu distanzieren, also zwischen Nacherleben und rationaler Durchdringung hin- und herzupendeln, kann ja Gemeinsamkeiten mit der spezifisch psychoanalytischen Methode nicht verleugnen. Ungewohnt war aber die Verwendung schriftlichen Materials, des Akteninhalts, zur Rekonstruktion historischer Ereignisse. Der Bezug zur Erlebnisrealität, der hier nur teilweise, nämlich nur soweit die reale Beteiligung jeweils eines Mitglieds der Arbeitsgruppe am historischen Prozeß reichte, hergestellt werden konnte, erwies sich für die Psychoanalytiker immer wieder als unzureichend. Die — mögliche — Beschränkung ihrer Funktion auf die Analyse der (Arbeits-)Gruppenprozesse erschien ebenfalls unbefriedigend. Der Beitrag der Psychoanalytiker ergab sich daher zunächst vor allem aus Überlegungen und Erklärungen zu der Frage, warum ihnen die vorliegenden schriftlichen Informationen nicht ausreichten, mit wem sie noch hätten sprechen wollen, wie ein solches Gespräch hätte ablaufen können, und welche Aufschlüsse ihnen im einzelnen für ihre eigene Entscheidung fehlten.

Für die *Soziologen,* aber auch für die nicht klinisch-praktisch arbeitenden *Psychologen* und *Erziehungswissenschaftler* war schon die Falldiskussion als solche ungewohnt. Für sie machte sich besonders bemerkbar, daß man sich im Vorfeld der Hypothesenbbildung befand, einem bisher wenig reflektierten Stadium des wissenschaftlichen Arbeitsprozesses, das meist eher dem Zufall, der „Intuition“ bzw. der indiviudellen Phantasie des Wissenschaftlers überlassen bleibt. Es lag daher von dieser Position aus besonders nahe, die Einzelfallanalyse eher rezeptiv als Quelle von Anregungen zur Hypothesenbildung und Methodenwahl zu nutzen. Der unmittelbare Beitrag bestand oftmals in dem Bemühen, aus theoretischem Wissen der Gefahr entgegenzusteuern, psychische Strukturen und Prozesse ausschließlich als Ergebnis individueller Lebensgeschichte zu begreifen und ihre historische Determinierung in größeren sozialen Zusammenhängen unberücksichtigt zu lassen. Freilich konnte dies meist nur in Form von stichwortartigen Theoriehinweisen, häufig nur durch die Artikulation „soziologischen Unbehagens" am Diskussionsverlauf geschehen, das Akzente verschob und Erfahrungen relativierte, da der individuelle Fall allein eben keine zwingenden Schlüsse auf soziale Determination erlaubt.

Der Beitrag des Verfahrens zur Erfassung der vormundschaftsgerichtlichen Praxis

Die Frage, in wieweit die Kommunikation in der Arbeitsgruppe, der reflektierte Nachvollzug des gerichtlichen Kommunikationsprozesses, diesem angemessen, also geeignet ist, seine spezifische Problematik zu erfassen, läßt sich eher beantworten, wenn man die Situation in der Arbeitsgruppe mit der des gerichtlichen Verfahrens genauer vergleicht.

Definiertes *Ziel* des vormundschaftsgerichtlichen Verfahrens ist es, die Probleme des Falles zu erfassen und darüber zu entscheiden. In der Arbeitsgruppe geht es demgegenüber nicht nur um die Problematik des Falles, sondern auch um die des Verfahrens, d.h. um die Erfassung der Kommunikationsmuster, und schließlich um die Reflexion des eigenen Umgangs mit den vorgefundenen Fall- und Verfahrensproblemen, also der eigenen Gewichtungs- und Bewertungstendenzen. Nicht richtig erschiene es mir, einen Unterschied dahingehend zu formulieren, daß die gerichtliche Fallösung ausschließlich unter juristischen Aspekten erfolge, während die Arbeitsgruppe auch psychologische und soziologische Aspekte einbeziehe. Auch der Richter sieht ja soziale und psychologische Probleme und versucht, sie im juristischen Entscheidungsprozeß zu verarbeiten. Allerdings sind Wahrnehmung und Artikulation dieser verschiedenen Aspekte in der Arbeitsgruppe auf verschiedene Personen, Repräsentanten der entsprechenden Disziplinen verteilt und können von ihnen ohne Einengung durch juristische Denkgewohnheiten oder Subsumtionsnotwendigkeiten thematisiert werden. Dies bedeutet einen für den Forschungsprozeß notwendigen Vorzug.

Definiertes *Motiv* für die Kommunikation im vormundschaftsgerichtlichen Verfahren sind normative Entscheidungs-, Beteiligungs- oder Unterwerfungszwänge. Gesetzlich verpflichtet ist der Richter zur Entscheidung, der Jugendamtsvertreter zur Stellungnahme. Anwälte und Gutachter sind durch Vertrag bzw. gerichtlichen Auftrag verpflichtet, ihren Verfahrensbeitrag zu leisten. Die Antragsteller sind in ihrem künftigen Handeln, meist in wichtigen familiären Dispositionen vom Ausgang des Verfahrens abhängig. Häufig genug sind darüber hinaus dritte Personen von der Entscheidung abhängig, ohne formell am Verfahren beteiligt zu sein, z.B. Pflegeeltern, die bisher im Auftrag desjenigen Elternteils, dessen Sorgerecht bestritten wird, für das Kind gesorgt haben. In der Arbeitsgruppe besteht dagegen kein Entscheidungszwang. Das sachliche Interesse ist in erster Linie auf die Erkenntnis der Zusammenhänge und Bestimmungsfaktoren des gerichtlichen Verfahrens ausgerichtet. Der Nachvollzug der Entscheidung ist nur Mittel zu diesem Zweck. Niemand ist davon abhängig, wie die Entscheidung ausfällt, ob sie mit der des Vormundschaftsgerichts übereinstimmt oder nicht. Dieser Unterschied, also der quasi „spielerische" Charakter der Diskussion in der Arbeitsgruppe macht es schwer, die Bedeutung des subjektiven Empfindens von Zwang und von Verantwortung voll zu erfassen. Andererseits bringt er eine größere Freiheit für kreatives Assoziieren und Phantasieren: Gewagte, extreme, am Rande liegende, ja absurde Möglichkeiten können eher ins „Spiel" gebracht werden, persönliche Empfindungen, Bewertungen und Einstellungen – auch aggressiver Art – werden leichter thematisiert. (Hierin scheint mir ein Vorteil auch gegenüber den Verfahren teilnehmender Beobachtung zu liegen, bei denen der Beobachter selbst mit Verantwortung trägt) (3). Im übrigen wurde dadurch, daß jeweils ein Gruppenmitglied auch an der realen Entscheidung beteiligt war, auch das subjektive Erleben des Entscheidungszwanges in einem gewissen Maße eingebracht.

Definierte *Rollen* haben im vormundschaftsgerichtlichen Verfahren alle Beteiligten. Sie hängen eng zusammen mit einer bestimmten Funktion, der Erwartung eines bestimmten Beitrages zum Verfahren. In der Arbeitsgruppe gibt es solche vordefinierten Rollen nicht. Funktion und erwartete Beiträge der einzelnen Mitglieder lassen sich im voraus nur vage im Hinblick auf ihre jeweilige fachspezifische Perspektive umschreiben. „Funktionsüberschreitungen" sind jederzeit möglich, ebenso der Wechsel in der Identifikation mit einzelnen Verfahrensbeteiligten. Auch das am realen Verfahren beteiligte Gruppenmitglied kann sich in der Gruppendiskussion jederzeit von seiner „realen" Rolle als Richter, Anwalt, Sachverständiger distanzieren. Daraus ergibt sich, daß in der Arbeitsgruppe der Einfluß von Rollenerwartungen auf Verhalten und Interaktion im Gerichtsverfahren leicht unterschätzt werden kann. Andererseits liegt ein unverkennbarer Vorteil darin, daß die Identifikation mit den Verfahrensbeteiligten nicht normativ festgelegt ist, sondern den jeweiligen persönlichen und fachspezifischen Tendenzen folgen kann.

Ein Unterschied zum gerichtlichen Verfahren muß allerdings nachdrücklich hervorgehoben werden: Es gibt in der Arbeitsgruppe keine Entscheidungs- und Verfahrensbetroffenen. Keines der Gruppenmitglieder war jemals in der Rolle des Betroffenen an einem zur Diskussion stehenden Verfahren real beteiligt und könnte diesen Part aus eigener Erfahrung darstellen. Zwar war es in einigen Fällen einzelnen Gruppenmitgliedern möglich, Gespräche mit Verfahrensbetroffenen zu führen. Dennoch fehlte in der Arbeitsgruppe die Konfrontation mit der persönlichen Präsenz des Betroffenen. Die Auseinandersetzung mit seinen Aktions- und Reaktionsweisen blieb stärker „vermittelt", sei es durch das Aktenmaterial, sei es durch Berichte der Gruppenmitglieder. Dem ist allerdings hinzuzufügen, daß der Unterschied zum gerichtlichen Verfahren nicht so gravierend ist, wie es auf den ersten Blick scheint. Nach vorläufigen Ermittlungen haben auch die Vormundschaftsrichter durchaus nicht regelmäßig persönlichen Kontakt mit den Betroffenen. In einer großen Zahl von Fällen, wenn nicht in der Mehrzahl kommt es gar nicht zu einer mündlichen Anhörung. Vielfach stützt sich der Richter auf Berichte des Jugendamtes, und nur der Jugendamtsmitarbeiter hat selbst mit Beteiligten gesprochen.

Schließlich wären noch die spezifischen Beschränkungen der Kommunikation zu vergleichen: Normbindung, Informationsmängel, Zeitdruck und Kontrolle.

Die Kommunikation im vormundschaftsgerichtlichen Verfahren ist an formale Regeln – Verfahrensnormen – gebunden, wenn es auch wenige sind im Vergleich zu anderen Verfahrensarten (s.o.). Neben der weniger bedeutsamen Beachtung von Fristen und Zuständigkeiten ist hier insbesondere an den Grundsatz des rechtlichen Gehörs zu denken, der den Richter nach neuerer, wenngleich umstrittener Meinung im förmlichen Beweisverfahren z.B. daran hindert, allein mit einem Zeugen oder Sachverständigen zu sprechen.

Schwerwiegender sind aber zweifellos die Einschränkungen, die sich mittelbar aus der Bindung des Richters ans materielle Recht bzw. an die durch die Rechtsprechung geschaffenen Maßstäbe und Kriterien ergeben. Kommunikation im gerichtlichen Verfahren wird unter dem Gesichtspunkt der Subsumtionsnotwendigkeit gesteuert und eingeschränkt. Solche Einschränkungen gehen vom Richter aus und treffen vor allem Zeugen und Sachverständige. Die Kommunikation in der Arbeitsgruppe ist von solchen Beschränkungen frei. Alternativen zur gesetzlich vorstrukturierten Kommunikatin im diskutierten Fall können jederzeit erwogen und – allerdings nur imaginär – durchgespielt werden.
Andererseits kann das Gericht – im Rahmen der erwähnten Normen – jede Ermittlungsidee in Ermittlungshandeln umsetzen, also versuchen, fehlende Informationen zu beschaffen. In der Arbeitsgruppe bestehen solche Möglichkeiten grundsätzlich nicht. Alternativen zum realen Ablauf können nur hypothetisch betrachtet werden. Nur ausnahmsweise könnten in Gesprächen mit den Beteiligten nachträglich zusätzliche Informationen beschafft werden. In diesem Zusammenhang ist jedoch wiederum zu berücksichtigen, daß die Informationsmöglichkeiten in der Praxis auch für den Richter enger begrenzt sind, als es der Theorie nach scheint. Vor allem der Kosten- und Zeitaufwand setzt hier Grenzen.
Unter Zeitdruck steht das Vormundschaftsgericht nicht nur – wie andere Gerichte auch – aus allgemein ökonomischen Gründen, sondern zusätzlich deshalb, weil die Fallprobleme selbst auf kurzfristige Regelung drängen. Vor allem, wenn es um kleine Kinder geht, sind schnelle Entscheidungen nötig, weil etwa der Wechsel der Bezugsperson die kindliche Entwicklung schwer schädigen kann, wenn der richtige Zeitpunkt dafür verpaßt ist. In der Arbeitsgruppe besteht kein solcher Zeitdruck. Welche Rolle er in der Praxis spielt, ist daher nicht unmittelbar zu ermessen. Andererseits ist die Freiheit von Zeitdruck gerade eine unabdingbare Voraussetzung für wissenschaftliche Arbeit in der hier praktizierten Form.
Schließlich bleibt zu erwähnen, daß das Vormundschaftsgericht sein Verfahren und seine Entscheidung der möglichen Kontrolle durch die höheren Instanzen ausgesetzt weiß. Das ist deshalb für die Erfassung der Praxis von Bedeutung, weil die Kontrolle häufig bereits antizipiert wird durch Orientierung an der höchstrichterlichen Rechtsprechung oder an den Entscheidungen der nächsthöheren Instanz. Irgendeine vergleichbare Form von Fremdkontrolle besteht für die Arbeitsgruppe nicht.
Aus alledem wird, glaube ich deutlich, daß das geschilderte Verfahren die üblichen empirischen Forschungstechniken einerseits wirkungsvoll ergänzen, andererseits aber diese nicht ersetzen kann. Sein wichtigster Vorzug liegt wohl in der Verbindung von identifikatorischen Nachvollzug des gerichtlichen Kommunikationsprozesses und distanzierter Reflexion seiner einzelnen Momente, unter Einschluß der Verbalisierung der dadurch angeregten Phantasien. Sie erlaubt eine relativ umfassende Annäherung an die komplexe Problematik, und zwar auf der intellektuellen wie auf der affektiven Ebene.
Eben darin liegt aber auch seine wichtigste Beschränkung: Die objektive und subjektive Identifikation mit den Verfahrensbeteiligten hat ihre Grenzen ebenso wie Phantasie und Realitätseinschätzungsfähigkeit in der Arbeitsgruppe. Standardisierte Interviews sowie einzelne Intensivgespräche mit Richtern, Jugendamtsmitarbeitern, Sachverständigen, Anwälten, vor allem aber mit Verfahrensbetroffenen bilden daher eine notwendige Ergänzung schon im Stadium der Projektvorberei-

tung. Die Verallgemeinerung der in diesem Verfahren gewonnenen Einsichten und Ergebnisse ist schon deshalb nicht möglich, weil die Stichprobe der diskutierten Fälle in keiner Weise repräsentativ sein kann. Einmal ist ihre Zahl zu gering (insgesamt fünf Fälle wurden in nunmehr zwei Jahren (3) analysiert), zum anderen wurden gezielt „materialreiche“ Fälle ausgewählt, d.h. längerdauernde Verfahren in komplizierten Fällen, deren Akten inhaltsreiche Schriftsätze, Gutachten und Stellungnahmen enthielten.

Annahmen, die daraus hergeleitet werden, müssen zunächst an Hand einer größeren systematisch ausgewählten Aktenstichprobe auf ihre Relevanz hin überprüft werden, bevor sie als Hypothesen fixiert werden.

Gerade der große Zeitaufwand ist natürlich schon für sich genommen ein Handicap des Verfahrens. Für interdisziplinäre Forschung auf unvorbereitetem Gelände scheint aber ein größerer Zeitraum ebenso unentbehrlich wie kontinuierliche Zusammenarbeit und eine geringe Fluktuation in der Arbeitsgruppe. Alle drei Faktoren begünstigen die Ausbildung differenzierter und intensiver Kommunikation. Der Ertrag dieses aufwendigen Verfahrens kann nicht allein in den nennbaren konkreten Ergebnissen gesucht werden, die – wie geschildert - der Ergänzung und Überprüfung bedürfen. Wichtiger noch scheint mir, ob und in wieweit auf diesem Wege die Voraussetzungen für interdisziplinäre Zusammenarbeit in einem Forschungsprojekt geschaffen werden können, ob es also zu Annäherung, Austausch und wechselseitiger Teilhabe an unterschiedlichen Denkansätzen kommt, die über das hinausgeht, was normalerweise durch individuelle Lektüre erreicht werden kann. Ein solcher Ertrag ist jeweils nur zu schätzen. Letztlich läßt er sich wohl nur am Verlauf und Ergebnis des Gesamtforschungsprozesses ablesen.

Summary

The author reports on a current interdisciplinary research project which deals with family court decisions for the "best interests of the child". Jurists, psychologists, psychoanalysts, sociologists and specialists in education are all taking part.

The goal of the project is to find ways to improve unsatisfactory conditions in such courts. Another purpose is to develop concepts, and investigate whether it is useful to integrate social science theories and legal decisions in this and other areas. To prepare for the project, therefore, particular attention has been given to the method of approaching it.

Interdisciplinary work is constantly hindered because different social sciences have such different points of view. These difficulties can be counteracted only by long-term dialogue among members of the research team, from the very beginning of a project. A colloquium has met for more than a year and a half, to define problems, devise methods, and discuss theoretical frameworks. The discussions turn on concrete cases concerning children, based on case files and outside information.

Judicial proceedings in general (and child cases in particular), are communication processes; in them psychological, sociological and juridical questions, though theoretically divisible, intertwine, in the form of a single concrete problem. One cannot deal with such complexities, by proposing specific hypotheses at the outset (drawn perhaps from organization or conflict theory), because this would skew the direction of research prematurely, before one is sure of the importance to be assigned to particular aspects of the cases.

Discussion of particular cases did turn out to be a satisfactory way to prepare the ground for hypthesis-building. The communications process of judicial procedure was, so to speak, replicated while theoretically important aspects of the perspectives of the various disciplines were sounded out. This "communication" approach to research has revealed both problems and possibilities; experience suggests its value in the framework of the total project.

Anmerkungen

1 Die Arbeitsgruppe setzt sich zusammen aus vier wissenschaftlich arbeitenden Juristen, einer Richterin, einer Anwältin, zwei Psychoanalytikern, einem Psychologen und drei Soziologen bzw. Erziehungswissenschaftlern.

2 Die Akten wurden uns mit freundlicher Unterstützung des Landgerichtspräsidenten, des Amtsgerichtspräsidenten sowie der zuständigen Richter in Frankfurt zur Verfügung gestellt.

3 In wöchentlichen Sitzungen, die allerdings während der Semesterferien in der Regel nicht stattfanden.

GPSR Compliance

The European Union's (EU) General Product Safety Regulation (GPSR) is a set of rules that requires consumer products to be safe and our obligations to ensure this.

If you have any concerns about our products, you can contact us on ProductSafety@springernature.com

In case Publisher is established outside the EU, the EU authorized representative is:

Springer Nature Customer Service Center GmbH
Europaplatz 3
69115 Heidelberg, Germany

Batch number: 10809468

Printed by Printforce, the Netherlands